T0189084

Rationale

The CCIS series is devoted to the publication of proceedings of computer science conferences. Its aim is to efficiently disseminate original research results in informatics in printed and electronic form. While the focus is on publication of peer-reviewed full papers presenting mature work, inclusion of reviewed short papers reporting on work in progress is welcome, too. Besides globally relevant meetings with internationally representative program committees guaranteeing a strict peer-reviewing and paper selection process, conferences run by societies or of high regional or national relevance are also considered for publication.

Topics

The topical scope of CCIS spans the entire spectrum of informatics ranging from foundational topics in the theory of computing to information and communications science and technology and a broad variety of interdisciplinary application fields.

Information for Volume Editors and Authors

Publication in CCIS is free of charge. No royalties are paid, however, we offer registered conference participants temporary free access to the online version of the conference proceedings on SpringerLink (http://link.springer.com) by means of an http referrer from the conference website and/or a number of complimentary printed copies, as specified in the official acceptance email of the event.

CCIS proceedings can be published in time for distribution at conferences or as postproceedings, and delivered in the form of printed books and/or electronically as USBs and/or e-content licenses for accessing proceedings at SpringerLink. Furthermore, CCIS proceedings are included in the CCIS electronic book series hosted in the SpringerLink digital library at http://link.springer.com/bookseries/7899. Conferences publishing in CCIS are allowed to use Online Conference Service (OCS) for managing the whole proceedings lifecycle (from submission and reviewing to preparing for publication) free of charge.

Publication process

The language of publication is exclusively English. Authors publishing in CCIS have to sign the Springer CCIS copyright transfer form, however, they are free to use their material published in CCIS for substantially changed, more elaborate subsequent publications elsewhere. For the preparation of the camera-ready papers/files, authors have to strictly adhere to the Springer CCIS Authors' Instructions and are strongly encouraged to use the CCIS LaTeX style files or templates.

Abstracting/Indexing

CCIS is abstracted/indexed in DBLP, Google Scholar, EI-Compendex, Mathematical Reviews, SCImago, Scopus. CCIS volumes are also submitted for the inclusion in ISI Proceedings.

How to start

To start the evaluation of your proposal for inclusion in the CCIS series, please send an e-mail to ccis@springer.com.

Communications
in Computer and Information Science   1901

Luca Longo

Editor

Explainable Artificial Intelligence

First World Conference, xAI 2023
Lisbon, Portugal, July 26–28, 2023
Proceedings, Part I

 Springer

Editor
Luca Longo ⓘ
Technological University Dublin
Dublin, Ireland

ISSN 1865-0929 ISSN 1865-0937 (electronic)
Communications in Computer and Information Science
ISBN 978-3-031-44063-2 ISBN 978-3-031-44064-9 (eBook)
https://doi.org/10.1007/978-3-031-44064-9

This Springer imprint is published by the registered company Springer Nature Switzerland AG
The registered company address is: Gewerbestrasse 11, 6330 Cham, Switzerland

Paper in this product is recyclable.

Preface

This is an exciting time to be a researcher in eXplainable Artificial Intelligence (xAI), a scholar's discipline that has undergone significant growth and development over the past few years. xAI has evolved from a mere topic within Artificial Intelligence (AI) to a multidisciplinary, interdisciplinary and transdisciplinary fermenting field of research. AI-driven technologies, Machine Learning (ML) and specifically Deep Learning (DL) applications have entered our everyday lives and society, with exponential, incessant growth. These have been successfully applied in various real-world contexts such as finance, education and healthcare, just to mention a few. The reasons are the great capability of these technologies to learn patterns from complex, non-linear multi-dimensional data, thus enabling the design of solutions for real-world problems such as forecasting, recommendation, classification, prediction and data generation. However, these solutions are often too opaque, non-transparent and non-interpretable, with a negative impact on the explainability of their inferences and outputs. As a consequence, this has led regulators and policymakers to increase pressure for the design of AI-based technologies that are better aligned with humans and our rights and that do not have a negative effect on society. This call for transparency, interpretability and ethics has made xAI an active and necessary research area. As a consequence, many reviews are published every year, and an abundance of theoretical and practical contributions are appearing every month, some application-dependent, some method or discipline-specific, and some context-agnostic. Similarly, various workshops around the world are organised by independent scholars at larger events, each focused on certain aspects of the explainability of AI-based systems. Unfortunately, these are scattered, often organised at a national level, thus attracting only local scholars. This motivated the creation of a larger event, the first World Conference on eXplainable Artificial Intelligence (xAI 2023). The aim was and is to bring together researchers, academics and professionals from different disciplines, and to promote the sharing and discussion of knowledge, new perspectives, experiences and innovations in xAI.

Against the initial expectations whereby a few dozen authors and attendees were forecasted, xAI 2023 broke several records. Firstly, more than 220 articles were submitted to the different tracks. Secondly, authors and attendees were from more than 35 countries, making this conference a truly world event. Thirdly, the acceptance rate of submitted articles was already relatively low (~40%), despite this being only the first edition of, hopefully, a long series of conferences, with 94 manuscripts being accepted. It is thus a great privilege to present the proceedings of the first World Conference on eXplainable Artificial Intelligence, held in Belem, Lisbon, Portugal, from the 26th to the 28th of July at the beautiful Cultural Congress Center of Belem. Split over three volumes, this book aggregates a collection of the best contributions received and presented at xAI 2023, describing recent developments in the context of theoretical and practical models, methods and techniques in eXplainable Artificial Intelligence. The accepted articles were selected through a strict, single-blind peer-review process. Each article received at least three reviews from scholars in academia and industry, with 99% of them holding a PhD in an area relevant to the topics of the conference. The general chair of the conference, along with the programme committee chairs, carefully selected the top contributions by ranking articles across several objective criteria and evaluating and triangulating the qualitative feedback left by the 188 international reviewers. The reviewing process was intensive, and it ensured that xAI 2023 adhered to the highest standards of quality. All accepted contributions are included in these proceedings and were invited to give oral presentations. Besides the main technical track, several special tracks were introduced, each proposed and chaired by one or more scholars, to allow the identification of highly innovative areas within the larger field of eXplainable Artificial Intelligence. Special track chairs were encouraged to be innovative in designing their topics to attract relevant scholars worldwide. Similarly, a parallel track was designed to give a chance to scholars to submit novel late-breaking pieces of work that are specific in-progress research studies relevant to xAI, and present them as posters during the main event. A demo track was also organised, providing a mechanism for scholars to demo software prototypes on explainability or real-world applications of explainable AI-based systems. A doctoral consortium was organised, with lectures delivered by renowned scientists to PhD scholars who submitted their doctoral proposals on future research related to eXplainable Artificial Intelligence. A separate programme committee was set up for the late-breaking work, demo and doctoral consortium tracks.

Finally, a panel discussion was held with renowned scholars in xAI and all in all, the 1st World Conference on eXplainable Artificial Intelligence offered a truly multidisciplinary view while inspiring the attendees to come up with solid recommendations to tackle hot-topic challenges of current technologies built with Artificial Intelligence. As the Monument of the Discoveries, right outside the conference centre, celebrates the Portuguese Age of Discovery during the 15th and 16th centuries, xAI 2023 symbolises a new mechanism for exploring and presenting novel directions for the design of the explainable intelligent systems of the future that are transparent, sustainable and ethical and have a positive impact on humans.

Luca Longo

Organizing Committee

General Chair

Luca Longo   Technological University Dublin, Ireland

Programme Committee Chairs

Francisco Herrera   Granada University, Spain
Javier Del Ser   Tecnalia & University of the Basque Country, Spain
Luca Longo   Technological University Dublin, Ireland

Doctoral Consortium Chairs

Luis Paulo Reis   University of Porto, Portugal
Sarah Jane Delany   Technological University Dublin, Ireland

Inclusion and Accessibility Chair

Alessandra Sala   Shutterstock, Ireland

Student Support Chair

Federico Cabitza   University of Milano-Bicocca, Italy

Programme Committee

Arianna Agosto   University of Pavia, Italy
Jaumin Ajdari   South East European University, Rep. of Macedonia
Jose M. Alonso   University of Santiago de Compostela, Spain
Andrea Apicella   Federico II University, Italy
Annalisa Appice   University Aldo Moro of Bari, Italy

Adrian Groza	Technical University of Cluj-Napoca, Romania
Riccardo Guidotti	University of Pisa, Italy
Miguel A. Gutiérrez-Naranjo	University of Seville, Spain
Mark Hall	Airbus, UK
Barbara Hammer	Bielefeld University, Germany
Yoichi Hayashi	Meiji University, Japan
Fredrik Heintz	Linköping University, Sweden
Jorge Henriques	University of Coimbra, Portugal
Jose Antonio Iglesias	Carlos III University of Madrid, Spain
Francesco Isgro	Università degli Studi di Napoli Federico II, Italy
Florije Ismaili	SEEU, Republic of Macedonia
Lundström Jens	Halmstad University, Sweden
Richard Jiang	Lancaster University, UK
Jose M. Juarez	Universidad de Murcia, Spain
Martin Jullum	Norwegian Computing Center, Norway
Zenun Kastrati	Linnaeus University, Sweden
Abhishek Kaushik	Dublin City University, Ireland
Hassan Khosravi	University of Queensland, Australia
Christophe Labreuche	Thales R&T, France
Markus Langer	Philipps-Universität Marburg, Germany
Thi Thu Huong Le	Pusan National University, South Korea
Philippe Lenca	IMT Atlantique, France
Andrew Lensen	Victoria University of Wellington, New Zealand
Francesco Leofante	Imperial College London, UK
David Lewis	Trinity College Dublin, Ireland
Paulo Lisboa	Liverpool John Moores University, UK
Weiru Liu	University of Bristol, UK
Henrique Lopes Cardoso	University of Porto, Portugal
Ana Carolina Lorena	Instituto Tecnológico de Aeronáutica, Brazil
Brian Mac Namee	University College Dublin, Ireland
Luis Macedo	University of Coimbra, Portugal
Lucie Charlotte Magister	University of Cambridge, UK
Giancladio Malgieri	Consiglio Nazionale delle Ricerche, Italy
Avleen Malhi	Bournemouth University, UK
Eleni Mangina	University College Dublin, Ireland
Francesco Marcelloni	University of Pisa, Italy
Stefano Mariani	Università di Modena e Reggio Emilia, Italy
Goreti Marreiros	ISEP/IPP-GECAD, Portugal
Manuel Mazzara	Innopolis University, Russia
Kevin McAreavey	University of Bristol, UK
Susan McKeever	Technological University Dublin, Ireland
Yi Mei	Victoria University of Wellington, New Zealand

Lucas Rizzo	Technological University Dublin, Ireland
Marcel Robeer	Utrecht University, The Netherlands
Mohammad Rostami	University of Southern California, USA
Araceli Sanchis	Universidad Carlos III de Madrid, Spain
Carsten Schulte	University of Paderborn, Germany
Christin Seifert	University of Marburg, Germany
Pedro Sequeira	SRI International, USA
Edwin Simpson	University of Bristol, UK
Carlos Soares	University of Porto, Portugal
Timo Speith	Universität Bayreuth, Germany
Gregor Stiglic	University of Maribor, Slovenia
Gian Antonio Susto	Università degli Studi di Padova, Italy
Jacek Tabor	Jagiellonian University, Poland
Nava Tintarev	University of Maastricht, The Netherlands
Alberto Tonda	Université Paris-Saclay, France
Alicia Troncoso	Universidad Pablo de Olavide, Spain
Matias Valdenegro-Toro	University of Groningen, The Netherlands
Zita Vale	GECAD - ISEP/IPP, Portugal
Jan Vanthienen	Katholieke Universiteit Leuven, Belgium
Katrien Verbert	Katholieke Universiteit Leuven, Belgium
Gianni Vercelli	University of Genoa, Italy
Giulia Vilone	Technological University Dublin, Ireland
Fabio Vitali	University of Bologna, Italy
Marvin Wright	Leibniz Institute for Prevention Research and Epidemiology - BIPS & University of Bremen, Germany
Arjumand Younus	University of Galway, Ireland
Carlos Zednik	Eindhoven University of Technology, The Netherlands
Bartosz Zieliński	Jagiellonian University, Poland

Acknowledgements

A thank you goes to everyone who helped in the organising committee for the 1st World Conference on eXplainable Artificial Intelligence (xAI 2023). A special thank you goes to the PC chairs, the doctoral committee chairs, the inclusion & accessibility chair and the student support chair. Also special thanks to the keynote speaker, Peter Flach, who, with Paolo Giudici and Grégoire Montavon took part in the conference's interesting panel discussion and provided their lectures during the doctoral consortium. A word of appreciation goes to the organisers of the special tracks, and those who chaired them during the conference. We are grateful to the members of the organisation and the volunteers who helped sort out the logistics and last-minute challenges behind organising such a large conference with great enthusiasm, effort and professionalism. A special thank you goes to the researchers and practitioners who submitted their work and committed to attending the event and turning it into an opportunity to meet and share findings and new avenues of research.

Contents – Part I

Model-Agnostic Explanations, Methods and Techniques for xAI, Causality and Explainable AI

Explainable AI in Finance, Cybersecurity, Health-Care and Biomedicine

Contents – Part II

Actionable eXplainable AI, Semantics and Explainability, and Explanations for Advice-Giving Systems

Contents – Part III

Human-Centered Explanations and xAI for Trustworthy and Responsible AI

Explainable and Interpretable AI with Argumentation, Representational Learning and Concept Extraction for xAI

Interdisciplinary Perspectives, Approaches and Strategies for xAI

XAI Requirements in Smart Production Processes: A Case Study

Deborah Baum[1(✉)], Kevin Baum[2(✉)], Timo P. Gros[3], and Verena Wolf[2,3]

[1] August-Wilhelm Scheer Institut für digitale Produkte und Prozesse gGmbH,
Uni-Campus Nord, 66123 Saarbrücken, Germany
deborah.baum@aws-institut.de

[2] Deutsches Forschungszentrum für Künstliche Intelligenz, Stuhlsatzenhausweg 3,
66123 Saarbrücken, Germany
{Kevin.Baum,Verena.Wolf}@dfki.de

[3] Modeling and Simulation Group, Saarland University, Saarland Informatics
Campus, Campus E1 3, Room 304, 66123 Saarbrücken, Germany
{timopgros,wolf}@cs.uni-saarland.de

Abstract. The increasing prevalence of artificial intelligence (AI) systems has led to a growing consensus on the importance of the explainability of such systems. This is often emphasized with respect to societal and developmental contexts, but it is also crucial within the context of business processes, including manufacturing and production. While this is widely recognized, there is a notable lack of practical examples that demonstrate how to take explainability into account in the latter contexts. This paper presents a real-world use case in which we employed AI to optimize an Industry 4.0 production process without considering explainable AI (XAI) requirements. Building on previous work on models of the relationship between XAI methods and various associated expectations, as well as non-functional explainability requirements, we show how business-oriented XAI requirements can be formulated and prepared for integration into process design. This case study is a valuable resource for researchers and practitioners seeking better to understand the role of explainable AI in practice.

Keywords: Explainable AI · Smart Factories · Smart Manufacturing · Smart Processes · Industry 4.0 · Human-Centric AI · Human Oversight

1 Introduction

The widespread adoption of artificial intelligence (AI) has had a profound impact on various sectors, including healthcare [4], finance [9], and many other fields

---

This paper is partially based on work funded by the Volkswagen Foundation grants AZ 98512 and 98514 "Explainable Intelligent Systems" (EIS), by the DFG grant 389792660 as part of TRR 248, by the European Regional Development Fund (ERDF) in context of the MoDigPro project, and by the European Digital Innovation Hub Saarland (GA: 101083337, PIC: 923810347).

L. Longo (Ed.): xAI 2023, CCIS 1901, pp. 3–24, 2023.
https://doi.org/10.1007/978-3-031-44064-9_1

[13]. As AI systems become more prevalent, the need for explainability and interpretability of their decision-making and decision-support processes becomes increasingly important. Explainable AI (XAI) aims to develop methods that make AI systems and their decisions understandable for human stakeholders [26], which requires fulfilling diverse expectations and requirements [36].

In this paper, we address the issue of explainability in the context of corporate AI applications, focusing on internal processes and practical applications [23]. We present a real-world case study where an AI system is employed to optimize an Industry 4.0 production process without considering XAI requirements. This case study enables us to identify situations where explainability is crucial and explore how business-oriented XAI requirements can be formulated and prepared for integration into process design [8,10,35].

Building on prior work in general models and non-functional software requirements, we provide valuable insights into the importance of explainable AI in smart manufacturing and formal business process development and into how corresponding requirements can be incorporated. This study is a resource for researchers and practitioners seeking better to understand the role of explainable AI in practice.

1.1   Related Work

That the lack of transparency, explainability, and understandability (or, more generally, perspicuity, as per [60]) in opaque AI models, known as black boxes [5], can lead to serious consequences is widely recognized [25,26,65]. In high-stakes contexts like healthcare and criminal justice, the consequences of using AI that lacks perspicuity become especially apparent, as decisions based on flawed or biased algorithms may harm individuals or communities on a large scale. Accordingly, XAI research dedicated to developing methods that make such systems understandable promises to help mastering various black-box-induced challenges [26,27,49,62].

In recent years, various methods and approaches have been developed to address the explainability of AI models, making them more interpretable and understandable for human stakeholders (for recent reviews, see [3,40,59]). Techniques such as local surrogate models like LIME [16,52] and SHAP [12,41] have emerged as popular tools for model-agnostic post-hoc interpretability. Another approach is to employ counterfactual explanations [63,64], which provide insights into AI decisions by presenting alternative scenarios where the outcome would have differed. Other techniques like TCAV or approaches exploiting the attention mechanisms are model-specific and try to look into the models' inner processes [34,47]. Alternatives such as [33] aim to explain models globally, i.e., to explain them (and their properties) as a whole rather than individual outputs.

XAI methods, however, are not an end in themselves but merely a means to an end. Thus, ever more and ever new XAI methods do not necessarily represent the solution to the identified black-box-induced challenges. From an application-oriented perspective, the usefulness of XAI methods hinges on the particular use context and in order to evaluate the suitability of XAI methods, one must understand the requirements, expectations, and needs of the relevant stakeholders that they are meant to fulfill [17,35,36,51,58,61] Most considerations regarding XAI requirements take either a broad societal perspective [15,19,56] or the perspective of specific stakeholders [21,29,38] , especially in high-stake fields [20,48,50]. Typical examples of concrete expectations connected to XAI are the improvement of unfairness detection [7,14,30], the resolution of accountability questions, the filling of responsibility gaps [6,44,57], and the improvement of trustworthiness assessments [32,42,43,55].

A long-standing consensus acknowledges the growing importance of explainability as AI systems become increasingly widespread. However, the significance of explainability is not restricted to societal contexts but extends to development and plays an instrumental role in AI-supported business processes, including manufacturing and production. Nevertheless, there remains a lack of concrete examples that practically substantiate these abstract considerations and clarify how to deal with the corresponding XAI requirements. More specifically despite the successful application of XAI techniques in various contexts, researchers still need to explore their significance in AI-driven production processes within companies sufficiently. Although international conferences have hosted workshops on the role of XAI in industry [22,28], books have featured it [11], and experts consider it central to the advancement of Industry 4.0 [2], tangible, real-world case studies demonstrating how to address explainability requirements in practice remain a rarity.

2 The Case Study

In the following, we will use a concrete case to show which XAI requirements one should consider when designing and planning AI-supported production processes. We will begin by presenting a real example that demonstrates the achievement of the actual optimization goal while overlooking specific user requirements. We then use this case as the basis for an XAI-oriented analysis.

2.1 The Case

Initial Situation. The factory of a big car producer constitutes our use case. The manufacturing process of a car is complex. Before it can take place, several components must be produced and prepared for assembly. While the bare bodies and some components are produced separately by the manufacturer, additional parts are produced by external suppliers and delivered to the factory. Finally, the workers assemble all parts of the vehicle. In what follows, we will look at the last part of that process.

The assembly of passenger cars involves two steps (for an overview, see Fig. 1): In the first step, the workers prepare the base bodies. More specifically, they add doors and paint them. In the second step, the final assembly, all other parts are

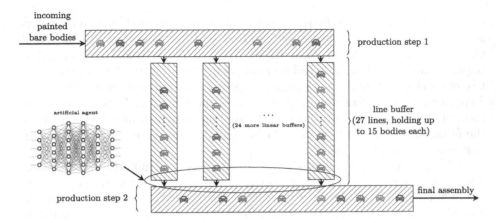

Fig. 1. The illustration depicts the on-site situation at the factory. The upper production line combines the bodies that are the result of the first assembly step, where the bare bodies are pre-assembled and painted. The production line at the bottom is leading to the final assembly. In between, buffering takes place in a line buffer that consists of 27 linear buffers with space for up to 15 painted bodies each. The AI agent described here makes recommendations for the outfeed, i.e., it recommends which painted bodies should go onto the conveyor belt of the final assembly line.

attached, from windows to the engine, transmission, axles, exhaust system and, finally, the interior.

During final assembly, the order in which workers assemble cars is crucial for the production process's effectiveness. The challenge becomes more complex as conveyors automatically move the bodies from one workstation to another on a fixed cycle. If a car part is missing or the work at some station goes too slow, production has to stop. Concerning the latter issue, it is vital to be aware that the cars have different characteristics, which bring different difficulties in the assembly process. If complex, difficult to assemble cars with similar characteristics are repeatedly assembled one after the other, the entire production may come to a standstill.

To optimize the production order, the car factory has a line buffer connecting the two stages. This buffer holds up to 15 bodies per line in up to 27 lines. When utilizing the line buffer, decision-makers must determine the line on which to store a car arriving from the base body assembly and painting area and the line from which to retrieve the next car for final assembly.

The second decision, from which line to take the next car body for final assembly, is made entirely manually through a human supervisor. Employees with a lot of experience make said decisions by trying to algorithmically follow a number of rules based on the stored car's features.

AI-Driven Solution. Employees can only apply and monitor the application of a limited number of relatively simple rules. Therefore, the approach, co-developed by some of the authors of this paper, aims at optimizing the second decision, i.e., which car body should go from the line buffer to final assembly, with the help of a learned AI agent. In addition to increasing efficiency through better and faster decision-making, the approach also aims to reduce the workload and cognitive load of the supervisors, who were not to be replaced but supported. To accomplish this, an AI was trained using reinforcement learning. Through self-play, without human supervision, this training was based on a simulation of the line buffer and the subsequent final assembly line. In order to obtain the appropriate rewards for reinforcement learning from the previously used rule-of-thumb-based method and these simulations, two approaches were combined:

1. Based on the existing rules of thumb, a large number of rules hierarchically ordered by importance are defined. We impose negative rewards on the AI agent, for rule violations, and assign more severe punishments to more critical rules. The AI agent was trained to minimize these punishments.
2. Based on a model of the final assembly line, one can simulate the production time, including possible events that would lead to a production stop. The AI agent was trained to maximize the number of cars produced, i.e., among other things, to minimize the time for which production has to be stopped.

Even early results of first experiments were impressive: in a toy example [24], the authors could show that the usage of an AI agent can significantly decrease the stopping time. Comparing historical data, i.e., results of real decisions about the order in which cars were produced, with the simulated results based on the AI suggestions showed a significantly increased plant productivity. Initial experience after deployment at the factory validated these experimental results – even though hurdles were encountered in practice.

Observation: A Lack of Adoption. In consultation with factory management and the works council, the system was never designed to make decisions fully automatically, i.e., independently. Instead, it was designed to make recommendations to a human overseer, i.e., a supervisor in the loop, who would then decide on their responsibility. However, when the system was deployed, it was observed that supervisors tended not to follow system recommendations, at least when they differed significantly from the decisions they would have made themselves.

Personal conversation in the field confirmed our suspicion that blindly following AI-based recommendations that do not match one's own assessment is perceived as unsatisfactory and therefore tends to be rejected. Although this is only anecdotal evidence that should be substantiated by qualitative and quantitative studies in future work, it should nevertheless be allowed to be regarded as sufficient motivation for our present work. This is all the more true because links between acceptance and trust on the one hand and XAI on the other hand have also been postulated in other theoretical papers (see also related work above and our analysis below).

Taking a step back, it becomes clear: We have discovered a step in an existing production process that can be significantly optimized through AI and have developed a corresponding solution. What should have been initially considered in addition, however, is that using an AI system leads to new human-machine relationships and alters existing relationships between stakeholders. Only if these relationships and the associated interactions are considered, AI use can unfold its true potential.

3   Identifying XAI Requirements

Examples like the case described above show that more than merely incorporating AI applications into existing business processes is required to reach the desired goals. It is crucial to realize that the potential change in the overall dynamics and decision-making within the process when introducing AI applications is reason to rethink the *entire* process rather than simply adding AI components or replacing parts of the process with them. AI may offer new insights and perspectives that challenge or improve traditional business decision methods. However, this might necessitate reevaluating and restructuring the process to fully unlock AI's capabilities. Thus, only true integration of AI, rather than merely the automation of tasks without considering broader implications and effects within the modified process, results in optimized outcomes. Most importantly, as we incorporate AI into our processes, it is crucial to consider the impact of this technology on communication and collaboration between humans and machines, as well as the overall effectiveness of the adapted process. For AI components to be effectively utilized, one must adapt the process to new requirements that emerge due to AI implementation in specific contexts, especially when human-computer collaboration becomes an integral part of the new overall system or process. Understanding these new requirements correctly or identifying them in the first place is much work. In particular, anticipating such requirements requires some experience and systematic approaches. However, if one runs into new challenges *after* already deploying an AI system (like in our case), it is crucial to analyze the observed deficiencies. Such situations are great opportunities to learn from mistakes and for future projects.

The present case lends itself to such an analysis, which is the main contribution of our work. We want to figure out how to design better and more efficient AI-driven business processes, especially concerning issues of *adoption*. Since we have no reason to believe that supervisors reject AI recommendations in principle, we hypothesize that the lack of adoption is due to a lack of information and understanding on the human side. This assumption is by no means intended to diagnose a lapse on the part of the human but to point to a flaw in the system. Apart from other transparency-related questions (cf. [60]), we assume a need for more explainability. As a result, the interaction between humans and machines, necessitated by the deployment of the AI components, introduces at least one new technical requirement: the need for AI to be explainable to the relevant human stakeholder.

Of course, this vague statement offers little concrete guidance concerning designing better and more efficient AI-driven business processes, specifically regarding adoption. Aiming for more transparency and more explainability means making concrete software engineering decisions. To tackle these challenges

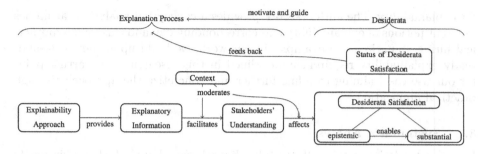

Fig. 2. The model of [36] that we use as the starting point of our analysis. We start by identifying the relevant stakeholders, which we consider the critical context factor. What the authors call "desiderata" we call "needs", and we derive them from the stakeholders. Furthermore, we do not consider concrete explanatory approaches, i.e., concrete XAI methods, but consider what kind of explanatory information seems expedient to fulfill the identified needs of the relevant stakeholders.

systematically, we build upon the groundwork laid by [36] (see also Fig. 2). The thus-gained understanding we then translate to concrete explainability requirements in the sense of [35]. By synthesizing the insights from both works, we aim to make steps toward a more comprehensive understanding of the challenges and opportunities presented by AI integration in business processes.

According to [36], we first need to understand what *de facto* needs (or, as called there, "desiderata") of the human stakeholders involved that were not met and how they connect to what XAI can deliver before we can then identify the suitable XAI methods. More specifically, their work investigates stakeholders' desiderata (needs) in the context of explainability approaches. They start from the observation that much of XAI literature claims that certain XAI methods help meet specific needs in an interdisciplinary way. The authors emphasize the lack of clarity about how exactly explanatory approaches can help satisfy the cited stakeholder needs. The authors provide a model that explicitly outlines the essential concepts and relationships to consider when evaluating, adjusting, selecting, and developing explainability approaches. We utilize this model to inform our analyses of stakeholders' needs in the context of AI explainability. In particular, the work of these authors prompts us to begin by looking at the concrete needs of stakeholder groups, to ask under what contextual conditions these needs would be met, and how, in principle, different XAI methods can help in achieving this.

Once these relationships have been understood, however, tangible forms are needed in practice to unambiguously express the requirements. This includes defining the conditions under which the requirements should be considered fulfilled and determining how to check whether conditions were met. The findings of [35] that investigates the elicitation, specification, and verification of explainability as a Non-Functional Requirement (NFR) offer a good starting point for doing so. They start by observing that a systematic and overarching approach to ensure explainability by design remains elusive while there is a growing demand for explainability. The author's work provides a conceptual analysis that unifies different notions of explainability and corresponding demands, using a hypothetical hiring scenario as an example. In our work, we build upon the rough-and-ready explainability requirements outlined in this research as a starting point for our use case, aiming to refine further and concretize the approach through practical application.

3.1 Systematic Analysis

In order to derive empirically testable hypotheses about which requirements result from the use of our AI system systematically, we draw on the model from [36] (see also Fig. 2). To do this, we analyze the situations in four steps. The first step is to determine the relevant stakeholder groups as crucial contextual factors.

We omit other factors beyond stakeholder identity because we could not identify any further critical factors (e.g., no time pressure).

We then attempt to identify the specific practical needs of these stakeholder groups, focusing on supervisors and their needs that may explain the lack adoption of AI recommendations. Thirdly, we consider the types of explanatory information that address the identified needs. Finally, the XAI methods that can provide this information are presented.

Stakeholders. To ensure the successful implementation and operation of an AI system within an assembly line setting, understanding and addressing the needs of the following three key stakeholder groups is essential:

Supervisors. Supervisors are responsible for deciding which car bodies leave the line buffer. Importantly, it is they who decide whether to follow the AI's recommendation.

Assembly Line Workers. The AI-supported decisions directly affect workers on the assembly line. They may encounter unexpected or potentially frustrating configurations.

Management. Managers must comprehend the underlying reasons in case of incidents and, most importantly, production halts.

All of these roles significantly influence the system's overall performance and are, in a sense, affected by the deployment of our AI system. Arguably, one can foster a more efficient, productive, and transparent AI-driven environment by catering to their requirements and addressing their concerns.

Needs. Upon closer examination, we find relatively similar needs for each class of stakeholder, which can thus be subsumed under three more general categories: needs for (adequate) *trustworthiness assessment*; needs for *responsibility*; and needs for *improvement*. Table 1 presents a general overview of the individual needs of supervisors, workers, and management we identified and show which categories they fall into. Below, we list the three relevant needs of supervisors whose frustrations could plausibly explain the lack of adoption of our system:

Trustworthiness Assessment. A lack of trust in the AI system and its results could explain why supervisors often do not follow pay to the generated recommendations. Drawing from the literature on organizational trust [45] and trust in automation [37], there could be several reasons for such a lack of trust. For example, the system could perform poorly, revealing its insufficient capability and thus disqualifying it from being a trustworthy system. Since our AI-driven system has been shown to perform better than the previous system, this is not a plausible explanation. Alternatively, the user's lack of trust might be a case of decalibrated trust [37], i.e., the incorrect assessment of a trustworthy system as non-trustworthy. Again, this could be explained by several factors [55], and the most likely one in our case is inadequate access to relevant cues and information by the supervisor. In other words, our system needs to allow supervisors to appropriately develop trust in the system by providing more information. Therefore it is rational, especially in the absence of experience, to not trust the system when its recommendations do not match one's expectations.

Responsibility. The human supervisor should not be a mere button pusher but a responsible decision-maker. This is not only the factory management's expectation but is also likely to correspond to the supervisor's self-image. However, our system could give the human in the loop an insufficient sense of self-efficacy, and it might indeed put them in a position where they cannot – and should not – take responsibility for their decisions. By this, we mean that if supervisors deviate from the traditional rules and their gut feeling in favor of AI recommendations, they may fear not being able to justify their decision. Especially in case of incidents like production stops, pointing to the computer and telling the management the computer said so is undoubtedly unsatisfactory. No one wants to find themselves in such a situation, so they might decide to follow the old rules rather than the AI recommendations. If so, the situation of the supervisors would be typical instances of only *apparent* responsibility in case of *de facto* responsibility gaps [6,44].

Improvement. Supervisors should regularly review the AI system's performance and contribute to its ongoing improvement. This involves assessing accuracy and reliability, analyzing data, comparing AI-generated recommendations with their traditional approaches, and identifying biases or errors. By continually staying informed about the AI system's strengths and weaknesses, supervisors can enhance their own skills, enabling them to make more informed decisions regarding the utilization of AI assistance in the future. This adaptation allows them to respond effectively to changing circumstances within the production context.

Even if we were to restrict our investigation to these three needs of the supervisors let alone considering all nine defined needs, (cf. Table 1) this would go beyond the scope of this work. As we believe that the most plausible barrier to using AI recommendations is that supervisors do not feel they can arrive at well-informed decisions themselves, we consider the need of responsibility to be

Table 1. Stakeholder's needs. In the paragraph on the stakeholder's needs, we explain the supervisor's needs, those in the top row, in more detail. Their non-fulfillment could explain the need for more adoption of AI recommendations.

	Trustworthiness Assessment	Responsibility	Improvement
Supervisors	*Trust Calibration:* being able to achieve an adequate level of trust in the AI and its recommendations	*Reasoned Decision-Making:* being able to weigh the pros and cons of AI recommendations and one's own judgments.	*Continuous Improvement:* being able to analyze AI recommendations and improve one's own decision-making
Workers	*Trust Calibration:* being able to achievie an adequate level of trust in the supervisor's evaluation and implementation of AI recommendations	*Voice:* being able to share concerns or feedback about the implemented decisions with the supervisor	*Adaptability:* being able to develop skills to anticipate and adjust to new patterns
Management	*Trust Calibration:* being able to achieve an adequate level of trust in that the AI system's recommendations align with overarching goals	*Risk Management:* being able to identify and mitigate potential risks associated with AI implementation	*Continuous Improvement:* being able to evaluate AI system performance and incorporating feedback for ongoing optimization and enhancement of processes

the best explanation for the observed lack of adoption. Thus, we restrict the further analyses to what we take to be the heart of that need.

In order to complete the analysis in terms of [36], we next need to ask ourselves what explanatory information is purposeful to meet the needs of the respective stakeholders to be addressed. From this, we can make a first educated guess concerning suitable XAI methods.

Explanatory Information. The model of [36] requires us to ask what *understanding* is required on the part of the stakeholders in order to fulfill their individual needs. Only then can one ask what information is needed for this so that the corresponding understanding can be obtained and actually will be obtained in practice. However, of course, we cannot base such analysis on fully developed, sophisticated theories of understanding from Philosophy or Psychology. However, this is not necessary for practical application, mainly because we cannot directly observe or measure understanding as a latent structure anyway. Instead, we ask ourselves how the respective understanding might show up in the behavior or capacity of a supervisor. What is it that the supervisor cannot do in the present case but should be able to do so that one can rightly say that the individual need is fulfilled?

In order to understand what is missing to enable supervisors to do this, it is helpful to take the perspective of the supervisors. Supervisors have so far made decisions based on specific rules of thumb and their gut feeling, which has developed from experience and is difficult to verbalize, explicate, and explain. This form of intuitive knowledge need not be inferior to explicable knowledge (a fact also known as Polanyi's paradox). Now, AI-based decision recommendations entered the picture, which have quite similar characteristics. Remember: Our AI system's recommendations result from a self-reinforcing learning process in which both said rules of thumb and the result of simulations (which might be understood as formalized work experience) go hand in hand. Similar to the decisions of humans, however, the system's recommendations cannot be easily cast into explanations. Only when these two different forms of implicit knowledge conflict does the problem arise. The following case distinction illustrates this:

– Either the recommendations are consistent with the rules of thumb and could be explained by them. However, they should be already similar to what the supervisor would decide. So this case is not interesting as it cannot be the basis for the observed lack of adoption.
– Alternatively, the AI's recommendations apparently conflict with the rules of thumb. In this case, the recommendation either conforms to what the supervisor would do or they do not:
  • In the first case, there is no disparity between the recommendation and the decision. Again, this case is of no interest as there is no disagreement between humans and machines.
  • However, if the system's recommendation does *not* correspond to what the supervisor would do, a relevant case is found.

Why should supervisors follow the recommendations of the system in that last case? If they follow their feeling, they can take responsibility as they can rationalize and verbalize their decision or at least partially justify it. However, if they follow the system's recommendation, the most they can do is point to the AI. In this case, they must fear others questioning whether they are essential to the decision process. In short, they would be mere "vicarious agents" of the AI, i.e., mere button-pushers.

This consideration leads to the fundamental question that the supervisor should be able to answer: Why did someone choose car A and not car B (or C or D or ...) as the next car for the conveyor? To answer this question, they must know *why* the AI suggested one car body and not another. Suppose the supervisor followed the recommendation of the AI. The supervisor must then be able to answer in the following form: "I would have chosen body X rather than A. However, the AI suggested choosing body A. At first, I was surprised, but in fact I learned from the system that E would have obtained otherwise." Whereas E should refer to a valid reason that supports choosing A instead of X. For example, E could be that choosing X would have made a production stoppage more likely. Alternatively, that A has been waiting in the buffer for a very long time and is blocking the buffer line where other car bodies are waiting for that should be able to be selected later for effective operation. From this, we conclude that at the core of the supervisor's need for responsibility lies the following expectation:

Reasoned Decision-Making: Being able to weigh the pros and cons of AI recommendations against the pros and cons of one's own judgments.

Thus, the required explanatory information should be *contrastive*. Contrastive explanations focus on comparing the outcome of interest with a reference outcome, highlighting the differences between the two. This approach seeks to answer questions like, "Why did the model choose option A over outcome B?" Contrastive explanations emphasize the specific features or factors that led the model to prefer one outcome over another. By providing this comparative perspective, contrastive explanations offer users a better understanding of the decision-making process and the relative importance of different factors.

Contrastive explanations are not necessarily *counterfactual* explanations. Instead, counterfactual explanations typically explain what minimal input feature variations would have led to other outputs. These explanations answer questions like, "What would need to change in the input for the model to produce a different outcome?" Counterfactual explanations present hypothetical situations where the model's decision would have differed if certain conditions or input features were altered. It is generally assumed that such dependence shows what part of the input is "causally most relevant" for the specific output. This approach helps grasp the sensitivity of the model's decisions to specific factors and understand the impact of those factors on the decision-making process.

However, counterfactual explanations can also be understood on the side of outputs rather than inputs: As explanations that function about what would otherwise have been the case. Of course, this is precisely the kind of explanation we need in this case: we need to show the supervisor the extent to which his favored choice would lead to different consequences than following the system's recommendations – and why those consequences would be better than the consequences of the supervisors favored choice. Supervisors can either accept this explanation, which is necessarily based on simulation results based on two different runs in the factory's digital twin, or reject it based on their experience and factual information. (Note, that in practice the information that is available to a human supervisor may well exceed that available to the AI system. For example, the supervisor may recognize that the workers at a particular workstation are performing better than usual or that a workstation is understaffed today and therefore considered too efficient in the simulation. This kind of estimation is precisely what the supervisor is supposed to be there for as a human in the loop.)

In summary, contrastive explanations in XAI emphasize the differences between the two outcomes. At the same time, counterfactual explanations explore alternative scenarios by modifying input features to explain AI models' decision-making processes better.

In our use case, a contrastive and counterfactual explanation, contrasting the consequences of following the option the supervisor would choose with the consequences of following the AI recommendations, seems particularly useful for the supervisor. Why choosing the body from one line is preferable to drawing a body from another can depend on highly non-trivial dependencies, for instance, about possible future choices and further uncertainties. This might make generating good explanations computationally expensive and their presentation non-trivial. However, supervisors need to be in a position to understand such dependencies, at least approximately, if they are meant to base their decisions on the pros and cons of the different alternatives.

This leaves the question of what kind of XAI approaches we need.

XAI Methods. While the specific choice and design of a concrete XAI approach are beyond the scope of this paper, the above considerations do make clear that post-hoc approaches to local explanation should be considered:

Ante-Hoc vs. Post-Hoc. Ante-hoc approaches focus on creating transparent and explainable systems that do not require additional procedures for understanding their inner workings or outputs. Models like decision trees, rule-based models, and linear approximations are inherently explainable, but this may only be useful for stakeholders with specific expertise. Using inherently explainable models often comes with a loss of accuracy.

Post-hoc approaches focus on extracting explanatory information from a system's underlying model, which is usually a black-box, i.e., an inherently opaque model.

Since, in our case, the AI system, a deep neural network, already exists and works very well, a post-hoc approach is demanded. Two reasons in particular suggest that there is no need to switch to ante-hoc explainable models. Firstly, the considerations above suggest that the kinds of explanations to be generated are likely to be simulation-based. Secondly, said considerations suggest that the specific decision criteria of the AI, if such a thing is encoded at all in a separable way in the internal structure of the deep neural network, are likely to be less relevant. Even if such criteria are not present at all or are present but cannot be extracted (which in the end is not even a proven impossibility), this does not necessarily speak against principally opaque models plus post-hoc XAI techniques.

Local vs. Global. In the field of XAI, *local* and *global* explanation approaches serve different purposes when it comes to understanding AI models. Local explanations provide insights into specific outputs. They should make it easier to comprehend why the model arrived at that specific conclusion.

Global explanations, on the other hand, provide an overall understanding of the AI model's behavior and decision-making process. They seek to convey a general understanding of how the model operates, including its patterns, relationships, and rules. Global explanations are valuable when stakeholders need a holistic view of the model or aim to identify potential biases, trends, or systemic issues in the model's functioning. In summary, local explanations clarify individual decisions made by an AI model, while global explanations offer a broader view of the model's behavior and decision-making patterns.

Considering that our primary objective is to enable the supervisor to understand individual system decisions and justify them (to themselves, the management, or the workers), we focus our attention on local explanations in this context.[1]

3.2   Derivation of Requirements and Conditions for Success

All the findings listed above as results of our analysis are systematic. However, they need a more *formal* structure to be explicitly fed into further development or used to design business processes. [35] proposed the following general structure for explainability requirements that are meant to serve such purposes:

Definition 1 (Explainability Requirement). *A system S must be explainable for target group G in context C with respect to aspect Y of explanandum X.*

This definition emphasizes two essential points: First, a system must be understandable to a particular target group (the stakeholders) in a particular context (that, remember, is assumed to be given in our case by the stakeholder's role alone); and second, an explanation always refers to a particular aspect of what is to be explained (i.e., the explanandum). In the present cases, the explanandum is not the AI system itself but its outputs, i.e., we are interested in local explanations. The aspect of the recommendation we are after is what makes it better than what the supervisor would otherwise choose, e.g., in the absence of the recommendation. Hence, we can derive the following specific requirement:

Definition 2 (Explainability Requirement: Supervisor's Responsibility). *The AI-based recommendation system must be explainable for supervisors with respect to what makes the system's recommendation better than the options the supervisor may favor initially.*

Finally, we need a success criterion, i.e., we need to specify the circumstances under which a certain kind of explanatory information fulfills the requirement. As previously mentioned, ensuring that the explanation is appropriate for the stakeholder is crucial. For this, we again make use of [35], which, quite similar to the model of [36], emphasizes both the stakeholder-relativity of explanations and the importance of understanding concerning measuring success:

---

[1] This focus is explicitly not meant to negate the potential relevance of global explanation and a global understanding of our model. In fact, there are good reasons to consider them as well. For example, knowledge about general limitations and also strengths of our system – "For configurations of this kind, our system tends to make certain mistakes more often..." etc. – may well enable the supervisor to better recognize critical situations or also to better assess his own weaknesses against those of the system. Local explanations are unlikely to be sufficient to ensure adequate, calibrated trust in the system, and a lack of global transparency may therefore fundamentally undermine trust and acceptance in AI systems. We thank an anonymous reviewer for rightly bringing this point to our attention.

Definition 3 (Explainable For). *E is an explanation of explanandum X with respect to aspect Y for target group G, in context C, if and only if the processing of E in context C by any representative R of G makes R understand X with respect to Y.*

So for our case-specific purposes, we get the following instance:

Definition 4 (Explainable For: Supervisor's Responsibility). *E is an explanation of the AI-based system's recommendations with respect to what makes the system's recommendation better than the options the supervisor may favor initially for the target group of supervisors if and only if the processing of E by any specific supervisor makes them understand the AI-based system's recommendation with respect to this contrastive regard.*

As before, we do not need a detailed, theoretical understanding of the concept of understanding as [35] aims at a practical, capability-oriented approach, precisely as argued for in the previous section. Ultimately, such an approach should allow the carrying out of concrete user studies to determine whether the requirement is fulfilled:

> Analyzing explanations in terms of understanding [...] enables leveraging results from psychology and the cognitive sciences to assess whether something is an explanation and how people react to different explanations. In particular, tying explainability to an understanding eventually enables verification through studies conducted with the relevant stakeholders [...] Overall, the idea is to enable the examination of explainability by measuring understanding, e.g., in psychological studies of whether the processing of specific explanations makes stakeholders understand the explanandum concerning the relevant aspect in relevant contexts. [35, pp. 365]

Thus, structured interviews and observational studies with supervisors should be conducted to assess the suitability of some approaches in the direction sketched in the last subsection. For instance, one should observe how the supervisors decide and ask them to justify their decisions for a given set of specific example choices, together with explanations.

Suppose these interviews reveal that the supervisors' choices are highly inaccurate and inefficient or that their answers are insufficiently based on the given explanations. In that case, the specific explanation approach obviously does not meet the requirement and needs to be revised.

4   Conclusion

This paper examined a real-world case study highlighting the importance of explainability in AI-driven decision-making processes. For this, we investigated the actual application of AI in a smart manufacturing context in which insufficient consideration was given to the new human-machine interaction arising from the AI deployment. In particular, we focused on the observed lack of adoption of the AI-generated recommendations by human supervisors.

To understand how to remedy this, we used the model of [36] and identified a set of stakeholders and their respective needs induced by AI deployment. We explained to what extent these needs are frustrated by a lack of explainability of the AI recommendations and how this frustration arguably explains the observed lack of adoption. From this, we inferred plausible types of explanatory information and identified potentially requisite types of explanatory methods. Based on this, we derived concrete explainability requirements based on prior work from [35] and described how to test their fulfillment in studies. However, carrying out the outlined program of work is beyond the scope of this paper.

In the following, we briefly point out how the knowledge and insights collected throughout this case study can be incorporated into the future development of AI-based business processes so that corresponding emerging explainability requirements can be anticipated rather than identified after deployment when problems arise. We then provide a brief outlook on future work that could build on our case study.

4.1   XAI in Business Process Management and Business Process Management Notation

Our analysis has shown that it is necessary to incorporate XAI techniques to ensure good trust, enable responsible decisions, and allow for continuous improvement and that one can systematically identify corresponding requirements "from the armchair". By anticipating the needs of stakeholders to understand AI-generated results at the design time of business process modeling in the form of explainability requirements as described in our work, the emergence of new hurdles, such as the lack of adoption discussed here, can be prevented or at least minimized from the outset. In light of these findings, considering XAI in the early stages of business process modeling is essential for organizations to realize the full potential of AI systems and address potential challenges. We are not alone in this view, even though the integration of XAI into business process modeling is still in its infancy [18,31].

Integrating XAI early on in the modeling process promises several advantages:

Adequate Trust and Acceptance: Understanding the rationale behind AI-driven decisions enables and fosters adequate trust (in the sense of [55]) and acceptance among stakeholders towards the AI system, including different groups of employees, managers, and regulators. Transparent decision-making processes can lead to better collaboration and more widespread adoption of AI systems within organizations.

Improved Decision-Making Quality: Incorporating XAI techniques during the design phase allows for more informed decision-making, as users can evaluate the AI system's reasoning, assumptions, and potential biases. This ensures that AI-generated outcomes align with organizational goals and possibly also moral standards.

Facilitating Compliance and Auditing: Ensuring transparency and explainability in AI systems from the outset aids in meeting regulatory requirements and addressing potential legal or ethical concerns. Organizations can more effectively demonstrate compliance with data protection and AI ethics regulations by explaining their AI-driven decisions.

Simplified Debugging and Optimization: The early integration of XAI enables easier identification of issues or shortcomings in AI systems, allowing for more efficient debugging and optimization processes. This, in turn, results in better-performing AI models that are tailored to meet specific business objectives.

Streamlining Knowledge Transfer: XAI facilitates knowledge transfer and employee training, offering a deeper understanding of the AI system's decision-making processes. This empowers employees to work effectively with AI systems and ensures the organization's smooth integration of AI technologies.

In conclusion, considering XAI from the initial stages of business process modeling is crucial for organizations seeking to harness the full potential of AI systems while addressing potential challenges. By integrating XAI early on, organizations can enhance trust, improve decision-making quality, and facilitate compliance, leading to more effective and ethically sound AI-driven business processes.

4.2 Future Work

In our future work, we primarily envision two areas of focus:

Firstly, conducting empirical studies involving decision-makers and stakeholders from our real-life case example is imperative. This will allow us to test our current theoretical considerations in practice and gain valuable insights into the practical implications of our findings.

Secondly, explainability can be explicitly integrated into the design of AI-driven processes. How and in what form can explainability requirements already be considered in the design of business processes? This may also require extensions to the corresponding modeling languages like BPMN.

Thirdly, our real-world case study shows that having a solid framework for building studies would help test the fulfillment of the derived explainability requirements. How could appropriate studies be systematically derived directly from the requirements? For instance, which kinds and types of abilities typically correspond to what needs of what sort of stakeholder? How do they relate to the various XAI methods and all sorts of explanatory information? Moreover, how could they be executed without employing entire teams of organizational psychologists? No such framework or guiding principles exist – although, of course, the need for such studies has long been recognized and their general structure has been described [17,28,54], a number of specific studies have been conducted (for a relatively recent overview, see [53]), and both contextual (and stakeholder) relevance and the need for interdisciplinarity have been emphasized [1,39,46]. While we hope to have underscored all of this in the context of industrial and business processes in this work, we intend future work to tie the development of such studies more closely to explicit, non-functional requirements such as those outlined here.

References

1. Adadi, A., Berrada, M.: Peeking inside the black-box: a survey on explainable artificial intelligence (XAI). IEEE Access **6**, 52138–52160 (2018). https://doi.org/10.1109/ACCESS.2018.2870052
2. Ahmed, I., Jeon, G., Piccialli, F.: From artificial intelligence to explainable artificial intelligence in industry 4.0: a survey on what, how, and where. IEEE Trans. Ind. Inform. **18**(8), 5031–5042 (2022)
3. Arrieta, A.B., et al.: Explainable artificial intelligence (XAI): concepts, taxonomies, opportunities and challenges toward responsible AI. Inf. Fusion **58**, 82–115 (2020)
4. Avati, A., Jung, K., Harman, S., Downing, L., Ng, A., Shah, N.H.: Improving palliative care with deep learning. BMC Med. Inform. Decis. Mak. **18**(4), 55–64 (2018)
5. Bathaee, Y.: The artificial intelligence black box and the failure of intent and causation. Harv. JL Tech. **31**, 889 (2017)
6. Baum, K., Mantel, S., Schmidt, E., Speith, T.: From responsibility to reason-giving explainable artificial intelligence. Philos. Technol. **35**(1), 12 (2022)
7. Biewer, S., et al.: Software doping analysis for human oversight. Formal Methods Syst. Des. (in press)
8. Brunotte, W., Chazette, L., Klös, V., Speith, T.: Quo vadis, explainability? – a research roadmap for explainability engineering. In: Gervasi, V., Vogelsang, A. (eds.) REFSQ 2022. LNCS, vol. 13216, pp. 26–32. Springer, Cham (2022). https://doi.org/10.1007/978-3-030-98464-9_3
9. Buchanan, B.: Artificial intelligence in finance (2019)
10. Chazette, L., Schneider, K.: Explainability as a non-functional requirement: challenges and recommendations. Requir. Eng. **25**(4), 493–514 (2020). https://doi.org/10.1007/s00766-020-00333-1
11. Chen, T.C.T.: Explainable Artificial Intelligence (XAI) in Manufacturing: Methodology, Tools, and Applications. Springer, Cham (2023). https://doi.org/10.1007/978-3-031-27961-4
12. Chromik, M.: Reshape: a framework for interactive explanations in XAI based on shap. In: Proceedings of 18th European Conference on Computer-Supported Cooperative Work. European Society for Socially Embedded Technologies (EUSSET) (2020)
13. Cioffi, R., Travaglioni, M., Piscitelli, G., Petrillo, A., De Felice, F.: Artificial intelligence and machine learning applications in smart production: progress, trends, and directions. Sustainability **12**(2), 492 (2020)
14. Confalonieri, R., et al.: What makes a good explanation? Cognitive dimensions of explaining intelligent machines. In: CogSci, pp. 25–26 (2019)
15. Deeks, A.: The judicial demand for explainable artificial intelligence. Columbia Law Rev. **119**(7), 1829–1850 (2019)
16. Dieber, J., Kirrane, S.: Why model why? Assessing the strengths and limitations of lime. arXiv preprint arXiv:2012.00093 (2020)
17. Doshi-Velez, F., Kim, B.: Towards a rigorous science of interpretable machine learning. arXiv preprint arXiv:1702.08608 (2017)

18. Elstermann, M., Bönsch, J., Kimmig, A., Ovtcharova, J.: Human-centered referential process models for AI application. In: Zimmermann, A., Howlett, R.J., Jain, L.C., Schmidt, R. (eds.) KES-HCIS 2021. SIST, vol. 244, pp. 56–65. Springer, Singapore (2021). https://doi.org/10.1007/978-981-16-3264-8_6
19. Farrow, R.: The possibilities and limits of XAI in education: a socio-technical perspective. Learn. Media Technol. 1–14 (2023)
20. Fiok, K., Farahani, F.V., Karwowski, W., Ahram, T.: Explainable artificial intelligence for education and training. J. Def. Model. Simul. 19(2), 133–144 (2022)
21. Förster, M., Klier, M., Kluge, K., Sigler, I.: Fostering human agency: a process for the design of user-centric XAI systems (2020)
22. Gade, K., Geyik, S.C., Kenthapadi, K., Mithal, V., Taly, A.: Explainable AI in industry. In: Proceedings of the 25th ACM SIGKDD International Conference on Knowledge Discovery & Data Mining, pp. 3203–3204 (2019)
23. Gerlings, J., Shollo, A., Constantiou, I.: Reviewing the need for explainable artificial intelligence (XAI). arXiv preprint arXiv:2012.01007 (2020)
24. Gros, T.P., Groß, J., Wolf, V.: Real-time decision making for a car manufacturing process using deep reinforcement learning. In: 2020 Winter Simulation Conference (WSC), pp. 3032–3044. IEEE (2020)
25. Gunning, D., Aha, D.: Darpa's explainable artificial intelligence (XAI) program. AI Mag. 40(2), 44–58 (2019)
26. Gunning, D., Stefik, M., Choi, J., Miller, T., Stumpf, S., Yang, G.Z.: XAI-explainable artificial intelligence. Sci. Robot. 4(37), eaay7120 (2019)
27. Hagras, H.: Toward human-understandable, explainable AI. Computer 51(9), 28–36 (2018)
28. Hall, M., et al.: A systematic method to understand requirements for explainable AI (XAI) systems. In: Proceedings of the IJCAI Workshop on eXplainable Artificial Intelligence (XAI 2019), Macau, China, vol. 11 (2019)
29. Haque, A.B., Islam, A.N., Mikalef, P.: Explainable artificial intelligence (XAI) from a user perspective: a synthesis of prior literature and problematizing avenues for future research. Technol. Forecast. Soc. Chang. 186, 122120 (2023)
30. Holstein, K., Wortman Vaughan, J., Daumé III, H., Dudik, M., Wallach, H.: Improving fairness in machine learning systems: what do industry practitioners need? In: Proceedings of the 2019 CHI Conference on Human Factors in Computing Systems, pp. 1–16 (2019)
31. Jan, S.T., Ishakian, V., Muthusamy, V.: AI trust in business processes: the need for process-aware explanations. In: Proceedings of the AAAI Conference on Artificial Intelligence, vol. 34, pp. 13403–13404 (2020)
32. Kästner, L., Langer, M., Lazar, V., Schomäcker, A., Speith, T., Sterz, S.: On the relation of trust and explainability: why to engineer for trustworthiness. In: 2021 IEEE 29th International Requirements Engineering Conference Workshops (REW), pp. 169–175. IEEE (2021)
33. Kim, B., Khanna, R., Koyejo, O.O.: Examples are not enough, learn to criticize! criticism for interpretability. In: Lee, D., Sugiyama, M., Luxburg, U., Guyon, I., Garnett, R. (eds.) Advances in Neural Information Processing Systems, vol. 29. Curran Associates, Inc. (2016). https://proceedings.neurips.cc/paper_files/paper/2016/file/5680522b8e2bb01943234bce7bf84534-Paper.pdf
34. Kim, B., Wattenberg, M., Gilmer, J., Cai, C., Wexler, J., Viegas, F., et al.: Interpretability beyond feature attribution: quantitative testing with concept activation vectors (TCAV). In: International Conference on Machine Learning, pp. 2668–2677. PMLR (2018)

35. Köhl, M.A., Baum, K., Bohlender, D., Langer, M., Oster, D., Speith, T.: Explainability as a non-functional requirement. In: Damian, D.E., Perini, A., Lee, S. (eds.) IEEE 27th International Requirements Engineering Conference, Piscataway, NJ, USA, pp. 363–368. IEEE (2019). https://doi.org/10.1109/RE.2019.00046
36. Langer, M., et al.: What do we want from explainable artificial intelligence (XAI)? – a stakeholder perspective on XAI and a conceptual model guiding interdisciplinary XAI research. Artif. Intell. **296**, 1–24 (2021). https://doi.org/10.1016/j.artint.2021.103473
37. Lee, J.D., See, K.A.: Trust in automation: designing for appropriate reliance. Hum. Factors **46**, 50–80 (2004)
38. Liao, Q.V., Varshney, K.R.: Human-centered explainable AI (XAI): from algorithms to user experiences. arXiv preprint arXiv:2110.10790 (2021)
39. Liao, Q.V., Zhang, Y., Luss, R., Doshi-Velez, F., Dhurandhar, A.: Connecting algorithmic research and usage contexts: a perspective of contextualized evaluation for explainable AI. In: Proceedings of the AAAI Conference on Human Computation and Crowdsourcing, vol. 10, pp. 147–159 (2022)
40. Linardatos, P., Papastefanopoulos, V., Kotsiantis, S.: Explainable AI: a review of machine learning interpretability methods. Entropy **23**(1) (2021). https://doi.org/10.3390/e23010018. https://www.mdpi.com/1099-4300/23/1/18
41. Lundberg, S.M., Lee, S.I.: A unified approach to interpreting model predictions. In: Advances in Neural Information Processing Systems, vol. 30 (2017)
42. Machlev, R., Perl, M., Belikov, J., Levy, K.Y., Levron, Y.: Measuring explainability and trustworthiness of power quality disturbances classifiers using XAI-explainable artificial intelligence. IEEE Trans. Industr. Inf. **18**(8), 5127–5137 (2021)
43. Marques-Silva, J., Ignatiev, A.: Delivering trustworthy AI through formal XAI. In: Proceedings of the AAAI Conference on Artificial Intelligence, vol. 36, pp. 12342–12350 (2022)
44. Matthias, A.: The responsibility gap: ascribing responsibility for the actions of learning automata. Ethics Inf. Technol. **6**(3), 175–183 (2004). https://doi.org/10.1007/s10676-004-3422-1
45. Mayer, R.C., Davis, J.H., Schoorman, F.D.: An integrative model of organizational trust. Acad. Manag. Rev. **20**(3), 709–734 (1995)
46. Miller, T.: Explanation in artificial intelligence: insights from the social sciences. Artif. Intell. **267**, 1–38 (2019). https://doi.org/10.1016/j.artint.2018.07.007. https://www.sciencedirect.com/science/article/pii/S0004370218305988
47. Mohankumar, A.K., Nema, P., Narasimhan, S., Khapra, M.M., Srinivasan, B.V., Ravindran, B.: Towards transparent and explainable attention models. In: Proceedings of the 58th Annual Meeting of the Association for Computational Linguistics, pp. 4206–4216 (2020)
48. Ohana, J.J., Ohana, S., Benhamou, E., Saltiel, D., Guez, B.: Explainable AI (XAI) models applied to the multi-agent environment of financial markets. In: Calvaresi, D., Najjar, A., Winikoff, M., Främling, K. (eds.) EXTRAAMAS 2021. LNCS (LNAI), vol. 12688, pp. 189–207. Springer, Cham (2021). https://doi.org/10.1007/978-3-030-82017-6_12
49. Páez, A.: The pragmatic turn in explainable artificial intelligence (XAI). Mind. Mach. **29**(3), 441–459 (2019)
50. Pawar, U., O'Shea, D., Rea, S., O'Reilly, R.: Incorporating explainable artificial intelligence (XAI) to aid the understanding of machine learning in the healthcare domain. In: AICS, pp. 169–180 (2020)
51. Preece, A., Harborne, D., Braines, D., Tomsett, R., Chakraborty, S.: Stakeholders in explainable AI. arXiv preprint arXiv:1810.00184 (2018)

52. Ribeiro, M.T., Singh, S., Guestrin, C.: "Why should i trust you?" Explaining the predictions of any classifier. In: Proceedings of the 22nd ACM SIGKDD International Conference on Knowledge Discovery and Data Mining, pp. 1135–1144 (2016)
53. Rong, Y., et al.: Towards human-centered explainable AI: user studies for model explanations. arXiv preprint arXiv:2210.11584 (2022)
54. Saeed, W., Omlin, C.: Explainable AI (XAI): a systematic meta-survey of current challenges and future opportunities. Knowl.-Based Syst. **263**, 110273 (2023). https://doi.org/10.1016/j.knosys.2023.110273. https://www.sciencedirect.com/science/article/pii/S0950705123000230
55. Schlicker, N., Uhde, A., Baum, K., Hirsch, M.C., Langer, M.: Calibrated trust as a result of accurate trustworthiness assessment-introducing the trustworthiness assessment model (2022)
56. Schraagen, J.M., Elsasser, P., Fricke, H., Hof, M., Ragalmuto, F.: Trusting the X in XAI: effects of different types of explanations by a self-driving car on trust, explanation satisfaction and mental models. In: Proceedings of the Human Factors and Ergonomics Society Annual Meeting, vol. 64, pp. 339–343. SAGE Publications Sage CA, Los Angeles (2020)
57. Santoni de Sio, F., Mecacci, G.: Four responsibility gaps with artificial intelligence: why they matter and how to address them. Philos. Technol. **34**, 1057–1084 (2021)
58. Sokol, K., Flach, P.: Explainability fact sheets: a framework for systematic assessment of explainable approaches. In: Proceedings of the 2020 Conference on Fairness, Accountability, and Transparency, pp. 56–67 (2020)
59. Speith, T.: A review of taxonomies of explainable artificial intelligence (XAI) methods. In: Proceedings of the 2022 ACM Conference on Fairness, Accountability, and Ransparency, FAccT 2022, pp. 2239–2250. Association for Computing Machinery, New York (2022). https://doi.org/10.1145/3531146.3534639
60. Sterz, S., Baum, K., Lauber-Rönsberg, A., Hermanns, H.: Towards perspicuity requirements. In: 2021 IEEE 29th International Requirements Engineering Conference Workshops (REW), pp. 159–163. IEEE (2021)
61. Tomsett, R., Braines, D., Harborne, D., Preece, A., Chakraborty, S.: Interpretable to whom? A role-based model for analyzing interpretable machine learning systems. arXiv preprint arXiv:1806.07552 (2018)
62. Verhagen, R.S., Neerincx, M.A., Tielman, M.L.: A two-dimensional explanation framework to classify AI as incomprehensible, interpretable, or understandable. In: Calvaresi, D., Najjar, A., Winikoff, M., Främling, K. (eds.) EXTRAAMAS 2021. LNCS (LNAI), vol. 12688, pp. 119–138. Springer, Cham (2021). https://doi.org/10.1007/978-3-030-82017-6_8
63. Wachter, S., Mittelstadt, B., Russell, C.: Counterfactual explanations without opening the black box: automated decisions and the GDPR. Harv. JL Tech. **31**, 841 (2017)
64. Warren, G., Keane, M.T., Byrne, R.M.: Features of explainability: how users understand counterfactual and causal explanations for categorical and continuous features in XAI. arXiv preprint arXiv:2204.10152 (2022)
65. Xu, F., Uszkoreit, H., Du, Y., Fan, W., Zhao, D., Zhu, J.: Explainable AI: a brief survey on history, research areas, approaches and challenges. In: Tang, J., Kan, M.-Y., Zhao, D., Li, S., Zan, H. (eds.) NLPCC 2019. LNCS (LNAI), vol. 11839, pp. 563–574. Springer, Cham (2019). https://doi.org/10.1007/978-3-030-32236-6_51

Perlocution vs Illocution: How Different Interpretations of the Act of Explaining Impact on the Evaluation of Explanations and XAI

Francesco Sovrano[1,2]([✉]) [iD] and Fabio Vitali[1] [iD]

[1] Department of Computer Science, University of Bologna, Bologna, Italy
francesco.sovrano@uzh.ch
[2] Department of Informatics, University of Zurich, Zurich, Switzerland

Abstract. This article discusses the concepts of illocutionary, perlocutionary, and locutionary acts, and their role in understanding explanations. Illocutionary acts concern the speaker's intended meaning, perlocutionary acts refer to the listener's reaction, and locutionary acts are about the speech act itself. We suggest a new way to categorise established definitions of explanation based on these speech act principles. This method enhances our grasp of how explanations work. We found that if you define explanation as a perlocutionary act, it requires subjective judgements. This makes it hard to assess an explanation objectively before the listener receives it. On the other hand, we claim that existing legal systems prefer explanations based on illocutionary acts. We propose that the exact meaning of explanation depends on the situation. Some kinds of definitions suit specific circumstances better. For example, in educational settings, a perlocutionary approach often works best, while legal settings call for an illocutionary approach. Additionally, we show how current measures of explainability can be grouped based on their theoretical support and the speech act they rely on. This categorisation helps us pinpoint which measures are best for assessing the results of Explainable AI (XAI) tools in legal or other settings. In simpler terms, we are explaining how to evaluate and improve XAI and explanations in different situations, such as in education and law. By understanding where and when to apply different explainability measures, we can make better and more specialised XAI tools. This will lead to significant improvements in AI explainability.

Keywords: Theories of explanation · Speech act theory · Evaluation of explanations · Explanations in law

1 Introduction

Explanations are essential in various fields, such as philosophy, cognitive science, Artificial Intelligence (AI), and law, as they facilitate understanding and promote effective communication. However, the absence of a universally agreed-upon

L. Longo (Ed.): xAI 2023, CCIS 1901, pp. 25–47, 2023.
https://doi.org/10.1007/978-3-031-44064-9_2

definition of explanations poses a significant challenge [50]. One field that highlights the importance of explanations is Explainable Artificial Intelligence (XAI), which focuses on developing explainable AI systems. In XAI, explanations often focus on causality [3,6,64], providing insight into how the AI system arrived at a particular decision or recommendation. The goal is to improve transparency and trust in AI systems, making them more accessible to users.

On the other hand, cognitive science employs explanations not just to address perceived gaps in mental models [27], but to better understand and analyse the underlying cognitive processes that enable individuals to form and manipulate their mental models of the world [29]. These mental models, representations of external reality, play a significant role in cognition, reasoning, and decision-making[1] [16,17]. In contrast, legal contexts prioritise providing sufficient information while adhering to regulations. In these contexts, explanations aim to meet legal requirements while ensuring that the information is properly structured, accessible and understandable to all parties involved [7,21,50].

The lack of a universally accepted definition of explanations raises questions about the applicability of a single definition to various domains [12,38]. Different fields have varying perspectives on explanations, with each field emphasising different aspects of explanations. As such, it may be necessary to adopt distinct definitions of explanations in different contexts, but without a clear understanding of which definition may apply, it is difficult to practically assess the quality of XAI and explanations.

In this paper, we suggest that understanding the distinctions between illocutionary, perlocutionary, and locutionary acts is crucial for understanding explanations and how to evaluate them in different contexts (e.g., education, law).

These speech acts are key in evaluating explanations and influence how explanations are generated, received, and assessed by different audiences. So, by examining the relationship between speech act principles and various types of explanations, we aim to provide a more comprehensive understanding of the explanation process in different contexts, especially in XAI.

In particular, our paper discusses how current explainability measures can be categorised based on the speech act they rely on. This categorisation helps us identify which measures are best suited for evaluating the results of XAI tools and explanations in various settings, such as legal and educational contexts. We show that certain explainability metrics are more suitable than others when it comes to evaluating the legal compliance of XAI outputs. Eventually, by understanding where and when to apply different explainability measures, one can create more effective and specialised XAI tools.

In summary, this paper contributes valuable insights into the nature and evaluation of explanations, also in the XAI field. It provides a novel perspective on the nature of explanations, discusses practical tools for evaluating and comparing different kinds of explanations, and underscores the role of context in shaping explanation definitions. Ultimately, the findings and contributions

---

[1] The exact mechanisms and implications of mental models in various aspects of cognition and decision-making are still areas of active investigation.

of this study will have practical implications for researchers, practitioners, and decision-makers in the wider XAI community.

This paper is organised as follows. First, in Sect. 2, previous research on explanations is reviewed. Next, Sect. 3 provides background information on speech act theory and explains the concepts of illocutionary, perlocutionary, and locutionary acts. It also provides insights into explanations in different contexts, such as European law. Section 4 presents a classification of established explanation theories based on illocution, perlocution, and locution. The section highlights the unique characteristics of each category. In Sect. 5, the context-dependent nature of explanation definitions is discussed, emphasising the importance of adaptable approaches in different settings. Section 6 explores the impact of speech acts on the evaluation of explanations. The section discusses how illocutionary, perlocutionary, and locutionary acts can affect the assessment process. To discuss and exemplify the analytical results presented in the previous sections, Sect. 7 delves into the findings and observations derived from the study of two real-world XAI systems: a heart disease predictor and a credit approval system. These systems are examined using various explanation evaluation metrics and analysed through speech acts. Finally, Sect. 8 summarises the main findings and suggests possible avenues for future research and improvements in the understanding and development of explanations across diverse domains.

2 Related Work

The concept of speech acts, which originated from Austin's work [5] and was further developed by Searle [48], has significantly influenced the understanding of explanations and explainability across various fields. Achinstein's Ordinary Language Philosophy [1] applies speech act theory to philosophical theories of explanation, emphasising explanations as illocutionary acts that concentrate on communicative and linguistic aspects. Our work not only takes into account the illocutionary perspective, but also extends this view by comparing and contrasting it with perlocutionary acts, analysing their implications for the evaluation of explanations.

The literature contains numerous categorisations of explanations, including those based on the mechanisms to achieve explainability, as presented in [2,4, 20,50,66]. These surveys explore different aspects of explainability techniques; some focus on the notion of explanation and the type of black-box system, like [20], while others, such as [66], centre on metrics to quantify the quality of explanation methods. Although these classifications provide valuable insights, our work offers a unique perspective by examining explanations through the lens of speech acts. Specifically, we focus on the distinctions between illocutionary and perlocutionary acts and their implications for the evaluation of explanations.

Our work builds upon, extends, and aligns closely with [50] in terms of its focus on the notion of explainability. Like their approach, we recognise the existence of multiple definitions of explainability, each potentially requiring its own unique set of metrics. This acknowledgement of diversity in explainability concepts enhances our understanding of the various aspects involved in the evaluation and interpretation of explanations. However, unlike [50], we further explore the application of speech acts in the context of explanations, concentrating on the distinctions between illocutionary and perlocutionary acts and their relationship to the evaluation of explanations, suggesting that the nature and definition of explanations may be context-dependent.

Our paper emphasises the importance of context and the distinction between perlocutionary and illocutionary acts, arguing that different situations necessitate different types of explanations. This approach aligns with the pluralist perspective presented in [12], which supports the idea of multiple concepts of explanation. While our paper categorises existing explanation definitions using speech act concepts and focuses on the implications of these distinctions for various domains, Colombo [12] delves into the philosophy and psychology of explanation, drawing on experimental philosophy and advocating for pluralism based on results from psychology and philosophy.

In summary, our work sets itself apart from related research by offering a comprehensive analysis of speech acts in the context of explanations and explainability, particularly focusing on the comparison of illocutionary and perlocutionary acts. We investigate their relationships with various philosophical theories of explanation and present a novel perspective that can inform the design and evaluation of explainable AI systems.

3 Background

The study of explanations spans various disciplines, including philosophy, cognitive science, artificial intelligence, and law. However, there is no consensus on a shared definition of explanation, with different fields emphasising different aspects. To better understand explanations, it is essential to explore the perspectives on the nature of explanations across different domains. This section provides background information on speech act theory, European law, and other contexts where explanations are commonly used.

3.1 Speech Act Theory: Illocution, Perlocution, and Locution

Speech Act Theory is a branch of pragmatics that aims to explain how people use language to perform actions in the world. According to this theory, when people use language, they not only convey information, but also perform actions such as making requests, giving orders, or making promises. These actions are known as speech acts, and they can have different effects on the listener depending on the context and the speaker's intention.

In the 1950s and 1960s, philosophers J.L. Austin [5] and John Searle [48] developed Speech Act Theory as a way to understand the complex nature of language use. Their work highlights the importance of considering the intention and context behind language use, rather than simply focusing on the literal meaning of words.

Speech Act Theory is essential for understanding communication because it provides a framework for analysing the various ways in which language is used to perform actions in the world. By considering the speaker's intention, the listener's interpretation, and the context in which a speech act is performed, Speech Act Theory enables a more nuanced understanding of communication. This deeper understanding can lead to better comprehension of how language is used in various domains, such as law, education, and XAI. Illocutionary, perlocutionary, and locutionary acts are key components of speech acts:

- **Illocutionary acts** refer to the speaker's intended meaning or purpose behind a speech act. For example, when someone says 'I promise to be there at 7 pm', they are performing the illocutionary act of making a promise.
- **Perlocutionary acts** pertain to the effect that a speech act has on the listener. Perlocutionary acts are the actual effects of a speech act, which can vary depending on the listener's interpretation, expectations, and context. For instance, if the listener believes the speaker is not trustworthy, the perlocutionary effect of the promise may be scepticism or doubt.
- **Locutionary acts** involve the actual words and sentences used in a speech act. For example, the locutionary act of the sentence 'I promise to be there at 7 pm' is the act of producing that particular string of words.

In everyday communication, one can easily find examples of illocutionary, perlocutionary, and locutionary acts. For instance, consider the scenario where a teacher says, 'Please open your textbooks to page 42'. Here, the illocutionary act is the teacher's intention to request that the students turn to a specific page in their textbooks. This act can differ from the literal meaning of the words spoken. Other examples of illocutionary acts include utterances such as:

- 'Can you please close the window?' (request),
- 'I would like to buy this dress' (proposal),
- and 'I forbid you to leave the house' (prohibition).

On the other hand, the perlocutionary act occurs when the students respond to the teacher's request by opening their textbooks to page 42. Examples of perlocutionary acts include expressions such as:

- 'Thank you for your help' (the listener feels appreciated),
- 'You're fired' (the listener feels upset),
- and 'I'm sorry for your loss' (the listener feels comforted).

Finally, the locutionary act is the teacher's actual utterance of the sentence, 'Please open your textbooks to page 42'. Other examples of locutionary acts include phrases like:

- 'The sky is blue',
- 'I am hungry',
- and 'The book is on the table'.

Understanding the differences between these three types of acts can help us gain a deeper understanding of language and its roles in communication. By analysing and interpreting how language is used to convey meaning and perform actions, we can refine our comprehension of communication across various domains and situations.

3.2 Explaining Automated Decision-Making: Regulatory Landscape and Challenges

Automated decision-making systems have become increasingly common, impacting various aspects of our lives. As a result, regulatory frameworks have emerged to ensure transparency, fairness, and accountability in these systems. This section discusses the right to explanation in the General Data Protection Regulation (GDPR)[2], the proposed AI Act[3], and the Platform-to-Business (P2B) Regulation[4], focusing on the challenges and opportunities they present for explaining automated decision-making systems.

The Right to Explanation in the GDPR. The GDPR introduced the *right to explanation*, allowing individuals to obtain explanations when their legal status is affected by a solely automated decision-making process. The GDPR outlines two types of explanations: *ex-ante* and *ex-post*. Minimal explanations required under the GDPR include causal, descriptive, and justificatory explanations [56]. While it is unclear whether user-centred personalized explanations are required, the GDPR mandates that data controllers provide 'meaningful information about the logic involved' in an automated decision. The Think Tank of the European Parliament suggests that a reasonable explanation should possess various qualities, including intelligibility and understandability [13].

The Proposed AI Act and its Role in Explainability. The proposed AI Act seeks to address the risks posed by AI systems by setting new obligations to ensure transparency, lawfulness, and fairness for high-risk AI systems listed in Annex IV. It aims to establish mechanisms to ensure quality throughout the AI system's life cycle while preserving fundamental rights and values. The AI Act promotes user-empowering and compliance-oriented explainability, enabling users to understand the AI system's operation and helping verify compliance with the many obligations set by the AI Act [51].

According to [51], user-empowering explainability is related to human oversight design obligations, while compliance-oriented explainability is evident in the technical documentation required by Article 11. The AI Act aims to minimize potential harmfulness through these explainability measures.

Transparency and Fairness in the P2B Regulation. The aim of the P2B Regulation is to address imbalances between online platforms and businesses by ensuring transparency in their terms and conditions. According to Article 5 of the 2019/1150 P2B Regulation, online marketplaces are required to provide explanations about the main parameters that determine the ranking of products and the reasons for their relative importance [21].

To meet these requirements, online marketplaces must provide easily accessible, up-to-date explanations in plain and intelligible language. If the possibility exists for any direct or indirect remuneration to influence ranking, providers must describe those possibilities and their effects on ranking. The explanations should help business and corporate website users understand how the ranking mechanism takes into account the characteristics of goods and services, their relevance to consumers, and website design characteristics. However, providers are not required to disclose algorithms or information that could enable consumer harm or deception.

3.3 Explaining as Answering Questions in XAI and Computer Science

Computer science, through XAI, has long studied the topic of explanations and how to generate them (e.g., for explaining complex software computations, for law compliance), frequently drawing from philosophy and social sciences [39]. Two distinct types of explainability are predominant in the literature of XAI: rule-based and case-based. Rule-based explainability is when explainable information is a set of formal logical rules describing information related to cause and effects. For example, the inner logic of a model, its causal chain, how it behaves, why that output gave the input, and what would happen if the input were different. While case-based explainability is when the explainable information is a set of input-output examples (or counter-examples) meant to give an intuition of the model's behaviour. For example, counterfactuals, contrastive explanations, or prototypes[5].

The idea of answering questions as explaining is familiar to XAI and compatible with everyone's intuition of what constitutes an explanation. In fact, despite the different types of explainability one can choose, it is always possible to frame the information provided by explainability with one or (sometimes) more questions. In particular, it is common to many works in the field [14,19,30,34,37,39,43,44,62] the use of generic (e.g., **why**, **who**, **how**, **when**) or more punctual questions to clearly define and describe the characteristics of explainability [32]. For example, Lundberg et al. [36] assert that the local explanations produced by their TreeSHAP (a XAI algorithm for estimating the importance of features as input to an AI model) might enable 'agents to predict **why** the customer they are calling is likely to leave' or 'help human experts understand **why** the model made a specific recommendation for high-risk decisions'.

---

[5] Prototypes are instances of the ground-truth considered similar to a specific input-output for which the similarity explains the model's behaviour.

Similarly, Dhurandhar et al. [14] state that they designed the Contrastive Explanation Method (CEM; a XAI algorithm for the generation of counterfactuals and other contrastive explanations) to answer the question 'why is input x classified in class y?'.

Several authors [19,34,39], analysing XAI literature, were able to hypothesise that a good explanation, about an automated decision-maker, answers at least the following questions:

- What did the system do?
- Why did the system do P?
- Why did the system not do X?
- What would the system do if Y happens?,
- How can one get the system to do Z, given the current context?
- What information does the system contain?

In particular, from a preliminary analysis, it appears that most classical XAI algorithms focus more on the production of explainable software and explanations that generally follow a one-size-fits-all approach, answering one (or sometimes a few) predefined questions well. However, one-size-fits-all explanations tend to lack user-centrality, usually failing to answer all the questions an explainee might have. This is also suggested by Liao et al. [33], who show that no single XAI seems to be able to cover all identified user needs and that various XAI algorithms may be needed to explain a system better. Indeed, users' needs in terms of explainability are multiple and challenging to capture [32], e.g., they may concern terminology, system performance, system outputs, and inputs.

3.4   Explanations in Education and Pedagogy

Explanations play a crucial role in education and pedagogy, contributing to effective teaching and learning, pedagogical practice, and understanding human behaviour and mental processes. Designing intelligent agents capable of providing explanations to people can draw upon models of how humans explain decisions and behaviour to each other, as the primary function of explanation is to facilitate learning [35,39,65]. Heider [22] suggests that people seek explanations to enhance their understanding of someone or something, developing stable models for prediction and control. Research supports this hypothesis, indicating that people tend to inquire about events or observations they consider abnormal or unexpected from their perspective [24,25,39].

Incorporating the principles of learner-centred education (LCE), promoted by UNICEF[6], can help create effective explanations that facilitate learners' understanding of complex concepts, ideas, and theories [18,58]. These explanations must be well-crafted, engaging, and tailored to learners' understanding and learning objectives, as LCE requires a high level of active control from learners over the content and process of learning [47]. Pedagogical practice involves

---

[6] https://www.unicef.org/esa/sites/unicef.org.esa/files/2019-08/
ThinkPiece_9_LearnerCentredEducation.pdf.

designing and implementing learning experiences that enable the acquisition of knowledge, skills, and attitudes while considering learners' needs, capacities, and interests [8]. Aligning learning objectives and explanations with LCE principles enables educators to create more personalised and meaningful learning experiences, empowering learners to actively engage in their education.

Crafting effective explanations in education and pedagogy can be challenging due to the need to adapt explanations to the person's understanding and the concepts being explained. However, advances in technology, such as multimedia and interactive tools, offer opportunities for delivering engaging and interactive explanations. Interdisciplinary collaborations can lead to innovative approaches for explaining complex concepts, ideas, and theories. Additionally, effective explanations can foster critical thinking, creativity, and problem-solving skills, promoting deeper understanding and lifelong learning.

4   An Explained Classification of Theories of Explanations in Terms of Illocution, Perlocution, and Locution

In this section, we provide an overview of various theories of explanation and explainability, highlighting key philosophical perspectives that shape our understanding of these concepts. Understanding the nature of explanations and explainable information is crucial for measuring explainability effectively.

In 1984, Hempel and Oppenheim published their 'Studies in the Logic of Explanation' [23], giving rise to what is considered the first theory of explanation: the deductive-nomological model. After this work, many modified, extended, or replaced this model, which was considered fatally flawed [9,46]. Indeed, Hempel's epistemic theory of explanations is not empiricist: it is concerned (mistakenly) only with logical form, so an explanation can be such regardless of the actual processes and entities conceptually required to understand it. Several more modern and competing theories of explanation have been the result of this criticism [38]. For example, Salmon's realist theory [46], called Causal Realism, emphasises that actual processes and entities are conceptually necessary to understand precisely why an explanation works. Instead, the Constructive Empiricism of Van Fraassen [59] relies more on a Bayesian interpretation of probability, framing explanation as a creative process of building models that are likely true.

In contrast to these theoretical and primarily scientific approaches, other philosophers have favoured a theory of explanation that is more grounded in how people perform explanations [38]. For example, Achinstein's theory [1], based on Ordinary Language Philosophy, emphasises the communicative or linguistic aspect of an explanation and its usefulness in answering questions and fostering understanding between individuals. The theory of Holland et al. [27] instead, based on Cognitive Science, frames the process of explaining as a purely cognitive activity and explanations as a certain kind of mental representation. Conversely, Sellars [49] suggests a different way of thinking about the epistemic meaning of the explanatory act, making it more of a utilitarian process of constructing a coherent belief system.

In particular, Hempel's, Salmon's, and Van Fraassen's theories frame the act of explaining more as a *locutionary act* [5], whereby an explanation is such because it utters something about causality. Differently, Achinstein's theory explicitly frames explaining as an *illocutionary act* [5] so that an explanation is such because of the intention to explain. The theories of Holland and Sellars, on the other hand, frame explaining more as a *perlocutionary act* [5], thus with an explanation being such because of the effects it produces in the interlocutor. For more details about locution, illocution and perlocution read Sect. 3.1.

Table 1. Philosophical definitions of explanation and explainable information.(This table extends a similar one in [50].) In this table, we summarise the definitions of *explanation* for each one of the identified theories of explanations. We also indicate which *speech act* they mostly refer to.

Theory	Definition of Explanation	Speech Act
Causal Realism	Descriptions of causality, expressed as chains of causes and effects.	Locution
Constructive Empiricism	Contrastive information that answers why questions, allowing one to calculate the probability of a particular event relative to a set of (possibly subjective) background assumptions.	Locution
Ordinary Language Philosophy	Answers to questions (not just why ones) given with the explicit intent of producing understanding in someone, i.e., the result of an illocutionary act.	Illocution
Cognitive Science	Mental representations resulting from a cognitive activity. They are information which fixes failures in someone's mental model.	Perlocution
Naturalism and Scientific Realism	Information which increases the coherence of someone's belief system, resulting from an iterative process of confirmation of truths aimed at improving understanding.	Perlocution

Thus, each of these theories devises different definitions of explanation and explainability, sometimes in a complementary way. A summary of these definitions is shown in Table 1, shedding light on the fact that there is no complete agreement on the nature of explanations. Nevertheless, according to [38], fundamental disagreements on the nature of explanations are just of two types, metaphysical and meta-philosophical, and mainly unrelated to their *logical* and *cognitive* structure. This gives room to understandings of 'explanations' that may be complementary, some focusing more on cognition and others on logic.

We observe that when explaining is not considered a locutionary act and thus it must satisfy someone's needs, explainability differs from explaining. Indeed, pragmatically satisfying someone (e.g., user-centrality) is achieved when explanations are designed for a specific person or audience. This implies that the same explainable pieces of information can be presented and re-elaborated differently across different individuals as different explanations. The type and order of explainable information matter and directly impact the quality of the resulting explanations. In simpler terms, not every combination of explainable information qualifies as an explanation according to illocutionary and perlocutionary theories.

The distinction between illocutionary and perlocutionary explainability lies in the explainer's intent and its impact on the explainee. Illocutionary explanations, as in Ordinary Language Philosophy, focus on the explainer's intention to create understanding in someone. For instance, in Ordinary Language Philosophy, an 'explanation' is used to answer questions about pertinent aspects, intending (i.e., illocution) to generate understanding in someone. On the other hand, perlocutionary explanations, as in Cognitive Science, emphasise the actual effects explanations have on explainees. In short, illocutionary explanations aim for a perlocutionary effect, but the intention doesn't always guarantee the desired outcome. Although Ordinary Language Philosophy highlights user-centrality, it doesn't focus on the user as much as Cognitive Science or other theories that treat explanations as perlocutionary acts.

When designing explainable systems from a prescriptive perspective, it is important to align illocutionary and perlocutionary explainability more closely. Designers should create systems that not only intend to provide meaningful explanations but also effectively achieve the desired impact on users. However, it is crucial to recognise that the explainer's intention may not always lead to the desired effect on the explainee. By considering both illocutionary and perlocutionary aspects, AI researchers and practitioners can develop more adaptable and user-centred systems, addressing the diverse needs and expectations of users.

5   Exploring the Contextual Nature of Explanations

To fully grasp the nature of explanations, it is important to understand not only their philosophical underpinnings but also the influence of the different kinds of speech acts on them. The distinctions between these speech acts have a significant impact on the evaluation of explanations, as they determine what is considered a valid or effective explanation in various scenarios. In this section, we will explore the nuances of these speech acts in different contexts, such as legal, educational, and XAI settings, and highlight the importance of tailoring explanations to better align with the specific needs and requirements of the domain or audience.

As discussed in Sect. 3.2, explanations in the legal context have a more justificatory connotation [50, 56]. They must be clear but do not necessarily need to be personalised for a child or different types of people (e.g., those who do not speak the official language). The essential aspect is that the necessary information to understand (for instance) the logic of an AI model is present and expressed in a common language that is easily understandable according to the law [61].

Conversely, in the educational context (cf. Sect. 3.4), an explanation is considered valid when it has an effect on the person. Thus, an 'explanation' may be suitable for an adult but not for a 3-year-old child. Therefore, it is not possible to explain Einstein's general relativity to a 3-year-old child in the same way it would be done with an undergraduate physics student or a high school student.

In general, in XAI (cf. Sect. 3.3), an explanation is considered valid when it reveals something about a black-box. Although it may not be user-centred (and therefore not optimal), it remains an explanation because it clarifies an aspect (any) of the black box. Consequently, this type of explanation is accepted regardless of its effects on the person or its ability to answer as many (archetypal) questions as possible.

Thus, in the three different contexts mentioned above, three different speech acts and therefore different definitions of explanation are applied. For laws, an illocutionary sense is used; for education, a perlocutionary sense is applied, while for XAI, a locutionary sense is adopted.

However, this does not imply that explanations in the context of law or XAI cannot have a perlocutionary effect. For instance, one notable sub-field of XAI, called Human-Centred XAI [33], focuses on developing tools that offer customised explanations to meet users' requirements. Therefore, the distinction lies not in the absence of perlocutionary explanations in XAI, but rather in the minimum act required for information to qualify as an explanation. For XAI, a locutionary act is sufficient, while the law necessitates an illocutionary act, and education and similar domains call for perlocutionary acts.

We observe a complexity hierarchy among the different explanatory acts. The occurrence of a locutionary act is necessary for the performance of an illocutionary act, and both of these acts can be crucial for the realisation of a perlocutionary act. In particular, the locutionary act can be better associated with the production of explainable information, while the other two acts can be better associated with the production of explanations. In the case of illocutionary acts, these explanations should aim to be useful for a majority of people by addressing a wide range of questions (cf. Sect. 4). On the other hand, perlocutionary acts should strive to be effective for a specific individual, tailored to their needs.

Based on the classification reported in Sect. 4, we find that different definitions of explanations are applicable to different contexts. Indeed, the definitions from Cognitive Science and Naturalism seem to align better with education and pedagogy, as they are perlocutionary. In contrast, the definition taken from Ordinary Language Philosophy is illocutionary and aligns better with the law (as suggested also by [50]). Meanwhile, the definitions from the remaining theories align more with most XAI practices, which often involve designing systems that provide understandable insights into their decision-making processes, answering well only one or few specific questions.

In essence, the definition of explanation depends on the context and the type of speech act that is deemed sufficient for a satisfactory explanation. Consequently, the evaluation criteria which can be used to assess the quality of explanations and XAI tools cannot be independent from the context, particularly in situations where adherence to the law is critical.

In the subsequent section, we will present a methodology to establish a connection between evaluation metrics for explanations and philosophical theories, and thereby, speech acts. Subsequently, in Sect. 7, we will engage in a comprehensive discussion of our findings and their implications for the evaluation of XAI.

6 Linking of Explanation Evaluation Metrics to Philosophical Theories

In this section, we explore the alignment of various explainability metrics with philosophical theories to provide a comprehensive understanding of their applicability across different needs and interpretations of explainability. We have reviewed the literature and selected a diverse range of metrics applicable to various types of explanations, including ex-ante and ex-post explanations. Our selection is based on their relevance, novelty, and applicability in the context of XAI.

We established a **method for correlating explanation metrics with the respective philosophical theories** that underpin them. This method hinges on the assumptions and viewpoints that guide the design and interpretation of each metric. Specifically, it involves the following steps:

1. **Determining the metric's goal**: First, we need to ascertain the objective of the metric. It could be to assess the quality of explanations, the fidelity of the model, the user satisfaction, or some other facet of explainability.
2. **Exploring the metric's methodology**: Next, we examine the strategy the metric adopts towards explainability. For instance, does it attempt to quantify causal relationships, or does it focus on user cognitive processes? Does it strive to build likely accurate models or emphasise the communicative aspects of the explanation?
3. **Associating the metric with the relevant philosophical theory**: Based on the metric's goal and methodology, we can then link it to the suitable philosophical theory. This includes:
   - Linking the metric to *Causal Realism* if it aims to quantify causal relationships.
   - Associating it with *Cognitive Science, Naturalism, and Scientific Realism* if it centres on cognitive processes and user understanding.
   - Relating it to *Constructive Empiricism* if it prioritises the development of likely accurate models.
   - Connecting it to *Ordinary Language Philosophy* if it focuses on the linguistic or communicative facets of explanation.

Table 2. Comparing Explainability Metrics(This table extends a similar one in [50].). The column labelled 'Source' provides references to the papers, while the 'Metrics' column lists the names of the metrics mentioned in the papers. The 'Subject-based' column indicates whether the metrics require subjective feedback from human subjects. Bold elements denote the best values within each column. Additional information includes what explanations are considered by the metric (e.g., rules) and the *Supporting Theory* of the metric, which refers to the philosophical theory that underlies the metric (e.g., Cognitive Science, Constructive Empiricism).

Source	Explanations are:	Closest Supporting Theory	Subject based	Metrics
[45]	Rules	Causal Realism	No	Performance Difference, Number of Rules, Number of Features, Stability
[60]	Rules	Causal Realism	No	Fidelity, Completeness
[31]	Rules	Causal Realism	No	Fidelity, Unambiguity, Interpretability, Interactivity
[28]	**Any text or image**	Causal Realism, Cognitive Science, Naturalism & Co.	Yes	System Causability Scale
[26]	**Any text or image**	Cognitive Science, Naturalism & Co.	Yes	Satisfaction, Trust, Mental Models, Curiosity, Performance
[15,40] [57,63] [10,42]	**Any text or image**	Cognitive Science, Naturalism & Co.	Yes	Usability: Effectiveness, Efficiency, Satisfaction
[41]	Contrastive Examples	Constructive Empiricism	No	Non-Representativeness, Diversity
[55]	**Any Natural Language Text**	Ordinary Language Philosophy	No	Degree of Explainability

Table 2 presents an overview of the metrics and their associated philosophical theories, which encompass Causal Realism, Cognitive Science, Naturalism, Scientific Realism, Constructive Empiricism, and Ordinary Language Philosophy. The sources of these metrics include recent papers that propose novel explainability metrics or evaluate existing ones. We discuss each metric in more detail below.

[45] introduce objective metrics to quantify explainability. It argues that many explanations are generated post-hoc, resulting in limited meaning due to their lack of transparency and fidelity. To address this issue, the paper proposes four metrics: Performance Difference between the explanation's logic and the agent's actual performance, Number of Rules outputted by the explanation, Number of Features used to generate the explanation, and Stability of the explanation. These metrics are grounded in Causal Realism as they focus on quantifying the causal relationships between variables to provide more meaningful explanations, emphasising the necessity of actual processes and entities for understanding.

[60] introduce a novel comparative approach to evaluate and compare rule sets produced by post-hoc rule extractors using six quantitative metrics. The goal is to identify superior methods capable of successfully modelling explainability. This work is connected to Causal Realism, as it assumes that an explanation can be evaluated in terms of how it discloses causal relationships between input and output, representing them as a set of inference rules that explain the underlying causal mechanisms of the system, taking into account the actual processes and entities required for understanding.

The metrics proposed by [31] for quantifying fidelity, ambiguity, and interpretability can be seen as aligned with Causal Realism because they are designed for evaluating the quality of compact decision sets that explain the black box model.

[28] propose the System Causability Scale, which combines aspects of causality, mental representations, and iterative understanding improvement. System Causability Scale is aligned to Causal Realism, Cognitive Science, and Naturalism and Scientific Realism theories. That is because this metric evaluates explanations in terms of their capacity to represent causal relationships, align with mental models, and facilitate the user's understanding of the underlying system, emphasising the importance of actual processes, entities, and cognitive aspects in creating meaningful explanations.

[26] propose Satisfaction, Trust, Mental Models, Curiosity, and Performance metrics, grounded in Cognitive Science, Naturalism and Scientific Realism theories. It focuses on the cognitive aspects of explanations and their impact on users' understanding and behaviour. These metrics assess how well explanations address user expectations, foster trust, align with mental models, stimulate curiosity, and improve overall performance, taking into account the cognitive processes involved in understanding and explaining.

[10, 15, 40, 42, 57, 63] propose usability metrics, such as Effectiveness, Efficiency, and Satisfaction connected to Cognitive Science, Naturalism and Scientific Realism theories. These metrics evaluate explanations from the perspective of users' cognitive processes and their overall experience with the system, assessing the quality of the explanations in terms of their utility, ease of use, and user satisfaction, emphasising the role of cognitive aspects in understanding and engaging with explanations.

[41] propose two metrics for example-based contrastive or counterfactual explanations: Non-Representativeness and Diversity. Non-Representativeness is a measure of fidelity of the explanation, and high non-representativeness can indicate factual inaccuracy. Diversity, on the other hand, is used to demonstrate the degree of integration of the explanation by measuring the spread of examples in the input space. These metrics align with Constructive Empiricism as they aim to quantify how likely is a contrastive explanation to explain something accurately. By monitoring the fidelity and diversity of the examples provided by the explanation method, they assess the quality of the explanation generated by the model in terms of its representativeness and variety.

[53,55] present a novel model-agnostic metric called Degree of Explainability, which objectively measures the explainability of correct information within complex systems. The metric is explicitly based on Achinstein's Theory of Explanations from Ordinary Language Philosophy, and it leverages deep language models for knowledge graph extraction and information retrieval.

Our analysis shows that most tools for evaluating XAI software align with causal realism and constructive empiricism, while tools for evaluating explanatory user interfaces are more aligned with the interpretation from Cognitive Science. In general, as shown in Table 2, theories such as Cognitive Science that define explanations as perlocutionary acts require an evaluation of the explanation that is inseparable from the user's opinion or subjective outcome, as the explanation is valid when it produces an effect on the user.

On the other hand, illocutionary definitions based on Ordinary Language Philosophy do not bind the explanation to the user's effects and therefore allow for a more objective evaluation in line with the law's requirements. Similarly, locutionary definitions do not require subjective evaluations but also do not require the explanatory tool (for example, an XAI) to answer as many questions as possible in a cohesive and coherent manner. It is sufficient that they correctly explain what is causing something, even if such explanation does not provide an in-depth understanding of the explanandum.

7   Findings and Discussion

This section synthesises the insights gathered in Sects. 6 and 5, analysing their practical implications for the actual evaluation of XAI systems. Our focus is on two specific XAI systems: a heart disease predictor and a credit approval system. These systems have been evaluated using various explainability metrics associated with distinct speech acts. The analytical tools introduced in this paper were instrumental in this analysis.

We dissect and discuss the results of three studies [52,54,55], centred on usability and XAI-specific metrics. The goal is to gain insights into the effectiveness and applicability of these metrics across various contexts.

The first XAI system, the heart disease predictor, is designed for healthcare applications. Its foundation is the XGBoost [11] and TreeSHAP [36] models, as detailed in Sect. 3.3. The second system, the credit approval system, employs a basic Artificial Neural Network in tandem with the Counterfactual Explanations Method (CEM) [14], also discussed in Sect. 3.3. Both systems fall under the category of *conventional XAI Explainers*. They generate explanations by supplementing the XAI output with comprehensive contextual information.

In two user studies [52,54], these conventional systems were compared with *Enhanced XAI Explainers* and *Interactive XAI Explainers*, verifying their *usability*, a measure influenced by Cognitive Science (cf. Sect. 6). The latter two types of explainers are able to provide expanded information about the XAI systems, with the Interactive Explainers specifically offering user-driven interactive explanations. Conversely, the third study [55] applied the *DoX* metric, based on Ordinary Language Philosophy (cf. Sect. 6), on all these XAI systems.

A fascinating pattern emerged when comparing usability metrics and DoX scores, aligning with our insights from Sect. 6: the tests showed that Interactive XAI Explainers excelled in usability over others, yet both the Interactive and the Enhanced XAI Explainers achieved identical DoX scores. This difference demonstrates a distinct divergence in focus: usability metrics measure user interaction and understanding (perlocution), while DoX measures information depth and completeness (illocution). This distinction aligns with the legal implications outlined by Wachter et al. [61], according to which the legal acceptability of an explanation depends more on the depth and breadth of information given, rather than on customisation or interactivity.

An additional observation arose in these tests, when it was found out that TreeSHAP, even when combined with XGBoost (which theoretically ensures accurate, high-quality explanations [36]), does not necessarily yield superior usability or DoX scores. This emphasises the argument that good explanations from a locutionary standpoint (i.e., those generated by TreeSHAP) may not meet illocutionary or perlocutionary goals, as demonstrated by the lower-scoring conventional XAI Explainers using TreeSHAP.

In this regard, TreeSHAP explanations, despite their mathematical rigour, do not solely determine effectiveness in explanations. This underscores that locutionary metrics may not be enough in all those contexts where effective explanations need to meet illocutionary or perlocutionary goals, not just locutionary ones. For example, usability might be crucial in user-centred environments such as education, while DoX scores might provide valuable insights into the illocutionary force of explanations in legal contexts.

In summary, the case studies highlight the usefulness of contemplating philosophical theories when selecting and applying explanation evaluation metrics. As suggested in Sects. 6 and 5, this approach can indeed augment our comprehension and practice of XAI.

8   Conclusions and Future Work

Throughout this paper, we have examined the distinctions between perlocutionary, illocutionary, and locutionary acts in the context of explanations and their implications for the evaluation of explanations. We have argued that the evaluation of explanations should be context-dependent and tailored to the specific needs of different situations and users, and our user testings [52,54,55] have indeed essentially confirmed our arguments.

In educational settings, a perlocutionary understanding of explanations may be more appropriate, as the primary goal is to facilitate understanding and learning for the individual. This necessitates considering the listener's background, prior knowledge, and cognitive abilities when crafting explanations.

Conversely, in other contexts such as the legal one, an illocutionary understanding of explanations is typically more desirable. In these settings, it is crucial to establish facts and determine the speaker's intended meaning while maintaining a certain level of objectivity. The focus is less on the listener's subjective understanding and more on the overall consistency and clarity of the explanation itself.

By acknowledging the distinctions between perlocutionary, illocutionary, and locutionary acts in the context of explanations, we can develop more effective strategies for evaluating and generating explanations in various domains. This understanding can be applied to enhance the quality of explanations in educational materials, legal documents, and scientific research.

Moreover, this contextual approach to explanations also has implications for the development of artificial intelligence and natural language processing systems. As these systems increasingly undertake tasks that involve generating explanations, comprehending the nuances of perlocutionary and illocutionary acts will be essential in creating more human-like and effective explanations tailored to specific situations and users.

For future research, we intend to explore the practical applications of our findings in various domains and investigate methods for systematically adapting explanations based on the context and the needs of the listener. This will enable the development of more effective and contextually appropriate explanations, ultimately benefiting a wide range of fields, from education and law to artificial intelligence and natural language processing.

References

1. Achinstein, P.: The Nature of Explanation. Oxford University Press, Oxford (1983). https://books.google.it/books?id=0XI8DwAAQBAJ
2. Adadi, A., Berrada, M.: Peeking inside the black-box: a survey on explainable artificial intelligence (XAI). IEEE Access **6**, 52138–52160 (2018). https://doi.org/10.1109/ACCESS.2018.2870052
3. Antoniadi, A.M., et al.: Current challenges and future opportunities for XAI in machine learning-based clinical decision support systems: a systematic review. Appl. Sci. **11**(11), 5088 (2021). https://doi.org/10.3390/app11115088, https://www.mdpi.com/2076-3417/11/11/5088
4. Arrieta, A.B., et al.: Explainable artificial intelligence (XAI): concepts, taxonomies, opportunities and challenges toward responsible AI. Inf. Fusion **58**, 82–115 (2020). https://doi.org/10.1016/j.inffus.2019.12.012
5. Austin, J., Urmson, J., Sbisà, M.: How to Do Things with Words. William James lectures, Clarendon Press (1975). https://books.google.it/books?id=XnRkQSTUpmgC

6. Beckers, S.: Causal explanations and XAI. In: Schölkopf, B., Uhler, C., Zhang, K. (eds.) 1st Conference on Causal Learning and Reasoning, CLeaR 2022, Sequoia Conference Center, Eureka, CA, USA, 11–13 April 2022. Proceedings of Machine Learning Research, vol. 177, pp. 90–109. PMLR (2022). https://proceedings.mlr.press/v177/beckers22a.html

7. Bibal, A., Lognoul, M., de Streel, A., Frénay, B.: Legal requirements on explainability in machine learning. Artif. Intell. Law **29**(2), 149–169 (2021). https://doi.org/10.1007/s10506-020-09270-4

8. Brandes, D., Ginnis, P.: A Guide to Student-centred Learning. Stanley Thornes (1996). https://books.google.ch/books?id=MTJSGGTAN3MC

9. Bromberger, S.: Why-questions. In: Colodny, R.G. (ed.) Mind and Cosmos - Essays in Contemporary Science and Philosophy, pp. 86–111. University of Pittsburgh Press (1966)

10. Buçinca, Z., Lin, P., Gajos, K.Z., Glassman, E.L.: Proxy tasks and subjective measures can be misleading in evaluating explainable AI systems. In: Paternò, F., Oliver, N., Conati, C., Spano, L.D., Tintarev, N. (eds.) 25th International Conference on Intelligent User Interfaces, IUI 2020, Cagliari, Italy, 17–20 March 2020, pp. 454–464. ACM (2020). https://doi.org/10.1145/3377325.3377498

11. Chen, T., Guestrin, C.: Xgboost: A scalable tree boosting system. In: Krishnapuram, B., Shah, M., Smola, A.J., Aggarwal, C.C., Shen, D., Rastogi, R. (eds.) Proceedings of the 22nd ACM SIGKDD International Conference on Knowledge Discovery and Data Mining, San Francisco, CA, USA, 13–17 August 2016, pp. 785–794. ACM (2016). https://doi.org/10.1145/2939672.2939785

12. Colombo, M.: Experimental philosophy of explanation rising: the case for a plurality of concepts of Explanation. Cogn. Sci. **41**(2), 503–517 (2017). https://doi.org/10.1111/cogs.12340

13. DG, E.: Understanding algorithmic decision-making: opportunities and challenges (2019). https://www.europarl.europa.eu/thinktank/en/document/EPRS_STU(2019)624261

14. Dhurandhar, A., et al.: Explanations based on the missing: towards contrastive explanations with pertinent negatives. In: Bengio, S., Wallach, H.M., Larochelle, H., Grauman, K., Cesa-Bianchi, N., Garnett, R. (eds.) Advances in Neural Information Processing Systems 31: Annual Conference on Neural Information Processing Systems 2018, NeurIPS 2018, pp. 3–8, 2018. Montréal, Canada, pp. 590–601 (2018). https://proceedings.neurips.cc/paper/2018/hash/c5ff2543b53f4cc0ad3819a36752467b-Abstract.html

15. Dieber, J., Kirrane, S.: A novel model usability evaluation framework (muse) for explainable artificial intelligence. Inf. Fusion **81**, 143–153 (2022). https://doi.org/10.1016/j.inffus.2021.11.017

16. Endsley, M.R.: Toward a theory of situation awareness in dynamic systems. Hum. Factors **37**(1), 32–64 (1995). https://doi.org/10.1518/001872095779049543

17. Gary, M.S., Wood, R.E.: Mental models, decision rules, and performance heterogeneity. Strateg. Manage. J. **32**(6), 569–594 (2011). https://doi.org/10.1002/smj.899

18. Geelan, D.: Teacher Explanations, pp. 987–999. Springer, Dordrecht (2012). https://doi.org/10.1007/978-1-4020-9041-7_65

19. Gilpin, L.H., Bau, D., Yuan, B.Z., Bajwa, A., Specter, M.A., Kagal, L.: Explaining explanations: an overview of interpretability of machine learning. In: Bonchi, F., Provost, F.J., Eliassi-Rad, T., Wang, W., Cattuto, C., Ghani, R. (eds.) 5th IEEE International Conference on Data Science and Advanced Analytics, DSAA 2018,

Turin, Italy, 1–3 October 2018, pp. 80–89. IEEE (2018). https://doi.org/10.1109/DSAA.2018.00018

20. Guidotti, R., Monreale, A., Ruggieri, S., Turini, F., Giannotti, F., Pedreschi, D.: A survey of methods for explaining black box models. ACM Comput. Surv. **51**(5), 93:1-93:42 (2019). https://doi.org/10.1145/3236009

21. Hacker, P., Passoth, J.: Varieties of AI explanations under the law. From the GDPR to the AIA, and beyond. In: Holzinger, A., Goebel, R., Fong, R., Moon, T., Müller, K., Samek, W. (eds.) xxAI 2020. LNCS, vol. 13200, pp. 343–373. Springer, Cham (2020). https://doi.org/10.1007/978-3-031-04083-2_17

22. Heider, F.: The Psychology of Interpersonal Relations. Psychology Press, London (1982)

23. Hempel, C.G., Oppenheim, P.: Studies in the logic of explanation. Philos. Sci. **15**(2), 135–175 (1948). https://doi.org/10.1086/286983

24. Hilton, D.J.: Mental models and causal explanation: judgements of probable cause and explanatory relevance. Think. Reason. **2**(4), 273–308 (1996). https://doi.org/10.1080/135467896394447

25. Hilton, D.J., Slugoski, B.R.: Knowledge-based causal attribution: the abnormal conditions focus model. Psychol. Rev. **93**(1), 75 (1986)

26. Hoffman, R.R., Mueller, S.T., Klein, G., Litman, J.: Metrics for explainable AI: challenges and prospects. CoRR abs/1812.04608 (2018). http://arxiv.org/abs/1812.04608

27. Holland, J., Holyoak, K., Nisbett, R., Thagard, P.: Induction: Processes of Inference, Learning, and Discovery. Bradford books, MIT Press (1986). https://books.google.it/books?id=Z6EFBaLApE8C

28. Holzinger, A., Carrington, A.M., Müller, H.: Measuring the quality of explanations: the system causability scale (SCS). Künstliche Intell. **34**(2), 193–198 (2020). https://doi.org/10.1007/s13218-020-00636-z

29. Horne, Z., Muradoglu, M., Cimpian, A.: Explanation as a cognitive process. Trends Cogn. Sci. **23**(3), 187–199 (2019). https://doi.org/10.1016/j.tics.2018.12.004, https://www.sciencedirect.com/science/article/pii/S1364661318302857

30. Jansen, P., Balasubramanian, N., Surdeanu, M., Clark, P.: What's in an explanation? characterizing knowledge and inference requirements for elementary science exams. In: Calzolari, N., Matsumoto, Y., Prasad, R. (eds.) COLING 2016, 26th International Conference on Computational Linguistics, Proceedings of the Conference: Technical Papers, 11–16 December 2016, Osaka, Japan, pp. 2956–2965. ACL (2016). https://aclanthology.org/C16-1278/

31. Lakkaraju, H., Kamar, E., Caruana, R., Leskovec, J.: Interpretable & explorable approximations of black box models. CoRR abs/1707.01154 (2017). http://arxiv.org/abs/1707.01154

32. Liao, Q.V., Gruen, D.M., Miller, S.: Questioning the AI: informing design practices for explainable AI user experiences. In: Bernhaupt, R., et al. (eds.) CHI Conference on Human Factors in Computing Systems, CHI 2020, Honolulu, HI, USA, 25–30 April 2020, pp. 1–15. ACM (2020). https://doi.org/10.1145/3313831.3376590

33. Liao, Q.V., Varshney, K.R.: Human-centered explainable AI (XAI): from algorithms to user experiences. CoRR abs/2110.10790 (2021). https://arxiv.org/abs/2110.10790

34. Lim, B.Y., Dey, A.K., Avrahami, D.: Why and why not explanations improve the intelligibility of context-aware intelligent systems. In: Jr., D.R.O., Arthur, R.B., Hinckley, K., Morris, M.R., Hudson, S.E., Greenberg, S. (eds.) Proceedings of the 27th International Conference on Human Factors in Computing Systems, CHI

2009, Boston, MA, USA, 4–9 April 2009, pp. 2119–2128. ACM (2009). https://doi.org/10.1145/1518701.1519023

35. Lombrozo, T.: The structure and function of explanations. Trends Cogn. Sci. **10**(10), 464–470 (2006). https://doi.org/10.1016/j.tics.2006.08.004, https://www.sciencedirect.com/science/article/pii/S1364661306002117

36. Lundberg, S.M., et al.: From local explanations to global understanding with explainable AI for trees. Nat. Mach. Intell. **2**(1), 56–67 (2020). https://doi.org/10.1038/s42256-019-0138-9

37. Madumal, P., Miller, T., Sonenberg, L., Vetere, F.: A grounded interaction protocol for explainable artificial intelligence. In: Elkind, E., Veloso, M., Agmon, N., Taylor, M.E. (eds.) Proceedings of the 18th International Conference on Autonomous Agents and MultiAgent Systems, AAMAS 2019, Montreal, QC, Canada, 13–17 May 2019, pp. 1033–1041. International Foundation for Autonomous Agents and Multiagent Systems (2019). http://dl.acm.org/citation.cfm?id=3331801

38. Mayes, G.R.: Theories of explanation (2001). https://iep.utm.edu/explanat/

39. Miller, T.: Explanation in artificial intelligence: insights from the social sciences. Artif. Intell. **267**, 1–38 (2019). https://doi.org/10.1016/j.artint.2018.07.007

40. Mohseni, S., Block, J.E., Ragan, E.D.: Quantitative evaluation of machine learning explanations: A human-grounded benchmark. In: Hammond, T., Verbert, K., Parra, D., Knijnenburg, B.P., O'Donovan, J., Teale, P. (eds.) 26th International Conference on Intelligent User Interfaces, IUI 2021, College Station, TX, USA, 13–17 April 2021, pp. 22–31. ACM (2021). https://doi.org/10.1145/3397481.3450689

41. Nguyen, A., Martínez, M.R.: On quantitative aspects of model interpretability. CoRR abs/2007.07584 (2020). https://arxiv.org/abs/2007.07584D

42. Poursabzi-Sangdeh, F., Goldstein, D.G., Hofman, J.M., Vaughan, J.W., Wallach, H.M.: Manipulating and measuring model interpretability. In: Kitamura, Y., Quigley, A., Isbister, K., Igarashi, T., Bjørn, P., Drucker, S.M. (eds.) CHI Conference on Human Factors in Computing Systems, CHI 2021, Virtual Event / Yokohama, Japan, 8–13 May 2021, pp. 237:1–237:52. ACM (2021). https://doi.org/10.1145/3411764.3445315

43. Rebanal, J.C., Combitsis, J., Tang, Y., Chen, X.A.: Xalgo: a design probe of explaining algorithms' internal states via question-answering. In: Hammond, T., Verbert, K., Parra, D., Knijnenburg, B.P., O'Donovan, J., Teale, P. (eds.) 26th International Conference on Intelligent User Interfaces, IUI 2021, College Station, TX, USA, 13–17 April 2021, pp. 329–339. ACM (2021). https://doi.org/10.1145/3397481.3450676

44. Ribera, M., Lapedriza, À.: Can we do better explanations? A proposal of user-centered explainable AI. In: Trattner, C., Parra, D., Riche, N. (eds.) Joint Proceedings of the ACM IUI 2019 Workshops co-located with the 24th ACM Conference on Intelligent User Interfaces (ACM IUI 2019), Los Angeles, USA, March 20, 2019. CEUR Workshop Proceedings, vol. 2327, p. 38. CEUR-WS.org (2019). http://ceur-ws.org/Vol-2327/IUI19WS-ExSS2019-12.pdf

45. Rosenfeld, A.: Better metrics for evaluating explainable artificial intelligence. In: Dignum, F., Lomuscio, A., Endriss, U., Nowé, A. (eds.) 20th International Conference on Autonomous Agents and Multiagent Systems, AAMAS 2021, Virtual Event, United Kingdom, 3–7 May 2021, pp. 45–50. ACM (2021). https://doi.org/10.5555/3463952.3463962, https://www.ifaamas.org/Proceedings/aamas2021/pdfs/p45.pdf

46. Salmon, W.: Scientific Explanation and the Causal Structure of the World. Book collections on Project MUSE, Princeton University Press (1984). https://books.google.it/books?id=2ug9DwAAQBAJ

47. Schweisfurth, M.: Learner-centred education in international perspective: whose pedagogy for whose development? Education, Poverty and International Development, Taylor & Francis (2013). https://books.google.ch/books?id=dT4jLusPp9AC

48. Searle, J.R.: Austin on locutionary and illocutionary acts. Philos. Rev. **77**(4), 405–424 (1968). http://www.jstor.org/stable/2183008

49. Sellars, W.: Science, Perception and Reality. Humanities Press, New York (1963)

50. Sovrano, F., Sapienza, S., Palmirani, M., Vitali, F.: A survey on methods and metrics for the assessment of explainability under the proposed AI act. In: Erich, S. (ed.) Legal Knowledge and Information Systems - JURIX 2021: The Thirty-fourth Annual Conference, Vilnius, Lithuania, 8–10 December 2021. Frontiers in Artificial Intelligence and Applications, vol. 346, pp. 235–242. IOS Press (2021). https://doi.org/10.3233/FAIA210342, https://doi.org/10.3233/FAIA210342

51. Sovrano, F., Sapienza, S., Palmirani, M., Vitali, F.: Metrics, explainability and the European AI act proposal. J **5**(1), 126–138 (2022). https://doi.org/10.3390/j5010010

52. Sovrano, F., Vitali, F.: From philosophy to interfaces: an explanatory method and a tool inspired by Achinstein's theory of explanation. In: Hammond, T., Verbert, K., Parra, D., Knijnenburg, B.P., O'Donovan, J., Teale, P. (eds.) 26th International Conference on Intelligent User Interfaces, IUI 2021, College Station, TX, USA, 13–17 April 2021, pp. 81–91. ACM (2021). https://doi.org/10.1145/3397481.3450655

53. Sovrano, F., Vitali, F.: An objective metric for explainable AI: how and why to estimate the degree of explainability. CoRR abs/2109.05327 (2021). https://arxiv.org/abs/2109.05327

54. Sovrano, F., Vitali, F.: Explanatory artificial intelligence (YAI): human-centered explanations of explainable AI and complex data. Data Min. Knowl. Disc. (2022). https://doi.org/10.1007/s10618-022-00872-x

55. Sovrano, F., Vitali, F.: How to quantify the degree of explainability: experiments and practical implications. In: 31th IEEE International Conference on Fuzzy Systems, FUZZ-IEEE 2022, Padova, 18–23 July 2022, pp. 1–9. IEEE (2022)

56. Sovrano, F., Vitali, F., Palmirani, M.: Modelling GDPR-compliant explanations for trustworthy AI. In: Kő, A., Francesconi, E., Kotsis, G., Tjoa, A.M., Khalil, I. (eds.) EGOVIS 2020. LNCS, vol. 12394, pp. 219–233. Springer, Cham (2020). https://doi.org/10.1007/978-3-030-58957-8_16

57. Szymanski, M., Millecamp, M., Verbert, K.: Visual, textual or hybrid: the effect of user expertise on different explanations. In: Hammond, T., Verbert, K., Parra, D., Knijnenburg, B.P., O'Donovan, J., Teale, P. (eds.) 26th International Conference on Intelligent User Interfaces, IUI 2021, College Station, TX, USA, 13–17 April 2021, pp. 109–119. ACM (2021). https://doi.org/10.1145/3397481.3450662

58. Thagard, P.: Analogy, explanation, and education. J. Res. Sci. Teach. **29**(6), 537–544 (1992). https://doi.org/10.1002/tea.3660290603, https://onlinelibrary.wiley.com/doi/abs/10.1002/tea.3660290603

59. Van Fraassen, B.C.: The Scientific Image. Clarendon Library of Logic and Philosophy, Clarendon Press (1980). https://books.google.it/books?id=VLz2F1zMr9QC

60. Vilone, G., Rizzo, L., Longo, L.: A comparative analysis of rule-based, model-agnostic methods for explainable artificial intelligence. In: Longo, L., Rizzo, L., Hunter, E., Pakrashi, A. (eds.) Proceedings of The 28th Irish Conference on Artificial Intelligence and Cognitive Science, Dublin, Republic of Ireland, 7–8 December 2020. CEUR Workshop Proceedings, vol. 2771, pp. 85–96. CEUR-WS.org (2020). http://ceur-ws.org/Vol-2771/AICS2020_paper_33.pdf

61. Wachter, S., Mittelstadt, B., Floridi, L.: Why a right to explanation of automated decision-making does not exist in the general data protection regulation. Int. Data Priv. Law **7**(2), 76–99 (2017)
62. Wachter, S., Mittelstadt, B., Russell, C.: Counterfactual explanations without opening the black box: automated decisions and the GDPR. Harvard J. Law Technol. **31**(2), 841 (2018). https://doi.org/10.2139/ssrn.3063289
63. Wang, X., Yin, M.: Are explanations helpful? A comparative study of the effects of explanations in AI-assisted decision-making. In: Hammond, T., Verbert, K., Parra, D., Knijnenburg, B.P., O'Donovan, J., Teale, P. (eds.) 26th International Conference on Intelligent User Interfaces, IUI 2021, College Station, TX, USA, 13–17 April 2021, pp. 318–328. ACM (2021). https://doi.org/10.1145/3397481.3450650
64. Warren, G., Keane, M.T., Byrne, R.M.J.: Features of explainability: How users understand counterfactual and causal explanations for categorical and continuous features in XAI. In: Heyninck, J., Meyer, T., Ragni, M., Thimm, M., Kern-Isberner, G. (eds.) Proceedings of the Workshop on Cognitive spects of Knowledge Representation Co-located with the 31st International Join Conference on Artificial Intelligence (IJCAI-ECAI 2022), Vienna, Austria, 23 July 2022. CEUR Workshop Proceedings, vol. 3251. CEUR-WS.org (2022). https://ceur-ws.org/Vol-3251/paper1.pdf
65. Williams, J.J., Lombrozo, T., Rehder, B.: The hazards of explanation: overgeneralization in the face of exceptions. J. Exp. Psychol.: General **142**(4), 1006 (2013)
66. Zhou, J., Gandomi, A.H., Chen, F., Holzinger, A.: Evaluating the quality of machine learning explanations: a survey on methods and metrics. Electronics **10**(5) (2021). https://doi.org/10.3390/electronics10050593, https://www.mdpi.com/2079-9292/10/5/593

Dear XAI Community, We Need to Talk!

Fundamental Misconceptions in Current XAI Research

Timo Freiesleben[1(✉)] and Gunnar König[2]

[1] Cluster of Excellence "Machine Learning in Science", Tübingen University,
Tübingen, Germany
timo.freiesleben@uni-tuebingen.de
[2] Department of Statistics, LMU Munich, Munich, Germany
gunnar.koenig@stat.uni-muenchen.de

Abstract. Despite progress in the field, significant parts of current XAI research are still not on solid conceptual, ethical, or methodological grounds. Unfortunately, these unfounded parts are not on the decline but continue to grow. Many explanation techniques are still proposed without clarifying their purpose. Instead, they are advertised with ever more fancy-looking heatmaps or only seemingly relevant benchmarks. Moreover, explanation techniques are motivated with questionable goals, such as building trust, or rely on strong assumptions about the 'concepts' that deep learning algorithms learn. In this paper, we highlight and discuss these and other misconceptions in current XAI research. We also suggest steps to make XAI a more substantive area of research.

Keywords: XAI · Interpretable Machine Learning

1 Introduction

This is an unusual paper from start to end. We don't start the paper with generic examples of great Machine Learning (ML) achievements. The thoughts in this paper are directed at people who are already working on eXplainable Artificial Intelligence (XAI), so we are long past promotional talks. Our goals with this paper are twofold: 1. to highlight misconceptions within parts of the XAI community in past and current research; 2. to provide constructive feedback and steps forward to make XAI a scientific discipline that actually improves ML transparency.

After wrapping our heads around XAI-related topics for a couple of years, we became increasingly frustrated whenever we attended a workshop or conference on the topic. We do not claim that no progress is being made or that no high-quality research is being conducted. However, we are saddened that many computational, intellectual, and financial resources are being poured into projects that, in our view, do not stand on solid grounds:

© The Author(s), under exclusive license to Springer Nature Switzerland AG 2023
L. Longo (Ed.): xAI 2023, CCIS 1901, pp. 48–65, 2023.
https://doi.org/10.1007/978-3-031-44064-9_3

- proposals for new interpretation techniques that serve no clear purpose
- anecdotal evidence from intuitive-looking heatmaps or "benchmarks" on seemingly relevant criteria are used as a substitute for a clear motivation
- explanations are generated that mislead humans into trusting ML models without the models being trustworthy

Instead of swallowing our frustration, we decided to canalize it into this paper with the hope of helping researchers avoid such projects that might be technically interesting but conceptionally unfounded. We believe that such a debate is especially urgent since funding for XAI research is inexorably high, and the community is ever-growing. Without clear purposes and proper conceptual foundations, the XAI boom could lead to a bubble endangered to implode. We would like to see our field become a pillar of ML transparency rather than the ML trust-washing machine.

The perspective we will take is more of a philosophical bird's eye view of XAI research. It is not our style to expose specific papers by pointing out their flaws. We also feel that this is not necessary because the misconceptions discussed are 'elephants in the room' in our community.

The thoughts presented in this paper reflect our opinion on the field. The paper is not intended as a review article on current XAI research, nor does it claim the systematicity in methodology or completeness of a review. Whenever possible, we will substantiate our claims with hints to related work.

In Sect. 3, we share our thoughts on key misconceptions in current XAI research, such as the idea that explanation techniques are purpose-free or that we can obtain benchmarks without a notion of ground-truth. In Sect. 4, we propose steps forward for XAI as a field; for instance, we describe how a purpose-oriented XAI can lead to benchmarks and discuss key questions that any new XAI technique should face. Before presenting our thoughts, however, we would like to refer the reader to work that had influenced our perspective on XAI, and that may help to underpin our arguments.

2   Related Work

Many papers criticize XAI on various grounds, and we believe many of the criticisms still apply to current XAI. We focus on the critiques that most impacted the community and/or our thoughts.

In his seminal paper, Zachary Lipton argues that XAI lacks a proper problem formulation and that this problem must be tackled to make progress as a field [35]. Instead of a well-defined goal, XAI offers a potpourri of motivations for explainability, such as increasing trust, fairness, or understanding. Summarized, he argues that: "When we have solid problem formulations, flaws in methodology can be addressed by articulating new methods. But when the problem formulation itself is flawed, neither algorithms nor experiments are sufficient to address the underlying problem." [35, p.8]

Finale Doshi-Velez and Been Kim highlight the problem of assessing the quality of explanations and comparing different explanation techniques. They describe three potential standards for evaluation: application, human, and functionally grounded interpretability. The first two rely on human studies, and the third on formal model properties [14]. The authors posit the intuitive principle that "the claim of the research should match the type of the evaluation." [14, p.9]

Cynthia Rudin provides examples of post-hoc explanations that can mislead the user because they are difficult to interpret [46]. She argues that this issue becomes particularly threatening when the stakes are high, and model authorities have a financial interest in model opacity. Rudin and her co-authors point out that: "interpretable models do not necessarily create or enable trust - they could also enable distrust. They simply allow users to decide whether to trust them." [47, p.6] In consequence, they argue in favor of inherently interpretable models.

Our views on XAI have also been strongly shaped by philosophical discussions around explanation and interpretability. Philosophers gave formal accounts of what constitutes an explanatory relationship, namely a statement about the phenomenon to be explained (called the *explanandum*), a statement about a phenomenon that explains the explanandum (called the *explanans*), and an *explanatory link* between explanans and explanandum [23,58]. For formalizing the explanatory link, especially causal accounts dominate, where the explanans is a difference maker with respect to the explanandum [57].

Krishnan rightfully highlights the importance of distinguishing the causal explanatory from the justificatory role of explanations. She notes that the two may often not align in the context of XAI as we might face explanations that do not justify decisions and justifications that do not explain them [31]. Others have emphasized the different explananda present in XAI, are we interested in explaining the model or the modeled real-world phenomenon [11,16,56]? Finally, Erasmus, Brunet, and Fisher argued that many statements may formally explain a phenomenon, however, it is often difficult to interpret these explanations correctly [15].

There are also several other papers that take a bird's eye view on XAI, but these mainly provide opinions on specific XAI subtopics such as model-agnostic techniques: Watson discusses conceptual problems in (model-agnostic) XAI and proposes a new approach to severely test explanations [56]; Molnar et al. discuss common pitfalls of interpreting model-agnostic interpretability techniques [40]; Schmid and Wrede provide a human-centered, interdisciplinary vision of XAI [49]; Krishna et al. demonstrate that practitioners lack a principled approach to resolve disagreements between state-of-the-art XAI methods [30]. In addition, there exist a large number of review articles that structure the field using conceptual frameworks and that often also provide an outlook on open challenges [1,5,12,38,53].

3   Misconceptions in XAI Research

In this section, we highlight the key misconceptions we see present in current XAI research and illustrate them in little caricatures. For some of these misconceptions, we are not the first to identify them. Because these misconceptions have persisted over time despite strong and convincing criticism, we see nothing wrong in repeating true things that are still ignored by parts of our community. However, where misconceptions have been discussed elsewhere, we will highlight this and refer the reader to those works.

Misconception 1: "Explanation Methods are Purpose-Free"

Many 'explanation methods' are presented as mathematical constructs without a conceptual or practical justification. Usually, such papers have the following storyline:

1. ML models are black-boxes
2. Explanations are needed because of [trust, transparency, detecting bugs, etc.]
3. Here are some formalisms, theorems, and the implementation
4. Look at the nice [images, text annotations, plots, etc.], don't they look exactly how you would expect them?
5. In this arbitrary benchmark we invented, our method is much better than all the others in 'explaining'.

However, it remains unclear why anyone should call these images or plots explanations in the first place. Worse, it even remains unclear what purpose these 'explanations' might serve and under what conditions they are helpful (Fig. 1).

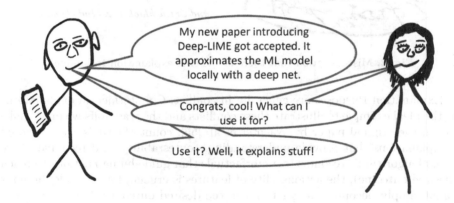

Fig. 1. Misconception that explanation methods are purpose-free

We do not claim that explanations can serve only one purpose, but rather that they should serve at least one purpose. Moreover, it should be shown, or at least clearly motivated, how exactly the proposed explanation technique serves this purpose. One may contend here that we do science for science's sake; the purpose is knowledge. However, as long as we do not have a widely accepted definition of explainability or interpretability [35], a purpose is the only way to connect explainability techniques with the real world. 'Explanation techniques' that are not motivated by any practical purpose should be suspicious to our community. If you cannot think of any context in which your explanation helps potential explainees (i.e. the recipients of explanations), this is a good indication that you should trash the technique.

Misconception 2: "One Explanation Technique to Rule Them All"

There is a persistent belief in our community that we only need to find and research the single best explanation technique (e.g., SHAP), choose the best hyperparameters (e.g., the ideal baseline), and then we will always have the best explanations that provide perfect understanding. However, as also argued by others [1,40,59], the goals we pursue with explanations are diverse: we may want to audit the model, learn something about the modeled phenomenon, debug models, or provide end-users with the ability to contest the model's decision or act based on it. Depending on the goal, an entirely different technique, with different hyperparameters choices and additional side constraints may be appropriate (Fig. 2).

One technique to explain it all,
One technique to find bugs,
One technique to convince them all
and in the black-box bind them.

Fig. 2. Misconception that there is one true explanation technique

Explanation Purposes are generally in conflict. Counterfactual explanations are the ideal example to illustrate these conflicts and the trade-offs we must make [29]. In the original paper by Wachter et al. [55], counterfactuals are presented as explanations that provide understanding, contestability, and recourse. If we think of algorithmic recourse (counterfactuals that guide human actions to reach a desired outcome), the actionability of features is crucial; for example, humans cannot simply become younger to reach the desired outcome. Thus, age is not part of counterfactuals tailored for recourse. Discrimination based on age, on the other side, might be a good reason to contest a decision. That is why, age can surely be part of a counterfactual tailored for contesting. Finally, for the vague purpose of understanding the ML model, counterfactuals might not be the right tool at all, as they only provide extremely limited insight into the model [46].

Misconception 3: "Benchmarks do not Need a Ground-Truth"

Benchmarks are meant to be objective comparisons between competitors according to a universally agreed standard. Machine learners love benchmarks. Benchmarks have been the bread and butter in ML research in the last decade and an important pillar for progressing the field. Because of the success of benchmarking in ML, the XAI community figured that benchmarks should be a central part of our field as well. Unfortunately, in XAI we generally lack the central element we have in supervised ML to make objective comparisons – a ground truth [24,56]. Without a ground-truth, it is hard to come up with metrics that quantify desirable properties and that are widely agreed upon (Fig. 3).

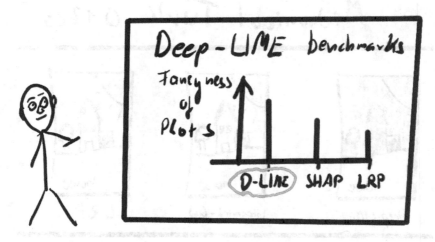

Fig. 3. Misconception that we can have benchmarks without ground-truth

Accepting the problem of the missing ground truth, there would have been two ways for progress in XAI: 1. abandon the idea of benchmarks in XAI altogether and move toward a more qualitative evaluation of explanations; 2. define benchmarks through the explanation purpose, i.e., how well does the explanation serve that purpose, which gives us again some notion of ground-truth. Parts of our community, however, have taken less rocky paths: Regardless of the explanation purpose, and with little conceptual motivation, they formally define properties that they are optimizing their explanations for. Other explanation techniques (often designed for completely different applications and optimized for distinct desiderata) are then compared according to their own standards. In this form, benchmarks lose their justification; they become advertisement space rather than an objective standard for comparison.

Misconception 4: "We Should Give People Explanations They Find Intuitive"

Many papers in our field use standards to motivate explanations that we find particularly questionable. For instance, explainees are given images or annotations that should convince them that the explanation technique actually highlights the right things. The images and annotations are tailored to look compelling and intuitive, conveying a message like – "You see, the model is actually looking at the parts of the object that you also look at when performing the task; you can trust this." As a consequence, we (over-)fit explanation techniques to human intuition; however, the question is whether these 'explanations' are still faithful to the explained ML model (Fig. 4).

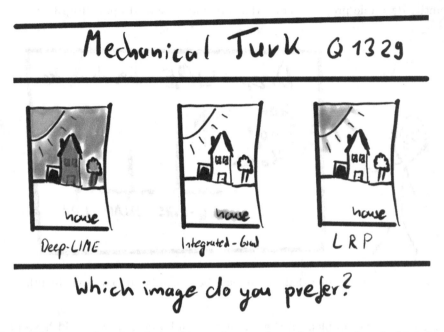

Fig. 4. Misconception that the goal is to give people explanations they find intuitive

We and also other researchers [3,31,46,47] think that a categorical mistake is made here; XAI should help make the model mechanism more transparent, not compel people into believing the system is good. Explanations provide grounds to decide whether to trust the model; they should not be designed to compel people into trusting the model. We should distinguish between an *explanation* of a decision and a *justification* of a decision. Justifications are good reasons for a decision; Explanations are the actual reasons for a decision [4,31]. They may align in decisions where the actual reasons for a decision can be ethically justified. In XAI, however, they very often diverge. Think of cases where an 'explainer' 'explains' the predictions of the prediction model without any access to it beyond the single prediction. Or, when the evaluation standard for explanations is which kinds of explanations people like better. Indeed, it can be argued that people also often provide only justifications for their actions, but do not provide their actual reasons or are often not even aware of them. However, this is not an argument for why we should accept the same for XAI explanations; instead, we should strive for higher standards, explanations that are faithful to the causal decision-making process [21].

Misconception 5: "Current Deep Nets Accidentally Learn Human Concepts"

Big parts of our field share the following, in our opinion unwarranted, presupposition: Deep neural nets learn the same concepts as humans. The idea is that early layers learn low-level concepts, such as edges in images or syllables in sound; Layers closer to the output on the other side learn high-level concepts, such as the concept of a wheel or the concept of a noun [43]. Concepts are assumed to be learned without explicitly forcing the model to learn such concepts, but only by optimizing the model to classify images or correctly complete sentences. The assumption is that the only way to solve complex tasks is to use exactly the concepts that humans use [8]. Thus, all we need to do is to train the network and then use XAI techniques like activation maximization or network dissection to discover/reveal which nodes in the network stand for which concept, and then – tada – we have a fully transparent model where every part of the model stands for something, and the model basically does logical reasoning again [42].

We agree that this would be fantastic; however, for the following reasons, we are far more pessimistic concerning the conceptual reasoning in neural nets:

– Many regularization techniques, for instance, dropout [51], explicitly force the model to represent in a distributed manner by punishing overreliance on individual neurons.
– Even though research showed that some nodes in the network co-activate in the presence of certain concepts (actually, the co-activation in percentage is far less impressive than one would think), the causal role of the concept is not shared [7,13,18,41,54]. That means that for instance cutting the neuron in a bird classifier that 'represents' wings or intervening on it does not or only marginally change the model's performance/prediction when birds with different wings are presented. Is this really what we mean when we talk about representing concepts?
– One of the reasons why humans have shared concepts is because they need to effectively communicate with other humans about the world [20,44]. However, effective communication has not been a constraint in the training of ML models. Also, humans do not face one but a variety of different tasks. For simple classifications, abstract concepts are not needed as there exist shortcuts [19] (Fig. 5).

Fancy images like those generated by activation maximization techniques [43] should not fool us in this regard: Just because the images generated have some wing-like elements does not mean that they represent wings. Not only are the images we get extremely sensitive to the source image on which we perform activation maximization [43], but they are likely to contain other forms and small shapes that we, as humans, blend out. For instance, research on adversarial examples indicates that deep nets use features in their classification that humans do not attend to [27]. It is questionable whether we as humans will ever understand the 'concepts' of ML models [10].

Fig. 5. Misconception that current deep nets accidentally learn human concepts

Misconception 6: "Every XAI Paper Needs Human Studies"

Many pointed to the importance of human studies in making progress on XAI [12,14,34]. We agree that evaluating the quality of explanations based on their impact on human performance on a particular task (to which the explanations are tailored) is reasonable and solid research. However, when it comes to explaining a specific phenomenon, at least two distinct questions must be addressed [36]: 1. What counts conceptually as an explanation for the phenomenon? 2. Which among the explanations for the phenomenon are good explanations for a specific explainee? While the latter question requires properly designed human studies, the former does not; instead, it's a philosophical/conceptual question that can be addressed with conceptual analysis and formal mathematical tools (Fig. 6).

Fig. 6. Misconception that every XAI paper needs human studies

Why is the conceptual definition of what counts as an explanation important at all? Why can't we go directly to the second step and test explanations in the real world, with real human explainees? In principle we could do that, but in practice the space of possible 'explanations' is unlimited. Conceptualizing what counts as an explanation for a phenomenon is building up the theory needed for an informed search for good explanations. In many cases where human studies are conducted, a more careful conceptual analysis would have been advisable.

More generally, not conducting human studies does not mean dismissing explanation evaluation. For instance, a purely formal evaluation of explanation techniques can be justified if human studies have already been conducted for that type of explanation. Also, not all purposes of XAI require conducting human studies. For example, if we want to use XAI to estimate a specific quantity using the model, the speed and accuracy by which this quantity is measured allows us to compare it with other estimators estimating the same quantity [39].

Misconception 7: "XAI Methods can be Wrong"

Many papers have recently shown how saliency-based or model-agnostic explanation techniques like SHAP, LIME, and counterfactuals can be 'tricked' to provide any desired explanation [2, 28, 33, 50]. This has been taken as major arguments against these techniques and led to arguments why the techniques are wrong or questioning their reliability [9, 12, 33, 37, 46, 47, 56]. To us, there seem to be misunderstandings concerning the consequences of these lines of research (Fig. 7).

Fig. 7. Misconception that XAI methods can be wrong

While we allow for arbitrary model and data complexity, we require that explanations be simple [36, 37]. Therefore, explanations will indeed not be faithful to every aspect of the model. In this sense, they do nothing wrong; they describe the formal aspects they describe. The fact that explanations are not faithful to every model aspect is the motivation for having different kinds of XAI techniques, each illuminating a different aspect while neglecting another.

You may be able to fool SHAP, you may be able to fool LIME, but you won't be able to fool all techniques all the time. It is difficult to find the right level of abstraction in a given context: Easily interpretable and local explanations like counterfactuals might have too little expressive power; they can be manipulated without changing much of the overall model behavior. More abstract and global explanations like partial dependence plots may zoom out too far, thereby allowing to hide problematic behavior in the specifics of the model.

The fact that small model modifications can mislead explanation techniques is nevertheless important – it shows that the XAI techniques we have and the explanations they provide are very hard to interpret. We may need more diverse evidence to draw conclusions based on XAI explanations. Our field should take this as a call for developing XAI techniques on all levels of abstraction, describing all aspects of behavior relevant to real-world purposes.

Misconception 8: "Extrapolating to Stay True to the Model"

Most XAI techniques rely on probing the ML model in one way or the other: LIME is locally sampling inputs, predicts them, and fits a linear model [45]; counterfactuals search for close input points from a desired predicted class [55]; Permutation feature importance (PFI) permutes the values in a specific feature and measures the drop in performance due to this permutation [17]; Activation maximization uses gradient descent to find an input that maximally triggers a specific unit [43]; integrated gradients approximate the integral over the path integral between the 'explained' image and a baseline image [52] (Fig. 8).

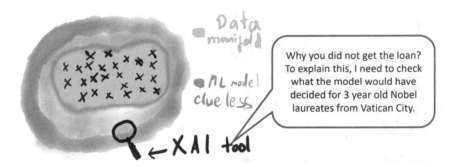

Fig. 8. Misconception that model evaluation in extrapolation regions is unproblematic

The problem is not THAT the model is probed, but WHERE – namely in areas where it has not seen any data, i.e., in areas where the model has to extrapolate [26]. ML models are notoriously bad at extrapolating to completely unseen instances [6,22]. In extrapolation regions, models disagree even when fitted to exactly the same data and achieve similar high performance on a test set [25]. Asking an ML model to extrapolate is like asking a five-year-old kid who hasn't gone to school about her insights into algebraic topology. You might get an answer, but that answer will not really help you.

Recent literature argues that explanations that rely on extrapolation are true to the model, while those that only probe the model within the data manifold are true to the data [11].[1] Clearly, since the model is defined for instances outside of the manifold, probing the model in these areas will give us further insight into the model (for purposes such as debugging or robustness checks) that we would not have gained otherwise. However, we believe that for most XAI purposes, we are interested in the behavior of the model in areas where it is (at least putatively) qualified. As soon as we leave the data manifold, the interpretation of explanation techniques becomes very blurry. We think it is highly problematic for the interpretation of current explanation methods that they rely so strongly on extrapolation.

4   Steps Forward

We hope that these misconceptions show: XAI is still a pre-paradigmatic discipline [32]. We cannot simply adopt some arbitrary assumptions and move on to paradigmatic scientific problem-solving. We must fight about the right conceptions of what the field is about, the language we should use, and the right evaluation strategies. We know that it is very easy to be critical while it is very difficult to be constructive. So we want to share at least some thoughts and intuitions about how we think the field should evolve to become a more substantive discipline.

Step 1: Go From Purpose to Benchmark

Explanation techniques should start with a purpose. Again, this does not mean that they can only serve one purpose, but they should show that they serve at least one purpose. A purpose is a goal humans have in mind when they ask for explanations. Once the purpose is fixed, the evaluation of the explanations follows naturally. Your explanation technique should enable debugging? Then the evaluation for the method should be a qualitative study of whether the method suits model developers and helps them to debug their models. If your global explanation technique is supposed to infer relevant properties of the data-generating mechanism, then show in a simulation how well and how resource efficient your technique approximates these properties. When your local explanation technique is designed to provide recourse options to end-users, then either carefully conceptually justify desiderata for recourse and base your evaluation upon these desiderata, or test the suitability of these recourse options in experiments.

The purpose determines the right evaluation metric; the evaluation metric(s) often allows for benchmarking. Different explanation techniques that are

---

[1] If we stay within the manifold, the model explanations can even be interpreted in terms of the data-generating mechanism [16].

designed for the same purpose can be judged by the same evaluation metric(s) and thus benchmarked. One simple example is when two methods are estimating the same quantity i.e. a quantifiable property of the model.

Step 2: Be Clear What You Need to Explain and by What

Every explanation comes with an explanation target, the so-called *explanandum*. The explanandum specifies what is to be explained and is determined by the explanation's purpose. Very often, confusion in XAI research arises because it is unclear what the explanandum is in a given context. For instance, confusions about the right sampling technique are often implicit confusions about the right explanandum [16,56]. XAI techniques may for instance aim to explain:

- the model prediction $\hat{Y}$,
- the predicted target Y, or
- an intermediate model element.

If you are clear about the explanandum, the second big question is by what you want to explain it – the so-called *explanans*. The explanans describes the factor(s) you are pointing to in order to account for the state of the explanandum. There are a variety of explanantia (plural of explanans) in XAI research such as:

- the model inputs $\overline{X}$,
- the predictors X,
- the dataset or a subset of it, or
- intermediate model elements.

Finally, be clear on the connection between the explanans and the explanandum. Explanations can be established by pointing to associations between the explanans and the explanandum [48]. Usually, however, the relationship we are interested in is causal, that is, the explanans makes a difference for the explanandum [57]. While causal explanations are more desirable than reference to mere associations, they are also more difficult to establish.

Step 3: Give Clear Instructions for How to Interpret Explanation Techniques

Interpreting the outputs of XAI techniques is extremely difficult. Rather than letting people figure out how to interpret XAI statements on their own, papers should provide clear guidance on how to do so. We believe that addressing the following questions in new proposals for XAI techniques would contribute to securing good usage:

- What purpose does this XAI technique serve and how should it be applied?
- Under which (model) conditions does the XAI technique enable a clear interpretation?
- How do the hyperparameters of the technique affect the interpretation?
- What is the intuitive meaning of extremes, namely high, close to zero, or negative values?
- In what way, does the explanation guide actions and decisions?
- When is it better to rely on other explanation techniques and why?

Step 4: XAI Needs Interdisciplinarity AND Expertise

XAI is a highly interdisciplinary field. XAI involves so many aspects that a single field would fail terribly; we need interaction. XAI needs to solve the following key questions, among others:

- **Conceptual:** What are relevant explanation purposes? What is required to establish an explanatory relationship between an explanans and an explanandum? What are general explanation desiderata for a specific purpose? How can explanations be conceptualized? How to interpret explanations?
- **Technical:** How to describe the conceptual definitions formally? What can be shown formally about the properties of these explanations? How to compute the explanations efficiently? How to implement explanations accessibly and correctly? How to interpret formalized explanations?
- **Psychological:** How to visualize explanations the right way? What makes a good explanation for a particular explainee? What are context and person-specific desiderata of explanations? What cognitive biases do people have when interpreting explanations? Is the explanation successful in serving the explanation purpose?
- **Social and Ethical:** Should we provide explanations and if yes, what are ethical desiderata? What are the risks with XAI in high-stakes decisions? How do explanations affect people's trust and actions? What level of transparency do we need?

Not every paper must involve researchers from each group. However, the questions between the different categories should be seen as closely tied: Formal XAI methods without a conceptual foundation should be disregarded; Conceptually solid XAI tools that experimentally fail in guiding humans should be modified and fine-tuned; Finally, XAI explanations that serve a purpose successfully but this purpose is morally questionable should be dismissed.

At the same time, nothing is wrong with XAI research that focuses on a narrow field-specific question such as providing a more efficient algorithm or testing a specific XAI method in human experiments concerning its success in finding model flaws. Every field has its expertise and it is important that conceptual foundations, algorithms, experiments, and ethical evaluations live up to the highest standards of the individual fields. Not every individual paper needs to cover the whole story from conceptual motivation to technical implementation to psychological experiments, such papers would probably look like books rather than fitting in a ten-page conference format. All we want to emphasize is that researchers should keep the bigger picture in mind and should not run around having blenders on.

5   Conclusion

This paper covered the key misconceptions in current XAI research. In our opinion, the most important one is the idea of purpose-free explanations. Fixing specific purposes will provide a way for evaluating and benchmarking XAI techniques objectively. The explanation purpose will also guide us: how XAI techniques must be constructed, when they should be used, and how they have to be interpreted. Overall, purpose-centered XAI research will help us make ML systems more transparent. Therefore, we hope that future researchers will start thinking more about the purpose of explanations before they make grand proposals for new methods.

Acknowledgements. This project has been supported by the German Federal Ministry of Education and Research (BMBF) and the Carl Zeiss Foundation (project on "Certification and Foundations of Safe Machine Learning Systems in Healthcare").

References

1. Adadi, A., Berrada, M.: Peeking inside the black-box: a survey on explainable artificial intelligence (XAI). IEEE Access **6**, 52138–52160 (2018)
2. Adebayo, J., Gilmer, J., Muelly, M., Goodfellow, I., Hardt, M., Kim, B.: Sanity checks for saliency maps. In: Advances in Neural Information Processing Systems, vol. 31 (2018)
3. Aïvodji, U., Arai, H., Fortineau, O., Gambs, S., Hara, S., Tapp, A.: Fairwashing: the risk of rationalization. In: International Conference on Machine Learning, pp. 161–170. PMLR (2019)
4. Alvarez, M.: Reasons for action: justification, motivation, explanation. In: Zalta, E.N. (ed.) The Stanford Encyclopedia of Philosophy. Metaphysics Research Lab, Stanford University, Winter 2017 (2017)
5. Arrieta, A.B., et al.: Explainable artificial intelligence (XAI): concepts, taxonomies, opportunities and challenges toward responsible AI. Inf. Fusion **58**, 82–115 (2020)
6. Barnard, E., Wessels, L.: Extrapolation and interpolation in neural network classifiers. IEEE Control Syst. Mag. **12**(5), 50–53 (1992)
7. Bau, D., Zhou, B., Khosla, A., Oliva, A., Torralba, A.: Network dissection: quantifying interpretability of deep visual representations. In: Proceedings of the IEEE Conference on Computer Vision and Pattern Recognition, pp. 6541–6549 (2017)
8. Beckmann, P., Köstner, G., Hipólito, I.: Rejecting cognitivism: Computational phenomenology for deep learning. arXiv preprint arXiv:2302.09071 (2023)
9. Bordt, S., Finck, M., Raidl, E., von Luxburg, U.: Post-hoc explanations fail to achieve their purpose in adversarial contexts. In: 2022 ACM Conference on Fairness, Accountability, and Transparency, pp. 891–905 (2022)
10. Buckner, C.: Understanding adversarial examples requires a theory of artefacts for deep learning. Nat. Mach. Intell. **2**(12), 731–736 (2020)
11. Chen, H., Janizek, J.D., Lundberg, S., Lee, S.I.: True to the model or true to the data? arXiv preprint arXiv:2006.16234 (2020)
12. Das, A., Rad, P.: Opportunities and challenges in explainable artificial intelligence (XAI): A survey. arXiv preprint arXiv:2006.11371 (2020)
13. Donnelly, J., Roegiest, A.: On interpretability and feature representations: an analysis of the sentiment neuron. In: Azzopardi, L., Stein, B., Fuhr, N., Mayr, P., Hauff, C., Hiemstra, D. (eds.) ECIR 2019. LNCS, vol. 11437, pp. 795–802. Springer, Cham (2019). https://doi.org/10.1007/978-3-030-15712-8_55
14. Doshi-Velez, F., Kim, B.: Towards a rigorous science of interpretable machine learning. arXiv preprint arXiv:1702.08608 (2017)

15. Erasmus, A., Brunet, T.D., Fisher, E.: What is interpretability? Philos. Technol. **34**(4), 833–862 (2021)
16. Freiesleben, T., König, G., Molnar, C., Tejero-Cantero, A.: Scientific inference with interpretable machine learning: Analyzing models to learn about real-world phenomena. arXiv preprint arXiv:2206.05487 (2022)
17. Friedman, J.H., et al.: Multivariate adaptive regression splines. Ann. Stat. **19**(1), 1–67 (1991). https://doi.org/10.1214/aos/1176347963
18. Gale, E.M., Martin, N., Blything, R., Nguyen, A., Bowers, J.S.: Are there any 'object detectors' in the hidden layers of CNNs trained to identify objects or scenes? Vis. Res. **176**, 60–71 (2020). https://doi.org/10.1016/j.visres.2020.06.007, https://www.sciencedirect.com/science/article/pii/S0042698920301140
19. Geirhos, R., et al.: Shortcut learning in deep neural networks. Nat. Mach. Intell. **2**(11), 665–673 (2020)
20. Grice, P.: Studies in the Way of Words. Harvard University Press, Cambridge (1989)
21. Günther, M., Kasirzadeh, A.: Algorithmic and human decision making: for a double standard of transparency. AI Society, 1–7 (2022)
22. Haley, P.J., Soloway, D.: Extrapolation limitations of multilayer feedforward neural networks. In: Proceedings 1992 IJCNN International Joint Conference on Neural Networks, vol. 4, pp. 25–30. IEEE (1992)
23. Hempel, C.G., Oppenheim, P.: Studies in the logic of explanation. Philos. Sci. **15**(2), 135–175 (1948)
24. Holzinger, A., Carrington, A., Müller, H.: Measuring the quality of explanations: the system causability scale (SCS) comparing human and machine explanations. KI-Künstliche Intell. **34**(2), 193–198 (2020)
25. Hooker, G., Mentch, L.: Please stop permuting features: An explanation and alternatives. arXiv e-prints pp. arXiv-1905 (2019)
26. Hooker, G., Mentch, L., Zhou, S.: Unrestricted permutation forces extrapolation: variable importance requires at least one more model, or there is no free variable importance. Stat. Comput. **31**(6), 1–16 (2021)
27. Ilyas, A., Santurkar, S., Tsipras, D., Engstrom, L., Tran, B., Madry, A.: Adversarial examples are not bugs, they are features. arXiv preprint arXiv:1905.02175 (2019)
28. Kindermans, P.J., et al.: The (un) reliability of saliency methods. Explainable AI: Interpreting, explaining and visualizing deep learning, pp. 267–280 (2019)
29. König, G., Freiesleben, T., Grosse-Wentrup, M.: Improvement-focused causal recourse (ICR). In: Proceedings of the AAAI Conference on Artificial Intelligence (2023)
30. Krishna, S., et al.: The disagreement problem in explainable machine learning: A practitioner's perspective. arXiv preprint arXiv:2202.01602 (2022)
31. Krishnan, M.: Against interpretability: a critical examination of the interpretability problem in machine learning. Philos. Technol. **33**(3), 487–502 (2020)
32. Kuhn, T.S.: The Structure of Scientific Revolutions, vol. 111. Chicago University of Chicago Press (1970)
33. Lakkaraju, H., Bastani, O.: "How do i fool you?" manipulating user trust via misleading black box explanations. In: Proceedings of the AAAI/ACM Conference on AI, Ethics, and Society, pp. 79–85 (2020)
34. Liao, Q.V., Varshney, K.R.: Human-centered explainable ai (xai): From algorithms to user experiences. arXiv preprint arXiv:2110.10790 (2021)
35. Lipton, Z.C.: The mythos of model interpretability: in machine learning, the concept of interpretability is both important and slippery. Queue **16**(3), 31–57 (2018)

36. Miller, T.: Explanation in artificial intelligence: insights from the social sciences. Artif. Intell. **267**, 1–38 (2019)
37. Mittelstadt, B., Russell, C., Wachter, S.: Explaining explanations in AI. In: Proceedings of the Conference on Fairness, Accountability, and Transparency, pp. 279–288 (2019)
38. Molnar, C.: Interpretable machine learning. Lulu. com (2020)
39. Molnar, C., Freiesleben, T., König, G., Casalicchio, G., Wright, M.N., Bischl, B.: Relating the partial dependence plot and permutation feature importance to the data generating process. arXiv preprint arXiv:2109.01433 (2021)
40. Molnar, C., et al.: General pitfalls of model-agnostic interpretation methods for machine learning models. In: Holzinger, A., Goebel, R., Fong, R., Moon, T., Muller, K.R., Samek, W. (eds.) xxAI 2020. LNCS, vol. 13200, pp. 39–68. Springer, Cham (2022)
41. Mu, J., Andreas, J.: Compositional explanations of neurons. Adv. Neural. Inf. Process. Syst. **33**, 17153–17163 (2020)
42. Olah, C., Cammarata, N., Schubert, L., Goh, G., Petrov, M., Carter, S.: Zoom in: an introduction to circuits. Distill **5**(3), e00024–001 (2020)
43. Olah, C., Mordvintsev, A., Schubert, L.: Feature visualization. Distill **2**(11), e7 (2017)
44. Pagel, M.: Q&a: what is human language, when did it evolve and why should we care? BMC Biol. **15**, 1–6 (2017)
45. Ribeiro, M.T., Singh, S., Guestrin, C.: Why should i trust you?: explaining the predictions of any classifier. In: Proceedings of the 22nd ACM SIGKDD International Conference on Knowledge Discovery and Data Mining, pp. 1135–1144. ACM (2016). https://doi.org/10.1145/2939672.2939778
46. Rudin, C.: Stop explaining black box machine learning models for high stakes decisions and use interpretable models instead. Nat. Mach. Intell. **1**(5), 206–215 (2019)
47. Rudin, C., Chen, C., Chen, Z., Huang, H., Semenova, L., Zhong, C.: Interpretable machine learning: fundamental principles and 10 grand challenges. Stat. Surv. **16**, 1–85 (2022)
48. Salmon, W.C.: Statistical explanation and statistical relevance, vol. 69. University of Pittsburgh Pre (1971)
49. Schmid, U., Wrede, B.: What is missing in XAI so far? KI-Künstliche Intell. **36** (2022)
50. Slack, D., Hilgard, S., Jia, E., Singh, S., Lakkaraju, H.: Fooling lime and shap: adversarial attacks on post hoc explanation methods. In: Proceedings of the AAAI/ACM Conference on AI, Ethics, and Society, pp. 180–186 (2020)
51. Srivastava, N., Hinton, G., Krizhevsky, A., Sutskever, I., Salakhutdinov, R.: Dropout: a simple way to prevent neural networks from overfitting. J. Mach. Learn. Res. **15**(1), 1929–1958 (2014)
52. Sundararajan, M., Taly, A., Yan, Q.: Axiomatic attribution for deep networks. In: International Conference on Machine Learning, pp. 3319–3328. PMLR (2017)
53. Vilone, G., Longo, L.: Explainable artificial intelligence: a systematic review. arXiv preprint arXiv:2006.00093 (2020)
54. Voss, C., et al.: Visualizing weights. Distill **6**(2), e00024–007 (2021)
55. Wachter, S., Mittelstadt, B., Russell, C.: Counterfactual explanations without opening the black box: automated decisions and the GDPR. Harv. JL Tech. **31**, 841 (2017)
56. Watson, D.S.: Conceptual challenges for interpretable machine learning. Synthese **200**(1), 1–33 (2022)

57. Woodward, J.: Making Things Happen: A Theory of Causal Explanation. Oxford University Press, Oxford (2005)
58. Woodward, J., Ross, L.: Scientific explanation. In: Zalta, E.N. (ed.) The Stanford Encyclopedia of Philosophy. Metaphysics Research Lab, Stanford University, Summer 2021 (2021)
59. Zednik, C.: Solving the black box problem: a normative framework for explainable artificial intelligence. Philos. Technol. **34**(2), 265–288 (2021)

Speeding Things Up. Can Explainability Improve Human Learning?

Jakob Mannmeusel[1] , Mario Rothfelder[2,3] , and Samaneh Khoshrou[4]([✉])

[1] Department of Digitalization, Kobaltblau Management Consultants,
Munich, Germany
jakob.mannmeusel@kobaltblau.com
[2] Amsterdam School of Economics, University of Amsterdam,
Amsterdam, The Netherlands
m.p.rothfelder@uva.nl
[3] Tinbergen Institute, Amsterdam, The Netherlands
[4] Department of Artificial Intelligence and Cognitive Science, Tilburg University,
Tilburg, The Netherlands
s.khoshrou@tiburguniversity.edu

Abstract. Active learning strategies have been employed when AI alone can not make an accurate prediction (e.g. due to concept drift, class evolution, etc.). In such circumstances, the algorithm requests a teacher, usually a human, to select or verify the system's prediction on the most informative points. The most informative usually refers to the instances that are the hardest for the algorithm to label. However, it has been proven that humans are more likely to make an accurate judgment, but the decision will not be error-free. In this article, we quantify to what extent explainable artificial intelligence can teach a human about the nuances of the data and help them to be better teachers for the machine in such complex circumstances. This is done via a within-subject experimental setup where human annotators are tasked with classifying queries (i.e. unknown texts) in a multi-class setting. The queries were chosen in an active learning setting. For the treatment condition, we provide the human annotators with LIME-explanations of the queries. We also carried out robustness checks controlling for the annotators' self-perceived level of expertise, in terms of AI and task knowledge. Our findings support the hypothesis that XAI can have lasting effects, even after the treatment is removed from the task. Moreover, we find that an increase in self-perceived AI or task knowledge does not change the outcomes qualitatively.

Keywords: Explainable Active learning · Human-centered
Computing · Text Classification · Empirical Studies

J. Mannmeusel and M. Rothfelder—These authors contributed equally to this work

1 Introduction

Recent advancements in technology made AI more accessible and ubiquitous than ever before, and it has been adopted in several domains, such as health care, finance, legal, and business. However, most of the AI solutions have focused on some idealized settings, where independent and identically distributed observations are drawn from a fixed yet unknown distribution(s), and fixed and known concepts are available. In practice, these assumptions are likely to be only partially true, which makes the technology impractical or suboptimal. In such circumstances, AI alone is no magic, and human needs to chip in and create a team to keep the system on track. Now the question arises of how humans and AI team up to solve such tasks. Current state-of-the-art calls for active learning (AL) strategies, which allow AI to query human experts to label the most informative instances interactively. Most of the AL literature has evolved around an algorithm-centric view and neglected the human dimension of the team. They assumed that human annotators are able to provide error-free annotations around the clock. This vision has faced significant criticism since it ignores the task characteristics, the annotators' individuality, and the interaction learning effect over time. Recently, there has been a growing effort to propose more human-centric strategies, which aim to improve and optimize the user and developers' experience side by side of algorithms' performance [12].

With the recent advancement in the field of explainable AI (XAI), common wisdom suggests that AI explanations can serve as complementary sources of information for end-users and developers and assist them in the decision-making process.

In this work, we aim to answer the following research questions:

- To what extent does XAI affect human annotation skills in an active learning setting?
- How does the XAI treatment episode affect individuals?

Despite the prevalence of text data across numerous industries, this is the first attempt to study the impact of XAL on human performance in multi-class text classification scenario.

The rest of the paper is organized as follows: in Sect. 2 we introduce the line of works related to this paper, Sect. 3 presents an overview of the learning framework, in Sect. 4 we discuss the experimental methodology, Sect. 5 places the findings within the XAI/XAL literature and Sect. 6 concludes the paper's contributions and indicate future research directions.

2 Background

2.1 XAI Journey: From Algorithmic-Centered to Human-Centered Explanations

Since the ability to interpret and understand AI systems is essential for various domains, XAI has emerged rapidly as a critical field of research to address the opacity and lack of transparency in complex machine learning models [15,32,40]. XAI has been researched in various domains and disciplines including: healthcare [10,23], business [16,41], law [6,39], social and cognitive science [4,7,25]. The field's primary focus was on algorithms to generate explanations for the output of machine learning models, rather than considering the individuals involved or the specific environment in which these systems were implemented and executed [19,20,24,26,30]. However, recently the focus shifts towards integrating human-centered principles into XAI methods [19], acknowledging that effective XAI methods can only be developed with a comprehensive grasp of people's requirements within a particular context [9,22]. The human-centered XAI aims to answer the following questions: "what, when, and how to explain to human end-users?" [33]. Recent work suggests that the combination of human-centered XAI and Human in the loop framework can create new design possibilities in human-AI collaboration [38].

2.2 XAI and Human-AI Collaboration

With the growing adoption of XAI in human-AI teams, there has a surge of studies on assessing XAI as a medium for improving human-AI teams. Numerous methods have been developed to incorporate XAI in human-AI teams under different scenarios, such as explainable active learning (XAL) [13,17,28], co-active learning [3,21], and interactive learning [36]. However, most of the research has focused on what "researchers can do rather than what users need or want" [1, 19]. Recently, there has been a growing interest in looking into end-user-friendly XAI either in the context of specific applications (e.g. health domain, language translation) or general [5,11,31,35]. One of the most exciting and recent findings is that people expect XAI strategies to help them improve their annotation skills [31]. They perceive XAI as an instructive entity who is able to educate them on nuances of data, particularly those that they have previously overlooked. This newfound knowledge is then can be utilized to enhance future decision-making processes.

The significance of potential learning effect of XAI is specially amplified in AL settings, where a human require to interactively provides the most accurate input in real-time. [8] has shown that individuals can acquire knowledge from recommendations and explanations generated by AI in a between subject setting. However, the study has been conducted in the chess playing domain, wherein the participants were actively engaged in the cognitive aspects of the game. As such, the extent to which these findings can be applied more broadly in real-world environment remains uncertain.

2.3 Human-Centeric XAI for Active Learning

In recent years, active learning has received increasing attention due to its potential for reducing data annotation costs and improving the performance of machine learning models [14]. Classic active learning refers to settings where an algorithm can interactively query a teacher to obtain the desired information (e.g., a label) for a set of queries [34]. The main body of the literature, until recently, has mainly focused on the algorithmic side of the framework and tried to find the best query set, which leads to higher performance with a minimum number of queries [19,29]. They assume that humans can provide error-free input around the clock, which is not always true. As the model matures over time, it becomes increasingly challenging for annotators to provide correct labels [13]. To improve the feedback quality, the explanations were provided for the annotators in [37]. However, the validity of the hypothesis has not been investigated. Later, Gai conducted an empirical study to assess the effects of explanation [13]. The experiments demonstrated that local explanations have an "anchoring effect" on annotators, and contrary to the expectation, human supported by explanation do not necessarily make a more accurate judgment. In this work, however, people were asked to perform a binary classification task on structured (i.e.tabular data), and the validity of the claims on multi-class classification of unstructured data (e.g. text) is unexplored. We specifically focus on the potential learning effects of episodic XAI on annotators in a real-world problem, a research question which will be explored for the first time. We further hypothesize how explanation affects different individuals in such settings. Moreover, [13] utilize a between-framework for their experimental design which does not allow for investigating the effects of episodic XAI since a given individual either receives the treatment or the control over the entire experiment.

3 Methodology

3.1 Data Set

The data for this study is the customer complaints data set from the Consumer Financial Protection Bureau (CFPB) and was downloaded on 19.03.2022 from the CPFB website[1]. It consists of complaints that consumers have filed against actors in the financial sector in the US, originally containing 924,187 observations with narratives, starting in December 2011. Due to the large size of the original data set, we make use of only the most recent 100,000 complaints, i.e. complaints recorded between 14.10.2021 and 19.03.2022. We chose this dataset as it contains real-world data and contexts, made by common individuals. Therefore, it seems natural to us to assume that participants in the experiment would intuitively understand the context of the presented data and we therefore expect that participants have a certain level of familiarity with the terminology used, having a task at hand which does not require the participants being actual subject-matter experts. Thus, we recruited the participants from a pool of university students with diverse backgrounds, ensuring sufficient English language skills to take part in the experiment.

The CFPB offers consumers nine categories and 79 different issues to select their complaint from. To facilitate the task of text classification for the participants and due to an overlap between different classes (e.g. vehicle, student or

---

[1] https://www.consumerfinance.gov/data-research/consumer-complaints/.

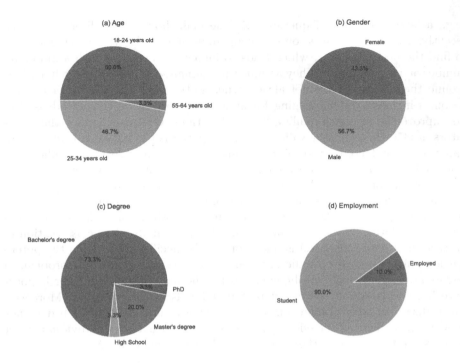

Fig. 1. Demographic information of the participants

payday loan), we grouped the complaints into three final categories: (i) credit reporting, (ii) mortgage loans debt collection and (iii) retail banking. The participant were then asked to assign a presented text to either one of these three classes and the result was recorded. Using the CFPB's own classification, we then identified whether a participant classified the text correctly or not, which will constitute one of our dependent variables. The dataset used in this study can be accessed through the following link: https://github.com/SamanehKh77/Human-centered-XAI (Fig. 1).

We process the raw text-data by first converting to lowercase letters and removing stopwords from the narratives. Then, we lemmatize and separate the texts by space [2]. Lastly, we remove duplicate texts to avoid redundancies. This results in the final dataset consisting of the product category, the original complaint as well as the pre-processed text documents. Finally, we employ the LIME explanation as one of the few model-agnostic methods that work for different data types. It provides "human-friendly" explanations (i.e. short and possibly contrastive), which makes them a perfect choice where the recipient of the explanation might be an unprofessional person or someone with limited time (i.e. which is the case in AL) [27].

Finally, following [13] we also asked participants to report their self-perceived a-priori experience with AI, respectively banking knowledge on a scale from 1 (being the lowest) to 4 (being the highest). We do so to have a proxy for participants' familiarity with the task and AI, since a higher familiarity with the task, respectively with AI is expected to yield better results, everything else being equal (Fig. 2).

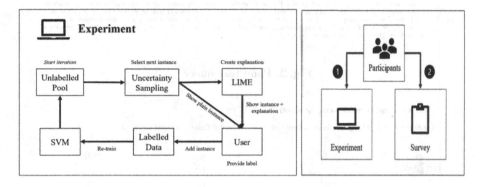

Fig. 2. Block diagram of the framework

3.2   AI-Experiment

An experiment presents an adequate choice to investigate the collaboration of humans and AI, as it gives due prominence to the focal role of humans. Each participant conducted the experiment remotely at their own computer and without supervision. To ensure that participants had received and understood all needed information, all were provided with initial written instructions about the experiment and their task, accompanied by verbal clarifications between experiment conductor and participant. Each participant received initial instructions about the task. They were also informed that the two best performing participants would be rewarded with 20€, as monetary incentives have shown to increase motivation and facilitate better focus on the task at-hand when conducting an experiment [18]. The participants acted as subject-matter experts on the presented task. In the beginning, the participants were presented with complaints as plain text to read and assign to either of the three categories (Fig. 3). This was repeated until ten complaints had been labelled. After the 10th iterations, the participants were informed that they would receive additional visualizations from that point on while the task remained the same. In addition to the plain text, they now also saw LIME-based explanations and the estimated class probabilities (Fig. 4). The participants annotated 20 instances with explanations before switching the condition again to plain text for another 10 complaints. After every 8th labelled instance, the model was re-trained with the provided data. After finishing the experiment, they were asked to fill in a brief questionnaire about their experiences and attitudes. Please refer to Appendix (Tables 5, 6, 7, 8) for additional details.

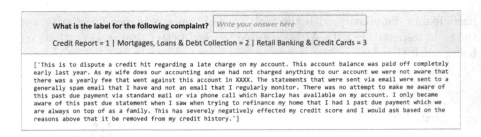

Fig. 3. Plain text query

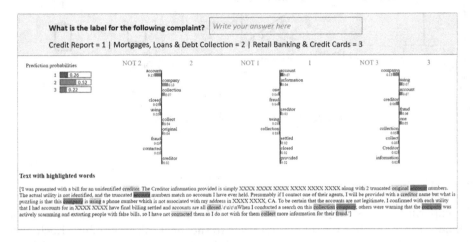

Fig. 4. Explanation and query presented in XAL condition

3.3   Experimental Set-Up

For the experiment, we use a 1 (CFPB data) × 2 (Conditions: *Plain text* and *Text with explanation*) within-subject experimental design. The two conditions are as follows. *Plain text* refers to the case where participants were asked to determine a label for a plain text without any AI-based information, whereas *Text with explanation* refers to the case in which participants received the text with LIME-based explanations. These explanations contained *i*) highlighted key terms within the text as decided by the classifier and *ii*) class probabilities for each of the three classes.

The conditions were presented to the participants ($N = 30$) in a 10 control – 20 treatment – 10 control scheme. That is, participants first received ten texts without additional AI explanations, the 20 texts with additional AI explanation and then again 10 text without additional AI explanation. We chose this design setting over a between-subject design in order to exploit the so-called ordering effect to identify learning and treatment effects in the current setting. To wit, in many real life settings, we are not necessarily interested in permanently presenting employees with additional AI explanations to support them doing their tasks. One reason for this is that the annotators become too reliant on the provided information and just take over the machines decision without adding human domain expertise. Thus, one would want to take the additional AI explanations away from the annotators after a training effect has been achieved[2].

Moreover, the participants received detailed instructions and a personal briefing on how to conduct the experiment, as well as background information on banking and the financial sector in the US. We also note that the experiment was conducted remotely without supervision and that participants were allowed to consult any additional information, such as the internet or translators. The idea behind this reasoning is to simulate the role of experts, which would also have unrestricted access to such information in real life settings.

Finally, we note that we consider three different dependent variables in case of task completion speed. For one, we use the originally recorded completion time in seconds. The problem which clearly arises with this is that different text-lengths will have different completion times. In order to account for this, we also consider the completion time (in seconds) per word and per character. The reason for the latter distinction is that a word-count is not necessarily a good measure since two sentences with the same text-length can have different completion times due to the fact that one sentence uses rather long words, whereas the other uses shorter words.

3.4 Empirical Strategy

Given the chosen 10-20-10 within-design, our baseline specification to identify potential effects of the XAL treatment on classification accuracy and speed is given by

$$y_{i,t} = \alpha + \beta_T \mathbf{1}\{11 \leq t \leq 30\} + \beta_{PoT} \mathbf{1}\{31 \leq t \leq 40\} + \mu_i + \epsilon_{i,t} \quad (1)$$

where $i = 1, ..., 30$ captures the subject and $t = 1, ..., 40$ the time period/text order within the experiment. μ_i captures unobserved subject specific effects which are constant over the experiment, such as financial knowledge, prior AI knowledge, aptitude, etc., $\epsilon_{i,t}$ is the error term and $y_{i,t}$ the outcome, being either the task duration or a binary indicator for correct task completion. Given that μ_i is independent of the only explanatory variables, the treatment/control-indicators, random effects estimation is, next to consistent, also efficient in this setting and thus, appropriate. Specifically, we use a linear random effects model

---

[2] We interpret such a training effect in such a way that the AI assisted highlights train the annotators focus to find relevant information faster/more accurately so that the annotators can perform their task faster/more accurately even after removing the AI explanations.

when $y_{i,t}$ is one of the three the task duration variables and a logit random effects model in case of classification accuracy.

Since $\mathbf{1}\{a \leq b\}$ denotes the indicator function taking value 1 if $a \leq b$ and 0 otherwise, we expect that $\beta_{PoT} = 0$, i.e. the effect on classification accuracy/speed after the XAL treatment has been removed is zero, if there were no task learning effects (i.e. participants becoming better at repeatedly executing a task over time) and lasting effects from the XAL treatment. On the other hand, $\beta_{PoT} \neq 0$ would imply that there are additional learning effects[3], be it via repeated task execution or due to lasting XAL effects. However, in this case we cannot readily disentangle these two effects by using the baseline model (1).

Similarly, β_T captures several competing effects as well. For one, it captures potential effects coming from the XAL treatment (expected positive sign in case of classification accuracy and expected negative sign in case of task completion speed). Additionally, it also captures task learning effects (same expected signs as for the a treatment effect) and it might also contain reverse effects deriving from initially getting used to the treatment and processing the new information[4]. In order to accommodate such behavior, we will split the periods of XAL-treatment into two sub-samples from periods 11 to period t^* and from $t^* + 1$ to period 30. If we were not to do so, the earlier described effects could off-set each other and affect the results. Since it is unclear to us how many periods it takes for participants to get accustomed to the XAL-treatment, we experiment with $t^* \in \{15, 17, 20\}$ so that there are enough observations in the first XAL-treatment period to reliable estimate the aforementioned potential effects. Thus, we formally extend the baseline model (2) as follows

$$y_{i,t} = \alpha + \beta_{PrT}\mathbf{1}\{5 \leq t \leq 10\} + \beta_{T,1}\mathbf{1}\{11 \leq t \leq t^*\} + \beta_{T,2}\mathbf{1}\{t^* \leq t \leq 30\}$$
$$+ \beta_{PoT,1}\mathbf{1}\{31 \leq t \leq 35\} + \beta_{PoT,2}\mathbf{1}\{36 \leq t \leq 40\} + \mu_i + \epsilon_{i,t} \qquad (2)$$

$\beta_{PrT} \neq 0$ gives an estimate/indication for a learning effect occurring during the immediate pre-XAL period, attributed to repeated task exercising. In particular, if such an effect happens, then classification accuracy, respectively task completion speed should improve in periods six through ten, compared to periods one through five. Compared to pre-XAL effects, one would expect the XAL1 and XAL2 effects to be larger in absolute value, as they indicate an effect size, if the XAL-treatment has a positive effect on participants' task completion[5]. Of course, one could easily imagine that introducing XAL from one period to another might not immediately yield positive effects for a participant's task completion, but rather has an initially detrimental effect since participants first need

---

[3] In case of classification accuracy we expect a positive sign, and in case of classification speed a negative sign.

[4] Even though the participants were briefed prior to the experiment, we would expect such an effect due to time delays between briefing and the actual task, akin to a surprise shock even though it was announced to happen.

[5] Recall, that all coefficients are relative to the benchmark of the first five texts. Thus, equality would mean there is no positive effect of XAL on a participant's task completion. If the effects were smaller, then XAL would actually have a detrimental effect.

to get used to the additional information provided[6]. In that case, we expect that the XAL1 effect is less or equal to the XAL2 effect in absolute values. However, we would also expect that the XAL2 effect is larger than the pre-XAL effect, if there is a positive effect of XAL on task completion, since participants should now be used to the treatment. If, on the other hand, there is no effect of the XAL-treatment on task completion, then we expect the XAL2 effect to be equal to the pre-XAL effect. Using similar reasoning, we expect that the post-XAL1 and post-XAL2 effects are smaller in absolute value than (at least) the XAL2 effects, if there is a treatment effect of XAL on task completion. In Table 1, we summarize the different effects in the augmented model (2).

Table 1. Summary of Effects in Model (2)

Coefficient	In-Text Reference	Explanation
β_{PrT}	pre-XAL	>0 indicates task learning effect during periods 6 through 10
$\beta_{T,1}$	XAL1	>0 indicates task learning effects and/or treatment effects due to presence of XAL condition during periods 11 through 20
$\beta_{T,2}$	XAL2	>0 indicates task learning effects and/or treatment effects due to presence of XAL condition during periods 21 through 30
$\beta_{PoT,1}$	post-XAL1	>0 indicates task learning effect and/or lasting XAL-treatment effect during periods 31 through 35
$\beta_{PoT,2}$	post-XAL2	>0 indicates task learning effect and/or lasting XAL-treatment effect during periods 36 through 40

[a] This table summarizes the effects in Model (2) and provides the used in-text references (column 2) for these effects.
[b] All effects are understood as relative to periods 1 through 5.

4 Results

We present the results for our baseline specification (1) in Table 2. We first note that there are no individual statistically significant effects (even on a 10% level) of the XAL condition on labeling accuracy[7]. On the other hand, we find

---

[6] As argued before, even though participants were briefed about the XAL condition prior to the experiment, the delay in time might cause some initial confusion/getting used the new environment.

[7] Note that the results do not imply that the participants are no better than chance since we have three text classes in the experiment. Thus, random classification would imply a success rate of 33%, whereas the results imply a success rate of 50%.

that participants perform the classification task faster over the course of the experiment. Moreover, testing whether $\mathbb{H}_0 : \beta_T = \beta_{PoT}$ vs. $\mathbb{H}_0 : \beta_T \neq \beta_{PoT}$ rejects the null hypothesis ($p \leq 0.01$) for all three specifications. Combined with their magnitudes we conclude from this base specification that there is a strong learning effect over time. However, given the results in Table 2, one might wonder whether this improvement is due only to carrying out the task repetitively, i.e. a learning effect. In order to try to answer this question, we now turn our focus onto specification (2), for which we display the results in Table 3. First, we note again that the XAL condition has no effect on correctly classifying the texts. In fact, there are also no measurable learning effects with respect to this task. On the other hand, we again observe that there are individually statistically significant (at the 1% level) effects on the task completion speed. We note that these results do not change qualitatively if we account for self-perceived AI, respectively task knowledge.

Table 2. Results for Specification (1)

	(1)	(2)	(3)	(4)
β_T	-21.618^{***}	-0.155^{***}	-0.026^{**}	0.095
	(3.167)	(0.059)	(0.010)	(0.143)
β_{PoT}	-31.873^{***}	-0.347^{***}	-0.063^{***}	-0.257
	(3.657)	(0.068)	(0.012)	(0.165)
Constant	64.397^{***}	0.750^{***}	0.135^{***}	0.081
	(4.592)	(0.061)	(0.011)	(0.123)

[a] *p < 0.1; **p < 0.05; ***p<0.01; standard errors in parentheses.
[b] Columns labeled (1) refer to the absolute task completion length, columns labeled (2) refer to per word task completion length, columns labeled (3) refer to the per character task completion length (all in seconds) and columns labeled (4) refer to classification accuracy as dependent variable.
[c] We carried out robustness checks by also including self-perceived AI, respectively financial knowledge to all specifications. Additionally, we also controlled for text length in case of classification accuracy (column 4). The results are not altered qualitatively. Thus, we do not report them for the sake of brevity.

From these results alone, we conclude that there is, at least, a learning effect. However, we cannot yet ascertain whether the XAL condition in itself has an effect on task completion speed. To do so, we conduct several hypotheses tests, summarized in Table 4, following the logic outlined in Sect. 3.4.

Before discussing the results, we note that we apply a Bonferroni correction for testing the seven hypotheses in Table 4 at the same time. Also, we focus the discussion on the per word, respectively per character normalized results.

Table 3. Results for Specification (2)

	(1)	(2)	(3)	(4)
$t^* = 15$				
β_{PrT}	−28.927***	−0.248***	−0.045***	0.217
	(5.096)	(0.096)	(0.017)	(0.232)
$\beta_{T,1}$	−22.607***	−0.084	−0.011	0.054
	(5.067)	(0.095)	(0.017)	(0.232)
$\beta_{T,2}$	−40.573***	−0.344***	−0.061***	0.253
	(4.137)	(0.078)	(0.014)	(0.190)
$\beta_{PoT,1}$	−45.100***	−0.437***	−0.078***	−0.163
	(5.067)	(0.095)	(0.017)	(0.233)
$\beta_{PoT,2}$	−47.573***	−0.504***	−0.092***	-0.135
	(5.066)	(0.095)	(0.017)	(0.233)
Constant	78.860***	0.874***	0.157***	−0.027
	(5.225)	(0.077)	(0.014)	(0.169)
$t^* = 17$				
β_{PrT}	−28.927***	−0.248***	−0.045***	0.217
	(5.096)	(0.096)	(0.017)	(0.232)
$\beta_{T,1}$	−27.160***	−0.162*	−0.026*	0.201
	(4.702)	(0.088)	(0.015)	(0.215)
$\beta_{T,2}$	−40.886***	−0.342***	−0.061***	0.204
	(4.226)	(0.079)	(0.014)	(0.194)
$\beta_{PoT,1}$	−45.100***	−0.437***	−0.078***	−0.163
	(5.079)	(0.095)	(0.017)	(0.233)
$\beta_{PoT,2}$	−47.573***	−0.504***	−0.092***	−0.135
	(5.079)	(0.095)	(0.017)	(0.233)
Constant	78.860***	0.874***	0.157***	−0.027
	(5.230)	(0.078)	(0.014)	(0.169)
$t^* = 20$				
β_{PrT}	−28.927***	−0.248***	−0.045***	0.217
	(5.096)	(0.096)	(0.017)	(0.232)
$\beta_{T,1}$	−31.980***	−0.254***	−0.044***	0.162
	(4.414)	(0.083)	(0.014)	(0.201)
$\beta_{T,2}$	−40.183***	−0.304***	−0.054***	0.244
	(4.414)	(0.083)	(0.014)	(0.202)
$\beta_{PoT,1}$	−45.100***	−0.437***	−0.078***	−0.163
	(5.096)	(0.096)	(0.017)	(0.233)
$\beta_{PoT,2}$	−47.573***	−0.504***	−0.092***	−0.135
	(5.096)	(0.096)	(0.017)	(0.233)
Constant	78.860***	0.874***	0.157***	−0.027
	(5.237)	(0.078)	(0.014)	(0.169)

[a] *p < 0.1; **p < 0.05; ***p<0.01; standard errors in parentheses.
[b] Columns labeled (1) refer to the absolute task completion length, columns labeled (2) refer to per word task completion length, columns labeled (3) refer to the per character task completion length (all in seconds) and columns labeled (4) refer to classification accuracy as dependent variable.
[c] Robustness checks including self-perceived AI, respectively financial knowledge and controlling for text length in case of classification accuracy did not alter the results qualitatively. Thus, these results are not reported.

First, we note that for splitting the XAL-treatment periods in period 20, most hypothesis indicating constant performance of participants during the experiment. The exception here is the hypothesis on identity between XAL- and post-XAL effects cannot be rejected, albeit weakly on a 10% significance level. For the remaining two cases, i.e. $t^* = 15$ and $t^* = 17$, we can reject the null hypothesis that the XAL- and post-XAL effects are equal on a 1%-level. Furthermore, we can only reject the null that the pre-XAL and XAL-effects are equal on a 5%-level for $t^* = 15$. Finally, we also reject the null of equality between the XAL1- and XAL2-effects on the 1% ($t^* = 15$), respectively 10%-level ($t^* = 17$) and we cannot reject the null that the post-XAL1 and post-XAL2-effects are equal. Combined with the regression results in Table 3 we conclude that there is, albeit weak, evidence for the following: i) A small detrimental effect of the XAL-treatment directly after its introduction. However, it is compensated for after the participants get accustomed to the XAL-treatment. ii) A small and lasting XAL-effect into the post-XAL periods. This last result could indicate that XAL can help human annotators beyond the actual treatment periods. That is to say, XAL-treatments need only be administered on a temporary basis rather than permanently.

5   Discussion of Findings

Human-centred XAI for the AL setting is a very young line of research. Ghai et el [13] utilized a between-framework for their experimental design to study the potential effects of XAI on the performance of the annotators in a binary classification problem on tabular data. However, the validity of their claims on the multi-class classification of unstructured data (e.g. text) needs to be explored. Given the massive number of applications generating text in the real-world and the evolving and unstructured nature of the text, we conducted our study on the complaint narrative of the customers to reflect a realistic setting. A very recent study [31] had highlighted an intriguing finding: individuals anticipated that XAI techniques would assist them in enhancing their annotation skills. Motivated by this discovery, we conducted our experiments to explore the potential learning effects of XAI on annotators in a real-world problem, a research question which explored for the first time.

Before discussing and putting our results into the broader context of XAI and XAL, we take a step back and briefly summarize our findings. First, our results suggest that there is no measurable effect of the XAL treatment on classification accuracy. However, there is a measurable effect on the task completion speed during the XAL-periods, compared to the first ten baseline periods. Second, there is an effect of the XAL-treatment on task completion speed, albeit weak, onto the last ten periods of the experiment where the XAL-treatment was taken away from the participants, without compromising classification accuracy. This suggests that XAL-treatment do not need to be permanently present for humans to reap the benefits of its support. Third, the results also suggest that there is an initial acclimatization period for the participants to get used to the XAL-

Table 4. Hypothesis Tests for Specification (2)

$\mathbb{H}_0$	(1)	(2)	(3)
	$t^* = 15$		
All effects equal	37.487***	24.251***	28.795***
pre-XAL = post-XAL1 = post-XAL2	15.980***	7.823	8.401
pre-XAL = XAL1 = XAL2	22.051***	11.387**	13.924***
XAL1 = XAL2 = post-XAL1	23.929***	15.634***	18.892***
XAL1 = XAL2 = post-XAL1 = post-XAL2	30.022***	22.535***	27.243***
XAL1 = XAL2	18.860***	11.213***	13.844***
post-XAL1 = post-XAL2	0.238	0.497	0.668
	$t^* = 17$		
All effects equal	31.832***	19.428***	22.987***
pre-XAL = post-XAL1 = post-XAL2	15.905***	7.790	8.360
pre-XAL = XAL1 = XAL2	16.468***	6.616	8.187
XAL1 = XAL2 = post-XAL1	18.337***	10.846**	13.131***
XAL1 = XAL2 = post-XAL1 = post-XAL2	24.402***	17.719***	21.442***
XAL1 = XAL2	13.293***	6.443*	8.108**
post-XAL1 = post-XAL2	0.237	0.495	0.665
	$t^* = 20$		
All effects equal	23.593***	13.459*	15.526**
pre-XAL = post-XAL1 = post-XAL2	15.796***	7.751	8.308
pre-XAL = XAL1 = XAL2	8.336	0.712	0.820
XAL1 = XAL2 = post-XAL1	10.192**	4.920	5.733
XAL1 = XAL2 = post-XAL1 = post-XAL2	16.215***	11.758*	13.991**
XAL1 = XAL2	5.182	0.539	0.741
post-XAL1 = post-XAL2	0.236	0.492	0.661

[a] $^*p < 0.1/7$; $^{**}p < 0.05/7$; $^{***}p < 0.01/7$, i.e. statistical rejection of an individual null-hypothesis is reported based on a Bonferroni correction for testing all seven null-hypotheses for a given model specification.
[b] Columns labeled (1) refer to the absolute task completion length, columns labeled (2) refer to per word task completion length and columns labeled (3) refer to the per character task completion length (all in seconds) as dependent variable.

treatment. This is evident from varying the cut-off t^* in specification (2)[8] and comparing the results, as indicated in Tables 3 and 4. Finally, at least in this

---

[8] Note that it is not clear where this cut-off should be put. Thus, putting it at random to some specific period can lead to misleading results. For example, the cut-off is set too far from the onset of the XAL-treatment, then the first treatment period covers the acclimatization period as well as the acclimatized period, thereby averaging the two counter-effects and diminishing the real effects. Similarly, if the cut-off is set too early. Thus, empirically one must compare several specifications as we did. This is commonly referred to as a break-point model.

setting and minor overall, there is also no difference between the per-word and per-character normalization of the task completion speed.

6   Conclusion and Future Work

In this article, we tackled the question of whether XAI can help humans become better annotators in an XAL environment. Our results suggest that this question can, partially, be affirmed. In particular, we find weak evidence that the XAL condition might have a lasting effect on the humans in terms of task completion speed. That is, even though administering the XAL condition does not have a direct effect on task completion speed, our results suggest that it does prime the human annotator to find the correct clues faster, when completing their task. Our results also suggest that this does not come at the cost of less classification accuracy.

For further investigating the effect of a XAL-treatment on classification, respectively task completion speed, we think it would be interesting to derive a measure for the "difficulty" of a given text. We want to do this since answering whether and when XAI and XAL can be helpful will crucially depend on such a notion; for example, one can expect that generally easier texts are easier/faster to classify without the help of XAI/XAL than more difficult texts. If we do not account for such a notion of difficulty in the analysis, it can very well be that the lack of this control blurs the overall picture and one underestimates/rejects the effects XAI/XAL has on human annotators. Similarly, we think that such a notion can be helpful in practice to pre-sort unknown texts according to difficulty and provide XAL treatment for human annotators only in case of difficult texts.

Additionally, we think it would be worth investigating the effects of several episodic periods of administering XAI/XAL-treatments. This way, practitioners can design optimal training schedules to keep their employees on a higher level with respect to task completion and there would be more insight into whether multiple episodes of XAI/XAL-treatments improve the annotators' performance in the long-run.

A   Appendix

Throughout the experiment, you were shown two types of text.

- Plain text without any annotations, highlights, etc.
- Explanations/Suggestions by the algorithm.

A.1   Questions About Explanations

This section will ask you about your experience and opinions for the explanations.

Table 5. Questionnaire about user's experience with explanations

The explanations were intuitive to understand						
Strongly disagree	Disagree	Somewhat disagree	Neither agree nor disagree	Somewhat agree	Agree	Strongly agree
The explanations have made the task easier						
Strongly disagree	Disagree	Somewhat disagree	Neither agree nor disagree	Somewhat agree	Agree	Strongly agree
The explanations supported my decision-making						
Strongly disagree	Disagree	Somewhat disagree	Neither agree nor disagree	Somewhat agree	Agree	Strongly agree
The explanations were helpful						
Strongly disagree	Disagree	Somewhat disagree	Neither agree nor disagree	Somewhat agree	Agree	Strongly agree
The explanations helped me classify the text better						
Strongly disagree	Disagree	Somewhat disagree	Neither agree nor disagree	Somewhat agree	Agree	Strongly agree
The explanations helped me classify the text faster						
Strongly disagree	Disagree	Somewhat disagree	Neither agree nor disagree	Somewhat agree	Agree	Strongly agree
In general, I relied a lot on the explanations						
Strongly disagree	Disagree	Somewhat disagree	Neither agree nor disagree	Somewhat agree	Agree	Strongly agree
In cases where I was very unsure, I made my decision based on the explanations						
Strongly disagree	Disagree	Somewhat disagree	Neither agree nor disagree	Somewhat agree	Agree	Strongly agree
I trust the algorithm to categorize the texts correctly						
Strongly disagree	Disagree	Somewhat disagree	Neither agree nor disagree	Somewhat agree	Agree	Strongly agree
The explanations were adequate for the purpose						
Strongly disagree	Disagree	Somewhat disagree	Neither agree nor disagree	Somewhat agree	Agree	Strongly agree
The explanations made the text better understandable						
Strongly disagree	Disagree	Somewhat disagree	Neither agree nor disagree	Somewhat agree	Agree	Strongly agree

A.2   Questions About Plain Text

Table 6. Questions about user's experience and opinions for the plain text.

With plain texts, I read the text more carefully						
Strongly disagree	Disagree	Somewhat disagree	Neither agree nor disagree	Somewhat agree	Agree	Strongly agree
I prefer explanations over plain text						
Strongly disagree	Disagree	Somewhat disagree	Neither agree nor disagree	Somewhat agree	Agree	Strongly agree

A.3   Task-Related Background

Table 7. Questionnaire about users level of experience for the task

How much knowledge about the financial sector and the respective terms did you already have?						
Strongly disagree	Disagree	Somewhat disagree	Neither agree nor disagree	Somewhat agree	Agree	Strongly agree
How experienced are you in the field of AI?						
Strongly disagree	Disagree	Somewhat disagree	Neither agree nor disagree	Somewhat agree	Agree	Strongly agree

A.4   Expert Learning

Table 8. Questionnaire about personal learning and experience.

I learnt more about the financial complaints with the explanations						
Strongly disagree	Disagree	Somewhat disagree	Neither agree nor disagree	Somewhat agree	Agree	Strongly agree
In the beginning, I found it difficult to categorize the complaints						
Strongly disagree	Disagree	Somewhat disagree	Neither agree nor disagree	Somewhat agree	Agree	Strongly agree
Towards the end, I found it difficult to categorize the complaints						
Strongly disagree	Disagree	Somewhat disagree	Neither agree nor disagree	Somewhat agree	Agree	Strongly agree

References

1. Adadi, A., Berrada, M.: Peeking inside the black-box: a survey on explainable artificial intelligence (XAI). IEEE Access **6**, 52138–52160 (2018)
2. Alpert, H.: Complaint content classification. https://github.com/halpert3/complaint-content-classification-nlp. Accessed 25 Apr 2023
3. Alufaisan, Y., Marusich, L.R., Bakdash, J.Z., Zhou, Y., Kantarcioglu, M.: Does explainable artificial intelligence improve human decision-making? In: Proceedings of the AAAI Conference on Artificial Intelligence, vol. 35, pp. 6618–6626 (2021)
4. Broniatowski, D.A., et al.: Psychological foundations of explainability and interpretability in artificial intelligence. Technical report, NIST (2021)
5. Cai, C.J., Winter, S., Steiner, D., Wilcox, L., Terry, M.: "Hello AI": uncovering the onboarding needs of medical practitioners for human-ai collaborative decision-making. Proc. ACM Hum. Comput. Interact. **3**(CSCW), 104:1–104:24 (2019). https://doi.org/10.1145/3359206
6. Chhatwal, R., Gronvall, P., Huber-Fliflet, N., Keeling, R., Zhang, J., Zhao, H.: Explainable text classification in legal document review a case study of explainable predictive coding. In: 2018 IEEE International Conference on Big Data (big Data), pp. 1905–1911. IEEE (2018)

7. Confalonieri, R., et al.: What makes a good explanation? Cognitive dimensions of explaining intelligent machines. In: CogSci, pp. 25–26 (2019)
8. Das, D., Chernova, S.: Leveraging rationales to improve human task performance. In: Proceedings of the 25th International Conference on Intelligent User Interfaces, pp. 510–518 (2020)
9. Ehsan, U., Riedl, M.O.: Human-centered explainable AI: towards a reflective sociotechnical approach. In: Stephanidis, C., Kurosu, M., Degen, H., Reinerman-Jones, L. (eds.) HCII 2020. LNCS, vol. 12424, pp. 449–466. Springer, Cham (2020). https://doi.org/10.1007/978-3-030-60117-1_33
10. Evans, T., et al.: The explainability paradox: challenges for XAI in digital pathology. Futur. Gener. Comput. Syst. **133**, 281–296 (2022)
11. Gajos, K.Z., Mamykina, L.: Do people engage cognitively with AI? Impact of AI assistance on incidental learning. In: 27th International Conference on Intelligent User Interfaces, pp. 794–806 (2022)
12. Ghai, B., Liao, Q.V., Zhang, Y., Bellamy, R.K.E., Mueller, K.: Explainable active learning (XAL): an empirical study of how local explanations impact annotator experience. CoRR abs/2001.09219 (2020)
13. Ghai, B., Liao, Q.V., Zhang, Y., Bellamy, R.K.E., Mueller, K.: Explainable active learning (XAL): toward AI explanations as interfaces for machine teachers. Proc. ACM Hum. Comput. Interact. 4(CSCW3), 1–28 (2020)
14. Gilyazev, R., Turdakov, D.Y.: Active learning and crowdsourcing: a survey of optimization methods for data labeling. Program. Comput. Softw. **44**, 476–491 (2018)
15. Guidotti, R., Monreale, A., Ruggieri, S., Turini, F., Giannotti, F., Pedreschi, D.: A survey of methods for explaining black box models. ACM Comput. Surv. (CSUR) **51**(5), 1–42 (2018)
16. Guo, Q., Zhuang, F., Qin, C., Zhu, H., Xie, X., Xiong, H., He, Q.: A survey on knowledge graph-based recommender systems. IEEE Trans. Knowl. Data Eng. **34**(8), 3549–3568 (2020)
17. Jia, S., Li, Z., Chen, N., Zhang, J.: Towards visual explainable active learning for zero-shot classification. IEEE Trans. Vis. Comput. Graph. **28**(1), 791–801 (2022)
18. Kazai, G., Kamps, J., Milic-Frayling, N.: An analysis of human factors and label accuracy in crowdsourcing relevance judgments. Inf. Retrieval **16**, 138–178 (2013)
19. Kim, S.S., Watkins, E.A., Russakovsky, O., Fong, R., Monroy-Hernández, A.: "Help me help the AI": understanding how explainability can support human-AI interaction. In: Proceedings of the 2023 CHI Conference on Human Factors in Computing Systems, pp. 1–17 (2023)
20. Kim, T.W., Routledge, B.R.: Why a right to an explanation of algorithmic decision-making should exist: a trust-based approach. Bus. Ethics Q. **32**(1), 75–102 (2022)
21. Lai, V., Tan, C.: On human predictions with explanations and predictions of machine learning models: A case study on deception detection. In: Proceedings of the Conference on Fairness, Accountability, and Transparency, pp. 29–38 (2019)
22. Liao, Q.V., Zhang, Y., Luss, R., Doshi-Velez, F., Dhurandhar, A.: Connecting algorithmic research and usage contexts: a perspective of contextualized evaluation for explainable AI. In: Proceedings of the AAAI Conference on Human Computation and Crowdsourcing, vol. 10, pp. 147–159 (2022)
23. Loh, H.W., Ooi, C.P., Seoni, S., Barua, P.D., Molinari, F., Acharya, U.R.: Application of explainable artificial intelligence for healthcare: a systematic review of the last decade (2011–2022). Comput. Methods Program. Biomed. 107161 (2022)
24. Lundberg, S.M., Lee, S.I.: A unified approach to interpreting model predictions. In: Advances in Neural Information Processing Systems, vol. 30 (2017)

25. Miller, T.: Explanation in artificial intelligence: insights from the social sciences. Artif. Intell. **267**, 1–38 (2019)
26. Mohebbi, H., Zuidema, W., Chrupała, G., Alishahi, A.: Quantifying context mixing in transformers (2023)
27. Molnar, C., Casalicchio, G., Bischl, B.: Interpretable machine learning – a brief history, state-of-the-art and challenges. In: Koprinska, I., et al. (eds.) ECML PKDD 2020. CCIS, vol. 1323, pp. 417–431. Springer, Cham (2020). https://doi.org/10.1007/978-3-030-65965-3_28
28. Mondal, I., Ganguly, D.: Alex: Active learning based enhancement of a classification model's explainability. In: Proceedings of the 29th ACM International Conference on Information & Knowledge Management, pp. 3309–3312 (2020)
29. Mosqueira-Rey, E., Hernández-Pereira, E., Alonso-Ríos, D., Bobes-Bascarán, J., Fernández-Leal, Á.: Human-in-the-loop machine learning: a state of the art. Artif. Intell. Rev. 1–50 (2022)
30. Ribeiro, M.T., Singh, S., Guestrin, C.: "Why should i trust you?" Explaining the predictions of any classifier. In: Proceedings of the 22nd ACM SIGKDD International Conference on Knowledge Discovery and Data Mining, pp. 1135–1144 (2016)
31. Saeed, W., Omlin, C.W.: Explainable AI (XAI): a systematic meta-survey of current challenges and future opportunities. Knowl. Based Syst. **263**, 110273 (2023)
32. Samek, W., Montavon, G., Vedaldi, A., Hansen, L.K., Müller, K.R.: Explainable AI: Interpreting, Explaining and Visualizing Deep Learning, vol. 11700. Springer, Heidelberg (2019). https://doi.org/10.1007/978-3-030-28954-6
33. Schoonderwoerd, T.A., Jorritsma, W., Neerincx, M.A., Van Den Bosch, K.: Human-centered XAI: developing design patterns for explanations of clinical decision support systems. Int. J. Hum. Comput. Stud. **154**, 102684 (2021)
34. Settles, B.: From theories to queries: active learning in practice. In: Active Learning and Experimental Design Workshop in Conjunction with AISTATS 2010, pp. 1–18. JMLR Workshop and Conference Proceedings (2011)
35. Suresh, H., Gomez, S.R., Nam, K.K., Satyanarayan, A.: Beyond expertise and roles: a framework to characterize the stakeholders of interpretable machine learning and their needs. In: Kitamura, Y., Quigley, A., Isbister, K., Igarashi, T., Bjørn, P., Drucker, S.M. (eds.) CHI 2021: CHI Conference on Human Factors in Computing Systems, Virtual Event/Yokohama, Japan, 8–13 May 2021, pp. 74:1–74:16. ACM (2021)
36. Teso, S., Alkan, Ö., Stammer, W., Daly, E.: Leveraging explanations in interactive machine learning: an overview. Frontiers Artif. Intell. **6** (2023)
37. Teso, S., Kersting, K.: "Why should i trust interactive learners?" Explaining interactive queries of classifiers to users (2018)
38. Tsiakas, K., Murray-Rust, D.: Using human-in-the-loop and explainable AI to envisage new future work practices. In: Proceedings of the 15th International Conference on PErvasive Technologies Related to Assistive Environments, pp. 588–594 (2022)
39. Vale, D., El-Sharif, A., Ali, M.: Explainable artificial intelligence (XAI) post-hoc explainability methods: risks and limitations in non-discrimination law. AI Ethics **2**, 1–12 (2022)
40. Vilone, G., Longo, L.: Explainable artificial intelligence: a systematic review. arXiv preprint arXiv:2006.00093 (2020)
41. Weber, P., Carl, K.V., Hinz, O.: Applications of explainable artificial intelligence in finance-a systematic review of finance, information systems, and computer science literature. Manage. Rev. Q. 1–41 (2023)

Statutory Professions in AI Governance and Their Consequences for Explainable AI

Labhaoise NiFhaolain$^{(\boxtimes)}$ (ID), Andrew Hines (ID), and Vivek Nallur (ID)

School of Computer Science, University College Dublin, Dublin, Ireland
labhaoise.ni.fhaolain@gmail.com, {andrew.hines,vivek.nallur}@ucd.ie

Abstract. Intentional and accidental harms arising from the use of AI have impacted the health, safety and rights of individuals. While regulatory frameworks are being developed, there remains a lack of consensus on methods necessary to deliver safe AI. The potential for explainable AI (XAI) to contribute to the effectiveness of the regulation of AI is being increasingly examined. Regulation must include methods to ensure compliance on an ongoing basis, though there is an absence of practical proposals on how to achieve this. For XAI to be successfully incorporated into a regulatory system, the individuals who are engaged in interpreting/explaining the model to stakeholders should be sufficiently qualified for the role. Statutory professionals are prevalent in domains in which harm can be done to the health, safety and rights of individuals. The most obvious examples are doctors, engineers and lawyers. Those professionals are required to exercise skill and judgement and to defend their decision making process in the event of harm occurring. We propose that a statutory profession framework be introduced as a necessary part of the AI regulatory framework for compliance and monitoring purposes. We will refer to this new statutory professional as an AI Architect (AIA). This AIA would be responsible to ensure the risk of harm is minimised and accountable in the event that harms occur. The AIA would also be relied on to provide appropriate interpretations/explanations of XAI models to stakeholders. Further, in order to satisfy themselves that the models have been developed in a satisfactory manner, the AIA would require models to have appropriate transparency. Therefore it is likely that the introduction of an AIA system would lead to an increase in the use of XAI to enable AIA to discharge their professional obligations.

Keywords: Artificial Intelligence · XAI · Governance · Regulation · Statutory Profession

This paper emanated from research funded by Science Foundation Ireland to the Insight Centre for Data Analytics (12/RC/2289_P2) and SFI Centre for Research Training in Machine Learning (18/CRT/6183). For the purpose of Open Access, the author has applied a CC BY public copyright licence to any Author Accepted Manuscript version arising from this submission.

1   AI Regulation and Challenges

Intentional and accidental harms arising from the use of AI have impacted the health, safety and rights of individuals [3]. While there is much pre-existing legislative regulation applicable to AI [48], and AI specific regulatory frameworks are being developed [16], there subsists a lack of consensus on the wider governance framework necessary to deliver safe AI [45]. An effective governance framework must include mechanisms to ensure compliance on an ongoing basis. To date, in terms of compliance mechanisms in AI regulation, the focus has been on seeking to make corporations and companies responsible and accountable. However, these entities are explicitly structured through incorporation to avoid personal liability [11]. Gaps in accountability in AI have been reviewed [22,44] and some work has been carried out on the dearth of practical proposals on how to move from principles to practice in AI governance [40]. Human oversight in relation to AI has been explored [30,43] as has the empowerment of employees through continuous education and change management to operationalise AI governance [33]. However there remains a lack of proposals on how to structure a system of accountability and associated enforcement that interacts with the legal system in a pragmatic manner. In effect, the operationalisation of accountability and attendant enforcement remains absent. The potential for XAI to contribute to the effectiveness of the governance of AI within the legal system is being increasingly examined [12]. In this paper we seek to establish the potential for combining XAI with personal obligations that underpin statutory professions to illustrate how they can contribute to the enforceable accountability for AI through regulation.

Regulation seeks to modify behaviour to achieve particular outcomes [42] and a regulatory framework encompasses norms along with monitoring and correction. While an AI regulatory framework is far from complete, regulatory norms for AI exist including ethics principles and codes of conduct [8], standards [50] and law (both applying existing law and proposals for Regulations [16]). These are all necessary components but are not sufficient. Operational and adherence mechanisms are also required. Voluntary guidelines, such as ethics principles and codes of conduct, require deep embedding for success [49], and rely on human actors. Standards require government oversight to deliver societal benefit [21]. For compliance with standards, Huising and Silbey [26] argue that individuals' conduct and personal responsibility is crucial for implementation. By design, corporate accountability limits personal responsibility and, in order to minimise harm, a regulatory system needs individuals who are responsible for preventing harm, and held accountable if harms do occur.

Regulation of professionals arises predominantly in domains with significant impact on health, safety and rights due to the fundamental importance of these areas to the individual and to society as a whole. While lawyers and doctors have been the subject of some form of governance for millenia, modern-day professions emerged in the late nineteenth and early twentieth centuries [28]. Statutory professions are those whose conduct is regulated by legislation, who can be subject to the rules (including educational requirements) and codes of conduct set out by a regulatory body, and who can be disciplined by the regulatory body and the judiciary for infractions. The EU Commission has defined a regulated profession as "A professional activity or group of professional activities, access to which, the pursuit of which, or one of the modes of pursuit of which is subject, directly or indirectly, by virtue of legislative, regulatory or administrative provisions to the possession of specific professional qualifications." [19]. In some jurisdictions the use of certain titles (known as *reserved titles*) is limited. Prerequisites for using the title may include prescribed qualifications and registration with the relevant body. However this falls short of a fully statutory profession. For example, the title of *software engineer* is a reserved one in every province and territory in Canada. Each of the ten provinces and three territories regulates the work of software engineering in a different way, under their own legislative provisions. Therefore while the title is limited in a uniform manner, the work is not controlled in a similar way. Indeed, it has been noted by Engineers Canada, an national umbrella body for provincial and territorial regulators, that the regulation of software engineering practice has been troublesome due to its overlap with software development [14].

In considering whether to create a new statutory profession, the governing question asked in most jurisdictions is whether there is the risk of harm to the public as a result of the professional's conduct [32]. In other domains, where individuals can be negatively affected by the conduct of service providers, those service providers are regulated. However, whilst computer scientists and software developers can impact the health, safety and rights of individuals across society when developing AI systems, individuals are not regulated.

We propose that a statutory profession framework, akin to the system for lawyers, doctors and engineers, be introduced as a necessary part of the AI regulatory framework, for compliance and monitoring purposes. We will refer to this statutory professional as an AI Architect (AIA). In this paper the term AIA is simply used as a working title for the proposed professional and the specific term is not of significance at this juncture.

2   XAI Interface Challenges

There is much discussion about *humans in the loop, on the loop* and *in command* and about the importance of the role from a legal perspective, though there is no legal definition of what these terms entail [13]. Indeed the *human in the loop* is "no panacea" for the concerns arising from AI [27], but as governance is a social structure, humans are central it.

The goal of XAI is to produce human-interpretable models [4] and to *justify* decisions which have been made, particularly when used in critical situations [29].

Ali et al. [4] categorise XAI techniques as follows: data explainability, model explainability, post-hoc explainability and assessment of explanations. The authors also outline the role of humans in the assessment of the explanations and set out post-hoc explainability methods as follows: attribution methods, visualisation methods, example based explanation methods, game theory

Table 1. Summary of regulated professions in Ireland with a requirement for professional indemnity insurance categorised by risk

Health	Rights	Safety
Medical (Anaesthesiology, Basic medical training - Ireland, Cardiology, Cardiothoracic surgery, Chemical pathology, Child and adolescent psychiatry, Clinical genetics, Dermatology, Emergency medicine, Endocrinology and diabetes mellitus, Gastro-enterology, General (internal) medicine, General Medical Practitioner, General surgery, Genito-urinary medicine, Geriatric medicine, Haematology (clinical and laboratory), Histopathology, Immunology (clinical and laboratory), Infectious diseases, Medical oncology, Microbiology, Nephrology, Neurology, Neurosurgery, Obstetrics and gynaecology, Occupational medicine, Ophthalmic surgery, Ophthalmology, Oral and maxillo-facial surgery, Otolaryngology, Paediatric Surgery, Paediatrics, Pharmaceutical Medicine, Plastic, reconstructive and aesthetic surgery, Psychiatry, Public health medicine, Radiation oncology, Radiology, Respiratory medicine, Rheumatology, Trauma and orthopaedic surgery) Veterinary Surgeon	Auctioneer Building Energy Rating (BER) Assessors Certified Public Accountant Chartered Accountant/Auditor Chartered Certified Accountant Chartered Tax Adviser Estate Agents Incorporated Public Accountant Letting Agents Liquidator Management Agent Personal Insolvency Practitioner Solicitor	Aeromedical Examiner (AME) Affiliate (engineering) Associate Engineer Architect Architect (acquired rights) Building Surveyor Chartered engineer Engineering Technician Quantity Surveyor Registered Electrical Contractor Transport Manager for a Road Transport Undertaking

methods, knowledge extraction methods and neural methods. These techniques are used by people in order to arrive at an explanation - therefore these methods can only be deployed in the context of a *human-computer interaction* [4].

Miller et al. [31] have identified that moving from technical aspects to the mindset of the user can be challenging for XAI designers. In proposing a process for the design of user-centric XAI systems as a means to avoid unwanted consequences, Förster et al. [20] recommend a higher user involvement in the process.

Given that the veracity of explanation is at the core of the future of XAI, challenges arise when explanations are provided which are guided by the explainer's agenda, rather than the individual impacted by the decision. Reference has been made to the rise of *altered* explanations in the field of XAI which pose problems in the field [7,41]. Examples of *altered* explanations being provided include in order to avoid intellectual property disclosure, or a bank employee denying loans for nefarious reasons, or companies using explanations to lure customers [41].

Doran et al. [10] have drawn the distinction between how "rules" of certain XAI systems can shed light on *how* decisions are made but they do not explain *why* the decision was made. The authors state that the annotations and visualisations produced within the XAI domain require "human-driven post processing under their own line of reasoning".

3   Regulated Professions in the EU

At a general level, there are different elements in systems of regulated professions. The professional has a legal/regulatory requirement to register with a prescribed body (regulatory body). The regulatory body is charged with assessing whether the individual has reached a requisite level of education/qualification (at admission to the profession and often on an ongoing basis) and the professional is subject to rules which govern their conduct (in their professional role, and sometimes outside of that role). If the professional breaches the rules of conduct, the regulatory body (usually in conjunction with the Court) can prevent the professional from practising in that regulated role.

Professional indemnity (PI) Insurance can provide indemnity against claims made by those impacted by the professional's conduct. It is designed to compensate for losses which have arisen from a professional's failures and is not entirely dependent on the professional's own financial assets [34]. Morgan and Hanrahan [34] have set out the overall purpose of PI insurance, stating that "The reasons for mandating PI insurance have public interest elements, encompassing both the protection of individual clients in the event of professional failure that results in a loss, and the creation and support of trust in the general body of professionals". Cannon and McGurk [5] have noted that the purpose of mandating this type of insurance is to protect the clients and those impacted by the professional's conduct, rather than protecting the professional.

Therefore society requires certain professionals to carry PI insurance due to their potential to cause serious damage to individuals. In order to examine the relevance for a regulated profession to enhance the governance of AI, we conducted a survey of regulated professions in Ireland as set out by the European Commission in the Regulated Professions Database [1]. That database contains the regulated professions of all EU countries and provides a search and filter function. Using web data extraction we filtered the results to include regulated professions from Ireland only. We then identified those professions for whom PI insurance is a prerequisite for practising in the area (e.g. solicitor [2]).

The total number of regulated professions in Ireland which appear on the European Database of Regulated Professions [1] is 229. Of those, 69 are required to carry PI insurance. We have set out these professions in Table 1. We examined that subsection and categorised them. The three risk areas into which these professions fall are very clearly identifiable as those of health, safety and rights. The impact on rights includes an impact on property rights (whether real property in the form of land and buildings or other property). It also includes the civil and political rights, along with economic, social and cultural rights dealt with by solicitors.

4   Proposal for AI Architect to Address Regulatory and XAI Challenges

We propose that AI regulation should be operationalised effected through a human actor, specifically by requiring through legislation, that certain AI solutions be 'signed off' by an AIA who is a member of a statutory profession, as previously proposed [36]. In the case of XAI, the AIA would be the person entitled to provide and sign off on the interpretation/explanation of the model. Like other domains, not all those working in computer science or software engineering would require regulation within a statutory profession, but AIA would be a protected title for those with the responsibility and accountability for sign-off. We have set out in Fig. 1 an outline of a Machine Learning Operations (ML Ops) pipeline. The top row sets out the instance of development and deployment of an ML solution, while the bottom row sets out deployment only. The middle row illustrates how the pipeline is punctuated with the involvement of an AIA.

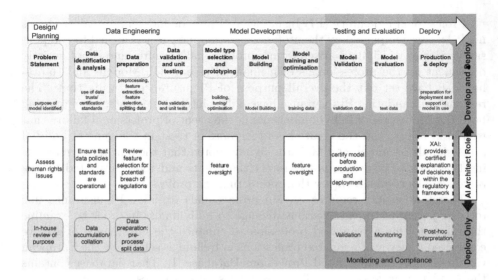

Fig. 1. Suggested functions of AI Architect in development of ML solution and in deployment of ML solution.

The AIA's role would be explicitly outlined and tightly coupled to the AI system's lifecycle. In this way, the AIA's obligations would be clearly delineated and bounded. The dotted blocks are references to the role of the AIA in the case of XAI, in respect of providing explanations of XAI within the regulatory framework. As can be seen from Fig. 1, the AIA role may be wide ranging. Much like the profession of *doctor* has evolved into sub-specialties, as can be seen from the first column in Table 1., a similar evolution would likely occur in the case of the AIA profession. Indeed, the field of AI engineering as a discipline is already being explored and is gaining momentum [6, 39].

The AIA would have a professional obligation to ensure that AI solutions being developed and deployed are safe, by ensuring that due diligence is performed on datasets, following best practices, and remaining up to date with technological developments. Crucially, professional obligations (given their statutory status) would take precedence over employee obligations. Tensions may arise between the desires of the company and the requirements of the regulations governing the AIA's conduct. Similar tensions arise in the case of solicitors who are employed by companies as *in-house solicitors*, where the companies are in effect their sole clients. Like solicitors, the AIA would be required to conduct themselves according to stipulated principles. The Solicitors Regulation Authority of England and Wales sets out the principles required of solicitors which include independence, honesty and integrity. In the event that the principles come into conflict with the client's interests, the principles which safeguard the wider public interest take precedence [46]. The question arises of the employment security of an AIA if they are obliged to make *unpopular* decisions. The AIA would benefit from the protection of the regulatory body system such that they cannot be dismissed from their employment for carrying out these professional and legally protected obligations. Any attempt to dismiss an employee could be deemed to be wrongful dismissal. This combined obligation and protection dynamic balances the power between individual professionals and large corporations.

Personal responsibility would be a component of the system for AIAs. This would not be a means to absolve corporations of responsibility, rather a recognition that the very rationale of the modern corporation is to avoid personal liability. This would address the ongoing challenge of making shareholders liable for the obligations of their corporation as *piercing the corporate veil* of limited personal liability is fraught with obstacles [35].

In order to deliver personal responsibility and accountability, legislation and codes of conduct exist by which the professionals must abide. Failure to comply can result in disciplinary procedures which are instigated by the errant professional's regulatory body. Mills et al. [32] have stated that "Professional-specific grounds for misconduct reflect the approach that professionals are, if the profession itself is to be trusted and well regarded, to be held to a different - typically higher - standard than non-professionals". In broad outline, following successful disciplinary proceedings, sanctions may be brought against the professional. The ultimate sanction, usually reserved for a disciplinary procedure which comes before a judge in court, is to strike the individual from the register of professionals, preventing them from practising in that professional role. Disciplinary sanctions can also have cross border implications. Under the EU Direction on the recognition of professional qualifications, certain professional regulators must notify parallel competent authorities in other member states when certain individual professionals have been restricted or prohibited in their practice [19].

In parallel with the disciplinary proceedings, legal claims for professional negligence can arise, this time brought by those who have been harmed by the conduct of the professional. In these cases the professional may make seek indemnity from their professional indemnity insurers. This twin track approach (a) protects society in general through the disciplinary process (through sanctions deterring or preventing the professional from causing similar harm again) and (b) restores the individual to the position they were in before the harm caused by the professional occurred (through an award of damages or through another restorative court order). Whether in the context of disciplinary proceedings or professional negligence claims, the professional is obliged to justify their conduct and the decisions they made to the satisfaction of experts in that field, rather than lay people.

In the case of AI, the role of AIA would be different from that of *ethical lead* and similar roles within AI development and deployment. Currently, without the statutory footing, it is open to companies to change their internal ethics guidelines or choose to disregard external ethics guidelines or standards, due to their voluntary nature. This can result the role of "ethical leads" being rendered ineffective, or indeed can result in the role being made redundant through termination of employment contracts.

A search of the internet will produce many results relating to certification of computer scientists including some calls for *regulation* of that role. To the best of our knowledge there are no specific, measurable and realistic proposals for exactly how this should be done. Our proposal calls for a fully regulated profession with statutory obligations for professional conduct, liability, indemnity insurance and disciplinary regimes which can result in the professional being before the Court for breaches of their duties and being prevented from practising in the role.

The AIA, as the regulated a human in the loop, at each stage of the development and deployment process would increase consumer/citizen confidence. This *farm to fork* style responsibility tracing would require that an AIA oversees substantive changes in the solution, or the deployment environment. An AIA system would benefit those corporations that see value in a market with legal certainty, while nefarious actors would be disadvantaged. Given that fast moving fields such as AI are difficult to legislate for, an agile AIA system would also facilitate better State protection of citizens.

The individual fulfilling the AIA role would have personal responsibility to ensure that explanations provided in XAI are accurate, rather than being driven by the deploying company. This would avoid the problem of *altered* explanations, referred to above. In addition, in the context of an increase in the interactions between technical teams and stakeholders in the development phases of XAI, those interactions could be mediated by the AIA, who can adopt a neutral stance between the two cohorts. The characteristics of XAI would mean that AIAs could more confidently ensure that the AI systems are developed in compliance with the relevant regulations. Therefore it is likely that the introduction of this regulated profession would garner an increase in the use of XAI techniques.

The AI Act may be a natural route through which to introduce the AIA into the regulatory system. Recital 48 of the draft AI Act compromise text requires "human oversight" in particular scenarios and requires that "natural persons to whom human oversight has been assigned have the necessary competence, training and authority to carry out that role". Article 14 requires high risk systems to have effective human oversight to prevent or minimise risks to health safety and rights of individuals. Under Article 29 the deployers of AI systems must "ensure that the natural persons assigned to ensure human oversight of the high-risk AI systems are competent, properly qualified and trained, and have the necessary resources in order to ensure the effective supervision of the AI system in accordance with Article 14". The requirements for human oversight would be fulfilled by an AIA while the transparency obligations under Article 13 may see an expansion of the use of XAI.

Many standards organisations continue their work in the field of AI [47]. While this form of governance has been criticised for being driven by industry, this has been acknowledged by the EU, resulting in a new strategy on Standardisation [17]. The AI Act makes explicit reference to the use of standards and the EU Commission has issued a draft standardisation request to the European Standardisation Organisations for standards in support of safe and trustworthy

AI [18]. This draft request mandates CEN-CENELEC to include human rights expertise and civil society involvement in the development of the standards. As with any standards, a method to ensure that they are being complied with will be necessary. Again, the AIA would contribute to ongoing monitoring and compliance rather than evaluating compliance ex-post.

The approach to bring the regulated profession of AIA into being would be multipronged. The process would include the creation of a regulatory body and a protected title through legislation [25]. That body would work to set out the educational requirements and the practices which would be reserved to the regulated professional. The introduction of an AIA may be unpalatable to technology companies as a costly overhead. However much like regulation in Pharma is a cost of doing business, so too would the inclusion of an AIA. The introduction of the professional to the market could be achieved through the requirement that an AIA be used in all cases of government procurement initially. This would create an incentive for corporations to bring AIAs into their operations. Phased introduction into other spheres could then proceed.

Regulatory impact assessments (RIAs) are used as evaluation tools for policy, laws and regulations at national [9], cross-national [15] and international levels [38]. These RIAs would be built into the regulatory framework to allow transparent assessment during the evolution of the profession within the wider regulatory context. Examples of ML pipelines which resulted, for example, in human rights breaches could be contrasted with a pipeline in which an AIA had defined tasks to be performed to consider whether the inclusion of the AIA reduced the incidence human rights breaches.

The statutory professions system is not a perfect solution but its longevity in the areas of medicine, law and civil engineering demonstrates its ability to deliver on the objectives of service and product quality standards and to adapt over many centuries to changing circumstances.

5   Conclusion

Governments around the world are signalling an appetite for AI regulation in AI strategies [37] and the EU has initiated work on a regulatory system [16]. When quality levels and rules are being determined, through ethics guidelines, standards and legislation, it is critical that monitoring and compliance mechanisms are developed in parallel. We propose that the inclusion of a statutory profession is a necessary, yet currently unconsidered, component of a sustainable and workable AI regulatory system. The concept of a computer science profession has been examined for decades [23,24]. While some advances have been made, for example through being chartered as an IT professional, the profession has not evolved into a regulated profession with authority and responsibilities underpinned by legislative status. There are sufficient examples of effective statutory regulation of professionals in other similar domains to indicate that an AIA is a promising candidate for statutory regulation in order to enhance the regulation of AI.

References

1. https://ec.europa.eu/growth/tools-databases/regprof/professions/bycountry
2. Regulated Professions Database/Ireland/Solicitor. https://ec.europa.eu/growth/tools-databases/regprof/regprof/3572
3. Acemoglu, D.: Harms of AI. (no. w29247). National Bureau of Economic Research (2021)
4. Ali, S., et al.: Explainable artificial intelligence (XAI): what we know and what is left to attain trustworthy artificial intelligence. Inf. Fusion **99**, 101805 (2023)
5. Cannon, M., McGurk, B.: Professional Indemnity Insurance, 2nd edn. Oxford University Press, Oxford (2016)
6. Carnegie Mellon University: Artificial Intelligence Engineering. https://www.sei.cmu.edu/our-work/artificial-intelligence-engineering/
7. Chromik, M., Eiband, M., Völkel, S.T., Buschek, D.: Dark patterns of explainability, transparency, and user control for intelligent systems. In: IUI Workshops, vol. 2327 (2019)
8. Council of Europe: AI Initiatives (2023). https://www.coe.int/en/web/artificial-intelligence/national-initiatives
9. Department of the Taoiseach, Government of Ireland: Revised RIA Guidelines: How to conduct a Regulatory Impact Analysis (2009). https://assets.gov.ie/43562/b2c5a78227834a96ad001b381456ab18.pdf
10. Doran, D., Schulz, S., Besold, T.R.: What does explainable AI really mean? A new conceptualization of perspectives (2018). https://arxiv.org/abs/1710.00794
11. Easterbrook, F.H., Fischel, D.R.: Limited liability and the corporation. Univ. Chicago Law Rev. **52**(1), 89–117 (1985)
12. Ebers, M.: Regulating explainable AI in the European Union. An overview of the current legal framework(s). In: Nordic Yearbook of Law and Informatics 2020–2021: Law in the Era of Artificial Intelligence. The Swedish Law and Informatics Research Institute (2021)
13. Enarsson, T., Enqvist, L., Naarttijärvi, M.: Approaching the human in the loop - legal perspectives on hybrid human/algorithmic decision-making in three contexts. Inf. Commun. Technol. Law **31**(1), 123–153 (2022)
14. Engineers Canada: Professional practice in software engineering (2023). https://engineerscanada.ca/sites/default/files/public-policy/professional-practice-software-engineering-en.pdf
15. EU Commission: Better Regulation Toolbox (2021)
16. EU Commission: Proposal for a Regulation laying down harmonised rules on artificial intelligence (Artificial Intelligence Act) (2021). https://eur-lex.europa.eu/legal-content/EN/TXT/?uri=CELEX%3A52021PC0206
17. EU Commission: An EU Strategy on Standardisation - Setting global standards in support of a resilient, green and digital EU single market (2022). https://ec.europa.eu/docsroom/documents/48598
18. EU Commission: Draft standardisation request to the European Standardisation Organisations in support of safe and trustworthy artificial intelligence (2022). https://ec.europa.eu/docsroom/documents/52376
19. EU Parliament and Council: Directive 2005/36/EC of the European Parliament and of the Council of 7 September 2005 on the recognition of professional qualifications. https://eur-lex.europa.eu/LexUriServ/LexUriServ.do?uri=OJ:L:2005:255:0022:0142:en:PDF

20. Förster, M., Klier, M., Kluge, K., Sigler, I.: Fostering human agency: a process for the design of user-centric XAI systems. In: ICIS 2020 Proceedings, p. 12 (2020)
21. Garvin, D.A.: Can industry self-regulation work? Calif. Manage. Rev. **25**(4), 37–52 (1983)
22. Hohma, E., Boch, A., Trauth, R., Lütge, C.: Investigating accountability for artificial intelligence through risk governance: a workshop-based exploratory study. Front. Psychol. **14**, 1073686 (2023)
23. Holmes, N.: The social implications of the Australian computer society. Aust. Comput. J. **6**(3), 124–128 (1974)
24. Holmes, N.: The profession and digital technology. Computer 114–116 (2011)
25. Huber, W.D.: Should the forensic accounting profession be regulated? Res. Account. Regul. **25**(1), 123–132 (2013)
26. Huising, R., Silbey, S.S.: Governing the gap: forging safe science through relational regulation. Regul. Govern. **5**(1), 14–42 (2011)
27. Krügel, S., Ostermaier, A., Uhl, M.: Algorithms as partners in crime: a lesson in ethics by design. Comput. Hum. Behav. **138**, 107483 (2023)
28. Law, M.T., Kim, S.: Specialization and regulation: the rise of professionals and the emergence of occupational licensing regulation. J. Econ. Hist. **65**(3), 723–756 (2005)
29. Meskea, C., Bundea, E., Schneiderb, J., Gersch, M.: Explainable artificial intelligence: objectives, stakeholders, and future research opportunities. Inf. Syst. Manag. **39**(1), 53–63 (2022)
30. Methnani, L., Aler Tubella, A., Dignum, V., Theodorou, A.: Let me take over: variable autonomy for meaningful human control. Front. Artif. Intell. **4**, 737072 (2021)
31. Miller, T., Howe, P., Sonenberg, L.: Explainable AI: beware of inmates running the asylum or: how I learnt to stop worrying and love the social and behavioural sciences. In: IJCAI-17 Workshop on Explainable AI (XAI) Proceedings, Melbourne (2017)
32. Mills, S., Ryan, A., Scott-Byrne, C.: Disciplinary Procedures in the Statutory Professions. Bloomsbury Professional (2023)
33. Mökander, J., Sheth, M., Gersbro-Sundler, M., Blomgren, P., Floridi, L.: Challenges and best practices in corporate AI governance: lessons from the biopharmaceutical industry. Front. Comput. Sci. **4**, 1068361 (2022)
34. Morgan, J.K., Hanrahan, P.: Professional indemnity insurance: protecting clients and regulating professionals. Univ. New South Wales Law J. **40**(1), 353–384 (2017)
35. Muchlinski, P.: Limited liability and multinational enterprises: a case for reform? Camb. J. Econ. **34**, 915–928 (2010)
36. NiFhaolain, L., Hines, A.: Could regulating the creators deliver trustworthy AI? In: Second Workshop on Implementing Machine Ethics, Dublin (2020)
37. NiFhaolain, L., Hines, A., Nallur, V.: Assessing the appetite for trustworthiness and the regulation of artificial intelligence in Europe. In: Proceedings of The 28th Irish Conference on Artificial Intelligence and Cognitive Science, Dublin, Ireland 7–8 December 2020 (2020)
38. OECD: Regulatory impact assessment (2020). https://www.oecd.org/gov/regulatory-policy/regulatory-impact-assessment-7a9638cb-en.htm
39. Ozkaya, I.: An AI engineer versus a software engineer. IEEE Softw. **39**(06), 4–7 (2022)
40. Palladino, N.: A 'biased' emerging governance regime for artificial intelligence? How AI ethics get skewed moving from principles to practices. Telecommun. Policy **47**, 102479 (2022)

41. Schneider, J., Meske, C., Vlachos, M.: Deceptive AI explanations: creation and detection. In: ICAART 2022–14th International Conference on Agents and Artificial Intelligence (2022)
42. Shaffer, G.C., Pollack, M.A.: Hard vs. soft law: alternatives, complements, and antagonists in international governance. Minnesota Law Rev. **94**(3), 706–799 (2010)
43. Santoni de Sio, F., van den Hoven, J.: Meaningful human control over autonomous systems: a philosophical account. Front. Robot. AI **5**, 15 (2018)
44. Santoni de Sio, F., Mecacci, G.: Four responsibility gaps with artificial intelligence: why they matter and how to address them. Philos. Technol. **34**, 1057–1084 (2021)
45. Smuha, N.A.: From a 'race to AI' to a 'race to AI regulation': regulatory competition for artificial intelligence. Law Innov. Technol. **13**, 57–84 (2021)
46. Solicitors Regulation Authority of England and Wales: SRA Principles. https://www.sra.org.uk/solicitors/standards-regulations/principles/
47. The Alan Turing Institute: AI Standards Database (2023). https://aistandardshub.org/ai-standards-search/
48. Viljanen, M., Parviainen, H.: AI applications and regulation: mapping the regulatory strata. Front. Comput. Sci. **3**, 141 (2022)
49. Webley, S., Werner, A.: Corporate codes of ethics: necessary but not sufficient. Bus. Ethics Eur. Rev. **17**(4), 405–415 (2008)
50. Winfield, A.: Ethical standards in robotics and AI. Nat. Electron. **2**(2), 46–48 (2019)

The Xi Method: Unlocking the Mysteries of Regression with Statistics

Valentina Ghidini[✉]

Department of Decision Sciences, Bocconi University, Milan, Italy
valentina.ghidini@unibocconi.it

Abstract. As machine learning models become increasingly complex, the ability to provide explanations for their predictions becomes more important. In this work, we propose the Xi method, a novel technique for providing pre hoc and post hoc explanations of black box regression models. The Xi method is based on distances between probability distributions, which can be interpreted as variable importance measures. Notably, the explanations provided by this method are backed by theoretical guarantees, as they are obtained through statistical estimators that are proven to be asymptotically consistent. Additionally, the Xi method is model and data agnostic, meaning that it can be applied to a wide range of machine learning models and data types. To demonstrate the potential of the Xi method, we provide applications that encompass three different data types: tabular, image, and text.

Keywords: Explainability · Post hoc explanations · pre hoc explanations · Variable Importance Measures

1 Introduction

The growing size and complexity of data structures and the simultaneous need of accurate predictions force analysts to employ black boxes rather than transparent machine learning models in an increasing number of applications [14,16]. While the success of such models extends the range of statistical applications, it also increases the need of methods that aid explainability. Most of the explainability methods in the literature are based (implicitly or explicitly) on scores known as variable importance measures in the statistical literature [2,4,13,15]. Variable importance measures are statistical techniques used to assess the relative contribution or significance of independent variables (also known as predictors, covariates or features) in explaining the variation in a target variable. These measures help to identify the influence of each covariate on the outcome: features with high variable importance are the most important ones to predict the target. There are different variable importance measures in the literature: a first class is provided by suitable coefficients of transparent models [16]. The first example that comes to mind are the absolute values of the estimated coefficients in a linear regression (or a suitable generalization): in general, larger coefficients suggest a stronger impact on the dependent variable. Moreover, in machine learning algorithms such as decision trees or random forests, feature importance measures assess the contribution of each feature to the overall predictive performance of the model [4]. These measures are based on the decrease in impurity or information gain when splitting the data based on each feature. An alternative approach to estimate the variable importance of a given model is provided by Sensitivity Analysis (SA). SA [17] involves the quantification of how the uncertainty in a target variable, whether observed or predicted by a model, can be attributed to different sources in a given set of input variables. Although SA and XAI have been developed independently, there is a significant overlap in their goals and techniques. Examples of methods which can be used in sensitivity analysis as well as to explain machine learning models include knockoffs [1] and model-X knockoffs [5]. In both techniques, the aim is to construct knockoff versions of the original features which allows to find the smallest subset $\mathcal{S}$ of variables $\{X_j\}_{j=1}^p$ such that the response Y is independent of all the other variables conditionally on $\{X_{j \in \mathcal{S}}\}$. This serves as a feature selection procedure, and the most recent version allows its application to high-dimensional settings. An alternative technique is the Sure Independence Screening (SIS) [8]: SIS is also a feature selection procedure which picks out a subset of covariates according to the magnitude coefficients of a componentwise regression. Recent works [7,9] have also tried to combine the idea of having a general, model-independent measure of feature importance, valid for an entire class of optimal models, with the objective of providing explanations for the overall role of each feature in the prediction task of a target variable. The focus is to overcome the potential bias associated with explanations pertaining to a specific model. Another classic choice in terms of variable importance measures are Sobol indices [17]. They provide a systematic and quantitative way to assess the importance of different input factors in a model by decomposing the variance of the target output into contributions from individual factors and their interactions.

In this work, we make the association between feature importance and explanations for regression models explicit, using variable importance measures defined through distances between probability distributions as the building blocks for our explainability method. We propose the Xi method in the context of regression models, a data and model-agnostic [14] technique which can provide pre hoc and, more interestingly, post hoc explanations. The Xi method was first introduced in the literature for explaining classifiers [3]. The rationale of the Xi method is to compute a distance between the probability distribution of the target Y (or of the model predictions $\widehat{Y}$) and the conditional probability distribution of Y ($\widehat{Y}$) given a set of variables X, in order to measure the influence of X on Y ($\widehat{Y}$).

The rest of this paper is organized as follows: in Sect. 2, we introduce the Xi method for regression models, along with some theoretical properties. Section 3 provides use cases for three different data formats: tabular, images and texts. Finally, in Sects. 4 and 5, we discuss our findings, the advantages and disadvantages associated to the Xi method, and some desirable future research directions.

2 Xi Method for Regression Models

Consider a dataset (X, Y) of N independent and identically distributed data points, where $X = [X_1, \ldots, X_p]$ are p variables of any type and Y is a numerical target variable (either continuous or discrete). Consider also the predictions $\widehat{Y} = g(X)$ from a machine learning model $g(X)$ [12], trained with a superset of X. Denote by P_Y ($P_{\widehat{Y}}$) the probability distribution of Y ($\widehat{Y}$), and by $P_{Y|X}$ ($P_{\widehat{Y}|X}$) the conditional distribution of Y ($\widehat{Y}$) given X. Finally, consider the space of the probability distributions $\mathcal{P}$ and a separation measurement $\zeta(P, Q)$ between two distributions $P, Q \in \mathcal{P}$. A separation measurement is a function $\zeta : \mathcal{P} \times \mathcal{P} \to \mathbb{R}$ such that a) $\zeta(P, Q) \geq 0 \ \forall P, Q \in \mathcal{P}$ and b) $\zeta(P, Q) = 0$ if and only if $P = Q$ in distribution [10]. Then, we can define the pre hoc and post hoc explanations provided by the Xi method as follows:

Definition 1. *The **pre hoc** explanations for the dataset (X, Y) are defined as*

$$\xi_X^Y = \{\xi_i^Y = \mathbb{E}_{X_i}[\zeta(P_Y, P_{Y|X_i})], \text{ for } i = 1, \ldots, p\}.$$

where each expectation is taken with respect to the features X_i, $i = 1, \ldots, p$.

Definition 2. *The **post hoc** explanations for a model predicting $\widehat{Y} = g(X)$ are defined as*

$$\xi_X^{\widehat{Y}} = \{\xi_i^{\widehat{Y}} = \mathbb{E}_{X_i}[\zeta(P_{\widehat{Y}}, P_{\widehat{Y}|X_i})], \text{ for } i = 1, \ldots, p\}.$$

where each expectation is taken with respect to the features X_i, $i = 1, \ldots, p$.

Hence, the explanations $\xi_X^Y, \xi_X^{\widehat{Y}}$ provided by the Xi method are basically p different non-negative scores, proportional to the importance of the covariate X_i, $i = 1, \ldots, p$ for the target Y or prediction $\widehat{Y}$ (the higher, the most important). Moreover, $\xi_i^Y = 0$ ($\xi_i^{\widehat{Y}} = 0$) if and only if X_i and Y ($\widehat{Y}$) are stochastically independent, i.e. X_i does not influence the target (the predictions) at all. Until now, we have implicitly assumed that each X_i is a single feature in the design matrix X, i.e. unidimensional. However, pre hoc and post hoc explanations in Definitions 1 and 2 are well-defined when each X_i has dimension r, with $r > 1$. In this case, the Xi method provides joint explanations which also take into account the dependency structure among the features, yielding a straightforward generalization to explanations of $r-$dimensional covariates. Nevertheless, care must be taken in providing explanations for multidimensional features: the cause is not the Xi method per se, but the curse of dimensionality that afflicts the estimation of the conditional distributions. The curse of dimensionality refers to the difficulties encountered when dealing with high-dimensional data, where the number of data points required to accurately estimate conditional distributions grows exponentially with the number of dimensions. More specifically, the number of data points N needed to maintain the same accuracy grows exponentially with r. Thus, to address this issue, it is important to carefully consider the trade-off between the desired level of accuracy in estimating conditional distributions and the amount of available data. Moreover, the

Xi method can have some resemblance with univariate and marginal regression methods, but it is fundamentally different. Besides the straightforward extension of the Xi method to multidimensional features, which allows the natural inclusion of dependence structures in the explanation process, the explanations provided by the proposed technique are model-independent and even prior to any model fitting, in the case of pre hoc explanations. The Xi method does not require to fit a simple or surrogate model to explain possibly complex relationships between X and Y ($\widehat{Y}$). Another notable advantage of the Xi method, compared to regression approaches, is that both pre hoc and post hoc explanations can be *localized* within a specific interval $\mathcal{I}$ of the support $\mathcal{Y}$ of the response variable Y. We can define the localized pre hoc explanations for the interval $\mathcal{I} \in \mathcal{Y}$ as $\xi_X^{Y_{\mathcal{I}}} = \{\xi_i^{Y_{\mathcal{I}}} = \mathbb{E}_{X_i}[\zeta(P_Y, P_{Y|X_i})|Y \in \mathcal{I}], \text{ for } i = 1, \ldots, p\}$ (and analogously for their post hoc counterpart). This set of values will provide explanations about the dependency between X and $Y, \widehat{Y}$ in a specific interval $\mathcal{I}$. For example, one may be interested in the most influential covariates for predicting a value of Y when it is low or high (e.g. over or under a certain threshold). Localized explanations are crucial from an applicative viewpoint due to several reasons. Firstly, their granularity enables a more in-depth comprehension of how variations in input variables impact the outcome within a specific context. Secondly, localized explanations offer more actionable insights that are directly relevant to a particular range or scenario. By focusing on specific intervals, decision-makers can identify the key variables that drive desired outcomes, allowing for targeted interventions. Lastly, localized explanations assist in identifying areas of stability and uncertainty. By examining the model's explanations within different intervals, it is possible to pinpoint regions where the impacts of the features on the model are consistent and reliable, as well as areas where uncertainty of the importance measures is more prevalent. This knowledge helps in making informed decisions based on the level of confidence associated with specific predictions.

2.1   Computational Framework

The explanations in Definitions 1–2 can be obtained via a set of estimators of $\mathbb{E}_{X_i}[\zeta(P_Y, P_{Y|X_i})]$, for $i = 1, \ldots, p$. In the remainder of this section, we will provide the estimation process for the pre hoc explanations ξ_X^Y, but the very same technique holds for the post hoc explanations $\xi_X^{\widehat{Y}}$, just replacing the target Y with the predictions $\widehat{Y}$. To this aim, consider a partition $\mathcal{K}_i = \{\mathcal{X}_i^1, \mathcal{X}_i^2, \ldots, \mathcal{X}_i^K\}$ of $\mathcal{X}_i$ (the support of the variable X_i), i.e. a countable collection of K subsets of $\mathcal{X}_i$ such that $\mathcal{X}_i = \bigcup_{k=1}^K \mathcal{X}_i^k$ and $\mathcal{X}_i^m \cap \mathcal{X}_i^l = \emptyset$, for all $m \neq l$. Then, an estimator for the explanation $\xi_i^Y = \mathbb{E}_{X_i}[\zeta(P_Y, P_{Y|X_i})] = \int_{\mathcal{X}_i} \zeta(P_Y, P_{Y|X=x}) \mathrm{d}P_X(x)$ is given by the following integral approximation:

$$\xi_i^Y(\mathcal{K}_i) = \sum_{k=1}^K p(X_i \in \mathcal{X}_i^k) \zeta(P_Y, P_{Y|X \in \mathcal{X}_i^k}). \tag{1}$$

Given the sample, we can estimate ξ_i^Y of Eq. (1) by plugging in consistent estimates of the probabilities involved

$$\widehat{\xi}_i^Y(K, N) = \sum_{k=1}^{K} \frac{N(\mathcal{X}_i^k)}{N} \zeta(\widehat{P}_Y, \widehat{P}_{Y|X\in\mathcal{X}_i^k}), \tag{2}$$

where $N(\mathcal{X}_i^k)$ denote the number of observations in $\mathcal{X}_i^k$, and $\widehat{P}_Y, \widehat{P}_{Y|X\in\mathcal{X}_i^k}$ are consistent estimators of the distributions $P_Y, P_{Y|X\in\mathcal{X}_i^k}$. There are various alternatives for estimating marginal and conditional distributions using consistent estimators. In our approach, we opted for histogram-based density estimators [18] implemented in standard Python packages. Another viable option is to employ kernel density estimators. The framework presented in this paper remains valid as long as the densities of interest are estimated through consistent estimators. In other words, the choice of estimator is flexible as long as it satisfies the property of consistency. Under some mild regularity conditions on the separation measurement, Proposition 1 proves that the estimator in Eq. (2) is consistent.

Proposition 1. *Let $\zeta(\cdot, \cdot)$ be a separation measure between probability distributions, continuous and bounded almost everywhere as X_i varies in $\mathcal{X}_i$. Let $\widehat{\xi}_i^Y(K, N)$ be defined by Eq. (2). Then, if X_i is discrete,*

$$\lim_{N\to\infty} \widehat{\xi}_i^Y(K, N) = \xi_i^Y.$$

If X_i is continuous,

$$\lim_{K\to\infty} \lim_{N\to\infty} \widehat{\xi}_i^Y(K, N) = \xi_i^Y. \tag{3}$$

Proposition 1 is based on Proposition 1 in [3]. A formal proof is provided in the Appendix.

3 Application

In Sect. 2 we defined the explanations obtained through the Xi method, and we provided a computational framework to calculate them. The framework introduced is quite general, that is, it holds for every separation measurement $\zeta(\cdot, \cdot)$ and every kind of data structure which can be coerced into a design matrix X. To further illustrate the data and model agnostic nature of the Xi method, we propose three different applications on tabular, image and text data. Three different models (XGboost, Convolutional Neural Network and Ridge regression) are estimated on a training set (including 70% of the original data), and the explanations are computed on the remaining observations, serving as test set. All the explanations in the remainder are based on the Kullback-Leibler separation measurement, that is $\zeta(P, Q) = \int_{\mathbb{R}} \log[dP(x)/dQ(x)]dP(x)$. Notice that in this case the resulting explanations are the mutual information between X and $Y, \widehat{Y}$. The partitions of the variables' supports are fixed, with a cardinality $K = 10$ and equipopulated elements.

3.1   Tabular Data

The first application makes use of an oceanographic dataset[1], the CalCOFI data. The dataset contains physical, chemical, and biological features collected on different water samples to study climatic cycles in the California current. In our application, after a proper data cleaning and an explorative data analysis, we define a XGboost model to predict the reported temperature of the water through some chemical properties, namely the silicate concentration (R_SIO3), phosphate concentration (PO4uM), nitrate quality (NO3q), reported oxygen (R_Oxy_μmol/kg), reported oxygen saturation (O2Sat), pressure quality code (P_qual), millimeters of oxygen per liter of seawater (R_02), dissolved oxygen (O2ml_L), ammonium (NH3q), potential density of water (R_SIGMA), Specific Volume Anomaly (R_SVA), salinity units of precision (S_prec), salinity of water (Salnty), dynamic height (R_DYNHT) and temperature units of precision (T_prec). The performance of the model is fairly good (with a mean absolute error of 0.005), but a complete performance analysis is out of the scope of this work. In Fig. 1 we report the pre hoc and post hoc explanations of the trained model, estimated on the test set: both ξ_X^Y and $\xi_X^{\widehat{Y}}$ are comparable and on the same scale, meaning that the XGboost model picks up the same dependencies as the original data generating process. The scatterplot in Fig. 1 is also interesting to look at: it shows that the values of the pre hoc and post hoc explanations are not so different (the points are close to the 0–1 line in red), and the ranking of importance of the features is preserved. This means that the most important covariate for the data generating process (Specific Volume Anomaly—R_SVA) is also the most important feature for the XGboost model, according to the Xi method, followed by the amount of oxygen in the water, both well-known impact factors in determining water temperature.

Figure 2 shows explanations for the prediction of a low or high temperature of the water, considering the localized explanations for the intervals $\mathcal{I}_1 = \{Y|Y < Q_{10}(Y)\}$ and $\mathcal{I}_2 = \{Y|Y > Q_{90}(Y)\}$, where $Q_p(Y)$ is the empirical percentile of Y of level p. In particular, the most important variable to predict water temperature below the 10th percentile is the dynamic height of the water, while the most impactful variable to predict a value of the target given that is over the 90th percentile seems to be specific volume anomaly. However, the values of $\xi_X^{Y_{\mathcal{I}_1}}, \xi_X^{Y_{\mathcal{I}_2}}$ are on quite different scales, and also provide different rankings of importance of the features, as highlighted in the scatterplot of Fig. 2.

Competitor: Variable Importance Measure. The XGboost model allows a natural and standard derivation of a variable importance measure, that is the relative importance of predictor variables (see reference [12], Section 10.13). We report such measure in Fig. 3, along with its comparison with the post hoc explanations provided by the Xi method. Both the methods agree on Specific Volume Anomaly (R_SVA) being the most important feature, however the relative importance measure has little variability, since the importance value for most variables

---

[1] https://www.kaggle.com/datasets/sohier/calcofi.

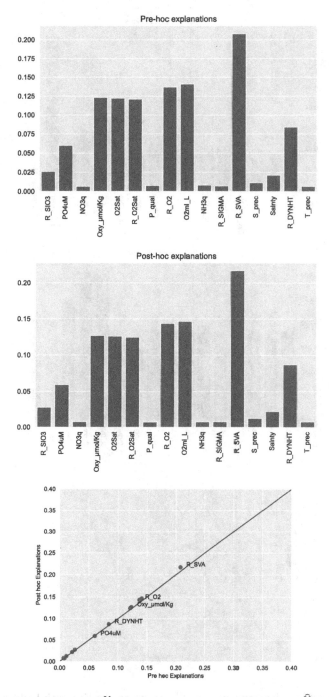

Fig. 1. Pre hoc explanations ξ_X^Y (top) and post hoc explanations $\xi_X^{\widehat{Y}}$ (middle) based on the Kullback-Leibler divergence; scatterplot of pre hoc versus post hoc explanations (bottom)—tabular data.

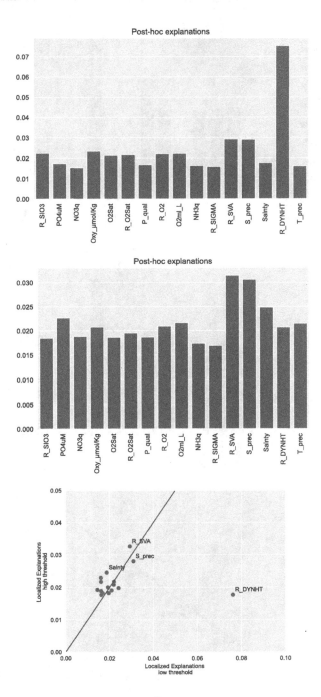

Fig. 2. Localized post hoc explanations $\xi_X^{\widehat{Y}_I}$ based on the Kullback-Leibler divergence, for low (top) and high (middle) predicted values of Y; scatterplot of localized explanations for low predicted values of Y versus localized explanations for high predicted values of Y (bottom)—tabular data.

is near zero. This scenario does not allow to infer a robust ranking of importance of the variables, and it only distinguishes between the super important covariate (R_SVA) and the other ones, overlooking some important factors commonly related to water temperature in the literature.

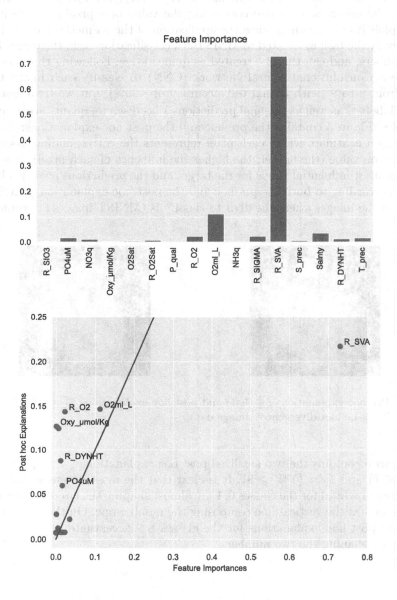

Fig. 3. Relative importance of predictor variables (top) and scatterplot of relative importance of predictor variables versus post hoc explanations (bottom)—text data.

3.2 Image Data

The MNIST dataset [6] has been used as a standard machine learning benchmark for more than twenty years. It contains 28×28 grayscale images of handwritten digits: in this scenario, the design matrix $X = \{X_1, \ldots, X_{28 \times 28}\}$ is composed by 28×28 columns, each one containing the value of a pixel for each image. We exploit it once again to show the application of the Xi method: even though technically the task associated to MNIST is a classification task, the target labels are numbers, and can then be treated as quantitative. Following this rationale, we use a Convolutional Neural Network (CNN) to classify each image into a label from 0 to 9 (with a final test accuracy of $\sim 99\%$), but we treat both the initial labels Y as well as the final predictions $\widehat{Y}$ as discrete, quantitative random variables. Figure 4 contains the pre hoc and the post hoc explanations: they are shown as a heatmap, where each pixel represents the corresponding associated explanation value (the lighter, the higher the influence of such pixel). It is clear that the most influential pixels for the target and the predictions provided by the model (according to both the pre hoc and the post hoc explanations) are in the center of the image, where the digit to classify is (MNIST images are centered).

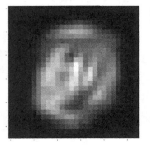 

Fig. 4. Pre hoc explanations ξ_X^Y (left) and post hoc explanations $\xi_X^{\widehat{Y}}$ (right) based on the Kullback-Leibler divergence—image data.

Figure 5 contains the two localized post hoc explanations $\xi_X^{Y_{\mathcal{I}_1}}, \xi_X^{Y_{\mathcal{I}_2}}$ for $\mathcal{I}_1 = \{Y | Y \leq 1\}$ and $\mathcal{I}_2 = \{Y | Y \geq 8\}$. It is clear that the most important pixels (in light grey or white) for the classes $0, 1$ are almost shaping the circular form of the zero as well as the vertical line composing the number one. On the contrary, the localized post hoc explanations for the classes $8, 9$ accentuate more the curves commonly shaping the two numbers.

 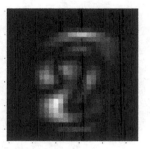

Fig. 5. Localized post hoc explanations $\xi_X^{\hat{Y}_\mathcal{I}}$ based on the Kullback-Leibler divergence, for low (left) and high (right) predicted values of Y—image data.

3.3 Text Data

In this application, a model is fit in order to predict the (log) price of a night in an Airbnb in New York City[2]. The chosen model is a Ridge regression [12] (with hyperparameters set through crossvalidation), and the design matrix contains different covariates, among which we can find the position of the Airbnb, the number of listings of the same host, the minimum number of nights, the number of reviews, number of reviews per month, and the days since the last review. What is actually of interest in this section though is the "name" of the listing: it is usually a short text, containing a brief description of the Airbnb (for example, *Hip Historic Brownstone Apartment with Backyard* or *Cute apt in artist's home*). This original column has been transformed using the Bag of Words vectorization [11], which counts the occurrences of words in each text entry. In this way, the order of appearance of the words is discarded, and since the name of the listings are short, the resulting feature space will be high-dimensional and sparse. Figure 6 shows the pre hoc and post hoc explanation values of the 50 covariates (all words) whose corresponding coefficients in the Ridge regression are the highest (in absolute value). Pre hoc and post hoc explanations are comparable, and in both cases the most important words according to the Xi method are *entire_home/apt* and *Manhattan*: thus, the two most important factors in determining the Airbnb price are whether it is located in Manhattan or whether the entire property is listed, or just a room. The scatterplot of Fig. 6 shows that in some cases the actual values of the pre hoc and post hoc explanations are different, but nevertheless the ranking of the importance of random variables is similar in the two cases.

Figure 7 shows explanations for the prediction of a low or high (log) price of an Airbnb, considering the localized explanations for the intervals $\mathcal{I}_1 = \{Y | Y < Q_{10}(Y)\}$ and $\mathcal{I}_2 = \{Y | Y > Q_{90}(Y)\}$, where $Q_p(Y)$ is the percentile of Y of level p. In this case, the most important words in the listing name, given a predicted price for the rental over the 90th percentile, indicate whether the entire property is for rent, if it is located in Manhattan or Tribeca, or if the Airbnb is a

---

[2] https://www.kaggle.com/datasets/dgomonov/new-york-city-airbnb-open-data..

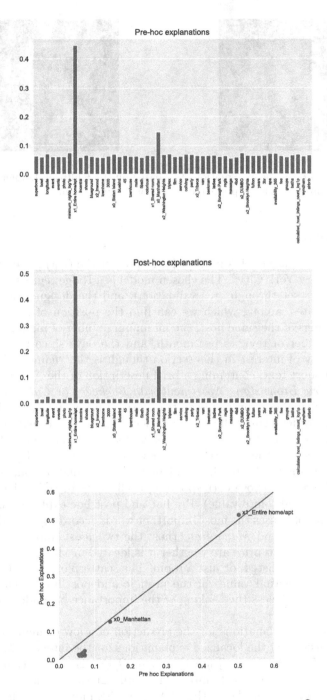

Fig. 6. Pre hoc explanations ξ_X^Y (top) and post hoc explanations $\xi_X^{\widehat{Y}}$ (middle) based on the Kullback-Leibler divergence; scatterplot of pre hoc versus post hoc explanations (bottom)—text data.

suitable set for a photoshoot. On the other hand, the most important covariate in predicting a rental price under the 10th percentile is whether the listing is about a shared room, which will be cheaper than a single room or an entire property. The scatterplot in Fig. 7 additionally shows the difference in the two localized explanations: the ranking of importance of the features is clearly not preserved in the two cases.

4   Discussion of Findings

In Sect. 3, we have shown three possible use cases of the Xi method for regression on tabular, image and text data. The models are diverse, with different levels of opacity: we have employed a XGboost, a CNN and a Ridge regression. Using statistically-based explainability techniques like the Xi method offers two significant advantages. Firstly, these techniques are grounded in solid theoretical foundations. The definitions and estimation procedures are well-defined, and the methodology comes with theoretical guarantees. As the number of observations increases, the estimated explanations converge to the true ones, defined in a probabilistic sense. This convergence ensures that the explanations become more accurate and reliable as more data becomes available. Moreover, it is possible to employ standard statistical techniques (e.g. bootstrap) to estimate the variability in the explanations [3]. Secondly, the explanations defined by techniques like the Xi method are highly flexible. While Sect. 3 illustrates explanations based on the Kullback-Leibler divergence, the framework allows for the use of various separation measurements $\zeta(\cdot, \cdot)$. By simply changing the separation measurement, a whole family of explanations can be obtained by employing different distances between probability distributions. This flexibility enables researchers and practitioners to tailor the explanation technique to suit their specific needs, preferences, or domain-specific requirements. However, while the Xi method provides a valuable approach for explaining regression models, there is much room for improvement. One potential area of enhancement is the computational scheme: improving the estimation procedure can lead to more accurate, reliable and faster estimates of the conditional distributions, enhancing the quality of the explanations provided by the Xi method. Furthermore, the extension of the Xi method to consider the joint importance measure of a set of features is immediate. This allows for the consideration of the dependence structure among the features within the explanations, providing a more comprehensive understanding of their collective importance. However, implementing the Xi method in the multidimensional case poses challenges and is not straightforward. The curse of dimensionality becomes more pronounced as the number of features increases, necessitating an exponentially larger number of data points to maintain the same level of accuracy. This trade-off between the cardinality of the feature set, the available data points, and the desired accuracy becomes an important consideration in practice. Lastly, it is important to acknowledge that Sect. 3 primarily consists of toy applications. The main purpose of these examples is to showcase the potential and versatility of the Xi method, rather than

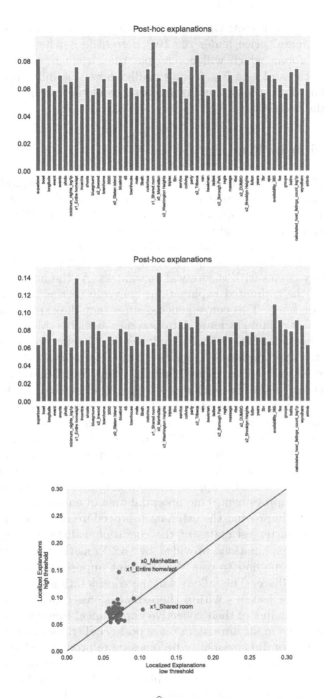

Fig. 7. Localized post hoc explanations $\xi_X^{\widehat{Y}_{\mathcal{I}}}$ based on the Kullback-Leibler divergence, for low (top) and high (middle) predicted values of Y; scatterplot of localized explanations for low predicted values of Y versus localized explanations for high predicted values of Y (bottom)—text data.

presenting significant or practical applications. Future research directions should include the application of the Xi method to real-world problems to offer meaningful insights and practical value, enhancing our understanding of the method's capabilities.

5   Conclusion

This work proposes the Xi method, a novel explainability technique for obtaining insights about regression models using distances between distributions. The usage of the Xi method is shown through three different examples, involving different models and data formats. The major advantage of such method is that the resulting explanations have theoretical guarantees of convergence to sensible importance measures, under minor assumptions on the separation measurement of choice. The Xi method also provides both pre hoc and post hoc explanations. The former allow us to gain some insights about the data generating process; the latter, give us information about which covariates influence the prediction of a black box model. Comparing them gives us insightful glimpses of possible divergences between the data generating process and the machine learning prediction task. Moreover, we can also obtain localized explanations in a suitable subset of the support of the target variable. An important disadvantage is the curse of dimensionality: in fact, the extension of the Xi method to obtain joint importance measures of a group of random variables for the target of interest is straightforward, but the number of data points needed to maintain the same accuracy in the estimation grows exponentially with the dimensionality of the group of random variables. This direction is worth exploring in future research.

Proofs

Proof (Proof of Proposition 1)
This proof follows and adapts the steps of the proof of Proposition 1 in [3] for the case of continuous target variables.

1) Discrete input case. Consider a p–dimensional discrete variable X_i with support

$$\mathcal{X}_i = \left\{ x_i^1, x_i^2, \ldots, x_i^K \right\}.$$

In this case, a natural choice for the partition of the support is the support itself, that is

$$\mathcal{K}_i = \left\{ \mathcal{X}_i^1, \mathcal{X}_i^2, \ldots, \mathcal{X}_i^K \right\},$$

with $\mathcal{X}_i^k = \{X_i : X_i = x_i^k\}$, for $k = 1, 2, \ldots, K$.

Now, the explanations $\xi_i^Y = \xi_i(\mathcal{X}_i) = \xi_i(\mathcal{K}_i)$ are defined as

$$\xi_i^Y = \xi_i(\mathcal{K}_i) = \sum_{k=1}^{K} p(X_i = x_i^k) \zeta(P_Y, P_{Y|X_i = x_i^k}). \tag{4}$$

Plugging in consistent estimators $\hat{P}_Y, \hat{P}_{Y|X_i=x_i^k}$, respectively for the marginal and the conditional distributions $P_Y, P_{Y|X_i=x_i^k}$ (which can be obtained for example using kernel density estimators or histogram estimators), and also noting that a well-behaved, unbiased and consistent estimator for $p(X_i = x_i^k)$ is $\hat{p}(X_i = x_i^k) = N(\mathcal{X}_i^k)/N$ (where $N(\mathcal{X}_i^k)$ denote the number of observations in $\mathcal{X}_i^k$), then an estimator for the explanations above is:

$$\hat{\xi}_i(K, N) = \sum_{k=1}^{K} \hat{p}(X_i = x_i^k)\zeta(\hat{P}_Y, \hat{P}_{Y|X_i=x_i^k}). \tag{5}$$

Thanks to the consistency of the involved estimators, we get $\hat{P}_Y \to P_Y$, $\hat{P}_{Y|X_i=x_i^k} \to P_{Y|X_i=x_i^k}$, $N(\mathcal{X}_i^k)/N \to p(X_i = x_i^k)$ for $N \to \infty$. Moreover, for the continuity of the separation measurement $\zeta(\cdot, \cdot)$, we have the following limit for $N \to \infty$:

$$\zeta(\hat{P}_Y, \hat{P}_{Y|X_i=x_i^k}) \to \zeta(P_Y, P_{Y|X_i=x_i^k}),$$

and thus

$$\sum_{k=1}^{K} \hat{p}(X_i = x_i^k)\zeta(\hat{P}_Y, \hat{P}_{Y|X_i=x_i^k}) \to \sum_{k=1}^{K} p(X_i = x_i^k)\zeta(P_Y, P_{Y|X_i=x_i^k}),$$

which implies $\hat{\xi}_i^Y(K, N) \to \xi_i^Y$ as $N \to \infty$.

2) Absolutely continuous input case. Consider now a p–dimensional absolutely continuous random variable X_i with support $\mathcal{X}_i$, and let $f_{X_i}(x_i)$ be the density of X_i. The explanation $\xi_i^Y = \xi_i^Y(\mathcal{X}_i)$ for such a variable is then equal to

$$\xi_i^Y(\mathcal{X}_i) = \int_{\mathcal{X}_i} \zeta(P_Y, P_{Y|X_i=x_i})f_{X_i}(x_i)dx_i.$$

The integral above can be seen as the limit of the following Riemann-Stieltjes sum (provided that it exists):

$$\xi_i(\mathcal{X}_i) = \lim_{\delta \to 0} \xi_i(\mathcal{K}_i^\delta) = \lim_{\delta \to 0} \sum_{k=1}^{K(\delta)} \zeta(P_Y, P_{Y|X_i \in \mathcal{X}_i^k(\delta)})p(X_i \in \mathcal{X}_i^k(\delta)),$$

where the set $\mathcal{X}_i^k(\delta)$ is a member of a partition $\mathcal{K}_i^\delta$ of $\mathcal{X}_i$, and where K and δ denote the cardinality and norm of the partition, respectively.

Consider now the observed features X and target variable Y, and fix a partition with K elements $\mathcal{K}_i(K) = \{\mathcal{X}_i^1, \ldots, \mathcal{X}_i^K\}$. As before, plugging in some consistent estimators $\hat{P}_Y, \hat{P}_{Y|X_i \in \mathcal{X}_i^k}$, $\hat{p}(X_i \in \mathcal{X}_i^k)$ for the probability laws involved, the estimator for the explanations is given by $\hat{\xi}_i^Y(K, N)$ can be written as

$$\hat{\xi}_i(K, N) = \sum_{k=1}^{K} \zeta(\hat{P}_Y, \hat{P}_{Y|X_i \in \mathcal{X}_i^k})\hat{p}(X_i \in \mathcal{X}_i^k).$$

Now, let $N \to \infty$. For the continuity of the separation measurement $\zeta(\cdot, \cdot)$, we can compute the following limit, using the same argument of the discrete case:

$$\lim_{N \to \infty} \widehat{\xi}_i^Y(K, N) = \lim_{N \to \infty} \sum_{k=1}^{K} \zeta\left(\widehat{P}_Y, \widehat{P}_{Y|X_i \in \mathcal{X}_i^k}\right) \widehat{p}\left(X_i \in \mathcal{X}_i^k\right)$$

$$= \sum_{k=1}^{K} \zeta\left(P_Y, P_{Y|X_i \in \mathcal{X}_i^k}\right) p\left(X_i \in \mathcal{X}_i^k\right) =: \xi_i^Y(K).$$

Furthermore, we consider a sequence of refining partitions of $\mathcal{X}_i$ such that $\mathcal{K}_i(K + 1)$ is finer than $\mathcal{K}_i(K)$ and such that $\lim_{K \to \infty} \mathcal{K}_i(K) = \mathcal{X}_i$ (that is equivalent to $\lim_{\delta \to 0} \mathcal{K}_i^\delta = \mathcal{X}_i$ with the notation above). Then, we can apply the Rohlin's disintegration theorem, to obtain $\widehat{P}_{Y|X_i \in \mathcal{X}_i^k} \to \widehat{P}_{Y|X_i = x_i^k}$ for almost every $x_i^k \in \mathcal{X}_i$. Finally, since the separation measurement $\zeta(\cdot, \cdot)$ is continuous and bounded, using the definition of Riemann-Stieltjes integral, we obtain

$$\lim_{K \to \infty} \xi_i^Y(K) = \xi_i^Y.$$

References

1. Barber, R.F., Candés, E.J.: Controlling the false discovery rate via knockoffs. Ann. Stat. **43**(5), 2055–2085 (2015)
2. Binder, A., Bach, S., Montavon, G., Müller, K.-R., Samek, W.: Layer-wise relevance propagation for deep neural network architectures. In: Information Science and Applications (ICISA) 2016. LNEE, vol. 376, pp. 913–922. Springer, Singapore (2016). https://doi.org/10.1007/978-981-10-0557-2_87
3. Borgonovo, E., Ghidini, V., Hahn, R., Plischke, E.: Explaining classifiers with measures of statistical association. Comput. Stat. Data Anal. **182**, 107701 (2023)
4. Breiman, L.: Random forests. Mach. Learn. **45**(1), 5–32 (2001)
5. Candés, E., Fan, Y., Janson, L., Lv, J.: Panning for gold: 'model-X' knockoffs for high dimensional controlled variable selection. J. R. Stat. Soc. Series B: Stat. Methodol. **80**(3), 551–577 (2018)
6. Deng, L.: The MNIST database of handwritten digit images for machine learning research. IEEE Signal Process. Mag. **29**(6), 141–142 (2012)
7. Dong, J., Rudin, C.: Exploring the cloud of variable importance for the set of all good models. Nat. Mach. Intell. **2**(12), 810–824 (2020)
8. Fan, J., Lv, J.: Sure independence screening for ultrahigh dimensional feature space. J. R. Stat. Soc. Series B: Stat. Methodol. **70**(5), 849–911 (2008)
9. Fisher, A., Rudin, C., Dominici, F.: All models are wrong, but many are useful: learning a variable's importance by studying an entire class of prediction models simultaneously. J. Mach. Learn. Res. **20**, 1–81 (2019)
10. Glick, N.: Measurements of separation among probability densities or random variables. Can. J. Stat. **3**(2), 267–276 (1975)
11. Goodfellow, I., Bengio, Y., Courville, A.: Deep Learning. MIT Press, Cambridge (2016)

12. Hastie, T.J., Tibshirani, R., Friedman, J.H.: The Elements of Statistical Learning. SSS, vol. 2. Springer, New York (2009). https://doi.org/10.1007/978-0-387-84858-7

13. Lundberg, S.M., Lee, S.I.: A unified approach to interpreting model predictions. In: Advances in Neural Information Processing Systems, vol. 2017, pp. 4766–4775 (2017)

14. Murdoch, W.J., Signh, C., Kumbier, K., Abbasi-Asl, R., Yu, B.: Definitions, methods and applications in interpretabile Machine Learning. Proc. Natl. Acad. Sci. **116**(44), 22071–22080 (2019)

15. Ribeiro, M.T., Singh, S., Guestrin, C.: "Why should I trust you?" Explaining the predictions of any classifier. In: Proceedings of the International Conference on Knowledge Discovery and Data Mining, pp. 1135–1144 (2016)

16. Rudin, C.: Stop explaining black-box Machine Learning models for high stakes decisions and use interpretable models instead. Nat. Mach. Intell. **1**(5), 206–215 (2019)

17. Saltelli, A., et al.: Global Sensitivity Analysis: The Primer. Wiley, Hoboken (2008)

18. Silverman, B.W.: Density Estimation for Statistics and Data Analysis. Chapman and Hall/CRC, Boca Raton (1986)

Do Intermediate Feature Coalitions Aid Explainability of Black-Box Models?

Minal Suresh Patil[✉][ID] and Kary Främling[ID]

Umeå universitet, Umeå, Sweden
{minalsp,kary.framling}@cs.umu.se

Abstract. This work introduces the notion of intermediate concepts based on levels structure to aid explainability for black-box models. The levels structure is a hierarchical structure in which each level corresponds to features of a dataset (i.e., a player-set partition). The level of coarseness increases from the trivial set, which only comprises singletons, to the set, which only contains the grand coalition. In addition, it is possible to establish meronomies, i.e., part-whole relationships, via a domain expert that can be utilised to generate explanations at an abstract level. We illustrate the usability of this approach in a real-world car model example and the Titanic dataset, where intermediate concepts aid in explainability at different levels of abstraction.

Keywords: Coalition Formation · Explainability · Trust in Human-Agent Systems

1 Introduction

A mathematical theory of coalition behavior is the theory of n-person cooperative games. Determining which of the potential coalitions may be anticipated to form and what will be the ultimate distribution of payoffs to each player is a fundamental problem in game theory. In the field of coalition games, research on coalition formation has consistently attracted attention. Often, it is implicitly assumed that any coalition may form and that all actors will share in the value of the grand coalition. It is possible that in some situations the players would want to organize themselves in another way because the coalition building issues could be influenced by a variety of variables (such as the sharing rule in use). Based on the factors that influence the nature of coalitions, the research on coalition formation in cooperative games can be divided into two categories.

First, it concentrates on cooperative games when player collaboration is constrained by predetermined social, technological, or other structures. The coalition structure was put forth by Aumann and Dreze [1] as a division of players into coalitions that are unrelated to one another. Negotiations are only permitted until the coalition structure has been established inside each coalition that makes up the structure. By presuming that eventually the grand coalition will form with the coalitions that make up the coalition structure as members, Owen

L. Longo (Ed.): xAI 2023, CCIS 1901, pp. 115–130, 2023.
https://doi.org/10.1007/978-3-031-44064-9_7

elaborates on the coalition structure [20]. Cooperative games with communication structures were first introduced by Myerson [18] where an undirected graph that represents players as nodes and enables for collaboration only amongst coalitions that are connected by the graph. In games with precedence constraints, where the set of players is organized according to some precedence relation, Faigle and Kern [5] considered only coalitions that aim to satisfy the constraints in the sense that if a player is a member of a coalition, all players who come before that player must also be members of the same coalition. Hyper-graph communication scenarios, in which the nodes are the players and the links are the subgroups of players who can communicate, were first described by Van den Nouweland et al. [19]. The assumption is that communication can only exist within a conference and that for communication to happen, all players must be present. A paradigm for cooperative games with levels structure was first presented by Winter [23]. A succession of coalition structures known as *levels structures* are generated from each other by aggregating coalitions each of which encompasses the numerous coalition cooperations of the prior coalition structure.

Second, a specific solution concept or a group of characteristic functions are utilized to construct the coalition. The notion of coalition formation motivated by a coalition structure was covered by Hart and Kurz [12]. In order to choose some coalition structures from a strategy profile that is a strong equilibrium [2], meaning, there is no straightforward payoff incentive for players to modify this structure, they first established a valuation criterion using the Owen value [20] for each individual player in a given coalition structure. A specific number of players who can provide specific payoffs via cooperation are termed a transferable utility cooperative game (TU). There are no restrictions on player cooperation; it is defined by the value that every coalition may achieve on its own. However, this setup is not feasible in all situations where cooperation is restricted. In order to model this, TU games were proposed by Aumann and Dreze [1] where the grand coalition was divided as disjoint prior unions and each of these unions were considered a whole without any interactions. However, Owen [20] relaxed this assumption and allowed players within a prior union to interact with other unions. The same rationale that compels players to unionize to boost their bargaining power during the distribution of the grand coalition's value should also motivate unions to form larger unions. The process can continue until the grand coalition emerges which leads to the formation of hierarchical or levels structure [23].

An example is an organisation with various levels of a structure while distributing resources at all levels. In a university, at the top-level faculties are grouped by the university and a level, we have multiple departments grouped by faculties, and lastly, lecturers are grouped by departments. TU games with a levels structure are appealing due to *level structure's* strong descriptive power. In this work, we focus on how intermediate concepts in machine learning can be represented as *levels structure* for explaining machine learning models.

2 Technical Preliminaries

2.1 Coalition Games

A pair for a cooperative game is denoted as (N, v), where $N = \{1, 2, \ldots, n\}$ represents the players and $v : 2^N \to \mathbb{R}_+$ with $v(\emptyset) = 0$ as the characteristic function. A subset $S \subseteq N$ is a *coalition* and $v(S)$ is the worth of S. For convenience, we write $\{i\}$ as i. If there is no ambiguity, we identify the game (N, v) with its characteristic function v. The set of all cooperative games over N is denoted by G^N. The restriction of a game (N, v) to a coalition $S \subseteq N$, denoted by (S, v_S), is defined by $v_S(T) = v(S \cap T)$ for all $T \subseteq S$. We represent (S, v) instead of (S, v_S) and $|\cdot|$ represents the number of players in a set.

- A *cooperative game* (N, v) is said to be zero-monotonic if $v(S \cup i) \geq v(S) + v(i)$ for any $S \subseteq N \backslash i$.
- A *cooperative game* (N, v) is said to be monotonic if $v(S) \geq v(T)$ for all $S, T \subseteq N, S \supseteq T$
- A *cooperative game* is superadditive if for all $S, T \subseteq N$ with $S \cap T = \emptyset$, it holds that $v(S \cup T) \geq v(S) + v(T)$ and SG^N represents the set of superadditive cooperative games.
- A *cooperative game* v is convex if $v(S \cup T) + v(S \cap T) \geq v(S) + v(T)$ for all $S, T \subseteq N$

Definition 1. *For any $\emptyset \neq T \subseteq N, (N, u_T) \in G^N$ is called a unanimity game, where for any $S \subseteq N$,*

$$u_T(S) = \begin{cases} 1 & \text{if } T \subseteq S \\ 0 & \text{otherwise.} \end{cases}$$

It is well established for any unanimity games $u_T, \emptyset \neq T \subseteq N$, form a basis for G^N, i.e., each game $(N, v) \in G^N$ can be expressed by $v = \sum_{T \subseteq N, T \neq \emptyset} \Delta_v(T) u_T$, where the coefficient $\Delta_v(T)$ is the Harsanyi dividend [11] of coalition T in the game, given as,

$$\Delta_v(T) = \sum_{S \subseteq T} (-1)^{|T| - |S|} v(S) \tag{1}$$

The solution concept of cooperative game theory deals with how to allocate the worth $v(N)$ of grand coalition N among the players. Formally, a payoff vector of a game v is an n-dimensional vector $x = (x_i)_{i \in N} \in \mathbb{R}^N$ allocating a payoff x_i to player $i \in N$.

Definition 2. *A payoff vector x for a game (N, v) satisfies ,*

- efficiency *if $\sum_{i \in N} x_i = v(N)$,*
- individual rationality *if the payoff to any player i is at least his own worth in the game, i.e., $x_i \geq v(\{i\})$ for each $i \in N$,*
- coalitional rationality *if every coalition $S \subseteq N$ receives from x at least the amount it can obtain by operating on its own, i.e., $x(S) = \sum_{i \in S} x_i \geq v(S)$*

The *imputation set* $I(N, v)$ of a game (N, v) is the set of all efficient and indi-vidually rational payoff vectors given as,

$$I(N, v) = \left\{ x \in \mathbb{R}^n \mid \sum_{i \in N} x_i = v(N), x_i \geq v(\{i\}) \text{ for each } i \in N \right\} \qquad (2)$$

A *solution* for a coalition game maps all the games to a set of payoff vectors.

The *core* of a cooperative game as the set of all payoff vectors that fulfill *efficiency* and *coalitional rationality*, for all $(N, v) \in G^N$.

$$C(N, v) = \left\{ x \in \mathbb{R}^N \mid \sum_{i \in N} x_i = v(N) \ and\, x(S) \geq v(S), \ for all \ S \subseteq N \right\} \qquad (3)$$

The coalition will not improve by leaving the grand coalition and cooperating on its own if the playoff vector belongs to *core* i.e. the elements of the core are stable payoffs.

2.2   Coalition Games with Levels Structure

A collection $\{B_1, B_2, \ldots, B_m\}$ of subsets of N is called a *partition* on N iff $B_1 \cup \cdots \cup B_m = N$ and $B_k \cap B_l = \emptyset$ for $k \neq l$. A coalition structure on N is a partition of N.

A *level structure* on N of degree h is a sequence $\mathscr{B} = \left(B^0, B^1, \ldots, B^h\right)$ of partitions of N with $B^0 = \{\{i\} \mid i \in N\}$ such that for each $k \in \{0, 1, \ldots, h-1\}$ and $S \in B^k$, there is $A \subseteq B^{k-1}$ such that $S = \bigcup_{T \in A} T$.

The grand coalition is represented as $B^h = \{N\}$ and the levels are represented as LS^N. B^k is called the kth level of $\mathscr{B}$ and each $S \in B^k$ is a union of level k. For any $T \in B^k$ and $S \subseteq T$, we use the notation B_S^k to represent the union of level k that contains the subset S, i.e., $B_S^k = T$. When $S = \{i\}$, we simply represent in $B_{\{i\}}^k$, i.e., B_i^k is the union of level k that includes player i.

For any $S = \bigcup_{T \in A} T$ for some $A \subseteq B$ and $N_B(S) = \{T : T \subseteq S, T \in B\}$ represent the *immediate players* of S w.r.t B. We represent the set of *immediate players* of $S \in B^{k+1}$ with respect to the kth level of $\mathscr{B}$ as $N_k(S)$. For a trivial case in a level structure of $\mathscr{B}$ on N, is represented as $\hat{N}$, if $h = 1$.

A triple $(N, v, \mathscr{B})$, where $(N, v) \in G^N$ and $\mathscr{B}$ is a level structure on N, represents a cooperative scenario with *level structure*, that describe the following cooperative scenario. The players first establish a coalition structure B^1 (level one of $\mathscr{B}$) as *bargaining groups* for the division of $v(N)$. Next, the coalitions in B^1 as players establish themselves again into the coalition structure B^2 (the second level of $\mathscr{B}$); and so on until the last level of $\mathscr{B}$ is reached. The set of cooperative games with level structures on N is denoted by LG^N. A solution on N for cooperative games with levels structures is a real-valued function $\Psi : LG^N \to \mathbb{R}^n$.

For each $k \in \{0, 1, \ldots, h\}$, we define a game with levels structure $\left(B^k, v/B^k, \mathscr{B}/B^k\right)$ on B^k, induced from $(N, v, \mathscr{B})$ by viewing unions of level k as indi-vidual players. Indeed, B^k is the set of players at level k in the k-level game $\left(B^k, v/B^k\right)$. The worth of a coalition of players of level k in the game $\left(B^k, v/B^k\right)$ is defined as the worth of the subset of all original players that it contains. Formally, the worth of the subset $\{S_1, S_2, \ldots, S_t\} \subseteq B^k$ of players at level k is defined to be $\left(v/B^k\right)\left(\{S_1, S_2, \ldots, S_t\}\right) = v\left(S_1 \cup S_2 \ldots \cup S_t\right)$. Generally, we denote a game as $(B, v/B)$ on a partition B of N, where for any $A \subseteq B, (v/B)(A) = \bigcup_{S \in A} v(S)$. And, $\mathscr{B}/B^k = \left(B^{k,0}, B^{k,1}, \ldots, B^{k,h-k}\right)$ is a levels structure of degree $h - k$ starting with the kth level of $\mathscr{B}$ given by: for all $r \in \{0, 1, \ldots, h- k\}, B^{k,r} = \left\{\{U : U \in B^k, U \subseteq U'\} : U' \in B^{k+r}\right\}$. For example, Let $\mathscr{B} = \left(B^0, B^1, B^2, B^3\right)$ be a levels structure of degree 3 given by $B^0 = \{\{1\}, \{2\}, \{3\}, \{4\}, \{5\}, \{6\}\}, B^1 = \{\{1,2\}, \{3,4\}, \{5,6\}\}, B^2 = \{\{1,2,3,, 4\}, \{5,6\}\}$, and $B^3 = \{\{1,2,3,4,5,6\}\}$. The levels structure $\mathscr{B}$ by viewing the unions of the first level as individuals is $\mathscr{B}/B^1 = \left(B^{1,0}, B^{1,1}, B^{1,2}\right)$ where $B^{1,0} = \{\{\{1,2\}\}, \{\{3,4\}\}, \{\{5,6\}\}\}, B^{1,1} = \{\{\{1,2\}, \{3,4\}\}, \{\{5,6\}\}\}$, and $B^{1,2} = \{\{\{1,2\}, \{3,4\}, \{5,6\}\}\}$.

The value for cooperative games with levels structure of cooperation is a solution concept in cooperative game theory that is used to determine how the total payoff of a cooperative game should be divided among the players, taking into account the levels or coalitions of players who have agreed to cooperate. In the context of machine learning, the value for cooperative games with levels structure of cooperation can be used as a way of forming intermediate concepts from features for machine learning models. For example, in a classification task, the features of a dataset can be grouped into different levels or coalitions based on their semantic meaning or relevance to the task. The value for cooperative games with levels structure of cooperation can then be used to assign a value or weight to each level, based on its contribution to the accuracy or utility of the machine learning model.

3   Levels Structure in Real-World Scenarios

In this section, we introduce five axioms that capture properties expected from coalition of features through levels structure when explaining black-box models. Let N be the set of features, and let $L = L_1, L_2, \ldots, L_m$ be the set of levels. For each $i = 1, 2, \ldots, m$, let L_i be the set of features in level i.

Definition 1 (*Efficiency*). $V(N) = v(L_1, L_2, \ldots, L_m) = \sum_{S \subseteq N} v(S)$

The value of the grand coalition is equal to the sum of the values of all coalitions.

Definition 2 (*Additivity*). $v(S \cup T) = v(S) + v(T)$ for all disjoint sets $S, T \subseteq N$
The value of the union of two disjoint coalitions is equal to the sum of their individual values.

Definition 3 (*Level independence*). $v(S) = v(S \cap L_1, S \cap L_2, \ldots, S \cap L_m)$ for all $S \subseteq N$
The value of a coalition depends only on the levels of the features in the coalition, and not on the specific values of the features.

Definition 4 *(Invariance under level-preserving relabeling). If σ_i is a permutation of L_i for each $i = 1, 2, ..., m$, then $v(S) = v(\sigma_1(S \cap L_1), \sigma_2(S \cap L_2), ..., \sigma_m(S \cap L_m))$ for all $S \subseteq N$ If the labels of the features within each level are permuted, but the levels themselves are not changed, then the value of each coalition should remain unchanged.*

Definition 5 *(Covariance). For any feature $i \in N$, and any constant $c > 0$, $v(S) = v(S \cup i) + c - v(S)$ for all $S \subseteq N \setminus i$*
If a feature's value is increased or decreased by a certain amount, then the value of each coalition should be increased or decreased by a proportional amount.

Naturally, the question arises, *how do we specify or define these feature coalitions in the context of the explainability of black-box models?* In this work, we employ knowledge engineering to collate features based on specific properties proposed by a knowledge engineer. It is important to note that there is no hard and fast rule or criterion to collate features since the end-user can be interested in explanations produced by different coalitions for the same predictive outcome. As a second example, consider a model that predicts car insurance claims. Then, the possible coalitions that can be engineered by a knowledge engineer (a car insurance expert) could be defined as follows:

- Customer profile - gender, age, profession, income, marital status, and years of driving experience.
- Customer history - claims made in the past ten years, license status.
- Vehicle profile - model, the monetary value of the vehicle, mileage covered, age of the car.

The intermediate concepts can be modelled for individuals and is capable of capturing the probability outcome of the insurance claim of each individual, thus allowing us to represent and collate implicit information in the data and generate explanation for each of the coalition.

3.1   Levels Structure Applied to Post-hoc Explainability

Explainability refers to understanding how individual agents make decisions and how their interactions lead to emergent behaviors. Achieving explainability involves using rule-based systems, decision trees, and other techniques to provide insights into agent behavior. Transparency and interpretability of agent actions and outcomes are essential for safe and trustworthy decision-making in MAS applications such as robotics, distributed control, and social simulations [14–16]. Contextual Importance and Utility (CIU) is a post-hoc explainability method proposed by Främling in [7,10]. CIU's origins are in Decision Theory and notably Multiple Criteria Decision Making as described in [8] and addresses the question of how human preferences can be expressed and modelled mathematically. The *intermediate concepts* presented in [6] correspond to coalitions of features with a level structure. In order to show this, we begin by studying the linear case where the additivity condition $v(S \cup T) = v(S) + v(T)$ holds. In this case, an N-attribute utility function is a weighted sum:

$$u(x) = u(x_1, \ldots, x_N) = \sum_{i=1}^{N} w_i u_i(x_i), \tag{4}$$

where $u_i(x_i)$ are the utility functions that correspond to the features $x_1, \ldots, x_N$. $u_i(x_i)$ are constrained to the range $[0,1]$, as well as $u(x)$ through the positive weights w_i. Since $u_i(x_i)$ are in the range $[0,1]$ and $u(x)$ is also constrained to the range $[0,1]$, the importance of feature i is $w_i / \sum_{i=1}^{N} w_i = w_i$ because $\sum_{i=1}^{N} w_i = 1$ by definition. This definition can be extended to the importance of a set of inputs $x_{\{i\}}$ versus another set of inputs $x_{\{I\}}$, where $\{i\}$ and $\{I\}$ are index sets and $\{i\} \subseteq \{I\} \subseteq 1, \ldots, N$. Then we have

$$w_{\{i\},\{I\}} = \frac{\sum w_{\{i\}}}{\sum w_{\{I\}}}. \tag{5}$$

This joint importance $w_{\{i\},\{I\}}$ of features in $\{i\}$ relative to features in $\{I\}$ defines how intermediate concepts can group features together into coalitions and level structures for providing higher levels of abstraction in the explanations through tree-like levels structures.

When studying super-additive cooperative games, a linear model is no longer adequate and the additivity condition no longer holds. This is the case for simple logical functions such as AND, OR etc. This is the case of most AI-based systems and notably for machine learning (ML) based models, whose outcomes and results we want to explain and justify. Model-agnostic XAI methods treat such models as black-boxes that define a presumably non-linear model $f(x)$. As there are no known w_i values for such functions, CIU defines *Contextual Importance (CI)* as the range of variation $[0, \omega_i]$, which we can estimate by observing changes in output values when modifying input values of the features in $\{i\}$ and keeping values of the features $\neg\{i\}$ constant at the ones defined by the instance x. This gives us an estimation of the range $[umin_{j,\{i\}}(x), umax_{j,\{i\}}(x)]$, where j is the index of the model output explain. CI is defined as:

$$\omega_{j,\{i\},\{I\}}(x) = \frac{umax_{j,\{i\}}(x) - umin_{j,\{i\}}(x)}{umax_{j,\{I\}}(x) - umin_{j,\{I\}}(x)}, \tag{6}$$

where we use the symbol ω for CI. Equation 6 differs from Eq. 5 by being a function of x, i.e., the instance to be explained. If the model $f(x)$ is linear, then $\omega_{j,\{i\},\{I\}}(x)$ should be the same for all/any instance x. If the model is non-linear, then $\omega_{j,\{i\},\{I\}}(x)$ depends on the instance x, which is the reason for calling it *contextual* importance.

The utility values $umin_j$ and $umax_j$ in Eq. 6 have to be mapped to actual output values $y_j = f(x)$. If f is a classification model, then the outputs y_j are typically estimated probabilities for the corresponding class, so we can consider that $u_j(y_j) = y_j$. The general form $u_j(y_j) = Ay_j + b$ is suitable also for dealing with most regression tasks. When $u_j(y_j) = Ay_j + b$, then CI can be directly calculated as:

$$\omega_{j,\{i\},\{I\}}(x) = \frac{ymax_{j,\{i\}}(x) - ymin_{j,\{i\}}(x)}{ymax_{j,\{I\}}(x) - ymin_{j,\{I\}}(x)}, \tag{7}$$

where $ymin_j()$ and $ymax_j()$ are the minimal and maximal y_j values observed for output j. However, the joint importance $w_{\{i\},\{I\}}$ can not be greater than one by definition:

Definition 3 (Joint importance of all features). *The joint importance of all features is one, i.e., when the index set* $\{i\} = \{1, \ldots, N\}$, *then* $\omega_{\{i\}} = 1$.

Contextual Utility (CU) corresponds to the factor $u_i(x_i)$ in Eq. 4. CU expresses to what extent the current values of features in $\{i\}$ contribute to obtaining a high output utility (i.e. payoff) $u_{j,\{i\}}$. CU is defined as

$$CU_{j,\{i\}}(x) = \frac{u_j(x) - umin_{j,\{i\}}(x)}{umax_{j,\{i\}}(x) - umin_{j,\{i\}}(x)}. \tag{8}$$

When $u_j(y_j) = Ay_j + b$, this can be written as:

$$CU_{j,\{i\}}(x) = \left| \frac{y_j(x) - yumin_{j,\{i\}}(x)}{ymax_{j,\{i\}}(x) - ymin_{j,\{i\}}(x)} \right|, \tag{9}$$

where $yumin = ymin$ if A is positive and $yumin = ymax$ if A is negative.

Contextual Influence can be calculated directly from CI and CU values and expresses how much current values of features in $\{i\}$ influence the output compared to a *baseline* or *reference value* ϕ_0:

$$\phi_{j,\{i\},\{I\}}(x) = \omega_{j,\{i\},\{I\}}(x)(CU_{j,\{i\}}(x) - \phi_0). \tag{10}$$

It should be emphasized that the baseline ϕ_0 of contextual influence is a utility value, so it can have a constant and semantic meaning, i.e., "averagely good/bad", "averagely typical", "best possible" *etc.*, that presumably makes sense to humans when used in explanations. In many cases, it intuitively makes sense to use the average utility value 0.5 as a baseline for all features. However, in many real-life use cases other values would make more sense. For instance, $\phi_0 = 0$ would be the expected value in an intrusion detection system, where every threat detection feature could only have positive influence.

4   Experiments

The experimental evaluation of using levels structures/intermediate concepts for producing post-hoc explanations is done using two data sets:

1. The Titanic data set, which is well-known and frequently used for assessing XAI methods. It has two outcome classes and seven features, of which some are numeric and others are categorical. Two intermediate concepts have been defined by the authors, "FAMILY" and "WEALTH".

2. The UCI Cars data set, for which the original authors built a ranking system using rules and intermediate concepts. The original rule set is unknown but a black-box model can be trained on the data set and explained using the original intermediate concepts of the authors.

All software for the experiments is written in R and is available as open-source on Github, including the source code for producing the results shown here at https://github.com/KaryFramling/ciu. The experiments were run using Rstudio Version 1.3.1093 on a MacBook Pro, with 2.3 GHz 8-Core Intel Core i9 processor, 16 GB 2667 MHz DDR4 memory, and AMD Radeon Pro 5500M 4 GB graphics card.

4.1 Titanic Data Set

The Titanic data set is a classification task with classes 'yes' or 'no' for the probability of survival. Our Random Forest model achieved 81.1% classification accuracy on the test set. The training/test set partition was 75%/25% of the whole data set. The Titanic data set only has seven features and two output classes but can be considered to be generic, while remaining manageable for presenting the results. The instance 'Johnny D' and model are the same as used by Biecek and Burzykowski [3]. A CIU bar plot explanation is shown in Fig. 1 for the probability of survival, which is 63.6%.

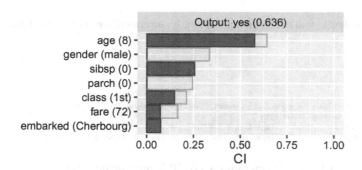

Fig. 1. CIU bar plot explanation for Titanic, instance 'Johnny D'. The transparent bar shows the CI value and the solid bar shows the relative CU value, i.e., how "favorable" the current value is.

We focus on intermediate concepts WEALTH that combines the input features 'fare' (price of ticket) and 'class' (cabin class) and FAMILY that combines 'sibsp' and 'parch'. The levels structure definition in R is:

```
wealth<-c(1,6);  family<-c(4,5)
gender<-c(2);  age<-c(3);  embarked <- c(7)
Titanic.voc <- list("WEALTH"=wealth,
   "FAMILY"=family, "Gender"=gender,
   "Age"=age, "Embarkment_port"=embarked)
```

Figs. 2, 3, 4 and 5 show textual CIU explanations using WEALTH and FAMILY. It is important to point out that **the CI of an intermediate concept is not simply the sum of its constituent CIs**. Therefore, the CI of FAMILY is not the sum of 'parch' and 'sibsp' CIs, nor is the CI of WEALTH the sum of 'class' and 'fare' CIs, unless the underlying model f is linear.

```
The value of output 'yes' for instance '1' is 0.636, which is good (CU=0.636).
Feature 'age' is extremely important (CI=0.642) and value '8' is very good (CU=0.897).
Feature 'gender' is very important (CI=0.334) and value 'male' is very bad (CU=0).
Feature 'sibsp' is very important (CI=0.256) and value '0' is very good (CU=0.992).
Feature 'parch' is important (CI=0.244) and value '0' is very bad (CU=0).
Feature 'class' is important (CI=0.212) and value '1st' is good (CU=0.698).
Feature 'fare' is important (CI=0.166) and value '72' is average (CU=0.434).
Feature 'embarked' is little important (CI=0.074) and value 'Cherbourg' is very good
   (CU=1).
```

Fig. 2. Basic textual explanation.eps

```
The value of output 'yes' for instance '1' is 0.636, which is good (CU=0.636).
Feature 'Age' is very important (CI=0.642) and value '8' is very good (CU=0.897).
Feature 'FAMILY' is important (CI=0.498) and value is average (CU=0.51).
Feature 'WEALTH' is slightly important (CI=0.388) and value is average (CU=0.526).
Feature 'Gender' is slightly important (CI=0.334) and value 'male' is very bad (CU=0).
Feature 'Embarkment port' is not important (CI=0.074) and value 'Cherbourg' is very go
od (CU=1).
```

Fig. 3. Top-level textual explanation with intermediate concepts FAMILY and WEALTH.

```
The value of intermediate concept 'FAMILY' for output 'yes', with instance '1'
 is average (CU=0.51).
Feature 'sibsp' is important (CI=0.514) and value '0' is very good (CU=0.992).
Feature 'parch' is important (CI=0.49) and value '0' is very bad (CU=0).
```

Fig. 4. Explanation for FAMILY intermediate concept

4.2 UCI Cars Evaluation Data Set

The UCI Cars Evaluation data set (https://archive.ics.uci.edu/ml/datasets/car+evaluation) evaluates how good different cars are based on six categorical features. There are four different output classes: 'unacc', 'acc', 'good' and 'vgood'. This signifies that both inputs and output are categorical. Figure 6 shows the basic results for a 'vgood' car (instance #1098). The model is Random Forest. CIU indicates that this car is 'vgood' because it has very good values for all important criteria. Having only two doors is less good but it is also a less important feature. In general, the CIU visualisation is well in line with

The value of intermediate concept 'WEALTH' for output 'yes', with instance '1'
is **average** (CU=0.526).
Feature 'fare' is **very important** (CI=0.66) and value '72' is **bad** (CU=0.281).
Feature 'class' is **important** (CI=0.546) and value '1st' is **good** (CU=0.698).

Fig. 5. Explanation for WEALTH intermediate concept.

the output value for all classes. The authors of the Cars data set used a rule set
with the intermediate concepts 'PRICE', 'COMFORT' and 'TECH', as reported
in [4]. The corresponding levels structure (vocabulary) is defined as follows:

```
price  <- c(1,2)
comfort  <- c(3,4,5)
tech  <- c(comfort, 6)
car  <- c(price, tech)
voc  <- list("PRICE"=price,"COMFORT"=comfort,
        "TECH"=tech,"CAR"=car)
```

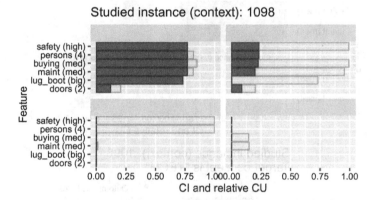

Fig. 6. CIU bar plot explanation for Car instance #1098. The transparent bar shows
the CI value and the solid bar shows the relative CU value, *i.e.* how "favorable" the
current value is.

The corresponding explanations are shown in Figs. 7 and 8.

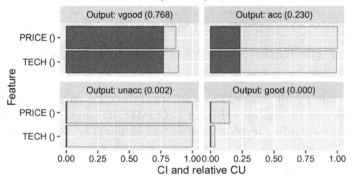

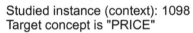

Fig. 7. Car explanation using highest level intermediate concepts.

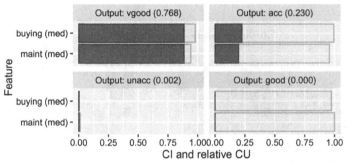

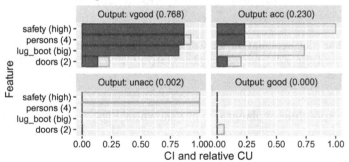

Fig. 8. Detailed explanations of the two intermediate concepts.

5   Discussion

The definition of joint importance in Eq. 5 only applies to weights w for linear models and to contextual importance ω. The equations for contextual utility (Eqs. 8 and 9) use the same $umin, umax, ymin, ymax$ values as the CI Eqs. 6 and 7, whereas the values $u_j(x)$ and $y_j(x)$ only depend on the output value for the instance x. Contextual influence is also defined for coalitions but we have not studied the use of intermediate concepts and levels structures for them for several reason. To begin with, influence values ϕ do not provide the kind of "counterfactual" (what-if) explanations as CI and CU in Fig. 1, for instance. Figure 9 shows the corresponding bar plot explanation using Contextual influence. For the FAMILY intermediate concept, we can see that the features 'sibsp' and 'parch' have opposite signs and would presumably eliminate each other. The same is true for WEALTH, where 'class' and 'fare' both have small influence values with opposite signs. The true joint Contextual influence values are $\phi_{FAMILY} = 0.08$ and $\phi_{WEALTH} = 0.04$, so they have close to zero influence on the outcome compared to the used baseline value $\phi_0 = 0.5$. This is correct but it would give the false impression that FAMILY and WEALTH do not have any importance for the outcome, which could be considered misleading. It is indeed a general challenge for influence-based methods that features with average values tend to have small influence values, even though the (contextual) importance of the feature can be significant. This is also the reason why we have not made any comparisons with the currently most well-known and used post-hoc explainability method, *i.e.* Shapley values [21]. Shapley values are also defined for coalitions. As shown in [17], Shapley values belong to a larger family of XAI methods that they call Additive Feature Attribution (AFA) methods. AFA methods construct an explanation model g that is a linear function of binary variables:

$$g(z') = \phi_0 + \sum_{i=1}^{M} \phi_i z_i', \tag{11}$$

where $z' \in \{0,1\}^M$, $M \leq N$ is the number of simplified input features, and $\phi \in \mathbb{R}$. For a linear function of the form $f(x) = w_0 + w_1 x_1 + \cdots + w_N x_N$, the Shapley value ϕ_i of the i-th feature on the prediction $f(x)$ is:

$$\phi_i(x) = w_i x_i - E(w_i X_i) = w_i x_i - w_i E(X_i), \tag{12}$$

where $E(w_i X_i)$ is the mean effect estimate for feature i [22]. Equation 12 is similar to the Contextual influence Eq. 10 when replacing x_i with $u_i(x_i)$ as shown in [9]. Therefore, AFA methods have the same limitations as Contextual influence.

Figure 10 shows the Shapley values for the Titanic experiment, where it is even clearer than in Fig. 9 that features with average values tend to get low influence values. Still, the use of coalitions for Shapley values has been proposed *e.g.* in the PartitionExplainer[1] and groupShapley approaches [13]. A general

---

[1] https://shap-lrjball.readthedocs.io/en/latest/generated/shap.PartitionExplainer.
html.

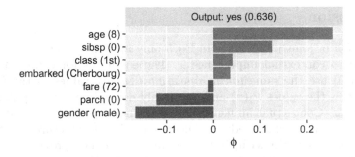

Fig. 9. Contextual influence bar plot explanation for Titanic, instance 'Johnny D'.

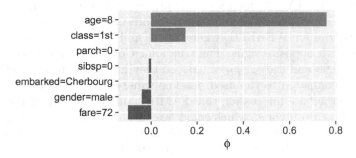

Fig. 10. Shapley value bar plot explanation for Titanic, instance 'Johnny D'.eps

challenge is how to deal with dependent features in appropriate ways. Therefore, using level structures for influence values is an ongoing topic and also a topic for future research.

6 Conclusion

The main contributions in our research can be summed up as follows:

- Establishing a well-founded link between coalitions in game theory, how they can be used for creating Levels Structures, and how they link with Intermediate Concepts.
- Provide the necessary theoretical (mathematical) framework towards Intermediate Concepts as defined for CIU.
- Show how such Intermediate Concepts enable the construction of more flexible and expressive explanations than what is possible with the current state-of-the-art post-hoc explainability methods.

References

1. Aumann, R.J., Dreze, J.H.: Cooperative games with coalition structures. Int. J. Game Theory **3**(4), 217–237 (1974)
2. Aumarm, R.J.: Acceptable points in general cooperative N-person games. Contrib. Theory Games (AM-40) **4**, 287 (2016)
3. Biecek, P., Burzykowski, T.: Explanatory Model Analysis. Chapman and Hall/CRC, New York (2021)
4. Bohanec, M., Rajkovič, V.: Knowledge acquisition and explanation for multi-attribute decision. In: 8th International Workshop on Expert Systems and Their Applications, Avignon, France, pp. 59–78 (1988)
5. Faigle, U., Kern, W.: The shapley value for cooperative games under precedence constraints. Int. J. Game Theory **21**(3), 249–266 (1992)
6. Främling, K.: Explaining results of neural networks by contextual importance and utility. In: Andrews, R., Diederich, J. (eds.) Rules and Networks: Proceedings of the Rule Extraction from Trained Artificial Neural Networks Workshop, AISB 1996 Conference, Brighton, UK (1996)
7. Främling, K.: Modélisation et apprentissage des préférences par réseaux de neurones pour l'aide à la décision multicritère. Ph.D. thesis, INSA de Lyon (1996)
8. Främling, K.: Decision theory meets explainable AI. In: Calvaresi, D., Najjar, A., Winikoff, M., Främling, K. (eds.) EXTRAAMAS 2020. LNCS (LNAI), vol. 12175, pp. 57–74. Springer, Cham (2020). https://doi.org/10.1007/978-3-030-51924-7_4
9. Främling, K.: Contextual importance and utility: a theoretical foundation. In: Long, G., Yu, X., Wang, S. (eds.) AI 2022. LNCS (LNAI and LNB), vol. 13151, pp. 117–128. Springer, Cham (2022). https://doi.org/10.1007/978-3-030-97546-3_10
10. Främling, K., Graillot, D.: Extracting explanations from neural networks. In: ICANN 1995 Conference, Paris, France (1995)
11. Harsanyi, J.C.: A simplified bargaining model for the n-person cooperative game. In: Harsanyi, J.C. (ed.) Papers in Game Theory. Theory and Decision Library, vol. 28, pp. 44–70. Springer, Dordrecht (1982). https://doi.org/10.1007/978-94-017-2527-9_3
12. Hart, S., Mas-Colell, A.: Bargaining and value. Econom.: J. Econom. Soc. 357–380 (1996)
13. Jullum, M., Redelmeier, A., Aas, K.: GroupShapley: efficient prediction explanation with shapley values for feature groups (2021). https://doi.org/10.48550/ARXIV.2106.12228, https://arxiv.org/abs/2106.12228
14. Patil, M.S.: Explainability in autonomous pedagogically structured scenarios (2022). arXiv:2210.12140, https://arxiv.org/pdf/2210.12140.pdf
15. Patil, M.S.: Towards preserving semantic structure in argumentative multi-agent via abstract interpretations (2022). arXiv:2211.15782, https://arxiv.org/pdf/2211.15782.pdf
16. Patil, M.S.: Modelling control arguments via cooperation logic in unforeseen scenarios (2022). arXiv:2210.12114, https://arxiv.org/pdf/2210.12114.pdf
17. Lundberg, S.M., Lee, S.I.: A unified approach to interpreting model predictions. In: Guyon, I., et al. (eds.) Advances in Neural Information Processing Systems, vol. 30, pp. 4765–4774. Curran Associates, Inc. (2017)
18. Myerson, R.B.: Conference structures and fair allocation rules. Int. J. Game Theory **9**(3), 169–182 (1980)
19. van den Nouweland, A., Borm, P., Tijs, S.: Allocation rules for hypergraph communication situations. Int. J. Game Theory **20**(3), 255–268 (1992)

20. Owen, G.: Values of games with a priori unions. In: Henn, R., Moeschlin, O. (eds.) Mathematical Economics and Game Theory. Lecture Notes in Economics and Mathematical Systems, vol. 141, pp. 76–88. Springer, Heidelberg (1977). https://doi.org/10.1007/978-3-642-45494-3_7
21. Shapley, L.S.: A value for n-person games. In: Kuhn, H.W., Tucker, A.W. (eds.) Contributions to the Theory of Games II, pp. 307–317. Princeton University Press, Princeton (1953)
22. Štrumbelj, E., Kononenko, I.: Explaining prediction models and individual predictions with feature contributions. Knowl. Inf. Syst. 41(3), 647–665 (2014)
23. Winter, E.: A value for cooperative games with levels structure of cooperation. Int. J. Game Theory 18(2), 227–240 (1989)

Unfooling SHAP and SAGE: Knockoff Imputation for Shapley Values

Kristin Blesch[1,2]([✉]) [iD], Marvin N. Wright[1,2,3] [iD], and David Watson[4] [iD]

[1] Leibniz Institute for Prevention Research and Epidemiology – BIPS,
Bremen, Germany
blesch@leibniz-bips.de
[2] Faculty of Mathematics and Computer Science, University of Bremen,
Bremen, Germany
[3] Department of Public Health, University of Copenhagen, Copenhagen, Denmark
[4] Department of Informatics, King's College London, London, UK

Abstract. Shapley values have achieved great popularity in explainable artificial intelligence. However, with standard sampling methods, resulting feature attributions are susceptible to adversarial attacks. This originates from target function evaluations at extrapolated data points, which are easily detectable and hence, enable models to behave accordingly. In this paper, we introduce a novel strategy for increased robustness against adversarial attacks of both local and global explanations: Knockoff imputed Shapley values. Our approach builds on the model-X knockoff methodology, which generates synthetic data that preserves statistical properties of the original samples. This enables researchers to flexibly choose an appropriate model to generate on-manifold data for the calculation of Shapley values upfront, instead of having to estimate a large number of conditional densities or make strong parametric assumptions. Through real and simulated data experiments, we demonstrate the effectiveness of knockoff imputation against adversarial attacks.

Keywords: XAI · Shapley Values · Adversarial Attacks · Knockoffs

1 Introduction

Explainable artificial intelligence (XAI) oftentimes strives to deliver insights on the underlying mechanisms of black-box machine learning models in order to generate trust in these algorithms. To do so, XAI methods themselves must be trustworthy.

Several popular XAI tools, such as SHAP [17] and LIME [19], are vulnerable to adversarial attacks [23]. The issue stems from how these approaches generate new data during the explanation process – typically by independently permuting feature values. Permute-and-predict methods force models to extrapolate beyond their training data, yielding off-manifold samples. This results in potentially misleading assessments [13] and enables adversaries to pass fairness audits

© The Author(s) 2023
L. Longo (Ed.): xAI 2023, CCIS 1901, pp. 131–146, 2023.
https://doi.org/10.1007/978-3-031-44064-9_8

even with discriminatory models. For example, an algorithm could fool the XAI method by using a fair model for queries on synthetic, extrapolated data during XAI evaluation in order to suggest the model would be fair even though it may produce discriminatory outcomes for non-synthetic, i.e. real data [23].

Robustness against such adversarial attacks can be achieved by reducing extrapolation during data generation. Ideally, conditional sampling procedures should be used, which ensures that the generated data is indistinguishable from the original data. Figure 1 visualizes data points generated through marginal in contrast to a conditional sampling method.

Fig. 1. Sampling of out-of-coalition features for a digit from $\{28 \times 28\}$ mnist data. The first 14 columns from the left are in-coalition, whereas the remaining 14 columns are sampled either from marginals (as in Kernel SHAP [17]) or deep knockoffs [21].

For Shapley values [22] – one of the most prominent XAI methods – conditional variants and their properties have been widely discussed in the literature [6,8,10,25,29]. Conditional Shapley values sample out-of-coalition features from a distribution conditioned on the in-coalition features. However, this requires knowledge about conditional distributions for all possible feature coalitions and, since estimating conditional distributions is generally challenging, there remains considerable room for improvement. However, to prevent adversarial attacks, calculating conditional Shapley values may be unnecessarily challenging. It suffices to minimize extrapolation, which is a strictly simpler task.

In that vein, we propose the model-X knockoff framework [5] in its full generality to sample out-of-coalition features for protection against adversarial attacks on Shapley value explanations. Knockoffs are characterized by two properties, formally defined below: (1) pairwise exchangeability with the original features; and (2) conditional independence of the response, given the true data. We argue that this makes them well-suited to serve as reference data in Shapley value pipelines. For example, property (1) allows us to estimate knockoffs upfront and use them to impute out-of-coalition features, which effectively avoids extrapolation and does not require the separate estimation of conditional distributions for any feature coalition. Knockoff imputed Shapley values balance on-manifold data sampling with maintaining utmost generality and flexibility in application.

The paper is structured as follows. First, we present the relevant background on Shapley values and model-X knockoffs in Sect. 2. We combine these approaches and study the theoretical properties of the resulting algorithm in Sect. 3. In Sect. 4, we present a series of experiments to demonstrate the effectiveness of our approach against adversarial attacks. We present a comprehensive discussion and directions for future research in Sects. 5 and 6, respectively.

2 Background and Related Work

2.1 Shapley Values

Originating from cooperative game theory, Shapley values [22] aim to attribute payouts fairly amongst a game's players. The basic idea is to evaluate the average change in output when a player is added to a coalition.

In XAI, we can think of the features $\mathbf{X} = \{X_1, \ldots, X_d\}$, where each X_j denotes a random variable, as a set of players $\mathcal{D} = \{1, \ldots, d\}$ who may or may not participate in a coalition of players $\mathcal{S} \subseteq \mathcal{D}$, i.e. $\mathcal{S}$ is a subset of $\mathcal{D}$. The value function v assigns a real-valued payout to each possible coalition, i.e. to every element of the power set of $\mathcal{D}$, which consists of $2^{|\mathcal{D}|} = 2^d$ elements, to a real value. This may be the expected output of a machine learning model f [17], or other quantities related to the model's prediction, such as the expected loss [8]. To compute the Shapley value ϕ_j for player j, we take a weighted average of j's marginal contributions to all subsets that exclude it:

$$\phi_j = \sum_{\mathcal{S} \subseteq \mathcal{D} \setminus \{j\}} \frac{|\mathcal{S}|!(|\mathcal{D}| - |\mathcal{S}| - 1)!}{|\mathcal{D}|!} \Big(v(\mathcal{S} \cup \{j\}) - v(\mathcal{S}) \Big). \tag{1}$$

It is not immediately obvious how to evaluate v on strict subsets of $\mathcal{D}$, since f requires d-dimensional input. One common solution is to use an expectation with respect to some reference distribution $\mathcal{R}$:

$$v(\mathcal{S}) = \mathbb{E}_{\mathcal{R}} \big[f(\mathbf{x}_{\mathcal{S}}, \mathbf{X}_{\bar{\mathcal{S}}}) \big]. \tag{2}$$

In other words, for the random variables $\mathbf{X}_{\mathcal{S}}$, which are the in-coalition features, we take the realized values $\mathbf{x}_{\mathcal{S}}$ as fixed and sample values for out-of-coalition features $\mathbf{X}_{\bar{\mathcal{S}}}$ according to $\mathcal{R}$. Common choices for $\mathcal{R}$ include the marginal distribution $P(\mathbf{X}_{\bar{\mathcal{S}}})$ and the conditional distribution $P(\mathbf{X}_{\bar{\mathcal{S}}} \mid \mathbf{X}_{\mathcal{S}} = \mathbf{x}_{\mathcal{S}})$.

Adversarial Attack Vulnerability. Taking the marginal distribution $\mathcal{R} = P(\mathbf{X}_{\bar{\mathcal{S}}})$ typically serves as an approximation to the conditional distribution $P(\mathbf{X}_{\bar{\mathcal{S}}} \mid \mathbf{X}_{\mathcal{S}} = \mathbf{x}_{\mathcal{S}})$ in order to facilitate computation, e.g. as in KernelSHAP [17]. However, marginal and conditional distributions only coincide when features are jointly independent, which is scarcely ever the case in empirical applications. A consequence from a violation of feature independence is that sampling a set of $\mathbf{x}'_{\bar{\mathcal{S}}}$ from marginals instead of conditional distributions will lead to generated instances $\mathbf{x}' = (\mathbf{x}_{\mathcal{S}}, \mathbf{x}'_{\bar{\mathcal{S}}})$ that are off the data manifold of original, i.e. real data observations $\mathbf{x} = (\mathbf{x}_{\mathcal{S}}, \mathbf{x}_{\bar{\mathcal{S}}})$. In such cases, it is possible to train a prediction model ω that successfully distinguishes real from generated data. In adversarial explanations, e.g. the strategy described by [23], such an out-of-distribution (OOD) detector ω that exposes synthetic data is the primary workhorse. If the data is synthetic, the adversary deploys a different model as with real data, which effectively fools the explanation.

We want to highlight that even though this fooling strategy was introduced and is typically discussed for local Shapley values [23,28], it can also be applied to global aggregates such as Shapley additive global importance (SAGE) [8].

Achieving Adversarial Attack Robustness. Avoiding the generation of extrapolated data protects against adversarial attacks by preventing ω from distinguishing real from generated data during Shapley value calculation.

Some approaches naturally circumvent the task of generating synthetic data altogether, for example by using surrogate models [10], retraining the model such that it adapts to missing features [8] or fitting a separate model for each coalition [25,29]. However, these approaches come at a high computational costs, since repeated model refitting is required.

Another approach is to calculate conditional Shapley values, for which we will give a brief overview of methods in the following paragraph. Working with conditional Shapley values, i.e. using $\mathcal{R} = P(\mathbf{X}_{\bar{\mathcal{S}}} \mid \mathbf{X}_{\mathcal{S}} = \mathbf{x}_{\mathcal{S}})$, is clearly the most rigorous way of enforcing on-manifold sampling of synthetic data, even though prior literature merely acknowledges the potential for preventing adversarial attacks. Several conditional Shapley value estimation procedures have been proposed, yet conditional feature sampling remains a challenging task and improvements are highly desirable.

A straightforward, empirical approach is to simply use the observed data that naturally satisfies the conditioning on the selected in-coalition features by using data points in close proximity to the instance to be explained [1,11]. For example, in Fig. 1, one could also sample the out-of-coalition features from other observations of digit zero in the data set. This approach, however, has the downside that the number of observations fulfilling the conditioning event might be very small, leading to only very few or even no appropriate observations available. Another approach to calculating conditional Shapley values is assuming a specific data distribution, e.g. a Gaussian distribution [1,7], for which conditional distributions are easy to derive, but this approach has the drawback of strong assumptions on the data generating process. Further, conditional generative models might be used [10,20], however, these models might be challenging to train and it is unclear whether they truly approximate the data well. In sum, conditional Shapley values are challenging to access and hence have limited applicability.

For the goal of preventing adversarial attacks, conditional Shapley values are sufficient but not necessary, since any method that avoids extrapolation will prevent the attack and hence related, but less strict frameworks provide another suite of promising methods. Such an idea is pursued by [28], where generative models use 'focused sampling' of new instances that are close to the original observations. However, this approach lacks theoretical guarantees and may fail depending on the fit of the generative models. We acknowledge that [28] investigate Gaussian knockoffs in conjunction with the so-called Interactions-based Method for Explanation (IME, [24]). However, the authors do not use model-X knockoffs for imputation in full generality, nor do they apply the strategy to SHAP or SAGE values directly. The authors even mention that the knockoff imputation idea merits further investigation as an approach, which is what the present paper contributes to.

2.2 Model-X Knockoffs

The model-X knockoff framework [5] is a theoretically sound concept to characterize synthetic variables with specific statistical properties. Intuitively speaking, knockoffs are synthetic variables that aim to copy the statistical properties of a given set of original variables, e.g. the covariance structure, such that they are indistinguishable from the original variables when the target variable Y is not looked at. Crucially, valid knockoffs ensure that original variables can be swapped with their knockoff counterparts without affecting the joint distribution.

Formally, in order for $\tilde{\mathbf{X}}$ to be a valid knockoff matrix for $\mathbf{X}$, two conditions have to be met:

1. Pairwise exchangeablility: For any proper subset $\mathcal{S} \subset \{1, \ldots, d\}$:

$$(\mathbf{X}, \tilde{\mathbf{X}})_{swap(\mathcal{S})} \overset{d}{=} (\mathbf{X}, \tilde{\mathbf{X}}), \qquad (3)$$

where $\overset{d}{=}$ represents equality in distribution and $swap(\mathcal{S})$ indicates swapping the variables in $\mathcal{S}$ with their knockoff counterparts.
2. Conditional independence:

$$\tilde{\mathbf{X}} \perp\!\!\!\perp Y \mid \mathbf{X}. \qquad (4)$$

Generating valid knockoffs is an active field of research and various sampling algorithms have been proposed, which ensures that practitioners can flexibly choose appropriate algorithms. For example, there are algorithms based on distributional assumptions [3,5,21], Bayesian statistics [12] or deep learning [14,16,18,26].

3 Combining Model-X Knockoffs with Shapley Values

This paper proposes to impute out-of-coalition features with model-X knockoffs for the calculation of Shapley value based quantities. Knockoffs come with strong theoretical guarantees that ensure avoiding extrapolation. Moreover, they provide a major computational boost, since knockoffs can be sampled upfront for the full data matrix instead of requiring separate models for each possible coalition. Since many methods are available for knockoff generation—including some that are essentially tuning-free—practitioners have a large collection of tools available for valid, flexible and convenient sampling of the out-of-coalition space that ensures robustness against adversarial attacks.

In detail, we propose Algorithm 1 to impute out-of-coalition features with knockoffs for Shapley values and Algorithm 2 (see Appendix A) for knockoff imputation with SAGE [8] values. In brief, the algorithms use N_{ko} knockoffs as the background distribution in the calculation of Shapley values. Note that for $N_{ko} = 1$, the Shapley values are with respect to a single knockoff baseline value, while for larger values of N_{ko}, Shapley values explain the difference between the selected instance and the expected value of the knockoff distribution.

Algorithm 1. Knockoff Imputed Shapley Values

Input: data matrix $(\mathbf{X}, Y)$, knockoff sampler $ko()$, model f, explanation instance
    $\mathbf{x}^0 = \{x_1^0, \ldots, x_d^0\}$, number of knockoffs N_{ko}, power set π of $\mathcal{D} \setminus \{j\}$
1: train knockoff sampler $ko(\mathbf{X})$
2: **for** feature j in $\mathcal{D}$ **do**
3:    initialize $\phi_j = 0$
4:    **for** i in N_{ko} **do**
5:       draw $\tilde{\mathbf{x}}^i = \{\tilde{x}_1^i, \ldots, \tilde{x}_d^i\}$ from $ko(\mathbf{X})$
6:       initialize $\Delta_j^i = 0$
7:       **for** $\mathcal{S}$ in π **do**
8:          out-of-coalition set $\bar{\mathcal{S}} = \mathcal{D} \setminus \mathcal{S}$
9:          $v(\mathcal{S}) = f(\mathbf{x}_\mathcal{S}^0, \tilde{\mathbf{x}}_{\bar{\mathcal{S}}}^i)$
10:        $\mathcal{S}' = \mathcal{S} \cup \{j\}$
11:        $\bar{\mathcal{S}}' = \bar{\mathcal{S}} \setminus \{j\}$
12:        $v(\mathcal{S}') = f(\mathbf{x}_{\mathcal{S}'}^0, \tilde{\mathbf{x}}_{\bar{\mathcal{S}}'}^i)$
13:        $\Delta_j^i = \Delta_j^i + \frac{|\mathcal{S}|!(|\mathcal{D}| - |\mathcal{S}| - 1)!}{|\mathcal{D}|!} \cdot \big(v(\mathcal{S}') - v(\mathcal{S}) \big)$
14:       **end for**
15:    **end for**
16:    $\phi_j = \frac{1}{N_{ko}} \sum_{i=1}^{N_{ko}} \Delta_j^i$
17: **end for**
18: **return** Shapley values $\phi = \{\phi_1, \ldots, \phi_d\}$

To understand the advantages of knockoff imputed Shapley values on a theoretical level, let us investigate the implications of the exchangeability property (Eq. 3) in more depth. This property ensures that we can swap *any* set $\mathcal{S} \subseteq \mathcal{D}$ of original variables $\mathbf{X}$ with knockoffs $\tilde{\mathbf{X}}$, while maintaining the same joint distribution. The same joint distribution guarantees that any generated data is indeed on the same data manifold, so for the prevention of adversarial attacks, it is both necessary and sufficient that $\mathbf{x}'_{\bar{\mathcal{S}}}$ is generated such that $P(\mathbf{X}_\mathcal{S}, \mathbf{X}_{\bar{\mathcal{S}}}) = P(\mathbf{X}_\mathcal{S}, \mathbf{X}'_{\bar{\mathcal{S}}})$. Conditional Shapley values ensure this by sampling $\mathbf{x}'_{\bar{\mathcal{S}}}$ from $P(\mathbf{X}_{\bar{\mathcal{S}}}|\mathbf{X}_\mathcal{S})$. Doing so, the original joint distribution is maintained by factorizing through $P(\mathbf{X}_\mathcal{S}) \cdot P(\mathbf{X}_{\bar{\mathcal{S}}}|\mathbf{X}_\mathcal{S}) = P(\mathbf{X}_\mathcal{S}, \mathbf{X}_{\bar{\mathcal{S}}})$, whereas knockoffs directly guarantee $P(\mathbf{X}_\mathcal{S}, \mathbf{X}_{\bar{\mathcal{S}}}) = P(\mathbf{X}_\mathcal{S}, \tilde{\mathbf{X}}_{\bar{\mathcal{S}}})$ by exchangebility.

That said, it becomes obvious that we can generate knockoff copies for $\mathbf{X}$ upfront and then swap in knockoffs for the out-of-coalition features $\mathbf{X}_{\bar{\mathcal{S}}}$ where needed. This is a clear advantage in contrast to conditional Shapley value methods that need access to $P(\mathbf{X}_{\bar{\mathcal{S}}}|\mathbf{X}_s)$ for all possible coalitions $2^{|\mathcal{D}|}$. Note that the pairwise exchangeability fulfilled by knockoffs is needed to guarantee on-manifold data in the imputation step, which is why other conditional sampling methods cannot be calculated upfront. This suggests a lower computational complexity for the knockoff imputed Shapley values in comparison to conditional Shapley values, however, the exact complexity will depend on the knockoff generating algorithm used. Further, even though we may want to sample N_{ko} knockoffs in advance to reduce bias, a reasonable number for N_{ko} is typically $N_{ko} \ll 2^{|D|}$.

However, the benefit of being able to sample knockoffs upfront comes at the cost of enforcing a restrictive set of conditioning events. At a first glance, knockoff imputation and calculating conditional Shapley values, i.e. using $\mathcal{R} = P(\mathbf{X}_{\bar{\mathcal{S}}} \mid \mathbf{X}_{\mathcal{S}} = \mathbf{x}_{\mathcal{S}})$, may appear interchangeable. However, knockoffs implicitly condition on all the feature values of the observation, which is inevitable since the exchangeability property must hold for *any* set of variables. This subtle difference yields the following expression for the game that uses knockoffs $\tilde{\mathbf{X}}_{\bar{\mathcal{S}}}$ as imputation for the out-of-coalition features in set $\bar{\mathcal{S}}$:

$$v_{\mathrm{ko}}(\mathcal{S}) = \mathbb{E}_{p(\tilde{\mathbf{X}}_{\bar{\mathcal{S}}} \mid \mathbf{x}_{\mathcal{S}}, \mathbf{x}_{\bar{\mathcal{S}}})} \left[f(\mathbf{x}_{\mathcal{S}}, \tilde{\mathbf{X}}_{\bar{\mathcal{S}}}) \right]. \tag{5}$$

To elaborate on the consequences of the expectation taken w.r.t. $P(\tilde{\mathbf{X}}_{\bar{\mathcal{S}}} \mid \mathbf{X}_{\mathcal{S}} = \mathbf{x}_{\mathcal{S}}, \mathbf{X}_{\bar{\mathcal{S}}} = \mathbf{x}_{\bar{\mathcal{S}}})$, imagine a dataset with three variables, i.e. X_1, X_2, X_3, where X_1 is in-coalition and the task is to impute values for the out-of-coalition features X_2 and X_3. When using knockoff $\tilde{X}_2$ for imputation, this knockoff has been generated from a knockoff sampler that was fitted on the observed values of all three variables in the dataset. For the Shapley value calculation however, the data for imputation is required to condition on the observed value of X_1 only. Hence, the procedure leaks information from the out-of-coalition feature X_3 during the imputation of X_2. As a consequence, the range of values sampled for imputing out-of-coalition values will be too narrow, i.e. conditioned on more features than necessary, which reduces the entropy of the predicted values in $f(\mathbf{x}_{\mathcal{S}}, \mathbf{x}_{\bar{\mathcal{S}}})$. To be clear, the generated data throughout Shapley value calculation will still be on the same data manifold as the original samples, so this procedure effectively defends against adversarial attacks, which is what we focus on in this paper. We can interpret the restrictive conditioning as a form of regularization imposed through the data sampling mechanism. We therefore expect estimated Shapley values of lower magnitude when using knockoff imputation. As a result, on the one hand, conditioning on variables in the out-of-coalition set may introduce bias due to information leakage from other covariates; on the other hand, this will also lead to a reduction in variance of Shapley values that are estimated by approximation instead of exact calculation, which may be advantageous. We encourage future research to investigate potential trade-offs.

4   Experiments

4.1   Unfooling SHAP

We start off the section on experiments by illustrating that knockoff imputed Shapley values indeed are able to prevent adversarial attacks that make use of extrapolation. We replicate and extend the German Credit [9] experiments conducted by [23], where the task is to determine whether clients will be good customers (GoodCustomer $= 1$) or not (GoodCustomer $= -1$). We demonstrate that with knockoff imputation, the adversarial attack is no longer successful.

The fooling strategy of [23] can be illustrated in an intuitive manner: Imagine an unethical bank that aims to exploit sensitive information, such as the Gender of the credit applicant, to assess creditworthiness with a prediction model f. However, in the country the bank operates in, credit assessment tools are legally required to pass a so-called fairness audit prior to model deployment. During the audit, black-box models will be evaluated via SHAP [17]. If high importance scores are attributed to sensitive features, the model fails the audit and its deployment is legally prohibited. In spite of this danger, the bank is determined to use the discriminatory model f in its daily business, and comes up with a strategy to fool the auditors and make them believe that the bank uses an innocent prediction algorithm ψ, which utilises the non-discriminatory feature LoanRateAsPercentOfIncome only.

To fool the explanation, a supervised classification algorithm ω, in this case a random forest [4], is trained to distinguish in-distribution from OOD data. For in-distribution data, the adversarial model α uses the discriminatory prediction algorithm f, but for OOD data, α makes predictions according to ψ. For simplicity, the prediction model f here makes use of only the discriminatory variable Gender, whereas prediction model ψ determines the predictions according to the non-discriminatory variable LoanRateAsPercentOfIncome, see further Fig. 2, Panel **A**.

Extending the experiments of [23], we evaluate the adversarial model α not only with SHAP using marginal imputation with $kmeans(10)$ to summarize the background distribution, but also with knockoff imputed SHAP. We use sequential knockoffs [15] due to the presence of both categorical and continuous features in the dataset and generate $N_{ko} = 10$ knockoffs for each test data point. In brief, sequential knockoffs [15] are generated through an iterative procedure that samples values from a Gaussian (for continuous features) or multinomial (for categorical features) distribution. The distribution parameters are estimated from a penalized linear or multinomial logistic regression of the feature for which a knockoff copy should be generated on the other features and already sampled knockoffs from earlier iterations.

Figure 2 Panel **B** replicates results of [23], where we can see the aggregated explanations across test data instances suggesting LoanRateAsPercentOfIncome as most relevant for the model, hence the adversarial attack is successful. On the contrary, we can see from Panel **C** that with knockoff imputation, the explanation reveals the true importance of Gender for the model's prediction in the majority of test data points.

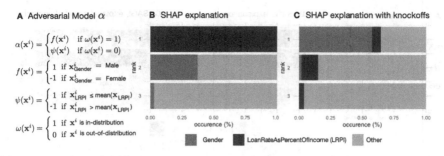

Fig. 2. Occurrences of features ranked amongst the top 3 features in SHAP explanations of test data, $N = 99$. Fidelity to detect real data as in-distribution with ω is 1.

Clearly, ω plays a crucial role for the success of the adversarial attack. In this experiment, we see that with knockoff imputation, ω is not able to detect OOD data as such, which is why the adversarial attack cannot unfold. At the same time, we have that ω always detects in-distribution data as such (fidelity = 1), so real world data will be reliably predicted with discriminatory model f. With this knowledge, advanced adversarial attackers might try to improve the model training of ω and optimize the decision threshold to reinstate a successful adversarial attack. However, with knockoff imputation – and conditional out-of-coalition-sampling in general – it is not possible to train an effective OOD classifier ω because the resulting data will lie on the same data manifold as the original data, hindering its detection as synthetic data. We discuss this issue further in Appendix B.

4.2   Unfooling SAGE

We now illustrate that global aggregates of Shapley values, SAGE values [8], suffer from the same vulnerability as local Shapley values and that knockoff imputation again can increase robustness. In this experiment, we simulate data, which further allows us to analyze key drivers in the data characteristics that affect the robustness against adversarial attacks.

We simulate data from $\mathbf{X}^{1000 \times 4} \sim N(\boldsymbol{\mu}, \boldsymbol{\Sigma})$, with $\boldsymbol{\mu} = [0, \ldots, 0]$ and correlation matrix $\boldsymbol{\Sigma}$ with correlation coefficient $\rho \in [0, 0.9]$ in all off-diagonal elements. The target variable Y is defined by $Y = \mathbf{X}\boldsymbol{\beta} + \epsilon$, where $\boldsymbol{\beta} = [1, \ldots, 1]$ and $\epsilon \sim N(0, \sigma^2)$, such that σ^2 guarantees a signal to noise ratio $SNR = \frac{Var(Y)}{\sigma^2} = 2$. The adversarial model α is given in Fig. 3 Panel **A**.

SAGE with marginal imputation uses a background distribution summarized by $kmeans(10)$ and SAGE with knockoff imputation uses $N_{ko} = 10$ Gaussian knockoffs for the background distribution of each observation. Gaussian knockoffs are generated through sampling from a multivariate Gaussian distribution with parameters estimated from the observed features, see [5] for further details.

Figure 3 reveals that SAGE can be fooled just as SHAP and that knockoff imputation again prevents the adversarial attack, i.e. unfools the explanation.

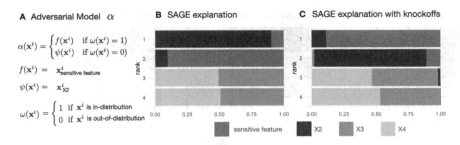

Fig. 3. Occurrences of features ranked amongst the top 4 in SAGE explanations with adversarial model α across 500 replicates. Correlation $\rho = 0.5$, fidelity of $\omega = 0.88$.

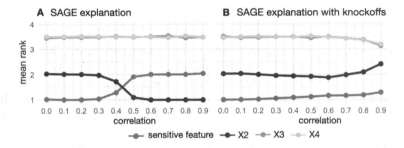

Fig. 4. Mean rank of features in SAGE explanations with adversarial classifier α across 500 replicates. We consider the adversarial attack successful if X_2 is ranked first, and unsuccessful if the sensitive feature is ranked first.

We can see from Fig. 4 that correlation strength plays a crucial role in the success of the attack. For marginal imputation (Fig. 4, Panel **A**), the adversarial attack is successful and hides the true rank of the sensitive feature (true rank is 1) for correlation levels greater than or equal to 0.5. Note that lower levels of correlation do not allow the adversarial attack to unfold regardless, because extrapolation is more pronounced and hence more likely to be detected by ω with medium or strongly correlated data (recall that $\rho = 0$ corresponds to feature independence). For SAGE with knockoffs (Fig. 4, Panel **B**), the model's usage of the sensitive feature is exposed for all levels of correlation. Hence, knockoff imputation effectively prevents the adversarial attack on SAGE explanations.

5   Discussion

We demonstrate that knockoff imputed Shapley values are robust against adversarial attacks that exploit extrapolated data. However, other adversarial attacks might be proposed. For example, because Shapley values are spread out across correlated features, the true importance of a sensitive feature could be toned down by adding correlated features to the model.

Further, the special characteristics of knockoffs may open up new trajectories in Shapley value research. One such example is SHAPLIT, which proposes conditional independence testing with FDR control for Shapley values [27]. Another promising approach could be to leverage the overly restrictive conditioning of knockoff imputed Shapley values for approximation tasks, where Shapley values are calculated with just a small fraction of all possible coalitions as opposed to exact Shapley value calculation. It is common in Shapley value software to optionally include some form of L_1 penalty on feature attributions to encourage sparse explanations, even when the underlying model f is not itself sparse [17]. Like many regularization methods, this effectively introduces bias in exchange for a decrease in variance. Knockoff imputed Shapley values may give a similar regularizing effect through the data sampling method rather than directly on the parameter estimation technique. This does not zero out feature attributions as the L_1 penalty does, but may serve to improve predictions for practitioners with limited computational budgets.

We want to emphasize that the use case for knockoff imputed Shapley values should be carefully chosen, since the method narrows down entropy of the target function, which may be disadvantageous in comparison to other methods when the computational capacity suffices to calculate exact conditional Shapley values.

Further, we want to highlight that a comparative benchmark study that analyzes variants for Shapley value calculation, including conditional Shapley value calculation, may be of great value for future research. For example, the knockoff-based approach proposed here could be compared with other conditional variants [1,2,20] both in terms of theory, e.g. analyzing the variance, and in empirical application, e.g. investigating the computational efficiency of the proposed algorithms and accuracy of estimates for different datasets. Such endeavors may further include novel methods that combine ideas from existing approaches. For example, one could use an overly strict conditioning set, as it is the case with knockoffs, for the conditional distribution based approaches to cut down the computational complexity of those approaches.

6   Conclusion

The paper presents an innovative approach to make Shapley explanations, such as SHAP [17] and SAGE [8], more robust against adversarial attacks by using model-X knockoffs. The discussion on theoretical guarantees and implications reveals that knockoffs can serve as a flexible and off-the-shelf methodology that effectively prevents extrapolation during Shapley value calculation. Through both real data and simulated data experiments, the paper demonstrates that vulnerability to adversarial attacks can be successfully reduced. It is worth emphasizing that the presented methodology can be used in conjunction with any valid knockoff sampling procedure and not only the deep [18], sequential [15] and Gaussian knockoffs [5] used in this paper, which further highlights the flexibility of the proposed approach. This, and the possibility to sample knockoffs upfront, which drastically reduces computational complexity, is a major advantage over conditional Shapley value calculation approaches that may otherwise be used for the prevention of adversarial attacks.

142   K. Blesch et al.

Acknowledgements. MNW and KB received funding for this project from the German Research Foundation (DFG), Emmy Noether Grant 437611051.

Data and Code availability. Reproducible code for the results presented in this paper is available at https://github.com/bips-hb/unfooling_shapley.

A Knockoff Imputed SAGE Values

Algorithm 2. Sampling-based approximation for SAGE values [8] with knockoff imputation

---
Input: data $(\mathbf{X}, Y)$, model f, loss function l, outer samples n, number of knockoffs N_{ko}, knockoff sampler $ko()$
1: Initialize $\hat{\phi}_1 = 0, \hat{\phi}_2 = 0, \ldots, \hat{\phi}_d = 0$
2: $\hat{y}_{\text{init}} = \frac{1}{N} \sum_{i=1}^{N} f(\mathbf{x}_i)$
3: train knockoff sampler $k(\mathbf{X})$
4: **for** i = 1 to n **do**
5:     Sample a data instance $(\mathbf{x}_i, y_i)$
6:     Sample instance π, a permutation of $\mathcal{D}$
7:     $\mathcal{S} = \emptyset$
8:     $\text{L}_{\text{prev}} = l(\hat{y}_{\text{init}}, \mathbf{y})$
9:     **for** j in $\mathcal{D}$ **do**
10:        $\mathcal{S} = \mathcal{S} \cup \{\pi[j]\}$
11:        $\hat{y} = 0$
12:        **for** $k = 1$ to N_{ko} **do**
13:           Sample $\tilde{\mathbf{x}}^k = \tilde{x}_1^k, \ldots, \tilde{x}_d^k$ from $ko(\mathbf{X})$
14:           $\hat{y} = \hat{y} + f(\mathbf{x}_{\mathcal{S}}, \tilde{\mathbf{x}}_{\bar{\mathcal{S}}}^k)$
15:        **end for**
16:        $\bar{\hat{y}} = \frac{\hat{y}}{N_{ko}}$
17:        $\text{L} = l(\hat{y}, y)$
18:        $\Delta = \text{L}_{\text{prev}} - \text{L}$
19:        $\hat{\phi}_{\pi[j]} = \hat{\phi}_{\pi[j]} + \Delta$
20:        $\text{L}_{\text{prev}} = \text{L}$
21:     **end for**
22: **end for**
23: **return** SAGE values $\frac{\hat{\phi}_1}{n}, \ldots, \frac{\hat{\phi}_d}{n}$

B The Role of ω

The detection of OOD data is the backbone of adversarial attacks which is why the performance of ω is crucial for the success of the attack. Let us take a closer look onto how ω is derived: In a first step, we take the training data and add the label $y = 1$ to it, because it is real world data. Then, we mimic the imputation procedure that occurs during Shapley value calculation. This means we treat some feature values as in-coalition, i.e. we take the actual value of these features for the respective observation, and impute the remaining out-of-coalition feature values with other quantities, for example, by sampling values from the marginal distribution. The resulting 'new' observations will then be labeled with $y = 0$, because this is generated data. In a second step, we fit a random forest classifier to distinguish in-distribution from OOD data, or technically speaking, to distinguish $y = 1$ from $y = 0$ data.

In the experiments of Sect. 4.1, we train ω exactly like [23], where we impute the out-of-coalition features with values from a background distribution that is characterised by the center points of a $kmeans(c = 10)$ clustering of the data. Note that this is the exact same background distribution which is used for the marginal imputation in the SHAP explanations later on. With this ω, the adversarial attack is successful for marginal imputation, but with the very same ω, SHAP explanations using knockoff imputation prevents the attack.

To some readers, it might have been clear from the beginning that an ω which is trained to detect OOD samples that are generated with $kmeans(c = 10)$ will not perform well in detecting OOD samples that occur when calculated knockoff imputed SHAP, where the background distribution consists of knockoffs and not $kmeans(c = 10)$ cluster centers. An advanced adversarial attacker strategy could be to train ω for detecting OOD samples from many different background distributions, including a knockoff background distribution. However, the crucial point is that with conditional out-of-coalition-sampling, for example knockoffs, it is not possible to train an effective OOD classifier ω because the $y = 1$ and $y = 0$ data points will lie on the same data manifold. In other words, there is no difference in in-distribution and OOD data, which hinders its detection as synthetic data. When training ω on such data, the classifier cannot learn reasonable information from the data.

The implications of this are illustrated in Fig. 5. There, we train ω on data that is generated by knockoff imputation. We vary the hyperparameters for the random forest classifier to force model ω to overfit, i.e. be less (Fig. 5, Panel **A**) or more (Fig. 5, Panel **B**) conservative in predicting data as OOD. This can be achieved by varying the number of trees in the random forest classifier, and the number of $y = 0$ training samples we generate. We denote the hyperparameters with ω(number of trees, number of samples generated).

For an adversarial attacker, the aim is high fidelity, i.e. a high percentage of true in-distribution classifications by ω and a high rank of the innocent feature `LoanRateAsPercentOfIncome` in the SHAP explanation. Different hyperparameter settings reveal that there is a trade-off between fidelity and the degree to which the innocent feature `LoanRateAsPercentOfIncome` is ranked up high. If the adversarial attacker is keen to predict real-world data with the discriminatory model, i.e. uses an ω that is conservative in classifying data as OOD, then knockoff imputed SHAP reveals the sensitive feature `Gender` as highly important (Fig. 5, Panel **B**). On the contrary, if the adversarial attacker prioritizes that the explanation should pretend that `LoanRateAsPercentOfIncome` is important, i.e.

uses an ω that is liberal in predicting data as OOD, then the fidelity of ω drops drastically (Fig. 5, Panel **A**). This is clearly in contrast to the overarching goal of adversarial attackers to use the discriminatory model for in-distribution (real world) applications, but fool the SHAP explanation such that the model appears innocent.

Consequently, when using knockoff imputed SHAP, the adversarial attacker is forced to use the fair model if the SHAP evaluation should suggest that the model is fair – in other words and recollecting the example stated in the main text before: The only way to pass a fairness audit that uses knockoff imputed SHAP explanations is using a fair model.

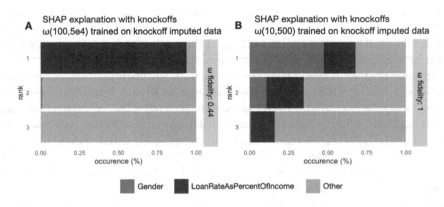

Fig. 5. Occurrences of features ranked amongst the top 3 features in SHAP explanations of $N = 99$ test data points.

References

1. Aas, K., Jullum, M., Løland, A.: Explaining individual predictions when features are dependent: more accurate approximations to Shapley values. Artif. Intell. **298**, 103502 (2021)
2. Aas, K., Nagler, T., Jullum, M., Løland, A.: Explaining predictive models using Shapley values and non-parametric vine copulas. Depend. Model. **9**(1), 62–81 (2021)
3. Bates, S., Candès, E., Janson, L., Wang, W.: Metropolized knockoff sampling. J. Am. Stat. Assoc. **116**(535), 1413–1427 (2021)
4. Breiman, L.: Random forests. Mach. Learn. **45**(1), 5–32 (2001)
5. Candès, E., Fan, Y., Janson, L., Lv, J.: Panning for gold: model-free knockoffs for high-dimensional controlled variable selection. J. Roy. Stat. Soc. Ser. B (Stat. Methodol.) **80**(3), 551–577 (2018)
6. Chen, H., Covert, I.C., Lundberg, S.M., Lee, S.I.: Algorithms to estimate Shapley value feature attributions. arXiv:2207.07605 (2022)
7. Chen, H., Janizek, J.D., Lundberg, S., Lee, S.I.: True to the model or true to the data? arXiv:2006.16234 (2020)

8. Covert, I., Lundberg, S.M., Lee, S.I.: Understanding global feature contributions with additive importance measures. In: Advances in Neural Information Processing Systems, vol. 33, pp. 17212–17223 (2020)
9. Dua, D., Graff, C.: UCI machine learning repository (2017)
10. Frye, C., de Mijolla, D., Begley, T., Cowton, L., Stanley, M., Feige, I.: Shapley explainability on the data manifold. arXiv:2006.01272 (2020)
11. Ghalebikesabi, S., Ter-Minassian, L., DiazOrdaz, K., Holmes, C.C.: On locality of local explanation models. In: Advances in Neural Information Processing Systems, vol. 34, pp. 18395–18407 (2021)
12. Gu, J., Yin, G.: Bayesian knockoff filter using Gibbs sampler. arXiv:2102.05223 (2021)
13. Hooker, G., Mentch, L., Zhou, S.: Unrestricted permutation forces extrapolation: variable importance requires at least one more model, or there is no free variable importance. Stat. Comput. 31(6), 1–16 (2021)
14. Jordon, J., Yoon, J., van der Schaar, M.: KnockoffGAN: generating knockoffs for feature selection using generative adversarial networks. In: International Conference on Learning Representations (2019)
15. Kormaksson, M., Kelly, L.J., Zhu, X., Haemmerle, S., Pricop, L., Ohlssen, D.: Sequential knockoffs for continuous and categorical predictors: With application to a large psoriatic arthritis clinical trial pool. Stat. Med. 40(14), 3313–3328 (2021)
16. Liu, Y., Zheng, C.: Auto-encoding knockoff generator for FDR controlled variable selection. arXiv:1809.10765 (2018)
17. Lundberg, S.M., Lee, S.I.: A unified approach to interpreting model predictions. In: Advances in Neural Information Processing Systems, vol. 30 (2017)
18. Romano, Y., Sesia, M., Candès, E.: Deep knockoffs. J. Am. Stat. Assoc. 115(532), 1861–1872 (2020)
19. Ribeiro, M. T., Singh, S., Guestrin, C.: Why should I trust you? Explaining the predictions of any classifier. In: Proceedings of the 22nd International Conference on Knowledge Discovery and Data Mining ACM SIGKDD 22, pp. 1135–1144 (2016)
20. Redelmeier, A., Jullum, M., Aas, K.: Explaining predictive models with mixed features using Shapley values and conditional inference trees. In: Proceedings of the 4th International Cross-Domain Conference for Machine Learning and Knowledge Extraction CD-MAKE, pp. 117–137 (2020)
21. Sesia, M., Sabatti, C., Candès, E.J.: Gene hunting with hidden Markov model knockoffs. Biometrika 106(1), 1–18 (2018)
22. Shapley, L.: A value for n-person games. In: Kuhn, H., Tucker, A. (eds.) Contributions to the Theory of Games II. Princeton University Press, Princeton (1953)
23. Slack, D., Hilgard, S., Jia, E., Singh, S., Lakkaraju, H.: Fooling LIME and SHAP: adversarial attacks on post hoc explanation methods. In: Proceedings of the AAAI/ACM Conference on AI, Ethics, and Society, pp. 180–186 (2020)
24. Štrumbelj, E., Kononenko, I.: An efficient explanation of individual classifications using game theory. J. Mach. Learn. Res. 11, 1–18 (2010)
25. Štrumbelj, E., Kononenko, I.: Explaining prediction models and individual predictions with feature contributions. Knowl. Inf. Syst. 41(3), 647–665 (2014)
26. Sudarshan, M., Tansey, W., Ranganath, R.: Deep direct likelihood knockoffs. In: Advances in Neural Information Processing Systems, vol. 33, pp. 5036–5046 (2020)

27. Teneggi, J., Bharti, B., Romano, Y., Sulam, J.: From Shapley back to Pearson: hypothesis testing via the Shapley value. arXiv:2207.07038 (2022)
28. Vreš, D., Robnik-Šikonja, M.: Preventing deception with explanation methods using focused sampling. Data Mining Knowl. Discov. (2022)
29. Williamson, B., Feng, J.: Efficient nonparametric statistical inference on population feature importance using Shapley values. In: International Conference on Machine Learning, pp. 10282–10291. PMLR (2020)

Strategies to Exploit XAI to Improve Classification Systems

Andrea Apicella[1,2,3]([📧]) [iD], Luca Di Lorenzo[1], Francesco Isgrò[1,2,3] [iD],
Andrea Pollastro[1,2,3,4] [iD], and Roberto Prevete[1,2,3] [iD]

[1] Dipartimento di Ingegneria Elettrica e delle Tecnologie dell'Informazione,
Università degli Studi di Napoli Federico II, Naples, Italy
andrea.apicella@unina.it
[2] Laboratory of Augmented Reality for Health Monitoring (ARHeMLab),
Naples, Italy
[3] Laboratory of Artificial Intelligence, Privacy and Applications (AIPA Lab),
Naples, Italy
[4] Lawrence Berkeley National Laboratory, Berkeley, CA 94720, USA
https://www.dieti.unina.it, https://arhemlab.dieti.unina.it,
http://aipa.dieti.unina.it

Abstract. Explainable Artificial Intelligence (XAI) aims to provide
insights into the decision-making process of AI models, allowing users
to understand their results beyond their decisions. A significant goal of
XAI is to improve the performance of AI models by providing explanations for their decision-making processes. However, most XAI literature focuses on how to explain an AI system, while less attention has
been given to how XAI methods can be exploited to improve an AI
system. In this work, a set of well-known XAI methods typically used
with Machine Learning (ML) classification tasks are investigated to verify if they can be exploited, not just to provide explanations but also to
improve the performance of the model itself. To this aim, two strategies
to use the explanation to improve a classification system are reported
and empirically evaluated on three datasets: Fashion-MNIST, CIFAR10,
and STL10. Results suggest that explanations built by Integrated Gradients highlight input features that can be effectively used to improve
classification performance.

Keywords: XAI · Machine Learning · DNN · Integrated Gradients ·
attributions

1 Introduction

Explainable Artificial Intelligence (XAI) aims to provide an understanding of
how AI models work and reasons beyond the decisions they make, allowing
users to understand their results. This is particularly important as AI becomes
more integrated into everyday life and critical decision-making processes such
as healthcare and finance. However, it is essential to note that a large part
of the current XAI literature proposes methods to provide explanations to AI

L. Longo (Ed.): xAI 2023, CCIS 1901, pp. 147–159, 2023.
https://doi.org/10.1007/978-3-031-44064-9_9

systems [1,2,12,13,16], but less attention is given on how XAI can be used to improve the performance of AI models. Indeed, the goal of XAI is not only to provide explanations but also to improve the AI model performance thanks to a more profound knowledge of the AI's decision-making strategies. This is a significant shortcoming in the context of such research studies, as XAI's overall goal is also to improve the performance of AI models thanks to a more profound knowledge of the AI's decision-making strategies. In fact, by explaining their decision-making processes, XAI techniques can help AI researchers better understand the mechanisms behind AI outputs, allowing them to identify errors in their design and/or implementation. Accordingly, in this paper, we explore several well-known XAI methods typically used for Machine Learning (ML) classification tasks to see if they can be exploited both to provide explanations and to improve the model itself. The single explanation of a given ML output may not be enough to improve the ML system: the ML researcher may not be able to use the explanation directly due to the complexity of the ML system (for example, a Deep Neural Network). It would be desirable to have an automatic process that uses explanations of the ML system behaviour to improve the ML system itself automatically, or ideally, the ML system should be able to improve itself in a feedback loop fashion using the explanations provided (see Fig. 1).

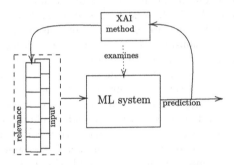

Fig. 1. General functional scheme of a Machine Learning architecture able to select/transform relevant input features relying on explanations provided by an XAI system.

The basic underlying idea is that explanations about the model outputs can help tune the ML system parameters better. In general, an explanation explains why an ML model returns a result given a specific input. However, building an explanation is particularly challenging if the model to inspect is a DNN, mainly for two reasons: i) DNNs offer excellent performances in several tasks, but at the price of high inner complexity of the models, leading toward low interpretability, ii) to help the ML user to understand the system behaviours, typical explanations have to be humanly understandable. However, we start from the simpler hypothesis that the knowledge given by the explanation can be used to understand the model's strengths and weaknesses, changing the ML model to adapt itself to different inputs better. In the XAI context, explanations are built using ML system behaviour to understand its input-output relationships. Therefore,

explanations of an ML system can be used to identify the critical characteristics of the input that caused a given output and thus use this knowledge to
adapt/modify the ML system itself.

Thus, this paper aims to investigate whether the relevant features highlighted
by an XAI method can be used with the input data to improve the classification
performance of an ML system. However, we also experimentally evaluate which
XAI methods can effectively highlight the most relevant features for our goal, as
the performance of existing XAI methods may depend on the specific problem.

2   Related Works

The internal workings of Modern ML approaches, such as Deep learning, are
typically opaque, letting to the AI scientist's ability to grasp the underlying processes that drive their behaviours. Subsequently, comprehending the connections
between outputs and inputs can be extremely difficult. The use of XAI methods
is becoming increasingly prominent for explaining various classification systems
that rely on multiple inputs, including, but not limited to, images [1,12,16],
natural language processing [10,14], clinical decision support systems [20], and
others. However, using XAI methods to improve the performance of ML models in classification problems is relatively scarce in current research. In [27], a
survey of the works leveraging XAI methods to improve classification systems is
reported. The authors of [7] provide a general framework to train a model both
with data and explanations with the aim of not only to get to the correct answer,
but also to provide a correct explanation. In general, the importance of involving the explanations in the ML pipeline has gaining attention in literature. For
instance, in [11] a dataset for a hate Speech detection including rationales about
their labels is described. In [19], a first study is proposed to use the relevance
produced by Deep Taylor Decomposition [13] to build a reliable classifier to build
a system able to detect the presence of orca whales in hydrophone recordings.
The relevance is used as a binary mask to select the most relevant input features.
Differently from [19], our study focuses on image classification tasks on publicly
available datasets, selecting an XAI strategy to build the relevance mask by a
preliminary study on a family of XAI methods available in the literature. In
[17], the training loss function is constrained to lead the classifier to focus only
on a prior-defined set of features. Similarly, in [25], LRP explanations [12] are
exploited to lead the training stage of an ML model to emphasize the important
features of a classification task. In [21], eXplanatory interactive Learning (XiL)
is proposed. XiL is a mechanism consisting of interactively querying the user (or
some other information source) during the training stage to obtain the desired
outputs of the data points. In particular, the model considers an input and predicts a label together with an explanation of its prediction. If necessary, the user
responds by correcting the learner and providing improved (but not necessarily
optimal) feedback to the model during its training.

In the biomedical field, [9,22] attempted to enhance the models' abilities to
select features by utilizing Correlation-based Feature Selection and Chaotic Spi-

der Monkey Optimization methods on biomedical data. Additionally, an occlusion sensitivity analysis technique [29] is suggested in [8] to identify the most pertinent cortical regions for a motor imagery task. The usage of XAI methods to interpret the outputs of Epilepsy Detection systems is also explored in [15]. In [3,4] an experimental analysis of several well-known XAI methods applied on an ML system trained on EEG data was carried out, showing that many components considered relevant by XAI methods are shared across the signal and can be potentially used to build a system able to generalize better. Instead, the main goal of the current study is to analyze the effectiveness of a set of selected XAI methods in improving the performance of a machine learning system for an image classification task. Additionally, this study explores various approaches to combining input and explanation to optimize the ML system's performance.

3   Method

We conducted a series of experiments with the following goals: i) testing the capability of a set of well-known selected XAI methods to provide information able to effectively improve the ML system performance in an image classification task on different datasets; ii) testing several strategies to combine input and explanation for improving the ML system performance.

i) Evaluating explanation methods

The following XAI methods have been tested and evaluated to detect an explanation method able to enhance the model performance positively: Saliency [23], Guided BackPropagation [24], and Integrated Gradients [26]. The explanations provided by these methods are evaluated by computing MoRF (Most Relevant First) curve and LeRF (Least Relevant First) curves, proposed in [5,18]. The MoRF curve is computed as follows: given a classifier, an input $\mathbf{x}$ and the respective classification output $C(\mathbf{x})$, the input features are iteratively replaced by zeros, following the descending order with respect to the relevance values returned by the explanation method. Therefore, the expected MoRF curve is such that the more relevant the identified components are for the classification output, the steepest the curve. Conversely, LeRF curves are built iteratively, removing the input features following the ascending order with respect to the relevance values returned by the explanation method. Consequently, we expect the classification output to be very close to the original value in the first iterations (corresponding to less relevant features removed), dropping quickly to zero as the process goes toward. While the MoRFs report how much the classifier output is altered by removing highly relevant components, LeRFs report how much the least relevant components leave the output intact. In the following of this subsection, the investigated XAI methods are described briefly.

Saliency: The saliency method [23] is a straightforward and intuitive way to explain a machine learning (ML) system. Originally presented in [23], Essentially, an explanation of the ML system's output $C(\mathbf{x})$ for an input $\mathbf{x} \in \mathbb{R}^d$ is created by generating a saliency map using the gradient $\frac{\partial C}{\partial \mathbf{x}}$. The gradient's magnitude indicates how much the features must be adjusted to impact the class score.

Guided BackPropagation: Guided BackPropagation (Guided BP) [24] is a method similar to the Saliency one, with the main difference being that in Guided BP, a gradient transformation is used preventing the backward flow of negative values, rather than using the real gradient. This method starts from the assumption that negative values may decrease the neuron activations and are not considered as important by the user. The main drawback is that it can failure to highlight inputs that negatively contribute to the output.

Integrated Gradients: [26] proposed an approach involving the average of all gradients between the original input $\mathbf{x}$ and a baseline input $\mathbf{x}^{ref}$, where $C(\mathbf{x}^{ref})$ results in a neutral prediction. This method, known as Integrated Gradient (IG), takes into account the magnitude of gradients of features of inputs closer to the baseline. The importance of each feature x_i is computed aggregating the gradients along the intermediate inputs on the straight-line between the baseline and the input by changing α over the range $[0, 1]$.

ii) Merging schemes

This work aims to propose a valid method to exploit an XAI explanation to improve the results of a classifier. However, it is important to highlight that we start from the assumption that, for a given input, an explanation of the model's output with respect to the correct target class is available. In real scenarios, where the correct class is not available for new input, this assumption is unrealistic. Despite this, this assumption is adopted to effectively explore the the improvement of classification performance exploiting the explanations. In other words, we try to answer the question, "If the explanation on how an ideal model should behave when fed with a given input, could it help the actual classifier?".

We propose two possible strategies to merge the explanations into the classification process: *binary mask* and *soft-masking* schema. These strategies are described in the following two sub-paragraphs.

Binary Mask Strategy: Similarly to [19], the first strategy starts from the assumption that the explanation's scores can be considered as a measurement of the "attention" that the model has to give to each feature to produce a certain output. In particular, given an input $\mathbf{x} \in \mathbf{R}^d$, and an explanation in terms of input relevance map $A(\mathbf{x}, C) \in \mathbf{R}^d$ for the output $C(\mathbf{x})$ of a classifier C, we use the following simple rule to construct a mask M:

$$M_i = \begin{cases} 1 & \text{if } A(\mathbf{x}, C)_i > 0, \\ 0 & \text{otherwise.} \end{cases}$$

In other words, the goal is fed the model C with only the features which contribute positively to the output. The aim is to understand if the feature highlighted by an explanation can actually lead the model toward the correct classification. Therefore, a masked version of the input $M * \mathbf{x}$, where $*$ is the dot-wise product, can be fed to the model C. Differently to [19], our study focuses on image classification tasks on well-known dataset, selecting as XAI strategy to build the relevance mask by a preliminary study on a family of XAI methods available in literature.

Soft-Masking Strategy: In the previous schema, features having negative relevance scores are removed from the input of the classifier. However, negative scores can be a source of information which could lead the classifier toward the right response, as well as the positive ones. The problem is how to integrate this kind of information into the input. Instead of defining a prior given merging rule, we consider to delegate a ML model to find the best one. In other word, we delegate the model to merge together relevance $A(\mathbf{x}, C)$ and the input $\mathbf{x}$. To this aim, a supplementary mixer network to merge together $\mathbf{x}$ and $A(\mathbf{x}, C)$ is adopted, connected to the classifier C as shown in Fig. 2. From now on, this network is called *Mixer*. We adopt two further networks, $E_{\mathbf{x}}$ and E_A to reduce the dimensionality of $E_{\mathbf{x}}$ and $A(\mathbf{x}, C)$ respectively. The $E_{\mathbf{x}}$ and E_A are then concatenated and fed to the Mixer. The resulting Mixer output can be considered as an input mask M and used for weighting the C input $\mathbf{x}$. Mixer, $E_{\mathbf{x}}$, and E_A can be learned freezing the C parameters and using classical training procedure on the remaining ones, corresponding to search for the best Mixer, $E_{\mathbf{x}}$, and E_A parameters able to reduce and join together $A(\mathbf{x}, C)$ and $\mathbf{x}$, for a given classifier C.

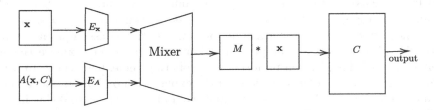

Fig. 2. Architecture of the soft-masking schema

4   Experimental Assessment

Fashion-MNIST, CIFAR10 and STL10 datasets were used as benchmark dataset. The Fashion-MNIST dataset contains images depicting various fashion articles [28]. It shares the same image size and training/testing splits of MNIST dataset. The dataset contains 60,000 training images and 10,000 test images, each of size 28×28 and grayscale in nature. There are ten classes in the dataset, including T-shirt/top, Trouser, Pullover, Dress, Coat, Sandal, Shirt, Sneaker, Bag, and Ankle boot.

CIFAR-10 is a collection of 60,000 color images grouped into ten categories, that are airplane, automobile, bird, cat, deer, dog, frog, horse, ship, and truck. The dataset offers 50,000 training images and 10,000 test images, all of size 32×32.

The STL10 dataset consists of images belonging to ten different classes, that are airplane, bird, car, cat, deer, dog, horse, monkey, ship, and truck. Each image has a size of 96×96 pixels.

As classifier C, we adopt a ResNet18 [6] pre-trained on ImageNet dataset for the CIFAR10 and STL10 dataset, and a custom model composed of two fully-connected layers with ReLU activation function for Fashion-MNIST dataset.

A first experiment to compute the baseline consisting in the fine tuning of C using the training set provided in each investigated dataset was carried out. Baseline models are then used to build the explanations of a model prediction for each input. Therefore, the produced explanations were evaluated computing the MoRF and the LeRF curves, as described in Sect. 3. The best explanation method found was used to evaluate the proposed merging schemes.

For the experiments involving binary masking scheme, the following two learning strategies have been used:

A. **fine tuning on masked data**: a fine tuning of C was made using only masked training data, as discussed in Sect. 3;
B. **fine tuning on both original and masked data**: a two-step fine tuning procedure was adopted, the former on the unaltered training data provided by the evaluated datasets, the latter on the masked training data.

Instead, in the soft-masking case, we adopt as $E_{\mathbf{x}}$ and E_A as two networks composed of 5 fully-connected layers equipped with ReLU activation function interspersed by Batch Normalization for experiments involving CIFAR10 and STL10, and of 2 fully-connected layers equipped with ReLU activation function interspersed by Batch Normalization for experiments involving Fashion-MNIST. Further details about the modules are reported in Table 1. The training consisted in two steps: firstly, a fine tuning of C was made using training data without any change on it. Secondly, the Mixer network, $E_{\mathbf{x}}$, and E_A are trained on the same data freezing the C parameters. The training was made with the Adam optimization algorithm. Best batch size and learning rate were found with a grid-search approach, testing batch sizes $\{64, 128, 256\}$ and learning rates in range $[0.001, 0.01]$ with step of 0.02. A validation set of 30% of the training data was adopted to stop the iterative learning process, with a maximum number of 100 iterations.

5   Results

In this section, results of the experimental assessments are reported.

5.1   Explanation Methods

In Fig. 3 the average MoRF and LeRF curves computed on the explanations obtained on Fashion-MNIST, CIFAR10, and STL10 test sets using the network models trained with the respective training sets are shown. Regarding the

Table 1. Architectures of the modules used. The numbers indicate how many neurons are employed in each fully-connected layer. The C module adopted for CIFAR10 and STL10 was a ResNet18 pretrained on ImageNet.

STL10 $E_{\mathbf{x}}, E_A$	Mixer	CIFAR10 $E_{\mathbf{x}}, E_A$	Mixer	F-Mnist $E_{\mathbf{x}}, E_A$	Mixer	C
4096	512	2048	512	512	512	128
batch norm.	batch norm.	batch norm.	batch norm.	batch norm.	batch norm.	
ReLU	ReLU	ReLU	ReLU	ReLU	ReLU	ReLU
2048	1024	1024	1024	256	784	64
batch norm.	batch norm.	batch norm.		batch norm.		
ReLU	ReLU	ReLU		ReLU		ReLU
1024	4096	512		128		10
batch norm.	batch norm.	batch norm.				
ReLU	ReLU	ReLU				
512	9216	256				
batch norm.		batch norm.				
ReLU		ReLU				
256		128				
batch norm.						
ReLU						
128						

Fashion-MNIST dataset, all the investigating methods produced good explanations respect to the MoRF and LeRF curves. This can be due to the simplicity of Fashion-MNIST dataset, leading the explanation methods to extract the actual real features in an easy way. Instead, for CIFAR10 dataset, it is easy to see that both MoRF and LeRF curves have the expected behavior only with Integrated Gradient. Indeed, it is evident that the Integrated Gradient MoRF curve quickly decreases toward zero, indicating that removing features reported as relevant by Integrated Gradient leads to a decrease in accuracy. On the other side, Integrated Gradient LeRF curve slowly tends to zero, indicating that removing features reported as not many relevant by the XAI method does not change the performance so much. Instead, in the Guided BackPropagation and Saliency method this behavior is not present, both for MoRF and LeRF curves. For STL10, Guided BackPropagation method produces poor explanations, accordingly with STL10 and CIFAR10 case. Integrated Gradient and Saliency produce similar results, but also in this case MoRF and LeRF curves are better in the former case respect to the latter. In conclusion, among the analyzed XAI methods, Integrated Gradient results the method providing the most reliable explanations among the analyzed datasets. Therefore, in the experiments dedicated to test how to merge input and explanations we adopted the Integrated Gradients method to build the explanations.

5.2   Merging Schema: Binary Masking

In Table 2 the results adopting the binary masks are reported for all the investigated datasets. Performance on the original-data fine-tuned model (baseline in the table) are reported on the original test set, differently from the masked-data

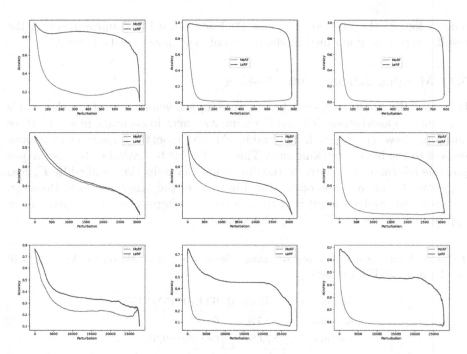

Fig. 3. Quantitative evaluation of the models' explanations on Fashion-MNIST (first row), CIFAR10 (second row) and STL10 (third row) test sets using Guided Back-Propagation (first column), Saliency (second column), and Integrated Gradient (third column). In each plot, MoRF (red) and LeRF (blue) curves are shown. (Color figure online)

fine-tuned models (cases A and B, described in Sect. 3). It is easy to see that the adoption of the relevance as masks can positively affect the model performance, leading the model toward an increment up to 10% points of accuracy in the case of CIFAR10 respect to the baseline and Fashion-MNIST, and 36% in case of STL10. In addition, it is interesting to notice that the data used during the fine-tuning stage, also if different from the data involved in the test stage, can affect the results. Interestingly, it seems that fine-tuning stage on the original

Table 2. Accuracy scores on test set using relevance as binary masks on CIFAR10, STL10 and Fashion MNIST test sets

Model	CIFAR10	STL10	F-MNIST
baseline	85.7%	66.3%	87.3%
binary masking (A)	90.9%	97.6%	97.4%
binary masking (B)	95.8%	98.2%	97.8%

data before of the masked one (case B) leads toward an improvement in the results respect to fine-tuned model using only the masked data (case A).

5.3   Merging Schema: Soft Masking

In Table 3 the results adopting the soft-masking schema are reported. Also in this case, the proposed strategies lead to an improvement in accuracy in all the three datasets. However, except that in Fashion-MNIST case, the improvement is lower respect to the binary-masking case. This can be due to several factors, such as a possible information loss due to the dimensionality reduction applied by $E_{\mathbf{x}}$ and E_A networks, or by a non optimal architecture of the Mixer network. However, the obtained results suggest that there is room for improvements adopting more appropriate Mixer and $E_{\mathbf{x}}, E_{\mathbf{A}}$ architectures.

Table 3. Accuracy scores on test set using relevance as soft masks on CIFAR10, STL10 and Fashion MNIST test sets

Model	CIFAR10	STL10	F-MNIST
baseline	85.7%	66.3%	87.3%
soft-masking	87.6%	68.6%	99.9%

6   Conclusions

This work reports an empirical analysis of three XAI techniques on the effectiveness of explanations for an image classification problem on three well-known datasets. Next, two strategies to merge explanations and input data to enhance the model's classification performance are provided. The former strategy consists of binary masking criteria to select the input features; the latter consists of letting the model find the better mixing strategy through a learning strategy. The results are promising in both cases, especially in the binary mask case. However, all the results are obtained under the hypothesis that the explanations on the right classes are available for the test data. This is an unrealistic hypothesis, since the right class of the testing data is unknown. Thus, the results of this research work can be exploited to improve the performance of a classifier by building a system capable of giving a good approximation of the explanations even in the test phase. We plan to pursue this line of research in our future works.

Acknowledgements. This work is supported by the European Union - FSE-REACT-EU, PON Research and Innovation 2014-2020 DM1062/2021 contract number 18-I-15350-2, and was partially supported by the Ministry of University and Research, PRIN research project "BRIO – BIAS, RISK, OPACITY in AI: design, verification and development of Trustworthy AI.", Project no. 2020SSKZ7R, and by the Ministry of Economic Development, "INtegrated Technologies and ENhanced SEnsing for cognition and rehabilitation" (INTENSE) project. Furthermore, we acknowledge financial support from the PNRR MUR project PE0000013-FAIR (CUP: E63C22002150007).

References

1. Apicella, A., Isgrò, F., Prevete, R., Sorrentino, A., Tamburrini, G.: Explaining classification systems using sparse dictionaries. In: ESANN 2019 - Proceedings, 27th European Symposium on Artificial Neural Networks, Computational Intelligence and Machine Learning, pp. 495–500 (2019)
2. Apicella, A., Giugliano, S., Isgrò, F., Prevete, R.: Exploiting auto-encoders and segmentation methods for middle-level explanations of image classification systems. Knowl.-Based Syst. **255**, 109725 (2022)
3. Apicella, A., Isgrò, F., Pollastro, A., Prevete, R.: Toward the application of XAI methods in EEG-based systems. In: Proceedings of the 3rd Italian Workshop on Explainable Artificial Intelligence co-located with 21th International Conference of the Italian Association for Artificial Intelligence(AIxIA 2022), Udine, Italy, 28 November–3 December 2022. CEUR Workshop Proceedings, vol. 3277, pp. 1–15. CEUR-WS.org (2022)
4. Apicella, A., Isgrò, F., Prevete, R.: XAI approach for addressing the dataset shift problem: BCI as a case study (short paper). In: Proceedings of 1st Workshop on Bias, Ethical AI, Explainability and the Role of Logic and Logic Programming (BEWARE 2022) co-located with the 21th International Conference of the Italian Association for Artificial Intelligence (AI*IA 2022), Udine, Italy, 2 December 2022. CEUR Workshop Proceedings, vol. 3319, pp. 83–88 (2022)
5. Bach, S., Binder, A., Montavon, G., Klauschen, F., Müller, K.R., Samek, W.: On pixel-wise explanations for non-linear classifier decisions by layer-wise relevance propagation. PLoS ONE **10**(7), e0130140 (2015)
6. He, K., Zhang, X., Ren, S., Sun, J.: Deep residual learning for image recognition. In: Proceedings of the IEEE Conference on Computer Vision and Pattern Recognition, pp. 770–778 (2016)
7. Hind, M., et al.: TED: teaching AI to explain its decisions. In: Proceedings of the 2019 AAAI/ACM Conference on AI, Ethics, and Society, pp. 123–129 (2019)
8. Ieracitano, C., Mammone, N., Hussain, A., Morabito, F.C.: A novel explainable machine learning approach for EEG-based brain-computer interface systems. Neural Comput. Appl. **34**(14), 11347–11360 (2022)
9. Laxmi Lydia, E., Anupama, C.S.S., Sharmili, N.: Modeling of explainable artificial intelligence with correlation-based feature selection approach for biomedical data analysis. In: Khamparia, A., Gupta, D., Khanna, A., Balas, V.E. (eds.) Biomedical Data Analysis and Processing Using Explainable (XAI) and Responsive Artificial Intelligence (RAI). ISRL, vol. 222, pp. 17–32. Springer, Singapore (2022). https://doi.org/10.1007/978-981-19-1476-8_2
10. Lei, T., Barzilay, R., Jaakkola, T.: Rationalizing neural predictions. arXiv preprint arXiv:1606.04155 (2016)
11. Mathew, B., Saha, P., Yimam, S.M., Biemann, C., Goyal, P., Mukherjee, A.: HateXplain: a benchmark dataset for explainable hate speech detection. In: Proceedings of the AAAI Conference on Artificial Intelligence, vol. 35, pp. 14867–14875 (2021)

12. Montavon, G., Binder, A., Lapuschkin, S., Samek, W., Müller, K.-R.: Layer-wise relevance propagation: an overview. In: Samek, W., Montavon, G., Vedaldi, A., Hansen, L.K., Müller, K.-R. (eds.) Explainable AI: Interpreting, Explaining and Visualizing Deep Learning. LNCS (LNAI), vol. 11700, pp. 193–209. Springer, Cham (2019). https://doi.org/10.1007/978-3-030-28954-6_10

13. Montavon, G., Lapuschkin, S., Binder, A., Samek, W., Müller, K.R.: Explaining nonlinear classification decisions with deep Taylor decomposition. Pattern Recogn. **65**, 211–222 (2017)

14. Qian, K., et al.: XNLP: A living survey for XAI research in natural language processing. In: 26th International Conference on Intelligent User Interfaces-Companion, pp. 78–80 (2021)

15. Rathod, P., Naik, S.: Review on epilepsy detection with explainable artificial intelligence. In: 2022 10th International Conference on Emerging Trends in Engineering and Technology-Signal and Information Processing (ICETET-SIP-22), pp. 1–6. IEEE (2022)

16. Ribeiro, M.T., Singh, S., Guestrin, C.: "Why should i trust you?" explaining the predictions of any classifier. In: Proceedings of the 22nd ACM SIGKDD International Conference on Knowledge Discovery and Data Mining, pp. 1135–1144 (2016)

17. Ross, A.S., Hughes, M.C., Doshi-Velez, F.: Right for the right reasons: training differentiable models by constraining their explanations. arXiv preprint arXiv:1703.03717 (2017)

18. Samek, W., Binder, A., Montavon, G., Lapuschkin, S., Müller, K.R.: Evaluating the visualization of what a deep neural network has learned. IEEE Trans. Neural Netw. Learn. Syst. **28**(11), 2660–2673 (2016)

19. Schiller, D., Huber, T., Lingenfelser, F., Dietz, M., Seiderer, A., André, E.: Relevance-based feature masking: improving neural network based whale classification through explainable artificial intelligence (2019)

20. Schoonderwoerd, T.A., Jorritsma, W., Neerincx, M.A., Van Den Bosch, K.: Human-centered XAI: developing design patterns for explanations of clinical decision support systems. Int. J. Hum Comput Stud. **154**, 102684 (2021)

21. Schramowski, P., et al.: Making deep neural networks right for the right scientific reasons by interacting with their explanations. Nat. Mach. Intell. **2**(8), 476–486 (2020)

22. Selvam, R.P., Oliver, A.S., Mohan, V., Prakash, N.B., Jayasankar, T.: Explainable artificial intelligence with metaheuristic feature selection technique for biomedical data classification. In: Khamparia, A., Gupta, D., Khanna, A., Balas, V.E. (eds.) Biomedical Data Analysis and Processing Using Explainable (XAI) and Responsive Artificial Intelligence (RAI). ISRL, vol. 222, pp. 43–57. Springer, Singapore (2022). https://doi.org/10.1007/978-981-19-1476-8_4

23. Simonyan, K., Vedaldi, A., Zisserman, A.: Deep inside convolutional networks: visualising image classification models and saliency maps. arXiv preprint arXiv:1312.6034 (2013)

24. Springenberg, J.T., Dosovitskiy, A., Brox, T., Riedmiller, M.: Striving for simplicity: the all convolutional net. arXiv preprint arXiv:1412.6806 (2014)

25. Sun, J., Lapuschkin, S., Samek, W., Zhao, Y., Cheung, N.M., Binder, A.: Explanation-guided training for cross-domain few-shot classification. In: 2020 25th International Conference on Pattern Recognition (ICPR), pp. 7609–7616. IEEE (2021)

26. Sundararajan, M., Taly, A., Yan, Q.: Axiomatic attribution for deep networks. In: International Conference on Machine Learning, pp. 3319–3328. PMLR (2017)

27. Weber, L., Lapuschkin, S., Binder, A., Samek, W.: Beyond explaining: opportunities and challenges of XAI-based model improvement. Inf. Fusion (2022)
28. Xiao, H., Rasul, K., Vollgraf, R.: Fashion-MNIST: a novel image dataset for benchmarking machine learning algorithms. arXiv preprint arXiv:1708.07747 (2017)
29. Zeiler, M.D., Fergus, R.: Visualizing and understanding convolutional networks. In: Fleet, D., Pajdla, T., Schiele, B., Tuytelaars, T. (eds.) ECCV 2014. LNCS, vol. 8689, pp. 818–833. Springer, Cham (2014). https://doi.org/10.1007/978-3-319-10590-1_53

Beyond Prediction Similarity: ShapGAP for Evaluating Faithful Surrogate Models in XAI

Ettore Mariotti[1]([envelope])[iD], Adarsa Sivaprasad[3][iD],
and Jose Maria Alonso Moral[1,2][iD]

[1] Centro Singular de Investigación en Tecnoloxías Intelixentes (CiTIUS),
Universidade de Santiago de Compostela, Rúa de Jenaro de la Fuente Domínguez
s/n, 15782 Santiago de Compostela, A Coruña, Spain
ettore.mariotti@usc.es
[2] Departamento de Electrónica e Computación, Universidade de Santiago de
Compostela, Rúa Lope Gómez de Marzoa, s/n, 15782 Santiago de Compostela, A
Coruña, Spain
[3] University of Aberdeen, Aberdeen, Scotland, UK

Abstract. The growing importance of Explainable Artificial Intelligence (XAI) has highlighted the need to understand the decision-making processes of black-box models. Surrogation, emulating a black-box model (BB) with a white-box model (WB), is crucial in applications where BBs are unavailable due to security or practical concerns. Traditional fidelity measures only evaluate the similarity of the final predictions, which can lead to a significant limitation: considering a WB faithful even when it has the same prediction as the BB but with a completely different rationale. Addressing this limitation is crucial to develop Trustworthy AI practical applications beyond XAI. To address this issue, we introduce ShapGAP, a novel metric that assesses the faithfulness of surrogate models by comparing their reasoning paths, using SHAP explanations as a proxy. We validate the effectiveness of ShapGAP by applying it to real-world datasets from healthcare and finance domains, comparing its performance against traditional fidelity measures. Our results show that ShapGAP enables better understanding and trust in XAI systems, revealing the potential dangers of relying on models with high task accuracy but unfaithful explanations. ShapGAP serves as a valuable tool for identifying faithful surrogate models, paving the way for more reliable and Trustworthy AI applications.

Keywords: Explainable Artificial Intelligence (XAI) · Fidelity
Measures · Surrogate Models · Interpretability · Black-box ·
White-box · Faithfulness · SHAP

© The Author(s) 2023
L. Longo (Ed.): xAI 2023, CCIS 1901, pp. 160–173, 2023.
https://doi.org/10.1007/978-3-031-44064-9_10

1   Introduction

Explainable Artificial Intelligence (XAI) aims to provide insights into the decision-making processes of complex machine learning models, particularly black-box models, which are often difficult to interpret due to their inherent complexity [2]. As the adoption of machine learning models in critical applications (e.g., healthcare, finance, or business decision-making) continues to increase, understanding their decision-making rationale becomes essential for building trust, ensuring fairness, and making informed decisions based on the output of the model [12].

Surrogate models, which are interpretable white-box (WB) models trained to approximate the behavior of black-box (BB) models, have emerged as a popular approach for providing explanations in XAI [21]. These surrogate models are particularly relevant in use cases where BB models are unavailable due to security or practical concerns or when stakeholders require explanations to support their decision-making processes. For instance, in healthcare, a BB model may predict the likelihood of a patient having a specific disease based on various symptoms and test results. A surrogate model that provides the same prediction but with a different rationale could lead medical professionals to focus on the wrong symptoms or tests, resulting in incorrect treatment or mismanagement of the patient's condition. In finance, a BB model might predict the probability of default for loan applicants based on their credit history, income, and other financial factors. A surrogate model that matches the BB model's predictions but with different reasoning could lead to unfair lending decisions or increased financial risk for the lending institution.

However, evaluating the faithfulness of these surrogate models remains challenging. Traditional fidelity measures such as accuracy focus on the similarity of the final predictions between the BB and surrogate models. This can lead to a significant limitation, as a surrogate model might be considered faithful even if it provides the same prediction as the BB model but with a completely different rationale. In critical applications like the ones mentioned above, this can be dangerous, as decision-makers might act on unfaithful explanations, leading to suboptimal or even harmful outcomes [14].

In this paper, we address this limitation by introducing a novel metric called ShapGAP, which assesses the faithfulness of surrogate models by comparing their reasoning paths, using SHAP explanations as a proxy. ShapGAP measures the average L2 distance between the SHAP explanations of BB and WB models, providing a more comprehensive evaluation of surrogate model faithfulness that goes beyond the similarity of final predictions. The main contributions are:

- We propose ShapGAP, a novel metric for evaluating surrogate model faithfulness that considers the reasoning paths of the models by comparing their SHAP explanations.
- We demonstrate the effectiveness of ShapGAP through experiments with real-world datasets, comparing it against traditional fidelity measures.

– We highlight the potential dangers and ethical concerns of relying on unfaithful explanations in critical applications, drawing on philosophical arguments for truthfulness and ethical AI.

By introducing ShapGAP, we aim to contribute to the ongoing research towards Trustworthy AI by providing a more effective method for evaluating surrogate model faithfulness that captures the essence of reasoning paths, enabling better understanding, trust, and ethical considerations in AI systems.

The rest of the manuscript is organized as follows. Section 2 introduces related work. Section 3 describes ShapGAP. Section 4 presents details about the experiments (i.e., experimental setting, datasets and models). Section 5 discusses the reported results. Section 6 goes in depth with some ethical concerns. Finally, Sect. 7 concludes the paper with final remarks and future work.

2   Related Works

The research field of XAI encompasses various approaches for extracting secondary models from primary models. Model distillation, for instance, often refers to the transfer of knowledge from a larger model (teacher) to a smaller one (student) with the aim of optimizing space and speed though not necessarily interpretability [4,13]. However, in our context, we pay major attention to distillation that results in a secondary model with greater interpretability than the primary one while maintaining most of its core characteristics in terms of both behaviour and performance.

In this domain, two main threads can be identified: local surrogates and global surrogates. Local surrogates ensure fidelity within a suitably defined neighborhood [17,21], resulting in multiple local models that collectively describe the global behavior. Conversely, global surrogates attempt to build a more interpretable model across the entire data domain, providing a bird's-eye view of the problem. Several methods have been proposed for distilling global surrogates:

– Pedagogical approach [6,8]: This method trains the surrogate on queries to the primary model, assuming availability of the primary model for evaluating arbitrary synthesized data points in order to obtain labels for training the secondary model.
– Audit approach [27]: When probing the model with new data is not possible, this approach trains the surrogate on predictions made by the primary model. This setup is sometimes more realistic in industrial scenarios where the primary model is unavailable due to security or practical concerns.

The quality of the secondary model is typically assessed using one or two metrics, which can be referred to as task accuracy and model accuracy. Task accuracy evaluates the accuracy of the secondary model concerning the true labels in the dataset, while model accuracy (sometimes called fidelity) measures the accuracy of the secondary model with respect to the labels provided by the primary model [7,8,15]. As an alternative, precision and recall are also used to evaluate the resulting rule system or Bayesian network trained with the pedagogical approach [23]. Bastani et al. [6] generalize this approach to non-classification domains, incorporating suitable metrics for regression and reinforcement learning tasks.

In addition to the aforementioned work, there are also studies that focus on alternative metrics for evaluating faithfulness of explanations in different contexts. For instance, Alvarez-Melis and Jaakkola [3] propose a self-explainable neural network that provides both prediction and self-relevance scores for feature or concept importance. Their faithfulness measure is based on the correlation between explanation vectors and probability drops from ablation studies, offering an alternative approach to assess faithfulness using explanation vectors. Although their setup is different from a global surrogate, it shares some similarity with ShapGAP in utilizing explanations for measuring faithfulness.

Alaa and van der Schaar [1] proposed another approach that employs feature importance for model comparison, although not necessarily in a global surrogate setting. They qualitatively compare the global feature importance of two models, demonstrating another perspective on assessing faithfulness and explanation quality between models. In addition, Dai et al. [9] proposed alternative fidelity measures such as ground truth fidelity, which can be adapted for comparing two models. This measure, which can be referred to as the "Top-k Percentage Accordance", calculates the percentage of top-k features from one explanation that are also in the top-k features of another explanation. While this metric might have limitations, it demonstrates another perspective on evaluating faithfulness between models.

It is worth noting that previous work does not directly address surrogation but contribute to the broader understanding of evaluating explanations and faithfulness in various settings. This context helps to clarify how ShapGAP fits into the larger landscape of XAI research.

3   Proposed Approach: ShapGAP

For giving context it is appropriate to recall some preliminary concepts before defining ShapGAP. Shapley values [25], originally derived from cooperative game theory, represent a strategy for allocating the payoff of a cooperative game among the players, based on their contributions. In the context of feature importance, each feature is considered as a player, and the prediction is the payoff. The Shapley value of a feature quantifies its average marginal contribution across all possible feature combinations. SHapley Additive exPlanations (SHAP) [17] combine Shapley values with a unified measure of feature importance for machine learning models. For a given prediction, SHAP assigns an importance value to each feature, such that the sum of all values equals the difference between the prediction and the average prediction for the dataset.

We define a BB model as a function $f_{bb} : X \rightarrow Y$, where X is the input space and Y is the output space, and a WB model as a function $f_{wb} : X \rightarrow Y$. Given a dataset D with n instances, we compute the SHAP values for each instance

x_i in D for both the BB and WB models. Let $S_{bb}(x_i)$ and $S_{wb}(x_i)$ represent the SHAP values for instance x_i for the BB and WB models, respectively.

To define a generic version of ShapGAP, we use a distance function $d(\cdot, \cdot)$ that measures the dissimilarity between the SHAP explanations of the BB and WB models for instance x_i. The ShapGAP metric is then the average of these distances across all instances in the dataset:

$$\text{ShapGAP}(D, d) = \frac{1}{n} \sum_{i=1}^{n} d(S_{bb}(x_i), S_{wb}(x_i)) \tag{1}$$

We can implement the distance function $d(S_{bb}(x_i), S_{wb}(x_i))$ using different distance measures, such as the L2 Euclidean distance and the Cosine distance. The L2 Euclidean distance, as shown in Eq. (2), is more precise and faithful to the final probability values, as the SHAP explanations sum up to the output of the model. This choice emphasizes the importance of the exact contribution of each feature in the explanation and is more sensitive to differences in magnitude between SHAP values associated to BB and WB models.

$$\text{ShapGAP}_{L2}(D) = \frac{1}{n} \sum_{i=1}^{n} ||S_{bb}(x_i) - S_{wb}(x_i)||_2 \tag{2}$$

However, it is noteworthy to mention some limitations of the L2 Euclidean distance. This method is sensitive to outliers, which means that a single instance with a large disparity in SHAP values can significantly affect the overall distance. Therefore, L2 Euclidean distance might not represent the overall similarity well in the presence of outliers.

On the other hand, the Cosine distance (see Eq. (3)) is more relaxed and focuses on the similarity in the direction of the SHAP explanations rather than their magnitude. This choice allows for finding out surrogate models with similar reasoning paths, even if the magnitude of their feature contributions differs. By being more scale-agnostic with respect to the magnitude of the explanations, the Cosine distance might be better suited for cases where the focus is on the general structure of the explanation, rather than the exact values of the SHAP contributions.

$$\text{ShapGAP}_{Cos}(D) = \frac{1}{n} \sum_{i=1}^{n} \left(1 - \frac{S_{bb}(x_i) \cdot S_{wb}(x_i)}{||S_{bb}(x_i)||_2 ||S_{wb}(x_i)||_2}\right) \tag{3}$$

By offering these two distance measures, the ShapGAP metric can accommodate different application requirements and preferences, providing more flexibility in the evaluation of surrogate model faithfulness.

To compute SHAP values, we use the widely adopted *shap* package[1], which offers efficient implementations for various types of models. For tree-like models such as random forests and decision trees, the package provides the fast TreeSHAP algorithm. Likewise, for linear models, an efficient method based on the

---

[1] https://github.com/slundberg/shap.

coefficients of the model is available. In cases where the BB model is neither tree-based nor linear, the package offers a model-agnostic method called KernelSHAP, which can be applied to any model at the expense of increased computational cost. By leveraging these implementations, we can calculate the ShapGAP metric for a diverse range of surrogate models, ensuring that the metric remains flexible and adaptable to various application scenarios.

4 Experimental Section

In this section, we present the experimental setting for using and validating both ShapGAP L2 and Cosine distance metrics, compared against Task Accuracy, Fidelity Accuracy (in the sense of model accuracy, i.e., the accuracy with respect to the labels predicted by the BB model), and ShapLength [18]. Shap-Length, a model-agnostic metric, enables the comparison of fundamentally different models, such as Logistic Regression and Decision Trees, in terms of their explanation complexity. By examining ShapLength, we can assess the trade-offs between faithfulness and simplicity in surrogate models, and gain insights into the complexity of models and their explanations, making our analysis more comprehensive and thorough.

To align with the problem suggested in the introduction, we use two popular datasets: the Breast Cancer dataset [26], which contains 569 instances with 30 features, and the German Credit score dataset from UCI [10], which includes 1,000 instances with 20 features. Both datasets are widely used for benchmarking machine learning models in the context of binary classification. For surrogating we employ the Audit approach and perform a 10-fold cross-validation. Then, we compute the quality metrics on the test set. The reported results represent the average across all the folds. To explore various surrogate models, we train Decision Trees by varying two parameters: max depth, which can take values of 3, 4, or 5, and ccp_alpha, a regularization parameter for cost complexity pruning, which takes values of 0.001, 0.01, and 0.1. For the Bank credit score dataset from UCI, which contains categorical columns, we preprocess the data by one-hot encoding the categorical columns.

For the sake of experimental reproducibility, everything required for running the experiments is available online[2].

5 Discussions of Results

Our analysis of the results on both the Breast Cancer (Fig. 1) and German Credit (Fig. 2) datasets reveal some important insights about the relationships between Task Accuracy, Fidelity Accuracy, Complexity, and ShapGAP. In both experiments, Logistic Regression (LR) performs better in terms of both Task Accuracy and Fidelity Accuracy compared to Decision Trees (DT). However, when we consider the ShapGAP metric, the LR model exhibits a very high ShapGAP

---

[2] https://gitlab.nl4xai.eu/ettore.mariotti/shapgap/.

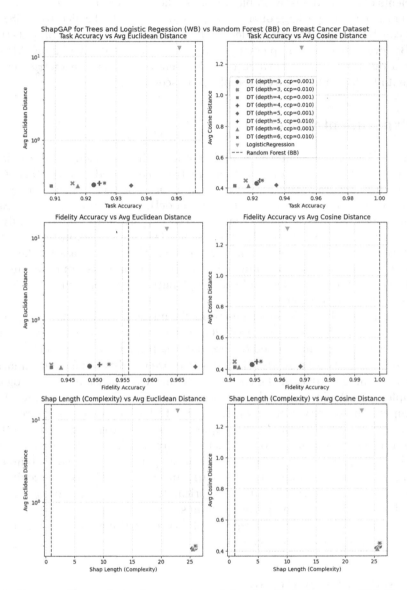

Fig. 1. Comparative analysis of surrogate models using Task Accuracy, Fidelity Accuracy, ShapGAP (L2 and Cosine distance), and ShapLength for the Breast Cancer dataset. The plot displays the performance of various Decision Trees (DT) and Logistic Regression models. The key findings show that although Logistic Regression has high Task Accuracy and Fidelity Accuracy, its large ShapGAP highlights the potential danger in using it as a global surrogate. Decision Trees with lower Fidelity Accuracy but smaller ShapGAP provide more faithful explanations.

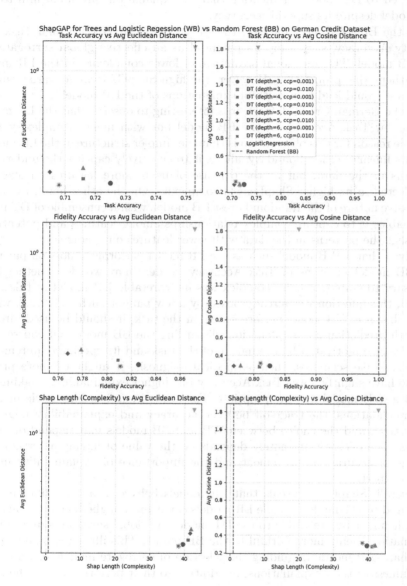

Fig. 2. Comparison of Task Accuracy, Fidelity Accuracy, ShapGAP (L2 and Cosine), and ShapLength for different surrogate models (Logistic Regression and Decision Trees) on the Bank credit score dataset. Each point represents a surrogate model, with its position determined by the respective metrics. The plot illustrates how Logistic Regression achieves similar Task Accuracy to the black-box model but has higher ShapLength complexity and significantly higher ShapGAP compared to Decision Trees, indicating that its explanations may be less faithful to the black-box model.

compared to DT models, indicating that its explanations are unfaithful to the BB model despite its superior accuracy.

In the Breast Cancer dataset, the LR model exhibits both high Task and Fidelity Accuracy, suggesting its potential as an effective global surrogate for the BB model. The additional advantage of lower complexity in the LR model strengthens this proposition. However, the high ShapGAP value warns against this, as it would lead to unfaithful explanations of the BB model.

In the German Credit dataset, it is interesting to observe that the LR model has similar Task Accuracy as the BB model but with higher complexity. One possible reason for this observation is that the simpler structure of the LR model, with its linear decision boundary, allows it to effectively capture the underlying patterns in the data, but at the expense of using more features on average, as reflected in its higher ShapLength complexity. On the other hand, the more expressive nature of the Random Forest BB model, with its ensemble of DT models, enables it to capture complex relationships among features and potentially represent the patterns in the data with fewer features on average.

Given that a WB model such as the LR model performs almost on par with the BB model in terms of Task Accuracy, readers may wonder whether it is necessary to employ a more complex less interpretable BB model in this case. Indeed, this question was already posed by a few papers, such as [19, 22], which argue that if a WB model performs well on the task, it should be used directly for both prediction and explanation, discarding the BB model. Of course, this choice is also motivated by the nature of the task and its specific requirements. For high-stake scenarios, such as medical diagnosis, it might be more preferable to have slightly lower Task Accuracy but higher explainability, making the use of a WB model more appropriate. For other scenarios, like movie or song recommendations, the trade-off between accuracy and explainability might be less critical, and the choice between WB and BB models may depend on other factors. The decision ultimately depends on the value of having a certain percentage of accuracy improvement and the importance of explainability in the given context.

Overall, ShapGAP reveals that LR models behave in a very different way compared to DT models. While LR models can achieve higher accuracy, in some cases, it might be preferable to use DT models as global surrogates due to their explanations being more faithful to the BB model. This illustrates the value of the ShapGAP metric in guiding the selection of surrogate models based on the faithfulness of their explanations, in addition to their performance on the task.

6   Ethical Considerations in Surrogate Explanations

The ethical implications of unfaithful surrogate explanations in critical applications are manifold. Unfaithful explanations can lead to misinformed decision-making, adversely affecting individuals' lives and well-being, especially in sensitive domains like healthcare, justice and finance [5]. This misalignment can also hinder the identification and correction of AI model shortcomings, exacerbating existing societal inequalities [20].

Accurate and reliable surrogate explanations are vital for ensuring AI systems align properly with ethical principles[3] guiding AI development. Such explanations enable users to understand and scrutinize model behavior, allowing them to make fully informed choices about the use of AI systems. Informed consent is a fundamental ethical principle that should be upheld in AI development and deployment, as it preserves users' autonomy and agency [11].

Unfaithful surrogate explanations can erode trust in AI systems, which is essential for the successful adoption of AI technologies [24]. Legal and liability issues can arise due to misaligned explanations, making responsibility attribution for errors or adverse outcomes challenging [28]. Furthermore, unfaithful explanations can mask biases and discrimination, perpetuating societal inequalities.

AI developers have an ethical obligation to provide truthful and accurate explanations. In summary, ShapGAP offers a means to evaluate and compare surrogate models, promoting responsible development and deployment of Trustworthy AI by helping developers in their pursuit of more faithful explanations. Ensuring truthfulness and accuracy in AI explanations is essential for preserving human values, promoting fairness, and fostering transparency and accountability in agreement with ethical guidelines [28].

7 Conclusions, Limitations, and Future Work

In this paper, we introduced the ShapGAP metric, a novel approach for evaluating the faithfulness of surrogate models by comparing their SHAP explanations with those of the black-box model. Through two illustrative case studies, we demonstrated the utility of ShapGAP in revealing the unfaithfulness of models that may otherwise appear as strong global surrogates based on Task Accuracy, Fidelity Accuracy, and complexity metrics like ShapLength.

The ShapGAP metric has the potential to improve the trustworthiness and utility of surrogate models, particularly in high-stakes applications such as healthcare and finance, where faithful explanations are crucial for decision-making. Our experimental results emphasize the importance of considering faithfulness as an essential criterion for surrogate model evaluation and selection.

While ShapGAP offers a promising approach for evaluating surrogate model faithfulness, there are some limitations to consider:

- **Computational Expense:** SHAP explanations can be computationally expensive to compute, especially for complex models or large datasets. Although various approximation methods exist, the computational cost of calculating SHAP values may still pose a challenge in some scenarios. Anyway, the utility of ShapGAP as an evaluation metric makes it worthwhile to consider these explanations despite the potential computational burden.
- **Approximate Nature:** though SHAP explanations are widely adopted in the XAI community, they are only approximations of the reasoning paths followed by the underlying models. Furthermore, the SHAP computation itself

---

[3] https://altai.insight-centre.org/.

yields approximations to the true Shapley values. Despite these limitations, we believe that a reasonable approximation is still useful for assessing surrogate model faithfulness, as it provides insights into the models' reasoning processes that are otherwise unavailable or incomparable.

– **Dependency on SHAP:** Our approach relies on SHAP explanations to compare reasoning paths, which may limit its applicability to other explanation methods. Although SHAP has gained widespread acceptance in the XAI community, future research could explore alternative approaches for evaluating surrogate model faithfulness using different explanation methods.

To address these limitations, future work could focus on expanding the scope of ShapGAP to incorporate other explanation methods or reduce the computational cost of producing SHAP explanations. Moreover, SHAP, as it stands, provides a first-order explanation, meaning it presents the impact of each individual feature without considering interactions between features. As a result, there might be missed nuances in feature relationships. To account for this, we plan taking into account SHAP interaction values [16], which consider the synergistic or antagonistic effects between feature pairs, as a basis for an enhanced ShapGAP. In Addition, more in-depth investigations into the factors that contribute to high or low ShapGAP scores, and how to optimize surrogate models for faithfulness, could be valuable. Further research might also delve into the role of ShapGAP in model selection and evaluation pipelines, its integration into automated machine learning (AutoML) frameworks, and its potential impact on the design or training of surrogate models for improved faithfulness. Moreover, further research could investigate potential biases or limitations in SHAP explanations on more datasets and explore methods to mitigate their impact on the evaluation of surrogate model faithfulness.

Acknowledgement. E. Mariotti and A. Sivaprasad are ESRs in the NL4XAI project which has received funding from the European Union's Horizon 2020 research and innovation programme under the Marie Skłodowska-Curie Grant Agreement No. 860621. In addition, this work is supported by Grant PID2021-123152OB-C21 funded by MCIN/AEI/10.13039/501100011033 and by "ESF Investing in your future", by Grant TED2021-130295B-C33 funded by MCIN/AEI/10.13039/501100011033 and by the "European Union NextGenerationEU/PRTR", and by the Galician Ministry of Culture, Education, Professional Training and University (grants ED431G2019/04, ED431C2022/19 co-funded by the European Regional Development Fund, ERDF/FEDER program).

References

1. Alaa, A.M., van der Schaar, M.: Demystifying black-box models with symbolic metamodels. In: Advances in Neural Information Processing Systems, vol. 32. Curran Associates, Inc. (2019)
2. Ali, S., et al.: Explainable Artificial Intelligence (XAI): what we know and what is left to attain trustworthy artificial intelligence. Inf. Fusion 101805 (2023). https://doi.org/10.1016/j.inffus.2023.101805. https://linkinghub.elsevier.com/retrieve/pii/S1566253523001148

3. Alvarez-Melis, D., Jaakkola, T.S.: Towards robust interpretability with self-explaining neural networks. In: Proceedings of the 32nd International Conference on Neural Information Processing Systems, NIPS 2018, pp. 7786–7795. Curran Associates Inc., Red Hook (2018)

4. Ba, J., Caruana, R.: Do deep nets really need to be deep? In: Advances in Neural Information Processing Systems, vol. 27. Curran Associates, Inc. (2014)

5. Barredo Arrieta, A., et al.: Explainable Artificial Intelligence (XAI): concepts, taxonomies, opportunities and challenges toward responsible AI. Inf. Fusion **58**, 82–115 (2020). https://doi.org/10.1016/j.inffus.2019.12.012

6. Bastani, O., Kim, C., Bastani, H.: Interpretability via model extraction (2018). http://arxiv.org/abs/1706.09773 [cs, stat]

7. Burkart, N., Huber, M.F.: A survey on the explainability of supervised machine learning. J. Artif. Intell. Res. **70**, 245–317 (2021). https://doi.org/10.1613/jair.1.12228. https://www.jair.org/index.php/jair/article/view/12228

8. Craven, M., Shavlik, J.: Extracting tree-structured representations of trained networks. In: Advances in Neural Information Processing Systems, vol. 8. MIT Press (1995)

9. Dai, J., Upadhyay, S., Aivodji, U., Bach, S.H., Lakkaraju, H.: Fairness via explanation quality: evaluating disparities in the quality of post hoc explanations. In: Proceedings of the 2022 AAAI/ACM Conference on AI, Ethics, and Society, pp. 203–214 (2022). https://doi.org/10.1145/3514094.3534159. http://arxiv.org/abs/2205.07277 [cs]

10. Dua, Dheeru and Graff, Casey: UCI Machine Learning Repository (2017). http://archive.ics.uci.edu/ml. University of California, Irvine, School of Information and Computer Sciences

11. Floridi, L., et al.: AI4People—an ethical framework for a good AI society: opportunities, risks, principles, and recommendations. Mind. Mach. **28**(4), 689–707 (2018). https://doi.org/10.1007/s11023-018-9482-5

12. Gunning, D., Vorm, E., Wang, J.Y., Turek, M.: DARPA's explainable AI (XAI) program: a retrospective. Appl. AI Lett. **2**(4), e61 (2021). https://doi.org/10.1002/ail2.61

13. Hinton, G., Vinyals, O., Dean, J.: Distilling the knowledge in a neural network (2015). http://arxiv.org/abs/1503.02531 [cs, stat]

14. Jacovi, A., Goldberg, Y.: Towards faithfully interpretable NLP systems: how should we define and evaluate faithfulness? In: Proceedings of the 58th Annual Meeting of the Association for Computational Linguistics, pp. 4198–4205. Association for Computational Linguistics, Online (2020). https://doi.org/10.18653/v1/2020.acl-main.386. https://www.aclweb.org/anthology/2020.acl-main.386

15. Lakkaraju, H., Kamar, E., Caruana, R., Leskovec, J.: Interpretable & explorable approximations of black box models (2017). http://arxiv.org/abs/1707.01154 [cs]

16. Lundberg, S.M., Erion, G.G., Lee, S.I.: Consistent Individualized Feature Attribution for Tree Ensembles (2018)

17. Lundberg, S.M., Lee, S.I.: A unified approach to interpreting model predictions. In: Advances in Neural Information Processing Systems, vol. 30. Curran Associates, Inc. (2017)

18. Mariotti, E., Alonso-Moral, J.M., Gatt, A.: Measuring model understandability by means of shapley additive explanations. In: 2022 IEEE International Conference on Fuzzy Systems (FUZZ-IEEE), Padua, Italy, pp. 1–8. IEEE (2022). https://doi.org/10.1109/FUZZ-IEEE55066.2022.9882773. https://ieeexplore.ieee.org/document/9882773/

19. Markus, A.F., Kors, J.A., Rijnbeek, P.R.: The role of explainability in creating trustworthy artificial intelligence for health care: a comprehensive survey of the terminology, design choices, and evaluation strategies. J. Biomed. Inform. **113**, 103655 (2021). https://doi.org/10.1016/j.jbi.2020.103655. https://www.sciencedirect.com/science/article/pii/S1532046420302835

20. Mittelstadt, B.D., Allo, P., Taddeo, M., Wachter, S., Floridi, L.: The ethics of algorithms: mapping the debate. Big Data Soc. **3**(2), 205395171667967 (2016). https://doi.org/10.1177/2053951716679679. http://journals.sagepub.com/doi/10.1177/2053951716679679

21. Ribeiro, M.T., Singh, S., Guestrin, C.: "Why should I trust you?": explaining the predictions of any classifier. In: Proceedings of the 22nd ACM SIGKDD International Conference on Knowledge Discovery and Data Mining, KDD 2016, pp. 1135–1144. Association for Computing Machinery, New York (2016). https://doi.org/10.1145/2939672.2939778

22. Rudin, C.: Stop explaining black box machine learning models for high stakes decisions and use interpretable models instead. Nat. Mach. Intell. **1**(5), 206–215 (2019). https://doi.org/10.1038/s42256-019-0048-x

23. Sanchez, I., Rocktaschel, T., Riedel, S., Singh, S.: Towards extracting faithful and descriptive representations of latent variable models (2015)

24. Selbst, A.D., Barocas, S.: The intuitive appeal of explainable machines. SSRN Electron. J. (2018). https://doi.org/10.2139/ssrn.3126971. https://www.ssrn.com/abstract=3126971

25. Shapley, L.S.: A value for n-person games. In: Kuhn, H.W., Tucker, A.W. (eds.) Contributions to the Theory of Games (AM-28), vol. II, pp. 307–318. Princeton University Press (1953). https://doi.org/10.1515/9781400881970-018

26. Street, N., Wolberg, W.H., Mangasarian, O.L.: Nuclear feature extraction for breast tumor diagnosis. In: Proceedings of the Conference on Biomedical Image Processing and Biomedical Visualization, vol. 1905 (1993). https://doi.org/10.1117/12.148698

27. Tan, S., Caruana, R., Hooker, G., Lou, Y.: Distill-and-compare: auditing black-box models using transparent model distillation. In: Proceedings of the 2018 AAAI/ACM Conference on AI, Ethics, and Society, pp. 303–310. ACM, New Orleans (2018). https://doi.org/10.1145/3278721.3278725. https://dl.acm.org/doi/10.1145/3278721.3278725

28. Wachter, S., Mittelstadt, B., Russell, C.: Counterfactual explanations without opening the black box: automated decisions and the GDPR. SSRN Electron. J. (2017). https://doi.org/10.2139/ssrn.3063289. https://www.ssrn.com/abstract=3063289

Model-Agnostic Explanations, Methods and Techniques for xAI, Causality and Explainable AI

iPDP: On Partial Dependence Plots in Dynamic Modeling Scenarios

Maximilian Muschalik[1,2]([✉])(iD), Fabian Fumagalli[3](iD), Rohit Jagtani[1](iD),
Barbara Hammer[3](iD), and Eyke Hüllermeier[1,2](iD)

[1] LMU Munich, Geschwister-Scholl-Platz 1, 80539 Munich, Germany
`maximilian.muschalik@ifi.lmu.de`
[2] Munich Center for Machine Learning (MCML), Munich, Germany
[3] CITEC, Bielefeld University, Inspiration 1, 33619 Bielefeld, Germany

Abstract. Post-hoc explanation techniques such as the well-established partial dependence plot (PDP), which investigates feature dependencies, are used in explainable artificial intelligence (XAI) to understand black-box machine learning models. While many real-world applications require dynamic models that constantly adapt over time and react to changes in the underlying distribution, XAI, so far, has primarily considered static learning environments, where models are trained in a batch mode and remain unchanged. We thus propose a novel model-agnostic XAI framework called incremental PDP (iPDP) that extends on the PDP to extract time-dependent feature effects in non-stationary learning environments. We formally analyze iPDP and show that it approximates a time-dependent variant of the PDP that properly reacts to real and virtual concept drift. The time-sensitivity of iPDP is controlled by a single smoothing parameter, which directly corresponds to the variance and the approximation error of iPDP in a static learning environment. We illustrate the efficacy of iPDP by showcasing an example application for drift detection and conducting multiple experiments on real-world and synthetic data sets and streams.

Keywords: Explainable Artificial Intelligence · Partial Dependence Plot · Incremental Learning · Data Streams

1 Introduction

Since machine learning (ML) models are increasingly applied in various high-stakes environments such as healthcare [45] or energy systems [21], models need

---

M. Muschalik and F. Fumagalli—denotes equal contribution.
We gratefully acknowledge funding by the Deutsche Forschungsgemeinschaft (DFG, German Research Foundation): TRR 318/1 2021 - 438445824.

Supplementary Information The online version contains supplementary material available at https://doi.org/10.1007/978-3-031-44064-9_11.

to be explainable. Often the best-performing models are less comprehensive than white-box alternatives resulting in a trade-off between performance and interpretability. Explainable artificial intelligence (XAI) research addresses this trade-off by providing explanations to uncover the internal logic of such black-box models [1]. Model-agnostic XAI methods can be applied to any ML model regardless of its structure. The model is treated as a black-box and is systematically probed with differently structured inputs to observe its output behavior. A special kind of global, model-agnostic explanation is the visualization of the *feature effects*. Feature effect methods such as the *Partial Dependence Plot* (PDP) [17] aim at marginalizing a model's output along a feature axis. This allows for visually inspecting the possibly complicated relationship between a model's outputs and feature values.

XAI research has traditionally focused on static learning environments, where models are trained on fixed data sets and ought to be stationary. However, ML models are increasingly applied in different dynamic learning environments such as *incremental learning* [33] from data streams or *continual lifelong learning* [42]. For instance, predictive maintenance models are often fitted on a constant stream of sensor information [13] or financial services providers benefit from online credit scoring models [11]. Such application scenarios often require incremental models to be updated efficiently one by one sequentially. Online models learn continuously from an ever-evolving stream of information where the learning task or the environment may change over time. Shifts in the data distributions, called *concept drift*, may arise from failing sensors or irregular readings in predictive maintenance applications [13], or because of pandemic-induced lockdowns in energy forecasting systems [43] or hospital admission criteria [15].

Similar to the static batch learning setting, high-stakes online learning applications require XAI approaches to enable the use of high-performance black-box models. However, in dynamic environments with ever-changing models, more than static explanations are required. To properly explain dynamic models at any point in time, special XAI approaches are required that are, like the incremental models, updated over time one by one [19,40]. In this work, we are interested in the well-established PDP to explain the dependencies of features in the model. The PDP is able to uncover changes in the model, which may remain undiscovered by measures based on changes in accuracy [40] or global feature importance [19,41]. We, thus, provide an incremental variant of PDP, referred to as iPDP, that efficiently computes a stream of PDPs over time. This stream can be viewed as an *explanation stream* or *interpretability stream*, which summarizes the data and the model efficiently at any point in time. In our experiments, we construct a synthetic data stream to highlight the benefits of iPDP over simple feature importance based methods. We further provide an example application that shows how this explanation stream of iPDP can be used to reliably detect changes in a real-world data stream setting.

Contribution. Our main contributions include:

- We introduce iPDP as a novel, model-agnostic explanation method that naturally retrieves the feature effects in non-stationary modeling scenarios, such as online learning from data streams. The iPDP incrementalizes the well-established XAI technique, PDP, and enables it to react to concept drift. It converts a data stream into an explanation stream, and we illustrate meaningful application domains, such as concept drift detection.

- We establish important theoretical guarantees for iPDP, such as that iPDP reacts properly to real drift and, in static settings, approximates the PDP.
- We demonstrate and validate the efficacy of iPDP by conducting experiments on synthetic and real-world online learning scenarios.
- We implement iPDP as part of an online learning XAI Python package[1].

Related Work. With the increasing use of streaming data, there is a growing need to develop methods that can accurately explain dynamic models. Since tree-based approaches are commonly applied in such streaming scenarios, model-specific approaches that compute global feature importance (FI) have been proposed [10,24]. Moreover, also model-agnostic variants exist that calculate FI for any model type trained on real-time streams of data [19,41]. Yet, the approach of using a single point estimate to model feature importance can conceal the underlying effects of a feature across the entire feature space, which could reveal additional insights. This could further enrich approaches aiming at describing concept drift through means of explanation [15,28,30,40,44].

For static, non-streaming, environments, several techniques to visualize single-feature effects exist. The PDP shows the marginal effect a set of features has on the predicted outcome of a ML model [17]. A PDP can show whether the relationship between the target and a feature is linear, monotonic or more complex [17,29,36]. PDPs have successfully been applied in various application domains across disciplines [5,16,39,46]. Application domains include, imbalanced classification costs as encountered in the criminal justice domain [5], animal-habitat factors in ecological research [16], congestion prediction for traffic planning [46], and hyperparameter optimization for automated ML pipelines [39].

Apart from visualizing the feature effects, the PDP can also be summarized in a FI score by computing the deviation between the individual feature scores in relation to the mean PD curve [25,36]. When significant interaction effects are present, the relationship between the response and predictors may vary considerably. Consequently, the use of an average curve, such as the PDP, may obscure the intricate nature of the modeled relationship, thereby masking the underlying complexity [29]. Individual Conditional Expectation (ICE) plots [22] refine the PDP by graphing the functional relationship between the predicted response and the feature for individual observations. Accumulated Local Effects (ALE) curves [3] present an alternative visualization approach to PDPs, which reduces extrapolation. ALE plots are far less computationally expensive than PDPs, however the interpretation of the resulting curves may be misleading in case of strongly correlated features [36]. To overcome the problem of feature interactions, stratifying PDPs by conditioning on a correlated and potentially interacting feature to group ICE curves was suggested [26]. VINE [9] achieves this by clustering ICE

---

[1] iPDP is part of the *iXAI* framework at https://github.com/mmschlk/iXAI.

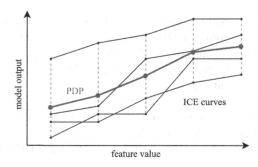

Fig. 1. Illustration of a PDP that reveals a positive effect for an arbitrary feature and model. The black lines denote individual ICE curves and the red line the PDP. (Color figure online)

curves with similar slopes. REPID [29] uses a tree-based approach to identify and cluster homogeneous ICE curves to produce individual effect curves for each unique cluster. Shapley dependence plots [35] use the SHAP value of a feature for the y-axis and the value of the feature for the x-axis. Thus, SHAP dependence plots capture vertical dispersion due to interaction effects in the model.

2   Theoretical Background

In the following, we introduce the notion of explaining black-box models through the features' effects as constructed with the PDP (Sect. 2.1) and briefly establish the problem setting of fitting time-dependent models on data streams (Sect. 2.2).

Notation. Given a d-dimensional feature space $\mathcal{X} \in \mathbb{R}^d$ and a target space $\mathcal{Y}$ (e.g., $\mathcal{Y} = [0,1]^c$ for a c-dimensional classification problem or $\mathcal{Y} = \mathbb{R}$ in case of regression) the corresponding ML model, which we aim to explain, is a prediction function $f : \mathcal{X} \rightarrow \mathcal{Y}$. We denote $(X^1, \ldots, X^d)$ and Y as the corresponding random variables for the feature and target spaces contained in the joint data distribution $\mathbb{P}(X,Y)$. A dataset $\mathcal{D} = \{(\mathbf{x}_i, y_i)\}_{i=1}^n$ consists of n samples drawn i.i.d. from $\mathbb{P}(X,Y)$. We denote the the i-th observation as $\mathbf{x}_i = (x_i^1, \ldots, x_i^d)$ and the realizations of the j-th feature X^j as $\mathbf{x}^j = (x_1^j, \ldots, x_n^j)$. We further denote a set of features indices with $S \subseteq \{1, \ldots, d\}$ and its complement as $\bar{S} = S^\complement$ and abbreviate the corresponding random variables with X^S and $X^{\bar{S}}$.

2.1   Estimating Feature Effects with Partial Dependence

Different approaches exist for retrieving the relationship of a feature on the underlying model's predictions. The *Partial Dependence Plot* (PD Plot, or PDP) [17] is a well-established method for retrieving the marginal effect of features on a model [29,36,37]. The PD function of a feature set S is defined as

$$f_S^{\mathrm{PD}}(\mathbf{x}^S) = \mathbb{E}_{X^{\bar{S}}}\left[f(\mathbf{x}^S, X^{\bar{S}}) \right].$$

The PD function marginalizes the underlying model over all features in $\bar{S}$. Since $\mathbb{P}$ is unknown, the PD function can be approximated via Monte-Carlo integration using all observed data points

$$\hat{f}_S^{\text{PD}}(\mathbf{x}^S) = \frac{1}{n} \sum_{i=1}^{n} f(\mathbf{x}^S, \mathbf{x}_i^{\bar{S}}). \tag{1}$$

The approximation therefore evaluates the model on the set of all n observations, where the values for features in $\bar{S}$ stem from the original data points and the feature values in S are replaced by values in $\mathbf{x}^S$. To visualize the PDP, m grid points $\mathbf{x}_1^S, \ldots, \mathbf{x}_m^S$ are used to construct a PD curve using the pairs $\{\mathbf{x}_k^S, \hat{f}_S^{\text{PD}}(\mathbf{x}_k^S)\}_{k=1}^m$. Grid points can be created in equidistance on the feature scale or based on the feature distribution [38]. As an additional layer of interpretation, the PDP can be enriched with ICE curves [22]. ICE curves show each observation's trajectory across the feature space revealing more complicated relationships because of feature interactions or correlations [22,29,37], i.e. a single term in the sum of (1). The PDP and its ICE curves are illustrated in Fig. 1.

Since, values for features in S are sampled independently of $\mathbf{x}^{\bar{S}}$, synthetic data points can be created that break the dependence between features in S and $\bar{S}$. Hence, the model is evaluated with unrealistic data points, which is also referred to as being *off-manifold* [18], sampled by the *marginal* expectation [32] or extrapolation.

2.2   Online Learning from Data Streams Under Drift

In many online learning settings from data streams, a dynamic model f_t learns from observations arriving sequentially over time such that the stream at time t consists of observations $(x_0, y_0), (x_1, y_1) \ldots (x_t, y_t)$. The model f_t is incrementally updated with each new observation (x_t, y_t) resulting in a new model $f_t \to f_{t+1}$ [20,33,34]. Compared to traditional batch learning settings, where models are trained on an accessible and static dataset, learning from data streams entails various challenges. First, data streams yield unbounded sets of training data resulting in new observations arriving in the future. Second, time intervals between new data points may be short, such that incremental models need to be updated efficiently to cope with the high frequency of arriving observations. Traditionally, the high capacity and frequency of the data prohibits exhaustively storing the complete stream. Hence, the model is ought to be evaluated and fitted only once on each new observation. Incremental updates can be realized by conducting a single gradient update for neural networks or linear/logistic regression models [33], or by updating split nodes in incremental decision trees [7,14,31]. Lastly, in most streaming scenarios, the data generating process is considered to be non-stationary leading to so-called *concept drift* [20,34].

Concept Drift. In general, concept drift can be defined as a shift in the joint distribution of the data generating process, i.e. there exist two time points t_1, t_2 such that $\mathbb{P}_{t_1}(X, Y) \neq \mathbb{P}_{t_2}(X, Y)$ [20]. Applying the Bayes rule to the joint distribution, concept drift can be further decomposed into $\mathbb{P}(X, Y) \propto \mathbb{P}(X)\mathbb{P}(Y \mid X)$. A change in the feature's distribution $\mathbb{P}(X)$ without affecting the dependencies between X and Y is referred to as *virtual drift*. Virtual drift thus, theoretically, does not affect the decision boundaries of a trained model f. In contrast, *real drift* refers to a change in the conditional distribution $\mathbb{P}(Y \mid X)$, which requires adaption of the learned model to reflect the novel functional dependency [34].

A shift can occur because of a real change in the functional relationship between the targets and features like exogenous events such as pandemic-induced lockdowns on energy consumption patterns [43] or hospital admission criteria [15]. Data distributions may shift smoothly from one concept into the other (gradual drift), or transition rapidly (sudden drift) [34]. The *effect* of a particular feature for predicting the target values may change substantially in all variants of concept drift.

3   Incremental Partial Dependence Plots

In an incremental learning setting on a data stream, the model is updated with every observation and may change fundamentally over time, if concept drift occurs. Providing insights into the model f_t at every time step with measures such as the PDP is a challenging, yet important, task to understand how the model's reasoning changes over time. In Sect. 3.1, we discuss the effect of concept drift on PDPs and identify two important challenges, caused by real and virtual concept drift. We then present, in Sect. 3.1, a novel and efficient algorithmic approach to compute incremental PDPs over time using minimal computational resources. Our approach results in an *interpretability* or *explainability* stream, which provides a stream of PDP values alongside the data stream, which can be further used in applications to understand how feature dependencies change over time. In Sect. 3.3, we analyze our approach theoretically and provide meaningful guarantees, which further support our algorithmic approach.

3.1   Partial Dependence Plots Under Concept Drift

We consider the incremental learning scenario described in Sect. 2.2, where we observe data points over time and update the current model with every new observation. Assuming that the model sufficiently approximates the underlying data generating distribution, we can distinguish between virtual and real drift and its effect on the PDPs over time.

PDP Under Real Drift. Real drift is usually reflected in a change in the model's decision boundaries. Such a change will often yield a change in the shape of the PDP, when compared with previously calculated PDPs, as illustrated in Fig. 2. Clearly, under real drift the model may change substantially and previously

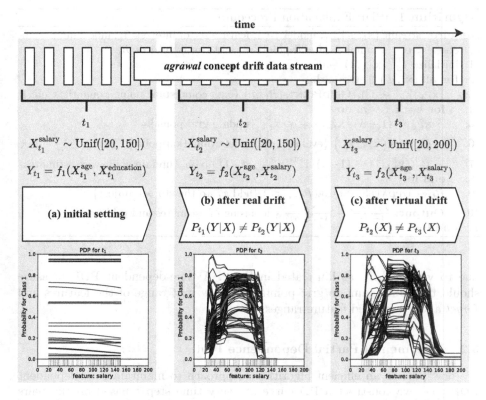

Fig. 2. An incremental model is fitted on a synthetic data stream based on the *agrawal* [2] concepts. The stream contains two concept drifts between three time intervals (t_1, t_2, t_3). The PDPs computed for the incremental model illustrate the drifts. At first the feature *salary* is not relevant for the classification task (a). Then a *real drift* (b) changes the classification problem and the feature becomes relevant. Lastly, a *virtual drift* (c) leads to a new feature range. Here, $f_1(X_t^{\mathrm{age}}, X_t^{\mathrm{education}})$ and $f_2(X_t^{\mathrm{age}}, X_t^{\mathrm{salary}})$ refer to the *agrawal* classification functions and not a model.

calculated PDPs will provide misleading insights into the model's behavior. A time-dependent PDP measure should therefore, ideally, recompute the PDP after every model update. However, in practice when working with rapid data streams, repeated computations quickly become infeasible, as at every time step computing (1) requires n model evaluations. To improve computational efficiency, previous model evaluations may be used but recent evaluations should be favored over outdated ones [19,40].

PDP Under Virtual Drift. In addition to changes in the decision boundaries due to changes in the correlation structure, virtual drift may also affect the grid points in which the PDP is visualized. In the static batch setting, the PDP is commonly calculated and shown based on equidistant grid points within the feature's range. While observing new data points, the feature's range may change

---

Algorithm 1. iPDP Explanation Procedure

Require: stream $\{\mathbf{x}_t, y_t\}_{t=1}^{\infty}$, model $f_t(.)$, feature set of interest S, smoothing parameter $0 < \alpha \leq 1$, number of grid points m, and storage object R_t

1: initialize $\hat{f}_S^{\mathrm{PD}}(\mathbf{x}_{0,k}^S, 1) \leftarrow 0$
2: **for all** $(\mathbf{x}_t, y_t) \in$ stream **do**
3:     $\{\tilde{\mathbf{x}}_{t,k}^S\}_{k=1}^m \leftarrow \mathrm{GETGRIDPOINTS}(R_t, m)$ {e.g., equidistant points, quantiles, etc.}
4:     **for** $k = 1, \dots, m$ **do**
5:         $\mathbf{x}_{t,k}^S \leftarrow (1 - \alpha) \cdot \mathbf{x}_{t-1,k}^S + \alpha \cdot \tilde{\mathbf{x}}_{t,k}^S$ {update grid point}
6:         $\hat{y}_k \leftarrow f_t\left(\tilde{\mathbf{x}}_{t,k}^S, \mathbf{x}_t^{\bar{S}}\right)$ {evaluate on model evaluation point}
7:         $\hat{f}_S^{\mathrm{PD}}(\mathbf{x}_{t,k}^S, t) \leftarrow (1-\alpha) \cdot \hat{f}_S^{\mathrm{PD}}(\mathbf{x}_{t-1,k}^S, t-1) + \alpha \cdot \hat{y}_k$ {update point-wise estimates}
8:     **end for**
9:     $R_t \leftarrow \mathrm{UPDATESTORAGE}(R_{t-1}, x_t^S)$ {add x_t^S to the storage object}
10:     **Output:** $\frac{\hat{f}_S^{\mathrm{PD}}(\mathbf{x}_{t,k}^S, t)}{1-(1-\alpha)^t}, \frac{\mathbf{x}_{t,k}^S}{1-(1-\alpha)^t}$ {debiasing of estimates and grid points}
11: **end for**

---

due to virtual drift, as illustrated in Fig. 2. A time-dependent PDP measure should therefore maintain grid points in the *current* range of the features and *forget* about outdated feature ranges.

3.2 Incremental Partial Dependence Plot

We now present an efficient algorithmic approach to maintain time-dependent PDPs, i.e. we construct a PD curve at every time step t based on the pairs $\{\mathbf{x}_{t,k}^S, \hat{f}_S^{\mathrm{PD}}(\mathbf{x}_{t,k}^S, t)\}_{k=1}^m$, where we denote $\mathbf{x}_{t,k}^S$ as the grid points constructed at time t. The main iPDP procedure is described in Algorithm 1, which includes a *debiasing* factor[2] in the output $(1 - (1 - \alpha)^t)^{-1}$ for both $\mathbf{x}_{t,k}^S$ and $\hat{f}_S^{\mathrm{PD}}(\mathbf{x}_{t,k}^S, t)\}$. We further distinguish between the *final grid points* $\mathbf{x}_{t,k}^S$ used for visualization of iPDP and *temporary model evaluation points* $\tilde{\mathbf{x}}_{t,k}^S$ used to evaluate the model at time t. Our approach is based on two mechanisms: At every time step, we compute $k = 1, \dots, m$ point-wise estimates for $\hat{f}_S^{\mathrm{PD}}(\mathbf{x}_{t,k}^S, t)$ by updating the previous estimates $\hat{f}_S^{\mathrm{PD}}(\mathbf{x}_{t-1,k}^S, t-1)$ using the current model evaluated at the model evaluation point $f_t(\tilde{\mathbf{x}}_{t,k}^S, \mathbf{x}_t^{\bar{S}})$, accounting for real drift. The grid points $\mathbf{x}_{t,1}^S, \dots \mathbf{x}_{t,m}^S$ used for visualization are then constructed by updating the previous grid points $\mathbf{x}_{t-1,1}^S, \dots \mathbf{x}_{t-1,m}^S$ based on the model evaluation point $\tilde{\mathbf{x}}_{t,k}^S$ obtained from the current feature's range, accounting for virtual drift. We now first describe the updating mechanism for the point-estimates and then discuss our approach of updating the grid points dynamically. Note that our approach may also be used, if the model does not change with every data point but only after a batch of data points.

---

[2] The debiasing factor ensures that for a constant sequence the exponential moving average remains constant and will be theoretically justified in Sect. 3.3.

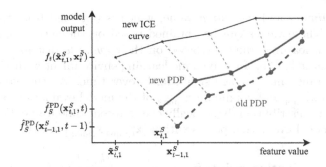

Fig. 3. The current PDP (red, dashed) is updated with a new ICE curve (black), which spans over a new feature range resulting in the updated PDP (red, solid) to slowly transition into the new feature range. (Color figure online)

Updating Point-Wise iPDP Estimates $\hat{f}_S^{\mathrm{PD}}(\mathbf{x}_{t,k}^S, t)$. Clearly, recomputing (1) at every time step using the current model f_t quickly becomes infeasible, as it requires n model evaluations for every grid point and feature set. Instead, to re-utilize previous model evaluations, we compute an exponential moving average for each grid point $\mathbf{x}_{t,k}^S$ (further described below), using the recursion

$$\hat{f}_S^{\mathrm{PD}}(\mathbf{x}_{t,k}^S, t) := (1 - \alpha) \cdot \hat{f}_S^{\mathrm{PD}}(\mathbf{x}_{t-1,k}^S, t-1) + \alpha \cdot f_t(\tilde{\mathbf{x}}_{t,k}^S, \mathbf{x}_t^{\bar{S}})$$

with $\hat{f}_S^{\mathrm{PD}}(\mathbf{x}_{0,k}^S, 0) := 0$ for $k = 1, \ldots, m$ and smoothing parameter $0 < \alpha < 1$. Here, $\mathbf{x}_{t,k}^S$ refers to the k-th grid point at time t, $\tilde{\mathbf{x}}_{t,k}^S$ refers to the k-th model evaluation point in the current feature's range (further described below), whereas $\mathbf{x}_t$ refers to the observed data point at time t. The model evaluations $\{f_t(\tilde{\mathbf{x}}_{t,k}^S, \mathbf{x}_t^{\bar{S}})\}_{k=1}^m$ can be viewed as an ICE curve of the current observation $\mathbf{x}_t$, and hence iPDP uses an exponential moving average of ICE curves of previous observations, as illustrated in Fig. 3. The main difference to (1) is that instead of evaluating f_t for n data points, we evaluate f_t for *only one* data point and utilize the previous calculations, which greatly reduces computational complexity. In Sect. 3.3, we theoretically justify our smoothing approach over grid points and model evaluation points by relating it to a local linearity assumption of f_t in the range of model evaluation points $\{\tilde{\mathbf{x}}_{s,k}^S\}_{s=1}^t$.

Updating iPDP Grid Points $\mathbf{x}_{t,k}^S$. Similarly to smoothing the point-wise estimates, we average each previous grid point $\mathbf{x}_{t-1,k}^S$ with a *model evaluation point* $\tilde{\mathbf{x}}_{t,k}^S$ (further described below) based on the current feature's distribution using an exponential moving average. Formally, the final iPDP grid points used for visualization are

$$\textbf{iPDP grid point: } \mathbf{x}_{t,k}^S := (1 - \alpha) \cdot \mathbf{x}_{t-1,k}^S + \alpha \cdot \tilde{\mathbf{x}}_{t,k}^S \tag{2}$$

at each time step t for $k = 1, \ldots, m$ and initial grid point $\mathbf{x}_{0,k}^S := 0$.

Dynamically Maintaining Model Evaluation Points $\tilde{\mathbf{x}}_{t,k}^S$. In the static batch setting, it is common practice to compute the PDP on equidistant grid points within a *minimum* and *maximum* value, which is obtained from the feature's distribution. These values can be obtained based on the actual minimum and maximum of a feature's range or based on their *quantile* distribution, e.g. 5% and 95% quantile [29,38]. In a dynamic learning environment with virtual drift, the feature's range may change significantly over time. We therefore maintain the minimum $\mathbf{x}_{t,\min}^S$ and maximum $\mathbf{x}_{t,\max}^S$ of the model evaluation points based on the feature's distribution dynamically over a recent time frame. Formally, the equidistant model evaluation points within $[\mathbf{x}_{t,\min}^S, \mathbf{x}_{t,\max}^S]$ are then given as

$$\textbf{Model evaluation point: } \tilde{\mathbf{x}}_{t,k}^S := \mathbf{x}_{t,\min}^S + \frac{k-1}{m-1}(\mathbf{x}_{t,\max}^S - \mathbf{x}_{t,\min}^S),$$

at each time step t for $k = 1, \ldots, m$. Our efficient implementation (Algorithm 2 in the appendix) of the rolling maximum (and minimum) is based on the observation that previous data points with lower values than a more recent observation can be discarded. We further provide an efficient implementation to store frequency distributions of features. Traditional streaming histograms [4] summarize the whole stream's distribution and cannot be applied to store rolling distributions, since old observations outside the window's range need to be forgotten. Instead, our frequency storage (Algorithm 3 in the appendix) extends on the geometric reservoir sampling procedure [19] by allowing observations to be skipped (i.e., $0 < p_{\text{inc}} < 1$) and enforcing an ordering on the reservoir. Based on this frequency storage, quantiles can be dynamically computed to obtain the $\mathbf{x}_{t,\min}^S$ and $\mathbf{x}_{t,\max}^S$ values. Furthermore, it is possible to use the dynamic quantiles instead as grid points depending on the application scenario [29,38].

3.3   Theoretical Guarantees

In this section, we provide theoretical results that further support our algorithmic approach. In particular, we show that iPDP, in expectation, is a weighted sum of previous PD function evaluations, which uses higher weight on recent evaluations to properly react to real drift, as required in Sect. 3.1. We further motivate the debiasing factor $(1 - (1 - \alpha)^t)^{-1}$ in Algorithm 1, which corrects the bias in a static environment. All proofs can be found in Appendix A.

Approximation of a Time-Dependent PD Function. In a dynamic environment, such as a data stream with concept drift, the data-generating distribution (X_t, Y_t) and the model f_t are not static and possibly noisy. Our first result shows that iPDP computes, in expectation, a weighted average of PD function evaluations, where recent evaluations receive a higher weight.

Theorem 1. *iPDP reacts to real drift and favors recent PD values, as*

$$\mathbb{E}[\hat{f}_S^{PD}(\mathbf{x}_{t,k}^S, t)] = \alpha \sum_{s=1}^{t} (1-\alpha)^{t-s} \underbrace{\mathbb{E}_{X_s^{\bar{S}}}\left[f_s(\tilde{\mathbf{x}}_{s,k}^S, X_s^{\bar{S}})\right]}_{\text{PD function at time } s}, \textit{ for } k = 1, \ldots, m.$$

By Theorem 1, iPDP estimates an exponential average of PD function evaluations, where recent evaluations receive a higher weight, which allows iPDP to react to real drift, as required in Sect. 3.1.

Guarantees in Static Environments. To establish further theoretical results, we restrict our analysis to a *static environment*, i.e. observations (x_t, y_t) are iid from a static distribution $\mathbb{P}(X, Y)$ and the model remains fixed over time $f \equiv f_t$. Clearly, these assumptions imply that the PD function does not change over time. If the sequence of $\{\tilde{\mathbf{x}}_{s,k}^S\}_{s=1}^t$ remains constant, then we can show that the expectation of $\hat{f}_S^{PD}(\mathbf{x}_{t,k}^S, t)$ is biased, which motivates the debiasing factor $(1 - (1 - \alpha)^t)^{-1}$.

Theorem 2. *Let observations* $(x_0, y_0), \ldots, (x_t, y_t)$ *be iid from* $\mathbb{P}(X, Y)$ *and* $f \equiv f_t$ *be a static model. Let further the sequence of model evaluation points be static, i.e.* $\tilde{\mathbf{x}}_k \equiv \tilde{\mathbf{x}}_{s,k}$ *for* $s = 1, \ldots, t$. *Then,*

$$\mathbb{E}[\hat{f}_S^{PD}(\mathbf{x}_{t,k}^S, t)] = \left(1 - (1 - \alpha)^t\right) f_S^{PD}(\tilde{\mathbf{x}}_k^S),$$

which motivates the debiasing factor for $\hat{f}_S^{PD}(\mathbf{x}_{t,k}^S, t)$ *in Algorithm 1.*

Clearly, assuming a fixed sequence of model evaluation points is restrictive. When no virtual drift is present, we may instead assume that the collection of temporary model evaluation points $\{\tilde{\mathbf{x}}_{s,k}^S\}_{s=1}^t$ remains in a close range. If these points remain close, then it is reasonable to assume that f behaves *locally linear* within this range. We can then show that the expectation of iPDP at time t is actually the PD function evaluated at the final grid point $\mathbf{x}_{t,k}^S$ used for visualization.

Theorem 3. *Let observations* $(x_0, y_0), \ldots, (x_t, y_t)$ *be iid from* $\mathbb{P}(X, Y)$ *and* $f \equiv f_t$ *be a static model. If* f *is locally linear in the range of temporary model evaluation points* $\{\tilde{\mathbf{x}}_{s,k}^S\}_{s=1}^t$ *for* $k = 1, \ldots, m$, *then*

$$\mathbb{E}\left[\hat{f}_S^{PD}(\mathbf{x}_{t,k}^S, t)\right] = f_S^{PD}\left(\mathbf{x}_{t,k}^S\right) \text{ and } \mathbb{E}\left[\frac{\hat{f}_S^{PD}(\mathbf{x}_{t,k}^S, t)}{1 - (1 - \alpha)^t}\right] = f_S^{PD}\left(\frac{\mathbf{x}_{t,k}^S}{1 - (1 - \alpha)^t}\right),$$

where the second equation justifies the debiasing factor for $\mathbf{x}_{t,k}^S$ *in Algorithm 1.*

We can further prove that the variance of iPDP is directly controlled by the smoothing parameter α and, in case of local linearity, controls the approximation error.

Theorem 4. *Let observations* $(x_0, y_0), \ldots, (x_t, y_t)$ *be iid from* $\mathbb{P}(X, Y)$ *and* $f \equiv f_t$ *be a static model. Then, the variance is controlled by* α, *i.e.* $\mathbb{V}[\hat{f}_S^{PD}(\mathbf{x}_{t,k}^S, t)] = \mathcal{O}(\alpha)$. *In particular, if* f *is locally linear in the range of temporary model evaluation points* $\{\tilde{\mathbf{x}}_{s,k}^S\}_{s=1}^t$ *for* $k = 1, \ldots, m$, *then for every* $\epsilon > 0$

$$\mathbb{P}\left(|\hat{f}_S^{PD}(\mathbf{x}_{t,k}^S, t) - f_S^{PD}(\mathbf{x}_{t,k}^S)| > \epsilon\right) = \mathcal{O}(\alpha).$$

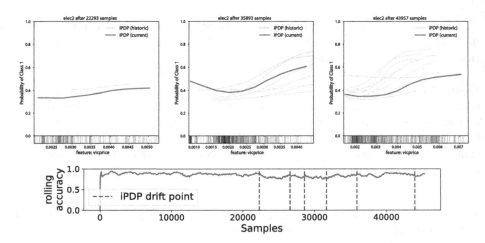

Fig. 4. Three iPDP explanations at different time points (after 22 293, 35 893, and 43 957 observations) for an ARF fitted on the *elec2* data stream. The iPDPs are computed for the *vicprice* feature. The time points for generating the explanations are detected by ADWIN based on the iPDP (blue lines). (Color figure online)

4   Experiments and Applications

We evaluate and show example use cases of iPDP in different experimental scenarios. First in Sect. 4.1, we explore how iPDP can be used to create a data stream of explanations, which can be further refined and used for dynamic explanations or drift detection. Second, in Sect. 4.2, we demonstrate how iPDP can be used in a dynamic learning environments to recover up-to-date feature effects which would be obfuscated by online FI measures. In Sect. 4.3, we validate our theoretical result and show how iPDP converges to the ground truth batch PDP in a static learning environment. In our experiments, values between $\alpha = 0.001$ (conservative) and $\alpha = 0.01$ (reactive) appeared to be reasonable, which we recommend for application.[3]

4.1   Use Case: Change Explanation Based on iPDP

iPDP creates time-dependent feature effect curves at any time. Therein, iPDP transforms the data stream on which a model is incrementally fitted into a stream of explanations. This stream of dynamic effect curves can be analyzed and monitored similar to other streams of information. Traditionally, concept drift detection algorithms are applied on streams of model performance values [34]. Yet, some performance-based drift detectors like ADWIN [6] can be applied

---

[3] All experiments are based on *sklearn*, *pytorch* and the *river* online learning framework. All datasets are publicly available and described in the supplement C.1. The code to reproduce the experiments can be found at https://github.com/mmschlk/iPDP-On-Partial-Dependence-Plots-in-Dynamic-Modeling-Scenarios.

on any numerical values streamed over time. Hence, we propose to analyze the explanation stream of incremental effect curves with classical drift detectors. This methodology can be used to detect and investigate changes in the underlying model more directly than by relying on the performance metrics [40].

To illustrate, how the iPDP stream can be monitored continuously, we fit and explain an Adaptive Random Forest (ARF) [23] with 10 trees as base learners on the well-established *elec2* [27] concept drift stream. We compute the iPDP with $\alpha = 0.001$ over 10 grid points yielding a curve at any time for each feature. The grid points are equidistant between quantiles Q_5 and Q_{95} as derived by Algorithm 3. To summarize the 10 individual grid points of the time-dependent PD curve, we condense the iPDP into a single FI score. The PDP-based importance score can be calculated as the deviation of each individual feature value from the average PD curve [25,36]. We apply ADWIN as a change detector on this stream of FI scores. With every drift detected by ADWIN (blue lines in Fig. 4), we plot the current iPDP and present the current model behavior to the user. Figure 4 shows a selection of three iPDP explanations at three different time points identified by ADWIN as change points. It shows, how the model behaves differently at different points in time. Until approximately 22 000 samples, the model has no effect given the *vicprice* feature of the stream, since the feature's value was constantly zero. After the concept drift, the *vicprice* value become relevant for the model in terms of a U-shaped effect on the predictions. Lastly, for a larger feature range the effect translates into a more linear relationship. A monitoring system like this can be used for various application domains, where decisions must be automated based on certain model characteristics.

4.2 iPDP in Dynamic Learning Environments

Similar to the previous example, we apply iPDP in different data stream scenarios. To illustrate the advantage of feature effects over mere FI values, we create a synthetic data stream called *hyperplane*, which refers to a simple classification function described by a rotating hyperplane. We will induce concept drift on this data stream and show that the FI values do not allow to detect the concept drift, while our iPDP estimates reveal the changes in the model. All observations on one side of the hyperplane are considered to be of class **1** and otherwise **0**. Let $X^{(1)} \sim \mathcal{N}(\mu_1, \sigma_1^2)$, $X^{(2)} \sim \mathcal{N}(\mu_2, \sigma_2^2)$ and error term $\epsilon \sim \mathcal{N}(\mu_\epsilon, \sigma_\epsilon^2)$ be random variables. We then define

$$Z = \beta_1 X^{(1)} + \beta_2 X^{(2)} + \epsilon \text{ and } Y = 1(\frac{1}{1 + \exp(-Z)} \geq \tau),$$

where $\beta_1, \beta_2 \in \mathbb{R}$ are scaling parameters, $0 < \tau < 1$ is a threshold value and **1** the indicator function, i.e. 1 if the condition is fulfilled and 0 otherwise. We initialize $\tau = 0.1, \mu_1 = 100, \mu_2 = 200, \sigma_1^2 = 20, \sigma_2^2 = 40, \beta^{(1)} = 1$, and $\beta^{(2)} = -0.5$ and induce a concept drift after 20 000 observations by switching to $\mu_1 = 200, \mu_2 = 100, \sigma_1^2 = 40, \sigma_2^2 = 20, \beta^{(1)} = -0.5$, and $\beta^{(2)} = 1$. We incrementally train a Hoeffding Adaptive Tree (HAT) [31] on this concept drift data stream and explain it with iPDP. The smoothing parameter is set to $\alpha = 0.001$ and

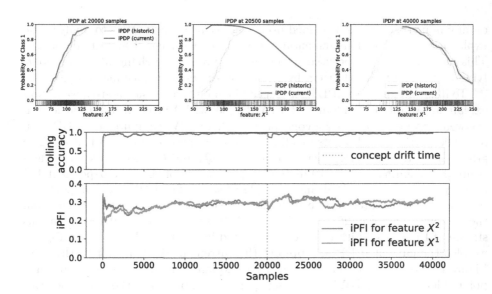

Fig. 5. iPDP and iPFI for an HAT model which is fitted over time on the synthetic *hyperplane* data stream. Unlike iPFI, iPDP can efficiently recover the change in feature effect direction and feature space (left to right: positive effect into negative effect).

20 equidistant grid points are spread out between the minimum and maximum values of the last 2 000 samples (cf. Algorithm 2 in the appendix). Moreover, we explain this HAT by measuring its incremental permutation feature importance (iPFI) [19] for this stream. iPFI computes the well-established PFI [8] score similar to iPDP for a non-stationary model and streaming data. Figure 5 shows, how the drastic concept drift may be detected by drift detection mechanism based on the model's performance or its iPFI scores. Yet, neither the change in the feature range (moving from $\mu_1 = 100$ to $\mu_1 = 200$), nor the switch in the classification function (moving from $\beta^{(1)} = 1$ to $\beta^{(1)} = -0.5$) can be derived from single point importance values. For a further example on the same data stream illustrated in Fig. 2, we refer to Appendix C.2.

4.3 Explaining in Static Environments

To validate the theoretical results, we compare iPDP and the traditional batch PDP in static modeling scenarios. We pre-compute different models in batch mode and then compute the traditional PDPs on the training data. We turn the same dataset into a data stream and compute iPDP. For an illustration, we fit a three layer NN (50, 100, and 5 neurons) regression model on the *california* housing data set. The regressor achieves a R^2 of 0.806 and a MSE of 0.077 on a 70%/30% train-test split with standard scaled features and log-scaled (base 10) prediction targets. The corresponding iPDP with $\alpha = 0.01$ and PDP for the *Longitude* feature are depicted in Fig. 6 using 20 grid points. Both, iPDP and PDP, show almost identical feature effects over the same feature range.

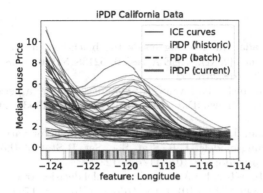

Fig. 6. iPDP (red) with $\alpha = 0.01$ and batch PDP (blue, dashed) for the *Longitude* feature of a NN trained on the *california* housing dataset. Note that the batch PDP is mostly hidden by the iPDP line. For both iPDP and PDP, 20 equidistant grid points are selected between the minimum and maximum value of the feature's range.

Both methods are computed with the same amount of model evaluations. The model has learned a, on average, positive relationship between the westwardness (more negative longitude) and the value of a property. This trend follows similar experiments conducted on this data set [29].

5   Conclusion and Future Work

We propose and analyze iPDP, a novel, model-agnostic XAI framework to compute feature effect plots in dynamic learning environments. Therein, iPDP is based on the well-established PDP for static models and datasets. We formally analyze iPDP and show that it approximates a time-dependent variant of the PDP that properly reacts to real and virtual concept drift. The time-sensitivity of iPDP is controlled by a single smoothing parameter α, which directly corresponds to the variance and the approximation error of iPDP in a static learning environment. In essence, iPDP transforms a model which is trained on an evolving data stream in a stream of explanations. We have demonstrated that this explanation stream can be analyzed with traditional online learning tools to detect and investigate behavior changes in dynamic models. We have further shown that such monitoring systems can detect changes in the model, which might otherwise be concealed in single valued importance scores, such as PFI. However, computing iPDP for every feature with high fidelity (larger grid sizes) might become infeasible for some application domains. In this case, a combination of iPDP and computationally more efficient approaches need to be explored. We further believe that our novel application of incremental XAI for drift detection could benefit from contrasting more complex Shapley-based single valued importance scores [12,41] with iPDP.

References

1. Adadi, A., Berrada, M.: Peeking inside the black-box: a survey on explainable artificial intelligence (XAI). IEEE Access **6**, 52138–52160 (2018). https://doi.org/10.1109/ACCESS.2018.2870052
2. Agrawal, R., Imielinski, T., Swami, A.: Database mining: a performance perspective. IEEE Trans. Knowl. Data Eng. **5**(6), 914–925 (1993). https://doi.org/10.1109/69.250074
3. Apley, D.W., Zhu, J.: Visualizing the effects of predictor variables in black box supervised learning models. J. R. Stat. Soc. Ser. B Stat Methodol. **82**(4), 1059–1086 (2020). https://doi.org/10.1111/rssb.12377
4. Ben-Haim, Y., Tom-Tov, E.: A streaming parallel decision tree algorithm. J. Mach. Learn. Res. **11**, 849–872 (2010). https://doi.org/10.5555/1756006.1756034
5. Berk, R.A., Bleich, J.: Statistical procedures for forecasting criminal behavior: a comparative assessment. Criminol. Public Policy **12**, 513 (2013)
6. Bifet, A., Gavaldà, R.: Learning from time-changing data with adaptive windowing. In: Proceedings of the Seventh SIAM International Conference on Data Mining (SIAM 2007), pp. 443–448 (2007). https://doi.org/10.1137/1.9781611972771.42
7. Bifet, A., Gavaldà, R.: Adaptive learning from evolving data streams. In: Adams, N.M., Robardet, C., Siebes, A., Boulicaut, J.-F. (eds.) IDA 2009. LNCS, vol. 5772, pp. 249–260. Springer, Heidelberg (2009). https://doi.org/10.1007/978-3-642-03915-7_22
8. Breiman, L.: Random forests. Mach. Learn. **45**(1), 5–32 (2001)
9. Britton, M.: VINE: visualizing statistical interactions in black box models. CoRR abs/1904.00561 (2019). http://arxiv.org/abs/1904.00561
10. Cassidy, A.P., Deviney, F.A.: Calculating feature importance in data streams with concept drift using online random forest. In: 2014 IEEE International Conference on Big Data (Big Data 2014), pp. 23–28 (2014). https://doi.org/10.1109/BigData.2014.7004352
11. Clements, J.M., Xu, D., Yousefi, N., Efimov, D.: Sequential deep learning for credit risk monitoring with tabular financial data. CoRR abs/2012.15330 (2020). https://arxiv.org/abs/2012.15330
12. Covert, I., Lundberg, S.M., Lee, S.: Understanding global feature contributions with additive importance measures. In: Advances in Neural Information Processing Systems 33: Annual Conference on Neural Information Processing Systems 2020 (NeurIPS 2020) (2020)
13. Davari, N., Veloso, B., Ribeiro, R.P., Pereira, P.M., Gama, J.: Predictive maintenance based on anomaly detection using deep learning for air production unit in the railway industry. In: 8th IEEE International Conference on Data Science and Advanced Analytics (DSAA 2021), pp. 1–10. IEEE (2021). https://doi.org/10.1109/DSAA53316.2021.9564181
14. Domingos, P., Hulten, G.: Mining high-speed data streams. In: Proceedings of International Conference on Knowledge Discovery and Data Mining (KDD 2000), pp. 71–80 (2000). https://doi.org/10.1145/347090.347107
15. Duckworth, C., et al.: Using explainable machine learning to characterize data drift and detect emergent health risks for emergency department admissions during COVID-19. Sci. Rep. **11**(1), 23017 (2021). https://doi.org/10.1038/s41598-021-02481-y
16. Elith, J., Leathwick, J.R., Hastie, T.: A working guide to boosted regression trees. J. Anim. Ecol. **77**(4), 802–813 (2008). https://doi.org/10.1111/j.1365-2656.2008.01390.x

17. Friedman, J.H.: Greedy function approximation: a gradient boosting machine. Ann. Stat. **29**(5), 1189–1232 (2001). http://www.jstor.org/stable/2699986
18. Frye, C., Mijolla, D.D., Begley, T., Cowton, L., Stanley, M., Feige, I.: Shapley explainability on the data manifold. In: International Conference on Learning Representations (ICLR 2021) (2021). https://openreview.net/forum?id=OPyWRrcjVQw
19. Fumagalli, F., Muschalik, M., Hüllermeier, E., Hammer, B.: Incremental permutation feature importance (iPFI): towards online explanations on data streams. CoRR abs/2209.01939 (2022). https://doi.org/10.48550/arXiv.2209.01939
20. Gama, J., Zliobaite, I., Bifet, A., Pechenizkiy, M., Bouchachia, A.: A survey on concept drift adaptation. ACM Comput. Surv. **46**(4), 44:1–44:37 (2014). https://doi.org/10.1145/2523813
21. García-Martín, E., Rodrigues, C.F., Riley, G., Grahn, H.: Estimation of energy consumption in machine learning. J. Parallel Distrib. Comput. **134**, 75–88 (2019). https://doi.org/10.1016/j.jpdc.2019.07.007
22. Goldstein, A., Kapelner, A., Bleich, J., Pitkin, E.: Peeking inside the black box: visualizing statistical learning with plots of individual conditional expectation. J. Comput. Graph. Stat. **24**(1), 44–65 (2015). https://doi.org/10.1080/10618600.2014.907095
23. Gomes, H.M., et al.: Adaptive random forests for evolving data stream classification. Mach. Learn. **106**(9), 1469–1495 (2017)
24. Gomes, H.M., Mello, R.F.D., Pfahringer, B., Bifet, A.: Feature scoring using tree-based ensembles for evolving data streams. In: 2019 IEEE International Conference on Big Data (Big Data 2019), pp. 761–769 (2019)
25. Greenwell, B.M., Boehmke, B.C., McCarthy, A.J.: A simple and effective model-based variable importance measure. CoRR abs/1805.04755 (2018). http://arxiv.org/abs/1805.04755
26. Grömping, U.: Model-agnostic effects plots for interpreting machine learning models. In: Reports in Mathematics, Physics and Chemistry: Department II. Beuth University of Applied Sciences Berlin (2020). http://www1.beuth-hochschule.de/FB_II/reports/
27. Harries, M.: SPLICE-2 comparative evaluation: electricity pricing. Technical report, The University of South Wales (1999)
28. Haug, J., Braun, A., Zürn, S., Kasneci, G.: Change detection for local explainability in evolving data streams. In: Proceedings of the 31st ACM International Conference on Information & Knowledge Management (CIKIM 2022), pp. 706–716. ACM (2022). https://doi.org/10.1145/3511808.3557257
29. Herbinger, J., Bischl, B., Casalicchio, G.: REPID: regional effect plots with implicit interaction detection. In: International Conference on Artificial Intelligence and Statistics, (AISTATS 2022). Proceedings of Machine Learning Research, vol. 151, pp. 10209–10233. PMLR (2022). https://proceedings.mlr.press/v151/herbinger22a.html
30. Hinder, F., Vaquet, V., Brinkrolf, J., Hammer, B.: Model based explanations of concept drift. CoRR abs/2303.09331 (2023). https://doi.org/10.48550/arXiv.2303.09331
31. Hulten, G., Spencer, L., Domingos, P.: Mining time-changing data streams. In: Proceedings of International Conference on Knowledge Discovery and Data Mining (KDD 2001), pp. 97–106 (2001). https://doi.org/10.1145/502512.502529

32. Janzing, D., Minorics, L., Blöbaum, P.: Feature relevance quantification in explainable AI: a causal problem. In: International Conference on Artificial Intelligence and Statistics (AISTATS 2020). Proceedings of Machine Learning Research, vol. 108, pp. 2907–2916. PMLR (2020). http://proceedings.mlr.press/v108/janzing20a
33. Losing, V., Hammer, B., Wersing, H.: Incremental on-line learning: a review and comparison of state of the art algorithms. Neurocomputing **275**, 1261–1274 (2018). https://doi.org/10.1016/j.neucom.2017.06.084
34. Lu, J., Liu, A., Dong, F., Gu, F., Gama, J., Zhang, G.: Learning under concept drift: a review. IEEE Trans. Knowl. Data Eng. 2346–2363 (2018). https://doi.org/10.1109/TKDE.2018.2876857
35. Lundberg, S.M., Erion, G.G., Lee, S.: Consistent individualized feature attribution for tree ensembles. CoRR abs/1802.03888 (2018). http://arxiv.org/abs/1802.03888
36. Molnar, C.: Interpretable Machine Learning, 2 edn. (2022). Lulu.com, https://christophm.github.io/interpretable-ml-book
37. Molnar, C., König, G., Bischl, B., Casalicchio, G.: Model-agnostic feature importance and effects with dependent features - a conditional subgroup approach. CoRR abs/2006.04628 (2020). https://arxiv.org/abs/2006.04628
38. Molnar, C., et al.: General pitfalls of model-agnostic interpretation methods for machine learning models. In: Holzinger, A., Goebel, R., Fong, R., Moon, T., Müller, K.R., Samek, W. (eds.) xxAI 2020. LNCS, vol. 13200, pp. 39–68. Springer, Cham (2020). https://doi.org/10.1007/978-3-031-04083-2_4
39. Moosbauer, J., Herbinger, J., Casalicchio, G., Lindauer, M., Bischl, B.: Explaining hyperparameter optimization via partial dependence plots. In: Advances in Neural Information Processing Systems 34: Annual Conference on Neural Information Processing Systems 2021 (NeurIPS 2021), pp. 2280–2291 (2021). https://proceedings.neurips.cc/paper/2021/hash/12ced2db6f0193dda91ba86224ea1cd8-Abstract.html
40. Muschalik, M., Fumagalli, F., Hammer, B., Hüllermeier, E.: Agnostic explanation of model change based on feature importance. Künstliche Intell. **36**(3), 211–224 (2022). https://doi.org/10.1007/s13218-022-00766-6
41. Muschalik, M., Fumagalli, F., Hammer, B., Hüllermeier, E.: iSAGE: an incremental version of SAGE for online explanation on data streams. CoRR abs/2303.01181 (2023). https://doi.org/10.48550/arXiv.2303.01181
42. Parisi, G.I., Kemker, R., Part, J.L., Kanan, C., Wermter, S.: Continual lifelong learning with neural networks: a review. Neural Netw. **113**, 54–71 (2019). https://doi.org/10.1016/j.neunet.2019.01.012
43. Rouleau, J., Gosselin, L.: Impacts of the COVID-19 lockdown on energy consumption in a Canadian social housing building. Appl. Energy **287**, 116565 (2021). https://doi.org/10.1016/j.apenergy.2021.116565
44. Susnjak, T., Maddigan, P.: Forecasting patient flows with pandemic induced concept drift using explainable machine learning. EPJ Data Sci. **12**(1), 11 (2023). https://doi.org/10.1140/epjds/s13688-023-00387-5
45. Ta, V.D., Liu, C.M., Nkabinde, G.W.: Big data stream computing in healthcare real-time analytics. In: Proceddings of International Conference on Cloud Computing and Big Data Analysis (ICCCBDA 2016), pp. 37–42 (2016). https://doi.org/10.1109/ICCCBDA.2016.7529531
46. Zhao, X., Yang, H., Yao, Y., Qi, H., Guo, M., Su, Y.: Factors affecting traffic risks on bridge sections of freeways based on partial dependence plots. Phys. A **598**, 127343 (2022). https://doi.org/10.1016/j.physa.2022.127343

SAC-FACT: Soft Actor-Critic Reinforcement Learning for Counterfactual Explanations

Fatima Ezzeddine[1,2]([✉]), Omran Ayoub[1], Davide Andreoletti[1],
and Silvia Giordano[1]

[1] University of Applied Sciences and Arts of Southern Switzerland,
Lugano, Switzerland
{fatima.ezzeddine,omran.ayoub,davide.andreoletti,
silvia.giordano}@supsi.ch
[2] Università della Svizzera italiana, Lugano, Switzerland
fatima.ezzeddine@usi.ch

Abstract. Explainable AI (XAI) techniques are essential for improving the interpretability of machine learning models, which are generally regarded as black boxes. Among the various XAI techniques, Counterfactual (CF) explanations have a distinctive advantage, as they can be generated post-hoc while still preserving the complete fidelity of the underlying model. The generation of feasible and actionable CFs is a challenging task, which is typically tackled by solving a constrained optimization problem. One of the primary difficulties lies in developing a system that is model-agnostic, capable of producing optimal CFs, and scalable to large datasets. While several methods, including linear programming and heuristic approaches, have been proposed to generate CFs, the potential of reinforcement learning (RL) in this task has not been thoroughly explored. This is particularly important as generating CFs requires handling complex constraints and exploring a large search space, which are challenges that RL may be well-suited to address. In this paper, we model the problem of generating CFs as an RL problem and exploit the Soft Actor-Critic (SAC) RL architecture to build an RL-based system for generating CFs. We refer to our SAC RL-based approach for generating CFs by SAC-FACT (Soft Actor-Critic for Counterfactual Explanations). We model the reward function of SAC-FACT to adhere to desirable characteristics of generating CFs such as diversity, proximity, sparsity and validity. We evaluate the effectiveness of the proposed approach by performing extensive experiments on four real-world datasets. We prove the effectiveness and convergence of the SAC. Moreover, we compare SAC-FACT state-of-the-art explainers, namely, DiCE and SingleCF, in terms of validity, diversity, and proximity. Experimental results show that SAC-FACT is an applicable option for generating CFs.

Keywords: Explainable AI · Counterfactual Explanations · Reinforcement Learning

© The Author(s), under exclusive license to Springer Nature Switzerland AG 2023
L. Longo (Ed.): xAI 2023, CCIS 1901, pp. 195–216, 2023.
https://doi.org/10.1007/978-3-031-44064-9_12

1   Introduction

In recent years, there has been a growing recognition within the Artificial Intelligence (AI) research community that predictive power alone is not sufficient in the development of AI solutions [1]. Rather, transparency of the Machine Learning (ML) models that provides clear and understandable reasons for their predictions or decisions, has become an equally important objective, particularly for high-risk decisions with social implications. Despite the importance of transparency, however, the utilization of inherently transparent models faced ongoing challenges due to their inability to match the predictive power of more complex, opaque models [2].

To enhance transparency without sacrificing predictive power, practitioners have turned to eXplainable AI (XAI) techniques to explain the decisions of opaque models in a post-hoc manner, which aims to provide insight into how a model arrived at its decision after it has made it [3,4]. While post-hoc explainability techniques are currently widely applied, their fidelity, i.e., how such techniques accurately reflect the underlying decision-making process of the AI model being explained, remains questioned [5,6]. Among the many XAI techniques, Counterfactual (CF) explanations have emerged as a promising technique because they remain truthful with respect to the underlying opaque model, exhibiting full fidelity [7,8].

CF explanations offer a hypothetical scenario that illustrates how a different decision or outcome could have arisen if the input data had been altered. In other words, they identify the variables that should have differed to observe a different outcome, enabling users to understand how changes in inputs would affect the model's output. This type of CF analysis have already proven to improve the interpretability of ML models in several domains such as healthcare and finance [9]. Nonetheless, despite the considerable efforts that has been made by the research community, the development of a time-efficient, scalable, and model-agnostic CF explainer that provides an accurate set of CFs is still an unresolved research question whose addressing is essential for the progress of XAI [10].

Many approaches have been proposed for generating CFs, relying on various types of optimization methodologies such as integer linear programming (ILP) [11,12], Genetic Algorithms [13,14], and Reinforcement Learning (RL) [15,16] to achieve comprehensive and accurate explanation. However, it is worth noting that while approaches such as ILP, heuristic and meta-heuristics have been extensively studied for generating CFs, less attention has been given to exploring the potential of RL strategies for this task in depth.

Against this backdrop, our primary goal is to investigate the potential of RL strategies for generating CF explanations for complex ML models. We recognize that the complexity of modern ML models presents significant challenges in terms of generating CFs that are both comprehensive and accurate. To address this challenge, we propose a novel formulation of the problem of generating CFs that leverages the unique strengths of RL, such as its ability to handle high-dimensional state and action spaces, learn from sparse rewards, and generalize to unseen scenarios. Specifically, we propose a Soft Actor-Critic (SAC) RL-based method named SAC-FACT (Soft Actor-Critic for Counterfactual Explanations) for generating CFs with a custom-designed reward function that adopts CF generation standards. By exploring this new architecture for generating CFs, we aim to demonstrate the effectiveness and efficiency of RL-based approaches in providing high-quality explanations that shed light on the behavior of complex models in a way that is both understandable and actionable for users.

We evaluate our approach using standard CFs evaluation metrics including sparsity, proximity, and validity, and then is compared to two baselines, Diverse Counterfactual Explanations (DiCE) [11] and SingleCF [7]. Through extensive experiments, we demonstrate the convergence of the SAC algorithm and its ability to achieve early convergence for most data points, providing highly accurate results for the optimal CF. We prove that SAC-FACT successfully generates valid and non-anomalous CFs with low proximity and sparsity scores.

The main contribution of our work is SAC-FACT, a novel solution for CF generation based on the SAC RL algorithm. This algorithm has been selected for its ability to efficiently explore complex feature spaces and which, to our knowledge, has never been used for the CF generation task. Another contribution is the design of the reward function that is used to train the SAC architecture. Specifically, we propose a custom reward function that accounts for the optimization of a set of metrics (such as proximity and sparsity) that are commonly used in the CF generation task. We compare the performance of SAC-FACT to two baseline methods by means of extensive simulations performed on four real-world datasets. In addition, we discuss the convergence of our proposed approach with the aim of contributing to a more comprehensive understanding of how RL can be leveraged to generate accurate and diverse CF explanations. We also discuss the main limitations of our approach, including its computational complexity, and present potential future directions for investigating RL-based approaches for generating CFs.

The remainder of this paper is organized as follows. Section 2 offers an in-depth review of the background and relevant literature on generating CF explanations. Section 3 provides a brief background to the necessary theoretical foundations of RL and SAC. Section 4 outlines the methodology of the proposed SAC-FACT explainer. Section 5 presents the experimental settings and discusses numerical results. Finally, in Sect. 6 we conclude our work and discuss future directions.

2 Preliminaries and Related Work

This section provides an overview of the fundamental concepts and prior research relevant to the concept of CF explanations. In addition, we introduce the necessary background knowledge and review the existing literature and highlight the gaps and limitations in the current state of research.

2.1   Counterfactual Explanations

A CF explanation is a type of explanation that provides a hypothetical scenario that, if it had been true, would have resulted in a different outcome from the one that actually occurred. CF analysis can enhance interpretability and explainability by revealing causal relationships between inputs and outcomes [7]. Through comparing the actual and its CFs, it is possible to evaluate the effects of specific factors, gain insights on how to modify these factors to achieve desired outcomes, and make informed decisions and take effective actions, thus providing actionability to the insights gained [7].

This user-friendly nature of CF explanations contributes to the field XAI by providing a clear and understandable framework for interpreting AI systems. By presenting users with specific changes needed to achieve a desired outcome, CF explanations bridge the gap between complex AI algorithms and human comprehension. CF explanations thus play a vital role in making AI more explainable, accountable, and ultimately more ethically and socially responsible [7].

Generating useful and interpretable CFs requires adherence to a set of requirements outlined in [17]. These guidelines highlight the importance of diversity, validity, proximity, sparsity, and user constraints in CF generation. We briefly discuss each of these aspects and their significance in creating effective CFs that benefit users as follows:

Diversity. CFs should exhibit diversity, meaning that they provide distinct ways of altering the model's outcome. This diversity is essential, as it provides users with multiple options to change the outcome. In various scenarios, it might be more beneficial to offer multiple explanations that encompass a wide range of diverse CFs associated with relevant or informative CFs. Instead, the relevance of CF explanations can be contingent on other factors specific to the case.

Validity. CFs must also be valid instances, ensuring that they are not anomalous. In other words, a CF must be feasible instances in a real-world settings so users can act upon them.

Proximity. Proximity of CFs quantifies how close are the CFs to the original input. By emphasizing proximity in generating CFs, we can obtain valuable insights into a model's decision-making process while minimizing unnecessary feature changes. Hence, it is desirable to perform the smallest changes necessary to alter the model's outputs. CFs that exhibit small proximity can have a significant impact on their usefulness in explaining a model's behavior and in providing feasible options to users willing to obtain a different outcome from the model.

Sparsity. Sparsity pertains to the extent to which features are modified compared to the original input, regardless of the magnitude of the changes. In simpler terms, a CF is considered more valuable and practical for users if it proposes modifications to a smaller number of features.

User Constraints. Allowing an approach for generating CFs complete freedom in deciding which features to modify and to what extent may lead to CFs that are not feasible or practical for users. For example, recommending a significant reduction or increase in the age feature may not align with the CF explanation objective. Therefore, an approach for generating CFs should be restricted, if required, to altering only a subset of the feature set of a given input x and modifying specified features within a pre-defined range. Such constraint goes in line with actionable CFs, which are CFs that users can act upon.

2.2 Related Work

Existing research on CF generation strategies is gaining increasing attention recently, as reflected by the vast corpus of literature in the field (see surveys [18–20] and [21]). Various surveys have proposed different taxonomies, which categorize existing approaches based on the problem type tackled (e.g., classification or regression) [20], the optimization method used to obtain the CFs (e.g., heuristic approaches or linear programming) [19], and whether the approach is model-specific or model-agnostic [19,20], i.e., whether the strategy used to generate CFs is applicable to all (resp., to specific) types of models. Arguably, the latter factor is the most fundamental from the operative point of view, as multiple models are generally considered when tackling an inference task. Hence, it is desirable to develop systems for CF generations that are as much generic as possible. Because of this, we focus on discussing some recent work that proposed model-specific or model-agnostic approaches for generating CFs.

As far as model-specific methods are concerned, CFs are obtained by optimizing a cost function that depends on the internal mechanisms of each model, e.g., on the gradients in the case of differentiable models [22,23], or on the internal structure of the learned trees in the case of tree-based models [24,25]. Various methods have been proposed to optimize the cost function, such as mixed integer programming [26], heuristic search strategies [27], and gradient descent [28]. For instance, [26] proposes a general method based on integer programming to generate CFs for linear models. While the proposed method works for a large family of cost functions, it is limited to binary classifiers only. [27] proposes a general model to obtain CFs of tree-based ensembles by minimizing a specific cost function, such as the euclidean or the cosine distances between original and modified inputs. By doing so, this approach can only optimize one single metric at a time (e.g., proximity). [28] proposes a method for CF generation in images, and obtains CFs by minimizing a cost function that can be defined for neural network models only. We observe that, besides the aforementioned limitations, in such works, the optimization performed to generate the CFs is strictly bonded to the internal structure of each model, which limits the applicability of the proposed optimization strategies to other families of models.

On the contrary, model-agnostic methods generalize to any type of model, as they obtain CFs by optimizing a cost function that does not depend on a specific model's internal structure, but rather only on its input/output pairs. Examples of model-agnostic methods are presented in Refs. [12,13,29,30]. The optimization of cost functions in model-agnostic methods is performed using various strategies, such as mixed-integer linear optimization [12], heuristic search strategies [29,31], and metaheuristic approaches, such as genetic algorithms [13,14] and RL [32,33]. For instance, [12] proposes a mixed-integer linear optimization approach to find an optimal CF considering minimal number of changes to features of original input and order of change. In [14] authors propose an approach based on a genetic algorithm considering as terms of fitness function the target prediction class, the number of changed features and the amount of change. In [29] authors minimize the cross-entropy loss between the predicted class probabilities and the class desired for the CF explanation, aiming at identifying explanations that lie directly on the decision boundary while constraining the number of features to alter with respect to the original input.

RL strategies, in particular, have gained significant attention recently, as CF generation can be modeled as the problem of an agent searching for the optimal policy to transition from a given data point to its corresponding CF. In this context, the ML model represents the environment the agent interacts with, and the policy is obtained by optimizing a reward function.

Several works have proposed RL-based approaches tailored for specific use cases. For instance, [33] proposes an RL-based approach for generating CFs considering as reward function the similarity between original input and candidate CF, however solely focusing on the specific use case of predicting drug-target affinity. Similarly, Refs. [34] and [32] employ RL to generate CFs focusing solely on the problem of sentiment analysis [34] and molecular analysis [32], respectively.

Other works have recently proposed RL as a general-purpose instrument to generate CFs [15,16]. For instance, [15] formulates the problem of generating CFs as an RL problem and proposes a deep RL with discrete-continuous hybrid action space to tackle it, considering weighted distance in the reward function and integrates a hierarchical curiosity-driven exploration mechanism. [16] uses deep RL to transform the optimization procedure into an end-to-end learnable process that incorporates encoding and embeddings. Although RL has been applied for CF generation, it is worth highlighting that while many existing works concentrate on specific scenarios or data, our approach stands out as case-agnostic as it is not limited to a specific case or scenario, allowing for broader applicability.

In our work, we present a novel model-agnostic CF explainer, prioritize selecting the appropriate RL algorithm, and focus on emphasizing the precise formulation of the reward function for the RL algorithm. The proposed approach is based on SAC RL and offers a distinctive problem formulation that takes into account various metrics, such as sparsity, proximity, and validity. The key advantage of SAC-FACT lies in its reward formulation, which leverages the SAC algorithm that balances exploration and exploitation and generates diverse CF explanations. This property makes SAC well-suited for generating diverse and informative CF explanations, as it can effectively navigate complex decision spaces and identify a range of plausible alternative scenarios. Another significant benefit of our proposed approach is its scalability to different datasets, making it a versatile tool for a wide range of applications.

3   Background on Actor-Critic RL

This section presents the fundamental concepts and principles of RL, along with the key components of the actor-critic (AC) RL framework.

3.1   Reinforcement Learning

The field of RL [35] takes inspiration from behavioral psychology, wherein an RL agent interacts with an environment to learn a policy that maximizes the expected sum of rewards over time. Typically, this environment is represented as a Markov Decision Process. The state space, referred to by S, and the action space, referred to by A, are defined, and a policy $\pi : S \rightarrow A$ that maps states to actions determines the behavior of the learning agent. The policy $\pi(a_t = a | s_t = s)$ is the probability of performing a certain action $a \in A$ when the agent is in a certain state $s \in S$ at time step t.

The objective of the RL agent is to maximize the expected sum of rewards R_t, known as the return, over a specific timeline T (Eq. 1). The return is calculated by considering the rewards obtained at each time step, denoted as r_k, and applying a discount factor $\gamma \in [0, 1]$. The value of the discount factor determines the significance of future rewards relative to immediate rewards.

$$R_t = \sum_{k=t+1}^{T} \gamma^{k-t-1} r_k \tag{1}$$

The value function of policy π, $V_\pi(s)$ can be expressed as the expected return when initiating from state s and following policy π, as in Eq. 2.

$$V_\pi(s) = \mathbb{E}_\pi(R_t | s_t = s) \tag{2}$$

Similarly, the action-state value function $Q_\pi(s, a)$, also known as Q value of policy π, is defined as the expected return when starting from state s and taking action a, following policy π, as shown in Eq. 3.

$$Q_\pi(s, a) = \mathbb{E}_\pi(R_t | s_t = s, a_t = a) \tag{3}$$

An RL algorithm can be either value-based or policy-based. Value-based methods focus on learning the optimal value function, which estimates the expected cumulative reward for each state or state-action pair and the goal is to find the policy that maximizes the value function. Policy-based methods, on the contrary, directly learn the optimal policy, which maps states to actions. Policy-based methods optimize the policy parameters by maximizing the expected cumulative reward under the policy.

3.2   Actor-Critic RL

AC is an RL architecture that is trained by optimizing both a policy (actor) and an estimate of the value function (critic) simultaneously [36]. The actor takes actions based on the current policy, while the critic evaluates the value of the actions taken by the actor and provides feedback to the actor on the quality of the actions. The policy is updated by the actor based on the feedback received from the critic. With respect to other RL algorithms, AC better handles scalability issues and slow learning for sparse environments (where the agent receives a low or infrequent amount of feedback or reward from the environment for its actions) [37]. In fact, AC combines the strengths of both value-based and policy-based RL methods, namely the ability to learn from high-dimensional input spaces and the ability to learn stochastic policies that can handle continuous action spaces. By exploiting both methods, AC algorithms can learn more efficiently and converge on optimal solutions faster than traditional RL. AC algorithms are also well-suited to tasks that involve continuous action spaces, as they can handle complex, high-dimensional action spaces more effectively [38,39].

However, the AC algorithm also comes with several limitations, such as sample inefficiency and policy entropy regularization. The former is the requirement for a large number of samples to accurately estimate the value function and update the policy, the latter is that the model may converge to a deterministic policy, which can result in a lack of exploration and a suboptimal solution. To tackle these issues, the Soft Actor-Critic was introduced [40]. In a SAC architecture, the actor aims to maximize both the expected reward and the entropy of the taken actions. As the entropy is a measure of the uncertainty or unpredictability of a random variable, its maximization induces a better balance of exploitation and exploration, which in turn prevents the learning of non-optimal policies.

The SAC architecture is composed of three distinct networks: a state value function V that is parameterized by ψ, a soft Q-function Q that is parameterized by θ, and a policy function π that is parameterized by ϕ. As described in [40], the approximation of V and Q facilitates the convergence of the algorithm. Hence, we consider function approximators and we optimize them as follows:

1) We train the Value network V by minimizing the squared difference between the prediction of the value network and the expected prediction of the Q function, plus the entropy of the policy function π (measured here by the negative log), across all states sampled from the experience replay buffer (past experiences). More formally, we minimize Eq. 4:

$$J_V(\psi) = \mathbb{E}_{s_t \sim D} \left[\frac{1}{2} (V_\psi(s_t) - \mathbb{E}_{a_t \sim \pi_\phi} [Q_\phi(s_t, a_t) - \log \pi_\phi(a_t|s_t)])^2 \right] \quad (4)$$

2) We train the Q network by minimizing the squared difference between the prediction of the Q function and the immediate (one-time-step) reward plus the discounted expected Value of the next state (computed with $\hat{Q}$), across all states sampled from the experience replay buffer (Eq. 5).

$$J_Q(\theta) = \mathbb{E}_{(s_t,a_t)\sim D}\left[\frac{1}{2}(Q_\theta(s_t,a_t) - \hat{Q}(s_t,a_t))^2\right] \qquad (5)$$

3) Train the Policy network π by minimizing the Kullback-Leibler (KL) divergence between the policy function's distribution and the distribution obtained by normalizing the exponentiation of the Q function with another function Z (Eq. 6).

$$J_\pi(\phi) = \mathbb{E}_{s_t\sim D}\left[D_{KL}\left(\pi(.|s_t)\left\|\frac{exp(Q_\theta(s_t,.))}{Z_\theta(s_t)}\right.\right)\right] \qquad (6)$$

RL approaches have proved their capability in solving static optimization problems, and are particularly valued for their capability of handling complex problems [41]. For the problem of CF generation, which is characterized by large action and state spaces, RL has been used before for CF generation and has shown success but was limited to some scenarios. Particularly, we chose the Soft Actor-Critic RL because it provides a better balance between exploration and exploitation. As for the latter, Soft Actor-Critic can handle high-dimensional state spaces, and it is therefore, suitable for problems with large amounts of data or complex input representations, which is the case for finding CFs for high-dimensional datasets.

We observe that the aforementioned properties make the SAC-RL architecture a very suitable tool for generating CFs. In fact, the generation of meaningful and diverse CFs requires efficiently exploring a wide range of possible actions, a task that in the SAC-RL architecture is accomplished by considering the entropy regularization term. Furthermore, SAC uses a soft Q-function, which allows the algorithm to estimate the expected return of a given state-action pair in a more robust manner than traditional RL methods, which eventually leads to generating CFs of a higher quality.

4 Methodology

This section presents the proposed approach for generating CFs. We first describe the procedure followed to train the SAC-FACT model, and then we describe the reward function, providing details for each of its components.

After training a machine learning model M, on a dataset $\mathcal{D}$, consisting of l data points represented as n-dimensional vectors (e.g., $v = (x_1, x_2, \ldots, x_n)$, where x_k is the k-th feature. The training of SAC-FACT for generating CFs, henceforth referred to as the explainer, requires the following inputs: i) the model M ii) the input data point to be explained, represented as a vector v_i, and iii) (optionally) the desired new output label. The training of the system consists in learning the policy that maximizes a reward function and is performed in a trial-and-error manner. In particular, an environment is defined, in which an actor performs actions to move within the state space, and receives a reward accordingly.

Note that during this stage of our research, it is necessary to train a distinct SAC-FACT model to provide an explanation for every individual data point. Sect. 5.4 discusses how to address this limitation in future work.

Specifically, the state space $\mathcal{S}$ is represented as an n-dimensional vector, whose initial value is the data point to explain, i.e., v_i. On the other hand, the action space $\mathcal{A}$ is represented as the bi-dimensional vector (f, q), where f is the index of the input feature to change, and q is the amount to change. Note that f is a discrete value, which can assume any of the feature indexes, i.e., $f \in \{1, ..., n\}$, while q is a continuous value representing the percentage of change with respect to the current feature value, i.e., $q \in [-100, 100]$. Taking action induces a change of state, and yields a certain reward. The process is iterated until convergence, i.e., monitoring the mean reward achieved by the policy. To detect the convergence timestep, we monitor the cumulative reward of each episode over a set number of steps (known as the patience parameter). If the cumulative reward remains stable during this period while still producing CFs, we consider the SAC model to have converged. We also monitor convergence plots of mean episode reward, length, and entropy over time to ensure that the models converge while maximizing reward and entropy and minimizing episode length.

In our proposed approach, the reward function is designed to optimize the validity, proximity, and sparsity of the generated CFs (following the guidelines for generating CFs discussed in Sect. 2.1). Equation 7 shows the reward function given by the transition between state s_t to s_{t+1}.

$$R(s_t, a, s_{t+1}) = \sigma - hamming(s_t, s_{t+1}) - gower(s_t, s_{t+1}) + anomaly(s_{t+1}) + \delta \quad (7)$$

The components of the reward function are described as follows. σ is a constant negative value, which favors the agent that takes as few actions as possible to achieve its goal. $hamming(s_t, s_{t+1})$ (Eq. 9) refers to the Hamming distance that measures the number of different features between the states at consecutive time instants, thereby promoting sparsity in the actions taken by the agent. $gower(s_t, s_{t+1})$ (Eq. 8) refers to the Gower distance, which quantifies the similarity between the states and the original input, thereby promoting proximity. $anomaly(s)$ is a penalty term for any anomaly detected during the process at a state s, thereby promoting validity. Anomalous instances are detected using a robust anomaly detection algorithm known as the Isolation Forest Anomaly detector [42], known for its effectiveness in identifying anomalies. Finally, the term δ indicates the attainment of the goal. The combination of these reward function components ensures that the actions taken by the agent are not only effective in achieving the goal, but also sparse, proximal, and valid.

$$gower(x_1, x_2) = 1 - \left(\frac{1}{p} \sum_{j=1}^{p} s_j(x_1, x_2)\right) \quad (8)$$

$$hamming(x_1, x_2) = count(changed\_features(x_1, x_2)) \quad (9)$$

Overall, our reward function is designed to encourage the agent to take the shortest path to the goal state (achieved by considering the σ term), minimize the number of features altered (achieved by minimizing the Hamming distance), maximize the between the current state and the CF explanation (achieved by minimizing the Gower distance), avoid generating anomalies (e.g., unrealistic explanations), and reach the objective of changing the prediction (achieved by means of the term δ).

5   Experiments and Results

In this section, we first introduce the experimental settings including the datasets utilized in our evaluations, models and explainer settings, and evaluation metrics. Then we discuss qualitative and quantitative results obtained through our evaluations. Finally, we briefly discuss the primary limitations of our approach and explore potential avenues for addressing them.

5.1   Experimental Settings

Datasets. We evaluate the generalizability of our approach by applying it to four publicly available datasets with varying numbers of features (ranging from 8 to 41). Our experiments focus exclusively on classification problems that involve numerical features. Table 1 provides a brief description of the datasets utilized in our evaluation, namely, Diabetes [43], Breast Cancer (BC) [44], Climate [45], and BioDeg [46]. The Diabetes dataset comprises patients signs of diabetes and has a total of 8 features. The BC dataset includes patients signs of breast cancer and consists of 9 features. The Climate dataset involves the simulation of crashes during uncertainty quantification ensembles and has 20 features. Finally, the BioDeg dataset comprises features that differentiate between ready and not-ready biodegradable molecules and has 41 features. By evaluating our approach on datasets with different numbers of features, we can assess its performance and determine its suitability for use in various contexts.

Table 1. Description of the datasets used in our evaluations.

Dataset	Description	Number of Features
Diabetes	patients signs of diabetes	8
BC	patients signs of breast cancer	9
Climate	simulation crashes during uncertainty quantification ensembles	20
BioDeg	features distinguishing ready/not ready biodegradable molecules	41

Models Settings. To train the classifiers that will serve as the underlying models, we employ the Gradient Boosting algorithm, known for its effectiveness in constructing highly **predictive models** for tabular data [47,48]. We utilize the scikit-learn library to implement the models and use its default parameters. The Diabetes, BC, Climate, and Biodeg classifiers attained respective accuracy scores of 77%, 83%, 95%, and 88%. For anomaly detection, we train an isolation forest **anomaly** detector for each dataset, using default parameters from the scikit-learn library.

Explainer Settings. We evaluate the performance of SAC models using two distinct architectures for the actor and the critic. The actor architecture comprised four hidden layers with 32, 64, 64, and 128 neurons, respectively, while the critic architecture consists of three hidden layers with 300, 200, and 100 neurons, respectively. A batch size of 512 and a buffer size of 500000 are used in the training process. The selection of these architectures is motivated by their ability to readily converge for a majority of the points.

We train our models on the Diabetes, BC, and Climate datasets for 30,000 timesteps to allow them to learn from the data and improve their performance. In contrast, due to the high dimensionality of the BioDeg dataset, we increase the training timesteps to 60,000 to ensure model convergence. To assess the performance of SAC-FACT on the datasets, we randomly select 40 datapoints from each dataset and train the models, monitoring their convergence timesteps to reach optimal performance levels (as describe in Sect. 4).

5.2   Evaluation Settings

Metrics. To assess the quality of our generated CF examples, we use three commonly used evaluation metrics: validity, proximity, and sparsity [17], which are frequently used to evaluate the effectiveness of CF generation methods.

Validity refers to the proportion of instances generated by a method that is truly CF, i.e., valid (nonanomalous) data points that result in an outcome different from the original input. This assessment focuses solely on distinct examples since a method may produce multiple identical instances. In our case, we report the percentage of valid CFs (non-anomalies) out of all CFs generated during the learning phase. The validity scores range from 0 (lowest validity) to 1 (highest validity). The determination of whether an instance is anomalous or non-anomalous relies on the output of the Isolation Forest anomaly detector model, which is integrated into the training process of SAC-FACT.

$$valid\_counter factuals = \frac{count(non\_anomalies)}{count(total\_counter factuals)} \quad (10)$$

Proximity refers to how similar input instance and relative CF are, based on some distance functions. In our work, proximity is computed as the average Gower distance (see Eq. 8) between the original input and the generated valid CFs ranging between 0 (similar) and 1 (maximally dissimilar) and hence, lower proximity is desired.

Sparsity is defined as the number of features that are changed in the generated CF. We compute sparsity as the average Hamming distance (see Eq. 9) over all the generated CFs for all data points explained (the lower the number of modified features, the lower the sparsity score).

Baselines. We compare SAC-FACT to two baselines:

1. DiCE (Diverse Counterfactual Explanations) [11]. DiCE is a method for generating a set of diverse CF examples that are both close to the original instance and provide explanations for the model's predictions. DiCE uses a combination of optimization and heuristics to generate CF examples that are both relevant to the user's goals and informative about the model's behavior. For the comparison, we generate 50 diverse CFs for each data point, in order to have a fair comparison since the SAC-FACT also generates a fair amount of CFs for each data point.
2. SingleCF [7]. SingleCF generates a single CF by optimizing for the difference in y-loss (i.e., the difference between the predicted outcome and the desired outcome) and proximity to the original instance. The goal of SingleCF is to generate a simple, interpretable explanation for the model's prediction.

The purpose of comparing SAC-FACT to other CF generation methodologies is not to establish superiority in a particular metric or aspect, nor is it to claim that one approach is universally better than others in all respects. Rather, the goal of the comparison is to demonstrate the potential of RL as a general and effective approach to solving a specific problem or task. By comparing the performance of RL against other existing methodologies, the study aims to establish the advantages and limitations of RL in relation to other approaches and to identify the specific conditions under which RL is most effective. Overall, the aim of the comparison is to provide a comprehensive evaluation of the different methodologies and to contribute to the ongoing discussion on the best practices and strategies for addressing the problem at hand.

5.3   Results and Discussion

In this section, we present the results of our evaluations. Specifically, we assess the convergence of SAC-FACT and verify its ability to learn and converge while avoiding getting lost in the action space. Next, we evaluate the quality of the generated CFs based on the predefined metrics discussed earlier, comparing the performance of SAC-FACT to those of baseline approaches. By analyzing these results, we can assess the effectiveness of SAC-FACT in generating informative and diverse CF explanations.

SAC-FACT Explainer Convergence. Figure 1 shows four violin plots reporting the density of the model's convergence for all data points explained, represented in terms of the number of timesteps taken by the SAC-FACT explainers to converge (i.e., to reach the CF with optimal reward), for the Diabetes, BC, Climate and BioDeg datasets, respectively.

For the Diabetes dataset (Fig. 1(a)), the plot shows a high density of the convergences between 0 and 10,000 timesteps with some convergence cases ranging up to 30,000 timesteps. For the BC dataset, the SAC mostly converges between 15,000 and 30,000 timesteps with only some cases of convergence with a relatively lower number of timesteps (e.g., 10,000). For the Climate Model dataset, number of timesteps for convergence mostly ranges between 10,000 and 20,000. Finally, for the BioDeg dataset, which is the most challenging considering the relatively high number of features, the plot shows two thick regions, between 0 and 20,000 timesteps and between 40,000 and 60,000 timesteps. Overall, results show that SAC-FACT has an acceptable convergence rate in most of the cases, independent of number of features of the data set, suggesting that it can applied in high-dimensional and complex input spaces.

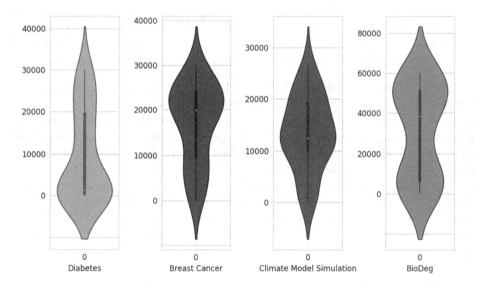

Fig. 1. Violin plots showing the convergence timestep distributions over the 4 datasets

In each of Fig. 2 and Fig. 3 we show the mean reward, the episode length and the entropy coefficient obtained by the agent over the episodes for a selected sample point of BioDeg dataset and Climate Model dataset, respectively. The plots provide an understanding of the agent's learning process and its ability to solve the given problem. Specifically, the mean reward plot allows observing the improvement in the agent's performance during the training process. The episode length allows us to understand how quickly the model learns and adapts to the problem and the entropy coefficient plot depicts how the entropy is maximized during training, which allows gaining insight into how the agent is able to explore the state space and improve its performance. For both examples, SAC-FACT

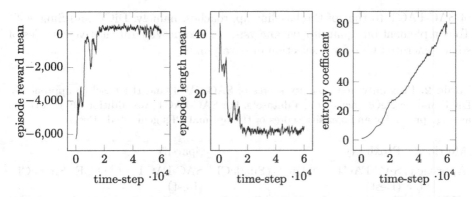

Fig. 2. Visualization of performance plots including episode mean, length, and entropy, for a sample point explanation in the Biodeg Dataset

shows clear convergence, with the episode reward mean increasing over time, indicating that the model is learning to adapt and maximize the cumulative reward. Over time, the mean length of each episode decreases, which suggests that the model is effectively accomplishing its objective and reducing the number of steps needed to reach convergence. Additionally, in both examples, the values of the entropy coefficient rise as time progresses. This confirms that the SAC-FACT explainer is maximizing both the reward and the entropy coefficient (this is desirable, as it can lead to better exploration of the action space and improved solutions). It also suggests that we can terminate or consider model convergence in some cases at earlier stages and with less timesteps.

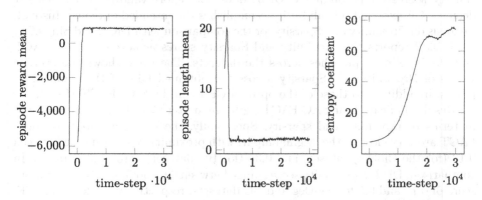

Fig. 3. Visualization of performance plots including episode mean, length, and entropy, for a sample point explanation in the Climate Dataset

Evaluating the Generated CFs. We now evaluate the quality of the generated CFs across the four datasets in terms of the evaluation metrics discussed in Sect. 5.2, namely, validity, proximity, and sparsity, and compare the performance of SAC-FACT to that of the baseline approaches, namely, DiCE and SingleCF. To complement our quantitative analysis, we also provide qualitative samples of some generated CFs for a selection of data points.

Table 2. Proximity and Sparsity scores of SAC-FACT and the baseline approaches, DiCE and SingleCF, across the 4 datasets. For SAC-FACT, we additionally report the average proximity and sparsity scores of the optimal CFs generated (Best).

Metric	Proximity			Sparsity		
Approach	SAC-FACT (Best)	DiCE	SingleCF	SAC-FACT (Best)	DiCE	SingleCF
Diabetes	0.33 (0.15)	0.7	0.85	2.7 (1.2)	5.2	7
BC	0.34 (0.12)	0.21	0.9	3.1 (1.14)	1.9	8
Climate	0.19 (0.1)	0.8	0.8	3.8 (2.0)	16	18
BioDeg	0.13 (0.05)	0.5	0.6	5.6 (2.2)	23	25

SAC-FACT achieves validity scores of 0.7, 0.8, 0.9, and 0.93 on the Diabetes, BC, Climate, and BioDeg datasets, respectively. It is worth noting that the RL models used in SAC-FACT may come across anomalous points and explore certain directions during CF generation, but they are trained to learn from these encounters and avoid them in future CF generations. SAC-FACT is effective in producing CFs that are non-anomalous in various domains and datasets. As for SingleCF, it generates only one CF explanation, and hence, we do not provide validity scores for it. Similarly, DiCE does not report validity scores since it deems a CF explanation valid if it accomplishes the intended outcome. Instead, we focus on Proximity and Sparsity for the comparison with DiCE and SingleCF.

Table 2 reports the Proximity and Sparsity scores achieved by SAC-FACT and the baseline approaches across the datasets. The table shows the average values of Proximity and Sparsity across the obtained CFs of the sampled 40 points, in addition to those of the optimal CF found by SAC-FACT (Best).

Results indicate that SAC-FACT performs better than DiCE and SingleCF in terms of proximity and sparsity. Specifically, the CFs generated by SAC-FACT are very close to the original input, with proximity scores ranging between 0.13 (for the BioDeg dataset) and 0.34 (for BC dataset) across all datasets. In comparison, DiCE's proximity scores range between 0.6 and 0.9, with a proximity score of 0.71 and 0.5 for BioDeg and BC datasets, respectively. As for SingleCF, it has a relatively high proximity ranging between 0.6 and 0.9. Furthermore, the proximity scores for SAC-FACT at convergence are between 0.05 and 0.15, indicating that the optimal CFs are very similar to the original input data points.

In terms of sparsity, SAC-FACT CFs have fewer modified features, with sparsity scores ranging from 2.7 (Diabetes Dataset) to 5.6 (BioDeg dataset) across all datasets. In comparison, DiCE's sparsity scores range between 1.9 and 23 for BC dataset and BioDeg datasets, respectively. As for signleCF, it has higher sparsity scores that range between 7 and 25, for the Diabetes and BioDeg datasets respectively. These results show that SAC-FACT outperforms the other methods in both metrics and in all cases except in terms of Sparsity for BC dataset. This also shows that SAC-FACT can scale to larger datasets and is able of producing more accurate and sparse CFs.

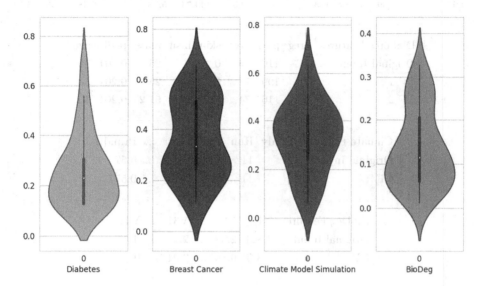

Fig. 4. Violin plots showing the proximity score distributions across the 4 datasets

We now examine in more detail the quality of the optimal CFs generated by SAC-FACT. Figure 4 shows the distribution of proximity scores for the generated CFs across the four datasets. Note that the range of proximity scores varies among the different datasets. Specifically, for Diabetes, BC, and Climate datasets, the proximity scores of the CFs range from 0 to 0.8, but for the BioDeg the CFs range between 0 and 0.4. For the Diabetes dataset, the majority of the CFs have proximity scores between 0.15 and 0.3, as indicated by the thick area in the violin plot. For the BC dataset, two thick areas are observed, one with CFs having proximity around 0.3 and a smaller region with proximity scores above 0.5. For the Climate dataset, there is one thick area indicating that the majority of generated CFs range between 0.2 and 0.4. Finally, for the BioDeg dataset, a thick region is observed around a proximity of between 0.05 and 0.2. In summary, these findings offer significant insights into the generated CFs quality and their diversity and differences. This information can be utilized to improve the algorithm's performance in generating more accurate and varied CFs.

Examples of Generated CFs. Table 3 shows example CFs generated for some data points from the different datasets. Starting with the Diabetes dataset, we show two CFs for a given original input data point. The first CF suggests changing only one feature, *plas*, by increasing its value from 116 to 199. The second

Table 3. Example of generated CFs for a data point selected from each of the four datasets. The table shows 4 sub-tables, with each table showing an example of a CF for a dataset.

BC Features	Age	BMI	Glucose	Insulin	HOMA	Leptin	Adiponectin	Resistin	MCP.1
Original Input	69	28.44	108	8.8	2.3	14.74	5.28	16.48	353.56
CF	69	38.57	108	8.8	2.3	14.74	5.28	16.48	353.56

Diabetes Features	preg	plas	pres	skin	insu	mass	pedi	age
Original Input	5	116	74	0	0	25	0.201	30
CF 1	5	199	74	0	0	25	0.201	30
CF 2	5	116	74	0	0	51.2	0.201	30

Climate Features	Study	Run	vconst corr	...	Prandtl
Original Input	2	11	0.2	...	0.57
CF	3	11	0.99	...	0.57

BioDeg Features	V1	V2	...	V31	...	V41
Original Input	4.821	2.58	...	2.2	...	0
CF	4.821	0.86	...	2.91	...	0

CF suggests modifying only *mass* by increasing its value from 25 to 51.2. For the BC dataset, we show one CF that suggests changing only one feature, *BMI*, increasing it from 28.44 to 38.57. For Climate dataset, the CF shown suggests modifying values of two features, *Study* (changed from 2 to 3) and *vconst corr* (decreased from 0.2 to 0.99). Finally, for the BioDeg dataset, the presented CF suggests altering the values of features *V2* and *V31*, reducing *V2* to 0.86 and increasing *V31* to 2.91. The qualitative examples presented serve to reinforce our previous observations concerning proximity and sparsity. By analyzing these examples, we can see that the SAC algorithm and metrics effectively incorporate proximity and sparsity in the reward function, as demonstrated by the generated CF explanations. They also demonstrate the effectiveness of the SAC algorithm and metrics in generating meaningful and interpretable CF explanations.

5.4   Limitations

Although SAC-FACT has demonstrated significant potential in generating CFs with relatively low proximity and sparsity scores across the four datasets we evaluated, we acknowledge that there are still some limitations that need to be addressed in future work. In the following, we outline three of these limitations and discuss possible solutions to overcome them.

1. Architecture-Dependent: The performance of SAC-FACT depends highly on its architecture. In fact, there is no rule of thumb for choosing the architecture of the SAC. This means that an architecture that is efficient and produces CFs of a desired quality for a specific scenario (use case or dataset) may not necessarily generalize to scenarios. This means that the architecture of the model, AC networks weights initialization, in addition to hyperparameters, need to be tuned for each specific scenario to produce optimal results. As future work, we aim to analyze the impact of different architectures and hyperparameters on the convergence time of SAC-FACT and the quality of CFs it produces.

2. Convergence Variability: As revealed by our experiments, the number of features that could be tuned in a dataset has a direct impact on the number of timesteps required by the explainer to converge (see Fig. 1). Similarly, the convergence timesteps may vary from one input data point to another. This variability adds to the time required to generate explanations. To address this limitation, we first plan to conduct a thorough analysis to understand what factors may delay convergence and then explore potential avenues to reduce the number of timesteps required for convergence.

3. Individual data-point model: Due to the nature of RL-based optimization, SAC-FACT necessitates the completion of a training procedure to generate CFs for each input data point. As a result, the amount of time required to generate CFs for a relatively large set of input data points may become unmanageable from a user experience standpoint. This limitation could be overcome by improving the convergence of the explainer. Additionally, we plan to explore methods to detect convergence as early as possible, explore more efficient RL algorithms and use parallelization techniques. Another promising direction is to investigate the feasibility of developing a single SAC model for a given scenario (model and dataset).

6   Conclusion

In this paper we focus on the problem of generating counterfactual (CF) explanations. We propose a novel approach based on Soft Actor-Critic (SAC) Reinforcement Learning (RL) architecture, referred to as SAC-FACT. SAC-FACT takes into account main guidelines for generating CFs such as the validity, proximity, and sparsity of the generated CFs by accounting for these terms in the reward function. We train SAC-FACT to learn a strategy for generating the CFs, specifically which features to alter and to what degree. We perform evaluations considering four real-world datasets and compare the performance of SAC-FACT to two baseline approaches, namely, Diverse Counterfactual Explanations (DiCE) and SingleCF. The experimental findings indicate that SAC-FACT surpasses the baselines, while also demonstrating the convergence of the SAC algorithm, achieving early convergence for most data points, and providing highly accurate results for the optimal CF. SAC-FACT was able to generate valid and non-anomalous CFs, with low proximity and sparsity scores, resulting in a Gower distance between 0.05 and 0.15 for the optimal CFs. Overall, the study shows that RL-based approaches like SAC-FACT are effective in generating meaningful CF explanations and contribute to the comprehension of the model's decision-making process. In future work, we plan to conduct additional strategies to accelerate convergence and improve the quality of the generated CFs on classification and regression tasks. One approach could be by analyzing impact of different hyperparameters on the quality of generated CFs. Another approach consists of incorporating surrogate models that can generate more accurate CFs and reduce timesteps required for convergence. Another potential avenue for improvement is to enhance the balance between exploration and exploitation, which could help improve the quality of the explanations. Finally, we plan to compare SAC-FACT to additional state-of-the-art methods to provide a more comprehensive comparison.

References

1. Jordan, M.I., Mitchell, T.M.: Machine learning: trends, perspectives, and prospects. Science **349**(6245), 255–260 (2015)
2. Lipton, Z.C.: The mythos of model interpretability: in machine learning, the concept of interpretability is both important and slippery. Queue **16**(3), 31–57 (2018)
3. Holzinger, A., Langs, G., Denk, H., Zatloukal, K., Müller, H.: Causability and explainability of artificial intelligence in medicine. Wiley Interdisc. Rev.: Data Min. Knowl. Disc. **9**(4), e1312 (2019)
4. Ribeiro, M.T., Singh, S., Guestrin, C.: Why should i trust you? explaining the predictions of any classifier. In: Proceedings of the 22nd ACM SIGKDD International Conference on Knowledge Discovery and Data Mining, pp. 1135–1144 (2016)
5. Alvarez-Melis, D., Jaakkola, T.S.: On the robustness of interpretability methods. arXiv preprint arXiv:1806.08049 (2018)
6. Samek, W., Wiegand, T., Müller, K.-R.: Explainable artificial intelligence: Understanding, visualizing and interpreting deep learning models. arXiv preprint arXiv:1708.08296 (2017)
7. Wachter, S., Mittelstadt, B., Russell, C.: Counterfactual explanations without opening the black box: automated decisions and the GDPR. Harv. JL Tech. **31**, 841 (2017)
8. Li, X., et al.: Interpretable deep learning: interpretation, interpretability, trustworthiness, and beyond. Knowl. Inf. Syst. **64**(12), 3197–3234 (2022)
9. Došilović, F.K., Brčić, M., Hlupić, N.: Explainable artificial intelligence: a survey. In: 2018 41st International Convention on Information and Communication Technology, Electronics and Microelectronics (MIPRO), pp. 0210–0215. IEEE (2018)
10. Höltgen, B., Schut, L., Brauner, J. M., Gal, Y.: Deduce: generating counterfactual explanations efficiently. arXiv preprint arXiv:2111.15639 (2021)
11. Mothilal, R.K., Sharma, A., Tan, C.: Explaining machine learning classifiers through diverse counterfactual explanations. In: Proceedings of the 2020 Conference on Fairness, Accountability, and Transparency, pp. 607–617 (2020)
12. Kanamori, K., Takagi, T., Kobayashi, K., Ike, Y., Uemura, K., Arimura, H.: Ordered counterfactual explanation by mixed-integer linear optimization. In: Proceedings of the AAAI Conference on Artificial Intelligence, vol. 35, no. 13, pp. 11564–11574 (2021)

13. Sharma, S., Henderson, J., Ghosh, J.: Certifai: Counterfactual explanations for robustness, transparency, interpretability, and fairness of artificial intelligence models. arXiv preprint arXiv:1905.07857 (2019)
14. Hashemi, M., Fathi, A.: Permuteattack: Counterfactual explanation of machine learning credit scorecards. arXiv preprint arXiv:2008.10138 (2020)
15. Chen, Z., Silvestri, F., Tolomei, G., Zhu, H., Wang, J., Ahn, H.: Relace: reinforcement learning agent for counterfactual explanations of arbitrary predictive models. arXiv preprint arXiv:2110.11960 (2021)
16. Samoilescu, R.-F., Van Looveren, A., Klaise, J.: Model-agnostic and scalable counterfactual explanations via reinforcement learning. arXiv preprint arXiv:2106.02597 (2021)
17. Verma, S., Boonsanong, V., Hoang, M., Hines, K.E., Dickerson, J.P., Shah, C.: Counterfactual explanations and algorithmic recourses for machine learning: A review. arXiv preprint arXiv:2010.10596 (2020)
18. Adadi, A., Berrada, M.: Peeking inside the black-box: a survey on explainable artificial intelligence (XAI). IEEE Access 6, 52138–52160 (2018)
19. Guidotti, R.: Counterfactual explanations and how to find them: literature review and benchmarking. Data Min. Knowl. Disc., 1–55 (2022)
20. Stepin, I., Alonso, J.M., Catala, A., Pereira-Fariña, M.: A survey of contrastive and counterfactual explanation generation methods for explainable artificial intelligence. IEEE Access 9, 11974–12001 (2021)
21. Arrieta, A.B., et al.: Explainable artificial intelligence (XAI): concepts, taxonomies, opportunities and challenges toward responsible AI. Inf. Fusion 58, 82–115 (2020)
22. Selvaraju, R.R., Cogswell, M., Das, A., Vedantam, R., Parikh, D., Batra, D.: Gradcam: visual explanations from deep networks via gradient-based localization. In: Proceedings of the IEEE International Conference on Computer Vision, pp. 618–626 (2017)
23. Wang, P., Vasconcelos, N.: Scout: self-aware discriminant counterfactual explanations. In: Proceedings of the IEEE/CVF Conference on Computer Vision and Pattern Recognition, pp. 8981–8990 (2020)
24. Stepin, I., Alonso, J. M., Catala, A., Pereira-Fariña, M.: Generation and evaluation of factual and counterfactual explanations for decision trees and fuzzy rule-based classifiers. In: 2020 IEEE International Conference on Fuzzy Systems (FUZZ-IEEE), pp. 1–8. IEEE (2020)
25. Lucic, A., Oosterhuis, H., Haned, H., de Rijke, M.: Focus: flexible optimizable counterfactual explanations for tree ensembles. Proc. AAAI Conf. Artif. Intell. 36(5), 5313–5322 (2022)
26. Ustun, B., Spangher, A., Liu, Y.: Actionable recourse in linear classification. In: Proceedings of the Conference on Fairness, Accountability, and Transparency, pp. 10–19 (2019)
27. Tolomei, G., Silvestri, F., Haines, A., Lalmas, M.: Interpretable predictions of tree-based ensembles via actionable feature tweaking. In: Proceedings of the 23rd ACM SIGKDD International Conference on Knowledge Discovery and Data Mining, pp. 465–474 (2017)
28. Dhurandhar, A., et al.: Explanations based on the missing: towards contrastive explanations with pertinent negatives. In: Advances in Neural Information Processing Systems, vol. 31 (2018)
29. Moore, J., Hammerla, N., Watkins, C.: Explaining deep learning models with constrained adversarial examples. In: Nayak, A.C., Sharma, A. (eds.) PRICAI 2019. LNCS (LNAI), vol. 11670, pp. 43–56. Springer, Cham (2019). https://doi.org/10.1007/978-3-030-29908-8_4

30. Goodfellow, I.J., Shlens, J., Szegedy, C.: Explaining and harnessing adversarial examples. arXiv preprint arXiv:1412.6572 (2014)
31. Martens, D., Provost, F.: Explaining data-driven document classifications. MIS Q. **38**(1), 73–100 (2014)
32. Numeroso, D., Bacciu, D.: Explaining deep graph networks with molecular counterfactuals. arXiv preprint arXiv:2011.05134 (2020)
33. Nguyen, T.M., Quinn, T.P., Nguyen, T., Tran, T.: Counterfactual explanation with multi-agent reinforcement learning for drug target prediction. arXiv preprint arXiv:2103.12983 (2021)
34. Li, J., Monroe, W., Jurafsky, D.: Understanding neural networks through representation erasure. arXiv preprint arXiv:1612.08220 (2016)
35. Sutton, R.S., Barto, A.G., et al.: Introduction to Reinforcement Learning, vol. 135. MIT press, Cambridge (1998)
36. Konda, V., Tsitsiklis, J.: Actor-critic algorithms. In: Advances in Neural Information Processing Systems, vol. 12 (1999)
37. Konda, V.R., Tsitsiklis, J.N.: Onactor-critic algorithms. SIAM J. Control. Optim. **42**(4), 1143–1166 (2003)
38. Lillicrap, T.P., et al.: Continuous control with deep reinforcement learning. arXiv preprint arXiv:1509.02971 (2015)
39. Sutton, R.S., McAllester, D., Singh, S., Mansour, Y.: Policy gradient methods for reinforcement learning with function approximation. In: Advances in Neural Information Processing Systems, vol. 12 (1999)
40. Haarnoja, T., Zhou, A., Abbeel, P., Levine, S.: Soft actor-critic: off-policy maximum entropy deep reinforcement learning with a stochastic actor. In: International Conference on Machine Learning, pp. 1861–1870. PMLR (2018)
41. Li, Y.: Deep reinforcement learning: An overview. arXiv preprint arXiv:1701.07274 (2017)
42. Liu, F.T., Ting, K.M., Zhou, Z.-H.: Isolation forest. In: 2008 Eighth IEEE International Conference on Data Mining, pp. 413–422. IEEE (2008)
43. Diabetes dataset. https://www.openml.org/d/37. Accessed 25 Apr 2023
44. Breast cancer dataset. https://archive.ics.uci.edu/ml/datasets/Breast+Cancer+Coimbra. Accessed 25 Apr 2023
45. Climate dataset. https://archive.ics.uci.edu/ml/datasets/Climate+Model+Simulation+Crashes. Accessed 25 Apr 2023
46. Biodeg dataset. https://openml.org/d/1494. Accessed 25 Apr 2023
47. Friedman, J.H.: Greedy function approximation: a gradient boosting machine. Ann. Stat., 1189–1232 (2001)
48. Chen, T., Guestrin, C.: Xgboost: a scalable tree boosting system. In: Proceedings of the 22nd ACM SIGKDD International Conference on Knowledge Discovery and Data Mining, pp. 785–794 (2016)

Algorithm-Agnostic Feature Attributions
for Clustering

Christian A. Scholbeck[1,2]($\boxtimes$) (iD), Henri Funk[1,2] (iD), and Giuseppe Casalicchio[1,2] (iD)

[1] LMU Munich, Munich, Germany
[2] Munich Center for Machine Learning (MCML), Munich, Germany
{christian.scholbeck,henri.funk,
giuseppe.casalicchio}@stat.uni-muenchen.de

Abstract. Understanding how assignments of instances to clusters can be attributed to the features can be vital in many applications. However, research to provide such feature attributions has been limited. Clustering algorithms with built-in explanations are scarce. Common algorithm-agnostic approaches involve dimension reduction and subsequent visualization, which transforms the original features used to cluster the data; or training a supervised learning classifier on the found cluster labels, which adds additional and intractable complexity. We present FACT (feature attributions for clustering), an algorithm-agnostic framework that preserves the integrity of the data and does not introduce additional models. As the defining characteristic of FACT, we introduce a set of work stages: sampling, intervention, reassignment, and aggregation. Furthermore, we propose two novel FACT methods: SMART (scoring metric after permutation) measures changes in cluster assignments by custom scoring functions after permuting selected features; IDEA (isolated effect on assignment) indicates local and global changes in cluster assignments after making uniform changes to selected features.

Keywords: Interpretable clustering · explainable AI · feature attributions · algorithm-agnostic · effect · importance · FACT · SMART · IDEA

1 Introduction

Recent efforts have focused on making machine learning models interpretable, both via model-agnostic interpretation methods and novel interpretable model types [27], which is referred to as interpretable machine learning or explainable artificial intelligence in different contexts. Unfortunately, success in addressing cluster interpretability has been limited [3]. In the context of our paper, feature attributions (FAs) either provide information regarding the importance of features for assigning instances to clusters (overall and to specific clusters); or how isolated changes in feature values affect the assignment of single instances or

---

C. A. Scholbeck and H. Funk—Contributed equally.

© The Author(s) 2023
L. Longo (Ed.): xAI 2023, CCIS 1901, pp. 217–240, 2023.
https://doi.org/10.1007/978-3-031-44064-9_13

the entire data set to each cluster. Interpretable clustering algorithms [3,23,31] provide some insight into the constitution of clusters, e.g., relationships between features within clusters, but often fall short of providing FAs. Furthermore, the range of interpretable clustering algorithms is limited. An alternative approach is to post-process the original data (e.g., via principal components analysis) and visualize the found clusters in a lower-dimensional space [17]. This obfuscates interpretations by transforming the original features used to cluster the data. A third option is to train a supervised learning (SL) classifier on the found cluster labels, which is interpreted instead. This adds additional and intractable complexity on top of the clustering by introducing an additional model.

Contributions: We present FACT[1] (feature attributions for clustering), a framework that is compatible with any clustering algorithm able to reassign instances to clusters (algorithm-agnostic), preserves the integrity of the data, and does not introduce additional models. As the defining characteristic of FACT, we propose four work stages: sampling, intervention, reassignment, and aggregation. Furthermore, we introduce two novel FACT methods: SMART (scoring metric after permutation) measures changes in cluster assignments by custom scoring functions after permuting selected features; IDEA (isolated effect on assignment) indicates local and global changes in cluster assignments after making uniform changes to selected features. FACT is inspired by principles of model-agnostic interpretation methods in SL, which detach the interpretation method from the model, thereby detaching the interpretation method from the clustering algorithm. In Fig. 1, we summarize how SMART and IDEA utilize select ideas from SL and how they innovate with new principles.

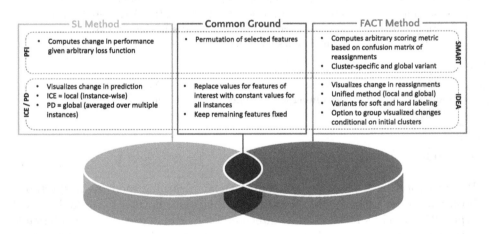

Fig. 1. Comparison of related concepts from SL (overlap in the center) with the clustering setting and novelties for FACT methods SMART and IDEA (right side).

---

[1] All presented methods are implemented in the R package **FACT** [13].

2 Notation and Preliminaries

2.1 Notation

We cluster a data set $\mathcal{D} = \{\mathbf{x}^{(i)}\}_{i=1}^{n}$ (where $\mathbf{x}^{(i)}$ denotes the i-th observation) into k clusters $\mathcal{D}^{(c)}$, $c \in \{1, \ldots, k\}$. A single observation $\mathbf{x}$ consists of p feature values $\mathbf{x} = (x_1, \ldots, x_p)$. A subset of features is denoted by $S \subseteq \{1, \ldots, p\}$ with the complement set being denoted by $-S = \{1, \ldots, p\} \setminus S$. With slight abuse of notation, an observation $\mathbf{x}$ can be partitioned into $\mathbf{x} = (\mathbf{x}_S, \mathbf{x}_{-S})$, regardless of the order of elements within $\mathbf{x}_S$ and $\mathbf{x}_{-S}$. A data set $\mathcal{D}$ where all features in S have been shuffled jointly is denoted by $\tilde{\mathcal{D}}_S$. The initial clustering is encoded within a function f that - conditional on whether the clustering algorithm outputs hard or soft labels[2] - maps each observation $\mathbf{x}$ to a cluster c (hard label) or to k soft labels:

$$\text{Hard labeling: } f : \mathbf{x} \mapsto c, \; c \in \{1, \ldots, k\}$$
$$\text{Soft labeling: } f : \mathbf{x} \mapsto \mathbb{R}^k$$

For soft clustering algorithms, $f^{(c)}(\mathbf{x})$ denotes the soft label for the c-th cluster. This notation is also used to indicate the cluster-specific value within an IDEA vector (see Sect. 3.2).

2.2 Interpretations of Supervised Learning Models

In recent years, the interpretation of model output has become a popular research topic [28]. Existing techniques provide explanations in terms of FAs (e.g., a value indicating a feature's importance to the model or a curve indicating its effects on the prediction), model internals (e.g., beta coefficients for linear regression models), data points (e.g., counterfactual explanations [39]), or surrogate models (i.e., interpretable approximations to the original model) [27]. Many model-agnostic methods are based on identical work stages: First, a subset of observations is sampled which we intend to use for the model interpretation (sampling stage). This is followed by an intervention in feature values where the instances from the sampling stage are manipulated in certain ways (intervention stage). Next, we predict with the trained model and this new, artificial data set (prediction stage). This produces local (observation-wise) interpretations which can be further aggregated to produce global or semi-global interpretations (aggregation stage) [35]. These work stages can be considered a sensitivity analysis (SA) of the model.

---

[2] A vector of soft labels represents the propensity of an observation being assigned to each cluster. A convenient representation corresponds to a vector of pseudo probabilities $[0, 1]^k$. We refrain from labeling any algorithm as a hard or soft clustering algorithm because often an algorithm can output both hard and soft labels, e.g., k-means - traditionally considered a hard clustering algorithm - could output soft labels in the form of Euclidean distances to each cluster centroid.

Established methods to determine FAs for SL models comprise the individual conditional expectation (ICE) [16], partial dependence (PD) [11], accumulated local effects (ALE) [2], local interpretable model-agnostic explanations (LIME) [33], Shapley values [26,37], or the permutation feature importance (PFI) [6, 9]. The functional analysis of variance (FANOVA) [18,34] and Sobol indices [36] of a high-dimensional model representation are powerful tools to quantify input influence on the model output in terms of variance but are limited by the requirement for independent inputs. Among the mentioned techniques, the following three are useful for the development of SMART and IDEA:

- **PFI:** Shuffling a feature in the data set destroys the information it contains. The PFI evaluates the model performance before and after shuffling and uses the change in performance to describe a feature's importance.
- **ICE:** The ICE function indicates the prediction of an SL model for a single observation x where a subset of values x_S is replaced with values $\tilde{x}_S$ while we condition on the remaining features x_{-S}, i.e., keep them fixed. For single features of interest, an ICE corresponds to a single curve.
- **PD:** The PD function indicates the expected prediction given the marginal effect of a set of features. The PD can be estimated through a point-wise aggregation of ICEs across all considered instances.

2.3   Interpretations for Clustering Algorithms

Unsupervised clustering has largely been ignored by this line of research. However, for high-dimensional data sets, the clustering routine can often be considered a black box, as we may not be able to assess and visualize the multidimensional cluster patterns found by the algorithm. It is, therefore, desirable to receive deeper explanations of how an algorithm's decisions can be attributed to the features. Interpretable clustering algorithms incorporate the interpretability criterion directly into the cluster search. One option is to find an interpretable tree-based clustering [5,10,12,14,15,24,25,30]. Interpretable clustering of numerical and categorical objects (INCONCO) [31] is an information-theoretic approach based on finding clusters that minimize minimum description length. It finds simple rule descriptions of the clusters by assuming a multivariate normal distribution and taking advantage of its mathematical properties. Interpretable clustering via optimal trees (ICOT) [3] uses decision trees to optimize a cluster quality measure. In [23] clusters are explained by forming polytopes around them. Mixed integer optimization is used to jointly find clusters and define polytopes.

The focus of this paper lies on algorithm-agnostic interpretations. In many cases, we wish to use a clustering algorithm that does not provide any explanations. Furthermore, even interpretable clustering algorithms often do not directly provide FAs, thus still requiring additional interpretation methods. Analogously to SL, we may define post-hoc interpretations (which are typically algorithm-agnostic) as ones that are obtained after the clustering procedure, e.g., by showing a subset of representative elements of a cluster or via visualization techniques such as scatter plots [22]. In most cases, the data is high-dimensional and requires the use of dimensionality reduction techniques such as principal component analysis (PCA) before being visualized in two or three dimensions. PCA creates linear combinations of the original features called the principal components (PCs). The goal is to select fewer PCs than original features while still explaining most of their variance. PCA obscures the information contained in the original features by rotating the system of coordinates. For instance, interpretable correlation clustering (ICC) [1] uses post-processing of correlation clusters. A correlation cluster groups the data such that there is a common within-cluster hyperplane of arbitrary dimensionality. ICC applies PCA to each correlation cluster's covariance matrix, thereby revealing linear patterns inside the cluster. One can also use an SL algorithm to post-process the clustering outcome which learns to find interpretable patterns between the found cluster labels and the features. Although we may use any SL algorithm, classification trees are a suitable choice due to naturally providing decision rules on how they arrive at a prediction [4]. Although this is a simple approach that can produce FAs via model internals or model-agnostic interpretation methods, it introduces intractable complexity through an additional model.

An algorithm-agnostic option that bypasses these issues is a form of SA where data are deliberately manipulated and reassigned to existing clusters. The global permutation percent change (G2PC) [8] indicates the percentage of change between the cluster assignments of the original data and those from a permuted data set. A high G2PC indicates an important feature for the clustering outcome. The local permutation percent change (L2PC) [8] uses the same principle for single instances.

3   FACT Framework and Methods

We first define a distinction of various FAs for the clustering setting: A *local FA* indicates how a feature contributes to the cluster assignment of a single observation; a *global FA* indicates how a feature contributes to the cluster assignments of an entire data set; a *cluster-specific FA* indicates how a feature contributes to the assignments of observations to one specific cluster. We introduce four work stages for FACT methods:

- **Sampling:** We sample a subset of observations that were previously clustered and shall be used to determine FAs. The larger this subset, the better our FA estimates. The smaller, the faster their computation.
- **Intervention:** Next, we manipulate feature values for the subset of observations from the sampling stage. This can be a targeted intervention (e.g., replacing current values with a pre-defined value) or shuffling values.
- **Reassignment:** This new, manipulated data set is reassigned to existing clusters through soft or hard labels. For each observation from the sampling stage, we receive a vector of soft labels or a single hard label.

- **Aggregation:** The soft or hard labels from the reassignment stage are aggregated in various ways, e.g., they can be averaged (soft labels) or counted (hard labels) cluster-wise.

The only prerequisite is an existing clustering based on an algorithm that can reassign instances to existing clusters through soft or hard labels. Methods only differ with respect to the intervention and aggregation stages. Next, we present our two novel FACT methods SMART and IDEA.

3.1 Scoring Metric After Permutation (SMART)

The intervention stage consists of shuffling values for a subset of features S in the data set $\mathcal{D}$ (i.e., jointly shuffling rows for a subset of columns); the aggregation stage consists of measuring the change in cluster assignments through an appropriate scoring function h applied to a confusion matrix consisting of original cluster assignments and cluster assignments after shuffling. When comparing original cluster assignments and the ones after shuffling the data, we can create a confusion matrix (see Appendix A) in the same way as in multi-class classification. One option to evaluate the confusion matrix is to directly use a scoring metric suitable for multiple clusters, e.g., the percentage of observations changing clusters after the intervention as in G2PC (found in all non-diagonal elements of the confusion matrix, see Eq. (1) for a definition). If one is interested in a scoring metric specifically developed for binary confusion matrices, the alternative is to consider binary comparisons of cluster c versus the remaining clusters. The results of all binary comparisons can then be aggregated either through a micro or a macro-averaged score (see Appendix B). Established scoring metrics based on binary confusion matrices include the F1 score (see Appendix B), Rand [32], or Jaccard [21] index. The micro-averaged score (hereafter referred to as micro score) is a suitable metric if all instances shall be considered equally important. The macro-averaged score (hereafter referred to as macro score) suits a setting where all classes (i.e., clusters in our case) shall be considered equally important. In general terms, the scoring function maps a confusion matrix to a scalar scoring metric. A multi-cluster scoring function is defined as:

$$h_{\text{multi}} : \mathbb{N}_0^{k \times k} \mapsto \mathbb{R}$$

A binary scoring function is defined as:

$$h_{\text{binary}} : \mathbb{N}_0^{2 \times 2} \mapsto \mathbb{R}$$

Let $M \in \mathbb{N}_0^{k \times k}$ denote the multi-cluster confusion matrix and $M_c \in \mathbb{N}_0^{2 \times 2}$ the binary confusion matrix for cluster c versus the remaining clusters (see Appendix A for details). SMART for feature set S corresponds to:

Multi-cluster scoring: $\text{SMART}(\mathcal{D}, \tilde{\mathcal{D}}_S) = h_{\text{multi}}(M)$

Binary scoring: $\text{SMART}(\mathcal{D}, \tilde{\mathcal{D}}_S) = \text{AVE}(h_{\text{binary}}(M_1), \ldots, h_{\text{binary}}(M_k))$

where AVE averages a vector of binary scores, e.g., via micro or macro averaging. In order to reduce variance in the estimate from shuffling the data, one can shuffle t times and evaluate the distribution of scores. Let $\tilde{\mathcal{D}}_S^{(t)}$ denote the t-th shuffling iteration for feature set S. The SMART point estimate is given by:

$$\overline{\mathrm{SMART}}(\mathcal{D}, \tilde{\mathcal{D}}_S) = \psi\left(\mathrm{SMART}(\mathcal{D}, \tilde{\mathcal{D}}_S^{(1)}), \ldots, \mathrm{SMART}(\mathcal{D}, \tilde{\mathcal{D}}_S^{(t)})\right)$$

where ψ extracts a sample statistic such as the mean or median.

We can demonstrate the equivalency between directly applying the G2PC scoring metric to the confusion matrix and micro averaging F1 scores[3]. Given a multi-cluster confusion matrix M (see Appendix A), G2PC is defined as:

$$\mathrm{G2PC}(M) = \frac{1}{n}\left(\sum_{i=1}^{k}\sum_{j=1}^{k} \#_{ij} - \sum_{l=1}^{k} \#_{ll}\right)$$

$$= \frac{1}{n}\left(n - \sum_{l=1}^{k} \#_{ll}\right)$$

$$= 1 - \frac{1}{n}\sum_{l=1}^{k} \#_{ll} \qquad (1)$$

The micro F1 score is equivalent to accuracy (for settings where each instance is assigned a single label), so the following relation holds (refer to Appendix D for a detailed proof):

Theorem 1 (Equivalency between SMART with micro F1 and G2PC).

$$1 - \mathrm{G2PC}(M) = \mathrm{AVE}_{\mathrm{MICRO}}(\mathrm{F1}(M_1), \ldots, \mathrm{F1}(M_k)) = \mathrm{F1}_{\mathrm{micro}}(M)$$

Proof sketch. In our utilization of confusion matrices, a "false classification" corresponds to a change in clusters after the intervention, and a "true classification" corresponds to an observation staying in the same cluster. It follows that accuracy (ACC) represents the global percentage of observations staying in the initial cluster after the intervention stage: $1 - \mathrm{ACC}(M) = \mathrm{G2PC}(M)$.

$\mathrm{AVE}_{\mathrm{MICRO}}(\mathrm{F1}(M_1), \ldots, \mathrm{F1}(M_k))$ can be directly derived from the multi-cluster matrix M and is denoted by $\mathrm{F1}_{\mathrm{micro}}(M)$. Let TP denote the number of true positive labels, FP the number of false positives, and FN the number of false negatives. For multi-class classification problems, FP = FN and thus:

$$\mathrm{F1}_{\mathrm{micro}}(M) = \frac{\mathrm{TP}}{\mathrm{TP} + \frac{1}{2}(\mathrm{FP} + \mathrm{FN})} = \frac{\mathrm{TP}}{\mathrm{TP} + \mathrm{FP}} = \mathrm{ACC}(M)$$

It follows that $1 - \mathrm{G2PC}(M) = \mathrm{F1}_{\mathrm{micro}}(M)$. $\square$

---

[3] Micro averaging refers to a strategy of aggregating binary comparisons where each instance is considered equally important. For the F1 score, the equivalency can be directly derived from the multi-cluster confusion matrix and involves summing up all diagonal elements (true positives) and remaining elements (false positives or false negatives). See Appendices B and D for details.

Micro F1 scores are unsuited for unbalanced classes in classification settings, as they treat each instance as equally important. From the direct dependency between G2PC and micro F1, it follows that for clusters that considerably differ in size (i.e., imbalanced clusters), G2PC does not accurately represent the importance of features, as it is dominated by larger clusters. SMART in turn allows more flexible interpretations than G2PC, e.g., by using macro F1 scores.

We can also directly evaluate binary comparisons of the found clusters to obtain cluster-specific FAs. Recall that a cluster-specific FA provides information regarding how a feature influences reassignments of instances to one specific cluster. Algorithms 1 and 2 describe the cluster-specific and global SMART algorithms, respectively. The algorithms are applied in Sects. 5 and 6. See Fig. 10 for visualized outcomes. Note that the resampling procedure to reduce the variance of estimates is optional and that global SMART can also involve binary comparisons (which requires running cluster-specific SMART), e.g., via macro averaging; we circumscribe all such different variants as the computation of the multi-cluster score h.

Algorithm 1. Cluster-Specific SMART

run clustering algorithm
for all iter $\in \{1, \ldots, t\}$ **do**
    shuffle columns S
    compute hard labels
    for all $c \in \{1, \ldots, k\}$ **do**
        create a binary confusion matrix
        compute score $h_c^{(\text{iter})}$ from confusion matrix
    end for
end for
for all $c \in \{1, \ldots, k\}$ **do**
    evaluate distribution of $\{h_c^{(\text{iter})}\}_{\text{iter}\in\{1,\ldots,t\}}$
end for

Algorithm 2. Global SMART

run clustering algorithm
for all iter $\in \{1, \ldots, t\}$ **do**
    shuffle columns S
    compute hard labels
    create a multi-cluster confusion matrix
    compute multi-cluster score $h^{(\text{iter})}$
end for
evaluate distribution of $\{h^{(\text{iter})}\}_{\text{iter}\in\{1,\ldots,t\}}$

3.2 Isolated Effect on Assignment (IDEA)

IDEA for soft labeling algorithms (sIDEA) indicates the soft label that an observation $\mathbf{x}$ with replaced values $\tilde{\mathbf{x}}_S$ is assigned to each c-th cluster. IDEA for hard labeling algorithms (hIDEA) indicates the cluster assignment of an observation $\mathbf{x}$ with replaced values $\tilde{\mathbf{x}}_S$. Both are described by the clustering (assignment) function f:

$$\text{IDEA}_{\mathbf{x}}(\tilde{\mathbf{x}}_S) = \text{sIDEA}_{\mathbf{x}}(\tilde{\mathbf{x}}_S) = \text{hIDEA}_{\mathbf{x}}(\tilde{\mathbf{x}}_S) = f(\tilde{\mathbf{x}}_S, \mathbf{x}_{-S})$$

sIDEA corresponds to a k-way vector:

$$\text{sIDEA}_{\mathbf{x}}(\tilde{\mathbf{x}}_S) = \left(f^{(1)}(\tilde{\mathbf{x}}_S, \mathbf{x}_{-S}), \ldots, f^{(k)}(\tilde{\mathbf{x}}_S, \mathbf{x}_{-S}) \right)$$
$$= \left(\text{sIDEA}_{\mathbf{x}}^{(1)}(\tilde{\mathbf{x}}_S), \ldots, \text{sIDEA}_{\mathbf{x}}^{(k)}(\tilde{\mathbf{x}}_S) \right)$$

Note that although IDEA is a local method, we typically compute it for a subset of observations selected in the sampling stage. The intervention stage consists of replacing $\mathbf{x}_S$ (for an observation $\mathbf{x}$) by $\tilde{\mathbf{x}}_S$. Algorithm 3 describes the computation of the local IDEA.

Algorithm 3. Local IDEA

---

run clustering algorithm
sample m vectors of feature values $\{\tilde{\mathbf{x}}_S^{(j)}\}_{j \in \{1,\ldots,m\}}$
for all $i \in \{1,\ldots,n\}$ **do**
    for all $j \in \{1,\ldots,m\}$ **do**
        generate hypothetical observation $\mathbf{x} = (\tilde{\mathbf{x}}_S^{(j)}, \mathbf{x}_{-S}^{(i)})$
        $\text{IDEA}_{\mathbf{x}^{(i)}}(\tilde{\mathbf{x}}_S^{(j)}) = f(\mathbf{x})$
    end for
end for

During the aggregation stage, we aggregate local IDEAs to a global function. For soft labeling algorithms, we can compute a point-wise average of soft labels for each cluster; for hard labeling algorithms, we can compute the fraction of hard labels for each cluster. The global IDEA is denoted by the corresponding data set $\mathcal{D}$. The global sIDEA corresponds to:

$$\text{sIDEA}_{\mathcal{D}}(\tilde{\mathbf{x}}_S) = \left(\frac{1}{n} \sum_{i=1}^{n} \text{sIDEA}_{\mathbf{x}^{(i)}}^{(1)}(\tilde{\mathbf{x}}_S), \ldots, \frac{1}{n} \sum_{i=1}^{n} \text{sIDEA}_{\mathbf{x}^{(i)}}^{(k)}(\tilde{\mathbf{x}}_S) \right) \quad (2)$$

where the c-th vector element is the average c-th element of local sIDEA vectors. The global hIDEA corresponds to:

$$\text{hIDEA}_{\mathcal{D}}(\tilde{\mathbf{x}}_S) = \left(\frac{1}{n} \sum_{i=1}^{n} \mathbb{1}_1(\text{hIDEA}_{\mathbf{x}^{(i)}}(\tilde{\mathbf{x}}_S)), \ldots, \frac{1}{n} \sum_{i=1}^{n} \mathbb{1}_k(\text{hIDEA}_{\mathbf{x}^{(i)}}(\tilde{\mathbf{x}}_S)) \right)$$
$$(3)$$

where the c-th vector element is the fraction of hard label reassignments to the c-th cluster. Algorithm 4 describes the computation of the global IDEA. See Sects. 5 and 6 for applications of the local and global IDEA and Figs. 6, 7, and 11 for visualizations.

A useful interpretation for hard labeling algorithms can be obtained by visualizing the percentage of all labels per isolated intervention. The fraction of the most frequent hard label indicates the – as we call it – "certainty" of the global IDEA function for hard labeling algorithms (see Fig. 6 on the left).

Whether the global IDEA can serve as a good description of the feature effect on the reassignment depends on the heterogeneity of underlying local effects. If substituting a feature set by the same values for all instances results in similar reassignments for most instances, the global IDEA is a good interpretation instrument. Otherwise, further investigations into the underlying local effects are required.

Algorithm 4. Global IDEA

---
run clustering algorithm
sample m vectors of feature values $\{\tilde{\mathbf{x}}_S^{(j)}\}_{j \in \{1,\dots,m\}}$
for all $i \in \{1,\dots,n\}$ **do**
    compute $\text{IDEA}_{\mathbf{x}^{(i)}}$ (see Algorithm 3)
end for
for $j \in \{1,\dots,m\}$ **do**
    for $c \in \{1,\dots,k\}$ **do**
        if soft labeling algorithm **then**
            compute $\text{sIDEA}_{\mathcal{D}}^{(c)}(\tilde{\mathbf{x}}_S^{(j)})$ (see Eq. 2)
        else
            compute $\text{hIDEA}_{\mathcal{D}}^{(c)}(\tilde{\mathbf{x}}_S^{(j)})$ (see Eq. 3)
        end if
    end for
end for

Initial Cluster Effect on IDEA: If there is a certain within-cluster homogeneity, we ought to see similar shapes of local IDEA functions depending on the observations' initial cluster (before the intervention stage). Let c_{init} denote the initial cluster index. We receive one aggregate IDEA per initial cluster (we refrain from using the word "global" here, as there is a separate, global IDEA independent from the initial cluster), which reflects the aggregate, isolated effect of an intervention in the feature(s) of interest on the assignment to cluster c **per initial cluster** c_{init}:

$$\text{IDEA}_{\mathcal{D}^{(c_{\text{init}})}}(\tilde{\mathbf{x}}_S) = \left(\text{IDEA}_{\mathcal{D}^{(c_{\text{init}})}}^{(1)}(\tilde{\mathbf{x}}_S), \dots, \text{IDEA}_{\mathcal{D}^{(c_{\text{init}})}}^{(k)}(\tilde{\mathbf{x}}_S) \right) \tag{4}$$

whose components correspond to (depending on the clustering algorithm output):

$$\text{sIDEA}_{\mathcal{D}^{(c_{\text{init}})}}^{(c)}(\tilde{\mathbf{x}}_S) = \frac{1}{n^{(c_{\text{init}})}} \sum_{i \,:\, \mathbf{x}^{(i)} \in \mathcal{D}^{(c_{\text{init}})}} \text{sIDEA}_{\mathbf{x}^{(i)}}^{(c)}(\tilde{\mathbf{x}}_S)$$

$$\text{hIDEA}_{\mathcal{D}^{(c_{\text{init}})}}^{(c)}(\tilde{\mathbf{x}}_S) = \frac{1}{n^{(c_{\text{init}})}} \sum_{i \,:\, \mathbf{x}^{(i)} \in \mathcal{D}^{(c_{\text{init}})}} \mathbb{1}_c(\text{hIDEA}_{\mathbf{x}^{(i)}}(\tilde{\mathbf{x}}_S))$$

where $n^{(c_{\text{init}})}$ corresponds to the number of observations within initial cluster c_{init}. This definition lends itself to a convenient visualization per initial cluster, which we showcase in Fig. 7.

4   Additional Notes on FACT

How to Generate Feature Values for Interventions: A simple option is to use a feature's sample distribution, i.e., all observed values. In classical SA of model output [34], one typically intends to explore the feature space as thoroughly as possible (space-filling designs). In SL, there are valid arguments against space-filling designs due to potential model extrapolations, i.e., predictions in areas where the model was not trained with enough data [19,29]. In clustering, the absence of model performance issues allows us to fill the feature space as extensively as possible, e.g., with unit distributions, random, or quasi-random (also referred to as low-discrepancy) sequences (e.g., Sobol sequences) [34]. In fact, assigning unseen data to the clusters serves our purpose of visualizing the decision boundaries between the clusters determined by the clustering algorithm.

Generating Feature Values for SMART and IDEA: For SMART, we evaluate a fixed data set and jointly shuffle values of the feature set S. For IDEA, we can either use observed values or strive for a more space-filling design. More values result in better FAs but higher computational costs.

Reassigning versus Reclustering: FACT aims to explain a given clustering of the data. The found clustering outcome is treated as "a snapshot in time", similarly to how explanations in SL are conditional on a trained model. FACT methods are therefore akin to model-agnostic interpretation methods in SL. It follows that we need a reassignment of instances to pre-found clusters instead of a reclustering (running the clustering algorithm from the ground up). Reclustering artificial data would result in a "concept drift" and different clusters, thus being counterproductive to our goals.

In Fig. 2 (left), we create an artificial data set using the Cartesian product of the original bivariate data that forms 3 clusters and reassign the artificially created observations to the found clusters of a cluster model fitted on the original bivariate data (grid lines). The right plot visualizes a reclustering of the same artificial data set, resulting in clearly visible changes in the shape and position of the clusters.

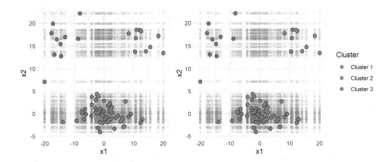

Fig. 2. Observations (solid points) and Cartesian product (transparent grid) reassigned (left plot) and reclustered (right plot).

How the FACT Framework is Algorithm-Agnostic: How to reassign instances differs across clustering algorithms. For instance, in k-means we assign an instance to the cluster with the lowest Euclidean distance; in probabilistic clustering such as Gaussian mixture models we select the cluster associated with the largest probability; in hierarchical clustering, we select the cluster with the lowest linkage value, etc. [8]. In other words, although the implementation of the reassignment stage differs across algorithms (the computation of soft or hard labels), FACT methods stay exactly the same. For FACT to be truly algorithm-agnostic, we develop variants to accommodate both soft and hard labeling algorithms.

Limitations: FACT is not suited for evaluating the quality of the clustering, i.e., whether clusters have a high within-cluster homogeneity and high between-cluster heterogeneity. Furthermore, we need an appropriate assignment function that assigns instances to existing clusters and which may frequently not be available. Particularly IDEA is limited by computational constraints for large data sets. Hence, we introduce a sampling stage for FACT, where only a subset of clustered observations can be selected to estimate FAs.

5   Simulations

5.1   Flexibility of SMART - Micro F1 versus Macro F1

In this simulation, we illustrate that the micro F1 score and therefore also the G2PC proposed in [8] is not useful for imbalanced cluster sizes. We also demonstrate the advantages of our more flexible SMART approach, which allows us to use the macro F1 score instead, a scoring metric better suited for imbalanced cluster sizes. We simulate a data set with two features consisting of 4 differently sized classes (see Fig. 3), where each class follows a different bivariate normal distribution. 60 instances are sampled from class 3 while 20 instances are sampled from each of the remaining classes. To capture the latent class variable, c-means is initialized at the 4 centers. The right plot in Fig. 3 displays the perfect cluster

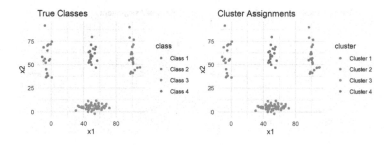

Fig. 3. Visualization of the data and the perfect clustering of c-means.

assignments found by c-means. We can see that x_1 is the defining feature of the clustering for 3 out of 4 clusters, i.e., for the clusters enumerated by 1, 2, and 4. Our goal is to analyze the c-means clustering model to discover which of the two features were more important for the clustering outcome.

We now compare the macro F1 score and micro F1 score (see Appendix B) for x_1 and x_2. Both features have micro F1 median scores of 0.58, suggesting equal importance for x_1 and x_2. Recall that the micro F1 score corresponds to 1 - G2PC (see Theorem 1). This implies that G2PC is unable to identify a meaningful feature importance ranking for x_1 and x_2 in this case. Macro F1 on the other hand is different for both features ($x_1 = 0.43, x_2 = 0.64$), indicating that x_1 is more important. Note that the F1 score is a similarity index. A low F1 score indicates a high feature importance, i.e., a high dissimilarity between the clustering outcome based on the original data and the clustering outcome after the feature of interest has been shuffled. These results stem from the fact that micro F1 accounts for each instance with equal importance (by globally counting true and false positives, see Appendix B). Cluster 3 is over-represented with three times as many instances as the remaining clusters. The macro F1 score accurately captures this by treating each cluster as equally important, regardless of its size.

5.2 Global versus Cluster-Specific SMART

Next, we demonstrate that even when using the macro F1 score for imbalanced clusters, the results may obfuscate the importance of features to specific clusters, which is where cluster-specific SMART becomes the method of choice. We simulate three visibly distinctive classes (left plot in Fig. 4) where each class follows a bivariate normal distribution with different mean and covariance matrices. 50 instances are sampled from class 2, and 20 instances are sampled from class 1 and class 3 each. We initialize c-means at the 3 mean values. As shown in Fig. 4, the cluster assignments capture all three classes almost perfectly, except for one instance of class 2 being assigned to cluster 1 and one to cluster 3.

We compare the global macro F1 (which weights the importance of clusters equally) to the cluster-specific F1 score. With a global macro F1 median of 0.62 for x_1 and 0.66 for x_2, there is no difference between the importance of both

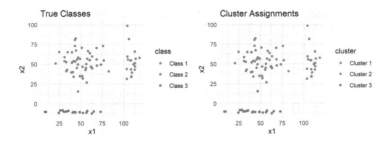

Fig. 4. Three classes with different distributions clustered by c-means. True classes (left) and clusters (right) almost perfectly match.

features for the overall clustering. In contrast, cluster-specific SMART offers a more detailed view of the contributions of each feature to the clustering outcome. Both features, x_1 and x_2, have an equal regional feature importance of 0.73 in forming cluster 2. For cluster 3, feature x_2 is considerably more important with a macro F1 score of 0.26, compared to 0.86 for feature x_1. Vice versa, feature x_1 is the defining feature of cluster 1 with a score of 0.24. In comparison, the importance of x_2 for cluster 1 is 1.0, implying that the permutation of feature x_2 had no effect on the assignment criteria for cluster 1.

5.3   How to Interpret IDEA

Here, we demonstrate how IDEA can visualize isolated, univariate effects of features on the cluster assignments of multi-dimensional data; how the heterogeneity of local effects influences the explanatory power of the global IDEA; and how grouping IDEA curves by initial cluster assignments reveals similar effects. We draw 50 instances from three multivariate normally distributed classes. To make them differentiable for the clustering algorithm, the classes are generated with an antagonistic mean structure. The covariance matrix of the three classes is sampled using a Wishart distribution (see Appendix C for details). The left plot in Fig. 5 depicts the three-dimensional distribution of the classes. We intend class 3 to be dense and classes 1 and 2 to be less dense but large in hypervolume. We initialize c-means at the 3 centers and optimize via the Euclidean distance. Figure 5 visualizes the perfect clustering. Figure 6 (left) displays an hIDEA plot for x_1 (see Sect. 3.2), indicating the majority vote of cluster assignments when exchanging values of x_1 by the horizontal axis value for all observations.

The curves in Fig. 6 (right) represent the cluster-specific components of the sIDEA function (local and global). Note that this refers to the effect of observations being reassigned to the c-th cluster and not the initial cluster effect, which we demonstrate below. The bandwidths represent the local IDEA curve ranges that were averaged to receive the respective global IDEA. We can see that - on average - x_1 has a substantial effect on the clustering outcome. The lower the value of x_1 that is plugged into an observation, the more likely it is assigned to cluster 1, while for larger values of x_1 it is more likely to be assigned to cluster

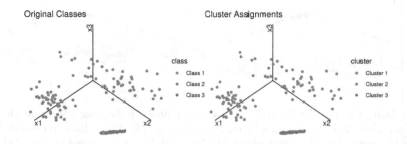

Fig. 5. Sampled classes (left plot) versus clusters (right plot).

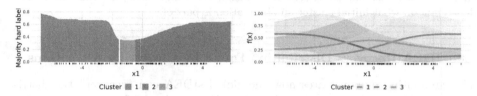

Fig. 6. Left: A plot indicating "certainty" of the global hIDEA function. On average, replacing x_1 by the axis value results in an observation being assigned to the color-indicated cluster. The vertical distance indicates how many observations are assigned to the majority cluster. **Right:** Cluster-specific global sIDEA curves. Each curve indicates the average soft label of observation being assigned to the c-th cluster if its x_1 value is replaced by the axis value. The bandwidths visualize the distribution of local sIDEA curves that were vertically averaged to the respective global, cluster-specific sIDEA.

2. For $x_1 \approx 0$, observations are more likely to be assigned to cluster 3. The large bandwidths indicate that the clusters are spread out, and plugging in different values of x_1 into an observation has widely different effects across the data set. Particularly around $x_1 \approx 0$, where cluster 3 dominates, the average effect loses its meaning due to the underlying local IDEA curves being highly heterogeneous. In this case, one should be wary of the interpretative value of the global IDEA. We proceed to investigate the heterogeneity of the local sIDEA curves for cluster 3 (see Fig. 7 on the left). The flat shape of the cluster-specific global sIDEA indicates that x_1 has a rather low effect on observations being assigned to cluster 3. However, the cluster-specific local sIDEA curves reveal that individual effects cancel each other out when being averaged.

Initial Cluster Effect: It seems likely that observations belonging to a single cluster in the initial clustering run would behave similarly once their feature values are changed. We color each sIDEA curve by the original cluster assignment (see Fig. 7 on the right) and add the corresponding aggregate curves. Our assumption - that observations within a cluster behave similarly once we make isolated changes to their feature values - is confirmed. The formal definition of this initial cluster effect is given by Eq. (4).

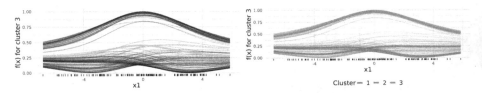

Fig. 7. Left: Cluster-specific IDEA (local and global), indicating effects on the soft labels for observations to be assigned to cluster 3. The black lines represent local effects; the yellow line the global effect. **Right:** sIDEA curves colored by initial cluster assignment. The thin curves represent local effects; the thick curves represent aggregate effects. We can see similar effects of replacing the values of x_1 on the soft labels, depending on what initial cluster an observation is part of.

5.4 IDEA Recovers Distribution Found by Clustering Algorithms

This simulation demonstrates how the global sIDEA can "recover" the distributions found by the clustering algorithm. We simulate 4 features and cluster the data into 3 clusters with FuzzyDBSCAN [20]. We illustrate soft labels for assignments to a single cluster in Fig. 8. The upper triangular plots display true bivariate marginal densities of features. The lower triangular plots display the corresponding bivariate global sIDEA estimates. Matching pairs of densities and sIDEA estimates "mirror" each other on the diagonal line. The diagonal plots visualize univariate marginal distributions (grey area) versus the corresponding estimated univariate global sIDEA curve (black line). The location and shape of sIDEA plots approximate the true marginal distributions. Note that for the correlated pairs (x_1, x_2) and (x_3, x_4), we recover the direction of the correlation.

6 Real Data Application

The Wisconsin diagnostic breast cancer (WDBC) data set [7] consists of 569 instances of cell nuclei obtained from breast mass. Each instance consists of 10 characteristics derived from a digitized image of a fine-needle aspirate. For each characteristic, the mean, standard error and "worst" or largest value (mean of the three largest values) is recorded, resulting in 30 features of the data set. Each nucleus is classified as malignant (cancer, class 1) or benign (class 2). We cluster the data using Euclidean optimized c-means. Figure 9 visualizes the projection of the data onto the first two PCs. The clusters cannot be separated with two PCs, and the visualization is of little help in understanding the influence of the original features on the clustering outcome.

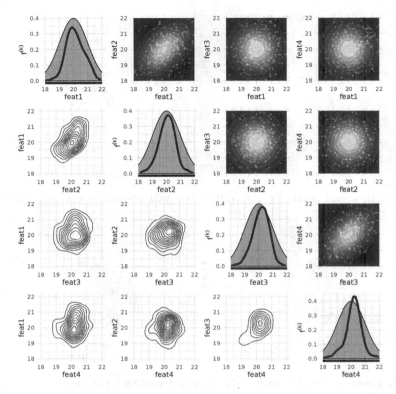

Fig. 8. Comparison of true bivariate marginal densities of features (upper triangular plots) with corresponding global bivariate sIDEA (lower triangular plots) and true univariate marginal densities of features (diagonal plots, grey area) with corresponding global univariate sIDEA (diagonal plots, black line). (Color figure online)

6.1   Aggregate FA for Each Cluster (SMART)

We first showcase how SMART can serve as an approximation of the actual reclustering. Measured on the latent target variable, the initial clustering run has an F1 score of 0.88. We then recluster the data, once with the 4 most important and once with the 4 least important features. Dropping the 26 least important features only reduces the F1 score by 0.03 to 0.85 (measured using the latent target). In contrast, using the 4 least important features reduces the F1 score by 0.55 to 0.33 and thus alters the clustering in a major way. This demonstrates that assigning new instances to existing clusters can serve as an efficient method for feature selection. To showcase the grouped feature importance, we jointly shuffle features and compare their importance in Fig. 10. Note that we use the natural logarithm of SMART here for better visual separability and to receive a natural ordering of the feature importance (due to F1 being a similarity index), where a larger bar indicates a higher importance and vice versa.

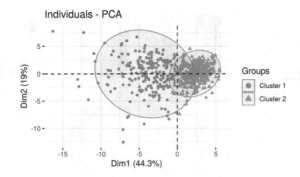

Fig. 9. First and second PCs of WDBC data with clusters of real target values.

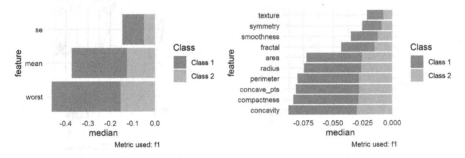

Fig. 10. Grouped SMART (using the natural logarithm) per cluster for groups of categories (left plot) and groups of characteristics (right plot) in the WDBC data set.

6.2 Visualizing Marginal Feature Effects (IDEA)

We now visualize isolated univariate and bivariate effects of features on assignments. Figure 11 plots the global IDEA curve for three features `concavity_worst`, `compactness_worst`, and `concave_points_worst`. The transparent areas indicate the regions where the local curve mass is located. A rug on the horizontal axis shows the distribution of the corresponding feature. For all three features, larger values result in observations being assigned to cluster 1, while lower values result in observations being assigned to cluster 2. The distribution of cluster-specific local IDEA curves is wide, reflecting voluminous clusters. All features have a strong univariate effect on the cluster assignments, which indicates a large importance of each feature to the constitution of each cluster.

Figure 11 (right) plots the two-dimensional sIDEA for `compactness_worst` and `compactness_mean`. The color indicates what cluster the observations are assigned to on average when `compactness_worst` and `compactness_mean` are replaced by the axis values. The transparency indicates the magnitude of the soft label, i.e., the "certainty" in our estimate. On average, the observations are assigned to cluster 2 when adjusting both features to lower values and to cluster 1 when adjusting both features to higher values.

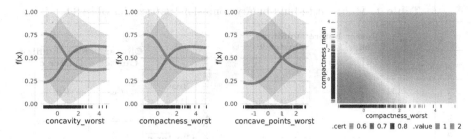

Fig. 11. Left: Univariate global sIDEA plots for the features `concavity_worst`, `compactness_worst`, and `concave_points_worst`. **Right:** Two-dimensional sIDEA for the features `compactness_worst` and `compactness_mean`. On average, an observation is assigned to cluster 1 for large values of both features, while it is assigned to cluster 2 for low values of both features.

7   Conclusion

This research paper proposes FACT, a framework to produce FAs which is compatible with any clustering algorithm able to reassign instances through soft or hard labels, preserves the integrity of the data, and does not introduce additional models. FACT techniques provide information regarding the importance of features for assigning instances to clusters (overall and to specific clusters); or how isolated changes in feature values affect the assignment of single instances or the entire data set to each cluster. We introduce two novel FACT methods: SMART and IDEA. SMART is a general framework that outputs a single global value for each feature indicating its importance to cluster assignments or one value for each cluster (and feature). IDEA adds to these capabilities by visualizing the structure of the feature influence on cluster assignments across the feature space for single observations and the entire data set.

Although explaining algorithmic decisions is an active research topic in SL, it is largely ignored for clustering algorithms. The FACT framework provides a new impetus for algorithm-agnostic interpretations in clustering. With SMART and IDEA, we hope to establish a foundation for the future development of FACT methods and spark more research in this direction.

A   Confusion Matrix for SMART

Transferring the concept of confusion matrices from classification tasks, a "true" classification would correspond to an observation staying within the same cluster after the intervention, and a "false" classification would result in a reassignment to a different cluster.

For the multi-cluster matrix on the left, let TP denote the sum of all true positives from all binary comparisons of cluster c versus the remaining clusters, FP the sum of all false positives, and FN the sum of all false negatives. It follows that $\sum_{l=1}^{k} \#_{ll} = \text{TP}$ and $n - \sum_{l=1}^{k} \#_{ll} = \text{FP} = \text{FN}$.

Table 1. Multi-cluster and binary confusion matrices for SMART.

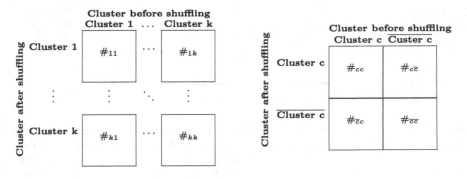

For the binary matrix on the right, let TP_c denote all true positives of cluster c versus the remaining clusters, FP_c all false positives, FN_c all false negatives, and TN_c all true negatives. It follows that $\#_{cc} = TP_c$, $\#_{c\bar{c}} = FP_c$, $\#_{\bar{c}c} = FN_c$, and $\#_{\bar{c}\bar{c}} = TN_c$.

B   Scores

F_β score: Balances false positives and false negatives. The F_β score of cluster c versus the remaining ones corresponds to:

$$F_{\beta,c} = \frac{(\beta^2 + 1) \cdot P_c \cdot R_c}{\beta^2 \cdot P_c + R_c}, \quad \text{where} \quad P_c = \frac{\#_{cc}}{\#_{cc} + \#_{\bar{c}c}} \quad \text{and} \quad R_c = \frac{\#_{cc}}{\#_{cc} + \#_{c\bar{c}}}$$

The F_1 (which we refer to as F1) score simplifies to:

$$F_{1,c} = 2\frac{P_c \cdot R_c}{P_c + R_c}$$

Given a multi-cluster confusion matrix M, let ϕ_c be an arbitrary binary scoring function dependent on TP, FP, FN, and TN. $\mathcal{S}_{\text{macro}}$ denotes the multi-cluster macro score that treats each cluster with equal importance. $\mathcal{S}_{\text{micro}}$ denotes the multi-cluster micro score that treats each instance with equal importance:

$$\mathcal{S}_{\text{macro}}(M) = \frac{1}{k}\sum_{c=1}^{k} \phi\left(TP_c, FP_c, FN_c, TN_c\right)$$

$$\mathcal{S}_{\text{micro}}(M) = \phi\left(\sum_{c=1}^{k} TP_c, \sum_{c=1}^{k} FP_c, \sum_{c=1}^{k} FN_c, \sum_{c=1}^{k} TN_c\right)$$

C   Wishart Distribution

We sample the covariance matrix M from the Wishart distribution with $M \sim$ Wishart$_3(3, \Sigma)$. Σ is constructed using $\Sigma_{\text{Class 1}} = 0.6I_3$, $\Sigma_{\text{Class 2}} = 0.3I_3$, and

$\Sigma_{\text{Class 3}} = 0.15I_3$, where I_3 refers to the 3×3 identity matrix. As a result, the variance of class 1 is the largest, the variance of class 3 is the lowest, and the variance of class 2 lies between the variances of classes 1 and 3.

D   Proofs

Proof (Theorem 1).
Recall the definition of G2PC with respect to a multi-cluster confusion matrix M (see Table 1 in Appendix A):

$$\text{G2PC}(M) = \frac{1}{n} \left(\sum_{i=1}^{k} \sum_{j=1}^{k} \#_{ij} - \sum_{l=1}^{k} \#_{ll} \right) = \frac{1}{n} \left(n - \sum_{l=1}^{k} \#_{ll} \right) = 1 - \frac{1}{n} \sum_{l=1}^{k} \#_{ll}$$

Let TP denote the number of true positive labels, FP the number of false positives, and FN the number of false negatives. The sum of diagonal elements corresponds to TP:

$$\sum_{l=1}^{k} \#_{ll} = \text{TP}$$

It follows that:

$$\text{G2PC}(M) = 1 - \frac{\text{TP}}{n}$$

TP divided by the absolute number of instances equals the percentage of "correctly classified instances" (the number of instances staying within the same cluster after the intervention in our case) which corresponds to accuracy (ACC):

$$\frac{1}{n} \sum_{l=1}^{k} \#_{ll} = \frac{\text{TP}}{n} = \text{ACC}(M)$$

It follows that:

$$\text{G2PC}(M) = 1 - \text{ACC}(M) \Leftrightarrow 1 - \text{G2PC}(M) = \text{ACC}(M) \tag{5}$$

The following relation holds by definition for the micro F1 score [38]:

$$\text{F1}_{\text{micro}}(M) = \frac{\text{TP}}{\text{TP} + \frac{1}{2}(\text{FP} + \text{FN})}$$

For multi-class classification it holds that FP = FN, as every false positive for one class is a false negative for another class. With $n = \text{TP} + \text{FP}$, it follows that:

$$\text{F1}_{\text{micro}}(M) = \frac{\text{TP}}{\text{TP} + \text{FP}} = \frac{\text{TP}}{n} = \text{ACC}(M) \tag{6}$$

From Eqs. (5) and (6), we have:

$$1 - \text{G2PC}(M) = \text{F1}_{\text{micro}}(M)$$

$\square$

References

1. Achtert, E., Böhm, C., Kriegel, H.P., Kröger, P., Zimek, A.: Deriving quantitative models for correlation clusters. In: Proceedings of the 12th ACM SIGKDD International Conference on Knowledge Discovery and Data Mining, KDD 2006, pp. 4–13. Association for Computing Machinery, New York, NY, USA (2006)
2. Apley, D.W., Zhu, J.: Visualizing the effects of predictor variables in black box supervised learning models. J. R. Stat. Soc. Ser. B **82**(4), 1059–1086 (2020)
3. Bertsimas, D., Orfanoudaki, A., Wiberg, H.: Interpretable clustering via optimal trees. ArXiv e-prints (2018). arXiv:1812.00539
4. Bertsimas, D., Orfanoudaki, A., Wiberg, H.: Interpretable clustering: an optimization approach. Mach. Learn. **110**(1), 89–138 (2021)
5. Blockeel, H., Raedt, L.D., Ramon, J.: Top-down induction of clustering trees. In: Proceedings of the Fifteenth International Conference on Machine Learning, ICML 1998, pp. 55–63. Morgan Kaufmann Publishers Inc., San Francisco, CA, USA (1998)
6. Breiman, L.: Random forests. Mach. Learn. **45**(1), 5–32 (2001)
7. Dua, D., Graff, C.: UCI machine learning repository (2019). http://archive.ics.uci.edu/ml
8. Ellis, C.A., Sendi, M.S.E., Geenjaar, E.P.T., Plis, S.M., Miller, R.L., Calhoun, V.D.: Algorithm-agnostic explainability for unsupervised clustering. ArXiv e-prints (2021). arXiv:2105.08053
9. Fisher, A., Rudin, C., Dominici, F.: All models are wrong, but many are useful: learning a variable's importance by studying an entire class of prediction models simultaneously. J. Mach. Learn. Res. **20**(177), 1–81 (2019)
10. Fraiman, R., Ghattas, B., Svarc, M.: Interpretable clustering using unsupervised binary trees. Adv. Data Anal. Classif. **7**(2), 125–145 (2013)
11. Friedman, J.H.: Greedy function approximation: a gradient boosting machine. Ann. Stat. **29**(5), 1189–1232 (2001)
12. Frost, N., Moshkovitz, M., Rashtchian, C.: ExKMC: Expanding explainable k-means clustering. ArXiv e-prints (2020). arXiv:2006.02399
13. Funk, H., Scholbeck, C.A., Casalicchio, G.: FACT: Feature Attributions for Clustering (2023). https://CRAN.R-project.org/package=FACT. R package version 0.1.0
14. Gabidolla, M., Carreira-Perpiñán, M.A.: Optimal interpretable clustering using oblique decision trees. In: Proceedings of the 28th ACM SIGKDD Conference on Knowledge Discovery and Data Mining, KDD 2022. pp. 400–410. Association for Computing Machinery, New York, NY, USA (2022)
15. Ghattas, B., Michel, P., Boyer, L.: Clustering nominal data using unsupervised binary decision trees: comparisons with the state of the art methods. Pattern Recognit. **67**, 177–185 (2017)
16. Goldstein, A., Kapelner, A., Bleich, J., Pitkin, E.: Peeking inside the black box: visualizing statistical learning with plots of individual conditional expectation. J. Comput. Graph. Stat. **24**(1), 44–65 (2015)
17. Hinneburg, A.: Visualizing clustering results. In: Liu, L., Özsu, M.T. (eds.) Encyclopedia of Database Systems, pp. 3417–3425. Springer, Boston (2009). https://doi.org/10.1007/978-0-387-39940-9_617
18. Hooker, G.: Generalized functional anova diagnostics for high-dimensional functions of dependent variables. J. Comput. Graph. Stat. **16**(3), 709–732 (2007)

19. Hooker, G., Mentch, L., Zhou, S.: Unrestricted permutation forces extrapolation: variable importance requires at least one more model, or there is no free variable importance. Stat. Comput. **31**(6), 82 (2021)
20. Ienco, D., Bordogna, G.: Fuzzy extensions of the DBScan clustering algorithm. Soft. Comput. **22**(5), 1719–1730 (2018)
21. Jaccard, P.: The distribution of the flora in the alpine zone. New Phytol. **11**(2), 37–50 (1912)
22. Kinkeldey, C., Korjakow, T., Benjamin, J.J.: Towards supporting interpretability of clustering results with uncertainty visualization. In: EuroVis Workshop on Trustworthy Visualization (TrustVis) (2019)
23. Lawless, C., Kalagnanam, J., Nguyen, L.M., Phan, D., Reddy, C.: Interpretable clustering via multi-polytope machines. ArXiv e-prints (2021). arXiv:2112.05653
24. Liu, B., Xia, Y., Yu, P.S.: Clustering through decision tree construction. In: Proceedings of the Ninth International Conference on Information and Knowledge Management, CIKM, pp. 20–29. Association for Computing Machinery, New York, NY, USA (2000)
25. Loyola-González, O., et al.: An explainable artificial intelligence model for clustering numerical databases. IEEE Access **8**, 52370–52384 (2020)
26. Lundberg, S.M., Lee, S.I.: A unified approach to interpreting model predictions. In: Proceedings of the 31st International Conference on Neural Information Processing Systems, NIPS 2017, pp. 4768–4777. Curran Associates Inc., Red Hook, NY, USA (2017)
27. Molnar, C.: Interpretable Machine Learning (2019). https://christophm.github.io/interpretable-ml-book/
28. Molnar, C., Casalicchio, G., Bischl, B.: Interpretable machine learning - a brief history, state-of-the-art and challenges. In: Koprinska, I., et al. (eds.) ECML PKDD 2020 Workshops, pp. 417–431. Springer International Publishing, Cham (2020). https://doi.org/10.1007/978-3-030-65965-3_28
29. Molnar, C., et al.: General pitfalls of model-agnostic interpretation methods for machine learning models. In: Holzinger, A., Goebel, R., Fong, R., Moon, T., Müller, K.R., Samek, W. (eds.) xxAI 2020. LNCS, vol. 13200, pp. 39–68. Springer, Cham (2022). https://doi.org/10.1007/978-3-031-04083-2_4
30. Moshkovitz, M., Dasgupta, S., Rashtchian, C., Frost, N.: Explainable k-means and k-medians clustering. In: III, H.D., Singh, A. (eds.) Proceedings of the 37th International Conference on Machine Learning. Proceedings of Machine Learning Research, vol. 119, pp. 7055–7065. PMLR (2020)
31. Plant, C., Böhm, C.: INCONCO: interpretable clustering of numerical and categorical objects. In: Proceedings of the 17th ACM SIGKDD International Conference on Knowledge Discovery and Data Mining, KDD 2011, pp. 1127–1135. Association for Computing Machinery, New York, NY, USA (2011)
32. Rand, W.M.: Objective criteria for the evaluation of clustering methods. J. Am. Stat. Assoc. **66**(336), 846–850 (1971)
33. Ribeiro, M.T., Singh, S., Guestrin, C.: "Why should I trust you?": explaining the predictions of any classifier. In: Proceedings of the 22nd ACM SIGKDD International Conference on Knowledge Discovery and Data Mining, KDD 2016, pp. 1135–1144. Association for Computing Machinery, New York, NY, USA (2016)
34. Saltelli, A., et al.: Global Sensitivity Analysis: The Primer. John Wiley & Sons Ltd, Chichester (2008)
35. Scholbeck, C.A., Molnar, C., Heumann, C., Bischl, B., Casalicchio, G.: Sampling, intervention, prediction, aggregation: a generalized framework for model-agnostic

interpretations. In: Cellier, P., Driessens, K. (eds.) ECML PKDD 2019. CCIS, vol. 1167, pp. 205–216. Springer, Cham (2020). https://doi.org/10.1007/978-3-030-43823-4_18

36. Sobol, I.: Global sensitivity indices for nonlinear mathematical models and their monte carlo estimates. Math. Comput. Simul. **55**(1), 271–280 (2001)
37. Strumbelj, E., Kononenko, I.: An efficient explanation of individual classifications using game theory. J. Mach. Learn. Res. **11**, 1–18 (2010)
38. Takahashi, K., Yamamoto, K., Kuchiba, A., Koyama, T.: Confidence interval for micro-averaged F1 and macro-averaged F1 scores. Appl. Intell. **52**(5), 4961–4972 (2022)
39. Wachter, S., Mittelstadt, B., Russell, C.: Counterfactual explanations without opening the black box: automated decisions and the GDPR. Harvard J. Law Technol. **31**(2) (2018)

Feature Importance versus Feature Influence and What It Signifies for Explainable AI

Kary Främling[1,2]($\boxtimes$) (iD)

[1] Umeå University, 901 87 Umeå, Sweden
kary.framling@cs.umu.se
[2] Aalto University, 02150 Espoo, Finland
https://www.umu.se/personal/kary-framling/

Abstract. When used in the context of decision theory, *feature importance* expresses how much changing the value of a feature can change the model outcome (or the *utility* of the outcome), compared to other features. Feature importance should not be confused with the *feature influence* used by most state-of-the-art post-hoc Explainable AI methods. Contrary to feature importance, feature influence is measured against a *reference level* or *baseline*. The Contextual Importance and Utility (CIU) method provides a unified definition of global and local feature importance that is applicable also for post-hoc explanations, where the *value utility* concept provides instance-level assessment of how favorable or not a feature value is for the outcome. The paper shows how CIU can be applied to both global and local explainability, assesses the fidelity and stability of different methods, and shows how explanations that use contextual importance and contextual utility can provide more expressive and flexible explanations than when using influence only.

Keywords: Explainable AI · Feature importance · Feature influence · Contextual Importance and Utility · Additive Feature Attribution

1 Introduction

Explainable Artificial Intelligence (XAI) is probably as old as AI itself and papers even from the 1970's such as [20] can still give valuable insight to XAI researchers. A relatively small but active XAI community existed in the 1990's, which tended to focus on building rule-based surrogate models of trained neural networks [1]. The *Contextual Importance and Utility (CIU)* method was presented in [7,8] at the same epoch and proposed a different approach, where only the outcome of the black-box model for a specific instance was justified and explained, which is nowadays often called *post-hoc explanation*. However, it seems like CIU was forgotten since then.

The work is partially supported by the Wallenberg AI, Autonomous Systems and Software Program (WASP) funded by the Knut and Alice Wallenberg Foundation.

This paper revisits the theoretical foundations of CIU and the core differences between CIU and current state-of-the-art methods. Notably, we show that "contextual importance" is compatible with the notion of "global feature importance" but extends it to the case of instance-level post-hoc explanation. We also show that influence values produced by so called Additive Feature Attribution (AFA) methods [15] are not compatible with global feature importance. Finally, we compare the methods experimentally using general-purpose criteria.

After this Introduction, Sect. 2 goes through the theory of global feature importance and AFA methods, followed by a presentation of CIU and new theory in Sect. 3. Section 4 experimentally compares CIU with the methods presented in Sect. 2, followed by Conclusions.

2   Background

When explaining the outcome of a model f, we are interested in how each feature (or possibly groups of features) affects the prediction of the instance being explained. For a linear model it is easy to identify the importance and influence of each feature, where the prediction for an instance x is:

$$f(x) = w_0 + w_1 x_1 + \cdots + w_N x_N. \tag{1}$$

Each x_i is a feature value, with $i = 1, \ldots, N$ and w_i is the weight associated with the feature i. Such linear models are considered understandable to humans and are therefore often used as so-called surrogate models g for explaining the outcome also for non-linear models, such as those produced by machine learning methods.

However, there are fundamental differences in how different XAI methods define *feature importance* in Eq. 1, versus *feature influence*. In decision theory and most other contexts, the feature importance for a linear model like Eq. 1 is considered to be w_i for feature i [5,11]. This is the definition that we adopt also in this paper. In *multi-attribute utility theory (MAUT)*, x_i is replaced by a *utility value* given by a *utility function* $u_i(x_i)$ [4].

On the other hand, the state-of-the-art XAI method Shapley value calculates an influence value ϕ_i for each feature. For a linear model as in Eq. 1, the Shapley value ϕ_i of the i-th feature on the prediction $f(x)$ is:

$$\phi_i(x) = w_i x_i - E(w_i X_i) = w_i x_i - w_i E(X_i), \tag{2}$$

where $E(w_i X_i)$ is the mean effect estimate for feature i [21]. This influence value $phi_i(x)$ depends on the instance x and is clearly not the same as the importance w_i.

The concepts of importance, utility, utility function and influence can be illustrated by an example of how the weighted average grade of a university student is calculated. The weight w_i of each course is the number of credits that can be obtained for the course and corresponds to the importance of the course. The utility value u_i of each course is the obtained grade in percent, *i.e.* normalized into range $[0, 1]$ by a utility function $u_i(x_i)$, where x_i is the original grade. The result $u = \sum_{i=1}^{N} w_i u_i(x_i)$ is normalized to the range $[0, 1]$ by dividing the weights w_i by the sum of all weights. Finally, the weighted average grade is scaled from the range $[0, 1]$ to the desired output range using the utility function $u(y)$, e.g. $[0, 1] \mapsto [4, 10]$. The desired output range tends to vary between schools, universities and countries.

The question is then: "where do we have 'influence' in the calculation of weighted average grade?". The answer is "nowhere", unless we introduce a baseline or reference level, which would normally be the average grade for the group of reference students that we want to compare with. The ϕ_i values from Eq. 2 would then indicate which courses had a negative or positive influence compared to the average of the reference population (e.g. students following the same cursus the same year), and a magnitude for that influence.

2.1   Global Feature Importance

In a machine learning context, global feature importance describes how much covariates contribute to a prediction model's accuracy, which differs from how decision theory defines it. However, both definitions are similar in practice as long as we only consider linear models, which is shown by the results in Sect. 4.

Estimating global feature importance can be done in many ways, as described e.g. in [6]. One commonly used method is the permutation-based feature importance (PFI) approach proposed in [3], which works by calculating the increase of the model's prediction error after permuting the feature values. A feature is "important" if permuting its values increases the model error, because the model relied on the feature for the prediction. A feature is "unimportant" if permuting its values keeps the model error unchanged, because the model ignored the feature for the prediction.

2.2   Additive Feature Attribution Methods

The concept of AFA methods was introduced in [15], where a set of XAI methods were identified that belong to this family. AFA methods use an *explanation model* g that is an interpretable approximation of the original model f, according to the following definition.

Definition 1. *AFA methods* *have an explanation model that is a linear function of binary variables:*

$$g(z') = \phi_0 + \sum_{i=1}^{M} \phi_i z'_i, \tag{3}$$

where $z' \in \{0, 1\}^M$, $M \leq N$ is the number of simplified input features, and $\phi \in \mathbb{R}$.

According to [14], Shapley values represent the only possible method in the broad class of AFA methods that will simultaneously satisfy three important properties:

local accuracy, *consistency*, and *missingness*. Local accuracy states that when approximating the original model f for a specific input x, the explanation's influence values should sum up to the difference $f(x) - \phi_0$.

The Shapley value is a solution concept that assigns a pay-off to each agent according to their marginal contribution [19]. Focusing on feature i, the Shapley value approach will test the accuracy of every combination of features not including feature i and then test how adding x_i to each combination improves the accuracy. Computing Shapley values is computationally expensive so most model-agnostic implementations only estimate approximate Shapley values, such as *Kernel SHAP* [15]. Kernel SHAP is essentially an adaptation of another AFA method, the Local Interpretable Model-agnostic Explanations (LIME) method [18], to estimate Shapley values. There are also model-specific methods for estimating Shapley values, such as Deep SHAP and Tree SHAP [14].

Shapley values are "local" in the sense that they are calculated for a specific instance x. However, in [14] it was suggested that $mean(|\phi_i|)$ could be used as a global feature importance estimate, when calculated over the entire training set and where influence values ϕ_i are Shapley values. They compare their approach with three well-known global feature importance methods and conclude that $mean(|\phi_i|)$ provides a better estimate of global feature importance. However, it can be questioned whether the use of influence values for estimating importance values is reasonable. As shown in this paper, contextual importance is mathematically similar to global feature importance. Different approaches for estimating global feature importance are used in Sect. 4 that highlight these differences.

Shapley value and LIME are presumably the most used methods for the moment within the category of model-agnostic post-hoc XAI. Shapley value seem to become the dominating method due to its mathematical properties, as explained above. However, for instance [13] recently pointed out several mathematical and human-centric issues with the use of Shapley value for XAI purposes. The mathematical issues concern how influence values are estimated and whether to use conditional or interventional distributions. Even in simple cases, the Shapley value is conceptually limited for non-additive models. Human-centric issues are mainly that Shapley value supports contrastive explanations only in comparison with the mean influence $E(w_i X_i)$ and are difficult to use for producing other kinds of counterfactual explanations. It is also noted that even when an individual lacks a correct mental model of the meaning of Shapley values, the explainee may use them to justify their evaluation anyways, whether or not this analysis is well-founded. In general, it is a problem if the explainability method is a black-box itself because then the explainee tends to interpret the explanations according to assumptions that might be false.

3   Contextual Importance and Utility

CIU is inspired from MAUT, which addresses the question of how humans can express their preferences and how they can be modelled mathematically in order to build human-understandable decision support systems. CIU uses core MAUT concepts of feature importance and utility value and specifies how they can be estimated for any model $f(x)$ and a specific instance or *Context* x. In MAUT, an N-attribute utility function is a weighted sum:

$$u(y) = u(x_1, \ldots, x_N) = \sum_{i=1}^{N} w_i u_i(x_i), \tag{4}$$

where $u_i(x_i)$ are the utility functions that correspond to the features $x_1, \ldots, x_N$. $u_i(x_i)$ are constrained to the range $[0,1]$, as well as $u(y)$ through the positive weights w_i.

When studying a general (presumably non-linear) model $f(x)$, there are no known w_i values, so we need a way to estimate those values.

Contextual Importance (CI). CI takes the range of variation of the output as the importance value to estimate, which we can do by observing changes in output values when modifying input values of the feature i and keeping the values of the other features at those given by the studied instance x. This principle can be extended to more than one feature and we will use the notion of input index set $\{i\}$ in the CIU equations that follow. For an input index set $\{i\}$, the values of the features $\neg\{i\}$ are defined by the instance x. We extend the definition further to the importance of $\{i\}$ versus another set of inputs $\{I\}$, where $\{i\} \subseteq \{I\} \subseteq 1, \ldots, N$. This gives us an estimation of the range $[umin_{j,\{i\},\{I\}}(x), umax_{j,\{i\},\{I\}}(x)]$, where j is the index of the model output to explain. CI is defined as:

$$\omega_{j,\{i\},\{I\}}(x) = \frac{umax_{j,\{i\}}(x) - umin_{j,\{i\}}(x)}{umax_{j,\{I\}}(x) - umin_{j,\{I\}}(x)}, \tag{5}$$

where we use the symbol ω for CI. If the model $f(x)$ is linear, then $\omega_{j,\{i\},\{I\}}(x)$ is identical for all/any instance x and is therefore also the global feature importance. If the model is non-linear, then $\omega_{j,\{i\},\{I\}}(x)$ depends on the instance x and is "local" or *contextual*.

Since the model f produces actual output values rather than utility values, the utility values $umin_j$ and $umax_j$ in Eq. 5 have to be mapped to actual output values $y_j = f(x)$. If f is a classification model, then the outputs y_j are typically estimated probabilities for the corresponding class, so the output value is also the utility value, i.e. $u_j(y_j) = y_j$. For many (or most) regression tasks, a utility function of the form $u_j(y_j) = Ay_j + b$ is applicable (and also applies to $u_j(y_j) = y_j$). When the utility function is of form $u_j(y_j) = Ay_j + b$, then CI can be calculated as:

$$\omega_{j,\{i\},\{I\}}(x) = \frac{ymax_{j,\{i\}}(x) - ymin_{j,\{i\}}(x)}{ymax_{j,\{I\}}(x) - ymin_{j,\{I\}}(x)}, \tag{6}$$

where $ymin_j()$ and $ymax_j()$ are the minimal and maximal y_j values observed for output j.

Contextual Utility (CU). CU corresponds to the factor $u_i(x_i)$ in Eq. 4. CU expresses to what extent the current values of features in $\{i\}$ contribute to obtaining a high output utility u_j. CU is defined as

$$CU_{j,\{i\}}(x) = \frac{u_j(x) - umin_{j,\{i\}}(x)}{umax_{j,\{i\}}(x) - umin_{j,\{i\}}(x)}. \tag{7}$$

When $u_j(y_j) = Ay_j + b$, this can be written as:

$$CU_{j,\{i\}}(x) = \left| \frac{y_j(x) - yumin_{j,\{i\}}(x)}{ymax_{j,\{i\}}(x) - ymin_{j,\{i\}}(x)} \right|, \tag{8}$$

where $yumin = ymin$ if A is positive and $yumin = ymax$ if A is negative.

Contextual Influence. Contextual Influence defines feature influence in a similar way as in Eq. 2 but using $w_i u_i(x_i)$ instead of $w_i x_i$. This gives us

$$\phi_i(x) = \omega_i(x)(u_i(x_i) - E(U(x_i))), \tag{9}$$

where $E(U(x_i)$ is the expected utility value for feature i. Since utility $u \in [0,1]$ for all features, it intuitively makes sense to use the average utility value 0.5 as a constant baseline for all features, even though it can be any value in the range $[0,1]$ that makes sense for the application. For consistency, this constant is called ϕ_0 as in Eq. 3. When including subset indices for CI and CU, we get the following equation for contextual influence:

$$\phi_{j,\{i\},\{I\}}(x) = \omega_{j,\{i\},\{I\}}(x)(CU_{j,\{i\}}(x) - \phi_0). \tag{10}$$

Contextual influence makes it possible to produce influence-based explanations like for AFA methods, in addition to the explanations based on CI and CU.

It should be emphasized that the baseline ϕ_0 of contextual influence has a constant and semantic meaning, *i.e.* "averagely good/bad", "averagely typical" *etc.*, that presumably makes sense to humans when used in explanations. It is also entirely data- and model-agnostic, which makes it different from the AFA baseline in Eq. 2.

Estimation of CI and CU. Most model-agnostic post-hoc XAI methods only attempt to estimate the importance/influence of one feature i on the output, with the assumption that features are independent. In this paper, we limit the scope to that case and do not consider coalitions of features or CIU's *intermediate concepts* as presented in [7–9][1]. Therefore, we only need to consider the case when $\{i\}$ has one single index and the case when $\{I\} = 1,\ldots,N$ in Eqs. 5, 7 and 10 (and Eqs. 6 and 8). $\{I\} = 1,\ldots,N$ signifies all inputs jointly, which by definition means that $umin_{j,\{I\}} = 0$ and $umax_{j,\{I\}} = 1$ for all instances x.

---

[1] Intermediate concepts also deal with dependencies between features. However, in this paper we assume that the features are independent, as is the case for Shapley value and LIME too.

Therefore, $umax_{j,\{I\}}(x) - umin_{j,\{I\}}(x) = 1$ $\forall x$. If we have a classification task where $u_i(y_j) = y_j$, then we also have $ymax_{j,\{I\}}(x) - ymin_{j,\{I\}}(x) = 1$ $\forall x$ and in a regression task with $u_j(y_j) = Ay_j + b$, $ymin_{j,\{I\}}$ and $ymax_{j,\{I\}}$ are calculated accordingly. If the actual model gives values outside this range, then the model is over-shooting at least in some parts of the input space.

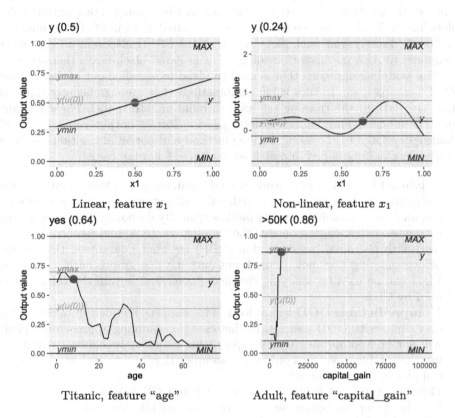

Fig. 1. Output value y as a function of one feature value for the four models, with illustration of CIU calculations. The red dot shows the x_i value of the instance to be explained for the feature i. The output range $[MIN, MAX]$ is $[0, 1]$ for all models, except for the "non-linear" model where it is $[-0.825, 2.29]$. The labels in the Figure are $MIN = ymin_j$, $MAX = ymax_j$, $ymin = ymin_{j,\{i\}}(x)$, $ymax = ymax_{j,\{i\}}(x)$, $y = y_j(x)$ and $y(u(0)) = ymin + \phi_0(ymax - ymin)$. (Color figure online)

The approach proposed in [10] is used for estimating $ymin$ and $ymax$[2]. For categorical features, the approach uses all possible values. For numerical features the model is sampled using a set of instances consisting of **1)** the instance x, **2)** the instance x with feature i value replaced by the smallest possible value for feature i (min_i), **3)** the instance x with feature i value replaced by the greatest

---

[2] The approach in [10] is applicable to any feature set $\{i\}$ and $\{I\}$, including $1, \ldots, N$.

possible value for feature i (max_i), and **4)** a set of instances where the value of feature i is replaced with a random value from the interval $[min_{\{i\}}, max_{\{i\}}]$. This approach guarantees exact values for $ymin_j$ and $ymax_j$ if $f(x)$ is monotonous, or in practice if $ymin_j$ and $ymax_j$ values are found at the input values $min_{\{i\}}$ and $max_{\{i\}}$. If $min_{\{i\}}$ and $max_{\{i\}}$ values are not pre-defined, then they can be determined from the training data set. The calculation of CI and CU values with different data sets and models is illustrated in Fig. 1 using input/output value plots like in [7], also called *ceteris paribus* or *what-if* plots in [2]. CIU values can be "read" directly from such plots, which makes CIU transparent at least when compared to AFA methods that might be considered black-boxes themselves.

The sampling approach that is used can lead to so called out of distribution (OOD) samples, *i.e.* feature value combinations that are significantly different from the data in the training set used to build an ML model. For such samples, the model f may be incapable to provide correct output values y_j. OOD challenges related to the used sampling method and potential solutions to those challenges can be grouped into at least the three following cases:

1. **Predictable OOD behaviour.** If OOD samples do not lead to undershooting of the $ymin$ value, nor to overshooting of the $ymax$ value, then OOD is not an issue. Ensemble learning models typically do not under- or overshoot even when extrapolating outside the training set. In [7] for instance, CIU was used with an radial basis function (RBF) net that guaranteed that under- or overshooting does not occur. Input-output value graphs such as those in Fig. 1 can be used for studying the model behaviour within the value ranges used by CIU.
2. **Non-predictable OOD behaviour.** This happens if under- or overshooting may occur with OOD samples. In that case the sampling approach used here will not be appropriate. Various approaches could be imagined for addressing this problem, such as only using samples that are "sufficiently" close to samples in the training set.
3. **Detecting model instability.** Since CI and CU values are in the range $[0, 1]$ by definition, obtaining values that are outside this range indicate that the model undershoots or overshoots the permissible range for one or more samples. This could be an indication that those samples should be removed or that the model should be corrected in order to increase its trustworthiness. A correction approach using what is called pseudo-examples was proposed in [8].

The second and third cases are considered to be out of scope for the current paper and remain topics of further research. It is also worth mentioning that similar OOD challenges exist for all model-agnostic XAI methods (at least for the permutation-based ones), including Shapley value and LIME. We do not consider model-specific methods here, such as TreeSHAP for Shapley values [14].

4   Results

All used software is written in R and is available as open-source on Github, including the source code for producing the results shown here. The caret package [12] is used for all machine learning models. The IML package is used for Shapley value calculations [16] and the 'lime' package for LIME [17]. The CIU implementation and results use the 'ciu' package [10] as a base. The default parameters are used for all packages unless stated otherwise. The experiments were run using Rstudio Version 1.3.1093 on a MacBook Pro, with 2.3 GHz 8-Core Intel Core i9 processor, 16 GB 2667 MHz MHz DDR4 memory, and AMD Radeon Pro 5500M 4 GB graphics card.

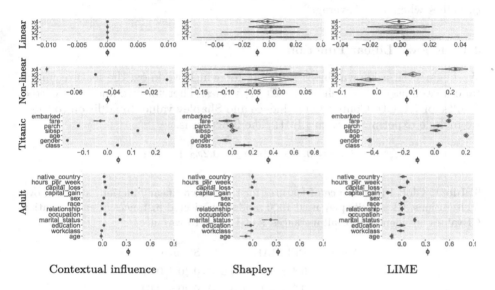

Contextual influence   Shapley   LIME

Fig. 2. Distribution of ϕ values from 50 runs with the studied data sets / models and the studied methods.

The "Elapsed" times shown in the results are indicated as "real time" ("elapsed" value of *system.time*() function) and have been collected for all methods during the same session in order to keep them as comparable as possible. Therefore, the exact values are not significant but only the ratio between the execution times of the different methods. It should also be emphasized that execution times do not depend only on the method itself but also on the used implementation and other factors. Parameters such as sample size have been set to be identical for all the methods. However, for sampling-based methods there is always a compromise between sample size (and execution time) versus the precision (variance) of the result. Therefore, the expectation is that the longer the execution time, the lower the variance. So a method with short execution time and low variance is preferred to a method with long execution time and high variance.

In order to make global feature importance values comparable, they have been normalised to the range $[0, 1]$ for PFI and Shapley value by dividing with the sum of importance of all features. CI values are by definition in the range $[0, 1]$. Unlike Shapley values, it doesn't seem like LIME values would have been used, or proposed to be used, for estimating global feature importance. Therefore LIME has not been included in the global feature importance experiments and results.

For the instance-specific experiments, instances that have average (or close to average) feature values have been chosen, except for the Titanic instance where we use the same instance as in [2]. The reason for this choice is that such instances illustrate the difference between importance and influence as clearly as possible. The importance ω_i of a feature does not depend on the feature's value x_i, whereas its influence value ϕ_i depends on x_i in a way that gives close to zero ϕ_i values when x_i is "average".

4.1   Known Linear Function

We begin with a known linear function, for which we know the feature importances (weights) w_i as well as the $E(X_i)$ values. Therefore we know the correct results for CI, CU, Contextual influence and Shapley value. In addition to these, we include experiments with LIME. The function is:

$$f(x) = 0.4x_1 + 0.3x_2 + 0.2x_3 + 0.1x_4$$

Table 1. Global importance of features for the known linear function, averaged over 50 iterations. CI and Shapley used 1000 randomly selected instances at each iteration. CI values are identical for all instances, so CI has zero variance.

Feature	PFI-MAE	CI	Shapley
x_1	0.4 ± 0.0	0.4 ± 0	0.40 ± 0.05
x_2	0.3 ± 0.0	0.3 ± 0	0.30 ± 0.04
x_3	0.2 ± 0.0	0.2 ± 0	0.20 ± 0.04
x_4	0.1 ± 0.0	0.1 ± 0	0.10 ± 0.02
Elapsed	*1460 ss.*	*713 s.*	*27786 s.*

CIU can use the function directly as the studied model, whereas the other methods require the availability of a training set and a trained model. The training data set consisted of all possible value combinations of the four features x_i in the range $[0, 1]$ with a step of 0.05, *i.e.* 194481 instances. The trained linear model achieved $R^2 = 1$. All results are reported for the trained linear model.

Table 2. Local importance, utility and influence values by different methods for the known linear function. The numbers show mean values over 50 iterations.

Feature	CI	CU	ϕ_{CIU}	$\phi_{Shapley}$	ϕ_{LIME}
$x_1 = 0.5$	0.4	0.5	0	0.004	−0.003
$x_2 = 0.5$	0.3	0.5	0	−0.001	0.001
$x_3 = 0.5$	0.2	0.5	0	−0.001	0.001
$x_4 = 0.5$	0.1	0.5	0	0.001	−0.002

Global Feature Importance. Table 1 shows results for the PFI method with the Mean Average Error (MAE) loss function, $mean(CI)$ and $mean|Shapley\ value|$. All methods retrieve the original weights of the linear model but with different accuracy and variance. CI values are identical for all instances in the case of linear models. Therefore, *importance as defined by CI is conceptually identical with global feature importance.* Even though Shapley values estimate instance-level influence it still gives similar values as the other methods but with a high variance, despite a significantly longer execution time.

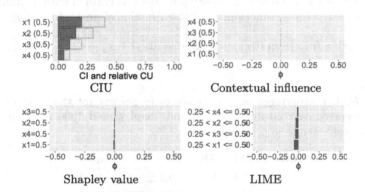

Fig. 3. Bar plot explanations for linear model and studied instance with different methods. For CIU and Contextual influence the plot is identical on consecutive runs. For Shapley value and LIME the plot changes on every run due to their variance.

Instance-Specific Results. We study the instance $x = 0.5, 0.5, 0.5, 0.5$ with $f(x) = 0.5$ for which ϕ_i values are zero by definition. Table 2 shows the CI, CU and ϕ values obtained. Figure 2 shows the same values and their variance over 50 runs for all the methods. CIU/Contextual influence has exactly zero variance. Shapley values and LIME have a great variance, so for the studied instance even the sign of ϕ_i values will change randomly from one explanation to the next. This signifies that the Shapley value and LIME plots in Fig. 3 are misleading. Furthermore, the influence-based explanations don't provide hardly any information, whereas the CIU plot does provide useful information about the model and the result.

The CIU plot in Fig. 3 illustrates how CI and CU can be combined into a more information-rich explanation than with influence alone. The length of the half-transparent bar corresponds to the CI value and shows how much modifying the value of the feature would modify the output. The solid bar illustrates the CU value so that a $CU = 1$ value will cover the transparent bar entirely, while $CU = 0$ gives a zero-length solid bar. Therefore, the solid bar shows "how good" the current value is compared with the worst and best possible values for the feature. CI and CU values can be visualised in many ways but the current one has been selected for its "counterfactual" aspect, which signifies that it indicates which features would have the greatest potential for improving the output utility. Such functionality is useful for instance if getting a negative credit decision and seeing what criteria could have the greatest effect if it would be possible to improve the values of those criteria.

4.2   Known Non-linear Function

In order to study the behaviour with a known, non-linear function we use the function in Eq. 11. It is worth noting that all features are independent in this function. A Stochastic Gradient Boosting model was trained with a similar training data as for the linear function, *i.e.* 194481 instances and achieved $R^2 = 0.992$.

$$f(x) = 0.7x_1 sin(10x_1) + 0.3x_2 sin(10x_2) + x_3^2 + (2x_4^4 - 1.5x_4^2) \qquad (11)$$

Table 3. Global importance of input features in percent for the known non-linear function, averaged over 50 iterations. CI and Shapley used 1000 randomly selected instances at each iteration.

Feature	PFI-MAE	CI	Shapley
x_1	30.5 ± 0.0	29.8 ± 0.1	29.4 ± 0.6
x_2	13.0 ± 0.0	11.7 ± 0.0	11.6 ± 0.3
x_3	36.4 ± 0.0	33.3 ± 0.1	39.5 ± 0.6
x_4	20.1 ± 0.0	25.2 ± 0.0	19.6 ± 0.5
Elapsed	*18611861ss.*	*618s.*	*35501s.*

Global Feature Importance. Based on the results in Table 3 it seems like all methods agree on the order of importance but it is not possible to say which one is the most "correct" one because they are all based on slightly different definitions of what global feature importance signifies. In [14] it is claimed that using average importance of all instances provides a better estimate of the global importance than PFI, for instance. That paper uses mean absolute Shapley values. However, as shown in this paper, CI provides a "true" importance measure, rather than the influence values given by Shapley values. CI is orders of magnitude faster than Shapley values and still gives lower variance.

Instance-Specific Results. We choose to study the instance $x = 0.63, 0.63, 0.59, 0.81$ with $f(x) = 0.235$, which is close to the average $f(x)$ value and therefore gives low expected ϕ_i values. Figure 2 shows that Contextual influence has close to zero variance, which is therefore true also for CI and CU. Influence-based methods all give close to zero ϕ_i values, resulting in explanations with a low information value, as shown in Fig. 4. The great variance of Shapley values may again cause the signs of ϕ_i to change from one run to the other, which is true also for LIME (Table 4).

Table 4. Local importance, utility and influence values given by different methods for the known non-linear function, averaged over 50 iterations.

Feature	CI	CU	ϕ_{CIU}	$\phi_{Shapley}$	ϕ_{LIME}
$x_1 = 0.63$	0.300	0.416	-0.025	-0.031	-0.049
$x_2 = 0.63$	0.128	0.416	-0.011	-0.015	-0.021
$x_3 = 0.59$	0.321	0.348	-0.049	0.011	0.095
$x_4 = 0.81$	0.251	0.202	-0.075	-0.040	0.216

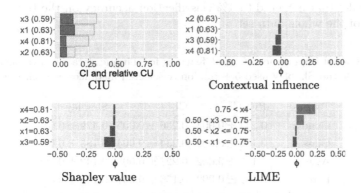

Fig. 4. Bar plot explanations for non-linear model and studied instance with different methods. For CIU and Contextual influence the plot is identical on consecutive runs. For Shapley value and LIME the plot changes on every run due to their variance.

4.3 Titanic

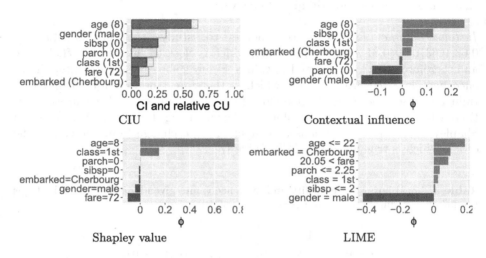

Fig. 5. Bar plot explanations of 63.6% survival probability of 8-year old boy 'Johnny D' on Titanic with different methods.

The Titanic data set is a classification task with classes 'yes' or 'no' for the probability of survival. The data set has 2179 instances. We used a Random Forest model that achieved 81.1% classification accuracy on the test set, which was 25% of the whole data set.

Table 5. Global importance of input features for Titanic data set, averaged over 50 iterations. CI and Shapley used 500 randomly selected instances at each iteration.

Feature	PFI-CE	CI	Shapley
Gender	0.244 ± 0.003	0.236 ± 0.005	0.479 ± 0.013
Class	0.163 ± 0.002	0.254 ± 0.004	0.185 ± 0.013
Age	0.157 ± 0.002	0.227 ± 0.003	0.142 ± 0.010
Fare	0.152 ± 0.002	0.156 ± 0.001	0.107 ± 0.007
Embarked	0.098 ± 0.001	0.059 ± 0.001	0.038 ± 0.003
Sibsp	0.096 ± 0.000	0.038 ± 0.002	0.033 ± 0.003
Parch	0.089 ± 0.000	0.029 ± 0.001	0.017 ± 0.002
Elapsed	*203s.*	*6463s.*	*15009s.*

Global feature importance. The class error (CE) loss function was used for PFI. Table 5 shows that all methods agree on the order of feature importance, even though the least important features get lower importance estimates with CI and Shapley than with the global importance method. The importance value 0.479 given by Shapley values to the 'gender' feature seems surprisingly high compared to the other methods. CI again has significantly lower variance than Shapley values and is faster (Table 6).

Table 6. Local importance/influence/utility estimations for Titanic instance 'Johnny D', averaged over 50 iterations.

Feature	CI	CU	ϕ_{CIU}	$\phi_{Shapley}$	ϕ_{LIME}
Gender	0.334	0	−0.334	−0.070	−0.419
Age	0.637	0.899	0.508	0.749	0.203
Class	0.212	0.698	0.084	0.116	0.030
Fare	0.210	0.373	−0.060	−0.056	0.090
Embarked	0.074	1	0.074	0.015	0.096
Sibsp	0.256	0.992	0.252	0.011	0.006
Parch	0.244	0	−0.244	−0.011	0.023

Instance-Specific Results. The studied instance is "Johnny D", an 8-year old boy from the Titanic that is also used and analyzed in [2]. Feature values and explanations by the different methods are shown as bar plots in Fig. 5 for the probability of survival, which is 63.6%. For Johnny D, the feature "age" has a clearly higher CI value than the global CI, which is normal because in the context of an 8-year old child the age is the most important feature, as shown by the input-output graph in Fig. 1. Figure 2 again shows that Contextual influence has close to zero variance. Shapley values and LIME again show great variance and seem to over-emphasize "age" (Shapley) and "gender" (LIME).

4.4   Adult Data Set

The Adult data set classifies people into the classes of yearly income in US dollars of "$<= 50K$" and "$> 50K$". A Stochastic Gradient Boosting model achieved 86.2% classification accuracy on the test set. The test set contained 25% of the whole data set. This data set is mainly included in order to validate the results with another "real-life" data set that has a greater number of features than Titanic. The Adult data set has 30162 instances, which is an order of magnitude more than for Titanic.

Global Feature Importance. Table 7 shows similar results as for Titanic. CI gives a much higher importance to "capital gain" and "capital loss" features, which can be understood when studying the input-output graphs for those features and realizing that good values for either one of those features greatly increases the probability of the class "$> 50K$" (see Fig. 1 for "capital_gain" of the studied instance). Shapley values give a high importance to "marital status" that is difficult to explain (Table 8).

Table 7. Global importance of input features in percent for Adult data set, averaged over 50 iterations. CI and Shapley used 500 randomly selected instances at each iteration.

Feature	PFI-CE	CI	Shapley
marital_status	10.0 ± 0.0	10.4 ± 0.2	22.7 ± 0.7
capital_gain	9.9 ± 0.0	29.9 ± 0.7	14.0 ± 1.2
education	8.9 ± 0.0	12.0 ± 0.2	17.8 ± 0.7
age	8.5 ± 0.0	7.8 ± 0.2	12.2 ± 0.5
occupation	8.3 ± 0.0	7.3 ± 0.2	12.8 ± 0.4
capital_loss	8.2 ± 0.0	17.2 ± 0.2	5.0 ± 0.5
hours_per_week	7.8 ± 0.0	5.8 ± 0.1	7.7 ± 0.3
relationship	7.7 ± 0.0	3.3 ± 0.1	2.4 ± 0.2
workclass	7.7 ± 0.0	2.3 ± 0.1	2.2 ± 0.2
sex	7.6 ± 0.0	1.5 ± 0.0	2.7 ± 0.2
native_country	7.6 ± 0.0	2.5 ± 0.1	0.5 ± 0.1
race	7.6 ± 0.0	0.0 ± 0.0	0.0 ± 0.0
Elapsed	*1291s.*	*3314s.*	*25111s.*

Table 8. Local importance/influence/utility estimations for Adult instance, averaged over 50 iterations.

Feature	CI	CU	ϕ_{CIU}	$\phi_{Shapley}$	ϕ_{LIME}
age	0.384	0.944	0.341	0.117	0.021
workclass	0.090	0.774	0.049	0.026	0.005
education	0.433	0.987	0.421	0.224	0.084
marital_stat	0.520	1.000	0.520	0.272	0.164
occupation	0.320	1.000	0.320	0.125	0.049
relationship	0.157	1.000	0.157	0.107	0.058
race	0.000	0.000	0.000	0.000	-0.001
sex	0.028	0.000	-0.028	-0.029	-0.030
capital_gain	0.241	0.218	-0.118	-0.012	-0.180
capital_loss	0.241	0.302	-0.088	-0.004	-0.014
hours_per_w	0.160	0.632	0.042	0.000	-0.075
native_count	0.060	0.794	0.035	0.003	0.018

Instance-Specific Results. The studied instance has a 86.3% probability of belonging to the class "$> 50K$". This particular instance has been chosen because the value "$age = 27$" is unusual for a person that belongs to the class "$> 50K$" and where the value for feature "capital_gain" is among the best possible and therefore makes this feature the most important/influential one. The high importance/influence of "capital_gain" is shown by CIU, Contextual influence and Shapley value in Fig. 6, whereas LIME shows radically different results. The Shapley values of many features are very close to zero, so it seems like the most influential features are over-emphasized in the same way as the "age" feature for the Titanic data set. Figure 2 again confirms the differences in variance between the methods.

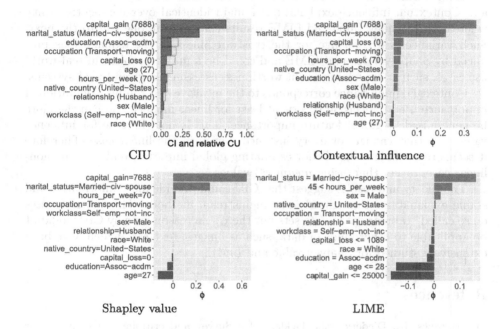

CIU

Contextual influence

Shapley value

LIME

Fig. 6. Bar plot explanations of 86.5% probability of belonging to the class "> 50K" with different methods.

5 Conclusions

As illustrated by the barplot "explanations" in Fig. 3, Fig. 4, Fig. 5 and Fig. 6 CI and CU values can provide a kind of counterfactual "what-if?" explanations that show what features have the greatest potential to change the outcome, while also providing an indication of what features have values that could be improved. Such information is missing in the influence-based explanations, which only indicate positive or negative influence compared with a reference value.

CI, CU and Contextual influence have known ranges and can therefore be interpreted directly. $CI = 1$ signifies that the output can be modified completely by modifying the feature value and $CI = 0$ signifies "no importance", so no effect on the output. $CU = 1$ signifies that the input value(s) are the best possible for obtaining a high-utility output value and $CU = 0$ signifies the worst possible input value(s). The value range for Contextual influence is $[-\phi_0, -\phi_0 + 1]$, so Contextual influence can also be interpreted directly. Shapley value and LIME don't have such pre-defined ranges, which may lead to misinterpretations of ϕ values, especially when ϕ values are close to zero.

CIU (and therefore also Contextual influence) values have no or small variance in the experimental results, whereas Shapley value and LIME show considerable variance on consecutive runs for the same instance. Therefore, CIU and Contextual influence explanations remain identical over consecutive runs, whereas the Shapley value and LIME results change from one run to the next. Such variance is a challenge for the trustworthiness of the explanations produced by Shapley value and LIME and could be a major problem in real-world use cases, such as explaining credit worthiness assessments given by AI systems.

Contextual importance corresponds to the intuitive and common definition of importance used in decision theory, at least for linear models, and can therefore be generalised to global feature importance. This is not the case for influence values (ϕ) that change for every instance x even in the linear case. Therefore it seems reasonable to use CI for estimating global importance also in the non-linear case, rather than using $mean(|\phi|)$ values.

The theory and results suggest that CIU could provide more informative and stable explanations than the studied mainstream methods. This paper focuses on so called "tabular data" data sets but there's no reason for why CIU wouldn't be applicable to other kinds of data, such as images, text *etc.*, which have been extensively studied for Shapley value and LIME.

References

1. Andrews, R., Diederich, J., Tickle, A.B.: Survey and critique of techniques for extracting rules from trained artificial neural networks. Know. Based Syst. **8**(6), 373–389 (1995)
2. Biecek, P., Burzykowski, T.: Explanatory Model Analysis. Chapman and Hall/CRC, New York (2021)
3. Breiman, L.: Random forests. Mach. Learn. **45**, 5–32 (2001)
4. Dyer, J.S.: Maut — multiattribute utility theory. In: Multiple Criteria Decision Analysis: State of the Art Surveys. ISORMS, vol. 78, pp. 265–292. Springer, New York (2005). https://doi.org/10.1007/0-387-23081-5_7
5. Fishburn, P.C.: Utility Theory and Decision Theory, pp. 303–312. Palgrave Macmillan, London (1990)
6. Fisher, A., Rudin, C., Dominici, F.: All models are wrong, but many are useful: learning a variable's importance by studying an entire class of prediction models simultaneously. J. Mach. Learn. Res. **20**(177), 1–81 (2019)
7. Främling, K.: Explaining results of neural networks by contextual importance and utility. In: Andrews, R., Diederich, J. (eds.) Rules and networks: Proceedings of the Rule Extraction from Trained Artificial Neural Networks Workshop, AISB 1996 Conference, Brighton, UK (1996)
8. Främling, K.: Modélisation et apprentissage des préférences par réseaux de neurones pour l'aide à la décision multicritère. Phd thesis, INSA de Lyon (1996)

9. Främling, K.: Decision theory meets explainable AI. In: Calvaresi, D., Najjar, A., Winikoff, M., Främling, K. (eds.) EXTRAAMAS 2020. LNCS, vol. 12175, pp. 57–74. Springer, Cham (2020). https://doi.org/10.1007/978-3-030-51924-7_4
10. Främling, K.: Contextual importance and utility in R: the 'ciu' package. In: Proceedings of 1st Workshop on Explainable Agency in Artificial Intelligence, at 35th AAAI Conference on Artificial Intelligence, 2–9 February 2021, pp. 110–114 (2021)
11. Keeney, R.L., Raiffa, H.: Decisions with Multiple Objectives: Preferences and Value Trade-Offs. Cambridge University Press, Cambridge (1993)
12. Kuhn, M.: Building predictive models in R using the caret package. J. Stat. Softw. Art. **28**(5), 1–26 (2008)
13. Kumar, I.E., Venkatasubramanian, S., Scheidegger, C., Friedler, S.: Problems with shapley-value-based explanations as feature importance measures. In: International Conference on Machine Learning, pp. 5491–5500. PMLR (2020)
14. Lundberg, S.M., Erion, G.G., Lee, S.I.: Consistent individualized feature attribution for tree ensembles. CoRR abs/1802.03888 (2018)
15. Lundberg, S.M., Lee, S.I.: A unified approach to interpreting model predictions. In: Guyon, I., Luxburg, U.V., Bengio, S., Wallach, H., Fergus, R., Vishwanathan, S., Garnett, R. (eds.) Advances in Neural Information Processing Systems, vol. 30, pp. 4765–4774. Curran Associates, Inc. (2017)
16. Molnar, C., Casalicchio, G., Bischl, B.: iml: an R package for interpretable machine learning. J. Open Source Softw. **3**(26), 786 (2018)
17. Pedersen, T.L., Benesty, M.: lime: Local Interpretable Model-Agnostic Explanations (2019). R package version 0.5.1
18. Ribeiro, M.T., Singh, S., Guestrin, C.: "Why should i trust you?" Explaining the predictions of any classifier. In: Proceedings of the 22nd ACM SIGKDD International Conference on Knowledge Discovery and Data Mining, pp. 1135–1144 (2016)
19. Shapley, L.S.: A value for n-person games. In: Kuhn, H.W., Tucker, A.W. (eds.) Contributions to the Theory of Games II, pp. 307–317. Princeton University Press, Princeton (1953)
20. Shortliffe, E.H., Davis, R., Axline, S.G., Buchanan, B.G., Green, C., Cohen, S.N.: Computer-based consultations in clinical therapeutics: explanation and rule acquisition capabilities of the MYCIN system. Comput. Biomed. Res. **8**(4), 303–320 (1975)
21. Štrumbelj, E., Kononenko, I.: Explaining prediction models and individual predictions with feature contributions. Knowl. Inf. Syst. **41**(3), 647–665 (2014)

ABC-GAN: Spatially Constrained Counterfactual Generation for Image Classification Explanations

Dimitry Mindlin[1]([✉])[ID], Malte Schilling[2][ID], and Philipp Cimiano[1][ID]

[1] Bielefeld University, Bielefeld, Germany
dimitry.mindlin@uni-bielefeld.de, cimiano@techfak.uni-bielefeld.de
[2] University of Münster, Münster, Germany
malte.schilling@uni-muenster.de
https://www.uni-bielefeld.de/fakultaeten/technische-fakultaet/ ,
https://www.uni-muenster.de/Informatik/

Abstract. There is a growing interest in methods that explain predictions of image classification models to increase algorithmic transparency. Counterfactual Explanations (CFEs) provide a causal explanation as they introduce changes in the original image that change the classifier's prediction. Current counterfactual generation approaches suffer from the fact that they potentially modify a too large region in the image that is not entirely causally related to a classifier's decision, thus not always providing targeted explanations. We propose a new method, Attention Based Counterfactuals via CycleGAN (ABC-GAN), that combines attention-guided object translation with counterfactual image generation via Generative Adversarial Networks. To generate an explanation, ABC-GAN incorporates both a counterfactual loss and the classifier's attention mechanism. By leveraging the attention map generated by GradCAM++, ABC-GAN alters regions in the image that are important for the classifier's prediction. This approach ensures that the generated explanation focuses on the specific areas that contribute to the change in prediction while preserving the background and non-salient regions of the original image. We apply our approach to medical X-ray datasets (MURA Bone X-Ray, RSNA Chest X-ray) and compare it to state-of-the-art methods. We demonstrate the feasibility and, in the case of the MURA dataset, the superiority of ABC-GAN in all the measured metrics with the highest percentage of counterfactuals (99% Validity) and image similarity. On the other dataset, our method outperforms the competitive methods in small changes and image similarity. We argue that ABC-GAN is thus beneficial for classification problems requiring precise and minimal CFEs.

Keywords: Counterfactuals · XAI · Generative Explanations

Funded by the *Deutsche Forschungsgemeinschaft* (DFG, German Research Foundation): TRR 318/1 2021 - 438445824.

1 Introduction

Artificial Intelligence (AI) and machine learning models are increasingly applied in various domains to support human decision-making. In medical image analysis, for example, there are already successful applications of such image-based machine learning methods as can be found in radiology [12], image segmentation of organs, and computer-aided diagnosis [15]. In autonomous driving, vision-based models are used to support navigation and benefit from explainability to avoid or determine the cause of an accident [5]. In these and other application domains, it is key to provide an explanation for the system's prediction so that model architects, users, and legal entities can gain confidence and trust in the model's output [35]. Most state-of-the-art explainability approaches for image data are based on saliency maps showing which areas are associated with a model's prediction [8,38]. Often gradient-based methods like CAM [44], GradCAM [32] or LIME [31] are applied after training of a model (post-hoc) to highlight the area that the model considers important for the prediction. Such approaches provide information on "where" an important area is located, but cannot provide a causal explanation which can be insufficient for domains where structure plays a crucial role [27]. Counterfactual Explanations (CFEs) are a valuable approach for addressing "why" questions and analyzing structural changes in images. In general, these explanations rely on counterfactual reasoning, which involves identifying the features that, if modified, would lead to different outcomes or predictions [28]. In the context of image analysis, counterfactuals modify specific features or regions of an image that bear causal responsibility for the model's prediction. Causality, within the framework of CFEs, pertains to the relationship between causes and their effects or outcomes [28]. It is important to note that this notion of causality differs from the traditional concept of causal modeling as discussed in Halpern and Pearl [16] since CFEs do not rely on explicit causal models or assumptions about interdependent variables [40]. CFEs, while closely associated with contrastive explanations and algorithmic recourse, offer a distinct perspective as described in Karimi et al. [19]. On the one hand, counterfactuals excel at identifying instances that exhibit interpretable differences and yield different predictions, providing unique insights into the model's decision-making process. on the other hand, contrastive explanations emphasize highlighting differences between a given and alternative event, while algorithmic recourse focuses on actionable recommendations.

An important property of CFEs mentioned in the literature is sparsity, referring to the fact that the changes in an image or input vector should be as minimal as possible to maximize interpretability by an end user [39,40]. Our contribution addresses the sparsity property, which is seldom explicitly tackled in the image domain, especially when employing methods like CycleGAN to generate counterfactual explanations. This requirement is particularly critical in domains like medical imaging, where distinguishing between diseases relies on identifying small and subtle differences. Existing approaches often face challenges in accurately identifying the minimal causally responsible areas, leading to widespread alterations throughout the entire image.

To alleviate this situation, we introduce our proposed method called "Attention Based Counterfactual via CycleGAN" (ABC-GAN). Our approach utilizes CycleGANs [45] for object translation while incorporating the attention map obtained from the classifier using GradCAM++ [6] and a counterfactual loss [27]. By combining these elements, we can accurately identify and modify the minimal region in an image required to flip the prediction of the classifier. ABC-GAN is specifically designed for "high precision explanatory contexts" where the detection of subtle changes and maintaining sparsity in the generated counterfactual explanations is of utmost importance.

We show that our method is effective in finding and visibly changing the causal area in experiments on a challenging dataset, the MURA dataset. It outperforms a state-of-the-art model, GANterfactual [27], in generating meaningful counterfactual images in this high-precision explanatory setting. The resulting counterfactuals have smaller changes (high sparsity) and higher accuracy in switching the classifier's prediction with the generated image, thus being a true counterfactual. Furthermore, aside from assessing our proposed method in a high-precision explanatory setting, we have also performed a comparative analysis against a state-of-the-art approach on the RSNA Chest X-ray dataset, which requires fewer subtle alterations.

Our contribution can be summarized as follows:

1. We utilize an attention-cropping mechanism to promote sparsity during image generation. Unlike related object translation approaches that employ additional attention networks, we leverage the attention generated by Grad-CAM++ from the classifier we aim to explain.
2. We combine the object translation with a counterfactual loss introduced by Mertes et al. [27] to generate counterfactual explanations.
3. To tackle the increased complexity introduced by attention maps and the counterfactual loss, we conduct experiments with various parameters and configurations to identify a stable solution that we can generalize to a second dataset.

2   Related Work

2.1   Counterfactual Explanations for Image Data

Counterfactual explanations for image data are generally designed to provide insights into the "why"behind a model's specific prediction by modifying the image and highlighting visible differences. This approach aligns with human reasoning, as individuals often employ counterfactual simulations to make causal judgments [28]. When it comes to computing counterfactuals through optimization, the process typically involves identifying the minimal perturbation necessary to alter the current instance [40]. However, it is important to consider that in certain cases, nearby instances may not be plausible, indicating that their occurrence is unlikely [9]. To tackle this issue, Kuhl et al. proposed the inclusion

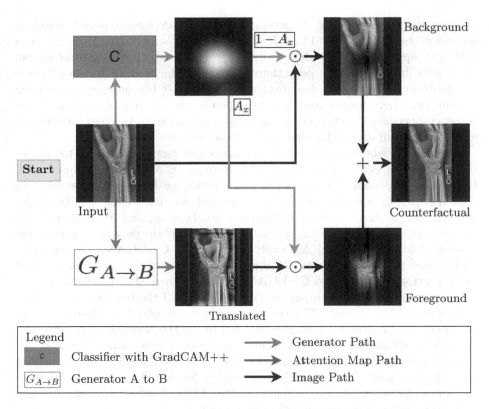

Fig. 1. The attention-based generation process in ABC-GAN is demonstrated using a MURA Wrist Image belonging to the "abnormality" class as an example. The blue arrows depict the path taken to create the attention map, where the input image is passed through the classifier (C), and the GradCAM++ algorithm is employed to generate the attention map A_x. To obtain the background, the attention map is multiplied with the input image. On the other hand, the Generator Path (red arrows) illustrates the translation step from the input image to a translated representation shows as "anslated". This translated image is then multiplied with the inverse of the attention map $1 - A_x$ to acquire the Foreground. Finally, the background and foreground images are combined through addition, resulting in the counterfactual. (Color figure online)

of a plausibility constraint, which helps generate counterfactual instances that are both minimal and plausible [23]. While these techniques prove effective for tabular data, perturbing individual pixels in images lacks semantic meaning and is unlikely to yield plausible counterfactuals.

For image data, patch-based swapping of small sections from a different class can be used to generate counterfactuals [14]. However, this technique may not yield realistic-looking images for more complex datasets, as demonstrated on the Caltech-UCSD Birds dataset [41]. The presence of misalignment between the patterns of birds and their surrounding natural backgrounds can result in counterfactual outcomes that appear implausible. In a recent study by Boreiko et al. [4], the authors the issue of sparse counterfactual explanations and introduce a novel perturbation method to induce changes in a focused area. However, even with this approach, subtle changes in the background may still occur as can be seen in their evaluation, potentially influencing the model's decision. This is less problematic in general domains like ImageNet [10] but becomes challenging in domains where precise and focused explanations are crucial, such as X-ray imaging. Specialized techniques are needed to minimize background interference and ensure accurate and focused explanations for such datasets.

In domains where small changes in images can significantly alter the classifier's prediction, counterfactuals should be proximate, plausible, and sparse [40]. Generative approaches using GANs can provide realistic-looking results, as demonstrated by Kenny et al. [21] on simple datasets like MNIST. In the realm of CFEs for medical Chest X-ray images, Singla et al. [33] leverage a conditional GAN [34] incorporating a loss function to retain patient-specific information. Additional research has explored the use of CycleGANs for generating CFEs using the Image-to-Image (I2I) generation framework. Narayanaswamy et al. [29] introduce a modified CycleGAN approach, where they incorporate a 1 x 1 convolutional path from input to output and model the functions as residual networks. GANterfactual [27] incorporates a counterfactual loss that penalizes the generator for producing images that fail to flip the classifier's prediction.

Guided diffusion models have shown promise in generating CFEs, as evidenced by recent studies [1,18]. However, these models require longer training and inference times since they rely on a lengthy Markov chain and employ more resources compared to older techniques like GANs. Furthermore, the work of [1,18] does not enforce minimal changes (sparsity).

While existing approaches utilizing CycleGAN aim to generate counterfactuals that closely resemble the input image, they often neglect the aspect of sparsity and may alter multiple regions of the image, as we will demonstrate in subsequent sections (see difference maps in Fig. 4). To address this limitation, we incorporate the classifier's attention to guide and refine the generation process, in addition to the counterfactual loss. The details of this approach will be elaborated upon in the following section, highlighting how it guides a CycleGAN toward generating more sparse and focused CFEs.

2.2   Attention-Guided GANs

Image-to-Image (I2I) approaches are designed to facilitate the translation of images from a source domain to a target domain while retaining the underlying content representation. Within the realm of I2I, there exists a particular scenario known as object transfiguration, wherein only selected objects undergo transformation into another domain. A notable challenge in object transfiguration involves the localization of the target object, and various solutions have been proposed utilizing the CycleGAN architecture. While certain methods rely on annotated attention masks to locate the relevant regions [24], alternative approaches can identify these regions without such annotations. A number of approaches train additional CNNs either jointly with the CycleGAN [26] or separately [7,20]. Other approaches modify the generator and discriminator of the CycleGAN to produce attention maps by a type of self-attention [43] or a built-in attention mechanism [37]. In the context of counterfactual image generation, object transfiguration serves as a means to induce sparse changes. However, the aforementioned approaches not only introduce additional networks or attention modules to the CycleGAN architecture, thereby increasing the parameter count, but they also do not consider the classifier that requires explanation. In our work, we incorporate the concept of object translation while obtaining the attention map through saliency map techniques like GradCAM++ [6]. This adaptation allows us to address these limitations and align our approach with the classifier to be explained.

3 Methods

Our objective is to generate plausible counterfactual image explanations by applying minimal changes to specific areas. The key innovation of our method lies in guiding the object translation location using the attention map of the classifier to be explained in combination with the counterfactual loss to penalize images that do not result in a flip in the classifier's prediction. In the following, we present the necessary parts of the architecture of our solution, ABC-GAN. We start with the image-to-image translation methodology and further explain how to incorporate the classifier's attention. As our method relies on the counterfactual loss to guide the generative process towards flipping the classifier prediction, it is explained lastly and the full objective function is shown.

3.1 Classifier Models

We trained a classifier for each dataset and show the evaluation metrics in Table 4. In the case of the MURA dataset, we use the InceptionV3 model for the classification of whether abnormalities are present in X-ray images. For the RSNA dataset, as we aim to create a comparative setting to the GANterfactual [27] experiment, we also use the AlexNET [22] classifier with the main modification to include L2 regularisation as suggested by the authors of GANterfactual. We further use their CycleGAN training configurations for both datasets as the two domains are close.

3.2 CycleGAN for Object Translation

Our approach builds upon the image-to-image (I2I) framework for image generation [27,29] and utilizes the CycleGAN [45] to generate CFEs. In order to establish the necessary groundwork for our approach, we provide an overview of the fundamental concepts and techniques that underpin our adaptation in the following.

We employ the original CycleGAN architecture, which consists of ResNet generators and Patch-GAN discriminators. In the following, we recap each component of the loss function. The objective function of CycleGAN consists of three parts that are combined to guide the training. First, the adversarial loss [13] $\mathcal{L}_{adv}$ for the mapping from A to B is defined as:

$$
\begin{aligned}
\mathcal{L}_{adv}(G_{AB}, D_B) = & \mathbb{E}_{b \sim p_{(B)}}[\log D_B(b)] \\
& + \mathbb{E}_{a \sim p_{(A)}}[\log(1 - D_B(G_{AB}(A)))].
\end{aligned}
\tag{1}
$$

During training, $\mathcal{L}_{adv}$ guides the generator to produce images indistinguishable from the real data. Since the CycleGAN trains two generators, the reverse mapping is analogous, and the complete adversarial loss is the combination of both.

Next, the identity loss [36] $\mathcal{L}_{id}$ guides the generators to preserve the identity of input images, preventing unnecessary changes to the coloration of the images. The loss is calculated as follows:

$$
\mathcal{L}_{id}(G_{AB}, G_{BA}) = \mathbb{E}b \sim p_{(B)}[\|G_{AB}(b) - b\|_1] + \mathbb{E}a \sim p_{(A)}[\|G_{BA}(a) - a\|_1]
\tag{2}
$$

Lastly, the cycle-consistency loss [45] $\mathcal{L}_{cyc}$ enforces that an image translated from A to B and back to A (cyclic translation) is similar to the initial input image. It is defined as:

$$
\begin{aligned}
\mathcal{L}_{cyc}(G_{AB}, G_{BA}) = & \mathbb{E}_{a \sim p_{(A)}}[\|G_{BA}(G_{AB}(a)) - a\|_1] \\
& + \mathbb{E}_{b \sim p_{(B)}}[\|G_{AB}(G_{BA}(b)) - b\|_1]].
\end{aligned}
\tag{3}
$$

These losses are used in the full objective function for this paper and can be seen in Eq. 7.

3.3 Attention-Guided Image-to-Image Translation

For an adequate counterfactual explanation, the resulting image should be similar to the input image with minor (sparse), visible changes, while flipping the classifier's prediction. Although previously proposed loss functions aim to restrict the altered area, there is no explicit constraint imposed on the generator to prevent extensive modifications across multiple parts of the image.

To overcome this, we utilize object transfiguration techniques to separate an image into its foreground (i.e., important area) and background [7,26,37]. This is achieved by leveraging spatial attention maps that highlight the regions of interest within the image. Unlike the object transfiguration methods outlined in the related work which use additional attention modules or CNNs to find the object to change, we employ GradCAM++ [6] for accomplishing this task. The attention maps returned by GradCAM++ are scaled to match the size of the input images and the importance of pixels in the classifier's decision is indicated by higher values, reaching a maximum of 1. To mitigate the issue of ill-fitting corners between the foreground object and the background, we represent the attention maps as continuous values within the range of 0 to 1. This approach facilitates the creation of gradual masks, ensuring that there is no overlap between the foreground and background regions [11].

The generation of counterfactual images utilizing our proposed approach, involving the attention map A_x obtained from the classifier, is described in Eq. 4. The process unfolds as follows: A trained classifier C predicts the class probabilities of an image x by $C(x) = (p(A), p(B))^T$. Here, $p(A)$ is the probability of x belonging to class A, and $p(B)$ is the probability of x belonging to class B. Let G_{AB} be the generator from domain A to B. Given an input sample x, the attention-map A_x is obtained by an XAI method I on the classifier:

$$A_x = I(C(x))$$

and the foreground and background are defined by

$$Foreground : A_x \odot x$$

$$Background : (1 - A_x) \odot x$$

Putting all together, the translated image x' is calculated by

$$x' = A_x \odot G_{AB}(x) + (1 - A_x) \odot x \tag{4}$$

An illustration of the generation step can be seen in Fig. 1. Intuitively, it consists of translating the whole image, cutting out the foreground, and putting it on the original background. This ensures that the background is unchanged, which leads to sparse changes. Mejjati et al. [26] also found that using the same attention technique for the discriminator improves the object translation, as only feedback for the translated part is given. We experiment with this idea by giving only the foreground of the image to the discriminator. As an XAI method to identify the important regions in the original image, we rely on GradCAM++ [6], which is better suited to locating multiple instances of an object compared to its predecessors. To include the attention map in the generative process, a custom training loop was implemented in the code base of CycleGAN Tensorflow 2[1].

3.4   Counterfactual Loss

Image-to-image applications do not aim to create CFEs. Therefore, we include the counterfactual loss [27], which guides the generator toward generating counterfactual images. This loss promotes generated images that successfully flip the prediction of the classifier.

---

[1] https://github.com/LynnHo/CycleGAN-Tensorflow-2.

Given a CycleGAN model with generators G_{AB} and G_{BA} responsible for mapping images between domain A and domain B, the generated CFEs should adhere to the following property with respect to a trained classifier C:

$$C(x) = A \Rightarrow C(G_{AB}(x)) = B$$

and

$$C(x) = B \Rightarrow C(G_{BA}(x)) = A \tag{5}$$

With the above property, Mertes et al. [27] define the counterfactual loss $\mathcal{L}_{cf}$ as:

$$\mathcal{L}_{cf}(G_{AB}, G_{BA}, C) = E_{a \sim p_{(A)}}[\|C_2(G_{AB}(a)) - \binom{0}{1}\|_2^2] \\ + E_{b \sim p_{(B)}}[\|C_2(G_{BA}(b)) - \binom{1}{0}\|_2^2] \tag{6}$$

where $\| \cdot \|_2^2$ is the squared L2 norm.
Finally, the complete objective function becomes the following:

$$\begin{aligned} \mathcal{L}(G_{AB}, G_{BA}, D_A, D_B, C) = {} & \alpha(\mathcal{L}_{adv}(G_{AB}, D_A, A, B) \\ & + \mathcal{L}_{adv}(G_{BA}, D_B, A, B)) \\ & + \lambda \mathcal{L}_{cyc}(G_{AB}, G_{BA}) \\ & + \mu \mathcal{L}_{id}(G_{AB}, G_{BA}) \\ & + \gamma \mathcal{L}_{cf}(G_{AB}, G_{BA}, C) \end{aligned} \tag{7}$$

where α is the Adversarial Loss Weight, λ is the Cycle-Consistency Loss Weight, μ is the Identity Loss Weight and γ is the Counterfactual Loss Weight.

4   Experiments

First, we tested our proposed architecture and performed a parameter search on the challenging MURA Wrist-Xray Images dataset. We also evaluated our approach against CycleGAN and GANterfactual on the RSNA Chest-Xray dataset to compare performance on a slightly different problem which GANterfactual was developed for.

4.1   Datasets

The MURA dataset [30] is a collection of 14,863 studies (40,561 images) of the upper body extremities from the Stanford Hospital that are binary labeled as *normal* or *abnormal* by board-certified radiologists. It contains 9,045 *normal* and 5,818 *abnormal* musculoskeletal radiographic studies. The dataset is one of the largest public radiographic image datasets and is commonly used for ML classification experiments. We consider in particular the subset of 10,411 wrist images that are quite balanced.

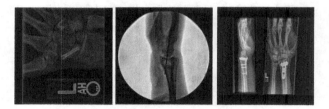

Fig. 2. Sample of difficult wrist images extracted from the MURA dataset. The images shown depict scenarios where there is a variation in wrist rotation and scale, the background colors are not consistent and several scans can be present in a single image.

We further evaluate our method on the RSNA dataset, where our comparative model, GANterfactual, was designed for. The RSNA dataset has X-ray images with various illnesses and abnormalities, such as pneumonia, emphysema, and lung cancer, and was made available for the Kaggle Pneumonia detection challenge.[2] We use the same data selection and split procedure as suggested by Mertes et al. [27], resulting in approximately 15,000 images that are split into training, validation, and test sets. The MURA dataset is more diverse and demanding than the RSNA dataset, as body parts and orientations are kept consistent throughout the latter. Some examples of challenging cases can be seen in Fig. 2.

Preprocessing. We use contrast limited histogram equalization (CLAHE) for the MURA dataset since it has been shown to increase model performance on medical X-ray images [2] and enhances the training of CNNs [17]. To improve model robustness, we use data augmentation techniques such as horizontal flipping, random gamma changes, and random brightness. We preprocess the RSNA dataset using steps similar to those in GANterfactual, which involve rescaling the images and scaling the pixel values.

4.2   Experimental Setup

The code of our implementation can be found online[3].

We perform end-to-end CycleGAN training with 20 epochs for both datasets. We use an Adam Optimizer with $\beta_1 = 0.5$ and $\beta_2 = 0.99$, a learning rate of 0.0001, and a batch size of 1 as originally suggested in Zhu et al. [45]. Each model uses the same objective function but with some weight values set to zero. Table 1 shows the loss weights for each model in the objective function presented in Eq. 7. The training was performed on GPU cores of the GTX (GTX 1080 Ti) architectures. The image size of 512 by 512 pixels as well as the data amount of around 10k-15k samples led to a training duration of approximately two days.

---

[2] https://www.kaggle.com/competitions/rsna-pneumonia-detection-challenge.
[3] https://github.com/dimitrymindlin/ABC-GAN.

Table 1. Loss weights of each model for Eq. 7.

Model Name	α	λ	μ	γ
CycleGAN	1	10	0	1
GANterfactual	1	10	1	1
ABC-GAN (Ours)	1	10	1	0

4.3 Evaluation Metrics

For a proper evaluation, we have to consider both, image quality and the flip in classifier prediction. For image quality, the Kernel Inception Distance (KID) [3] and Structure Similarity Index (SSIM) [42] are used. KID measures the similarity in feature space between a set of generated and original images, with the help of the InceptionV3 model's encoding layers. The KID value is multiplied by 100. We generate counterfactuals for the test set and evaluate the KID with randomly sampled images from the training set in five splits. SSIM directly compares the generated with the original image on pixel level and is widely used as a metric to evaluate the image quality of generated images. SSIM has a maximum of 1, indicating perfect similarity. To evaluate if the counterfactuals are flipping the classifier's prediction, the Target Validity Score (TCV) [25] can be used. This score captures the percentage of counterfactuals that successfully flip the prediction.

5 Results

5.1 ABC-GAN Settings Experiments

We conducted extensive experiments on the MURA dataset to optimize the ABC-GAN settings. Our findings indicate that the best model configuration is achieved by incorporating attention in the discriminator step, setting the weight of the identity loss to 0, and commencing the attention process after the halfway point of training. (See Appendix B). Among the seven alternative settings, this particular model, referred to as ABC-GAN, demonstrated superior performance and outperformed the others. The same architecture was used for both datasets, to show the generalisability of the settings.

5.2 Comparison to Competitive Approach and Baseline

We compared ABC-GAN to CycleGAN as a baseline and a state-of-the-art method, GANterfactual [27], on the MURA and RSNA datasets. In the case of the MURA dataset, we observe a consistent trend in both directions of domain translation. As a result, we only present the average results in the corresponding tables for clarity and conciseness. However, for the RSNA dataset, it is crucial to examine each direction separately, as one direction may exhibit better performance than the other.

In terms of image quality, ABC-GAN outperformed the other competitive methods, as indicated by its lower Kernel Inception Distance (KID) and higher Structural Similarity Index (SSIM) values. This superior performance in generating counterfactual explanations that closely resemble the original images is consistent across both the MURA and RSNA datasets.

We showcase the mapping from MURA abnormal to normal images, with a specific focus on hardware abnormalities. This choice aims to ensure that the results are interpretable and accessible to non-professionals, enabling a wider understanding of the generated outcomes. However, interpreting the reverse mapping from normal to abnormal images is challenging due to the presence of multiple diseases within the abnormality class. (See Appendix D). To provide an overview of the performance of our model, as well as the competitive models and the ablation study, we handpicked representative images and present them in Fig. 3. Upon close observation, we note that in cases where our method fails to remove the abnormality, the alternative methods also encounter difficulties in effectively eliminating the abnormality. Conversely, when our system successfully removes the abnormality, the other approaches struggle to achieve the same level of effectiveness. This observation highlights the consistency of our method's performance relative to the alternatives and underscores its ability to generate more accurate and reliable counterfactual explanations.

In our analysis, we further employed difference maps to evaluate the size of the area of change between ABC-GAN and the competing models. By visualizing these difference maps, we could observe and assess the subtle alterations in the generated counterfactual explanations. This analysis enabled us to determine the sparsity of the changes made by each method and gain insights into the level of precision and specificity in the generated counterfactuals. The generated images in Fig. 4 show that ABC-GAN only alters the attended area, while GANterfactual and CycleGAN alter the whole image. The high SSIM and low KID values achieved by ABC-GAN indicate that the generated counterfactual images are visually realistic and close to the input image. In these images, the hardware abnormality is made less prominent while preserving the overall appearance of the rest of the image. In contrast, GANterfactual tends to apply changes to a larger portion of the image, in combination with a failure to effectively remove the abnormalities. The higher KID values obtained by GANterfactual reflect the dissimilarity of the generated images to the target class in the feature space. In the case of the RSNA dataset, we observed that ABC-GAN occasionally generated counterfactual images where certain parts of the image still retained characteristics of the other domain. This observation is supported both quantitatively by the lower True Counterfactual Validity (TCV) scores and visually in the provided Appendix D. Conversely, GANterfactual and CycleGAN demonstrated more success in translating the expected parts of the image, encompassing a larger portion of the abnormalities (Tables 2 and 3).

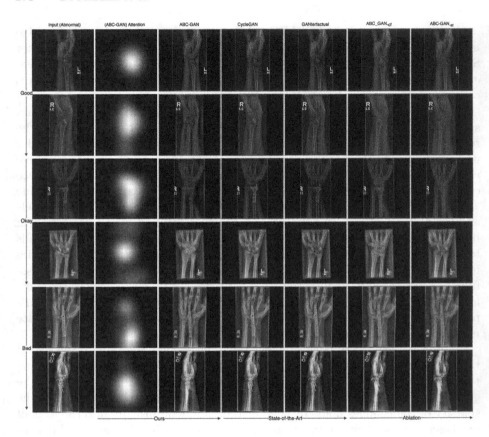

Fig. 3. MURA abnormal to normal mapping on selected samples to showcase good, okay, and bad performance. Comparing ABC-GAN with GANterfactual and models from the ablation study. Green borders show that image flipped classifiers prediction while red borders show that the generated image still belongs to the source class. (Color figure online)

Table 2. Evaluation Table for the MURA dataset. Showing averaged values of both domain mapping directions. KID: Lower is better, TCV and SSIM: Higher is better.

Approach	↓ KID	↑ TCV	↑ SSIM
CycleGAN	0.36	0.53	0.89
GANterfactual	0.38	0.99	0.84
ABC-GAN (Ours)	0.24	0.99	0.88

Table 3. Evaluation Table for the RSNA dataset. KID: Lower is better, TCV and SSIM: Higher is better.

Approach	↓ KID	↑ TCV	↑ SSIM
Averages			
CycleGAN	1.27 ± 0.03	0.56	0.65
GANterfactual	1.60 ± 0	0.95	0.56
ABC-GAN (Ours)	0.56 ± 0.02	0.86	0.75
Normal to Pneumonia			
CycleGAN	1.15 ± 0.05	0.34	0.71
GANterfactual	1.0 ± 0	0.98	0.65
ABC-GAN (Ours)	0.4 ± 0	0.95	0.72
Pneumonia to Normal			
CycleGAN	1.4 ± 0	0.77	0.58
GANterfactual	2.2 ± 0	0.91	0.47
ABC-GAN (Ours)	0.72 ± 0.04	0.78	0.77

5.3 Ablation Study

We perform an ablation study to justify the inclusion of classifier attention and counterfactual loss, resulting in two models to evaluate:

1. Ablating the counterfactual loss, the model results in a CycleGAN with our proposed attention strategy (ABC-GAN (Ours)$_{-cf}$).
2. Ablating the attention mechanism and leaves the approach similar to Mertes et al. [27] yet without the identity loss (ABC-GAN (Ours)$_{-at}$).

The full ablation study table can be found in Table 6. Without the counterfactual loss, we observe that TCV is going down as expected and in the case of the translation from abnormal to normal, it drops dramatically. When the classifier's attention is removed from the process, we observed a drop in the TCV. In our analysis, we found that the similarity scores are higher when excluding one of the components, which may indicate that the generated images undergo minimal changes. While higher similarity values are generally desirable, it is important to note that values close to 1 suggest that the changes made to the images are so subtle that they may not be visibly noticeable upon qualitative evaluation. Moreover, the absence of the attention map makes changes all over the image as can be seen in GANterfactual and CycleGAN in Fig. 4. Visual results for both versions are shown in Fig. 3.

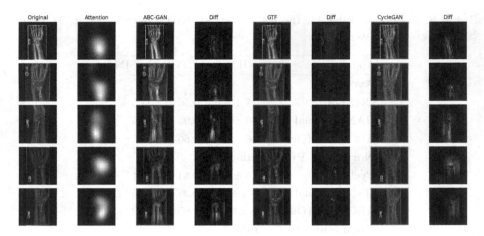

Fig. 4. MURA abnormal to normal mapping on random samples. Comparative analysis of model performances. Accompanying each model, the difference between the original image and the counterfactual image is displayed on the right for visualization of the altered areas ("Diff" column). A green border is indicative of the successful prediction of the target class by the classifier, while a red border denotes otherwise. The attention column showcases the classifier's focus on the original image. (Color figure online)

6   Discussion

Our work focuses on sparse counterfactual image explanations in high-precision scenarios and has proposed ABC-GAN as a novel approach combining two key elements: the incorporation of the attention map of the classifier into the generative process of CycleGANs and the utilization of the counterfactual loss. This combination enables the generation of sparse CFEs, where only minimal and relevant changes are made to the input image. The optimal settings found by various experiments were by excluding the identity loss in CycleGAN, initiating the attention mechanism halfway through training, and employing both the attentive generator and attentive discriminator components. ABC-GAN's ability to perform small changes compared to other models is reflected in the KID and SSIM scores in both datasets. Although the TCV demonstrates near-perfect performance on the MURA images, the worse performance on the RSNA dataset can be attributed to the fact that the attention map did not capture the entire significant region. The RSNA dataset comprises diseases with a wider spread in terms of anatomical localization, and thus, focused and restricted changes might not be sufficient to remove the disease that spreads over the whole lung. The tested attention map of the classifier guides toward small changes, which are not always sufficient to switch the classifier's prediction, making it less suited for tasks requiring changes to broad areas of images. Nevertheless, this is not surprising as it was designed to apply small targeted changes. The limitations of our work include the evaluation and interpretability of the visual results on the given datasets. We utilize standard metrics that are accepted as proxies, but the actual effectiveness remains unclear and requires expert evaluation. This will be addressed in future work, where we plan experiments with medical professionals.

Regarding the interpretability of the visual results, we acknowledge that the chosen domain may pose challenges for readers outside the medical field. To address this issue, we specifically focused on hardware abnormalities, which are considered to be relatively easier to interpret. By comparing the visual methods for these cases, we aimed to provide a more accessible and understandable evaluation. However, we are aware that this approach may limit the qualitative evaluation to a certain extent.

It is important to note that our study is the first to tackle the MURA dataset for generating counterfactual explanations. Given the nature of the dataset and the absence of ground truth annotations for counterfactuals, obtaining a more comprehensive evaluation without the involvement of medical professionals can be challenging. Nonetheless, our approach contributes to the technical exploration of counterfactual explanations in the medical domain, paving the way for future research in this field.

7   Future Work

In our future work, we plan to explore several avenues to enhance and expand upon our research. Firstly, we aim to analyze the tradeoff between True Counterfactual Validity (TCV) and image similarity, as it is crucial to strike a balance between generating meaningful counterfactual explanations and preserving the overall visual similarity to the original images. This analysis will help us fine-tune our approach and optimize the model's performance.

Additionally, we intend to investigate the use of different saliency map algorithms to further improve the interpretability of our generated counterfactual explanations. By incorporating alternative methods for generating attention maps, we can explore different approaches to highlighting important regions in the image and providing more insightful visual explanations.

To ensure the effectiveness and usability of our approach, we plan to conduct user studies with domain experts in the medical field. Their feedback and insights will be valuable in validating the interpretability and utility of our generated counterfactual explanations.

Lastly, we recognize the importance of evaluating our method against more recent techniques such as Diffusion Models [1]. By conducting comparative evaluations, we can gain a better understanding of the strengths and limitations of different approaches in generating counterfactual explanations.

8   Conclusion

In conclusion, our research addresses the need for sparse counterfactual image explanations in high-precision scenarios by presenting ABC-GAN, a novel approach to generating traceable, minimal CFEs for image classifiers. Our findings show that ABC-GAN successfully incorporates attention maps and a counterfactual loss to generate counterfactual images with a spatial constraint, making explanations more sparse and traceable. Through our experiments, we show that our method learns meaningful translations despite added complexity through attention maps and a counterfactual loss. Overall, ABC-GAN has the potential to provide useful explanations for high-precision scenarios, and further research on CNN attention maps as well as image translation will improve its performance.

A   Classifier Evaluation

Table 4. Classifier evaluation results per dataset. The MURA row describes the results for the InceptionV3 model and the RSNA row for the ResNet model.

Dataset	AUC	Precision	Recall	F1 Score
MURA	0.91	0.87	0.84	0.85
RSNA	0.93	0.98	0.87	0.86

B   ABC-GAN Parameter Search

(See Table 5).

Table 5. MURA parameter and architecture search results sorted by KID. The first three columns indicate which settings are chosen, where 'AD.' uses the Attentive Discriminator, L_{id} sets identity loss weight to 1, and 'LA.' is 'Yes' if attention begins after half of training. The optimal settings are located in the bottom rows, where omitting identity loss and delaying attention achieve the lowest KID value.

AD	L_{id}	LA	KID	TCV	SSIM
Yes	Yes	No	0.38	0.99	0.84
Yes	No	No	0.34	0.97	0.85
Yes	Yes	Yes	0.31	0.99	0.86
No	No	No	0.27	0.97	0.90
No	Yes	No	0.26	0.93	0.90
No	Yes	Yes	0.25	0.99	0.89
No	No	Yes	0.24	0.99	0.88
Yes	No	Yes	0.24	0.99	0.88

C   ABC-GAN Ablation Study

Table 6. Ablation study of ABC-GAN (Ours). The first ablation removes the counterfactual loss and the second removes the attention mechanism. Results show that the full model achieves the highest TCV value, suggesting that all components are needed to produce CFEs.

Approach	↓ KID	↑ TCV	↑ SSIM
Normal to Abnormal			
ABC-GAN (Ours)$_{-cf}$	0.38 ± 0.04	0.95	0.87
ABC-GAN (Ours)$_{-at}$	0.2 ± 0	0.86	0.93
ABC-GAN (Ours)	0.26 ± 0.05	1	0.86
Abnormal to Normal			
ABC-GAN (Ours)$_{-cf}$	0.2 ± 0	0.22	0.92
ABC-GAN (Ours)$_{-at}$	0.1 ± 0	0.74	0.95
ABC-GAN (Ours)	0.22 ± 0.04	0.99	0.90

D   Visual Examples on MURA and RSNA Datasets

(See Figs. 5 and 6).

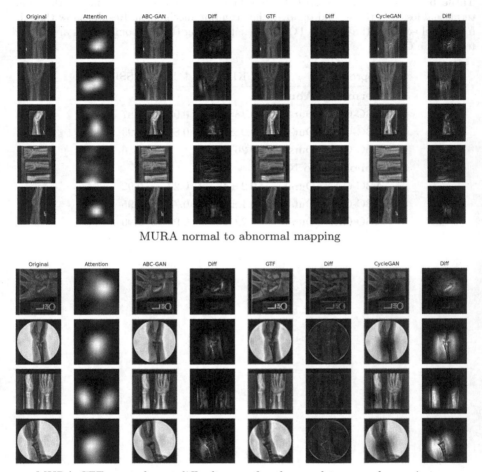

MURA normal to abnormal mapping

MURA CFE examples on difficult cases for abnormal to normal mapping.

Fig. 5. Image grids comparing different models for MURA Images. Next to each model, on the right, the difference image between the original and the counterfactual is shown to see where changes were applied ("Diff" column). A green border indicates that the classifier prediction is flipped, otherwise, a red border is shown. The "Attention" column shows the classifier's attention toward the original image. (Color figure online)

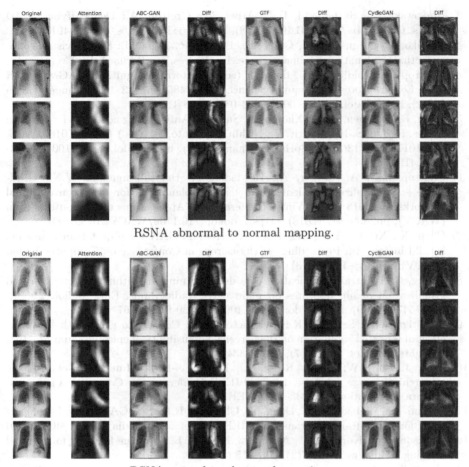

RSNA abnormal to normal mapping.

RSNA normal to abnormal mapping.

Fig. 6. Image grids comparing different models for RSNA data. The same color coding and column order applies as in other image grids.

References

1. Augustin, M., Boreiko, V., Croce, F., Hein, M.: Diffusion visual counterfactual explanations. CoRR **abs/2210.11841** (2022). https://doi.org/10.48550/arXiv.2210.11841
2. Bhat, M., Patil, T.: Adaptive clip limit for contrast limited adaptive histogram equalization (CLAHE) of medical images using least mean square algorithm. In: 2014 IEEE International Conference on Advanced Communications, Control and Computing Technologies, pp. 1259–1263. IEEE (2014)

3. Binkowski, M., Sutherland, D.J., Arbel, M., Gretton, A.: Demystifying MMD GANs. CoRR **abs/1801.01401** (2018). http://arxiv.org/abs/1801.01401
4. Boreiko, V., Augustin, M., Croce, F., Berens, P., Hein, M.: Sparse visual counterfactual explanations in image space. In: Andres, B., Bernard, F., Cremers, D., Frintrop, S., Goldlücke, B., Ihrke, I. (eds.) Pattern Recognition, DAGM GCPR 2022. Lecture Notes in Computer Science, vol. 13485, pp. 133–148. Springer, Cham (2022). https://doi.org/10.1007/978-3-031-16788-1_9
5. Chan, F.-H., Chen, Y.-T., Xiang, Yu., Sun, M.: Anticipating accidents in dashcam videos. In: Lai, S.-H., Lepetit, V., Nishino, K., Sato, Y. (eds.) ACCV 2016. LNCS, vol. 10114, pp. 136–153. Springer, Cham (2017). https://doi.org/10.1007/978-3-319-54190-7_9
6. Chattopadhay, A., Sarkar, A., Howlader, P., Balasubramanian, V.N.: Gradcam++: Generalized gradient-based visual explanations for deep convolutional networks. In: 2018 IEEE Winter Conference on Applications of Computer Vision (WACV), pp. 839–847 (2018). https://doi.org/10.1109/WACV.2018.00097
7. Chen, X., Xu, C., Yang, X., Tao, D.: Attention-GAN for object transfiguration in wild images. In: Proceedings of the European Conference on Computer Vision (ECCV), pp. 164–180 (2018)
8. Cheng, C.-T., et al.: Application of a deep learning algorithm for detection and visualization of hip fractures on plain pelvic radiographs. Eur. Radiol. **29**(10), 5469–5477 (2019). https://doi.org/10.1007/s00330-019-06167-y
9. De Brigard, F., Szpunar, K.K., Schacter, D.L.: Coming to grips with the past: effect of repeated simulation on the perceived plausibility of episodic counterfactual thoughts. Psychol. Sci. **24**(7), 1329–1334 (2013)
10. Deng, J., Dong, W., Socher, R., Li, L.J., Li, K., Fei-Fei, L.: ImageNet: a large-scale hierarchical image database. In: 2009 IEEE Conference on Computer Vision and Pattern Recognition, pp. 248–255. IEEE (2009)
11. Emami, H., Aliabadi, M.M., Dong, M., Chinnam, R.B.: Spa-GAN: spatial attention GAN for image-to-image translation. IEEE Trans. Multimedia **23**, 391–401 (2020)
12. Erickson, B.J., Korfiatis, P., Akkus, Z., Kline, T.L.: Machine learning for medical imaging. Radiographics **37**(2), 505–515 (2017)
13. Goodfellow, I., et al.: Generative adversarial networks. Commun. ACM **63**(11), 139–144 (2020)
14. Goyal, Y., Wu, Z., Ernst, J., Batra, D., Parikh, D., Lee, S.: Counterfactual visual explanations. In: International Conference on Machine Learning, pp. 2376–2384. PMLR (2019)
15. Haleem, A., Javaid, M., Khan, I.H.: Current status and applications of artificial intelligence (AI) in medical field: an overview. Current Med. Res. Pract. **9**(6), 231–237 (2019)
16. Halpern, J.Y., Pearl, J.: Causes and explanations: a structural-model approach. Part I: Causes. British J. Philos. Sci. (2005)
17. Ikhsan, I.A.M., Hussain, A., Zulkifley, M.A., Tahir, N.M., Mustapha, A.: An analysis of x-ray image enhancement methods for vertebral bone segmentation. In: 2014 IEEE 10th International Colloquium on Signal Processing and its Applications, pp. 208–211. IEEE (2014)
18. Jeanneret, G., Simon, L., Jurie, F.: Diffusion models for counterfactual explanations. CoRR **abs/2203.15636** (2022). https://doi.org/10.48550/arXiv.2203.15636
19. Karimi, A.H., Barthe, G., Schölkopf, B., Valera, I.: A survey of algorithmic recourse: contrastive explanations and consequential recommendations. ACM Comput. Surv. **55**(5), 1–29 (2022)

20. Kastaniotis, D., Ntinou, I., Tsourounis, D., Economou, G., Fotopoulos, S.: Attention-aware generative adversarial networks (ATA-GANs). In: 2018 IEEE 13th Image, Video, and Multidimensional Signal Processing Workshop (IVMSP), pp. 1–5. IEEE (2018)

21. Kenny, E.M., Keane, M.T.: On generating plausible counterfactual and semi-factual explanations for deep learning. In: Proceedings of the AAAI Conference on Artificial Intelligence, vol. 35, pp. 11575–11585 (2021)

22. Krizhevsky, A., Sutskever, I., Hinton, G.E.: ImageNet classification with deep convolutional neural networks. Commun. ACM **60**(6), 84–90 (2017)

23. Kuhl, U., Artelt, A., Hammer, B.: Keep your friends close and your counterfactuals closer: improved learning from closest rather than plausible counterfactual explanations in an abstract setting. In: 2022 ACM Conference on Fairness, Accountability, and Transparency, pp. 2125–2137 (2022)

24. Liang, X., Zhang, H., Xing, E.P.: Generative semantic manipulation with contrasting GAN. arXiv preprint arXiv:1708.00315 (2017)

25. Mahajan, D., Tan, C., Sharma, A.: Preserving causal constraints in counterfactual explanations for machine learning classifiers. CoRR **abs/1912.03277** (2019). http://arxiv.org/abs/1912.03277

26. Mejjati, Y.A., Richardt, C., Tompkin, J., Cosker, D., Kim, K.I.: Unsupervised attention-guided image-to-image translation. In: Bengio, S., Wallach, H.M., Larochelle, H., Grauman, K., Cesa-Bianchi, N., Garnett, R. (eds.) Advances in Neural Information Processing Systems 31: Annual Conference on Neural Information Processing Systems 2018, NeurIPS 2018, 3–8 December 2018, Montréal, Canada, pp. 3697–3707 (2018). https://proceedings.neurips.cc/paper/2018/hash/4e87337f366f72daa424dae11df0538c-Abstract.html

27. Mertes, S., Huber, T., Weitz, K., Heimerl, A., André, E.: Ganterfactual-counterfactual explanations for medical non-experts using generative adversarial learning. Front. Artif. Intell. **5**, 825565 (2022)

28. Miller, T.: Explanation in artificial intelligence: insights from the social sciences. Artif. Intell. **267**, 1–38 (2019)

29. Narayanaswamy, A., et al.: Scientific discovery by generating counterfactuals using image translation. In: Martel, A.L., et al. (eds.) MICCAI 2020. LNCS, vol. 12261, pp. 273–283. Springer, Cham (2020). https://doi.org/10.1007/978-3-030-59710-8_27

30. Rajpurkar, P., et al.: Mura: large dataset for abnormality detection in musculoskeletal radiographs. arXiv preprint arXiv:1712.06957 (2017)

31. Ribeiro, M.T., Singh, S., Guestrin, C.: "Why should i trust you?" Explaining the predictions of any classifier. In: Proceedings of the 22nd ACM SIGKDD International Conference on Knowledge Discovery and Data Mining, pp. 1135–1144 (2016)

32. Selvaraju, R.R., Cogswell, M., Das, A., Vedantam, R., Parikh, D., Batra, D.: Grad-CAM: visual explanations from deep networks via gradient-based localization. In: Proceedings of the IEEE International Conference on Computer Vision, pp. 618–626 (2017)

33. Singla, S., Eslami, M., Pollack, B., Wallace, S., Batmanghelich, K.: Explaining the black-box smoothly-a counterfactual approach. Med. Image Anal. **84**, 102721 (2023)

34. Singla, S., Pollack, B., Chen, J., Batmanghelich, K.: Explanation by progressive exaggeration. arXiv preprint arXiv:1911.00483 (2019)

35. Suresh, H., Gomez, S.R., Nam, K.K., Satyanarayan, A.: Beyond expertise and roles: a framework to characterize the stakeholders of interpretable machine learning and

their needs. In: Proceedings of the 2021 CHI Conference on Human Factors in Computing Systems, pp. 1–16 (2021)

36. Taigman, Y., Polyak, A., Wolf, L.: Unsupervised cross-domain image generation. arXiv preprint arXiv:1611.02200 (2016)

37. Tang, H., Xu, D., Sebe, N., Yan, Y.: Attention-guided generative adversarial networks for unsupervised image-to-image translation. In: 2019 International Joint Conference on Neural Networks (IJCNN), pp. 1–8. IEEE (2019)

38. Varma, M., et al.: Automated abnormality detection in lower extremity radiographs using deep learning. Nature Mach. Intell. 1(12), 578–583 (2019)

39. Verma, S., Boonsanong, V., Hoang, M., Hines, K.E., Dickerson, J.P., Shah, C.: Counterfactual explanations and algorithmic recourses for machine learning: a review

40. Wachter, S., Mittelstadt, B., Russell, C.: Counterfactual explanations without opening the black box: automated decisions and the GDPR. Harv. JL Tech. 31, 841 (2017)

41. Wah, C., Branson, S., Welinder, P., Perona, P., Belongie, S.: The Caltech-UCSD Birds-200-2011 Dataset. Technical report CNS-TR-2011-001, California Institute of Technology (2011)

42. Wang, Z., Bovik, A.C., Sheikh, H.R., Simoncelli, E.P.: Image quality assessment: from error visibility to structural similarity. IEEE Trans. Image Process. 13(4), 600–612 (2004). https://doi.org/10.1109/TIP.2003.819861

43. Zhang, H., Goodfellow, I., Metaxas, D., Odena, A.: Self-attention generative adversarial networks. In: International Conference on Machine Learning, pp. 7354–7363. PMLR (2019)

44. Zhou, B., Khosla, A., Lapedriza, A., Oliva, A., Torralba, A.: Learning deep features for discriminative localization. In: Proceedings of the IEEE Conference on Computer Vision and Pattern Recognition, pp. 2921–2929 (2016)

45. Zhu, J.Y., Park, T., Isola, P., Efros, A.A.: Unpaired image-to-image translation using cycle-consistent adversarial networks. In: Proceedings of the IEEE International Conference on Computer Vision, pp. 2223–2232 (2017)

The Importance of Time in Causal Algorithmic Recourse

Isacco Beretta and Martina Cinquini(✉)

University of Pisa, Pisa, Italy
{isacco.beretta,martina.cinquini}@phd.unipi.it

Abstract. The application of Algorithmic Recourse in decision-making is a promising field that offers practical solutions to reverse unfavorable decisions. However, the inability of these methods to consider potential dependencies among variables poses a significant challenge due to the assumption of feature independence. Recent advancements have incorporated knowledge of causal dependencies, thereby enhancing the quality of the recommended recourse actions. Despite these improvements, the inability to incorporate the temporal dimension remains a significant limitation of these approaches. This is particularly problematic as identifying and addressing the root causes of undesired outcomes requires understanding time-dependent relationships between variables. In this work, we motivate the need to integrate the temporal dimension into causal algorithmic recourse methods to enhance recommendations' plausibility and reliability. The experimental evaluation highlights the significance of the role of time in this field.

Keywords: Algorithmic Recourse · Causality · Consequential Recommendations

1 Introduction

Counterfactual explanations are becoming one of the most promising solutions to explainability in Machine Learning due to their compliance with legal requirements [23], their psychological benefit for the individual [22], and their potential to explore "what-if" scenarios [4]. A possible circumstance in which such explanations are required is when a credit scoring model denies a loan to an applicant, and the individual desires to understand what should be different to change the outcome of the AI system (i.e., to have the loan accepted). Comprehending an unfavorable decision adds new information about the facts, enhancing human trust in automated decision-making systems. Additional advantages from the user perspective could be gained by learning what *actions* take to reach a different outcome. A novel research area [9], referred to as *Algorithmic Recourse* (AR), aims at suggesting actionable recommendations that should be performed to reverse unfavorable decisions in the future. Among extensive literature, recent work [2] highlights that a significant drawback of AR methods is the implicit

L. Longo (Ed.): xAI 2023, CCIS 1901, pp. 283–298, 2023.
https://doi.org/10.1007/978-3-031-44064-9_16

assumption of examining features as independently manipulable inputs. Since the individual's attributes change may have downstream effects on other features, observing and identifying causal mechanisms is crucial in analyzing real-world scenarios to avoid sub-optimal or infeasible actions. From this perspective, Karimi et al. [10,11] propose a fundamental reformulation of the recourse problem, incorporating knowledge of causal dependencies into the process of recommending recourse actions. The ability to assess the causal relationships explicitly guarantees plausible counterfactuals [3] and improves the user's perception of a decision's quality since it reflects the tendency of human beings to think in terms of cause-effect [16].

Despite the recent progress in this field, a significant limitation of current methods is their inability to incorporate the temporal dimension. Neglecting the temporal interdependencies between features and actions can result in erroneous identification of the feature that requires modification at a particular moment, leading to ineffective or sub-optimal recourse actions. As a result, there is a need to devise causal AR techniques that can incorporate temporal information to provide explanations that precisely reflect the complex dynamics of the system and to guarantee that the recommendations offered are reliable and plausible.

This work investigates the usefulness of integrating the temporal dimension into a causal AR problem by incorporating the topological information of the causal graph in the cost function evaluation. Besides, it discusses the necessity of interpreting the causal model as a representation of a dynamical process i.e., one that involves the evolution of its instances over time.

The rest of the paper is organized as follows. Section 2 describes the state-of-the-art related to causal AR. Section 3 recalls basic notions for understanding our proposal. Section 4 motivates for our proposal by presenting a brief methodological discussion and a practical example. The cost function evaluation is presented in Sect. 5, while Sect. 6 reports the experimental results. Section 7 examines the impact of findings on the progress of the XAI field, Sect. 8 summarizes our contributions and discusses open research directions.

2   Related Works

Most of the existing approaches in the AR literature [8,9,20] derive recourse actions through solving an optimization problem that minimizes changes to the individual's feature vector, subject to various plausibility, diversity, and sparsity constraints. In [10] is presented a paradigm shift from recourse via nearest counterfactual explanations. The objective is to find recourse through minimal interventions attempting to use a causal probabilistic framework grounded on Structural Causal Models (SCMs) that fit in the class of additive noise models. Specifically, to seek the minimal cost set of actions in the form of structural interventions that would favorably change the prediction if acted upon, authors exploit structural counterfactual computed deterministically in closed-form by applying the Abduction-Action-Prediction procedure proposed in [15]. A significant drawback of this formulation is the extraction of SCM from the observed data. Indeed, assuming the knowledge of the true causal graph and the structural equations is very challenging and, in some cases, could be unrealistic [17]. Therefore, in [11] is presented two probabilistic approaches that relax such assumption. In both cases, authors suppose the knowledge of the causal graph a priori or postulated by an expert. The first method, referred to as *individualized recourse via GP-SCMs*, consists of using additive Gaussian noise and Bayesian model averaging to estimate the counterfactual distribution. The second approach, also known as *subpopulation-based recourse via CATE*, removes any assumptions on the structural equations by computing the conditional average treatment effect of an intervention on individuals similar to the factual subject.

Recently, there has been a growing interest in extending the formulation of actions and their consequences to incorporate them into a sequential context. This is due to the fact that, in reality, most changes do not occur instantaneously but are part of a process. For instance, in [13], the authors propose a model-agnostic method for generating sequential counterfactuals that have the ability to discover multiple optimal solution sequences of varying sequence lengths.

Furthermore, another novel research direction related to AR entails distinguishing the factors that influence the change in model prediction (i.e., acceptance) from those that contribute to the state of the real world (i.e., improvement) [2]. In [12] is tackled this subject by introducing the first approach that specifically focuses on promoting improvement rather than mere acceptance.

However, to the best of our knowledge, no state-of-the-art methods account for the *temporal relationship* between features and actions. This work aims to fill such a gap by incorporating this crucial dimension, which in turn enables us to provide more precise recommendations that reflect the reality of decision-making processes. Specifically, our approach evaluates the cost of an action taken by a particular node, considering its position within the causal graph and the required time frame for the decision to have an effect. This is particularly relevant, as certain decisions can have an immediate impact, while others may require a longer implementation period.

3   Setting the Stage

Causality. Given a set $\mathbf{X}$ of n random variables $X_1, \ldots, X_n$, a Structural Causal Model (SCM) is a tuple $(\mathbf{F}, p_U)$ where $\mathbf{F} = \{X_i := f_i(\mathbf{PA}_i, U_i)\}_{i=1}^n$ is a set of n structural equations and $p_U(U_1, \ldots, U_n)$ is a joint distribution over the noise variables $\{U_i\}_1^n$. f_i are deterministic functions computing each variable X_i from its causal parents $\mathbf{PA}_i \subseteq \mathbf{X} \setminus \{X_i\}$ and its noise variable U_i.

In each SCM, the variables within the system are partitioned into two sets: the *exogenous* (unobserved) variables denoted by $\mathbf{U}$ and the *endogenous* (observed) variables denoted by $\mathbf{X}$. Endogenous variables are those whose values are influenced by other variables within the system, while exogenous variables are determined by factors outside of the model [1]. Besides, an SCM induces a causal graph $\mathcal{G} = \{N, E\}$ where $N = \{N_1, \ldots, N_n\}$ is the set of nodes for which N_i represents X_i, while E is the set of the edges E_{ij} where $E_{ij} \in E \iff X_i \in \mathbf{PA}_j$.

Moreover, it induces an observational distribution over $\mathbf{X}$ to describe what is passively seen or measured, it can also generate many interventional distributions to describe active external manipulation or experimentation. Furthermore, it provides counterfactual statements about what would or could have been, given that something else was observed. These three modes of reasoning are referred to as the three layers of the "ladder of causation" [16].

Action Cost. Identifying the optimal action in the causal AR problem necessarily requires defining a notion of "intervention cost", typically using a function $c : \mathbf{X} \times \mathbb{A} \to \mathbb{R}^+$ where $X \in \mathbf{X}$ is the individual.

We use the notation $\mathbb{A}_\delta \in \mathbb{A}$ to denote an action that changes X by an amount δ. The cost associated with actions that result in greater changes to X is intuitively expected to be higher. In other words, we expect the function c to increase in $|\delta|$ monotonically. The choice of c determines the optimization outcome, regardless of whether the problem is formulated at the observational, interventional, or counterfactual level. The most widely used cost function in the literature is the ℓ_p norm [9], defined as

$$c_{\ell_p}(X, \mathbb{A}_\delta) = ||\delta||_{\ell_p} = \sqrt[p]{\sum_{i=1}^{n} |\delta_i|^p}.$$

c_{ℓ_p} is often replaced by its normalised variant

$$c_{\ell_p n}(X, \mathbb{A}_\delta) = \sqrt[p]{\sum_{i=1}^{n} \left(\frac{|\delta_i|}{\sigma_i} \right)^p}, \quad \text{where} \quad \sigma_i^2 = Var(X_i),$$

to guarantee scale invariance on the features of X.

Despite the constraints inherent in this formulation, it is widely considered a rational and viable choice, mainly due to the inherent challenges of formulating an effective cost function without access to supplementary information.

Actionable Recourse. The problem of AR can be formulated as a constrained optimization in the following terms: given a binary classification model $h : \mathbf{X} \to \{0, 1\}$, and a specific instance X for which $h(X) = 0$, the aim is to identify the action $\mathbb{A}_{\delta*}$ satisfying

$$\delta^* = \left[\arg\min_{\delta} c(X, \mathbb{A}_\delta) \quad s.t. \quad h(\mathbb{A}_\delta(X)) = 1 \right].$$

In other words, the objective is to identify the minimal cost action that alters the decision of the model from unfavorable to favorable.

The distinction between AR and the "*causality-aware*" variant is defined by the manner in which the action $\mathbb{A}_\delta$ operates on a particular instance X. In the former $\mathbb{A}_\delta(X) := X + \delta$, whereas in the latter, the action is considered as a causal intervention

$$\mathbb{A}_\delta(X) := \mathbf{F}_{\mathbb{A}_\delta}(X), \quad \text{where} \quad \mathbf{F}_{\mathbb{A}_\delta} = \{X_i := f_i(\mathbf{PA}_i, U_i) + \delta_i\}_{i=1}^{n}.$$

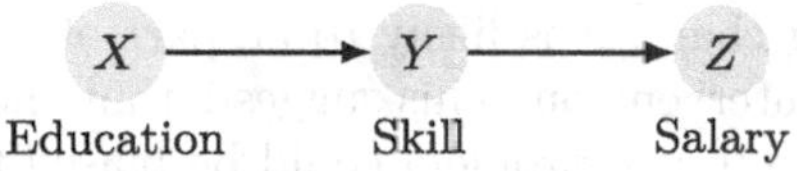

$$X \longrightarrow Y \longrightarrow Z$$

Education   Skill   Salary

Fig. 1. A causal graph illustrating the relationship between college education, individual skill, and job salary discussed in [5].

4 Motivation

In everyday experiences, we typically observe a temporal ordering between the cause and the effect, where the former precedes the latter. This relation could be exemplified by turning on a light switch in a room, where the action of flipping the switch serves as the cause of the light turning on. In the context of causal graphs applied to cross-sectional data, time is often ignored, leaving room for other notions of dependence between variables. However, in the framework of AR, it seems natural to include time as a relevant parameter in defining the cost of a specific action. We typically assume that *a change in the value of one variable in the causal graph instantaneously affects the descendant variables*. In short, probability distributions, including interventional ones, represent a static and unchanging phenomenon of a fundamentally descriptive type. From another perspective, when considering a physical system, its structural equations describe the system's behavior in response to specific physical interventions, ultimately leading to a new and distinct equilibrium state. However, the propagation of the effects of these interventions to the downstream variables may not occur immediately. For example, Fig. 1 reports a causal graph consisting of three variables, X, Y, and Z, representing a person's college education, skill, and job salary, respectively. We can assume that the system is described by a linear model with additive noise, which can be expressed by the following structural equations:

$$X := U_X, \quad Y := aX + U_Y, \quad Z := bY + U_Z.$$

where, U_X, U_Y, and U_Z represent noise terms, and a and b are constants. Such a model implies that a college education generally leads to better preparation and a higher salary. However, the process leading from X to Y can take time (in this case, years), but the model lacks this kind of temporal information and thereby is incapable of considering it. Suppose a person wants to increase his salary Z and queries the model for advice on achieving this goal. The alternatives are only two: the person can improve their skills Y by taking a training course, or they can attend college X to obtain skills as a result of the action. The optimal action would likely be to take a training course. However, the model may not be able to detect this fact. In particular, if the coefficient a that links X to Y is sufficiently large, according to [11], the optimal action would be to intervene on X, rather than on Y. Generally, whenever a node has many children and/or is the beginning of a long chain, it is likely to be part of the intervention set i.e., the set of variables to intervene on. This suggests that the actual formulation of the causal algorithmic recourse problem could be biased towards *root nodes*.

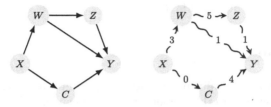

Fig. 2. An example of a causal graph and a simple way to incorporate time information over it. A wavy edge weight τ_{ij} is meant to represent time between intervention over node i and the observed effect on node j.

5   The Role of Time

A possible approach to consider the temporal aspect as a relevant parameter of the process is to use the topological information of the graph as an indicator of the time interval between the action and its consequences. One way to integrate the model with the missing information is to manually assign additional weights to each edge of the graph, incorporating information about the *characteristic response time* of the child variable w.r.t. the change of the parent variable. This allows for analyzing the dynamic flow of the causal effect over time.

Given $\mathcal{G} = \{N, E\}$, we reformulate the cost function of an action $\mathbb{A}_\delta$ over X *to obtain an effect over Y*, as

$$c(X, \mathbb{A}_\delta, Y) = c_s\left(X, \mathbb{A}_\delta\right) + \lambda c_{t(\mathcal{G})}\left(S(\mathbb{A}_\delta), Y\right),$$

where $S(\mathbb{A}_\delta) \subseteq N$ is the support of $\mathbb{A}_\delta$, i.e. the set of variables **directly** modified by $\mathbb{A}_\delta$. We add the parameter λ as a free variable to explicitly adjust the balance between the two components of the cost function, namely c_s that denotes the cost function in the feature space and $c_{t(\mathcal{G})}$ that reflects the time part. It should be noted that the parameters of c_s represent features and their values, while $c_{t(\mathcal{G})}$ involves the topological properties of the graph and thus depends on nodes and their graph relationships. In the following, we provide an example of a cost function considering the temporal dimension:

$$c(X, \mathbb{A}_\delta, Y) = ||\delta|| + \lambda \sup_{V \in S(\mathbb{A}_\delta)} d_{lp}^{\mathcal{G}}(V, Y), \qquad ||\delta|| = \sqrt{\sum_{V \in S(\mathbb{A}_\delta)} \delta_V^2},$$

where $d_{lp}^{\mathcal{G}}(V, Y)$ denotes the longest path distance between node V and Y over $\mathcal{G}$.

Figure 2 illustrates the graphical example of the above formula. Assuming for simplicity that each edge has a weight of 1, we consider an action over the set $\{W, X\}$, observing different directed paths towards Y. By applying c and focusing on the *time* part of the formula, we obtain

$$c_t = \sup_{V \in \{X, W\}} d_{lp}(V, Y) = d_{lp}(X, Y) = 3.$$

The *sup* operation is motivated by the following observation: when we act on some variables and interpret the process as a dynamic information flux from them to the target, the total causal effect will be observed after every single process finishes, equivalently, after the last one does. This proposal for c_t may be overly simplistic and lacking flexibility, as adding a single edge with a high weight can radically change the cost function regardless of its causal effect. A less rigid formulation of c_t could consider the average response time across the multitude of causal processes involved, each of which can be represented by a causal path between the intervention variable and the target. The average could be weighted by the causal impact of each process, ensuring that minor processes do not excessively skew the evaluation.

Consider the case of linear models with additive noise characterized by SCMs of the following form:

$$X_j := \sum_{X_i \in \mathbf{PA_j}} \beta_{ij} X_i + U_j.$$

In this setting, the path impact can be assessed by calculating the product of the coefficients β_{ij} associated with its edges. Furthermore, the total causal effect of a cause X over Y is the sum of the effects attributed to the paths between X and Y. Suppose we also have information regarding the response times associated with edges in $\mathcal{G}$, as depicted in Fig. 4. We denote these quantities as τ_{ij}. Considering the set of all these paths and defining the weight of each path π as $w_\pi := \prod_{E_{ij} \in \pi} \beta_{ij}$, we define the following:

$$c_t(X, Y) = \frac{1}{Z_{XY}} \sum_{\pi | X \xrightarrow{\pi} Y} w_\pi t_\pi, \quad Z_{XY} := \sum_{\pi | X \xrightarrow{\pi} Y} w_\pi, \quad t_\pi := \sum_{E_{ij} \in \pi} \tau_{ij}.$$

In brief, t_π represents the propagation time of the causal effect *through* π, and c_t is the weighted average of t_π, weighted by the relative importance of the causal effect of each path on the overall process. The value of c_t in this revised formulation intuitively represents the time at which a significant portion of the causal effect becomes observable, rather than necessarily capturing its entirety. In this sense, it offers greater robustness and flexibility compared to a cost that relies solely on calculating the longest path.

General Remarks. We have presented some formulations to incorporate temporal dimension within the causal AR framework. However, it is essential to recognize that a general solution is insufficient in resolving the issue across diverse contexts. Instead, deeper considerations must be given to the unique demands of the user and the specific properties inherent in the problem being addressed.

If the user needs to complete the action within a time constraint, e.g., purchase a house and move in within two months of applying for a loan, instead of directly adding the term c_t to the total cost, an alternative approach could be to use it as a constraint in the optimization problem. This approach would redefine the problem as finding the most cost-effective action, where the effects are achieved within a predetermined maximum time, leading to a favorable decision.

Furthermore, the problem could be such that τ_{ij} is not a predetermined fixed value, but rather it may depend on the specific instance x under consideration. For instance, in the context of achieving fitness through a diet and exercise program, the required time would vary based on factors such as the user's age, gender, and current weight. In such cases, it would be necessary to enrich the data structure and fit τ based on available data.

Lastly, the nature of the data can have a significant impact on the formulation of the problem. As an example, where data provides relevant information regarding the temporal dimension, the choice of c_t may inherently depend on it. In particular, when working with a time series dataset, it may be possible to construct a more nuanced c_t that aligns with specific practical contexts.

Regarding the aforementioned consideration, this issue is complex and multifaceted, presenting an intriguing and fruitful research area. While it is beyond the scope of this work to fully tackle it, the development of effective methods necessitates applying our proposal to real-world problems.

6   Experiments

The experimental evaluation[1] aims to show that the current formulation of causal AR may have a bias towards root nodes as postulated in Sect. 4, thus highlighting the significance of the role of time in this field.

Experimental Setup

We consider a semi-synthetic SCM based on the German Credit dataset[2]. While the corresponding causal graph is shown in Fig. 3, the loan approval SCM consists of the following structural equations and noise distributions:

$$
\begin{aligned}
(Gender) \quad & G := U_G, & U_G &\sim \text{Bernoulli}(0.5) \\
(Age) \quad & A := -35 + U_A, & U_A &\sim \text{Gamma}(10, 3.5) \\
(Education) \quad & E := G + A + U_E, & U_E &\sim \mathcal{N}(0, 1) \\
(Job) \quad & J := G + 2A + 4E + U_J, & U_J &\sim \mathcal{N}(0, 2) \\
(Loan\ Amount) \quad & L := A + 0.5G + U_L, & U_L &\sim \mathcal{N}(0, 3) \\
(Loan\ Duration) \quad & D := G - 0.5A + 2L + U_D, & U_D &\sim \mathcal{N}(0, 2) \\
(Income) \quad & I := 0.5G + A + 4E + 5J + U_I, & U_I &\sim \mathcal{N}(0, 4) \\
(Savings) \quad & S := 5I + U_S & U_S &\sim \mathcal{N}(0, 2)
\end{aligned}
$$

---

[1] The code is available here: https://github.com/marti5ini/time-car/.
[2] https://www.kaggle.com/datasets/uciml/german-credit.

The target Y is obtained according to:

$$Y \sim \sigma(2I + 3S - L - D).$$

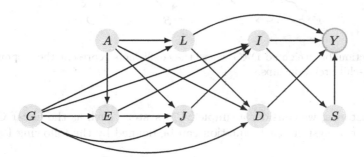

Fig. 3. The *German Credit* inspired causal DAG.

We model *Age*, *Gender* and *Loan Duration* as non-actionable variables but consider the latter to be mutable, i.e., it cannot be manipulated directly but is allowed to change (e.g., as a consequence of an intervention on *Loan Amount*). Our analysis specifically focuses on *Education* and *Income*, as we suppose that these two variables may display the most significant bias. The reason behind our belief is that both variables lie on the same causal pathway. Moreover, from a semantic perspective, one would anticipate that education is a way slower process compared to an income increase. A potential illustration of this idea is depicted in Fig. 4, in which edges starting from *Education* have quite significant weights compared to the others.

Notably, the structural equations used in [11] differ from those defined in our work. The rationale for the variation is rooted in the observation that the SCM used had excessive noise to each variable, thus rendering the causal effect of any reasonable intervention practically irrelevant and precluding the possibility of testing alternative scenarios. Moreover, while the original structural equations accounted for both linear and nonlinear relationships, it was deemed sufficient for us to only consider the linear ones. Indeed, for the scope of our work, studying systems other than linear was unnecessary because the time dimension is independent of the SCM form.

Proper Variance. As stated in Sect. 3, the cost function used in [11] is the normalized ℓ_1 norm. Such normalization is required because if the distributions of the variables being manipulated have different scales, this could result in different costs. Figure 5 depicts a possible scenario that describes the aforementioned phenomenon. The blue-colored distribution has a smaller σ, while the red has a larger one. As a result, the intervention cost in the case of the first distribution is higher than that of the second, given the same amount of δ.

Although this formulation is commonly used, we believe it may not be sufficient, given that it entails critical aspects that we endeavor to explain below.

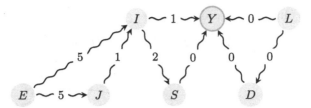

Fig. 4. Actionable weighted DAG where the coefficients represent the response times for parent-child relationships.

For instance, we consider a simple SCM system, such as the linear Gaussian model. In this system, each equation can be defined by the following formula:

$$X_i := \sum_{X_j \in \mathbf{PA_i}} a_{ji}X_j + U_i, \quad U_i \sim \mathcal{N}(0, \hat{\sigma}_i^2), \quad a_{ji} \in \mathbb{R}.$$

$\hat{\sigma}_i^2$ can be interpreted as the variability of X_i due to the exogenous variables of the system. Specifically, we consider it as the *proper variance* of X_i. Such variance is useful to observe that $\hat{\sigma}_i^2$ and $\sigma_i^2 = Var(X_i)$ are not the same quantity since the latter inherits the variability of the parents of X_i. An approximation of the magnitude of σ_i^2 - assuming for simplicity independence among the components X_j - can be obtained using the formula

$$\sigma_i^2 = Var(X_i) \approx \sum_{X_j \in \mathbf{PA_i}} a_{ji}\sigma_j^2 + \hat{\sigma}_i^2,$$

We observe that $\sigma_i \geq \hat{\sigma}_i$ holds. Furthermore, if X_i is an ancestor of X_j, the structural equation of X_j can be rewritten as a regression containing the term $a_{ij}X_i$ and other terms. If $a_{ij} \geq 1$, we have a *avalanche effect* of the variances. This means that the variables become increasingly spread along the causal order. A comprehensive discussion on this topic can be found in [18,19], where this property is exploited to infer the causal structure of a directed acyclic graph.

When considering AR, we argue that using the normalized ℓ_1 norm in relation to σ_i^2 as a cost function can lead to significant distortions if applied to the system being studied. This is because interventions become less expensive as one moves down the graph's topological order, regardless of each variable's internal properties. To address this issue, *we have decided to normalize the cost function based on the proper variances $\hat{\sigma}_i^2$*.

Dataset. Using the loan approval SCM described above, we have generated a synthetic observational dataset $\mathcal{D}$ with 10000 samples. For each feature X_i, we applied an intervention described by:

$$X_i \rightarrow X_i + \alpha \hat{\sigma}_i, \quad \text{where} \quad \alpha \in \mathbb{R}^+,$$

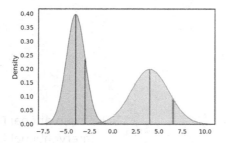

Fig. 5. Example of possibly different costs based on the scale of distributions considered.

generating for each intervention an interventional dataset $\mathcal{D}_{X_i}$[3]. To estimate the "derivative" of the causal effect, we have utilized the following formula:

$$\frac{\overline{Y}_{\mathcal{D}_{X_i}} - \overline{Y}_{\mathcal{D}}}{\alpha}. \tag{1}$$

6.1 Results

In Table 1, we report each feature's estimated Causal Effects Derivative (CED) obtained by applying Eq. 1 respectively to the SCM reported in [11] and the one proposed in this work. With regard to the former, it can be observed that nearly every CED is close to zero, giving rise to an unrealistic problem.

For instance, the absence of any importance of variables such as *Gender*, *Age* and *Education* in the context of credit score prediction appears highly unusual. One possible explanation could be related to the previous discussion on the use of variance as a normalization coefficient. If the variance increases along the causal direction (multiplying at each edge), variables that are further away from the target will have a smaller variance and, therefore, a higher intervention cost. Conversely, those closer to the

Table 1. Comparison between the estimated Causal Effect Derivative (CED) of the SCM used in [11] and the ones we proposed. Non-actionable variables are in red, best estimated actionable values are in bold.

Feature	CED in [11]	Our CED
Gender	0.004	0.273
Age	-0.016	0.329
Education	0.000	**0.181**
Loan Amount	-0.018	-0.099
Job	0.015	0.087
Duration	-0.021	-0.037
Income	**0.058**	0.137
Savings	0.038	0.066

target will have a larger variance and a lower cost. In fact, the four variables with the highest CED are at a distance of 1 from Y, while all those at a distance of at least 2 have lower CED values.

---

[3] Note that the cost of the action is equal to $\frac{\alpha \hat{\sigma}_i}{\hat{\sigma}_i} = \alpha$, regardless of the variable on which the action is executed. Given the same cost, we are interested in determining which action has the greatest impact on the target variable Y.

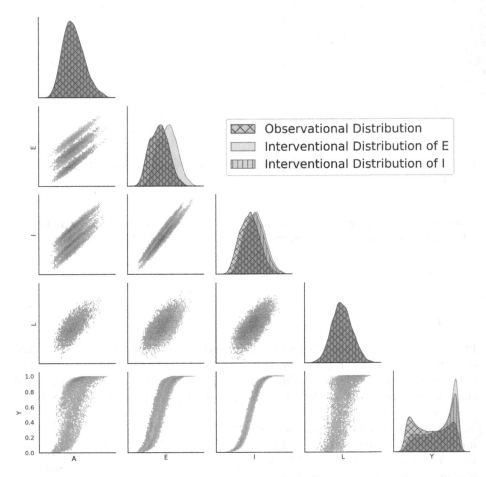

Fig. 6. Pair plot representing observational and interventional distributions of SCM described in Sect. 6. The results indicate that intervening on *Education* is more effective than intervening on *Income* when it comes to improving the outcome of *Y*, as depicted in the bottom-right subplot.

Figure 6 presents the pair plot of the SCM system described in Sect. 6, for three different distributions: Observational, Interventional on *Education*, and Interventional on *Income*. Due to space constraints, only a subset of variables was selected, focusing on the two treatment variables and on *Y*. We added *Age* and *Loan Amount* to provide a clearer view of the system's structure and how interventions modify instances. Regarding *Loan Amount*, it is observed that since it does not depend on either *Education* or *Income*, its distribution remains the same in all cases. The same applies to *Age*, which provides additional insight: the pair plots (*Age, Education*) and (*Age, Income*) show a bimodal distribution, explainable through the presence of fork paths $A \rightarrow E \leftarrow G$ and $A \rightarrow E \rightarrow I \leftarrow G$, revealing the presence of a gender gap in *Education* and *Income* of individuals described by the SCM. Finally, the most significant observation pertains to the *Target* variable Y. Notably, it is evident that for the same cost, *Education* has a stronger causal effect than *Income*. As a result, the recommended action for addressing the unfavorable outcome through recourse would involve prioritizing the improvement of *Education*, confirming the bias towards the root nodes we hypothesized in Sect. 4.

7   Discussion

Broader Impact. A crucial aspect emphasized by the XAI community is the user's demand for plausible explanations [7,21]. In the context of AR, *plausibility* refers to the perceived consistency and reasonableness of the recommendations provided by recourse approaches. From a psychological perspective, providing plausible explanations enables users to form mental models that align with their prior knowledge and reasoning abilities [14]. When the temporal dimension is incorporated into causal reasoning, an AR approach could ensure that the actions suggested are psychologically congruent with human intuitions and mental frameworks. This compatibility fosters a sense of trust and confidence in the algorithmic system, thereby facilitating user acceptance and engagement.

Furthermore, *actionability* is considered one of the crucial aspects in a counterfactual generation process, as highlighted in [6]. We propose expanding the concept beyond the notion of *being able to act upon* to include the ability to do so within a reasonable timeframe. In fact, if the action required to implement a recommendation is excessively time-consuming or impractical, the recommendation becomes unhelpful for the user.

In conclusion, the findings of this study could have significant implications for the XAI field. By incorporating the temporal dimension into causal AR reasoning, the plausibility of explanations is enhanced, aligning them more closely with user expectations and cognitive processes. Moreover, the consideration of actionability addresses the user's need for practical and timely actions. These insights highlight that time-aware causal recourse approaches are a valuable advancement, as they bridge the gap between human intuition, psychological congruence, and efficient decision-making processes.

Prediction vs Improvements. Another point necessary to clarify is the relationship between the predicted outcome ($\hat{Y}$) and the actual outcome (Y). ML models are typically statistical in nature and do not inherently capture causal relations. $\hat{Y}$ may behave very differently from Y. For example, consider the diagnosis of a disease in the medical field. Suppose we have several variables that indicate the presence or absence of certain symptoms in a patient. The predicted outcome, $\hat{Y}$, will utilize the correlation between these symptoms and the disease in order to enhance the predictive capability of the model. If the patient were to take a drug capable of suppressing some of these symptoms, $\hat{Y}$ could change significantly, regardless of whether the drug is effective in curing the underlying disease. However, the presence or absence of the disease Y would not change at all. From a causal viewpoint, taking action on effects does not have any impact on causes. For a more comprehensive analysis of this aspect, we recommend referring to [12]. In our work, we defined a predictive model aware of the causal relationships between variables, so that $\hat{Y}$ aligns with Y, allowing us to treat them as a unified entity. From this perspective, it is worth noting that the outcome is not directly influenced by all the variables within the system, but rather by a specific subset of them. Regarding *Gender, Age, Education, Job*, their impact on the outcome Y is only indirect and mediated through other variables. A purely statistical and non-causal model would ignore entirely these variables, as it would observe, for instance, that $\hat{Y}$ is independent of J given I.

8   Conclusions

In this work, we discussed the problem of Algorithmic Recourse from a causal perspective, focusing on incorporating the temporal dimension into the evaluation of the cost of an action. Firstly, we justified this integration methodologically by discussing its connection with the causal graph's topological structure and proposing a new *time-aware* causal AR formulation. Then, we tested our theoretical intuition through an experiment inspired by the credit score model on the German Credit Dataset, confirming our expectations: if the causal model is unaware of the response times between variables, it could recommend actions that, although optimal considering only the SCMs, would require too much time to be practically viable in most applications. These results serve as a strong motivation for future work to develop and evaluate causal algorithms that effectively incorporate temporal information to enhance the quality of recommendations.

As a final remark, we would like to point out how incorporating the temporal dimension into AR is a conceptually distinct problem from its causal formulation. A very similar discussion to the one presented in this work could be made under different causal knowledge conditions, up to the absence of it. In our opinion, the advantage of the causal framework stems from the use of the graph structure as a support for the finer estimation of the temporal relationships between the system's variables, requiring at least knowledge of the causal graph.

Acknowledgments. Work supported by the European Union's Horizon 2020 research and innovation programme under the Excellent Science European Research Council (ERC) programme for the XAI project (g.a. No. 834756), and by the FAIR (Future Artificial Intelligence Research) project, funded by the NextGenerationEU program within the PNRR-PE-AI scheme (M4C2, investment 1.3, line on Artificial Intelligence). This work reflects only the authors' views and the European Research Executive Agency (REA) is not responsible for any use that may be made of the information it contains.

References

1. Bareinboim, E., Correa, J.D., Ibeling, D., Icard, T.: On Pearl's hierarchy and the foundations of causal inference, 1st edn., pp. 507–556. Association for Computing Machinery, New York (2022)

2. Barocas, S., Selbst, A.D., Raghavan, M.: The hidden assumptions behind counter-factual explanations and principal reasons. In: FAT*, pp. 80–89. ACM (2020)
3. Byrne, R.M.J.: Counterfactuals in explainable artificial intelligence (XAI): evidence from human reasoning. In: IJCAI, pp. 6276–6282. ijcai.org (2019)
4. Chou, Y.L., Moreira, C., Bruza, P., Ouyang, C., Jorge, J.: Counterfactuals and causability in explainable artificial intelligence: theory, algorithms, and applications. Inf. Fusion **81**, 59–83 (2022)
5. Glymour, M., Pearl, J., Jewell, N.P.: Causal Inference in Statistics: A Primer. Wiley, Hoboken (2016)
6. Guidotti, R.: Counterfactual explanations and how to find them: literature review and benchmarking. Data Min. Knowl. Discov. 1–55 (2022)
7. Guidotti, R., Monreale, A., Ruggieri, S., Turini, F., Giannotti, F., Pedreschi, D.: A survey of methods for explaining black box models. ACM Comput. Surv. **51**(5), 93:1–93:42 (2019)
8. Joshi, S., Koyejo, O., Vijitbenjaronk, W., Kim, B., Ghosh, J.: Towards realistic individual recourse and actionable explanations in black-box decision making systems. arXiv preprint arXiv:1907.09615 (2019)
9. Karimi, A.H., Barthe, G., Schölkopf, B., Valera, I.: A survey of algorithmic recourse: definitions, formulations, solutions, and prospects. arXiv preprint arXiv:2010.04050 (2020)
10. Karimi, A., Schölkopf, B., Valera, I.: Algorithmic recourse: from counterfactual explanations to interventions. In: Elish, M.C., Isaac, W., Zemel, R.S. (eds.) FAccT 2021: 2021 ACM Conference on Fairness, Accountability, and Transparency, Virtual Event/Toronto, Canada, 3–10 March 2021, pp. 353–362. ACM (2021)
11. Karimi, A.H., Von Kügelgen, J., Schölkopf, B., Valera, I.: Algorithmic recourse under imperfect causal knowledge: a probabilistic approach. In: Advances in Neural Information Processing Systems, vol. 33, pp. 265–277 (2020)
12. König, G., Freiesleben, T., Grosse-Wentrup, M.: Improvement-focused causal recourse (ICR). CoRR abs/2210.15709 (2022)
13. Naumann, P., Ntoutsi, E.: Consequence-aware sequential counterfactual generation. In: Oliver, N., Pérez-Cruz, F., Kramer, S., Read, J., Lozano, J.A. (eds.) ECML PKDD 2021. LNCS (LNAI), vol. 12976, pp. 682–698. Springer, Cham (2021). https://doi.org/10.1007/978-3-030-86520-7_42
14. Panigutti, C., Beretta, A., Giannotti, F., Pedreschi, D.: Understanding the impact of explanations on advice-taking: a user study for AI-based clinical decision support systems. In: CHI, pp. 568:1–568:9. ACM (2022)
15. Pearl, J.: Causality. Cambridge University Press, Cambridge (2009)
16. Pearl, J., Mackenzie, D.: The Book of Why: The New Science of Cause and Effect. Basic Books (2018)
17. Peters, J., Janzing, D., Schölkopf, B.: Elements of Causal Inference: Foundations and Learning Algorithms. The MIT Press, Cambridge (2017)
18. Reisach, A., Seiler, C., Weichwald, S.: Beware of the simulated DAG! causal discovery benchmarks may be easy to game. In: Advances in Neural Information Processing Systems, vol. 34, pp. 27772–27784 (2021)
19. Reisach, A.G., Tami, M., Seiler, C., Chambaz, A., Weichwald, S.: Simple sorting criteria help find the causal order in additive noise models. CoRR abs/2303.18211 (2023)
20. Sharma, S., Henderson, J., Ghosh, J.: CERTIFAI: counterfactual explanations for robustness, transparency, interpretability, and fairness of artificial intelligence models. arXiv preprint arXiv:1905.07857 (2019)

21. Ustun, B., Spangher, A., Liu, Y.: Actionable recourse in linear classification. In: FAT, pp. 10–19. ACM (2019)
22. Venkatasubramanian, S., Alfano, M.: The philosophical basis of algorithmic recourse. In: Proceedings of the 2020 Conference on Fairness, Accountability, and Transparency, pp. 284–293 (2020)
23. Wachter, S., Mittelstadt, B., Russell, C.: Counterfactual explanations without opening the black box: automated decisions and the GDPR. Harv. JL & Tech. **31**, 841 (2017)

Explaining Model Behavior with Global Causal Analysis

Marcel Robeer[1,2](✉) ⒾⒹ, Floris Bex[2,3] ⒾⒹ, Ad Feelders[2] ⒾⒹ,
and Henry Prakken[2,4] ⒾⒹ

[1] Netherlands Police Lab AI, Netherlands Police, The Hague, The Netherlands
[2] Department of Information and Computing Sciences, Utrecht University, Utrecht,
The Netherlands
m.j.robeer@uu.nl
[3] Tilburg Institute for Law, Technology, and Society, Tilburg University, Tilburg,
The Netherlands
[4] Faculty of Law, University of Groningen, Groningen, The Netherlands

Abstract. We present GLOBAL CAUSAL ANALYSIS (GCA) for text classification. GCA is a technique for global model-agnostic explainability
drawing from well-established observational causal structure learning
algorithms. GCA generates an explanatory graph from high-level human-
interpretable features, revealing how these features affect each other and
the black-box output. We show how these high-level features do not
always have to be human-annotated, but can also be computationally
inferred. Moreover, we discuss how the explanatory graph can be used for
global model analysis in natural language processing (NLP): the graph
shows the effect of different types of features on model behavior, whether
these effects are causal effects or mere (spurious) correlations, and if and
how different features interact. We then propose a three-step method for
(semi-)automatically evaluating the quality, fidelity and stability of the
GCA explanatory graph without requiring a ground truth. Finally, we
provide a detailed GCA of a state-of-the-art NLP model, showing how
setting a global one-versus-rest contrast can improve explanatory relevance, and demonstrating the utility of our three-step evaluation method.

Keywords: Explainable Machine Learning (XML) · Causal
explanation · Model-agnostic explanation · Natural Language
Processing (NLP)

1 Introduction

Explaining the global behavior of a machine learning (ML) model remains a difficult and laborious task. It is hard to distinguish features with directed influences
from ones related through (spurious) correlations. Causal explanations could
help in this regard, providing explanations discerning causal effects from correlational ones [9]. Even when these can be distinguished, then generalizing—in a
human-understandable way—if and how features relate to the model behavior

© The Author(s), under exclusive license to Springer Nature Switzerland AG 2023
L. Longo (Ed.): xAI 2023, CCIS 1901, pp. 299–323, 2023.
https://doi.org/10.1007/978-3-031-44064-9_17

over a large input space remains challenging. Providing a human-understandable explanation inevitably requires selection (e.g. limiting the features under consideration by setting a contrast between outputs) and an appropriate level of explanation (e.g. abstracting detailed behavior into high-level tasks) [36].

Sani, Malinsky and Shpitser [48] proposed a method to explain the global behavior of black-box prediction methods using well-established causal graphical model learning techniques. Their method summarizes the behavior of a black-box model (e.g. a convolutional neural network) using low-level features (e.g. pixels) to predict a label (e.g. bird species), with a graph of high-level 'human-interpretable' features (e.g. the belly color, and wing pattern and shape). The generated global (causal) graph shows the (in)dependence relations amongst the high-level features themselves and with the predicted label, and how these are affected by unobserved confounders. Sani et al. illustrate the utility of their approach on image classification tasks with human-annotated high-level features: a simulated dataset, bird classification and pneumonia detection from X-rays. However, they were unable to (a) infer/select features with computational approaches for the image modality—thus always requiring expensive and time-consuming human annotation—and (b) assess the causal graph quality and faithfulness to the model—providing no guarantee that the explanatory model generalizes well over the data and is actually telling of model behavior.

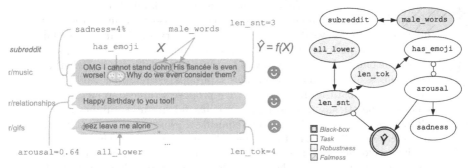

(a) Example data with predictions and inferred features   (b) GCA explanatory graph

Fig. 1. Explaining the global behavior of a black-box predictor of emotions on Reddit comment data, with a (causal) explanatory graph for multi-aspect analysis of high-level features related to the task, robustness and fairness.

In this paper, we show how to computationally infer high-level features and how to use them to study multiple aspects of model behavior. We introduce a method to evaluate the quality and faithfulness of the explanatory model without requiring a ground-truth reference. Additionally, we enhance explanatory relevance through class-wise contrastive explanations. GLOBAL CAUSAL ANALYSIS (GCA)[1] summarizes black-box model behavior in a single graphical overview,

---

[1] https://github.com/MarcelRobeer/GlobalCausalAnalysis.

showing (directed) feature interactions, and if and how they influence the black-box decision function. Key to GCA is our proposed (semi-)automatic evaluation method, which supports in estimating (a) how telling the features are of model behavior and (b) the quality of the explanatory graph.

Figure 1 illustrates the example case in this paper, explaining the behavior of a black-box predictor $\hat{Y} = f(X)$ for sentiment analysis of Reddit comments X over a dataset (e.g. the test set). The inferred high-level features (e.g. the presence of male_words, arousal score and number of tokens [len_tok]) and the human-annotated ones (e.g. subreddit) are combined in a global explanatory (causal) graph, showing features with a direct influence on prediction $\hat{Y}$ ($\cdot \rightarrow \hat{Y}$), indirectly related features (with a directed path to $\hat{Y}$), correlated features ($\leftrightarrow$ indicates a confounder $\cdot \leftarrow U \rightarrow \cdot$) and uncertain directed relations ($\circ$ indicates an end can be < or −). In summary, we make the following contributions:

1. We introduce the idea to use GCAs to describe model-agnostic black-box behavior to the area of **natural language processing** (NLP)—which has a well-established body of work on linguistic phenomena and methods for inferring them [4]—;
2. we extend the human-labelled features with **inferred high-level features**—considering model behavior with features related to multiple aspects, such as features related to the task at hand, robustness (generalizability) and fairness (protected attributes)—;
3. we propose a three-step method to (semi-)automatically **evaluate the quality, fidelity, and stability** of the explanatory graph—which does not rely on a ground truth as these are unavailable for a black box [22]—, and;
4. we study improving the relevance of high-level features by applying concepts from **global (type-level) contrastive explanation** [35,37,60].

The remainder of this paper is structured as follows. Section 2 discusses the background, techniques & evaluations of model-agnostic global explanation and causal models, and details the technique in [48]. Section 3 describes our extension for the NLP domain, and the experimental set-up. Section 4 discusses the results of the experiment, and illustrates GCA with three detailed analyses. Finally, Section 5 summarizes our findings and provides avenues for future research.

2   Background: Model-Agnostic Global Explanation and Causal Models

We describe the background on model-agnostic global explanation and causal models, and provide a detailed description of how causal models can be applied for model-agnostic global explanation. *Global explanation* (sometimes referred to as *model explanation*) aims to provide insights into the entire machine learning (ML) model it aims to explain [5]. It is distinguished in scope from *local explanation* (*instance explanation*; with well-known techniques such as LIME [44] and SHAP [34]) where the aim is to explain individual outputs by the ML model [5,23]. Their counterparts in causal explanation are *type-level* causality (akin to global explanation it describes general relations amongst variables) and *token-level* causality (like local explanation, focusing on individual events) [61].

2.1 Model-Agnostic Global Explanation

In our work, we focus on *model-agnostic* explanations: querying a black-box on its input-output behavior to derive an explanation. Unlike model-specific explanations, model-agnostic explanations have the benefit of being applicable to any type of ML model for a task type (e.g. classification or regression), and provide flexibility regarding the explanation and its representation [43]. Model-agnostic explanations are a type of post-hoc (pedagogical) explanation [5]. These are explanations that are applied after training the ML model [5].

Some well-known model-agnostic global explanation methods (an overview is given by [23] and [5]) are ones that study the relation between individual features and a model output (typically in tabular data)—*Partial Dependence Plots* (PDPs) [17], *Individual Conditional Expectation* (ICE) plots [21] and *Average Local Effect* (ALE) plots [1]—model-agnostic global feature importance scores—e.g. *Model Class Reliance* (MCR) [16]—, and global surrogates that approximate a black-box $f(\cdot)$ with a more interpretable model $g(\cdot)$ and use that directly for explainability—e.g. TREPAN [12,13], *Model Extraction* [3], *Black-Box Explanations through Transparent Approximations* (BETA) [30] and *Transparent Model Distillation* [54]. In addition, specifically relevant to our work are *Variable Interaction Networks* (VINs) [28] (evaluating the importance of non-additive tabular feature interactions with a graph), causal interpretations of black-box models [64] (showing how PDPs can be used in conjunction with a known causal graph) and LEWIS [18] (analyzing model behavior on tabular data with plots, including the influence of contextual factors such as sex).

Definitions. In ML, we train a model (e.g. a classifier) $f : \mathcal{X}^q \mapsto \mathcal{Y}$ taking inputs $X \in \mathcal{X}^q$ (e.g. texts) and transforming them into outputs $Y \in \mathcal{Y}$ (e.g. class labels). Training can be done in many ways, such as the supervised paradigm—where we provide it with a dataset $D = (X, Y)$ with example input-label pairs—, or clustering—assigning instances X to k clusters based on their similarity. To illustrate our idea, in our paper we focus on supervised classification models.

The *model-agnostic global explanation problem* involves finding an explanatory function $g(\cdot)$ that explains the behavior of $\hat{Y} = f(X)$ over some dataset $D' = (X, \hat{Y})$ [23].[2] From this function (e.g. a surrogate decision tree for global behavior), we then extract a set of explanations E (e.g. rules from the decision tree) that model the behavior of $f(\cdot)$ in a human-understandable way [23].

---

[2] Note that the dataset D' used for explanation does not have to be the same as the dataset D used for training, but can be e.g. the test set [5].

Evaluation. Several properties are important when considering the quality of a global explanation. Perhaps the most important property of an explanation method is its *fidelity* (faithfulness) to the model it aims to explain [6,29]. If the explanatory model $g(\cdot)$ is also a predictive model (e.g. a decision tree or sparse linear regressor), fidelity is typically estimated by calculating the predictive performance of the predicted labels $\hat{Y}' = g(X)$ of the surrogate model on the predicted labels of black-box $\hat{Y} = f(X)$ [13,44]. Another important property is the explanation *stability* (robustness) [6]. Stability is an indicator for the reliability and generalizability of the explanation [6,58]. A stable explainable ML method minimizes the effect of randomness and sampling on its performance [6]. Stability is either evaluated by applying small perturbations δ to the inputs X and taking the mean distance between $g(X)$ and $g(X + \delta)$ [58], or by drawing subsamples from the data to measure the effect of data distribution shifts [31].

2.2 Causal Graphs

Graphical Markov models use a graph consisting of nodes V and edges E to represent (conditional) independence relations among a set of variables [46]. We discuss four well-established types of graphical Markov models (two assuming no latent variables and two indicating the effect of latent confounders), search algorithms for causal structure learning, and how these algorithms are evaluated.

Graphs Assuming Causal Sufficiency. *Directed acyclic graphs* (DAGs) $\mathcal{G} = (V, E)$ consist of directed edges $V_i \rightarrow V_j$ between nodes (at most one between any two nodes), and are not allowed to contain cycles [46]. DAGs imply conditional independencies amongst the variables, where conditional independence $X_i \perp\!\!\!\perp X_j \mid \mathbf{X}$ indicates that the set of elements $\mathbf{X}$ blocks all paths between X_i and X_j.[3] An example DAG is provided in Fig. 2a, with nodes $V = \{$Age, Education, IQ, Length of Application Letter, Occupation, Sex$\}$. The graph implies independencies $\{$Age $\perp\!\!\!\perp$ Occ $\mid$ (Edu, Sex), Age $\perp\!\!\!\perp$ Sex, Edu $\perp\!\!\!\perp$ IQ $\mid$ Age, IQ $\perp\!\!\!\perp$ Occ $\mid$ Age, IQ $\perp\!\!\!\perp$ Occ $\mid$ (Edu, Sex), Len $\perp\!\!\!\perp \{$Age, Edu, IQ, Sex$\}\}$.

DAGs are Markov equivalent if they imply the same independencies. A *completed partially directed acyclic graph* (CPDAG) $\mathcal{C}_{[\mathbf{G}]}$ is a unique representation of the Markov equivalence class (MEC) of DAGs $[\mathbf{G}]$ that have the same skeleton graph (the same graph, where the edge marks are removed from the edges) and *v*-structures (subgraphs with structure $V_i \rightarrow V_k \leftarrow V_j$). CPDAGs can contain two types of edges: (1) a *directed edge* $V_i \rightarrow V_j$ indicates that $V_i \rightarrow V_j$ in all DAGs in the equivalence class, and; (2) an *undirected edge* $V_i - V_j$ indicates that in some DAGs in $[\mathbf{G}]$ there is an edge $V_i \rightarrow V_j$ and in others an edge $V_i \leftarrow V_j$.

---

[3] $X_i \perp\!\!\!\perp X_j$ is a short-hand for $X_i \perp\!\!\!\perp X_j \mid \emptyset$ (i.e. $\mathbf{X} = \emptyset$). $X_i \perp\!\!\!\perp \{X_m, X_n\}$ implies $X_i \perp\!\!\!\perp X_m$ and $X_i \perp\!\!\!\perp X_n$.

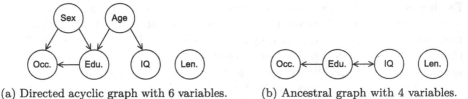

(a) Directed acyclic graph with 6 variables.   (b) Ancestral graph with 4 variables.

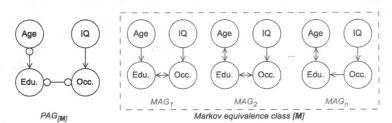

(c) Partial ancestral graph (PAG) for 4 variables and the corresponding Markov equivalence class (MEC) of maximal ancestral graphs (MAGs) it describes.

Fig. 2. Example causal graphs.

Graphs with Confounders. A *mixed graph* is a graph that can contain *directed* edges → and *bidirected* edges ↔ [62]. In the case of graphical Markov models, bidirection $V_i \leftrightarrow V_j$ indicates that there are unmeasured (latent) confounders $V_i \leftarrow U \rightarrow V_j$ (where U may be a single confounder U or represent a network of variables). Graphical Markov models allowing bidirected edges can therefore convey the information that there is a (set of) latent node(s) (i.e. variables not captured in the graph) that influence the (in)dependence relations within the graph. Formally stated, they do not assume *causal sufficiency*—the assumption that there are no unobserved confounders. A mixed graph is an *ancestral graph* if (a) there are no directed cycles, and (b) whenever there is an edge $V_i \leftrightarrow V_j$ then there is no other path from V_i to V_j or from V_j to V_i that is directed. Figure 2b shows an example ancestral graph of the DAG in Fig. 2a where Age and Sex are unmeasured. This graph implies independencies $\{$Edu $\perp\!\!\!\perp$ Len, IQ $\perp\!\!\!\perp$ Len, Occ $\perp\!\!\!\perp$ IQ | Edu, Occ $\perp\!\!\!\perp$ Len$\}$.

An ancestral graph is said to be maximal—i.e. a *maximal ancestral graph* (MAG) $\mathcal{M}$—if for every pair of nonadjacent nodes (V_i, V_j) there exists a set $\mathbf{W}$ $(V_i, V_j \notin \mathbf{W})$ such that $V_i \perp\!\!\!\perp V_j | \mathbf{W}$ [46]. That is, each absent edge corresponds to a conditional independency. Several MAGs can encode the same conditional independencies, forming an MEC of MAGs [**M**] described uniquely by a *partial ancestral graph* (PAG) $\mathcal{P}_{[\mathbf{M}]}$. PAG $\mathcal{P}_{[\mathbf{M}]}$ (a) has the same adjacencies as any member of [**M**] does; (b) contains a mark of an arrowhead (<) iff it is shared by all MAGs in [**M**], and; (c) contains a mark of a tail (−) iff it is shared by all MAGs in [**M**]. Arrows may contain a circle (∘) at an end to indicate that this end is in some MAGs in [**M**] an arrowhead (<) and in some a tail (−). Figure 2c depicts an example PAG implying independencies $\{$Age $\perp\!\!\!\perp$ IQ, Age $\perp\!\!\!\perp$ Occ $\mid$ Edu, Edu $\perp\!\!\!\perp$ IQ $\mid$ Occ$\}$, and the MAGs in the Markov equivalence class it describes.

Causal Structure Learning. Many authors have studied the problem of inferring causal models. Causal structure learning (sometimes called *causal search* or *causal (structure) discovery*) has the goal to infer a causal model from purely observational data, interventional data (e.g. interventions in randomized controlled trials) or a mixture of both [19,59]. These causal models also include causal structures beyond the aforementioned graphical Markov models, such as the popular *structural causal models* (SCMs; also known as *non-parametric structural equation models* [NPSEMs]) [24,25]. We outline some general strategies for causal structure learning from observational data.[4] We describe some causal structure learning algorithms for mixed data in our future work (Sect. 5).

Generally, we distinguish three types of learning methods for causal models: constraint-based, score-based and functional. *Constraint-based* methods use a series of statistical (conditional) independence tests to search for an MEC of graphs that satisfies these independencies [59]. Well-established algorithms in this category include the Peter-Clarke (PC) algorithm [52] that learns a CPDAG $\hat{\mathcal{C}}$[5] from observational data, and the (really) Fast Causal Inference ((r)FCI) algorithm [10,63] for learning a PAG $\hat{\mathcal{P}}$ from observational data. *Score-based* methods aim to maximize a scoring function to find the best graph among candidates [59]. *(Fast) Greedy Equivalence Search* ((f)GES) [8,42] learns a CPDAG $\hat{\mathcal{C}}$ from observational data by iteratively adding edges based on a scoring function, such as the Bayesian Information Criterion (BIC) for continuous variables. *Functional* methods search for *Functional Causal Models* (FCMs)—describing a causal network as a set of functions between variables, e.g. linear relationships and additive noise—by exploiting structural asymmetries in the data when assuming the parametric form of the given FCM (e.g. linearity). An example early FCM is the *Linear Non-Gaussian Acyclic Model* (LiNGAM) [51], which uses statistical analysis to search for a linear SCM when the data is assumed to be non-Gaussian.

Evaluation. Once a causal graph has been generated from the structural learning algorithm, how can it be evaluated? In the case of graphical Markov models, results (e.g. a PAG $\hat{\mathcal{P}}$) are typically evaluated relative to some ground-truth model (e.g. the DAG $\mathcal{G}$ used for data generation). A popular metric is the Structural Hamming distance (SHD) [56] between the two graphs, which is the number of edge insertions, deletions and flips required to change from one graph to another.[6] Other statistics for evaluations are computed based on the confusion matrices of the adjacencies or edges of the two graphs, with the assumption that

---

[4] For an in-depth overview, we refer the interested reader to [19] and [59].

[5] We use $\mathcal{P}$ as a short-hand for PAG $\mathcal{P}_{[M]}$ and $\mathcal{C}$ as a short-hand for CPDAG $\mathcal{C}_{[D]}$.

[6] Note that the SHD was originally defined on CPDAGs, but a similar approach can be applied to other types of graphical Markov models as well.

both graphs include the same features (nodes). Adjacency statistics use the *skeleton graphs* of the two graphs (where all types of edges in a graph are replaced by an undirected edge $-$, thereby reducing each node pair to two types of possible edges), and include statistics such as Adjacency Precision (AP) and Adjacency Recall (AR) [41]. Edge statistics compare the exact edges of the two models (e.g. {*no edge*, $-$, $\leftarrow$, $\rightarrow$} for a CPDAG) to evaluate performance. Arrowhead or tail statistics compare one end of each edge, the head or the tail respectively, and include statistics such as the Arrowhead Precision (AHP) and Arrowhead Recall (AHR) [41]. Note that for each of these statistics, other (computed) statistics of the confusion matrix could be reported instead, such as the number of true positives, the accuracy or the F_1-score.

2.3   Causal Graphs for Model-Agnostic Global Explanation

Sani, Malinsky and Shpitser [48] propose a *global* (type-level) method to summarize the behavior of a black-box model (e.g. a convolutional neural network [CNN]) that uses low-level features $X \in \mathcal{X}$ (e.g. pixels) to predict a label $Y \in \mathcal{Y}$ (e.g. a type of bird). Instead of explaining in the original feature space, the behavior of learned function $\hat{Y} = f(X)$ is explained with the (causal) relationships between some high-level 'human-interpretable' features $Z \in \mathcal{Z}$ (e.g. the belly color, wing pattern & shape, and bill shape & size) and predicted label $\hat{Y} \in \mathcal{Y}$.

In summary, the method works as follows. First, train a black-box $X \rightarrow \hat{Y}$ in a supervised manner with pairs (X, Y) to obtain predictions $\hat{Y}$. Here, $X = (X_1, X_2, \ldots, X_q)$ are the values in input space $\mathcal{X}^q$, $Y \in \mathcal{Y}$ the labels, and $f : \mathcal{X}^q \mapsto \mathcal{Y}$ a black-box function with predictions $\hat{Y} \in \mathcal{Y}$. Next, to explain the global behavior of $f(\cdot)$, estimate a causal *partial ancestral graph* (PAG) $\hat{\mathcal{P}}$ over $V = (Z, \hat{Y})$ with the FCI algorithm [10,63].[7] Other causal estimation methods and graphs (Sect. 2) may be used here instead, but note that PAGs are a good fit for explanation since we can minimize the set of selected variables (PAGs do not assume causal sufficiency) and places where confounding is present are made explicit. $Z = (Z_1, Z_2, \ldots, Z_p)$ $(p \ll q)$ is a set of interpretable features that are given with the data (e.g. additional human-interpretable labels for a bird classifier, or meta-descriptors of the image such as lighting descriptions or when the picture was taken) . The learned PAG forms a family of causal models that indicate (in)dependence relations amongst the selected features $V = (Z, \hat{Y})$, and places for confounding and correlation with the following notation:

- *direction* $Z_i \rightarrow \hat{Y}$ indicates that Z_i causes $\hat{Y}$;
- *bidirection* $Z_i \leftrightarrow \hat{Y}$ indicates Z_i and $\hat{Y}$ share a latent cause $Z_i \leftarrow U \rightarrow \hat{Y}$;
- *partial direction* $Z_i \circ\!\!\rightarrow \hat{Y}$ indicates $Z_i \rightarrow \hat{Y}$, $Z_i \leftrightarrow \hat{Y}$, or both, and;
- *partial bidirection* $Z_i \circ\!\!-\!\!\circ \hat{Y}$ indicates $Z_i \rightarrow \hat{Y}$, $Z_i \leftarrow \hat{Y}$, $Z_i \leftrightarrow \hat{Y}$, or any combination thereof.

---

[7] The only restriction given to FCI is that $\hat{Y}$ is a non-ancestor of any variable in Z, i.e. all elements in Z can cause each other and $\hat{Y}$ but they cannot be caused by $\hat{Y}$.

The method is evaluated in the computer vision domain with (1) a global PAG for images generated from a known causal diagram; (2) a bird-classification task where a CNN is trained on images with human-annotated features for nine types of bird; (3) a binary pneumonia CNN classifier with annotated features by radiologists, and; (4) a comparison of their techniques' outputs to a sample of local explanations by LIME [44] and SHAP [34].

While promising, the method of Sani, Malinsky and Shpitser [48] has two shortcomings. First, it relies on human-annotated high-level features for explanations. Human annotation is an expensive and time-consuming process. For the image modality, the authors were unable to apply computational methods for inferring high-level features (e.g. using visual object recognition) to address this issue. Second, they do not assess two key properties of global explanations (Sect. 2.1): if the explanatory graph is actually telling of model behavior (*fidelity*) and the generalizability of the explanatory graph (*stability*).

3   Experimental Set-Up

Natural language processing (NLP) has properties similar to computer vision, but has a more well-established body of work we can draw from to computationally infer features. Therefore, we apply GLOBAL CAUSAL ANALYSIS (GCA) to a state-of-the-art black-box text classifier on the GoEmotions [14] dataset. Importantly, we also evaluate the stability and faithfulness of the explanatory graph to the black-box model it aims to explain with our novel evaluation method.

Like computer vision, NLP typically uses a large input space $\mathcal{X}^q$ for its tasks. For example, the RoBERTa model [33] studied here converts the input texts into a sequence of tokens from a 30,000 word vocabulary. Using a small set of high-level features would therefore greatly benefit global explanations for NLP. We draw from the extensive literature on computationally inferring linguistic phenomena (from simple methods such as word presence to morphological, syntactic, and semantic information [4]), and illustrate how these features can be related to multiple aspects affecting model behavior (e.g. task-, robustness- and/or fairness-related features). In addition, we take the concept of contrastive explanation and use it to enhance explanatory relevance. Contrastive explanation is applied in local explanation to improve explanatory relevance by setting a one-versus-all class-wise contrast [37,60]. We apply the contrasts globally to limit the edges in the graph to features relevant for a specific class. As a key contribution, we propose a three-step evaluation method that requires no ground-truth causal graph for evaluation—as for black boxes the ground truth is unknown [22]. The method (1) quantifies how faithful GCA is to the model it aims to explain, and (2) evaluates the structural fit and stability of the explanatory graph.

3.1   Data Preprocessing and Model Training

GoEmotions [14] is a dataset containing 58,009 English-language Reddit comments. Each instance comprises a unique identifier, comment text, author, subreddit the comment was posted on, timestamp when it was posted, and a reference to its parent (if applicable). To anonymize the texts, proper names are replaced with a [NAME] token and religions with a [RELIGION] token [14].

Table 1. GoEmotions dataset descriptives of the high-level sentiment groupings ('positive', 'negative', 'ambiguous', 'neutral') after removing instances with non-unique high-level sentiments, and their corresponding emotion labels.

Sentiment	Emotion label(s)	Train	Test	Validation
Positive	*admiration, amusement, approval, caring, desire, excitement, gratitude, joy, love, optimism, pride, relief*	15216	1863	1941
Negative	*anger, annoyance, disappointment, disapproval, disgust, embarrassment, fear, grief, nervousness, remorse, sadness*	8133	1070	1014
Ambiguous	*confusion, curiosity, realization, surprise*	3858	488	459
Neutral	*neutral*	12823	1606	1592
	+	40030	5027	5006

Table 2. GoEmotions dataset excerpt with Reddit comment `text`, `subreddit` and human-annotated `emotion_labels` and high-level sentiment `label`.

text	subreddit	emotion_labels	label
You have a nice bro	pettyrevenge	[admiration]	positive
[NAME] ruled out due to injury. [NAME] starts	rugbyunion	[neutral]	neutral
I would hope the guy is genuine and honest, but	dating	[optimism]	positive
Hi, [NAME]! I thought I would stop by and	atheism	[caring, love, opt.]	positive
Ghost them. It'll drive them crazy and give you	TrueOffMyChest	[neutral]	neutral
Wow, an [NAME] sighting	timberwolves	[surprise]	ambig
i love how the caption implies that the only un	Instagramreality	[amusement]	positive

Each comment in the dataset is labelled by 3–5 human annotators with 27 fine-grained emotions or with the *neutral* label (28 fine-grained labels in total). Of the instances, 83% have one label assigned, 15% two labels, 2% three labels and .2% four or more [14]. All fine-grained labels belong to one of four high-level sentiment labels 'positive' (12 fine-grained labels), 'negative' (11), 'ambiguous' (4) or 'neutral' (1) [14]. For our experiments, we aggregate the 28 fine-grained labels into the four high-level sentiments, where instances that end up with multiple high-level sentiment labels are excluded from further analysis (resulting in 50,063 instances). Furthermore, the data is divided into the predefined 80%–10%–10% train-test-validation splits [14]. Table 1 shows the four high-level sentiment labels, the corresponding fine-grained labels that are grouped under these labels, and per dataset split the number of instances assigned each senti-ment label. Moreover, Table 2 depicts seven example instances, with their corre-sponding subreddit, human-annotated fine-grained label and inferred high-level sentiment.

For the black-box model, we finetune `DistilRoBERTa-base`: a distilled [47] version of English large language model RoBERTa [33]. We finetune it on the training split with the task to predict labels Y (`label`; 'positive', 'negative', 'neutral', 'ambiguous') based on Reddit comments X (`text`).[8] The most accurate model on the validation split is chosen as the final model. After finetuning, the model achieves an accuracy score of 73.1% (macro-weighted F_1-score 70.3%) on the test split.[9] The black-box model assigned the label 'positive' 1932 times, 'neutral' 1546 times, 'negative' 1002 times, and 'ambiguous' 547 times.

3.2   Procedure: Inferring Features and Global Contrastive Explanation

We extend the human-annotated high-level feature `subreddit` with 22 computa-tionally inferred high-level features. These features serve as an example, to illus-trate what type of features one could construct when applying GCA. We group them into three example groupings (so-called *aspects*) relevant for model analy-sis, where we use GCA to study their effect on model behavior separately, and in conjunction to show how GCA can provide an integrated multi-aspect model behavior analysis. Moreover, we propose to apply contrastive explanation—used to minimize the explanatory factors to the ones distinguishing the actual output from a contrast case in local explanation [37], e.g. by setting a contrast between one class label and all others [60]—to improve GCA's explanatory relevance.

Inferring Features. We study three example aspects of global model behavior: *task-*, *robustness-* and *fairness-*related features. GCA can be applied to study these aspects separately, or an integrated analysis of multiple of these aspects can be performed. Table 3 overviews the human-annotated and inferred features for each aspect, their data type (<u>boolean, categorical, integer, floating</u> point), their description, and if they are human-annotated. What features (and aspects) are relevant in applying GCA depend on the task and application (area).

Task-related features relate to the task at hand. For sentiment analysis, we study the subreddit ('Does sentiment generally differ between subreddits?') and presence of emojis ('Does the model use emojis?') as potential factors. We also include three components traditionally distinguished for word meaning in emo-tion detection: valence (positiveness-negativeness), arousal (active-passive) and

---

[8] The model is finetuned for 3 epochs, with a (linear) learning rate of 5×10^{-5}, AdamW optimizer ($\beta_1 = 0.9$, $\beta_2 = 0.999$, $\epsilon = 1 \times 10^{-8}$), a GPU batch size of 16, with seed 42. The Python finetuning uses `Transformers` 4.27.4 with `PyTorch` 2.0.0, `Datasets` 2.11.0 and `Tokenizers` 0.13.2, and is conducted on a Tesla T4 GPU (CUDA 12.0).

[9] The goal is not to get a well-performing model, but to explain model behavior.

dominance (dominant-submissive) [38]. In addition, we include eight basic emotion categorizations by Plutchik [40], with a well-balanced distribution amongst sentiments [39]: anger, anticipation, disgust, fear, joy, sadness, surprise and trust.

Robustness-related features test model sensitivity to noise, distributional artifacts and spurious correlations that may all negatively affect model generalizability [20]. GCA could be used to check if these features are (in)directly related with the black-box output. We include features known to affect earlier sentiment analysis models [32]: the text length (characters, word-level tokens, sentences) and readability (reading grade). In addition, we include features for studying the effect of comment voice (active/passive) and character case (all lowercase).

Table 3. An overview of all included high-level features (grouped by aspect of analysis), their data type, description, and if they are human-annotated.

Aspect	Feature	Type	Description	Annot.
Task	subreddit	cat	Subreddit the comment is from	✓
	has_emoji	bool	Any emoji in comment[*]	
	NRC_valence	float	Mean valence score[†]	
	NRC_arousal	float	Mean arousal score[†]	
	NRC_dominance	float	Mean dominance score[†]	
	NRC_anger	int	# tokens labelled with anger[‡]	
	NRC_anticip.	int	# tokens labelled with anticipation[‡]	
	NRC_disgust	int	# tokens labelled with disgust[‡]	
	NRC_fear	int	# tokens labelled with fear[‡]	
	NRC_joy	int	# tokens labelled with joy[‡]	
	NRC_sadness	int	# tokens labelled with sadness[‡]	
	NRC_surprise	int	# tokens labelled with surprise[‡]	
	NRC_trust	int	# tokens labelled with trust[‡]	
Robust.	len_chr	int	Length in number of characters	
	len_tok	int	Length in number of tokens[§]	
	len_snt	int	Length in number of sentences[‖]	
	is_active	bool	All sentences are in active voice[¶]	
	all_lower	bool	All characters are lowercase	
	flesch_grade	float	Flesch-Kincaid reading grade[**]	
Fairness	has_name	bool	Mention of [NAME]	
	has_religion	bool	Mention of [RELIGION]	
	male_words	int	Number of male-indicative words[††]	
	female_words	int	Number of female-indicative words[††]	
	non-binary_wor.	int	Number of words indicative of non-binary gender[††]	

[*] If any character is a valid emoji according to emoji. [†] Mean human rating of NRC valence/arousal/dominance (VAD) for words [38]. [‡] According to the tokens in NRC *Emotion Lexicon* (EmoLex) [39]. [§] Total number of tokens over all sentences, according to the spaCy tokenizer (en_core_web_sm) [27]. [‖] Number of sentences according to spaCy [27]. [¶] No passive sentences (PassivePy [50]) [**] Calculated with textstat, where $FKGL = 0.39(\text{words/sentences}) + 11.8(\text{syllables/words}) - 15.59$. [††] According to the English *Gender Bias Tool* (GenBit) wordlist [49].

Fairness-related features can be indicative of potential bias with respect to protected attributes [20]. The link between fairness research and NLP explainability has for the most part been limited to local explanations applied to hate speech detection [2], while we focus on global explanations for sentiment analysis. We consider features related to the protected attributes religion (which has been replaced with the [RELIGION] token), a person's name (replaced with the [NAME] token), and a person's gender (with words indicative of the male, female or non-binary, e.g. waiter versus waitress or herself versus themselves [49]).[10]

Class-Wise Global Contrastive Explanation. Since the relevant features within each aspect may differ for each class label, in addition to describing the overall behavior of the black-box in distinguishing all four classes ($\hat{Y}$) we also perform class-wise global analysis [35]. Contrastive explanation is usually applied to local explanations, where explanatory relevance is increased by setting a one-versus-rest class-wise contrast (e.g. "Why classify X_i as 'positive' rather than 'not positive'?") [37,60]. The explanation can then be limited to factors for distinguishing this class from all others [60]. For example, the task-related feature NRC_joy may be indicative in distinguishing the 'positive' label, and less informative for 'neutral'. For each class, we perform a one-versus-rest analysis where the class of interest is encoded as one (1) and the remaining classes as zero (0).[11]

Procedure. For the test split of GoEmotions (containing 5,027 instances) we let the black-box (Sect. 3.1) predict class labels for each instance $\hat{Y} = f(X)$. We then estimate a GCA explanatory graph with the χ^2 independence test, with $\alpha = 0.05$ and the restriction that $\hat{Y}$ may not have a direct arrow towards any variable $Z_i \in Z$ [48] (i.e. $\hat{Y} \not\to Z_i$ and $\hat{Y} \not\leftrightarrow Z_i$) . We do this separately for each aspect (Z_{task}, Z_{robust}, Z_{fair}) and all aspects combined ($Z = Z_{task} \cup Z_{fair} \cup Z_{robust}$), both for one-versus-rest on each predicted class ($\hat{Y}_{positive}$, $\hat{Y}_{negative}$, $\hat{Y}_{ambiguous}$, $\hat{Y}_{neutral}$) and over all classes ($\hat{Y}$). To work with the χ^2 independence test, non-integer continuous features are binned into 10 equal-sized intervals. In addition, to speed up FCI the subreddit feature is re-coded into the 10 most frequently occurring subreddits and the remainder is placed in a category 'other'.

3.3   Evaluation

We propose a three-step evaluation method for applying GCA in practical applications and for our experiments. The method aids domain experts and analysts

---

[10] We stress that the inferred fairness features here merely serve as an illustration— e.g. of indicators of protected attributes that one can study—, as the actual relevant features depend heavily on the intended application (area) of the ML model.

[11] Note that this same class-contrastive approach to binary encode outputs [60] can also be used to apply GCA to other types of black-boxes, such as ones providing probabilistic class scores, regression analysis and clustering.

in picking a set of variables Z, and indicates the domain fit, faithfulness and stability of the explanatory graph without requiring a ground-truth reference.

1. Z-fidelity The fidelity (faithfulness) of the global explanatory model $g(\cdot)$ is typically estimated with the predictive performance of the predicted labels $\hat{Y}' = g(X)$ of the surrogate on the labels $\hat{Y} = f(X)$ of the black-box it aims to explain [13,29,44] (Sect. 2.1). However, as in this case we use PAGs as an explanatory model—capturing (in)dependence relations among variables rather than being predictive models—we cannot compute $\hat{Y}'$. Nevertheless, fidelity is still important because if there is no good fit between the features in Z and $\hat{Y}$, then it might not be telling on how they are related.

To get a general sense of the explanatory power of the set of variables Z on $\hat{Y}$, we fit an ML model that is generally well-performing (predictive accuracy) and has few assumptions on the data: a Random Forest.[12] The Random Forest is merely instrumental in measuring how much information the high-level features contain about the black-box output; other methods can be used here instead. The model is trained with stratified k-fold cross validation (we use 5 folds), and estimates $\hat{Y}'$ on the folds are compared to predictions $\hat{Y}$ of the black-box model. We report the F_1-score as an estimate for Z-fidelity (other metrics can be used here instead).[13] Note that this step should be performed before fitting the global (causal) explanatory model, and can even be informative in feature selection.

2. Sanity Checks. Once the GCA explanatory graph has been estimated, we first perform some general sanity checks. We distinguish two types: (1) *automatic* checks ensure that the *background knowledge* imposed on the PAG generation algorithm is indeed in the final GCA explanatory graph (e.g. there are no edges from $\hat{Y}$ to Z,[14] or if a directed edge that is required is indeed there), and; (2) *manual* checks consider the GCA explanatory graph and if the expected relations amongst Z (according to e.g. a domain expert or when the functions are known) are indeed present, regardless of their effect on $\hat{Y}$ (e.g. the number of words and number of characters will be related regardless of whether the model uses these as causal influence or not). In our results, we discuss the manual and automatic sanity checks for three example cases.

3. Structural Fit and Stability. *Modal Value of Edges Existence* (MVEE) is a method for evaluating the quality of generated PAGs when no ground-truth graph is known [26]. It is an extension of *Intersection-Validation* (InterVal) [57], which evaluates the quality of generated CPDAGs $\mathcal{C} = \{\mathcal{C}_1, \ldots, \mathcal{C}_n\}$ learned by n different algorithms on the same dataset. In InterVal, the idea is to generate an *agreement graph*—obtained by taking the strict intersection between graphs

---

[12] The Random Forest uses default hyperparameters for `scikit-learn` 1.2.2 (100 trees, Gini impurity) with seed 42.

[13] We use F_1-score to account for non-equal distributions of predicted labels (Sect. 3.1).

[14] That is, the outdegree of $\hat{Y}$ for the GCA explanatory graph should always be zero.

$\mathcal{C}$: copy an edge (or the absence thereof) iff it is agreed upon by all graphs, else place a special edge ($\cdots$)—that is then used as proxy for the ground-truth graph. Evaluation metrics of CPDAGs (Sect. 2.2) are then computed relative to the agreement graph: for our experiments we use the SHD [56] towards the agreement graph, called the *Partial Hamming Distance* (PHD) [57].

MVEE [26] takes the notion of agreement graphs from InterVal, but addresses the issue that since there are three more types of edges possible for PAGs, InterVal may be too strict. The edge values for any pair of variables for a CPDAG can take on four values $\{no\ edge, \text{—}, \leftarrow, \rightarrow\}$, while in a PAG the edges between a pair of nodes can take on seven $\{no\ edge, \circ\!-\!\circ, \leftarrow, \leftarrow\!\circ, \rightarrow, \circ\!\rightarrow, \leftrightarrow\}$. Instead of the strict intersection between graphs, MVEE finds a *skeleton* agreement graph using a majority vote from the set of skeletons of a set of input graphs [26]. First, for each PAG $\mathcal{P}$ the skeleton S is calculated (i.e. removing the ends of the edges, such that each pair of nodes can only have an edge value of $\{no\ edge, \text{—}\}$), and then for these the InterVal method is applied to obtain an agreement graph.

To measure the structural fit & stability (in absence of a ground-truth PAG) we compute the PHD of the GCA explanatory graph with MVEE, where the agreement graph is generated from five explanatory graphs fitted on random 80% subsamples of $(Z, \hat{Y})$ (stability within subsamples; see Sect. 2.1). For MVEE, the PHD indicates the number of edge deletions and additions ($\downarrow$ lower is better) between the explanatory graph and the agreement graph. Since the number of nodes differs for the aspects in our experiment (and thereby the total possible number of edges between nodes), we report the *relative partial Hamming distance* with the MVEE strategy (*relative* MVEE; ranging from 0 to 1; $\uparrow$ higher is better):

$$1 - \frac{\text{MVEE}}{n_{nodes} \times (n_{nodes} - 1)/2} \tag{1}$$

where n_{nodes} is the number of nodes in the GCA explanatory graph and $\binom{n_{nodes}}{2} = n_{nodes} \times (n_{nodes} - 1)/2$ the maximum number of edge values over all nodes.

4   Results and Discussion

We generate GCA explanatory graphs for different sets of high-level features Z (*task*-related, *robustness*-related, *fairness*-related, and all combined) for each predicted label (for each class separately, and all four combined) to explain the behavior of the finetuned `DistilRoBERTa` model on the test split of GoEmotions (Sect. 3.1 & Sect. 3.2).[15] We evaluate their Z-fidelity and structural fit & stability (Sect. 3.3), and discuss three example graphs in detail.[16]

---

[15] The mean wall-time to generate the GCA explanatory graphs is 0.12s for the fairness aspect (5 features), 0.72s for the robustness aspect (6 features), 2.37s for the task aspect (13 features), and 220.11s for all aspects combined. Wall-time was measured with `causal-learn` 1.3.3 (no depth limit) on Python 3.9.16, on a MacBook Pro with macOS Monterey 12.6.3 (16 GB 2.3 GHz 8-Core Intel Core i9).

[16] Source code available at https://github.com/MarcelRobeer/GlobalCausalAnalysis.

4.1   Quantitative Results

Table 4 summarizes the Z-fidelity scores for our experiments and Table 5 the relative MVEE scores. In summary, we observe the following findings: (1) a high Z-fidelity for the behavior on $\hat{Y}$ (all four aspects), the 'positive' one-versus-rest label (each aspect except fairness), 'neutral' label (each aspect except fairness) and 'negative' label (Z and Z_{task}) shows that for these combinations the selected features Z are very informative of model behavior, and (2) a mean relative MVEE of 0.988 ($SD = 0.016$) over all aspect-label combinations indicates that the method is structurally well-fitting and stable.

Table 4. Z-fidelity ($\uparrow$ F_1-score, 0–100%) as an estimate for the explanatory power of the chosen variables in Z on $\hat{Y}$. Higher scores indicate that the variables are more telling of $\hat{Y}$, and thereby of the (absence) of edges in the explanatory graph.

Aspect	features	label ($\hat{Y}$)	positive	neutral	negative	ambiguous
all	24	41.95	59.80	32.27	31.79	3.48
fairness	5	21.33	1.11	10.27	0.00	0.00
robustness	6	28.48	40.67	32.43	13.02	8.31
task	13	39.04	57.99	32.69	34.14	6.60

Table 5. The GCA method has a high structural fit & stability ($\uparrow$ relative MVEE, 0–1) for all combinations of aspects and predicted class labels.

Aspect	label ($\hat{Y}$)	positive	neutral	negative	ambiguous
all	0.98	0.99	0.98	0.99	0.98
fairness	1.00	1.00	0.93	1.00	1.00
robustness	1.00	1.00	1.00	1.00	1.00
task	0.97	0.99	0.99	0.99	0.99

Z-fidelity. Table 4 cross-tabulates the Z-fidelity for the aspects (task-, robustness- & fairness-related features, and all features combined) and the predicted class label behaviors (four contrastive one-versus-rest and one combined). Especially the global behavior of the black-box on the 'positive' class ($\hat{Y}_{positive}$) can be captured well with all features (F_1-score of 59.80%) and just the task-related high-level features (57.99%). Describing its behavior with few features (24 and 13 respectively) is commendable given the black-box model complexity: the `DistilRoBERTa-base` input space is large as the model uses a vocabulary of 30,000 tokens, the model itself consists of 82 million parameters, and the model was pretrained on five datasets totalling 160GB of text [33]. The same can be said for the Z-fidelity of the features in distinguishing all four labels (label $\hat{Y}$), where all features (41.95%) and the task-related features (39.04%) are able to capture a large portion of the overall behavior (distinguishing four classes). The explanatory graph for each of these combinations should therefore provide valuable insights into what features are (not) related to model behavior.

Moreover, interestingly the model seems to be barely affected by any indicators for protected attributes (fairness aspect) for the one-versus-rest model behavior. This indicates that any arrows towards $\hat{Y}$ in the explanatory graph do not represent a substantial predictive value. The same low Z-fidelity scores hold for the 'ambiguous' label. However, in this case it indicates we have not selected/inferred variables telling of model behavior. Features to study the robustness aspect, however, seem to have a relatively large effect on model behavior—especially across the 'positive' and 'neutral' classes. These scores indicate that robustness-related (unlike fairness-related) features might substantially affect black-box model behavior. Studying the explanatory graphs in more detail can help in distinguishing if these effects are directed or merely due to confounding.

Structural Fit and Stability. The generated GCA explanatory graphs are very stable and have a high structural fit. Table 5 shows the relative MVEE scores (ranging from 0 to 1; higher is better) for all aspect-label combinations. Across all combinations, the mean relative MVEE is 0.988 ($SD = 0.016$). Nine out of 20 combinations are perfectly stable and have a good fit (relative MVEE 1.00), while 11 combinations have a near-one relative MVEE score. Note that the lowest scoring combination (0.93; fairness-related features for the 'neutral' label) has an absolute MVEE of 1 (one edge insertion/deletion to the agreement graph).

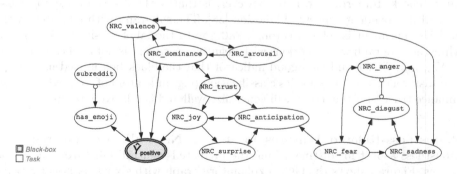

Fig. 3. GCA explanatory graph for task-related features Z_{task} on the 'positive' label $\hat{Y}_{positive}$ (one-versus-rest). The features directly related ($Z_i \rightarrow \hat{Y}_{positive}$) to $\hat{Y}_{positive}$ are NRC_valence and NRC_joy, while $\hat{Y}_{positive}$ is related due to confounding ($\leftrightarrow$) with has_emoji and NRC_dominance.

4.2   Empirical Results

We discuss three GCA explanatory graphs in detail, where we consider the three-step evaluation method, the resulting graph and how these interrelate.

Task-Related Features for Label 'Positive'. Figure 3 depicts the explanatory graph for the 13 task-related features for the 'positive' label (one-versus-rest). The features are able to capture the black-box behavior on distinguishing 'positive' ($\hat{Y}_{positive}$) from other classes very well. The model has a Z-fidelity of 57.99 (Table 4) and high structural fit & stability (relative MVEE 0.99; Table 5). $\hat{Y}_{positive}$ does not have any outgoing arrows and thus passes the automatic sanity check.

The class-wise contrast for the 'positive' label does not only quantitatively improve the explanatory relevance, but studying the explanatory graph in detail also provides additional qualitative insights. Two features have a direct effect ($\rightarrow$) on $\hat{Y}_{positive}$: NRC_joy (number of words indicative of 'joy' according to NRC EmoLex [39]) and NRC_valence (mean human scores of positiveness-negativeness [38]). NRC_trust has an indirect effect on $\hat{Y}_{positive}$ through NRC_joy, and NRC_arousal through NRC_dominance and NRC_valence. In addition, has_emoji (presence of any emojis) and NRC_dominance (inferred based on mean human score of dominant-submissive [38]) share unmeasured confounders with $\hat{Y}_{positive}$ ($\leftrightarrow$), possibly providing spurious correlations with model outputs.

Separate from model behavior, we also observe strong interrelatedness between indicators of VAD scores (NRC_valence, -arousal and -dominance), between emotions with a positive sentiment focus (NRC_trust, -joy, -anticip.), and between emotions with a relatively negative sentiment (NRC_anger, -disgust, -fear and -sadness). These subgroups largely correspond to the positive and negative sentiment emotions [40], indicating expected behavior from the manual sanity check. Important to note, however, is that VAD scores are usually considered independent aspects of emotion [38]. The subgraph with emotions with positive sentiment is related through NRC_joy to the label 'positive' ($\hat{Y}_{positive}$), while the subgraph with emotions with negative sentiment is not on a causal path to $\hat{Y}_{positive}$. This could be a good indicator that the black-box indeed uses positive task-related features for its classification (e.g. indicators of joy), which may enhance trust that the model will generalize well and is relatively robust.

Robustness-Related Features for Label 'Neutral'. We also study the robustness aspect for distinguishing the predicted 'neutral' label from all other classes. Figure 4 shows the GCA explanatory graph with six robustness features and $\hat{Y}_{neutral}$. The graph has a Z-fidelity of 32.43 and a relative MVEE of 1.00. It passes the automatic sanity check that $\hat{Y}_{neutral} \not\rightarrow Z_i$ and $\hat{Y}_{neutral} \not\leftrightarrow Z_i$.

Two features are independent from model behavior ($\hat{Y}_{neutral}$) and from all other robustness-related features: all_lower (if all characters are lowercase) and is_active (if all sentences in the comment are in active voice). The length in number of sentences (integer len_snt) is directly indicative of the 'neutral' label.

The number of characters (len_chr), number of tokens (len_tok), the number of sentences (len_snt) and the Flesch-Kincaid reading grade (flesch_grade; calculated based on number of syllables, words and sentences) form a clique. This is as expected, as the lengths all positively correlate (longer comments consist of more characters, tokens and sentences) and the reading grade is functionally related to the lengths. Thus, the graph passes the manual sanity check.

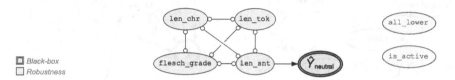

Fig. 4. GCA explanatory graph for robustness-related features Z_{robust} on $\hat{Y}_{neutral}$. len_snt is directly related ($Z_i \rightarrow \hat{Y}_{neutral}$) to $\hat{Y}_{neutral}$. all_lower and is_active are independent from $\hat{Y}_{neutral}$ and all other features in Z_{robust}.

FCI cannot distinguish the direction of this relationship ($Z_i \rightarrow Z_j$, $Z_i \leftrightarrow Z_j$ or $Z_i \leftarrow Z_j$) and if there are any confounders. It assigns a partial bidirection relationship between all four variables $Z_i \circ\!\!-\!\!\circ Z_j$. Including additional robustness features or combining the analysis with other aspects (e.g. fairness-related or task-related features) may help in clarifying these relations, and to see how strong the connection is between the robustness features and the 'neutral' label.

Task-, Fairness- and Robustness-Related Features Combined. Figure 5 shows the GCA explanatory graph over all aspects combined, for the whole black-box model behavior (distinguishing all four labels). The graph scores a Z-fidelity of 41.95 and a relative MVEE (structural fit & stability) of 0.98. The graph passes the sanity check that $\hat{Y}$ has no outgoing directed arrows. To foster multi-aspect analysis, the features related to different aspects in the explanatory graph are color-coded, and the node $\hat{Y}$ is shown in gray with a double bolded border.

Three things immediately stand out. First, the model behavior is directly affected by the mean arousal score (inferred based on the NRC VAD Lexicon [38]), the mean dominance score (also inferred using [38]) and the sentence length. Second, male_words (fairness-related), has_name (fairness), female_words (fairness) and subreddit (task-related) form a subgraph, with behavior separate from the behavior of $\hat{Y}$. Male- and female-indicative words, and the presence of the [NAME] token are indicative of the subreddit. Third, several task-, robustness- and fairness-related features are unconnected in the explanatory graph: has_emoji, is_active, all_lower, non-binary_words and has_religion.

Many features either share a common confounder or have a directed relationship in line with expected behavior (as studied in detail in Fig. 3 and Fig. 4). For

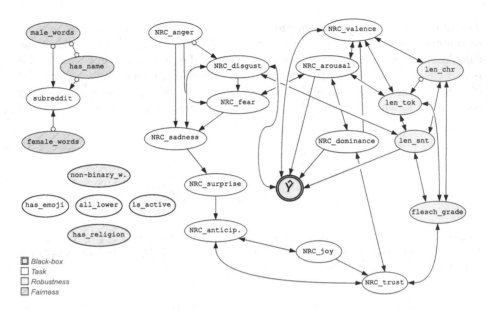

Fig. 5. GCA explanatory graph for all features $Z = Z_{task} \cup Z_{fair} \cup Z_{robust}$ (24 high-level features) on the overall black-box predictive behavior $\hat{Y}$ (four classes). The features directly related ($Z_i \rightarrow \hat{Y}$) to $\hat{Y}$ are NRC_arousal, NRC_dominance and len_snt. NRC_disgust and NRC_valence are directly related due to confounding ($\leftrightarrow$) with $\hat{Y}$. has_emoji, is_active, all_lower, non-binary_words and has_religion are independent from $\hat{Y}$ and all other features in Z.

task-related features, we observe strong connections with negative emotion features (NRC_anger, -disgust, -sadness and -fear), the VAD components of emotions (NRC_valence, -arousal and -dominance), and the three features catered towards positive emotions (NRC_joy, -anticip. and -trust). For robustness, the lengths in characters (len_chr), tokens (len_tok) and sentences (len_snt) are correlated as expected, and the reading grade (flesch_grade) also functionally relates to the instance length. Moreover, we observe how many task-related and robustness features share confounders: {NRC_disgust $\leftrightarrow$ len_snt, NRC_valence $\leftrightarrow$ len_chr, NRC_arousal $\leftrightarrow$ len_tok, NRC_trust $\leftrightarrow$ flesch_grade}.

5   Conclusion and Future Work

We presented GLOBAL CAUSAL ANALYSIS (GCA) as a method for global model-agnostic explanations for text classification, explaining model behavior with a causal explanatory graph. The GCA explanatory graph interprets black-box functioning over a dataset with high-level human-interpretable features (either over all classes or contrastively by setting a one-versus-rest class-wise contrast), revealing if and how these features affect each other and the black-box output.

GCA is a strong addition to global explanation methods. GCA can distinguish causal relations from effects due to (spurious) correlations, and explicitly shows where latent confounders are. The explanatory graph not only shows relations with the model output, but also between the high-level features themselves. We show how these features can be inferred computationally, avoiding costly human annotation to explain model behavior at a higher level of abstraction.

The three-step evaluation method that is a key part of GCA (1. Z-fidelity; 2. Sanity checks; 3. Structural fit & stability) proves useful in quantitatively and empirically assessing (a) the explanatory power of the selected high-level features and (b) the quality of the explanatory graph. GCA can summarize large parts of model behavior with few human-interpretable features, is structurally stable and well-fitting, and has high explanatory relevance with its ability to explain behavior over all classes or with class-wise one-versus-rest contrasts.

We consider three interesting avenues for future research. The first is using *global interventions* to provide a stronger link with causality research. NLP offers several computational approaches (e.g. [20,45,53]) to intervene upon specific attributes (e.g. for gender replacing all female names with male ones). GCA can then be applied with a mixed causal learning method (e.g. [11,15,55]), and then further enhanced by estimates of the effect sizes and directions (positive/negative) of features (e.g. *Average Causal Effect* [7]). Second, we want to study applying causal high-level feature explanations to *local explanations*. We could benefit from the wealth of desiderata, definitions and methods for counterfactuals and contrastive explanation at the local level (see [9]). Moreover, we could simplify local explanations by summarizing behavior with high-level features, study them from multiple aspects, and also explore locally explaining at various levels of linguistic structures (e.g. explanations at the phrase or word level). Third, we want to apply GCAs in practical contexts to perform *human evaluations* with domain experts, model developers and model end-users.

Acknowledgements. This study has been partially supported by the Dutch National Police. The authors would like to thank Elize Herrewijnen and Gizem Sogancioglu for their valuable feedback on earlier versions of this work.

References

1. Apley, D.W., Zhu, J.: Visualizing the effects of predictor variables in black box supervised learning models. J. Royal Stat. Soc. Ser. B: Stat. Methodol. **82**(4), 1059–1086 (2020). https://doi.org/10.1111/rssb.12377
2. Balkir, E., Kiritchenko, S., Nejadgholi, I., Fraser, K.: Challenges in applying explainability methods to improve the fairness of NLP models. In: Proceedings 2nd Workshop on Trustworthy Natural Language Processing (TrustNLP 2022), pp. 80–92. ACL, Seattle, U.S.A. (2022). https://aclanthology.org/2022.trustnlp-1.8
3. Bastani, O., Kim, C., Bastani, H.: Interpreting Blackbox models via model extraction. CoRR abs/1705.08504 (2017)
4. Belinkov, Y., Glass, J.: Analysis methods in neural language processing: a survey. Trans. Assoc. Comput. Linguist. **7**, 49–72 (2019). https://doi.org/10.1162/tacl_a_00254

5. Burkart, N., Huber, M.F.: A survey on the explainability of supervised machine learning. J. Artif. Intell. Res. **70**, 245–317 (2021). https://doi.org/10.1613/jair.1. 12228

6. Carvalho, D.V., Pereira, E.M., Cardoso, J.S.: Machine learning interpretability: a survey on methods and metrics. Electronics **8**(8), 832 (2019). https://doi.org/10. 3390/electronics8080832

7. Chattopadhyay, A., Manupriya, P., Sarkar, A., Balasubramanian, V.N.: Neural network attributions: a causal perspective. In: International Conference on Machine Learning, pp. 981–990. PMLR (2019)

8. Chickering, D.M.: Optimal structure identification with greedy search. J. Mach. Learn. Res. **3**, 507–554 (2002)

9. Chou, Y.L., Moreira, C., Bruza, P., Ouyang, C., Jorge, J.: Counterfactuals and causability in explainable artificial intelligence: theory, algorithms, and applications. Inf. Fusion **81**, 59–83 (2022). https://doi.org/10.1016/j.inffus.2021.11.003

10. Colombo, D., Maathuis, M.H., Kalisch, M., Richardson, T.S.: Learning high-dimensional directed acyclic graphs with latent and selection variables. Ann. Stat. **40**(1), 294–321 (2012). https://doi.org/10.1214/11-AOS940

11. Cooper, G.F., Yoo, C.: Causal discovery from a mixture of experimental and observational data. In: Proceedings of the 15th Conf. on Uncertainty in Artificial Intelligence, pp. 116–125. Morgan Kaufmann Publishers Inc., San Francisco, CA, USA (1999)

12. Craven, M.W., Shavlik, J.W.: Using sampling and queries to extract rules from trained neural networks. In: Eleventh International Conference on Machine Learning (ICML), Proceedings, pp. 37–45 (1994). https://dl.acm.org/doi/10.5555/ 3091574.3091580

13. Craven, M.W., Shavlik, J.W.: extracting tree-structured representations of trained neural networks. In: Advances in Neural Information Processing Systems (NIPS), vol. 8, pp. 24–30 (1996)

14. Demszky, D., Movshovitz-Attias, D., Ko, J., Cowen, A., Nemade, G., Ravi, S.: GoEmotions: a dataset of fine-grained emotions. In: 58th Annual Meeting of the Association for Computational Linguistics (ACL), pp. 4040–4054. Online (2020). https://doi.org/10.18653/v1/2020.acl-main.372

15. Eaton, D., Murphy, K.: Exact Bayesian structure learning from uncertain interventions. In: Artificial Intelligence and Statistics, pp. 107–114. PMLR (2007)

16. Fisher, A., Rudin, C., Dominici, F.: All models are wrong, but many are useful: learning a variable's importance by studying an entire class of prediction models simultaneously. J. Mach. Learn. Res. **20**, 1–81 (2019)

17. Friedman, J.H.: Greedy function approximation: a gradient boosting machine. Ann. Stat. **29**(5), 1189–1232 (2001). https://doi.org/10.1214/aos/1013203451

18. Galhotra, S., Pradhan, R., Salimi, B.: Explaining black-box algorithms using probabilistic contrastive counterfactuals. In: Proceedings of the 2021 International Conference on Management of Data, pp. 577–590. SIGMOD 2021, Association for Computing Machinery, New York, NY, USA (2021). https://doi.org/10.1145/3448016. 3458455

19. Glymour, C., Zhang, K., Spirtes, P.: Review of causal discovery methods based on graphical models. Front. Genet. **10**, 524 (2019)

20. Goel, K., Rajani, N.F., Vig, J., Taschdjian, Z., Bansal, M., Ré, C.: Robustness gym: unifying the NLP evaluation landscape. In: Proceedings of the 2021 Conference of the North American Chapter of the Association for Computational Linguistics (NAACL): Human Language Technologies: Demonstrations, pp. 42–55. ACL, Online (2021). https://doi.org/10.18653/v1/2021.naacl-demos.6

21. Goldstein, A., Kapelner, A., Bleich, J., Pitkin, E.: Peeking inside the black box: visualizing statistical learning with plots of individual conditional expectation. J. Comput. Graph. Stat. **24**(1), 44–65 (2015). https://doi.org/10.1080/10618600.2014.907095
22. Guidotti, R.: Evaluating local explanation methods on ground truth. Artif. Intell. **291**, 103428 (2021). https://doi.org/10.1016/j.artint.2020.103428
23. Guidotti, R., Monreale, A., Ruggieri, S., Turini, F., Giannotti, F., Pedreschi, D.: A survey of methods for explaining black box models. ACM Comput. Surv. **51**(5), 1–42 (2018). https://doi.org/10.1145/3236009
24. Halpern, J.Y.: A modification of the Halpern-Pearl definition of causality. In: International Joint Conference on Artificial Intelligence (IJCAI), pp. 3022–3033 (2015)
25. Halpern, J.Y., Pearl, J.: Causes and explanations: a structural-model approach - Part I: Causes. In: 17th Conference on Uncertainy in Artificial Intelligence, Proceedings, pp. 194–202. Morgan, San Francisco, CA (2001). https://doi.org/10.1093/bjps/axi147
26. Handhayani, T., Cussens, J.: Kernel-based approach for learning causal graphs from mixed data. In: Jaeger, M., Nielsen, T.D. (eds.) Proceedings of the 10th International Conference on Probabilistic Graphical Models. Proceedings of the Machine Learning Research, vol. 138, pp. 221–232. PMLR (2020). https://proceedings.mlr.press/v138/handhayani20a.html
27. Honnibal, M., Montani, I., Van Landeghem, S., Boyd, A.: spaCy: industrial-strength natural language processing in Python (2020). https://doi.org/10.5281/zenodo.1212303
28. Hooker, G.: Discovering additive structure in black box functions. In: Proceedings of the 10th ACM SIGKDD International Conference on Knowledge Discovery and Data Mining (2004)
29. Jacovi, A., Goldberg, Y.: Towards faithfully interpretable NLP systems: how should we define and evaluate faithfulness? In: Proceedings of the 58th Annual Meeting of the Association for Computational Linguistics (ACL), pp. 4198–4205. ACL, Online (2020). https://doi.org/10.18653/v1/2020.acl-main.386
30. Lakkaraju, H., Kamar, E., Caruana, R., Leskovec, J.: Interpretable & explorable approximations of black box models. In: KDD 2017 Workshop on Fairness, Accountability, and Transparency in Machine Learning (2017)
31. Lakkaraju, H., Arsov, N., Bastani, O.: Robust and stable black box explanations. In: Proceedings of the 37th International Conference on Machine Learning (ICML). JMLR.org (2020). https://proceedings.mlr.press/v119/lakkaraju20a/lakkaraju20a.pdf
32. Li, L., Goh, T.T., Jin, D.: How textual quality of online reviews affect classification performance: a case of deep learning sentiment analysis. Neural Comput. Appl. **32**(9), 4387–4415 (2018). https://doi.org/10.1007/s00521-018-3865-7
33. Liu, Y., et al.: RoBERTa: a robustly optimized BERT pretraining approach. CoRR abs/1907.11692 (2019)
34. Lundberg, S.M., Lee, S.I.: A unified approach to interpreting model predictions. In: Advances in Neural Information Processing Systems, pp. 4765–4774 (2017)
35. Madsen, A., Reddy, S., Chandar, S.: Post-hoc interpretability for neural NLP: a survey. ACM Comput. Surv. **55**(8), 1–42 (2022). https://doi.org/10.1145/3546577
36. Miller, T.: Explanation in artificial intelligence: insights from the social sciences. Artif. Intell. **267**, 1–38 (2019). https://doi.org/10.1016/j.artint.2018.07.007
37. Miller, T.: Contrastive explanation: a structural-model approach. Knowl. Eng. Rev. **36**, e14 (2021). https://doi.org/10.1017/s0269888921000102

38. Mohammad, S.: Obtaining reliable human ratings of valence, arousal, and dominance for 20,000 English words. In: Proceedings of the 56th Annual Meeting of the Association for Computational Linguistics (Volume 1: Long Papers), pp. 174–184. ACL, Melbourne, Australia (2018). https://doi.org/10.18653/v1/P18-1017
39. Mohammad, S.M., Turney, P.D.: Crowdsourcing a Word-Emotion Association Lexicon. Comput. Intell. **29**(3), 436–465 (2013)
40. Plutchik, R.: A general psychoevolutionary theory of emotion. In: Theories of Emotion, pp. 3–33. Elsevier (1980). https://doi.org/10.1016/b978-0-12-558701-3.50007-7
41. Raghu, V.K., Poon, A., Benos, P.V.: Evaluation of causal structure learning methods on mixed data types. In: Le, T.D., Zhang, K., Kıcıman, E., Hyvärinen, A., Liu, L. (eds.) Proceedings of the 2018 ACM SIGKDD Workshop on Causal Disocvery. Proceedings of the Machine Learning Research, vol. 92, pp. 48–65. PMLR (2018). https://proceedings.mlr.press/v92/raghu18a.html
42. Ramsey, J., Glymour, M., Sanchez-Romero, R., Glymour, C.: A million variables and more: the fast greedy equivalence search algorithm for learning high-dimensional graphical causal models, with an application to functional magnetic resonance images. Int. J. Data Sci. Anal. **3**(2), 121–129 (2017). https://doi.org/10.1007/s41060-016-0032-z
43. Ribeiro, M.T., Singh, S., Guestrin, C.: Model-agnostic interpretability of machine learning. In: 2016 ICML Workshop on Human Interpretability in Machine Learning (WHI 2016), pp. 91–95 (2016)
44. Ribeiro, M.T., Singh, S., Guestrin, C.: "Why should i trust you?": explaining the predictions of any classifier. In: 22nd ACM SIGKDD Intl. Conf. on Knowledge Discovery in Data Mining (KDD 2016), Proceedings, pp. 1135–1144 (2016). https://doi.org/10.1145/2939672.2939778
45. Ribeiro, M.T., Wu, T., Guestrin, C., Singh, S.: Beyond accuracy: behavioral testing of NLP models with CheckList. In: Proceedings of the 58th Annual Meeting of the Association for Computational Linguistics, pp. 4902–4912. ACL, Online (2020). https://doi.org/10.18653/v1/2020.acl-main.442
46. Richardson, T., Spirtes, P.: Ancestral graph Markov models. Ann. Stat. **30**(4), 962–1030 (2002). http://www.jstor.org/stable/1558693
47. Sanh, V., Debut, L., Chaumond, J., Wolf, T.: DistilBERT, a distilled version of BERT: smaller, faster, cheaper and lighter. In: 33rd Conference on Neural Information Processing Systems (NeurIPS 2019) (2019)
48. Sani, N., Malinsky, D., Shpitser, I.: Explaining the behavior of black-box prediction algorithms with causal learning. CoRR abs/2006.02482 (2020)
49. Sengupta, K., Maher, R., Groves, D., Olieman, C.: GenBiT: measure and mitigate gender bias in language datasets. Microsoft J. Appl. Res. **16**, 63–71 (2021)
50. Sepehri, A., Markowitz, D.M., Mir, M.: PassivePy: a tool to automatically identify passive voice in big text data (2022). https://doi.org/10.31234/osf.io/bwp3t
51. Shimizu, S., Hoyer, P.O., Hyvärinen, A., Kerminen, A.: A linear non-gaussian acyclic model for causal discovery. J. Mach. Learn. Res. **7**(72), 2003–2030 (2006). http://jmlr.org/papers/v7/shimizu06a.html
52. Spirtes, P., Glymour, C.N., Scheines, R., Heckerman, D.: Causation, Prediction, and Search. MIT Press, Cambridge (2000)
53. Tan, S., Joty, S., Baxter, K., Taeihagh, A., Bennett, G.A., Kan, M.Y.: Reliability testing for natural language processing systems. In: Proceedings of the 59th Annual Meeting of the Association for Computational Linguistics (ACL) and the 11th International Joint Conference on Natural Language Processing, pp. 4153–4169. ACL, Online (2021). https://doi.org/10.18653/v1/2021.acl-long.321

54. Tan, S., Caruana, R., Hooker, G., Lou, Y.: Distill-and-compare: auditing black-box models using transparent model distillation. In: Proceedings of the 2018 AAAI/ACM Conference on AI, Ethics, and Society, pp. 303–310. AIES 2018, Association for Computing Machinery, New York, NY, USA (2018). https://doi.org/10.1145/3278721.3278725

55. Tian, J., Pearl, J.: Causal discovery from changes. In: Proceedings of the Seventeenth Conference on Uncertainty in Artificial Intelligence, pp. 512–521. UAI 2001, Morgan Kaufmann Publishers Inc., San Francisco, CA, USA (2001)

56. Tsamardinos, I., Brown, L.E., Aliferis, C.F.: The max-min hill-climbing Bayesian network structure learning algorithm. Mach. Learn. **65**(1), 31–78 (2006). https://doi.org/10.1007/s10994-006-6889-7

57. Viinikka, J., Eggeling, R., Koivisto, M.: Intersection-Validation: a method for evaluating structure learning without ground truth. In: Storkey, A., Perez-Cruz, F. (eds.) Proceedings of the 21st International Conference on Artificial Intelligence and Statistics. Proceedings of the Machine Learning Research, vol. 84, pp. 1570–1578. PMLR (2018). https://proceedings.mlr.press/v84/viinikka18a.html

58. Vilone, G., Longo, L.: A quantitative evaluation of global, rule-based explanations of post-hoc, model agnostic methods. Front. Artif. Intell. **4**, 717899 (2021). https://doi.org/10.3389/frai.2021.717899

59. Vowels, M.J., Camgoz, N.C., Bowden, R.: D'Ya like DAGs? a survey on structure learning and causal discovery. ACM Comput. Surv. **55**(4), 1–36 (2022). https://doi.org/10.1145/3527154

60. van der Waa, J., Robeer, M., van Diggelen, J., Neerincx, M., Brinkhuis, M.: Contrastive explanations with local Foil Trees. In: 2018 Workshop on Human Interpretability in Machine Learning (WHI) (2018)

61. Woodward, J.: Making Things Happen. Oxford University Press, Oxford (2004)

62. Zhang, J.: Causal reasoning with ancestral graphs. J. Mach. Learn. Res. **9**(47), 1437–1474 (2008). http://jmlr.org/papers/v9/zhang08a.html

63. Zhang, J.: On the completeness of orientation rules for causal discovery in the presence of latent confounders and selection bias. Artif. Intell. **172**(16), 1873–1896 (2008). https://doi.org/10.1016/j.artint.2008.08.001

64. Zhao, Q., Hastie, T.: Causal interpretations of black-box models. J. Bus. Econ. Stat. **39**(1), 272–281 (2019). https://doi.org/10.1080/07350015.2019.1624293

Counterfactual Explanations for Graph Classification Through the Lenses of Density

Carlo Abrate[1,3]([✉]) [iD], Giulia Preti[1] [iD], and Francesco Bonchi[1,2] [iD]

[1] CENTAI, Turin, Italy
{carlo.abrate,giulia.preti,bonchi}@centai.eu
[2] EURECAT, Barcelona, Spain
[3] Sapienza University, Rome, Italy

Abstract. Counterfactual examples have emerged as an effective approach to produce simple and understandable post-hoc explanations. In the context of graph classification, previous work has focused on generating counterfactual explanations by manipulating the most elementary units of a graph, i.e., removing an existing edge, or adding a non-existing one. In this paper, we claim that such language of explanation might be too fine-grained, and turn our attention to some of the main characterizing features of real-world complex networks, such as the tendency to close triangles, the existence of recurring motifs, and the organization into dense modules. We thus define a general *density-based counterfactual search* framework to generate instance-level counterfactual explanations for graph classifiers, which can be instantiated with different notions of dense substructures. In particular, we show two specific instantiations of this general framework: a method that searches for counterfactual graphs by opening or closing triangles, and a method driven by maximal cliques. We also discuss how the general method can be instantiated to exploit any other notion of dense substructures, including, for instance, a given taxonomy of nodes. We evaluate the effectiveness of our approaches in 7 brain network datasets and compare the counterfactual statements generated according to several widely-used metrics. Results confirm that adopting a semantic-relevant unit of change like density is essential to define versatile and interpretable counterfactual explanation methods.

1 Introduction

Graphs provide a flexible, expressive, and powerful data representation paradigm to model complex systems made of entities and relationships between them, such as users in social networks, regions in the brain, and proteins in an organism. A widely studied task on graph-structured data is *graph classification*, which involves assigning labels or categories to graphs based on their structural properties or node features. Graph classification has benefited greatly from the many recent technical advances, especially thanks to *graph neural networks* (GNN). However, as AI techniques become more complex, it becomes challenging to understand their output [69]. This opacity can lead to uninformed decisions,

© The Author(s), under exclusive license to Springer Nature Switzerland AG 2023
L. Longo (Ed.): xAI 2023, CCIS 1901, pp. 324–348, 2023.
https://doi.org/10.1007/978-3-031-44064-9_18

complicate the audit process, and ultimately limit the trust in AI techniques, and thus their adoption. In these regards, post-hoc explanation methods have emerged as an approach to make black-box models more interpretable [5,19]. Explanations of black-box models can help to build trust in AI systems by enabling users to understand the decision-making process and assess the reliability of the system. While this is particularly important in applications that impact people's lives, such as healthcare, finance, and justice [4,27], explaining AI models is also of uttermost importance in biological domains in which, more than the mere classification accuracy, it is important for the scientist to understand which modules play a role in a specific pathology or biological condition. For instance, in brain networks analysis, the neuroscientist needs to understand which are the regions of the brain whose interactions discriminate between disordered and healthy individuals [22,62].

Counterfactual explanations [41,58] are a method for providing post-hoc explanations of individual instance classification. These explanations consist in a counterfactual example, which is a modified version of the instance that leads to a different classification. They take the form of a counterfactual statement, such as *"If X had been different, Y would not have occurred"*, which is typically concise and easy to understand [24]. Defining and generating optimal counterfactuals is a challenging task, especially when working with graph data. This is due to the large space of interdependent features and the complex interconnections between the nodes, which can make determining which features to modify difficult and time-consuming. Additionally, some states within the feature space may be too complex for humans to fully comprehend or may be difficult to explain using the same semantic associated with the type of data under consideration.

Graph Classification for Brain Networks. In this work, without loss of generality, we adopt as the main application example, the binary classification of brain networks [10,30,37,40,59,65]. Brain networks can be modeled as undirected graphs, with nodes denoting *regions of interest* (ROIs), and edges indicating correlations of activation. In brain networks classification we are given two groups of individuals, e.g., a condition group and a control group, where each individual is represented by a graph $G_i = (V, E_i)$, defined over the same set V of nodes (corresponding to the ROIs). The set of edges E_i represents the connections, either structural or functional, between the ROIs of the observed G_i. The goal is to learn a binary classifier $f : \mathcal{G} \to \{0, 1\}$ which, given an unseen brain network $G_n = (V, E_n)$, predicts to which of the two groups it belongs.

Besides brain networks, this specific type of graph classification task, i.e., graph classification *with node identity awareness* [3,21,28,67], occurs whenever the identity of the node is an important information which identifies the same entity across all the input graphs. This is, for instance, the case in *"omics"* domains, such as in gene co-expression networks [29,31], protein-protein interaction networks [20,45], or gene regulatory networks [26,54].

Density-Based Graph Counterfactuals. Intuitively, given a specific graph G and a binary classifier f, a *counterfactual graph* [1] is a graph G' such that $f(G') = 1 - f(G)$, while being as close as possible to G. Previous work has focused on generating counterfactual explanations for graphs by changing the most elementary unit of a graph, i.e., an existing edge that might be removed, or a non-existing edge that might be added [1]. However, as other researchers have observed [47], an explanation language based on the most fundamental unit of a graph structure, might be too fine-grained for producing interesting explanations. Aiming at a higher-order language for producing counterfactual graphs, we turn our attention to some of the main characterizing features of real-world complex networks. In fact, social and technological networks, as well as biological networks (such as brain networks, metabolic and regulatory networks), are all characterized by some common structural features, such as: *network transitivity*, which is the property that two nodes that are both neighbors of the same third node have a high probability of also being connected (a.k.a. *triadic closure*), the existence of *repeated local motifs* and, more importantly, the organization into *communities* or dense modules [17,38,44]. Indeed, the extraction of dense substructures in networks, such as *maximal cliques*, *quasi-cliques*, *k-plex*, *k-club*, etc., has received substantial attention in the algorithmic literature (see [7,12,13,16,33,63] for surveys). Finding groups of nodes that are densely connected inside and sparsely connected with the outside, is a key concept that has been approached under several different names, including *graph clustering*, *graph partitioning*, *spectral clustering*, and *community detection* [6,14,36,43,51].

Following this observation, in this work, we propose to produce counterfactual graphs based on the alteration of dense substructures. For our purposes, we define a general *density-based counterfactual search* framework to generate instance-level counterfactual explanations for graph classifiers, which can be instantiated with different notions of dense substructures. This framework identifies the most informative regions of the graphs and manipulates them by adding or removing dense structures until a counterfactual is found. We then instantiate the general framework to specific special cases. In Sect. 4.1, we present a method (TRI) that, inspired by network transitivity, searches for counterfactual graphs by opening or closing triangles. Then in Sect. 4.2, we move to a counterfactual search driven by maximal cliques (CLI).

Our framework can be instantiated with any notion of a dense structure, or region of interest: for instance, in the context of brain networks, ROIs are usually grouped into distinct partitions (*brain parcellation*), according to several properties such as structural and functional markers. Counterfactual graphs generated using the language of density w.r.t. these coarser-grain and well-established taxonomies, might produce explanations that are more consistent with the terminology used to describe the organization of the brain, and thus more comprehensible for the neuroscientists. In fact, deviations in the functional connections among the brain regions from the normal pattern of connectivity are typically associated with functional impairments: as a consequence, the notions of *hyperconnectivity* or *hypo-connectivity* within and between specific regions, are heavily adopted by neuroscientists as fingerprints of specific disorders. Subgraphs that are dense in one class and sparse in the other, have also been proven effective in discriminating between a condition group and a control group [30].

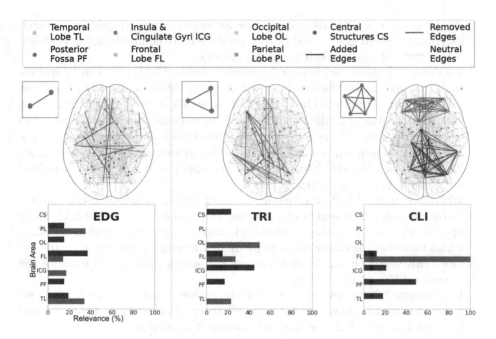

Fig. 1. Graph counterfactuals found by EDG [1], TRI, and CLI, for the brain network of patient 9 of the AUT dataset (see Sect. 5 for details). For each counterfactual, we highlight the edges added and removed in the input network. The boxplots aggregate the changes by brain region for more concise explanations.

Figure 1 showcases an example of our proposal over a brain network from the Autism Brain Image Data Exchange (ABIDE) dataset [8] (more details in Sect. 5). Nodes in different brain areas are denoted with different colors. In particular, the figure shows three different counterfactual graphs for the same brain network (patient 9): the leftmost one is generated using [1] (edge-based), the central one is produced using TRI, and the right-most one is created by CLI. In each counterfactual graph, red edges identify the regions sparsified (*removed edges*), while blue edges indicate the regions densified (*added edges*). The counterfactual statement corresponding to the counterfactual graph produced by CLI can be expressed in English as follows:

> *Patient X is classified as Autism Spectrum Disorder. If X's brain had less activation in the* FRONTAL LOBE *and more co-activation between the* POS-TERIOR FOSSA, INSULA CINGULATE GYRI, *and the* TEMPORAL LOBE *then X would have been classified as Typically Developed.*

Summary of Contributions and Roadmap. The contributions of this paper can be summarised as follows:

- We propose to use the language of dense substructure to guide the search for counterfactual graphs and thus to produce more comprehensible post-hoc counterfactual explanations for graph classifiers.
- We define a general and flexible framework, dubbed DCS, that can be instantiated to find counterfactual graphs leveraging different notions of a dense substructure of interest. Our framework is highly modular, providing users with a great deal of flexibility in defining the various parameters involved in the search process. Users can specify how to densify and sparsify (i.e., dense structures of interest), how to rank the nodes to identify the regions to modify, which black-box classifier to use, and whether the search should be refined via perturbation as post-processing.
- We showcase in detail two instantiations of DCS: a triangle-based counterfactual search (TRI) and a clique-based counterfactual search (CLI). Both approaches can be further customized, and we present a variation, RCLI, which identifies relevant regions to modify by leveraging the brain's parcellation. This variation can further improve the search process and enhance the interpretability of the explanations.
- We evaluate DCS in seven brain networks datasets and compare it with two baseline methods, demonstrating the efficiency of the proposed method and the high interpretability of the explanations it generates.

After an overview of the related work (Sect. 2), we introduce the density-based counterfactual search problem (Sect. 3). Section 4 presents our framework to generate counterfactual graphs adhering to the proposed density-oriented language, while Sect. 4.1 and Sect. 4.2 describe two implementations with customizable parameters. Finally, Sect. 5 shows our experimental evaluation of the framework and Sect. 6 discusses advantages and limitations.

2 Related Work

Post-hoc explanation methods have become essential for understanding the behavior of black-box machine learning models. One such method is counterfactual explanations [58], which produces example-based explanations by means of a counterfactual instance for each instance being classified. More specifically, counterfactual explanations need to exhibit two key characteristics: they must be *similar* to the original instance while being classified in the opposite class of the original instance. Numerous methods have been proposed to generate counterfactual explanations that possess these critical characteristics [18].

Explanations for Graph Classifiers. There has been a growing interest in addressing the challenge of explaining graph classifiers, resulting in a surge of the number of proposed methods, providing either local or global explanations. A recent survey [69] categorizes the main (local or) instance-level techniques into four main classes. *Gradient/feature-based methods*, such as SA and Guided BP [2], and CAM and Grad-CAM [48], aim to evaluate the relevance of each feature in the classification task. *Perturbation-based methods*, such as GNNExplainer [66], PGExplainer [35], ZORRO [15], GraphMask [52], RC-Explainer [60],

SubgraphX [70], measure the impact of the perturbation of the input features on the output of the classifier, to detect the most important features. Among them, GraphShap [47] generates graph-level explanations by ranking a set of input motifs according to their Shapley values.

Decomposition methods for graph neural networks, such as LRP [2], Excitation BP [48] and GNN-LRP [53], generate feature importance scores by back-propagating decomposed prediction scores to the input layer of the network. *Surrogate methods*, such as GraphLime [23], RelEx [71], and PGM-Explainer [57], fit an interpretable model in the neighborhood of the input graph.

Only a few works provide (global or) model-level explanations. Among them, XGNN [68] is based on graph generation.

Counterfactual Explanations for Graph Classifiers. DBS and OBS [1] propose heuristics to locally perturb a generic input graph. Specifically, they consider two types of modifications: edge addition and edge removal. The counterfactual explanations are found using a bidirectional search approach that first identifies a feasible counterfactual graph, and then modifies the candidate graph to make it more similar to the input graph. On the other hand, targeted approaches have been proposed for molecular graphs [34,61], which are graphs where nodes represent atoms and edges are bonds.

CF-GNNExplainer [34] is a counterfactual version of GNNExplainer [66] that returns relevant subgraphs as explanations. This method removes edges using a matrix sparsification technique that minimizes the number of edges changed. MMACE [61] generates counterfactuals for molecular graphs by exploring the chemical space vis the Superfast Traversal, Optimization, Novelty, Exploration and Discovery (STONED) method. In addition, the method uses DBSCAN to generate multiple counterfactuals.

This work proposes a more general framework for counterfactual graph generation that goes beyond existing approaches such as DBS, OBS [1] and CF-GNNExplainer [34]. While previous works primarily focused on modifying the structure of the original graph by adding or removing one edge at a time, our framework provides more fine-grained control over the graph modifications, as it operates on the dense and sparse regions of the graph. This opens up possibilities for generating counterfactuals for various scenarios.

3 Preliminaries

Given a set of nodes V we denote $\mathcal{G}$ the set of all possible graphs defined over V. Given one such graphs $G = (V, E) \in \mathcal{G}$, a *subgraph* of G is a graph $H = (V_H, E_H)$ such that $V_H \subseteq V$ and $E_H \subseteq E$. A subgraph H is a *k-clique* iff $|V_H| = k$ and $E_H = V_H \times V_H$. The *density*[1] $\delta(H)$ of a subgraph H is defined as its number of edges, i.e., $\delta(H) = |E_H|$.

---

[1] Density is usually defined as the number of edges over the number of possible edges. W.l.o.g. we omit the denominator.

We assume we are given a binary graph classification model $f : \mathcal{G} \to \{0, 1\}$, that assigns a label in $\{0, 1\}$ to each graph in $\mathcal{G}$. We assume that f **(i)** is a trained machine learning model whose internal structure is not known (black-box model), **(ii)** can be queried at will, and **(iii)** does not change from one query to the other one (i.e., it is static).

Given a specific graph $G \in \mathcal{G}$ a *counterfactual graph* is another graph $G' \in \mathcal{G}$ such that $f(G) = 1 - f(G')$. Depending on the domain at hand, several desired properties might guide the search for counterfactuals, such as, e.g., *similarity* between the original and the counterfactual instance, *sparsity* (the change affects only a few features), *efficiency* (the search should be fast), and the *feasibility* (to generate a feasible instance). We will discuss some of these measures in Sect. 5. For the moment, we only need to define the *distance* $\mathsf{d}(G, G')$ between two graphs G and G' as the symmetric difference between their edge sets:

$$\mathsf{d}(G, G') = |E \setminus E'| + |E' \setminus E| \ . \tag{1}$$

We next introduce a novel framework to generate counterfactual graphs based on the manipulation of dense substructures, which become the fundamental units of the vocabulary of the explanations produced.

4 Density-Based Counterfactual Search

We next introduce our general *Density-based Counterfactual Search* framework (DCS), which builds instance-level counterfactual explanations by iteratively searching for sparse regions to densify and for dense regions to sparsify. Pseudocode of DCS is provided in Algorithm 1.

Algorithm 1. DCS

Require: Binary Graph Classifier f; Graph G
Ensure: Counterfactual G'
 1: $G' \leftarrow G$
 2: **while** $f(G) = f(G')$ **do**
 3:     DENSIFY a sparse region in G'
 4:     SPARSIFY a dense region in G'
 5: **return** G'

The algorithm iteratively changes the input graph G until the modified graph G' is classified in the opposite class of G. At each iteration, it adds a dense structure to a sparse region in G' and removes a dense structure from a dense region in G'. Since two different regions of the graph undergo changes at each iteration, G' gradually diverges from the original graph G as the number of iterations increases. In generating counterfactual graphs, a commonly desired objective is to produce graphs that closely resemble the input graphs. This is because such counterfactual graphs are more likely to provide a concise and interpretable explanation. For this reason, the algorithm returns the counterfactual graph found in the smallest number of iterations.

Algorithm 1 can accommodate any definition of a dense substructure. In the rest of this section, we introduce two alternative approaches for defining the operations of densification and sparsification. The first approach, TRI, is based on triadic closure; while the second approach, CLI, is based on maximal cliques.

4.1   Triangle-Based Counterfactual Search

The *Triangle-based Counterfactual Search* (TRI) is illustrated in Algorithm 2. In addition to the original graph G and the classifier f, TRI takes as input a sorted list of candidate edges to remove E_- (to destroy triangles) and a sorted list of candidate edges to add E_+ (to create triangles) in the counterfactual graph. These lists are prepared using Algorithm 3 (discussed below). TRI iterates over the two lists until the graph becomes a counterfactual graph for G. At each iteration i, it selects the next best edge to add (e_+) and to remove (e_-) from the current graph G_i. If all the possible wedges have been closed, or if all the possible triangles have been opened (i.e. there are no more edges available in either E_- or E_+), but G_i is still classified in the same class as G, the algorithm returns $\emptyset$, indicating that a counterfactual could not be found.

Algorithm 2. TRI

Require: Binary Graph Classifier f; Graph G
Require: Sorted lists of candidate edges to remove E_- and to add E_+
Ensure: Counterfactual G' if found; $\emptyset$ otherwise
1: $G_0 \leftarrow G$; $i \leftarrow 1$
2: **while** $f(G_{i-1}) = f(G)$ **and** $i \leq \min(|E_-|, |E_+|)$ **do**
3:     $e_- \leftarrow \text{NEXTBEST}(E_-)$; $e_+ \leftarrow \text{NEXTBEST}(E_+)$
4:     $E_i \leftarrow E_{i-1} \setminus \{e_-\} \cup \{e_+\}$; $i \leftarrow i+1$
5: **if** $f(G_i) \neq f(G)$ **then return** G_i
6: **else return** $\emptyset$

Given a graph G, Algorithm 3 first computes a score for each feasible edge $(u, v) \in V \times V$, and then partitions the edges into two lists: a list of existing edges that could be removed (E_-) and a list of non-existing edges that could be added (E_+). Finally, the algorithm sorts both lists based on the number of triangles in G that contain the vertices of each edge. In particular, E_- is sorted in ascending order, while E_+ is sorted in descending order. This sorting strategy ensures that TRI adds triangles in sparse regions of G, and removes triangles from the dense regions.

4.2   Clique-Based Counterfactual Search

The *Clique-based Counterfactual Search* (CLI), illustrated in Algorithm 4, follows a structure similar to Algorithm 1 but employs several heuristics to speed up

---

Algorithm 3. TRIANGLE SCORE

Require: Graph G
Ensure: Sorted lists of candidate edges to remove E_- and to add E_+
1: $\mathsf{T}(v) \leftarrow$ number of triangles including v, $\forall v \in V$
2: $E_- \leftarrow E_+ \leftarrow \emptyset$
3: **for** $(v, u) \in V \times V$ **do**
4:     $s_v \leftarrow \mathsf{T}(v)$; $s_u \leftarrow \mathsf{T}(u)$
5:     **if** $(v, u) \in E$ **then** $E_- \leftarrow E_- \cup \{(s_v + s_u, (v, u))\}$
6:     **else** $E_+ \leftarrow E_+ \cup \{(s_v + s_u, (v, u))\}$
7: $Sort_s(E_-)$ in ascending order of score;
8: $Sort_s(E_+)$ in descending order of score;
9: **return** (E_-, E_+)

---

the search for a counterfactual graph G' for G. The algorithm receives in input two additional parameters: the maximum number of iterations max_I, and the list of nodes in G ranked according to a metric that gives more importance to nodes that belong to dense regions in G. At each iteration i, the algorithm adds a clique to a sparse region of the current graph G_i around the next worst node in the ranking $\bar{n}_h$ and removes a maximal clique from a dense region in G_i around the next best node in the ranking $\bar{n}_l$. The algorithm terminates when either G_i is classified in the opposite class of G or the maximum number of iterations max_I is reached. The densification of a sparse region is carried out by Algorithm 6 (DENSIFYCLI) and the sparsification by Algorithm 5 (SPARSIFYCLI). In the following, a clique is represented by its set of vertices, as its set of edges is the set of all the possible edges between such nodes.

Algorithm 4. CLI

Require: Binary Graph Classifier f; Graph G
Require: Max Num Iteration max_I; Sorted list of vertices $\bar{V}$
Ensure: Counterfactual G' if found; $\emptyset$ otherwise
1: $D[v] \leftarrow 0$, $\forall v \in V$
2: $G_0 \leftarrow G$; $\mathcal{L} \leftarrow \emptyset$; $i \leftarrow 1$
3: **while** $f(G_{i-1}) = f(G)$ **and** $i \leq \mathsf{max}_I$ **do**
4:     $\bar{n}_l, \bar{n}_h \leftarrow$ NEXTBEST$(\bar{V})$, NEXTWORST$(\bar{V})$
5:     $G_i \leftarrow$ SPARSIFYCLI$(G, G_{i-1}, \bar{n}_l, D, \mathcal{L})$
6:     $d_h \leftarrow 0$; $s \leftarrow d_l \leftarrow \mathsf{d}(G_{i-1}, G_i)$
7:     **while** $f(G_i) = f(G)$ **and** $d_l > d_h$ **do**
8:         $s \leftarrow s - d_h$
9:         $G^h \leftarrow$ DENSIFYCLI$(G_i, \bar{n}_h, D, s)$
10:         $d_h \leftarrow \mathsf{d}(G_i, G^h)$; $G_i \leftarrow G^h$
11:     $i \leftarrow i + 1$
12: **if** $f(G_i) \neq f(G)$ **then return** G_i
13: **else return** $\emptyset$

Procedure SPARSIFYCLI identifies a maximal clique in the input graph G surrounding a given node n, and removes all the edges in that clique in the candidate counterfactual graph G'. The algorithm operates by identifying the largest clique in G including n that has the lowest overlap with the cliques removed in prior iterations. By choosing the largest, lowest-overlap clique, the algorithm sparsifies one of the densest regions in G'. Note that the cliques considered by the algorithm are found in the original graph G, and some of their edges may have already been removed from G' in previous iterations of SPARSIFYCLI. After the desired clique C has been identified, the algorithm removes all its edges from G' and stores C in the set of cliques removed $\mathcal{L}$. Finally, the counts associated with each node in the clique are incremented by 1.

Algorithm 5. SPARSIFYCLI

Require: Graph G; Candidate Counterfactual G'
Require: Node n; Dictionary D; Set of Cliques $\mathcal{L}$
Ensure: G' with a clique removed
1: $\mathcal{C} \leftarrow$ cliques in G including n
2: **if** $\mathcal{L} = \emptyset$ **then return** largest clique in $\mathcal{C}$
3: $O \leftarrow \emptyset$
4: **for** $C \in \mathcal{C}$ **do**
5:   $o \leftarrow \max_{L \in \mathcal{L}} (|C \cap L|); O \leftarrow O \cup \{(o, C)\}$
6: $C \leftarrow$ clique in O with lowest value o
7: $\mathcal{L} \leftarrow \mathcal{L} \cup \{C\}$
8: $D[v] \leftarrow D[v] + 1$ for each v in C
9: **return** $G' \setminus \{$ edges in $C \}$

Algorithm 6. DENSIFYCLI

Require: Graph G; Node n; Dictionary D; Size s
Ensure: G with a clique added
1: $\Gamma_G(n) \leftarrow$ 2-hop neighborhood of n in G sorted according to D (ascending)
2: $W \leftarrow V \setminus \Gamma_G(n)$ sorted according to D (ascending)
3: $C \leftarrow$ CONCAT$(\Gamma_G(n), W)$; $V_s \leftarrow$ first s nodes in C
4: $D[v] \leftarrow D[v] - 1$ for each $v \in V_s$
5: **return** $G \cup \{$ edges between the nodes in $V_s \}$

Procedure DENSIFYCLI is iteratively called until the dense region added to the candidate counterfactual graph has at least as many edges as the dense region removed by Algorithm 5[2]. This ensures that the size of the counterfactual

---

[2] In our experiments we constrained the max deviation between the number of edges added and removed in terms of the max number of nodes b that a clique added can have with respect to the number of nodes in the clique removed, and set $b = 10$.

is similar to that of the original graph. At each iteration, the algorithm identifies a sparse region of size s around the given node n and adds all the possible edges between the s nodes. The size of the region s is determined by subtracting the number of edges added in the previous iterations from the number of edges removed by Algorithm 5. To avoid densifying a region that has just been sparsified, the algorithm selects a sparse region involving nodes that are not present in many cliques added in previous iterations. To achieve this, the algorithm uses a dictionary D, which keeps track of the number of times each node has been part of a clique added to the candidate counterfactual. Given a node n, DENSIFYCLI sorts both the 2-hop neighborhood $\Gamma_G(n)$ of n and the rest of the vertices W according to their counts in D (Algorithm 6 lines 1–2). Then, it adds to G the clique C consisting of the first s nodes in the concatenation between $\Gamma_G(n)$ and W, and updates D by decreasing the counts associated with the nodes in C.

Further Customizability of the Framework. In Algorithm 4, we made specific design choices that, however, can be customized and adapted to meet the needs of the application at hand.

Firstly, Algorithm 4 receives as input the list $\bar{V}$ of nodes in G ranked according to a metric that prioritizes nodes in dense regions for Algorithm 5 and nodes in sparse regions for Algorithm 6. In our implementation of CLI used in the experiments in Sect. 5 we sort the nodes in $\bar{V}$ based on the number of triangles in which each node participates. However, alternative measures could be used to rank the nodes, such as the node clustering coefficient or other features at node level. The key is to select a ranking that allows for traversing in one direction to be a good heuristic for sparsifying regions while traversing in the other direction is a good heuristic for densifying regions.

When domain-specific information is available, it is important to customize the algorithm to take such information into consideration. In the case of brain networks, for instance, nodes can be partitioned into well-defined and distinct regions (i.e. the brain lobes). In Sect. 5, we explore a variation of CLI that selects the regions to sparsify/densify based on the brain lobes, which we refer to as RCLI. The RCLI algorithm uses a two-level ranking strategy that first ranks the brain lobes according to the density of the subgraph induced by their nodes (regions having higher density ranked higher) and then, within each region, ranks the nodes according to the number of triangles in which they participate. This two-level ranking allows RCLI to conduct the edge changes within a lower number of brain regions and thus generate more interpretable explanations.

Secondly, for the sake of *feasibility* of the counterfactual, i.e., keeping its density similar to the original graph, we alternate between Algorithm 5 and Algorithm 6, meaning that we call them the same number of times. However, while this strategy is effective in most cases, it may not be the optimal approach. An alternative approach might let the density of the original graph govern the calls to Algorithm 5 and Algorithm 6, so that when the graph is very sparse, Algorithm 6 is called more often than Algorithm 5, and the other way around.

5   Experimental Evaluation

We next showcase the application of density-based counterfactuals in the context of brain networks, highlighting the high interpretability of such counterfactuals.

5.1   Brain Networks

Brain networks can be constructed using non-invasive techniques such as Functional Magnetic Resonance Imaging (fMRI) in resting-state patients. By measuring blood flow, fMRI exploits the link between neural activity and blood flow and oxygenation, to associate a time series of activation scores at voxel level. The voxels' signals are parcellated into Regions of Interest (ROIs) (*nodes of the graph*) using specific templates, such as the Automated Anatomical Labeling (AAL) [56] or the 200 [9] parcellation scheme. Then, interactions between ROIs (*edges of the graph*) are identified by looking at the correlation between the corresponding time series. Finally, relevant interactions are selected by applying a threshold (edge pruning), to obtain the brain's functional connectome. ROIs can be further aggregated into areas associated with the lobes of the brain. As discussed before, this aggregation can be exploited to express interpretable density-based counterfactual explanations.

We consider seven publicly available brain network datasets.

AUT is a dataset gathered within the Autism Brain Image Data Exchange (ABIDE) [8] project. This dataset includes brain network data from 49 patients with Autism Spectrum Disorder (ASD, condition group) and 52 Typically Developed (TD, control group) patients, all under the age of 9 years old.

BIP dataset about lithium response in type I bipolar disorder patients [50].

ADHD, ADHDM come from the Multimodal Treatment of Attention Deficit Hyperactivity Disorder project[3], which investigated the impact of cannabis use on adults with or without a childhood diagnosis of ADHD. In the ADHD dataset, subjects are labeled as either "ADHD" or "TD", while in the ADHDM dataset, they are labeled as "Marijuana use" or "Marijuana not used".

OHSU, PEK, KKI[4] are datasets constructed for three brain classification tasks: Attention Deficit Hyperactivity Disorder classification (OHSU), Hyperactive Impulsive classification (PEK), and gender classification (KKI) [46].

Data is preprocessed following the literature for converting time series to correlation matrices[5]. To generate the graph dataset, correlation matrices are transformed into adjacency matrices by setting edges when the correlation between the two nodes is higher than a fixed threshold. The threshold is selected based

---

[3] http://fcon_1000.projects.nitrc.org/indi/ACPI/html/acpi_mta_1.html.

[4] https://github.com/GRAND-Lab/graph_datasets.

[5] See http://preprocessed-connectomes-project.org/abide/dparsf.html for AUT and BIP, and https://ccraddock.github.io/cluster_roi/atlases.html for ADHD and ADHDM. For OHSU, PEK, and KKI, the data was already preprocessed.

on the distribution of the correlation matrix values, using the 90th percentile for ADHD and AUT, and 80th for BIP. All the preprocessed graph datasets are available in our repository[6].

Table 1 reports, for each dataset, the number of networks, the percentage of networks in class 1 (since we deal with binary classification, we report values for one class only), the total number of vertices and edges in the networks, and the accuracy and F1 score of the binary classifier trained on the dataset (see below).

Table 1. Num. of graphs $|\mathcal{G}|$, percentage of graphs in class 1, num. of nodes $|V|$, average num. of edges per graph avg$|E|$, and accuracy ACC and F1 score of the binary classifier, for each dataset.

Dataset	$|\mathcal{G}|$	$|Y_{=1}|$	$|V|$	avg$|E|$	ACC	F1
AUT	101	48%	116	665	0.92	0.90
BIP	118	46%	116	667	0.66	0.54
ADHD	123	32%	116	667	0.80	0.59
ADHDM	123	50%	116	667	0.93	0.93
OSHU	79	56%	190	199	0.68	0.72
PEK	85	42%	190	77	0.71	0.58
KKI	83	55%	190	48	0.66	0.68

Classifier. The proposed framework is model-agnostic, making it suitable for explaining any kind of binary classifier. In our experiments, we consider a binary classifier designed for graph classification that exploits the *Spectral Features* (SF) [32] of the graph to determine class memberships. Let $A \in \{0,1\}^{|V| \times |V|}$ be the adjacency matrix of the graph, D be the diagonal matrix of node degrees, and $L = I - D^{-1/2}AD^{-1/2}$ be the normalized Laplacian of A. The SF of the graph is a vector consisting of the k smallest positive eigenvalues of L, sorted in ascending order. We trained a KNN classifier with various parameter settings and selected the optimal configuration based on the accuracy (ACC) and F1 score using 5-fold cross-validation. The values of ACC and F1 of the configurations selected are reported in the last two columns of Table 1.

5.2   Metrics

Various metrics have been proposed to evaluate the quality of counterfactual explanations [18]. The selection of which measures to prioritize over others depends on factors such as the data type, the black-box models considered, and the vocabulary used to formulate the counterfactual statements. We consider three measures specifically proposed to evaluate graph counterfactuals [49].

---

[6] https://github.com/carlo-abrate/Counterfactual-Explanations-for-Graph-Classification-Through-the-Lenses-of-Density.git.

Flip Rate: measures the percentage of graphs in the dataset for which the algorithm was able to find a counterfactual explanation [42,49].

Edit Distance: measures how *different* is a graph G from its counterfactual G', and, in our case, is defined as the ratio between the symmetric difference of the edge sets of G and G' (Eq. (1)) and $|E \cup E'|$:

$$d_{\%}(G, G') = \frac{d(G, G')}{|E \cup E'|}.$$

Calls: run-time complexity of a counterfactual search method measured in terms of the number of calls to the black-box model (C).

5.3   Baselines

We compare the performance of TRI, CLI, and RCLI against three baseline methods. The first baseline, EDG [1], utilizes an edge-based language to generate counterfactual explanations. The second baseline, DAT, is an instance-level counterfactual search method proposed in [18]. This method searches for the closest graph in the dataset that is classified by the black-box model in the opposite class and returns it as a counterfactual explanation for the input graph.

Following [1] we also equip the RCLI and DAT methods with a *backward search* phase which tries to refine the counterfactual found by modifying the edges in the symmetric difference between the edge set of the input graph and that of the counterfactual graph, with the aim of reducing the distance between the two graphs. The resulting methods are named RCLI+BW and DAT+BW respectively.

All the methods are implemented in Python and the code is made publicly available[7] together with the datasets used in our analysis, and a supplemental material document containing further experimental results.

5.4   Qualitative Analysis

In this section, we compare the counterfactual graphs generated by three instantiations of DCS, namely TRI, CLI, and RCLI, with those produced by the three baseline methods, EDG, DAT, and DAT+BW, for specific patients in three datasets. All the results presented pertain to brain networks for which the classifier accurately predicted the class.

AUT Dataset. Figure 2 shows the counterfactual graphs for patient 9 in AUT. This patient is classified as "Autism Spectrum Disorder". For each method, the left figure shows the connectome of the patient overlaid on the brain glass schematics, where ROIs are projected onto a 2D space of the image, and different colors represent ROIs in different brain lobes. Blue edges indicate edges added to

---

[7] https://github.com/carlo-abrate/Counterfactual-Explanations-for-Graph-Classification-Through-the-Lenses-of-Density.

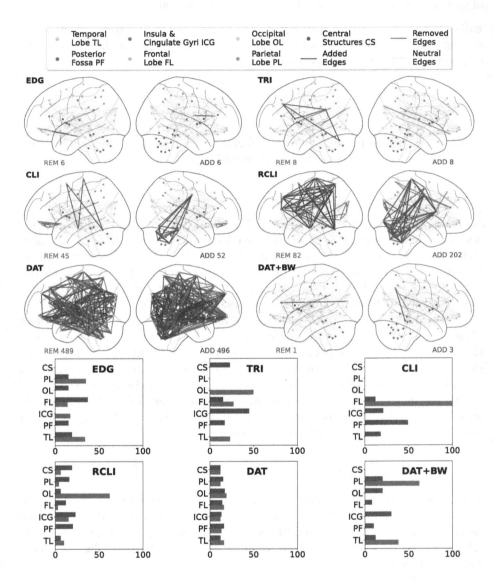

Fig. 2. Counterfactual graphs found by each method for patient 9 in AUT. The upper illustrations show the connectome of the patient where red edges indicate *connections to remove*, and blue edges indicate *connections to add* to generate the counterfactual (REM and ADD are the total numbers). The lower barplots show to which brain lobes the ROIs of the edges added (in blue) and removed (in red) belong (as percentages). (Color figure online)

the counterfactual graph, while red edges denote edges removed from the counterfactual graph. In addition to the connectome visualization, the right barplots illustrate the distribution of changes among brain lobes. For each brain lobe, the bars report the percentage of the nodes involved in the added (blue) and removed (red) edges that belong to that lobe. By examining these barplots, we can gain insights into which brain regions are most affected by each method's counterfactual graph generation process. We first observe that each method perturbed different regions of the brain. This is due to the fact that the set of changes identified by each method depends on a range of factors, including the method's underlying assumptions, its optimization criteria, and its specific implementation. The choice of counterfactual generation method should take into account the specific properties of the input data and the desired goals of the counterfactual analysis. One of the desiderata is interpretability. In general, the larger the number of regions changed and the more homogeneously the changes are distributed within the regions, the less human-interpretable the counterfactual explanation becomes. Of the methods examined, DAT produced the most complex explanation, with almost the same number of edges added and removed from each brain lobe. The DAT+BW method provides a partial solution to this issue by removing edges mainly from the Parietal Lobe and the Temporal Lobe, which reduces the heterogeneity of edge removals across the brain lobes. However, the edge additions still span across many regions, limiting the interpretability of the solution. The EDG method suffers from similar limitations in that its counterfactual graph involves changes spanning across most of the brain lobes. In contrast, TRI and CLI provide simpler explanations, as they perturbed a lower number of regions and concentrated most of the changes in the same regions. Specifically, TRI mainly sparsified the Occipital Lobe and densified the Insula & Cingulate Gyri, while CLI sparsified only the Frontal Lobe and added most of the edges in the Posterior Fossa. This results in a more focused and interpretable explanation. In fact, the output of CLI can be summarized by the following simple *counterfactual statement*:

> *Patient X is classified as Autism Spectrum Disorder. If X's brain had less activation in the* FRONTAL LOBE *and more co-activation in the* POSTERIOR FOSSA, INSULA CINGULATE GYRI, *and the* TEMPORAL LOBE *then X would have been classified as Typically Developed.*

BIP Dataset. Figure 3 shows the counterfactual graphs and the distributions of edges changed among the brain lobes, for patient 9 in the BIP dataset. This patient is classified as "Typically Developed". This example serves to confirm the effectiveness of TRI and CLI in generating more compact and interpretable explanations. Specifically, TRI produces a counterfactual graph that closely resembles the input network, with only 10 edges added and 10 edges removed. On the other hand, CLI concentrates its changes in two specific regions: the Parietal Lobe (with connections removed) and the Posterior Fossa (with connections added). The output of TRI can be summarized by the following simple *counterfactual statement*:

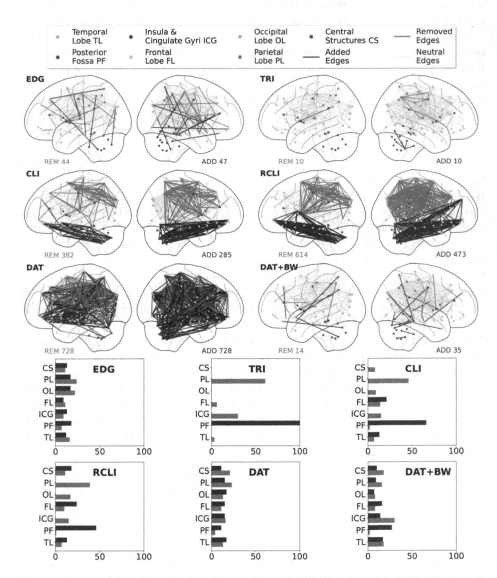

Fig. 3. Counterfactual graphs found by each method for patient 9 in BIP. The upper illustrations show the connectome of the patient where red edges indicate *connections to remove,* and blue edges indicate *connections to add* to generate the counterfactual (REM and ADD are the total numbers). The lower barplots show to which brain lobes the ROIs of the edges added (in blue) and removed (in red) belong (as percentages). (Color figure online)

Patient X is classified as Typically Developed. If X's brain had less activation in the PARIETAL LOBE *and the* INSULA CINGULATE GYRI, *and more co-activation in the* POSTERIOR FOSSA, *then X would have been classified as Bipolar.*

Given the Cerebellum's crucial role in emotional regulation, it's worth noting that the Posterior Fossa, which houses the Cerebellum, is an important area of study in bipolar disorder research [11, 25, 39].

In contrast, EDG and DAT generate sparser explanations that involve all the brain regions, making them more complex. The same is true for the backward search method (DAT+BW). Based on these results, we can conclude that the baseline methods are less effective at producing counterfactual explanations that are consistent with the terminology used to describe the organization of the brain.

ADHD Dataset. As a last example, Fig. 4 depicts the counterfactual graphs and the distributions of edges changed among the brain lobes, for patient 22 in the ADHD dataset, who is classified by ADHD. In this case, the counterfactuals generated by TRI and CLI are quite similar, with edges removed from the Occipital Lobe and added primarily in the Temporal Lobe. Additionally, CLI adds connections in the Posterior Fossa, while TRI adds them in the Frontal Lobe. It's worth noting that several studies on the structural and functional neuroimaging of ADHD patients have shown alterations in Occipital Regions [55, 64]. The output of CLI can be summarized by the following simple *counterfactual statement*:

Patient X is classified as ADHD. If X's brain had less activation in the OCCIPITAL LOBE, *and more co-activation in the* POSTERIOR FOSSA *and the* TEMPORAL LOBE, *then X would have been classified as Typically Developed.*

5.5 Quantitative Comparison

We next present a comparison of the various counterfactual generation methods, using the metrics outlined in Sect. 5.2.

Figure 5 reports the distribution of $d_\%$ and C values (the latter in logarithmic scale) at the class level for each method across three datasets (AUT, BIP, and ADHDM). Results for the remaining datasets can be found in the supplementary material shared in our repository. Computation complexity, which is measured as the number of calls to the black-box classifier, varies across the different methods tested, with DAT and DAT+BW being the most time-consuming due to the need to compare the input network with each graph classified in the opposite class. We note that DAT+BW requires slightly more calls to the oracle C because it also performs a backward search. CLI tends to find solutions more quickly than the other methods due to its tendency to make larger changes in the regions of the network, whereas EDG and TRI may require more iterations (and thus calls to the oracle) to achieve the same change.

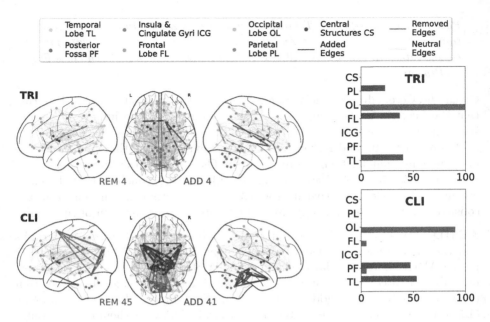

Fig. 4. Counterfactual graphs found by each method for patient 22 in ADHD. The left illustrations show the connectome of the patient where red edges indicate *connections to remove*, and blue edges indicate *connections to add* to generate the counterfactual (REM and ADD are the total numbers). The right barplots show to which brain lobes the ROIs of the edges added (in blue) and removed (in red) belong (as percentages). (Color figure online)

We next examine the proximity of the counterfactual graphs to the corresponding input networks. As we observed in the previous section, the explanations generated by DAT differ significantly from the input networks, as it searches for counterfactuals among the graphs in the dataset (which can vary considerably from each other) rather than perturbing the network itself. The application of the backward search on top of DAT results in counterfactuals that are much closer to the original networks compared to other methods. Interestingly, applying a backward search after RCLI does not significantly alter the resulting counterfactuals, suggesting that these solutions are more robust than those generated by DAT. Finally, since both TRI and EDG change a few edges at each iteration, the corresponding distributions of symmetric differences are comparable.

Methods such as CLI and RCLI operate on the maximal cliques in the network, which causes them to change a larger number of edges at each iteration, resulting in counterfactuals that are more distant than those obtained by EDG and TRI. It is important to stress that CLI and RCLI, by design, are expected to induce larger changes when producing a counterfactual as they use a coarser-grain vocabulary in the explanation (dense regions), w.r.t. the fine-grain approaches of EDG and TRI. As motivated in Sect. 1, we aim to have explanations at the level of regions

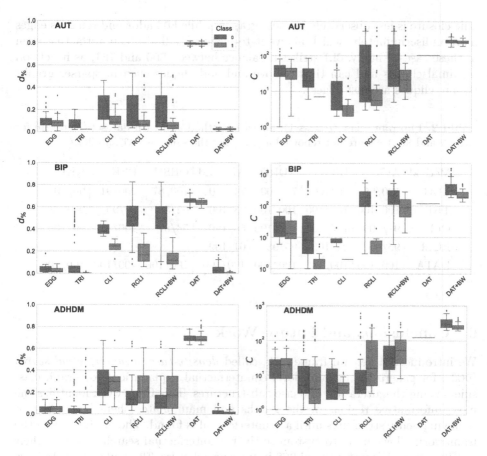

Fig. 5. Distribution of symmetric differences between original and counterfactual graphs ($d_\%$) and of calls to the oracle (C), for each counterfactual generation method, for AUT (1st row), BIP (2nd row), and ADHDM (3rd row).

(in which the changes are concentrated), because these are more interpretable for the domain expert than a simple list of flipped edges.

We finally report the flip rate per class (class 0/class 1) for each dataset (columns) and each method (rows) in Table 2. We remind that RCLI was tested only in the datasets where the brains' parcellations were available (i.e., all but OHSU, PEK, and KKI). By definition, the flip rate of DAT is always 100%, as it picks the closest counterfactual among the graphs in the database. The other methods, instead, did not achieve a perfect score, as they were run for a fixed number of iterations. In particular, TRI is run for at most $\min(|E_-|, |E_+|)$ iterations, CLI and RCLI for at most $\max_I = 200$ iterations, and EDG for st most 2000 iterations. We observe that TRI converges to a counterfactual more frequently than the other methods, even in the unbalanced ADHD dataset. However, it struggles in the three sparsest networks (OHSU, PEK, KKI), likely because triadic closure is less observable in these graphs, while EDG adds and removes edges more indiscriminately, which allows it to eventually find a counterfactual even in these cases. Finally, CLI strikes a balance between EDG and TRI, as it acts on maximal cliques and can thus remove and add cliques even in sparser graphs (where cliques are just edges).

Table 2. Flip rate (class 0/class 1), for each method and each dataset. Flip rate for DAT+BW and RCLI+BW are not reported as they are the same as DAT and RCLI.

Method	AUT	BIP	ADHD	ADHDM	OHSU	PEK	KKI
EDG	100/85	70/100	75/100	74/100	100/87	100/91	90/100
TRI	100/100	100/100	100/100	98/100	62/58	89/96	90/71
CLI	91/100	100/100	100/100	56/100	53/87	100/91	90/100
RCLI	96/93	94/100	95/98	61/100	–	–	–
DATA	100/100	100/100	100/100	100/100	100/100	100/100	100/100

6   Conclusions and Future Work

We introduced a general framework, called *density-based counterfactual search* (DCS), for generating instance-level counterfactual explanations for graph classifiers using the alteration of dense substructures. This framework identifies the most informative regions of the graphs and manipulates them by adding or removing dense structures until a counterfactual is found. The modularity of the framework allows users to customize their counterfactual search based on their specific needs. We instantiated DCS in two special cases: TRI and CLI. In TRI, we search for counterfactual graphs by opening or closing triangles, while in CLI, we move to a counterfactual search driven by maximal cliques. Additionally, we showed a variation of CLI, called RCLI, which leverages the brain's parcellation to rank the nodes and encourage changes within the same lobes of the brain. This variation generates more interpretable explanations for brain networks.

As further work, we plan to address the feasibility and robustness constraints, pivotal in many counterfactual search scenarios. The feasibility constraint arises because, for certain types of data, some counterfactuals may not be feasible or may not exist at all. For example, not all the counterfactuals generated for molecule graphs may be chemically feasible structures. On the other hand, robustness to noise, i.e., when small perturbations to the counterfactual do not change its predicted class, makes the counterfactual explanation more trustworthy and is thus a desirable characteristic.

References

1. Abrate, C., Bonchi, F.: Counterfactual graphs for explainable classification of brain networks. In: SIGKDD, pp. 2495–2504 (2021)

2. Baldassarre, F., Azizpour, H.: Explainability techniques for graph convolutional networks. arXiv preprint arXiv:1905.13686 (2019)
3. Barabási, A.L., Oltvai, Z.N.: Network biology: understanding the cell's functional organization. Nat. Rev. Genet. **5**(2), 101–113 (2004)
4. Bhatore, S., Mohan, L., Reddy, Y.R.: Machine learning techniques for credit risk evaluation: a systematic literature review. J. Bank. Financ. Technol. **4**(1), 111–138 (2020). https://doi.org/10.1007/s42786-020-00020-3
5. Biran, O., Cotton, C.: Explanation and justification in machine learning: a survey. In: IJCAI-17 Workshop on Explainable AI (XAI), vol. 8, pp. 8–13 (2017)
6. Buluç, A., Meyerhenke, H., Safro, I., Sanders, P., Schulz, C.: Recent advances in graph partitioning. In: Kliemann, L., Sanders, P. (eds.) Algorithm Engineering. LNCS, vol. 9220, pp. 117–158. Springer, Cham (2016). https://doi.org/10.1007/978-3-319-49487-6_4
7. Chang, L., Qin, L.: Cohesive Subgraph Computation over Large Sparse Graphs: Algorithms, Data Structures, and Programming Techniques. Springer Series in the Data Sciences, Springer, Heidelberg (2018). https://doi.org/10.1007/978-3-030-03599-0
8. Craddock, C., et al.: The neuro bureau preprocessing initiative: open sharing of preprocessed neuroimaging data and derivatives. Front. Neuroinform. **7**, 27 (2013)
9. Craddock, R.C., James, G.A., Holtzheimer III, P.E., Hu, X.P., Mayberg, H.S.: A whole brain fMRI atlas generated via spatially constrained spectral clustering. Hum. Brain Mapp. **33**(8), 1914–1928 (2012)
10. Du, Y., Fu, Z., Calhoun, V.D.: Classification and prediction of brain disorders using functional connectivity: promising but challenging. Front. Neurosci. **12**, 525 (2018)
11. Ewald, V., et al.: Posterior fossa sub-arachnoid cysts observed in patients with bipolar disorder: a retrospective cohort study. Cerebellum **22**, 1–9 (2022)
12. Fang, Y., Wang, K., Lin, X., Zhang, W.: Cohesive Subgraph Search over Large Heterogeneous Information Networks. SpringerBriefs in Computer Science, Springer, Heidelberg (2022). https://doi.org/10.1007/978-3-030-97568-5
13. Faragó, A., Mojaveri, Z.R.: In search of the densest subgraph. Algorithms **12**(8), 157 (2019)
14. Fortunato, S.: Community detection in graphs. Phys. Rep. **486**(3–5), 75–174 (2010)
15. Funke, T., Khosla, M., Anand, A.: ZORRO: valid, sparse, and stable explanations in graph neural networks. TKDE (2021)
16. Gionis, A., Tsourakakis, C.E.: Dense subgraph discovery: KDD 2015 tutorial. In: SIGKDD, pp. 2313–2314 (2015)
17. Girvan, M., Newman, M.E.J.: Community structure in social and biological networks. Proc. Natl. Acad. Sci. **99**(12), 7821–7826 (2002)
18. Guidotti, R.: Counterfactual explanations and how to find them: literature review and benchmarking. Data Min. Knowl. Discov. 1–55 (2022)
19. Guidotti, R., Monreale, A., Ruggieri, S., Turini, F., Giannotti, F., Pedreschi, D.: A survey of methods for explaining black box models. ACM CSUR **51**(5), 1–42 (2018)
20. Gulfidan, G., Turanli, B., Beklen, H., Sinha, R., Arga, K.Y.: Pan-cancer mapping of differential protein-protein interactions. Sci. Rep. **10**(1), 1–12 (2020)
21. Gutiérrez-Gómez, L., Delvenne, J.-C.: Unsupervised network embeddings with node identity awareness. Appl. Netw. Sci. **4**(1), 1–21 (2019). https://doi.org/10.1007/s41109-019-0197-1

22. Ha, S., Sohn, I.J., Kim, N., Sim, H.J., Cheon, K.A.: Characteristics of brains in autism spectrum disorder: structure, function and connectivity across the lifespan. Exp. Neurobiol. **24**(4), 273 (2015)
23. Huang, Q., Yamada, M., Tian, Y., Singh, D., Chang, Y.: GraphLIME: local interpretable model explanations for graph neural networks. TKDE (2022)
24. Karimi, A.H., Barthe, G., Schölkopf, B., Valera, I.: A survey of algorithmic recourse: definitions, formulations, solutions, and prospects. arXiv preprint arXiv:2010.04050 (2020)
25. Kim, D., et al.: Posterior cerebellar vermal deficits in bipolar disorder. J. Affect. Disord. **150**, 499–506 (2013). https://doi.org/10.1016/j.jad.2013.04.050
26. Kim, Y., Hao, J., Gautam, Y., Mersha, T.B., Kang, M.: DiffGRN: differential gene regulatory network analysis. IJDMB **20**(4), 362 (2018)
27. Kononenko, I.: Machine learning for medical diagnosis: history, state of the art and perspective. Artif. Intell. Med. **23**(1), 89–109 (2001)
28. Koutrouli, M., Karatzas, E., Paez-Espino, D., Pavlopoulos, G.A.: A guide to conquer the biological network era using graph theory. Front. Bioeng. Biotechnol. **8**, 34 (2020)
29. Lai, Y., Wu, B., Chen, L., Zhao, H.: A statistical method for identifying differential gene-gene co-expression patterns. Bioinformatics **20**(17), 3146–3155 (2004)
30. Lanciano, T., Bonchi, F., Gionis, A.: Explainable classification of brain networks via contrast subgraphs. In: SIGKDD (2020)
31. Lanciano, T., Savino, A., Porcu, F., Cittaro, D., Bonchi, F., Provero, P.: Contrast subgraphs allow comparing homogeneous and heterogeneous networks derived from omics data. GigaScience **12** (2023)
32. de Lara, N., Pineau, E.: A simple baseline algorithm for graph classification. arXiv preprint arXiv:1810.09155 (2018)
33. Lee, V.E., Ruan, N., Jin, R., Aggarwal, C.: A survey of algorithms for dense subgraph discovery. In: Aggarwal, C., Wang, H. (eds.) Managing and Mining Graph Data. Advances in Database Systems, vol. 40, pp. 303–336. Springer, Boston (2010). https://doi.org/10.1007/978-1-4419-6045-0_10
34. Lucic, A., Ter Hoeve, M.A., Tolomei, G., De Rijke, M., Silvestri, F.: CF-GNNExplainer: counterfactual explanations for graph neural networks. In: AISTATS, pp. 4499–4511 (2022)
35. Luo, D., et al.: Parameterized explainer for graph neural network. Adv. Neural. Inf. Process. Syst. **33**, 19620–19631 (2020)
36. Malliaros, F.D., Vazirgiannis, M.: Clustering and community detection in directed networks: a survey. Phys. Rep. **533**(4), 95–142 (2013)
37. Meng, L., Xiang, J.: Brain network analysis and classification based on convolutional neural network. Front. Comput. Neurosci. **12**, 95 (2018)
38. Milo, R., Shen-Orr, S., Itzkovitz, S., Kashtan, N., Chklovskii, D., Alon, U.: Network motifs: simple building blocks of complex networks. Science **298**(5594), 824–827 (2002)
39. Minichino, A., et al.: The role of cerebellum in unipolar and bipolar depression: a review of the main neurobiological findings. Riv. Psichiatria **49**, 124–31 (2014). https://doi.org/10.1708/1551.16907
40. Misman, M.F., et al.: Classification of adults with autism spectrum disorder using deep neural network. In: AiDAS, pp. 29–34 (2019)
41. Moraffah, R., Karami, M., Guo, R., Raglin, A., Liu, H.: Causal interpretability for machine learning-problems, methods and evaluation. ACM SIGKDD Explor. Newsl. **22**(1), 18–33 (2020)

42. Mothilal, R.K., Sharma, A., Tan, C.: Explaining machine learning classifiers through diverse counterfactual explanations. In: Proceedings of the 2020 Conference on Fairness, Accountability, and Transparency, pp. 607–617 (2020)
43. Nascimento, M.C., de Carvalho, A.C.: Spectral methods for graph clustering - a survey. Eur. J. Oper. Res. **211**(2), 221–231 (2011)
44. Newman, M.E.J.: Modularity and community structure in networks. Proc. Natl. Acad. Sci. **103**(23), 8577–8582 (2006)
45. Nibbe, R.K., Chowdhury, S.A., Koyutürk, M., Ewing, R., Chance, M.R.: Protein-protein interaction networks in the biology of disease. WIREs Syst. Biol. Med. **3**(3), 357–367 (2011)
46. Pan, S., Wu, J., Zhu, X., Long, G., Zhang, C.: Task sensitive feature exploration and learning for multitask graph classification. IEEE Trans. Cybern. **47**(3), 744–758 (2016)
47. Perotti, A., Bajardi, P., Bonchi, F., Panisson, A.: GRAPHSHAP: motif-based explanations for black-box graph classifiers. arXiv preprint arXiv:2202.08815 (2022)
48. Pope, P.E., Kolouri, S., Rostami, M., Martin, C.E., Hoffmann, H.: Explainability methods for graph convolutional neural networks. In: CVPR, pp. 10772–10781 (2019)
49. Prado-Romero, M.A., Prenkaj, B., Stilo, G., Giannotti, F.: A survey on graph counterfactual explanations: definitions, methods, evaluation. arXiv preprint arXiv:2210.12089 (2022)
50. Sani, G., et al.: Association between duration of lithium exposure and hippocampus/amygdala volumes in type i bipolar disorder. J. Affect. Disord. **232**, 341–348 (2018)
51. Schaeffer, S.E.: Graph clustering. Comput. Sci. Rev. **1**(1), 27–64 (2007)
52. Schlichtkrull, M.S., De Cao, N., Titov, I.: Interpreting graph neural networks for NLP with differentiable edge masking. In: ICLR (2020)
53. Schnake, T., et al.: Higher-order explanations of graph neural networks via relevant walks. arXiv preprint arXiv:2006.03589 (2020)
54. Singh, A.J., Ramsey, S.A., Filtz, T.M., Kioussi, C.: Differential gene regulatory networks in development and disease. Cell. Mol. Life Sci. **75**(6), 1013–1025 (2018)
55. Sörös, P., et al.: Inattention predicts increased thickness of left occipital cortex in men with ADHD. Front. Psychiatry **8**, 170 (2017). https://doi.org/10.3389/fpsyt.2017.00170
56. Tzourio-Mazoyer, N., et al.: Automated anatomical labeling of activations in SPM using a macroscopic anatomical parcellation of the MNI MRI single-subject brain. Neuroimage **15**(1), 273–289 (2002)
57. Vu, M., Thai, M.T.: PGM-explainer: probabilistic graphical model explanations for graph neural networks. Adv. Neural. Inf. Process. Syst. **33**, 12225–12235 (2020)
58. Wachter, S., Mittelstadt, B., Russell, C.: Counterfactual explanations without opening the black box: automated decisions and the GDPR. Harv. JL Tech. **31**, 841 (2017)
59. Wang, S., He, L., Cao, B., Lu, C.T., Yu, P.S., Ragin, A.B.: Structural deep brain network mining. In: Proceedings of the 23rd ACM SIGKDD International Conference on Knowledge Discovery and Data Mining, KDD 2017, pp. 475–484 (2017)
60. Wang, X., Wu, Y., Zhang, A., Feng, F., He, X., Chua, T.S.: Reinforced causal explainer for graph neural networks. Trans. Pattern Anal. Mach. Intell. **45**(2), 2297–2309 (2023)
61. Wellawatte, G.P., Seshadri, A., White, A.D.: Model agnostic generation of counterfactual explanations for molecules. Chem. Sci. **13**(13), 3697–3705 (2022)

62. Weston, C.S.: Four social brain regions, their dysfunctions, and sequelae, extensively explain autism spectrum disorder symptomatology. Brain Sci. **9**(6), 130 (2019)
63. Wu, Q., Hao, J.K.: A review on algorithms for maximum clique problems. Eur. J. Oper. Res. **242**(3), 693–709 (2015)
64. Wu, Z., Luo, Y., Gao, Yu., Han, Y., Wu, K., Li, X.: The role of frontal and occipital cortices in processing sustained visual attention in young adults with attention-deficit/hyperactivity disorder: a functional near-infrared spectroscopy study. Neurosci. Bull. **36**(6), 659–663 (2020). https://doi.org/10.1007/s12264-020-00492-9
65. Yan, Y., Zhu, J., Duda, M., Solarz, E., Sripada, C., Koutra, D.: GroupINN: grouping-based interpretable neural network for classification of limited, noisy brain data. In: Proceedings of the 25th ACM SIGKDD International Conference on Knowledge Discovery & Data Mining, KDD 2019, pp. 772–782 (2019)
66. Ying, R., Bourgeois, D., You, J., Zitnik, M., Leskovec, J.: GNN explainer: a tool for post-hoc explanation of graph neural networks. arXiv preprint arXiv:1903.03894 (2019)
67. You, J., Gomes-Selman, J.M., Ying, R., Leskovec, J.: Identity-aware graph neural networks. In: AAAI Conference on Artificial Intelligence, pp. 10737–10745 (2021)
68. Yuan, H., Tang, J., Hu, X., Ji, S.: XGNN: towards model-level explanations of graph neural networks. In: SIGKDD, pp. 430–438 (2020)
69. Yuan, H., Yu, H., Gui, S., Ji, S.: Explainability in graph neural networks: a taxonomic survey. IEEE Trans. Pattern Anal. Mach. Intell. **45**, 5782–5799 (2022)
70. Yuan, H., Yu, H., Wang, J., Li, K., Ji, S.: On explainability of graph neural networks via subgraph explorations. In: ICML, pp. 12241–12252 (2021)
71. Zhang, Y., Defazio, D., Ramesh, A.: ReLEx: a model-agnostic relational model explainer. In: AIES, pp. 1042–1049 (2021)

Ablation Path Saliency

Justus Sagemüller$^{(\boxtimes)}$ (ID) and Olivier Verdier (ID)

Western Norway University of Applied Sciences, Bergen, Norway
{jsag,olivier.verdier}@hvl.no

Abstract. Various types of saliency methods have been proposed for explaining black-box classification. In image applications, this means highlighting the part of the image that is most relevant for the current decision.

Unfortunately, the different methods may disagree and it can be hard to quantify how representative and faithful the explanation really is. We observe however that several of these methods can be seen as edge cases of a single, more general procedure based on finding a particular *path* through the classifier's domain. This offers additional geometric interpretation to the existing methods.

We demonstrate furthermore that ablation paths can be directly used as a technique of its own right. This is able to compete with literature methods on existing benchmarks, while giving more fine-grained information and better opportunities for validation of the explanations' faithfulness.

Keywords: Explainability · Classification · Saliency · Neural Networks · Visualisation · Gradient Descent

1 Introduction

The basic idea of *saliency* or *attribution* is to provide insights as to why a neural network produces a given output (for instance, a classification) for a given input (for instance, an image). There is no clear consensus in the literature as to what saliency should exactly be, but various properties that such a method should fulfill have been proposed. All the methods discussed here start out by contrasting the given input (also called *current target*) with another one, called *baseline*, which should be neutral in at least the sense of not displaying any of what causes the target image's classification. The saliency problem then amounts to finding out what the features of the target are which cause it to be classified differently from the baseline.

In [15] the authors give axioms attempting to make it precise what that means. Of these, *sensitivity* captures most of the notion of saliency, namely, that the features on which the output is most sensitive should be given a higher saliency value. The authors give further axioms to narrow it down: implementation invariance, completeness, linearity and symmetry preservation. They obtain a corresponding method: the Integrated Gradient method. Despite the attempt

L. Longo (Ed.): xAI 2023, CCIS 1901, pp. 349–372, 2023.
https://doi.org/10.1007/978-3-031-44064-9_19

to thus narrow down the choice of saliency method, Integrated Gradient has not established itself as a default in the community. Indeed the axioms used to justify it are not altogether self-evident.

In [6], a method is provided whose construction is quite different. Instead of following axioms about the properties a method should have, they produce a result that has direct meaning associated to it, namely as a mask that preserves only certain parts of the input and removes others, optimised so that the classification is retained even at high degrees of ablation, i.e., when the mask only keeps small part of the target image. This method is highly appealing, but in practice the optimisation problem is ill-conditioned and can only be solved under help of regularization techniques. That prevents this technique, too, from being a definite saliency method or "the" saliency method.

Various other methods from the literature are in a broadly similar position, all with certain arguments for their use but also various practical limitations and no clear reason to favour them over the alternatives. In some cases there are evident mathematical relationships between the methods, but they have not been investigated thoroughly yet or exploited for a unifying generalization.

This is what our paper provides: it introduces *ablation paths*, which take up and extend the idea of integrating from the baseline to the target image. It combines this with the notion of ablation/masks, in that each step along the path can constitute a mask highlighting progressively smaller portions of the image. The main purpose of this is mathematical unification and better (meta-) understanding of the various methods, but ours can also be used as a saliency method by itself.

A summary how the method works: suppose first that images are defined over a domain Ω, which can be regarded as the set of pixels in the discrete case, or as a domain such as a square, for the image at infinite resolution. We define *ablation paths* as parameter dependent smooth masks $\varphi\colon [0,1] \to \mathcal{C}(\Omega, \mathbb{R})$, with the further requirement that the mask at zero, $\varphi(0)$, should be zero over the domain Ω, and the mask at one, $\varphi(1)$, should be one over the domain Ω. We also impose that, at each pixel, the mask value increases over time (see Fig. 1), and that this happens with a constant area speed: the area covered by the mask should increase linearly over time (see Sect. 3). Let F be the classifier, which outputs a probability between zero and one. We choose a current image of interest x_0 and a *baseline image* x_1. The objective function $P_\uparrow$ is then $P_\uparrow(\varphi) := \int_0^1 F(x_0 + \varphi(t)(x_1 - x_0))\, \mathrm{d}t$ (see Sect. 4). Assuming that $F(x_0) \simeq 1$ and $F(x_1) \simeq 0$, maximising the objective function means that we try to find an ablation path that stays as long as possible in the decision region of x_0. Intuitively, we try to replace as many pixels of x_0 by pixels of x_1 while staying in the same class as x_0.

2   Related Work

[13] defines a saliency map as the gradient of the network output at the given image. This would appear to be a sensible definition, but the resulting saliency is very noisy because the network output is roughly constant around any particular

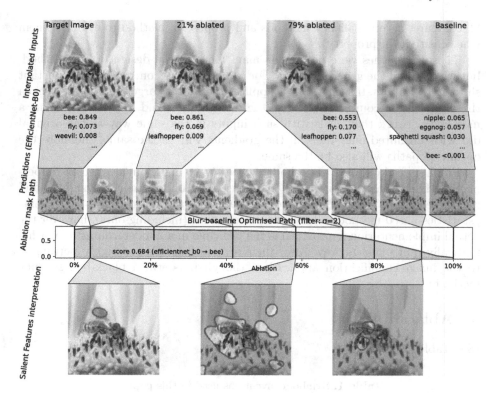

Fig. 1. Example of how an ablation path (sequence of masks, middle row) gives rise to a transition between a current target (a bee from ImageNet) and a baseline (blurred version of the same image).

image. Grad-CAM [12] improves the situation by separating the convolutional and fully connected layers. This is, however, not a black-box method such as the one we propose. [8] computes an *influence function*, that is, a function that measures how the parameters would be changed by a change in the training data. Although it is a black-box method, it is not a saliency method per se. They use the gradient of the network output to find the pixel most likely to have a high saliency. The pixels that have most effect are given a higher saliency.

By contrast, RISE [9] proposes to directly evaluate the saliency by finding out which pixels are most likely to affect the output, similarly to Meaningful Perturbations [6], but through statistical means instead of iterative optimisation. These methods can be seen as different ways of solving similar optimisation problems, the solution of which produces a mask (cf. Sect. 3.1) highlighting features of importance.

There are also a number of meta-studies of saliency methods. [1] lists essential properties, for instance the requirement that the results should depend on the training data in a sense that perturbing *model parameters* should change the saliency. [7] proposes a number of properties that saliency methods should satisfy.

[2] compares several saliency methods and proposes a method to evaluate them (the sensitivity-n property).

These properties were not in the main focus of the design of our method, but we do fulfill the general criteria. For example, [7] is concerned with constant shifts in the inputs. If such a shift is applied to both the target and baseline, then the modification commutes through the interpolation and if we then assume a modified network that deals with such inputs in the same way as the original did with unshifted ones then all the gradients will be the same, therefore the optimised paths will also be the same.

Finally, [3] developed a method to recursively mask out ever finer "super-pixels". Their construction claims to be based on solid causality principles, and it does seem to largely avoid the adversarial issues that perturbation-/gradient-/statistics-based methods all have to content with (including ours), however the actual implementation approximates the principle in a nondeterministic, mathematically quite unclear way. Also, their technical details are highly pertaining to the image-classification application, though it is still a black-box saliency method.

3   Ablation Paths

(See Table 1).

Table 1. Symbol conventions used in this paper.

$\Omega, V, \mathcal{M}, \mathcal{I}, \mathcal{P}$	Domains, see below
x, x_0, x_1	Dataset-samples/images
F	Classifier
θ	Masks
φ	Ablation paths
P	Score functions
σ, ζ, λ	Hyperparameters

3.1   Images and Masks

We assume data is represented by functions on a compact domain Ω. Examples for Ω may be $\Omega = \{1, \ldots, n\} \times \{1, \ldots, m\}$ (for pixel images), or a continuous domain $\Omega = [0, a] \times [0, b]$. What matters to us is that Ω is equipped with a positive measure. Without loss of generality, we assume the mass of that measure is one, i.e., $\int_\Omega 1 = 1$.

The data itself consists of functions on Ω with values in a vector space V (typically, the dimensions of V may be the *colour channels*). For the space of images, we choose

$$\mathcal{I} := \mathcal{C}(\Omega, V).$$

For our method to work, we need a space of *masks*, denoted $\mathcal{M}$, whose role is to select features between x_0 and x_1. We associate to each mask $\theta \in \mathcal{M}$ an *interpolation operator* between two images x_0 and x_1, denoted by $[x_0, x_1]_\theta$. This interpolator should have the property that $[x_0, x_1]_0 = x_0$ and $[x_0, x_1]_1 = x_1$. We will thus use the shorthand notation:

$$x_\theta := [x_0, x_1]_\theta \qquad \theta \in \mathcal{M} \quad (x_0, x_1 \in \mathcal{I}).$$

The specific choice of masks and interpolation we make in this paper is

$$\mathcal{M} := \mathcal{C}(\Omega, \mathbb{R}), \qquad [x_0, x_1]_\theta := (1 - \theta)x_0 + \theta x_1, \qquad \theta \in \mathcal{M}, \quad x_0, x_1 \in \mathcal{I}$$

Remark 1. Another example of interpolation is what in [5] is called the *pyramid of blur* perturbations. We also explored this possibility for our method, but we obtain better results with the affine interpolation (called "fade perturbation" in [5]). A possible reason that this blur perturbation technique did not work well is our start state, which in that case contains none of the highest-frequency components at all. This makes it likely for the classifier to behave completely different from the target input.

3.2   Ablation Paths

Definition 1. *We define the set $\mathcal{A}$ of ablation paths as the set of functions $\varphi \colon [0, 1] \to \mathcal{M}$ fulfilling the following properties:*

Boundary conditions $\varphi(0) = 0$ *and* $\varphi(1) = 1$
Monotonicity $t_1 \leq t_2 \implies \varphi(t_1) \leq \varphi(t_2) \qquad t_1, t_2 \in [0, 1]$
Constant speed $\int_\Omega \varphi(t) = t \qquad t \in [0, 1]$.

We will call monotone paths *the paths that fulfill the first two conditions but not the third.*

Note that the set $\mathcal{A}$ of ablation paths is a *convex subset* inside the set of possible paths denoted by $\mathcal{P} := \mathcal{L}^\infty([0, 1], \mathcal{M})$.

Some comments on each of those requirements are in order. (i) 0 and 1 denote here the constant functions zero and one (which corresponds to the zero and one of the algebra $\mathcal{M}$) (ii) $\varphi(t_1) \leq \varphi(t_2)$ should be interpreted as usual as $\varphi(t_2) - \varphi(t_1)$ being pointwise nonnegative. (iii) If $t \mapsto \int_\Omega \varphi(t)$ is differentiable, this requirement can be rewritten as $\frac{\mathrm{d}}{\mathrm{d}t} \int_\Omega \varphi(t) = 1$, so it can be regarded as a *constant speed* requirement. This requirement is more a normalisation convention than a necessity, as is further detailed in Remark 3.

The simplest (requirement-fulfilling) ablation path is the *affine interpolation* path:

$$\ell(t) := t. \tag{1}$$

The mask is thus constant in space at each time t. This path is implicitly used in [15]: its image-application corresponds to affine interpolation between target- and baseline image.

Note that a monotone path without the constant-speed property can always be transformed into one that fulfils it. The proof is in Appendix A.

Remark 2. In the sequel, we will abuse the notations and write φ as a function of one or two arguments depending on the context, that is, we will identify $\varphi(t) \equiv \varphi(t, \cdot)$. For instance, in Definition 1 above, $\int_\Omega \varphi(t) \equiv \int_\Omega \varphi(t, \cdot) \equiv \int_\Omega \varphi(t, \mathbf{r}) \, d\mathbf{r}$.

Remark 3. If the ablation path φ is differentiable in time, the requirements in Definition 1 admit a remarkable reformulation. Define $\psi(t) := \frac{d}{dt}\varphi(t)$. All the requirements in Definition 1 are equivalent to the following requirements for a function $\psi \colon [0,1] \times \Omega \to \mathbb{R}$:

$$\psi(t, \mathbf{r}) \geq 0, \quad \int_\Omega \psi(t, \mathbf{r}) \, d\mathbf{r} = 1, \quad \int_{[0,1]} \psi(t, \mathbf{r}) \, dt = 1 \qquad t \in [0,1], \mathbf{r} \in \Omega$$

The corresponding ablation path φ is then recovered by $\varphi(t) := \int_0^t \psi(s) \, ds$.

4   Score of an Ablation Path

We now define the *retaining score function* $P_\uparrow \colon \mathcal{P} \to \mathbb{R}$ from paths to real numbers by the integral

$$P_\uparrow(\varphi) := \int_0^1 F(x_{\varphi(t)}) dt. \tag{2}$$

Note that, as F is bounded between zero and one, so is $P_\uparrow(\varphi)$ for any ablation path $\varphi \in \mathcal{A}$. The main idea here is that $F(x_0) \simeq 1$ and $F(x_1) \simeq 0$, and $F(x) \leq 1$ holds always. So a high value of $P_\uparrow$ means that the classification stays similar to that of x_0 over most of the ablation path, which is another way of saying that the characteristics of the original image are retained as best as possible whilst other features of the image are ablated away. See Sect. 6 for caveats.

Another score to consider is the *dissipating score*

$$P_\downarrow(\varphi) := 1 - \int_0^1 F(x_{\varphi(t)}) dt \tag{3}$$

which instead takes high values for paths that ablate crucial features for the current classification as quickly as possible. Optimisation of $P_\downarrow$ corresponds roughly to what [6] call "deletion game", whereas $P_\uparrow$ corresponds to their "preservation game", the difference to this work being that they optimise individual masks rather than constrained paths.

Intuitively, the first features to be deleted in a $P_\downarrow$-optimal path $\varphi_\downarrow$ should correspond roughly to the ones longest preserved in a $P_\uparrow$-optimal path $\varphi_\uparrow$, meaning that a feature that is potent at retaining the classification should be removed early on if the objective is to change the classification. More generally, one would expect $\varphi_\downarrow(t)$ to be similar to $1 - \varphi_\uparrow(1 - t)$.

We observe this to be often *not* the case: specifically, there are many examples where either the classification is so predominant that it is almost indeterminate what features should be preserved longest (because any of them will be sufficient to retain the classification), or vice versa the classification is so brittle that it is indeterminate which ones should be removed first. It is however possible to *enforce* features to be considered simultaneously in a sense of their potency to preserve the classification when they are kept, and changing it when removed. This is achieved by optimising a path with the combined objective of retaining for the path itself and dissipating for its opposite: this is expressed by optimising the *contrastive score*

$$P_{\updownarrow}(\varphi) := P_{\uparrow}(\varphi) + P_{\downarrow}(1 - \varphi). \tag{4}$$

This too corresponds to ideas already used in previous work, called "hybrid game" or "symmetric preservation" [4,6].

A related possibility is to train both a retaining and a dissipating path in tandem, but with additional constraints to keep them in correspondence. Here, it is most useful to keep them not opposites of each other, but rather to keep them as similar as possible. (Cf. Fig. 4.) This is achieved by a score of the form

$$P_{\uparrow\downarrow}(\varphi_{\uparrow}, \varphi_{\downarrow}) := P_{\uparrow}(\varphi_{\uparrow}) + P_{\downarrow}(\varphi_{\downarrow}) + \lambda_{\pm} \|\varphi_{\uparrow} - \varphi_{\downarrow}\|, \tag{5}$$

where $\|\cdot\|$ could refer to various distance notions on the space of paths, and $\lambda_{\pm}$ parameterizes the degree to which this distance is penalized. We call the corresponding optimisation problem the *boundary-straddling method*, since (in the ideal of a classifier with exact decision boundaries) it rewards $\varphi_{\uparrow}$ staying in the domain of x_0 as much as possible and $\varphi_{\downarrow}$ in the domain of x_1 as much as possible, i.e. on the other side of the decision boundary but as close as possible. Thus, $\varphi_{\uparrow}$ and $\varphi_{\downarrow}$ effectively pinch the decision boundary between them.

For all the above score functions it is straightforward to compute the differential, e.g. $dP_{\uparrow}$, on the space of paths $\mathcal{P}$:

$$\langle dP_{\uparrow}, \delta\varphi \rangle = \int_0^1 \langle \underbrace{dF_{x_{\varphi(t)}}}_{\in \mathcal{I}^*}, \underbrace{(x_1 - x_0)}_{\in \mathcal{I}} \underbrace{\delta\varphi(t)}_{\in \mathcal{M}} \rangle \, dt \qquad \delta\varphi \in \mathcal{P}.$$

So if we define the product of $D \in \mathcal{I}^*$ and $x \in \mathcal{I}$ producing an element in $\mathcal{M}^*$ by $\langle xD, \varphi \rangle := \langle D, x\varphi \rangle$ as is customary[1], we can rewrite this differential as

$$\langle dP_{\uparrow}, \delta\varphi \rangle = \int_0^1 \langle (x_1 - x_0)dF_{x_{\varphi(t)}} \, \delta\varphi(t) \rangle \, dt.$$

Note that we know that any ablation path is bounded, so $\varphi \in \mathcal{L}^{\infty}([0,1], \mathcal{M})$, so the differential of $P_{\uparrow}$ at φ can be identified with the function $dP_{\uparrow_{\varphi}} = [t \mapsto (x_1 - x_0)dF_{x_{\varphi(t)}}]$ in $\mathcal{L}^1([0,1], \mathcal{M}^*)$.

4.1 Relation with the Integrated Gradient Method

When this differential is computed on the interpolation path ℓ (1) and then *averaged*, then this is exactly the integrated average gradient [15]. More precisely, the

---

[1] For instance in the theory of distributions.

integrated gradient is exactly $\int_0^1 \mathrm{d}P_{\uparrow \ell(t)} \mathrm{d}t$. Note that this is in fact an integrated *differential*, since we obtain an element in the dual space $\mathcal{I}^*$, and this differential should be appropriately smoothed along the lines of Sect. 5.1.

4.2   Relation to Pixel Ablation

Given any saliency function $\sigma \in \mathcal{M}$ (for example an integrated gradient, meaningful-perturbation, or grad-CAM result) we can define a path by

$$\tilde{\varphi}(t) := \mathbf{1}_{\sigma \leq \log(t/(1-t))} \text{ when } t \in (0,1) \tag{6}$$

and $\tilde{\varphi}(0) := 0$, $\tilde{\varphi}(1) := 1$. This path is a monotone path, except in the module of images $\mathcal{I} = \mathcal{L}^2(\Omega, V)$, equipped with the ring of masks $\mathcal{M} = \mathcal{L}^\infty(\Omega)$. To be an ablation path, it still needs to be transformed into a constant speed path, which is always possible as explained in Appendix A.

That results in a generalisation of the pixel-ablation scores used in [9] and [14]. In that case, the set Ω would be a discrete set of pixels, which are being sequentially switched from "on" to "off" by the (binary) mask.

Note that in the ranking, pixels with the same saliency would be ranked in an arbitrary way and added to the mask in that arbitrary order. In the method of Eq. 6, we add such pixels all at once, which seems preferrable because it does not incur an arbitrary bias between pixels. The time reparameterisation keeps the function constant longer to account for however *many* pixels were ranked the same. As long as the ranking is strict (no two pixels have the same saliency), the method is the same as discrete pixel ranking.

4.3   Relation to Meaningful Perturbations

In the saturated case, that is, if F only takes values zero and one (or in the limit towards this), our method reduces to finding the interpolation with the largest mask on the boundary, equivalent to the approach of [6]. This is a result of the following: suppose that the ablation path φ crosses the boundary at time t^*. It means that $F(x_{\varphi(t)})$ has value one until t^* and zero afterwards, so the score $P_\uparrow$ defined in (2) is $P_\uparrow(\varphi) = t^*$. By the constant speed property, $t^* = \int_\Omega \varphi(t^*)$, so we end up maximising the mask area on the boundary.

4.4   Relation with RISE

The method used in [9] does not explicitly involve an optimisation problem like here, though they do use pixel ablation as some validation for the results. It does nevertheless resemble specifically the boundary-straddling method in the sense that it evaluates F for many different inputs on both sides of the decision boundary, and uses the classification results to weigh the features involved.

5   Optimisation Problem and Algorithm

We proceed to define the optimisation problem that we propose as a saliency method, and how to solve it numerically.

Conceptually we try to find the ablation path[s] (see Definition 1) that maximises one of the scores $P_\uparrow(\varphi)$, $P_\downarrow(\varphi)$, $P_\updownarrow(\varphi)$, or $P_{\uparrow\downarrow}(\varphi_\uparrow, \varphi_\downarrow)$:

$$\max_{\varphi \in \mathcal{A}} P(\varphi).$$

Recall that the set $\mathcal{A}$ of ablation paths is convex; however, since any of objective functions are not convex, this is not a convex optimisation problem.

The method we suggest is to follow a gradient direction. Such an approach is in general not guaranteed to approximate a global maximum, a common problem with many practical applications. However, empirical results (see Sect. 7) suggests that gradient descent does often manage to approximate global maxima, particularly obvious in the unregularised near-perfect scores.

5.1   Gradient and Metric

In order to perform gradient descent, we need to be able to compute gradient vectors (sometimes called "natural gradients" in the literature). Strictly speaking the *differential* is an element of the dual space $\mathcal{M}^*$. In the Euclidean case that space is canonically isomorphic to $\mathcal{M}$, thus the common practice to use it directly as a *gradient* in $\mathcal{M}$, which is usable as contribution to a state update. In general, this requires first a map from that space to $\mathcal{M}$, and even in a discretised realisation it is prudent to consider this map explicitly, since the implied one depends on the (pixel) basis choice. A reasonable choice is the covariance operator associated to a smoothing operation. For a measure $\mu \in \mathcal{M}^*$, $\langle K\mu, \theta \rangle := \langle \mu, \int_\Omega k(\cdot - \mathbf{r})\theta(\mathbf{r})\,\mathrm{d}\mathbf{r}\rangle$, where k is a suitable smoothing function. We use here the same Gaussian blurring filter that is also applied between the optimisation steps for regularisation.

Since the optimisation problem is *constrained* (the ablation path φ being constrained by the requirements in Definition 1), following the gradient direction will in general leave the set $\mathcal{A}$. Because the constraints are convex, it is straightforward enough to project each gradient-updated version back to something that does fulfill them, and indeed that is the idea behind our algorithm (see Appendix C for the technical details). However, in addition to the hard constraints there are also properties that are desirable but cannot directly be enforced. This is the subject of the next section.

5.2   Mask Saturation

Recall that the masks we use in this paper are functions $\theta\colon \Omega \to [0,1]$. The interpretation is that if $\theta(\mathbf{r}) = 0$, the pixel $\mathbf{r} \in \Omega$ of the reference image x_0 is used, whereas if $\theta(\mathbf{r}) = 1$, the pixel $\mathbf{r}$ of the baseline image x_1 is used instead. Typically though, masks take value between zero and one. We notice that such intermediate values of masks produce blending of different images which lie far away from the natural distribution of images. What is problematic is that the classifier may put such blends of images in totally different classes. As analogy in human vision, an image of a person half-blended into an image of a hallway would not be seen as person present at 50 %, but rather as something completely different; for instance, to a human, this half-present person would look more like a ghost than a person.

In order to alleviate this potential problem, our algorithm intersperses gradient descent in $\mathcal{P}$ with both (hard) projections onto $\mathcal{A}$, as well as *soft projections* of the masks onto $\mathcal{M}_{\{0,1\}}$, the set of *saturated masks*, that is, masks taking value in the set $\{0, 1\}$. Concretely, this is done by tweaking the ablation path pointwise with a sigmoidal function[2] that brings values lower than $\frac{1}{2}$ slightly closer to 0, and values greater than $\frac{1}{2}$ slightly closer to 1.

$$\varphi \leftarrow \Pi_{\text{sat}}(\varphi) := \frac{1}{2}\left(\frac{\tanh((\varphi \cdot 2 - 1) \cdot \zeta_{\text{sat}})}{\tanh(\zeta_{\text{sat}})} + 1\right). \tag{7}$$

The parameter ζ_{sat} determines how strongly this affects the path.

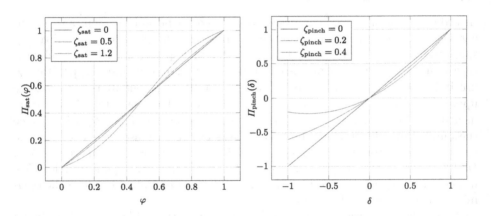

Fig. 2. The pointwise soft-projection functions for saturation and pinching.

5.3   Boundary-Pinching

For the boundary-straddling method there is another requirement: making $\varphi_\uparrow$ and $\varphi_\downarrow$ similar to each other can be achieved by explicitly penalizing their distance in the score function, but in our implementation this too is done by a dedicated algorithm step that manipulates the masks pointwise to become more similar. For interpretability purposes it is particularly desirable for $\varphi_\uparrow(t)$ to contain only few features that $\varphi_\downarrow(t)$ does not, since that allows direct comparison

---

[2] The exact definitions of Π_{sat} and Π_{pinch} are largely arbitrary, what matters are their attractive fixpoints; see Fig. 2

between two images showing how inclusion of these features bring the classification into the target class. The exact difference in strength of features meanwhile is less relevant (even when the masks themselves are not boolean). Accordingly, we suggest a *pinching tweak* that diminishes specifically the smaller positive differences between $\varphi_\uparrow$ and $\varphi_\downarrow$, in addition to any negative differences. The concrete form in our experiments is this: (recall that values close to 1 correspond to masked-*away* features)

$$\varphi_\downarrow(t, \mathbf{r}) \leftarrow \varphi_\uparrow(t, \mathbf{r}) + \Pi_{\text{pinch}}\big(\varphi_\downarrow(t, \mathbf{r}) - \varphi_\uparrow(t, \mathbf{r})\big) \tag{8}$$

where $\Pi_{\text{pinch}} : [-1, 1] \to [-1, 1], \delta \mapsto \Pi_{\text{pinch}}(\delta)$ is a continuous function with an attractive fixpoint at $\delta = 0$ (which is responsible for squelching unsubstantial contrasts between $\varphi_\uparrow$ and $\varphi_\downarrow$), and a repulsive one at $\delta = 1$ (which allows the most salient features of $\varphi_\uparrow$ to stay absent from $\varphi_\downarrow$, as necessary for a high $P_{\uparrow\downarrow}$).

The concrete definition of Π_{pinch} is uncritical, in our experiments we used

$$\Pi_{\text{pinch}}(\delta) := \delta(1 - \zeta_{\text{pinch}}) + \delta^2 \zeta_{\text{pinch}}.$$

Notice that in Eq. 8, $\varphi_\uparrow$ is not affected by $\varphi_\downarrow$, only vice versa. But conceptually, the update is performing a change to δ, i.e. the difference between the paths, rather than either of them individually.

6 Stability and Adversarial Effects

So far it was more or less taken for granted that a high-scoring ablation path owes its score to good highlighting of the features that were also responsible for the classification of x_0. This assumption would be reasonable if any masked version of that image were classified either the same for the same reasons as the original, or else classified differently. For a black-box model, there is however no way of verifying this, and in fact it is simply not true in general.

It is well known [6] that sufficiently pathological masks can act as *adversarial attacks* [16] on an image, i.e. that masking out very minor parts of an image may affect the classification disproportionally and in ways that involve completely different neural activations (or whatever other concept is appropriate for the classifier architecture at hand). Gradient descent approaches tend to produce such examples easily. Although the study of adversarial effects is an important matter of its own right, they are hardly relevant for saliency purposes, because they do not necessarily involve the features that caused the classification of the original image.

A standard technique [6,9] employed to avoid that masks affect images adversarially is to regularize them in some sense of smoothness, e.g. by adding a total variation penalty. Intuitively, this at least prevents the masked image from featuring sharp edges or similar details not present in x_0 that the classifier might latch onto. We implemented this in terms of a simple Gaussian filter applied to each mask in the path after each optimisation step. Empirically, strong enough smoothing does largely avoid adversarial classification, but unfortunately there is no a-priori way of telling how smooth it needs to be. And too strong smoothing can also have detrimental effects. Not only does it prevent the exact localization of small, salient features, but it can even bias the outcome: in Fig. 3, the strongly regularised saliency is not only condensed to a single location, but also specifically to a corner of the image. Our interpretation is that this happens because it reduces the total variation (since $\frac{3}{4}$ of the gradient of the mask lies outside of the image). And although the mask still contains enough of the dog's head to keep the classification, its maximum lies misleadingly in front of the nose.

$\sigma_{\text{reguBlur}} = 0.5$ $\sigma_{\text{reguBlur}} = 2$ $\sigma_{\text{reguBlur}} = 8$

Fig. 3. Example of how both too little and too much regularisation can be detrimental for interpretability. Image from VOC2007 test set; saliency is class transition of a $P_{\uparrow}$-optimal path.

Adversarialness, or generally instability of the mask-classification interaction, can also be viewed in terms of a decision boundary that is fractal-like crinkled in the high-dimensional image space, such that small exclaves of a class domain may reach far closer to x_0 than the bulk of that domain. This suggests that it would help to evaluate for many different masks rather than gradient-optimising a single one. Particularly the RISE method [9] benefits from this, by evaluating the classifier for a whole large random selection of masks. The reference implementation of [5] also optimises (individually) multiple masks of different sizes. This does not so much avoid adversarial examples as average out their contributions, whereas stable, faithfully-salient masks tend to agree.[3]

Our experiments show that the use of paths does by itself not prevent the optimisation from reaching adversarial (non-)explanations. The scores $P_{\uparrow}$ and $P_{\downarrow}$ are particularly prone to procuring such paths, but we observe them also when optimising for $P_{\updownarrow}$. This implies that the irregularity of the decision boundary is not necessarily of a disconnected nature with "islands" of adversarial examples, but rather akin to a connected but highly branched (or even fractal) space as sketched in Fig. 4.

By comparison, $P_{\updownarrow}$ seems to be more reliable in practice. An intuitive reason is that the two paths have less possibility to simultaneously follow adversarial masks for the classes of both x_0 and x_1, whilst also staying close to each other. That is certainly not inconceivable either, though.

---

[3] This still requires also dedicated mask regularity, as otherwise the adversarial contributions overwhelm and the result appears as mere noise.

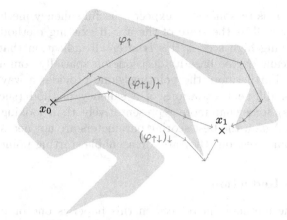

Fig. 4. Low-dimensional sketch of how irregularities in the decision boundary between two images can affect optimised paths. The blue region represents the class-domain of x_0. The $P_\uparrow$-optimised path takes a detour along a strong outlier ($\approx$adversarial branch of the class) that allows it to stay almost completely in-domain, which causes the final section to approach x_1 from a completely different direction. The pair of $P_{\uparrow\downarrow}$-optimised paths are still somewhat affected by outliers, but the pinching term causes them to mostly follow a more regular and consistent section of the boundary. N.B.: this represents only very crudely the behaviour in real image classification applications, as inevitable with low-dimensional visualisations. In particular, the monotonicity condition is not represented at all here, and the pinching is here a symmetric L^2-reduction, which is quite different from Eq. 8. (Color figure online)

7 Pointing Game

We evaluate our saliency algorithm using the pointing game. This method was introduced in [19] and used, for instance, in [6,12]. It checks whether the maximum pixel of a saliency heatmap agrees with the location of a human-annotated[4] object of the class of interest.

Assessments like the pointing game have their caveats for benchmarking saliency methods. One can for instance argue that the cases when the saliency points somewhere outside the bounding box are the most insightful ones, as they indicate that the classifier is using information from an unexpected part of the image (for instance, the background). Another caveat is that, if winning at the pointing game is the goal, a saliency method is only as good as its underlying classifier is. For these reasons, a pointing game score should not be considered as the predominant criterion for a good saliency method.

---

[4] The pointing game is generally used under the assumption that neither the classifier nor the saliency method have any direct training knowledge about the position annotations, i.e. it is not a test of how well a trained task generalizes but of an extrinsic notion of saliency.

Nevertheless, it is reasonable to expect a useful saliency method to perform at least similarly well as the state of the art: if existing methods have proven capable of achieving high scores, this is after all indication that the classifier does to a significant degree base its decisions on spatially confined features of the real objects. Furthermore the pointing game provides a way of comparing the behaviour of different variations of a saliency method (such as different hyperparameters) somewhat more representatively than looking at individual image examples. Again, the best-scoring parameters are not necessarily the best for attribution purposes, but they are a reasonable starting point.

7.1   Heatmap Reduction

The result of the methods introduced in this paper is one or multiple paths, whereas the pointing game expects a single heatmap. There are multiple ways of reducing to such a map:

Averaging. One can simply average over all the masks in a $P_\uparrow$-optimal path. This operation is (modulo a time renormalisation) left inverse to the pixel ablation of a saliency map (Sect. 4.2).

$$\overline{\varphi_\uparrow} := \int_0^1 \varphi(t)\mathrm{d}t. \tag{9}$$

This works well in some cases, but the result can be disproportionally affected by low-discriminate contrasts of masks generated far from a decision boundary, which are unstable in a similar way to plain gradient methods.

Class Transition. Taking the point of view that the decision boundary is what matters, one can seek the position where the path crosses it by tracking the classifier outputs along the path.

Empirically, this gives better results than averaging (both for the pointing game and, to our eyes, ease of interpretation), but it hinges on the assumption of there being a single boundary-crossing. In general, there may be multiple crossings, or the classifier might have a far more gradual transition, or (in case an explanation for a class different from the prediction for x_0 is sought) it might not cross a boundary at all. In our implementation, we therefore make a case distinction:

- If there exist t such that $F(\varphi(t))$ is dominated by the target class, then we select the largest of these t. In other words, we select the most confined mask that results in the classification of interest. Here (unlike the rest of the paper) we consider the full multi-class output of F, and by "dominate" we mean that the target class ranks higher than all others.
- If no such t exists, we select simply $\arg\max_t F(\varphi(t))$.

This may not be the best strategy in all applications, but it does guarantee always getting a result that can be compared in the pointing game. In critical applications it is likely better to discard paths that do not cross a boundary, and consult a different method in such a case.

Contrastive Averaging. For the two paths optimizing $P_{\uparrow\downarrow}$, the property of interest is that they pinch the decision boundary between them. That means that for each t, the normal direction of the boundary is approximated by $\varphi_\uparrow(t) - \varphi_\downarrow(t)$ (at least coarsely, cf. Fig. 4). This suggests averaging between these values, i.e.

$$\overline{\varphi_{\uparrow\downarrow}} := \int_0^1 \big(\varphi_\uparrow(t) - \varphi_\downarrow(t)\big)\,\mathrm{d}t. \qquad (10)$$

Indeed this appears to give comparatively good, stable results in practice. Our interpretation is that on any indiscriminate parts of the path, the pinching tweak Eq. 8 reduces $\varphi_\uparrow(t) - \varphi_\downarrow(t)$ so these parts do not contribute to the result like they would in Eq. 9. The reason for this behaviour is that indiscriminate parts do not have a consistent F-gradient that would keep $\varphi_\uparrow(t)$ and $\varphi_\downarrow(t)$ apart during optimisation. On the other hand, stably-salient differences do keep them apart and therefore prevail in $\overline{\varphi_{\uparrow\downarrow}}$.

8 Experimental Results

We initially ran a custom implementation of the pointing game on individual classes (synsets) from the ImageNet dataset. In some cases even simple $P_\uparrow$-optimal paths perform well, e.g. 83 % on the "Bee" synset with EfficientNet classifier, which is better than the result with saliency methods from the literature. These experiments turned however out to be not very representative: on larger and mixed datasets, we were not able to find hyperparameters that avoided high instability in the optimisation and consequently lower scores, especially in case of $P_\uparrow$.

For fair and representative comparison with the literature, we present here the result on a benchmark that was already used in [5]. Specifically, we used their TorchRay suite [17] to evaluate the saliency-result of our method (reduced to a heatmap), explaining the classifications by ResNet50 on the COCO14 validation dataset. We did not have the computational resources to run the whole set, so used the first 1000 images[5] for a comparison to the literature state of the art of

---

[5] By "first 1000" we mean the 1000 images with the lowest ids. Note that the VOC and COCO sets are in random order, so that this should be a reasonably representative and reproducible selection. Comparing the score of Grad-CAM to the one on the full datasets confirms this.

The astute reader may notice that on the other hand, with only the first 100 images the results are systematically worse. This is less due to these images being more difficult, than artifact of the way the TorchRay benchmark gathers the results: specifically, it counts success rate for each class separately and averages in the end, but rates classes that are not even present in the smaller subset as 0% success.

our best-scoring result (Table 2), which was in turn determined among variations of our method on the first 100 images (Table 3). For each image, a saliency is obtained for each of the annotated objects, so for example the 100 COCO images correspond to 310 optimised paths.

Table 2. *Left*: the highest-scoring results for the pointing game over 1000 images with ResNet50 classifier, for comparison with the state of the art. *Right*: excerpt from table 1 in [5] (theirs is the Extr method), which contains the scores of more methods from the literature for the complete datasets. The "All/Diff" refer to a "difficult" subset of the data chosen in [19]. The "Ctr." method does not compute saliency but always points at the center, as a trivial null-score.

Method	*VOC07 Test* (All%/Diff%)	*COCO14 Val* (All%/Diff%)	Method	*VOC07 Test* (All%/Diff%)	*COCO14 Val* (All%/Diff%)
Ctr.	70.9/41.9	26.0/15.4	RISE	86.4/78.8	54.7/50.0
GCAM	90.5/80.4	57.1/49.2	GCAM	90.4/82.3	57.3/52.3
Ours	84.3/64.8	49.3/41.0	Extr	88.9/78.7	56.5/51.5

The top scores for our method are close to the state of the art, but do not quite reach the pointing accuracy of Grad-CAM, nor of extremal perturbation or RISE. It is not clear whether this is a result of fundamental limitations of our approach, of remaining stability problems that could be fixed with e.g. other regularisation means, or whether it is even a deficiency at all. Clearly the method does work in principle, and it is by construction faithful, so the somewhat higher mismatch rate could also be construed as higher sensitivity to aberrant or unstable behaviour of the classifier.

Table 3. Some of our results for the pointing game over 100 images with ResNet50 classifier.

Method	opt.crit	intp.spc	ζ_{sat}	$\sigma_{reguBlur}$	postproc	*VOC07 Test* (All%/Diff%)	*COCO14 Val* (All%/Diff%)
Ctr.						71.4/36.6	26.5/11.2
GCAM						90.4/64.2	48.9/35.2
Abl.Path	$P_\uparrow$	blur-fade	0.8	8.0 px		44.0/38.1	30.2/23.2
Abl.Path	$P_\updownarrow$	blur-fade	0.8	2.0 px		73.8/46.9	38.8/26.4
Abl.Path	$P_\updownarrow$	blur-fade	0.8	7.0 px		52.4/40.0	32.5/23.1
Abl.Path	$P_\updownarrow$	blur-fade	0.8	7.0 px	window	76.4/48.9	40.6/26.7
Abl.Path	$P_\updownarrow$	blur-fade	0	7.0 px	window	80.5/46.1	46.2/31.0
Abl.Path	$P_{\uparrow\downarrow}$	blur-fade	0.8	7.0 px		72.2/47.5	48.3/34.8
Abl.Path	$P_{\uparrow\downarrow}$	pyramid	0.8	8.0 px		75.2/47.1	39.5/26.5

Different variations of our methods also perform quite differently. We cannot describe all the observations that could be made from these experiments here, nor is this necessarily useful (many of the trends here likely do not generalize to other data), but a selection that may be noteworthy:

- The simple single-path retaining (or dissipating) methods compete badly. See Sect. 6 for some possible explanations.
- The boundary-straddle method performs best on the COCO dataset, and also relatively good on the difficult subset of VOC. We propose that this is typically the best of our methods, though in particular on the simple subset of VOC its results are quite dissappointing.
- The contrastive method performs well in particular on the simple subset of VOC, but only with very particular regularisation settings; see Sect. 8.1. With e.g. strong blurring and saturation but no windowing, it may perform worse than even the trivial center method, evidently an artifact of the effect shown in Fig. 3.

8.1 Hyperparameter Choice

Most of the saliency methods from the literature have some hyperparameters[6], as does ours. The ideal choice of these parameters is little discussed. Unlike when training a machine learning model, there is no objective on which this choice should unambiguously be based, but it appears that several authors have used the pointing game for this purpose. Apart from the aforementioned caveats, this also has the problem that the required position-annotations are simply not available for most applications.

In our case, there *is* an additional score with a clear meaning available: the ablation path score. And though it is evidently not the case that the hyperparameters leading to the highest ablation score give the best saliency results, we propose that studying only the ablation score can nevertheless provide some guidance for a good choice.

Specifically, the regularisation parameter is responsible for avoiding adversarial masks, which can be identified by a large population of paths with very high score. Observe in Fig. 5 that the histograms at low $\sigma_{\mathrm{reguBlur}}$ have an upper bulge ($P_{\uparrow\downarrow} > 0.5$). After $\sigma_{\mathrm{reguBlur}}$ has been increased to a size of 5 pixels, the adversarial population vanishes, and accordingly the pointing game score rises towards its maximum at $\sigma_{\mathrm{reguBlur}} = 7$.

Because the path score is a property without application-specific dimension, this phenomen can also be expected in applications where very different regularisation is required compared the image classification examples here. This is therefore a possible criterion for hyperparameter choice when the pointing game or an analog is not available. Some care needs to be taken though: Fig. 5 also shows an example where the pointing game with unmodified masks has a steadily

---

[6] The authors in [5] emphasize that their method avoids hyperparameters, yet their examples rely on no fewer than 5 hard-coded number constants.

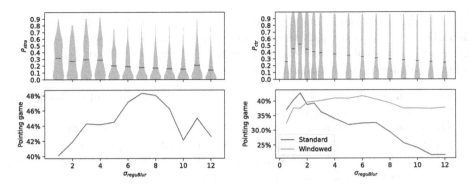

Fig. 5. Dependence on the size of the regularization filter, for both the distribution of boundary-straddling ablation-path scores and the pointing game score. *Left*: evaluated with contrastive averaging as per Sect. 7.1. *Right*: With paths optimised for the contrastive score; pointing game evaluated on both standard class-transition masks (Sect. 7.1), and with a boundary-suppressing window applied. Based on ResNet50 and 100 images from the COCO14 dataset.

decreasing score as the regularization is increased. We have identified the problem as stemming from the tendency of the regularization to push the argmax to the image boundary (cf. Fig. 3). This particular effect can be prevented by post-processing the masks with a window that suppresses the boundaries[7], in which case the rule suggested above is valid again.

9   Conclusion

We demonstrated that the ablation path formalism provides a usable saliency method that combines ideas from several previous methods within a single mathematical framework. The ablation path method can stand in for each of these methods to some extent, and is with suitable parameter choices also able to produce results that score similarly well in the pointing game.

This is a nontrivial result, because these methods appear quite different in their original formulations. And even though ours has strong similarity to [5,6], it was a priori not obvious that the restriction to a path instead of individual masks would still leave the optimisation problem solvable in practice. Indeed, for some inputs our method still struggles to converge on a human-reasonable explanation, even when other methods accomplish this. It is possible that in some cases there simply exist no paths that the classifier can follow in a well-behaved way. But for most of the examples we tested on, this does not seem to be a fundamental issue.

---

[7] This can be interpreted as applying prior knowledge of the location of objects in the dataset. However, there *are* also examples of objects close to the boundary. The window post-processing prevents these from being properly localised, which is why the top pointing-game score is still lower.

The main practical advantage of an ablation path, which is most evident when interactively browsing through it and tracking the exact classifier response, is the added information: unlike each of the previous methods, an ablation path offers a whole sequence of fine-grained changes to an input image. It thus offers a more thorough insight to the classification, while still ensuring the explanations form a consistent picture thanks to the monotonicity condition. Because each point in a path is associated with a concrete input to the network whose result can directly be inspected, we argue the method is *faithful* [18], whilst also being easy and intuitive to use. A caveat is that without suitable parameters (in particular regularisation), the explanations may highlight only the adversarial behaviour of a classifier, or even respond to spoofing by a classifier designed to detect the artificial inputs ("Volkswagening"). This possibility is to our knowledge common to all black-box saliency methods, so their use in critical applications should be considered carefully [10].

A disadvantage of our specific approach, in addition to the stability issues, is the rather high computational effort. A path requires many (ca. 50) optimisation steps, each of which require several classifier evaluations (ca. 20). Computing an ablation path for one image takes thus on the order of $\frac{1}{2}$ to 10 minutes (depending on the model and hyperparameters) on a consumer-grade GPU. This should be acceptable for use cases where individual, important decisions need explanation. Running the method over an entire large dataset is expensive, but should not be necessary for most users (even if they train a model on such a dataset).

For reasons of both slightly lower pointing-game score and performance, our method is perhaps best used in tandem with another one, for example Grad-CAM which is fast and stable but lacks the possibility of assessing faithfulness.

An open-source PyTorch implementation of our method is available [11].

Appendix A Canonical Time Reparametrisation

The function $m\colon [0,1] \to \mathbb{R}$ defined by $m(t) := \int_\Omega \varphi(t)$ is increasing and goes from zero to one (since we assume that $\int_\Omega 1 = 1$).

Note first that if $m(t_1) = m(t_2)$, then $\varphi(t_1) = \varphi(t_2)$ from the monotonicity property. Indeed, supposing for instance that $t_1 \leq t_2$, and defining the element $\theta := \varphi(t_2) - \varphi(t_1)$ we see that on the one hand $\int_\Omega \theta = 0$, on the other hand, $\theta \geq 0$, so $\theta = 0$ and thus $\varphi(t_1) = \varphi(t_2)$.

Now, define $\mathsf{M} := m([0,1]) = \{ s \in [0,1] \mid \exists t \in [0,1]\, m(t) = s \}$. Pick $s \in [0,1]$.

If $s \in \mathsf{M}$ we define $\psi(s) := \varphi(t)$ where $m(t) = s$ (and this does not depend on which t fulfills $m(t) = s$ from what we said above). We remark that $\int_\Omega \psi(s) = \int_\Omega \varphi(t) = m(t) = s$.

Now suppose that $s \notin \mathsf{M}$. Define $s_1 := \sup(\mathsf{M} \cap [0,s])$ and $s_2 := \inf(\mathsf{M} \cap [s,1])$ (neither set are empty since $0 \in \mathsf{M}$ and $1 \in \mathsf{M}$). Since $s_1 \in \mathsf{M}$ and $s_2 \in \mathsf{M}$, there are $t_1 \in [0,1]$ and $t_2 \in [0,1]$ such that $m(t_1) = s_1$ and $m(t_2) = s_2$. Finally define $\psi(s) := \varphi(t_1) + (s - s_1)\frac{\varphi(t_2) - \varphi(t_1)}{s_2 - s_1}$. In this case, $\int_\Omega \psi(s) = m(t_1) + (s - s_1)\frac{m(t_2) - m(t_1)}{s_2 - s_1} = s$. The path ψ constructed this way is still monotone, and it has the constant speed property, so it is an ablation path.

Appendix B $\mathcal{L}^\infty$-Optimal Monotonicity Projection

The algorithm proposed in Appendix C for optimising monotone paths uses updates that can locally introduce nonmonotonicity in the candidate $\hat{\varphi}_1$, so that it is necessary to project back onto a monotone path φ_1. The following routine[8] performs such a projection in a way that is optimal in the sense of minimising the $\mathcal{L}^\infty$-distance[9], i.e.,

$$\sup_t \left| \varphi_1(t, \mathbf{r}) - \hat{\varphi}_1(t, \mathbf{r}) \right| \leq \sup_t \left| \vartheta(t, \mathbf{r}) - \hat{\varphi}_1(t, \mathbf{r}) \right|$$

for all $\mathbf{r} \in \Omega$ and any other monotone path ϑ.

The algorithm works separately for each $\mathbf{r}$, i.e., we express it as operating simply on continuous functions $p : [0, 1] \to \mathbb{R}$. The final step effectively *flattens*

Algorithm 1. Make a function $[0, 1] \to \mathbb{R}$ nondecreasing

$\cup_i [l_i, r_i] \leftarrow \{\, t \in [0, 1] \mid p'(t) \leq 0 \,\}$ ▷ Union of intervals where p decreases
for i **do**
  $m_i \leftarrow \frac{p(l_i) + p(r_i)}{2}$
  $l_i \leftarrow \max\{\, t \in [r_{i-1}, l_i] \mid p(t) \leq m_i \,\}$
  $r_i \leftarrow \min\{\, t \in [r_i, l_{i+1}] \mid p(t) \geq m_i \,\}$
end for
for i, j **do**
  if $[l_i, r_i] \cap [l_j, r_j] \neq \emptyset$ **then**
    if $m_j < m_i$, merge the intervals and recompute m as the new center
  end if
end for
return $t \mapsto \begin{cases} p(t) & \text{if } t \notin \cup_i [l_i, r_i] \\ m_i & \text{if } t \in [l_i, r_i] \end{cases}$

---

out, in a minimal way, any region in which the function was decreasing.

In practice, this algorithm is executed not on continuous functions but on a PCM-discretised representation; this changes nothing about the algorithm except that instead as real numbers, l, r and t are represented by integral indices.

---

[8] It is easy to come up with other algorithms for monotonising a (discretised) function. One could simply *sort the array*, but that is not optimal with respect to any of the usual function norms; or clip the derivatives to be nonnegative and then rescale the entire function, but that is not robust against noise perturbations.

[9] Note that the optimum is not necessarily unique.

Appendix C Path Optimisation Algorithm

As said in Sect. 5, our optimisation algorithm is essentially gradient descent of a path φ: it repeatedly seeks the direction within the space of all paths that (first ignoring the monotonicity constraint) would affect the largest increase to $P(\varphi)$ as per Sect. 4, for any of the defined score functions. Algorithm 2 shows the details of how this is done in presence of our constraints. In case of $P_{\uparrow\downarrow}$, the state φ is understood to consist of the two paths $\varphi_\uparrow$ and $\varphi_\downarrow$.

As discussed before, the use of a gradient requires a metric to obtain a vector from the covector-differential, which could be either the implicit ℓ^2 metric on the discretised representation (pixels), or a more physical kernel/filter-based metric. In the present work, we base this on the regularisation filter.

Unlike with the monotonisation condition, the update can easily be made to preserve speed-constness by construction, by projecting for each t the gradient $\mathbf{g}$ on the sub-tangent-space of zero change to $\int_\Omega \varphi(t)$, by subtracting the constant function times $\int_\Omega \mathbf{g}(t)$. Note this requires the measure of Ω to be normalised, or else considered at this point.

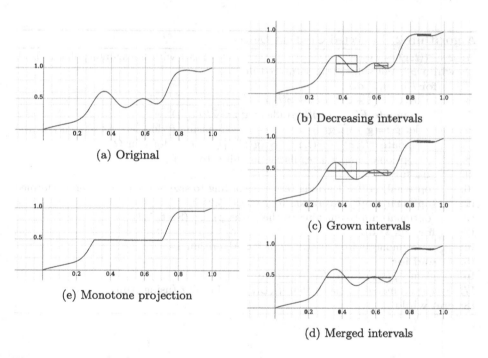

(a) Original

(b) Decreasing intervals

(c) Grown intervals

(e) Monotone projection

(d) Merged intervals

Fig. 6. Example view of the monotonisation algorithm in practice. (a) contains decreasing intervals, which have been localised in (b). For each interval, the centerline is then extended to meet the original path non-decreasingly (c). In some cases, this will cause intervals overlapping; in this case merge them to a single interval and re-grow from the corresponding centerline (d). Finally, replace the path on the intervals with their centerline (e).

Then we apply these gradients time-wise as updates to the path, using a scalar product in the channel-space to obtain the best direction for φ itself (as opposed to the corresponding image composite $x_{\varphi,t}$).

The learning rate γ can be chosen in different ways. What we found to work best is to normalise the step size in a $\mathcal{L}^\infty$ sense, such that the strongest-affected pixel in the mask experiences a change of at most 0.7 per step. This is small enough to avoid excessively violating the constraint, but not so small to make the algorithm unnecessarily slow (Fig. 6).

Appendix D Baseline Choice

The baseline image is prominently present in the input for much of the ablation path, and it is therefore evident that it will have a significant impact on the saliency. In line with previous work, we opted for a blurred baseline for the examples in the main paper, but even then there is still considerable freedom in the choice of blurring filter. Figure 7 shows two examples, where the result is not fundamentally, but still notably different.

Algorithm 2. Projected Gradient Descent

1: $\varphi \leftarrow ((t, \mathbf{r}) \mapsto t)$ ▷ Start with linear-interpolation path
2: **while** φ is not sufficiently saturated **do**
3:     **for** t in $[0, 1]$ **do**
4:         $x_{\varphi,t} := (1 - \varphi(t)) x_0 + \varphi(t) x_1$
5:         compute $F(x_{\varphi,t})$ with gradient $\mathbf{g} := \nabla F(x_{\varphi,t})$
6:         let $\hat{\mathbf{g}} := \mathbf{g} - \int_\Omega \mathbf{g}$ ▷ ensure $\hat{\mathbf{g}}$ does not affect mass of $\varphi(t)$
7:         update $\varphi(t, \mathbf{r}) \leftarrow \varphi(t, \mathbf{r}) - \gamma \langle \hat{\mathbf{g}}(\mathbf{r}) \mid |x_1 - x_0 \rangle$, for $\mathbf{r}$ in Ω
8:         (optional) apply a regularisation filter to $\varphi(t)$
9:     **end for**
10:    (optional) adjust learning rate γ according to size of the actual step performed
11:    (optional) apply saturation to φ (Sect. 5.2)
12:    (optional) apply pinching to the paths $\varphi_\uparrow, \varphi_\downarrow$ (Sect. 5.3)
13:    **for** $\mathbf{r}$ in Ω **do**
14:        re-monotonise $t \mapsto \varphi(t, \mathbf{r})$, using Algorithm 1
15:    **end for**
16:    clamp $\varphi(t, \mathbf{r})$ to $[0, 1]$ everywhere
17:    re-parametrise φ, such that $\int_\Omega \varphi(t) = t$ for all t (using Appendix A)
18: **end while**

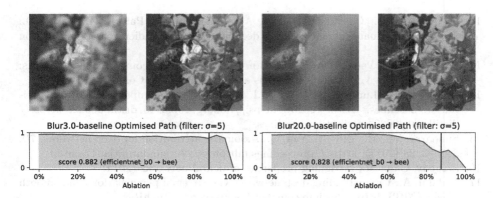

Fig. 7. An example of paths obtained with different-size blur baselines.

References

1. Adebayo, J., Gilmer, J., Muelly, M., Goodfellow, I., Hardt, M., Kim, B.: Sanity checks for saliency maps. In: Bengio, S., Wallach, H., Larochelle, H., Grauman, K., Cesa-Bianchi, N., Garnett, R. (eds.) Advances in Neural Information Processing Systems, vol. 31, pp. 9505–9515. Curran Associates, Inc. (2018). https://papers.nips.cc/paper/8160-sanity-checks-for-saliency-maps.pdf
2. Ancona, M., Ceolini, E., Öztireli, C., Gross, M.: Towards better understanding of gradient-based attribution methods for deep neural networks. CoRR (2017)
3. Chockler, H., Kroening, D., Sun, Y.: Explanations for occluded images. In: Proceedings of the IEEE/CVF International Conference on Computer Vision (ICCV), pp. 1234–1243 (2021)
4. Dabkowski, P., Gal, Y.: Real time image saliency for black box classifiers. In: Guyon, I., et al. (eds.) Advances in Neural Information Processing Systems, vol. 30. Curran Associates, Inc. (2017). https://proceedings.neurips.cc/paper/2017/file/0060ef47b12160b9198302ebdb144dcf-Paper.pdf
5. Fong, R., Patrick, M., Vedaldi, A.: Understanding deep networks via extremal perturbations and smooth masks, pp. 2950–2958 (2019)
6. Fong, R.C., Vedaldi, A.: Interpretable explanations of black boxes by meaningful perturbation (2017)
7. Kindermans, P.-J., et al.: The (un)reliability of saliency methods. In: Samek, W., Montavon, G., Vedaldi, A., Hansen, L.K., Müller, K.-R. (eds.) Explainable AI: Interpreting, Explaining and Visualizing Deep Learning. LNCS (LNAI), vol. 11700, pp. 267–280. Springer, Cham (2019). https://doi.org/10.1007/978-3-030-28954-6_14
8. Koh, P.W., Liang, P.: Understanding black-box predictions via influence functions. **70**, 1885–1894 (2017). https://proceedings.mlr.press/v70/koh17a.html
9. Petsiuk, V., Das, A., Saenko, K.: Rise: randomized input sampling for explanation of black-box models. CoRR (2018)
10. Rudin, C.: Stop explaining black box machine learning models for high stakes decisions and use interpretable models instead. Nat. Mach. Intell. **1**(5), 206–215 (2019). https://doi.org/10.1038/s42256-019-0048-x
11. Sagemüller, J.: Pytorch implementation of the ablation path saliency method (2023). https://github.com/leftaroundabout/ablation-paths-pytorch

372   J. Sagemüller and O. Verdier

12. Selvaraju, R.R., Cogswell, M., Das, A., Vedantam, R., Parikh, D., Batra, D.: Grad-CAM: visual explanations from deep networks via gradient-based localization (2017)
13. Simonyan, K., Vedaldi, A., Zisserman, A.: Deep inside convolutional networks: visualising image classification models and saliency maps. CoRR (2013)
14. Sturmfels, P., Lundberg, S., Lee, S.I.: Visualizing the impact of feature attribution baselines. Distill (2020). https://doi.org/10.23915/distill.00022. https://distill.pub/2020/attribution-baselines
15. Sundararajan, M., Taly, A., Yan, Q.: Axiomatic attribution for deep networks. **70**, 3319–3328 (2017). https://proceedings.mlr.press/v70/sundararajan17a.html
16. Szegedy, C., et al.: Intriguing properties of neural networks (2014)
17. Vedaldi, A.: Understanding deep networks via extremal perturbations and smooth masks (2019). https://github.com/facebookresearch/TorchRay
18. Weller, A.: Transparency: motivations and challenges. In: Samek, W., Montavon, G., Vedaldi, A., Hansen, L.K., Müller, K.-R. (eds.) Explainable AI: Interpreting, Explaining and Visualizing Deep Learning. LNCS (LNAI), vol. 11700, pp. 23–40. Springer, Cham (2019). https://doi.org/10.1007/978-3-030-28954-6_2
19. Zhang, J., Bargal, S.A., Lin, Z., Brandt, J., Shen, X., Sclaroff, S.: Top-down neural attention by excitation backprop. Int. J. Comput. Vis. **126**(10), 1084–1102 (2017). https://doi.org/10.1007/s11263-017-1059-x

IxDRL: A Novel Explainable Deep Reinforcement Learning Toolkit Based on Analyses of Interestingness

Pedro Sequeira$^{(\boxtimes)}$ and Melinda Gervasio

SRI International, 333 Ravenswood Ave., Menlo Park, CA 94025, USA
{pedro.sequeira,melinda.gervasio}@sri.com

Abstract. In recent years, advances in deep learning have resulted in a plethora of successes in the use of reinforcement learning (RL) to solve complex sequential decision tasks with high-dimensional inputs. However, existing systems lack the necessary mechanisms to provide humans with a holistic view of their competence, presenting an impediment to their adoption, particularly in critical applications where the decisions an agent makes can have significant consequences. Yet, existing RL-based systems are essentially competency-unaware in that they lack the necessary interpretation mechanisms to allow human operators to have an insightful, holistic view of their competency. Towards more explainable Deep RL (xDRL), we propose a new framework based on analyses of *interestingness*. Our tool provides various measures of RL agent competence stemming from interestingness analysis and is applicable to a wide range of RL algorithms, natively supporting the popular RLLib toolkit. We showcase the use of our framework by applying the proposed pipeline in a set of scenarios of varying complexity. We empirically assess the capability of the approach in identifying agent behavior patterns and competency-controlling conditions, and the task elements mostly responsible for an agent's competence, based on global and local analyses of interestingness. Overall, we show that our framework can provide agent designers with insights about RL agent competence, both their capabilities and limitations, enabling more informed decisions about interventions, additional training, and other interactions in collaborative human-machine settings.

Keywords: Explainable AI · Reinforcement Learning · Interestingness Analysis · Global and Local Explanations · Applications of xAI

1 Introduction

Reinforcement Learning (RL) is a machine learning technique for training autonomous agents to perform complex tasks through trial and error interactions with dynamic and uncertain environments. Recently, deep RL has achieved phenomenal successes, allowing agents to achieve—and even surpass—the performance level of human experts on various tasks, *e.g.*, [31,44,47]. In addition to

© The Author(s), under exclusive license to Springer Nature Switzerland AG 2023
L. Longo (Ed.): xAI 2023, CCIS 1901, pp. 373–396, 2023.
https://doi.org/10.1007/978-3-031-44064-9_20

Fig. 1. Our framework for analyzing the competence of deep RL agents through interestingness analysis.

solving complex tasks in simulated environments, RL has also been applied in real-life, industrial settings (see [29]) for a recent survey). However, an impediment to the wider adoption of RL techniques for autonomous control, especially in critical settings, is that deep learning-based models are essentially black boxes, making it hard to assess their competency in a task, and identify and understand the conditions that affect their behavior.

In deciding whether to delegate a task to an autonomous agent, a human needs to know that the agent is capable of making the right decisions under the various conditions to adequately accomplish the task. The challenge with an RL agent is that after being trained and deployed, it will always select one action at each step, as informed by its policy—but the why (and why not) behind its decisions cannot be retrieved from the agent's model. And while we can test RL agents prior to deployment and gather statistics about their performance on the task, or identify the actions they will select under certain circumstances, a more complete understanding of agents' competence—both in terms of its capabilities and limitations—remains essential to their acceptance by human collaborators.

Instead of capturing the agent's competence in terms of the specific decisions it makes under certain circumstances or its performance according to particular external metrics, we seek to characterize competence through self-assessment (introspection) over its history of interaction with the environment to capture distinct aspects that help explain its behavior. To do that, we analyze trained RL policies along various *interestingness* dimensions following the work in [42], *i.e.*, information that has the potential to be "interesting" in helping humans understand the competence of an RL agent. The interestingness analyses capture aspects of agent competence such as whether an agent is confident in its action selections, or whether it recognizes risky or unfamiliar situations, among other things. Overall, the goal is to direct end-users of the RL system towards appropriate intervention by providing deeper insight into the agent's competence, *e.g.*, identifying sub-task competency (the situations in which the agent is more/less competent), or highlighting the situations requiring more training or direct guidance.

In this paper, we describe a novel framework for **I**nterestingness analysis for explainable **D**eep **RL** that we refer to as **IxDRL**, and use it to investigate the various forms by which we can use interestingness analyses to better understand the competency of different deep RL agents. The focus is on the quantitative and qualitative analyses over interestingness data, and on the insights about an agent's behavior that our framework can provide to potential end-users of our system. Figure 1 depicts our IxDRL framework for competency-aware deep RL agents. The input to our system is a trained deep RL policy that provides a set of *learned models* that depends on the underlying RL algorithm, but typically corresponds to policy and value deep neural networks. Then, we test the agent by deploying it in the environment a number of times under different initial conditions, resulting in a set of traces. As the agent interacts with the environment, we probe the learned models and collect various information about the agent's behavior and internal state, *e.g.*, the value attributed to a state, or the probability each action has of being selected; we refer to all this information as the *interaction data*. We then perform interestingness analysis along several dimensions, resulting in a scalar value for each timestep of each trace—the *interestingness data*. Finally, we perform competency assessment based on interestingness using various techniques. Our contributions are as follows:

- A new set of interestingness dimensions designed to cover different families of deep RL algorithms. Our implementation of the interestingness framework is compatible with popular RL toolkits[1].
- A method to analyze an RL agent's behavior in a task by clustering traces based solely on interestingness. The method enables the identification of distinct competency-controlling conditions that in different behavior patterns.
- A method to discover which task elements impact agent's behavior the most and under which circumstances. We conduct feature importance analysis via SHapley Additive exPlanations (SHAP) [26] to perform global and local interpretation for competency assessment.

We present the results of a computational study where we trained RL agents for three different scenarios of varying complexity: Hopper, Atari Breakout, and a custom combat task running on the StarCraft II (SC2) platform. We used our interestingness framework to analyze the resulting agents' behavior and task competencies. We show that by going beyond trying to capture what an agent will do when and how well it will do it, our interestingness framework can provide human operators and partners a more complete picture of an RL agent's competence. Furthermore, the trace clusters (obtained based on interestingness data) expose disparate challenges resulting in distinct agent behaviors, allowing the identification of different sub-tasks within the general task and distinct competency-controlling conditions. In addition, our feature importance analysis via SHAP provides insights about the "sources" of interestingness in the environment that most impact the agent's competence, while also helping explain the contributions of each task element on particular situations having "abnormal" values of interestingness. Altogether, the higher-level competency modeling enabled by interestingness can provide human users with a more complete understanding of an agent's competencies, allowing them to make better decisions regarding the agent's use, providing insights on the agent's limitations in the task, and suggesting directions for improving agent behavior.

---

[1] The IxDRL toolkit code is available at: https://github.com/SRI-AIC/ixdrl.

2   Related Work

In recent years, many approaches to explainable RL (xRL) have been proposed for explaining various aspects of learned policies [14,34]. These include: identifying the regions of the input that most affect an agent's decisions [11,51], providing example trajectories [18], highlighting key decision moments to summarize an agent's behavior [1,17,23], extracting high-level descriptions of an agent's policy [7,16,22,40], and generating counterfactual explanations to help in understanding an agent's behavior [27,30,50]. Here we focus on the approaches that attempt to provide a more complete view of RL agent competence in a form understandable to humans.

Some approaches try to identify key moments of the agent's interaction that help explain its behavior in the task. For example, [1] proposes some heuristics to select important states that are then used to summarize an agent's policy. A similar heuristic is presented in [17]. [23] takes a slightly different approach to behavior summarization, identifying important trajectories to be shown to an end-user. Although these approaches provide deeper insight into agent competence than the previously work, they still provide only a limited view of competence and can only be applied to specific families of *tabular* RL methods.

Some approaches focus on explaining behavior in the form of queryable models that let users analyze agent behavior under different conditions. For example, [13] finds correlations between conditions and actions and lets users query the model through templated questions around identifying conditions for actions, predicting what an agent will do, and explaining expectation violations. Meanwhile, [49] uses simulation to predict sequences of future actions to answer user questions about the consequences of actions/policy.

Another body of work attempts to characterize agent behavior by extracting diverse structural models to represent agent strategies. For example, [7,16] use probabilistic graphical modeling to learn finite-state models of strategy for the StarCraft domain, while [40] infers strategies in the form of logical task specifications from agent traces using information-theoretic techniques to capture the conditions under which different behaviors occur. These approaches are focused solely on characterizing agent behavior and do not attempt to capture other aspects of the agent's decision-making.

In earlier work on interestingness analysis [41], we performed a user study that involved showing users short video clips highlighting different interestingness moments of agent interactions with the environment for RL agents with different capabilities and limitations on the task. The results revealed that some dimensions are better than others at conveying agent competence and that the diversity of aspects captured by the different interestingness dimensions helped users better understand an agent's task competencies. This paper builds upon our previous work [41,42], expanding it through a novel set of analyses that can extract interestingness from deep RL policies and not just tabular data. In addition, we go beyond summarizing behavior through the extraction of highlights, making use of interestingness for behavior clustering and local and global explanations of agent competence.

3 Interestingness Analyses

In this section we detail our framework for analyzing RL agent competence through interestingness, starting by providing the necessary background on RL.

3.1 Reinforcement Learning

We are interested in characterizing the competence of RL agents (we refer to [45] for a more thorough description of the problem and main approaches). RL is a machine learning technique allowing autonomous agents to learn sequential decision tasks through trial-and-error interactions with dynamic, uncertain environments [45]. RL problems can be framed under the *Markov decision process* (MDP) formulation [35], denoted as tuple $\mathcal{M} = (\mathcal{S}, \mathcal{A}, \mathsf{P}, \mathsf{R}, \gamma, \rho_0)$, where: $\mathcal{S}$ is the set of environment states; $\mathcal{A}$ is the set of agent actions; $\mathsf{P}(s' \mid s, a)$ is the probability of the agent visiting state s' after executing action a in state s; $\mathsf{R}(s, a) \in \mathbb{R}$ is the reward function, that dictates the reward that the agent receives for performing a in s; $\gamma \in [0, 1]$ is a discount factor denoting the importance of future rewards; ρ_0 is the starting state distribution.

The goal of an RL algorithm is to learn a policy, denoted by $\pi(a|s)$, mapping from states to actions, that maximizes the expected return for the agent, *i.e.*, the discounted sum of rewards it receives during its lifespan. The optimization problem can be formulated by $\pi^* = \arg\max_\pi \mathbb{E}\left[\sum_t \gamma^t R_t\right]$, where R_t is the reward received by the agent at discrete timestep t, and π^* is termed the optimal policy. Often, RL algorithms use an auxiliary structure while learning a policy called the value function, corresponding to $V^\pi(s) = \mathbb{E}\left[\sum_t \gamma^t R_t)|S_0 = s\right]$, that provides an estimate of the return the agent will receive by being in state s and following policy π thereafter. In deep RL, policies and other auxiliary structures are represented by neural networks whose parameters are adjusted during training to change the agent's behavior via some RL algorithm. As indicated in Fig. 1, we refer to all such networks optimized via deep RL as the *learned models*.

3.2 Interaction Data

Given a trained policy, the next step in our framework is the extraction of *interaction data* given a trained RL agent. We collect these data by "running" the agent in the environment for a number of times[2], collecting samples from the environment and probing the learned models at each step. The result is a set of *traces* comprising the agent's history of interaction with the environment from which the agent's competence will be analyzed.

Distinct RL algorithms make use of different models to optimize the agent's policy during training. Our framework extracts data from four main families of RL algorithms:

---

[2] Without loss of generality, here we deal with episodic tasks.

Policy gradient approaches (*e.g.*, [12,39,45]) that provide a stochastic policy, $\pi(a|s)$, *i.e.*, a function mapping from observations to distributions over the agent's actions;

Value-based approaches (*e.g.*, [28,38]) that compute a (state) value function, $V(s)$, that indicates how good it is for the agent to be in a situation, or an action-value function, $Q(s,a)$, asserting the value of executing some action given a state;

Model-based approaches (*e.g.*, [6,19]) that learn a model of the environment's dynamics, $P(s',r|s,a)$, *i.e.*, a function mapping from observations and actions to expected next observation and reward, that is used as a surrogate of the environment to collect samples and update the agent's policy;

Distributional RL approaches (*e.g.*, [3]) whose auxiliary structures, *e.g.*, the Q function, output distributions over values instead of point predictions, allowing the capture of uncertainty around the estimates.

Interaction data then comprises everything we can extract at each timestep given the learned models provided by the RL agent. In addition to this internal agent data, we also collect external (observable) data, *i.e.*, the reward received by the agent, the selected action, and the agent's observation.

3.3   Interestingness Dimensions

As mentioned earlier, the goal of interestingness analysis is to characterize RL agents' competence along various dimensions, each capturing a distinct aspect of the agent's interaction with the environment. The dimensions of analyses are inspired by what humans—whether operators or teammates—might seek when trying to understand an agent's competence in a task. Each dimension provides distinct *targets of curiosity* whose values might trigger a human to investigate the agent's learned policy further [15]. As such, our system provides a means for the agent to perform competency self-assessment, where we use the data resulting from the interestingness analyses to identify cases that a human should be made aware of, and where user input might be needed.

Computationally, an analysis is given interaction data for each trace as input (see Fig. 1) and, for each timestep, produces a scalar value in the $[-1, 1]$ interval denoting the "strength" or "amount" of competence as measured by that interestingness dimension. Further, with the goal of enabling the analyses to be computed online, *i.e.*, *while* the agent is performing the task, we restrict analyses to have access only to the data provided up to a given timestep. In this work, we designed and implemented a novel set of interestingness analyses that are applicable to a wide range of tasks and cover most of the existing deep RL algorithms. Notwithstanding, each RL algorithm allows the collection of only a subset of the interaction data mentioned in Sect. 3.2, which results in only a subset of the interestingness analyses being performed for any particular RL agent. Our IxDRL Python implementation is compatible with popular RL toolkits, including RLLib [25], an open-source library offering support for production-level, highly distributed RL workloads (20+ RL algorithms), which can foster wider adoption of our toolkit. We now describe the goal behind each interestingness analysis and their mathematical realization in our framework.

Value: characterizes the long-term importance of a situation as ascribed by the agent's value function. It can be used to identify situations where the agent is near its goals (maximal value) or far from them (low value). Given the agent's value function associated with policy π, denoted by V^π, we compute *Value* at discrete timestep t using: $\mathcal{V}(t) = 2\left(V^\pi_{[0,1]}(s_t)\right) - 1$, where $V_{[0,1]}$ is the normalized value function obtained via min-max scaling across all timesteps of all traces.

Confidence: measures the agent's confidence in its action selection, helping identify good opportunities for requesting guidance from a human user or sub-tasks where the agent may require more training. For discrete action spaces, where a stochastic RL policy is applicable, corresponding to a discrete probability distribution over the possible actions, we compute *Confidence* at timestep t with $\mathcal{C}(t) = 1 - 2J\left(\pi(\cdot|s_t)\right)$, where $J(X)$ is Pielou's evenness index [33], corresponding to the normalized entropy of a discrete distribution X, which is given by $J(X) = -\frac{1}{\log n}\sum_i P(x_i)\log P(x_i)$. Our implementation also computes confidence for continuous action spaces, where policies typically parameterize a multivariate Gaussian distribution. When that is the case, we use the relative entropy-based dispersion coefficient proposed in [21] to replace the J evenness index above.

Goal Conduciveness: assesses the desirability of a situation for the agent given the context of the decision at that point, *i.e.*, the preceding timesteps leading up to the current state. Intuitively, this computes how "fast" the agent is moving towards or away from the goal. Decreasing values can be particularly interesting, but we can also capture large differences in values, which potentially identify external, unexpected events that would violate operator's expectations and where further inspection may be required. We compute *Goal Conduciveness* at timestep t directly from the first derivative of the value function with respect to time at t, namely using: $\mathcal{G}(t) = \sin\left(\arctan\left(\rho\frac{d}{dt}V_{[0,1]}(s_t)\right)\right)$, where the sine of the angle generated by the slope (in an imaginary unit circle centered at $V_{[0,1]}(s_t)$) is used for normalization and ρ is a scaling factor to make the slope more prominent. In our implementation, we use $\rho = 100$, and resort to a finite difference numerical method to approximate $\frac{d}{dt}V(s_t)$ given the value function of the 3 previous timesteps[3].

Incongruity: captures internal inconsistencies with the expected value of a situation, which may indicate unexpected situations, *e.g.*, where the reward is stochastic or very different from the one experienced during training. In turn, a prediction violation identified through incongruity can be used to alert a human operator about possible deviations from the expected course

---

[3] This corresponds to using the *backward* finite difference coefficient with accuracy 2 [10]. A higher-order accuracy could be used if we wish to capture how the value function is changing for the computation of Goal Conduciveness, by using information from timesteps further back in the trace.

of action. Formally, we capture *Incongruity* via the temporal difference (TD) error [45], *i.e.*, $\mathcal{I}(t) = r_t + \gamma V^\pi(s_t) - V^\pi(s_{t-1})^4$. We then normalize $\mathcal{I}(t)$ by dividing it with the reward range observed from the task.

Riskiness: quantifies the impact of the "worst-case scenario" at each step, highlighting situations where performing the "right" vs. the "wrong" action can dramatically impact the outcome. This dimension is best computed for value-based RL algorithms by taking the difference between the value of the best action, $\max_{a \in \mathcal{A}} Q(a|s_t)$ and the worst, $\min_{a \in \mathcal{A}} Q(a|s_t)$. However, here we use a policy-gradient algorithm that updates the policy directly. As such, we compute *Riskiness* using $\mathcal{R}(t) = 2 \left(\max_{a_1 \in \mathcal{A}} \pi(a_1|s_t) - \max_{a_2 \in \mathcal{A}} \pi(a_2|s_t)\right) - 1, a_1 \neq a_2$. This will usually result in a value similar to that of Confidence, but may help identify situations where *one* of the actions is particularly undesirable (low-probability) compared to all the others, which can be used by an operator to further specify the conditions in which an action should never be executed.

Stochasticity: captures the environment's *aleatoric* uncertainty. This is the statistical uncertainty representative of the inherent system stochasticity, *i.e.*, the unknowns that differ each time the same experiment is run [6,19]. Here, we capture the uncertainty around what happens when we execute the same action in the same state on different occasions. This analysis requires an algorithm that models the uncertainty of the agent's environment, *e.g.*, , an algorithm implementing distributional RL [3]. For learned models parameterizing discrete distributions of the Q-function, we compute stochasticity using $\mathcal{S}(t) = \frac{1}{|\mathcal{A}|} \sum_{a \in \mathcal{A}} 1 - 4|D\left(Q^\pi(\cdot|s_t)\right) - 0.5|$, where $D(P) = 2 \sum_{k=0}^{K} \frac{d_k}{K-1}$ is Leik's ordinal dispersion index [24], with $d_k = \begin{cases} c_k, & c_k \leq 0.5 \\ 1 - c_k, & \text{otherwise.} \end{cases}$, and $c_k = \sum_{i=0}^{k} P(x_i)$. This can be used to identify inherently stochastic regions of the environment, where different agent behavior outcomes may occur[5].

Familiarity: estimates the agent's *epistemic* uncertainty, corresponding to the subjective uncertainty, *i.e.*, due to limited data or lack of experience with the environment. We follow approaches in the model-based RL literature [6,19,32,43] where epistemic uncertainty is measured by estimating the level of disagreement between different predictive models, forming an ensemble, that are trained independently, usually by random sub-sampling of a common replay buffer. Formally, an ensemble comprises a set of K bootstrapped forward models, where each model, denoted by $f_\theta^k(s_{t+1}, r_{t+1}|s_t, a_t)$, estimates the next-step state, s_{t+1}, and reward, r_{t+1}, given the current state, s_t, and action a_t taken by the agent. We then compute the agent's familiarity using $\mathcal{F}(t) = 1 - \frac{2}{K^2} \sum_{i,j}^{K} d(s_{t+1}^i, s_{t+1}^j)$, where s_{t+1}^k is the predicted next state vector from model k in the ensemble, and $d(x, y) \in [0, 1]$ is any suitable standardized distance function between two state vectors predicted by the models.

---

[4] This quantity is also known as the *one-step TD* or *TD(0) target*.

[5] Our framework also computes stochasticity from models parameterizing continuous distributions, using an appropriate coefficient of variation in place of Leik's D.

In our work we use the cosine distance. This analysis computes the level of (dis)agreement between the observations predicted by the models in the ensemble, and can thus be used to identify less-explored, unfamiliar parts of the environment where the agent might be more uncertain about what to do. It also identifies good intervention opportunities as it indicates regions that need further exploration[6].

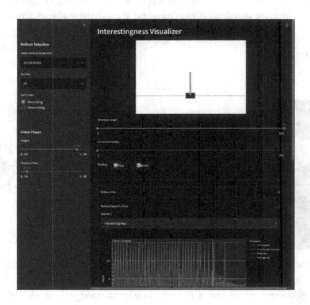

Fig. 2. Interestingness and agent behavior visualization tool.

To help potential end-users of our framework analyze the behavior of agents and interestingness resulting from the several analyses, we built an interactive graphical tool (see Fig. 2) that allows visualizing videos of traces (replays), select a dimension and sort traces by mean interestingness value, and see the various plots automatically produced by our framework during interaction data extraction and interestingness analysis.

4   Experiments and Results

To validate our framework and understand the insights it can provide to potential end-users, we performed a computational study where we extracted interestingness data and applied different methods for interpreting the agent's competency

---

[6] Our implementation also computes familiarity from an ensemble of predictive models parameterizing distributions instead of outputting point predictions, in which case we use divergence measures between prediction distributions to replace for d.

in three distinct scenarios with varying degrees of control complexity. Although we do not perform a user study, our experiments are a necessary first step to identify the types of insights about RL agent competence that interestingness can provide. For each scenario, we describe the goal and environment dynamics, and the RL algorithm used to train each agent used for interestingness analysis[7]. We then illustrate the capability of our framework in analyzing the overall competence of the trained RL agents. Due to space restrictions, here we provide some statistics of the agents' behaviors and interestingness analyses and highlight only a few examples of the agents' capabilities and limitations.

4.1   Environments

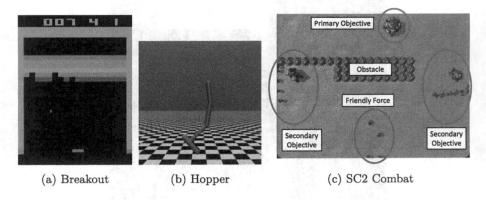

(a) Breakout   (b) Hopper   (c) SC2 Combat

Fig. 3. Screenshots of the different scenarios used in our experiments.

Breakout: [8] The agent controls the horizontal movement of a paddle at the bottom of the screen (see Fig. 3a), with the goal of hitting a bouncing ball into a colored brick wall at the top of the screen until it is fully destroyed. As more bricks are destroyed, the speed of the ball increases. The agent has five lives, and a life is lost whenever the ball falls into the ground (bottom part of the screen) without the paddle hitting it. Rewards (positive) are given when bricks are destroyed. We used the Arcade Learning Environment (ALE) implementation [2] with RLLib, where there are four discrete actions available (*noop, fire, right, left*), while the observations correspond to four time-consecutive stacked 84×84 grayscale frames transformed from the RGB game images. We trained an agent in RLLib for 2×10^6 timesteps using the distributional Q-learning approach as described in [3] where the Q function of each action is approximated using a discrete distribution over 51 values in the $[-10, 10]$ interval.

---

[7] All configurations used to train the RL agents, as well the data for each scenario, are available at: https://github.com/SRI-AIC/23-xai-ixdrl-data.

[8] https://gymnasium.farama.org/environments/atari/breakout/.

Hopper: [9] The agent controls a one-legged simplified robotic structure (see Fig. 3b) that consists of four main body parts: the *torso* at the top, the *thigh* in the middle, the *leg* in the bottom, and a *foot* on which the entire body rests. The goal of the agent is to make hops that move the robot forward in the environment by applying torques (continuous values) on the three hinges connecting the four body parts, *i.e.*, there are three action factors. Observations are 11-dimensional, consisting of positional values of the different body parts and their velocities. We trained an agent in the MuJoCo [46] Hopper implementation using the Model-Based Policy Optimization (MBPO) algorithm [19][10] that learns an ensemble of dynamics models, each predicting the parameters of a multivariate Gaussian distribution over the next-step observation and reward given the current state and performed action. The policy is optimized from rollouts produced by the learned models using Soft Actor-Critic (SAC) [12], where the idea behind using an ensemble is to prevent the policy from exploiting inaccuracies in any single model. The agent was trained for 15×10^4 timesteps, with 10^3 initial steps of exploration used to train the dynamics models.

StarCraft II Combat: [11] To test our interestingness framework on a more complex control task, we implemented a custom combat scenario in *Starcraft II* [4] using the pySC2 library [48] to interface with the game engine. The agent controls the Blue force, which starts at the bottom of the map (see Fig. 3c). The agent's goal is to destroy the Primary Objective, which is a Command-Center (CC) building located at the top of the map. The map is divided into three vertical "lanes," each of which may be blocked by obstacles. The two side lanes contain Secondary Objectives, which are buildings guarded by Red forces. Destroying the Red force defending one of the secondary objectives causes the building to be removed from the map and replaced with additional Blue units (reinforcements), with the type of reinforcements determined by the type of the building destroyed. Different types of units have distinct capabilities. The starting Blue force consists of infantry (Marines or Marauders), but Blue can gain SiegeTanks (armored ground units) by capturing a Factory building, or Banshees (ground attack aircraft) by capturing a Starport. The Banshees are especially important because they can fly over ground obstacles and Red has no anti-air units to defend the primary objective.

The initial state, including the number and type of Blue starting units, locations of obstacles, number of enemies, etc. is randomized to create a *scenario* distribution. In addition, Red sometimes receives reinforcements at a random time step, and capturing a secondary objective sometimes does not grant Blue reinforcements. The agent observes the world as a top-down view corresponding to three semantic layers of size 192×144, each encoding a distinct property of objects/units at each location. The action space is factored over the four unit types that Blue can have. A joint action assigns an order separately to each unit

---

[9] https://gymnasium.farama.org/environments/mujoco/hopper/.

[10] We used the implementation at: https://github.com/JannerM/mbpo.

[11] A more detailed description of our SC2 task is provided in [40].

type, and all units of that type execute the same order. The available orders are to *target* the nearest Red unit of a specified type, to *move* to one of 9 fixed locations while ignoring any enemies encountered, or to *do nothing*. The reward is a linear combination of five factors: a large reward for capturing the CC, rewards for gaining and losing Blue forces and for destroying Red forces in proportion to the resource cost of the units gained or lost, and a per-timestep cost. We trained an agent using a distributed implementation of the VTrace (actor-critic) algorithm [9] based on the open-source SEED-RL implementation [8].

4.2   Interaction Data and Interestingness Analysis

After training an RL agent for each scenario, we analyzed their competence using our IxDRL framework. We started by sampling 1,000 traces by running each policy on the corresponding environment, which was randomly initialized where applicable. Overall, we configured the training regime such that the agents do not attain optimal performance in the corresponding task. This resulted in agents with different levels of competence. The Hopper agent attains a very good performance, resulting in a mean cumulative reward of $3,415 \pm 105$. Conversely, the Breakout agent's performance is not very consistent, attaining a mean cumulative reward of 110 ± 143. Often, it reaches a state where most bricks are destroyed but it is unable to destroy the remaining ones, bouncing the ball through empty space and walls in a continuous loop. As for the SC2 Combat agent, it achieved its primary objective (destroying the CC) 36% of time and was defeated (no Blue units left) in 25% of traces (remaining 39% of traces timed out). The mean count of agent (Blue) units is 4.23 ± 3.47 while the count for opponent (Red) units is 13.34 ± 5.59. These results indicate that there appear to be task conditions for which the agents learned a strategy capable of achieving the task objectives, whereas others posed challenges that the agent could not overcome, and in which further training or guidance might be needed. These make the trained agents ideal candidates for interestingness analysis of competence.

After sampling the behavior traces, we collected interaction data as explained in Sect. 3.2 for each of the 1,000 sampled traces. Table 1 shows which interestingness dimensions were produced for each scenario. Due to the types of observation and action spaces and RL algorithm used for each scenario, each scenario only allowed for the analysis of interestingness along particular dimensions. Only Hopper allows analysis for all the dimensions described in Sect. 3.3 since, in addition to learning an ensemble of dynamics models, the models are distributional, which allows capturing both Familiarity and Stochasticity. For Hopper and the SC2 Combat scenario, because there are multiple action factors that the agent simultaneously controls at each timestep, Confidence can be computed for each factor separately. In the case of the SC2 task, Riskiness is also computed per action factor since the action space is discrete. We also compute the mean values for Confidence and Riskiness across action factors, thus resulting in a total number of dimensions higher than the number of analyses for these scenarios.

Table 1. The interestingness dimensions extracted for each scenario. The "Total" row indicates the total number of dimensions extracted. See text for details.

Dimension	Breakout	Hopper	SC2 Combat
Value	×	×	×
Confidence	×	×	×
Goal Cond.	×	×	×
Riskiness	×	×	×
Incongruity	×	×	×
Stochasticity	×	×	
Familiarity		×	
Total	6	10	13

4.3 Overall Competence Assessment

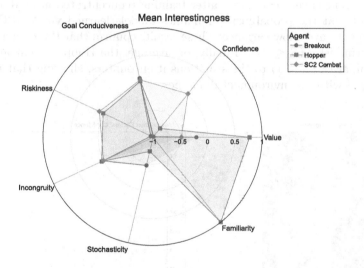

Fig. 4. Interestingness profiles for each agent in the different scenarios.

We start by assessing the agents' overall competency in the tasks as ascribed by the different interestingness dimensions. Fig. 4 shows a radar chart for the mean interestingness (across all timesteps of all traces) resulting from analyzing each agent. Each shape represents the interestingness profile or "signature" for the behavior of the corresponding agent. As we can see, different scenarios lead to distinct profiles. On average, the SC2 agent has a medium level of Confidence ($\mathcal{C} \approx 0$) while the other agents are not so confident in the selection of actions. This is expected since the Breakout and Hopper tasks are more cyclic and the differences between the action values or associated probabilities are not that high (*e.g.*, moving the paddle left or right in Breakout only has impact when hitting the ball). In contrast, the SC2 task is more strategic and the agent needs to understand better which action to select at each step. Conversely, the Hopper agent attributes a higher Value to situations it encounters ($\mathcal{V} > 0.5$) compared to the other agents who value situations negatively on average. This is also expected since the Hopper agent has the best performance overall, whereas the Breakout agent has a medium performance and the SC2 agent only values situations highly when in possession of the Banshees since, as explained earlier, they provide a winning advantage, although this does not happen frequently. Furthermore, all agents attribute on average a neutral level of Incongruity ($\mathcal{I} \approx 0$), which is explained by the lack of reward stochasticity in all scenarios. The reward the agent receives is expected compared to the values associated with the previous and current observations. In the SC2 task, high Incongruity occurs when the agent receives the Banshees and/or the enemy receives reinforcements, but those situations seldom occur. For the same reason, the Goal Conduciveness results show that on average there are no abrupt changes to the agents' value functions ($\mathcal{G} \approx 0$). As for Stochasticity, results show that the value attributed by the Breakout agent is very consistent after training (concentrated around a specific value) and that the probabilistic dynamics models learned via MBPO by the Hopper agent have a low variance. These results confirm that these scenarios are very deterministic ($\mathcal{S} \leq 0.5$). Finally, on average, the Hopper agent attributes high Familiarity ($\mathcal{F} \approx 1$) to the situations it encounters, showing that it is well experienced with its environment dynamics.

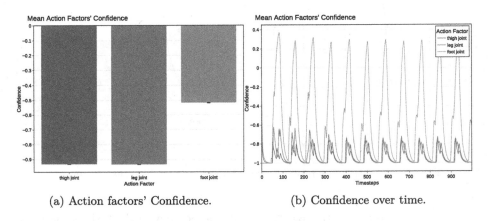

(a) Action factors' Confidence.   (b) Confidence over time.

Fig. 5. Results of interestingness analysis for the Hopper scenario.

While this analysis allows us to gain insights about the characteristics of each task and provides an overview of each agent's competence, we can use our framework to assess competence at a deeper level. Since Hopper generates interestingness for all dimensions, we use it here as an example to analyze the agent's competence over time and across different actuators. Figure 4 shows that the agent has on average very low confidence in selecting actions (mean $C = -0.8 \pm 0.27$) but Fig. 5a shows that confidence varies greatly with the action factor. Here, we see that the agent is more confident about selecting values for the *foot joint* actuator compared to the others. Figure 5b shows another level of detail by depicting how Confidence varies over the length of a trace for each action factor. It reveals a cyclic pattern where the agent is actually quite confident at times in selecting values for the *foot joint* (peaks at $C \approx 0.3$). An empirical analysis of the videos associated with the traces reveals that Confidence increases when the agent is preparing to jump and reaches its lowest values when the agent is in mid-air, which makes sense since at that point controlling the foot joint has little effect. Overall, we can see that depending on the scenario and agent's policy, interestingness can vary over time and across different action factors. Next, we investigate whether interestingness can be used to identify different sub-tasks that might denote distinct behaviors and conditions.

4.4 Trace Clustering Based on Interestingness

With the goal of using interestingness to identify distinct, meaningful patterns—which would indicate that an agent has achieved some level of competence—we clustered agents' traces using only the interestingness data. Our hypothesis is that each cluster will highlight different behaviors and represent distinct aspects of competence as captured by interestingness. For the purpose of this investigation we used the data generated with the Breakout scenario. Since each interestingness analysis computes a value for each timestep of a trace, the result is a set of sequences of numeric data. Since we noted a high variance in the length of the Breakout traces, to allow clustering the traces we first computed the mean value of each interestingness dimension for each trace. We then computed the Euclidean distances between each pair of traces[12], which were then fed to a Hierarchical Clustering [20] algorithm with a complete linkage criterion.

Table 2. Characteristics of the trace clusters found for the Breakout scenario.

Cluster	Size	Lives	Score	Length
0	451	3.53 ± 0.75	11.53 ± 13.47	247.92 ± 238.26
1	226	3.72 ± 0.45	318.42 ± 28.82	2878.58 ± 1131.26
2	70	1.00 ± 0.00	359.00 ± 0.00	740.00 ± 0.00
3	190	0.33 ± 0.47	29.28 ± 15.23	331.82 ± 181.09
4	63	2.00 ± 0.00	37.00 ± 0.00	166.00 ± 0.00

To select the number of clusters, we compute the Silhouette coefficient [36]. While the best partition according to this metric resulted in 14 clusters, for

---

[12] For traces with similar length, alternative methods such as Dynamic Time Warping (DTW) [37] could be used to align and compute the distances between traces.

illustrating the results of clustering by interestingness we chose 5 clusters since it provided the best balance between number of clusters and cluster sizes. Table 2 shows various agent performance metrics and characteristics of the traces in each resulting cluster. **Score** corresponds to the cumulative reward collected by the agent *during* the trace, which might be different from the total game (in Breakout, a trace ends whenever the agent loses a life). As we can see, each cluster captures different competency-controlling conditions and different stages of the Breakout game. This table is complemented by Fig. 6 showing the different interestingness profiles resulting for each cluster, where we see that profiles differ mainly in the Value and Stochasticity dimensions. Together with an analysis of the traces' videos in each cluster, this provides an understanding of the distinct challenges faced by the agent.

In particular, cluster 0 is characterized by the agent being in an early stage of the Breakout game where many lives are still available and the agent is unable to make much progress (low score, short trace lengths). Cluster 1 captures situations occurring in early stages of the game similar to cluster 0 but where the agent is able to make good progress on the task, which translates to the agent achieving a very high score, resulting in longer traces. In Fig. 6, we see that the agent assigns a higher Value on average to cluster 1 compared to cluster 0. As for cluster 2, all traces capture the exact same strategy of destroying the bricks on both sides of the wall, making the ball bounce on the top part of the environment and destroying the wall from above, resulting in the highest average score among clusters. This cluster is also characterized by the highest Value among clusters as well as the highest Stochasticity, presumably because the agent's actions have no effect while the ball is bouncing on the top, so the agent receives different rewards (whenever the ball hits a brick) on seemingly the same situation, resulting in stochasticity as experienced by the agent. In contrast, cluster 3 occurs at late stages of the game where there are only a few bricks left and the agent eventually fails to destroy all of them before losing its last remaining lives. As seen in Fig. 6, this is also the cluster with the lowest associated mean Value. Finally, cluster 4 captures situations where the behavior of the agent follows the exact the same pattern in each trace: the agent already has a relatively high game score, there are a few bricks left, and the agent loses a life when the ball is deflected on the right side of the environment near the bottom.

Overall, the scenarios in some clusters are indicative of situations where agent behavior can be improved, while others highlight situations where the agent behaves optimally (achieves its objectives), thereby denoting additional competency-controlling conditions. Furthermore, we note that the clusters were discovered using solely the interestingness analyses and did not rely on any external information such as game scores or remaining lives.

4.5   Global and Local Analysis of Feature Importance

So far, we have showed how we can use interestingness to better understand how interestingness correlates with agent behavior patterns and how we can cluster traces based on interestingness to identify different sub-tasks within a scenario,

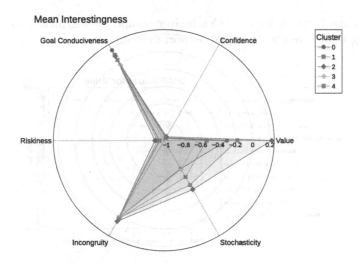

Fig. 6. Interestingness profiles for each trace cluster in the Breakout scenario.

denoting distinct competency-controlling conditions. Feature importance analysis allows us to gain deeper insight into which task elements most affect an agent's competence, how they affect the agent's behavior as measured by interestingness, and where (in which situations) this occurs.

For this analysis we use the SC2 Combat scenario since it is the one where the elements of the task (different buildings, unit types) could affect interestingness the most. To perform feature importance analysis, we first need a set of high-level, interpretable features whose influence on each dimension of analysis we can predict and explain. Given that the pySC2 interface provides semantic but still relatively low-level information, we utilized the high-level SC2 feature extractor described in [40], which provides numeric descriptions for the task elements (types and properties of units, amount and size of forces, etc.) and abstracts the agent's local behavior (movement of groups of units relative to the opponent, the orders assigned to each unit type, etc.).

To identify which features impact each interestingness dimension the most, we used SHapley Additive exPlanations (SHAP) [26]. SHAP values provide explanations by computing the impact of each feature's value on the prediction of a target variable, given a trained predictive model. For ease of analysis and SHAP computation, we used XGBoost (eXtreme Gradient Boosting) machines [5], which minimize the loss iteratively by adding weak learners (in our case, small decision trees) using a gradient-descent-like procedure. We trained regressors from our SC2 numeric high-level features (529 total) to each of the 13 interestingness dimensions using RMSE loss. We used the 1,000 traces sampled from our SC2 agent, randomly selecting 80% of the timesteps to get $\approx 13 \times 10^5$ training instances. By looking at the mean absolute error of the models tested on the remaining 20% of the data, we observed that most models achieve good prediction accuracy except for Goal Conduciveness and Incongruity[13], so we refrain from using these models for feature importance analysis.

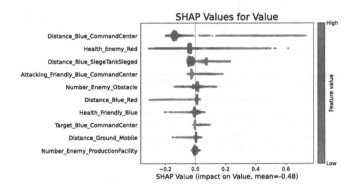

Fig. 7. SHAP density plot for Value. (Color figure online)

Global Interpretation: The goal of the global interpretation of interestingness is to understand how distinct aspects of the task influence interestingness in general. We computed the mean SHAP values for the test set ($\approx 3 \times 10^5$ instances), which provides a good estimate of the features' importance for the prediction of each interestingness variable. As an example, Fig. 7 shows the SHAP density plot for the model of Value for the 10 most predictive features (y-axis). Colored dots represent datapoints (prediction instances), stacked vertically when they have a similar SHAP value for a feature (x-axis). The color represents the corresponding feature's value, from blue (low feature values) to red (high feature values). Together, they represent how much a feature's value contributes to the prediction of Value, relative to the mean Value. As we can see, the top features show that the distance to CC (and enemy in general), the health of both forces, and whether the agent is attacking the CC have the most impact on the predicted magnitude of Value. We also see that when the agent is attacking the CC, the closer it is, the higher the Value; and that the healthier the agent/the weaker the enemy is, the higher the Value.

Local Interpretation: Global interpretation allows us to identify the task elements influencing an agent's task competency the most, indicating possible factors influencing the agent's capabilities and limitations. However, as discussed earlier, a good competency-aware system needs to model the situations one would expect a human operator to be curious about, ones in which a knowledge gap occurs and where further information is needed to make sense of the event [15].

---

[13] Because these dimensions rely on information from multiple timesteps, a more robust model, making use of past information, is likely required to provide good predictions.

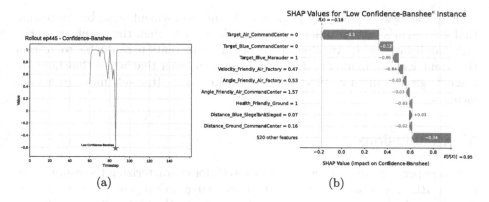

Fig. 8. Local interpretation for a trace with low Confidence in using Banshees: (a) the Confidence in using Banshees throughout the trace; (b) SHAP values for the low Confidence situation.

These provide opportunities for self-explanation, requesting feedback, counterfactual reasoning, etc. As such, we use local interpretation of interestingness to understand particular "key" moments for the agent. Specifically, for each dimension, we identified the timesteps (across all the 1,000 sampled traces) where the interestingness value was significantly different from the average (identified via the interquartile range method). Then, for each situation deemed "abnormal," we computed the SHAP values to identify which task elements might be responsible for the agent's high or low task competency.

Here we illustrate the usefulness of local interpretation with one example. Figure 8a plots the agent's Confidence in using Banshees for one trace, where we observe a sudden drop at around timestep 85. From previous results, we know that the agent is usually highly confident about using Banshees. Watching the episode's replay reveals that this happened when the aerial units stopped targeting the CC and turned away from it (in the direction of the Factory) and the Blue units started targeting the Red Marauders. This information is also reflected in the SHAP values for each feature, as illustrated in the waterfall plot in Fig. 8b, which indicates how the value of the 10 most impactful features (y-axis) contributed to the large deviation of Confidence from the mean (x-axis). This explains why the agent suddenly had low confidence in using the Banshees: even though Banshees usually target the CC alone since they cannot be defeated, here they were "forced" to help the ground units. Although this particular situation may be rare, it may still lead to undesirable consequences, e.g., to the loss of ground units.

By analyzing other examples of (extremely) low Confidence in using Banshees, we noted patterns in the SHAP values of those instances, as well as observed similar scenarios when watching the corresponding replays. In the future, we will automatically identify these patterns e.g., by clustering the outliers based on the SHAP values for a given dimension. Additionally, end-users of our system could use the patterns to recommend alternative courses of action or remedy the agent's policy by guiding it during deployment, *e.g.*, by suggesting that the agent's ground units not engage the enemy when the agent has aerial units at its disposal. An alternative human intervention could be to retrain the agent *e.g.*, by modifying its reward function, such that when Banshees are present, ground units never engage the enemy, or, better yet, move to a safer location.

5   Conclusions

In this paper, we presented a novel framework for characterizing the competence of deep RL agents based on interestingness analysis. Competency assessment is done by analyzing an agent's behavior along seven distinct interestingness dimensions: Value, Confidence, Goal Conduciveness, Incongruity, Riskiness, Stochasticity and Familiarity. Each dimension captures competence along a distinct aspect of the agent's interaction with the environment, making use of internal information by probing the models that are optimized by the algorithm during RL training. Our implementation supports a wide range of deep RL algorithms and is natively compatible with popular RL toolkits.

We conducted a computational study where we trained agents for different game scenarios using different RL algorithms. We applied our framework to each trained agent by extracting interestingness data from traces produced by each agent policy. We then used different methods to analyze the agents' competence based on interestingness. Our results show that different RL agents trained on distinct scenarios leads to different interestingness profiles and that analyzing temporal patterns of interestingness across traces reveals how an agent's behavior correlates with interestingness. In addition, we demonstrated how clustering traces based only on interestingness enables the discovery of distinct behaviors, applied under different competency-controlling conditions. Global interpretation of feature importance shows how we can identify which (and how) task factors affect an agent's competence along each dimension. Finally, local interpretation helps determine the contribution of each task element of a particular scene—identified as having an "abnormal" interestingness value—which allows gaining insights into an agent's limitations, and helps identify measures that might need to be taken to improve its performance.

Our current framework is directed at agent designers who are RL experts by providing a more holistic view of an RL agent's competence, without which it is harder to understand an agent's capabilities and limitations, identify potential barriers for optimal performance, or realize what interventions are needed to help the agent—and its human operators and teammates—achieve their goals. Currently, in addition to exploring ways to make better use of the interpretation mechanisms, we are developing user interfaces to facilitate the use of our competency awareness tool. Namely, since all of our interestingness analyses can be computed online based solely on interaction data collected up to the current timestep, we are exploring ways in which our tools can be used to guide (non-technical) operators during agent deployment, alerting them in situations in which operator-specified conditions or goals would be violated, and requesting their input in order to improve the agent's performance.

Acknowledgements. This material is based upon work supported by the Defense Advanced Research Projects Agency (DARPA) under Contract No. HR001119C0112. Any opinions, findings and conclusions or recommendations expressed in this material are those of the author(s) and do not necessarily reflect the views of the DARPA.

References

1. Amir, O., Doshi-Velez, F., Sarne, D.: Summarizing agent strategies. Auton. Agent. Multi-Agent Syst. **33**(5), 628–644 (2019). https://doi.org/10.1007/s10458-019-09418-w
2. Bellemare, M.G., Naddaf, Y., Veness, J., Bowling, M.: The arcade learning environment: an evaluation platform for general agents. J. Artif. Intell. Res. **47**, 253–279 (2013). https://doi.org/10.1613/jair.3912
3. Bellemare, M.G., Dabney, W., Munos, R.: A distributional perspective on reinforcement learning. In: Precup, D., Teh, Y.W. (eds.) Proceedings of the 34th International Conference on Machine Learning. Proceedings of Machine Learning Research, vol. 70, pp. 449–458. PMLR (2017). https://proceedings.mlr.press/v70/bellemare17a.html
4. Blizzard Entertainment: StarCraft II official game site (2022). https://starcraft2.com. Accessed 23 Aug 2022
5. Chen, T., Guestrin, C.: Xgboost: a scalable tree boosting system. In: Proceedings of the 22nd ACM SIGKDD International Conference on Knowledge Discovery and Data Mining, pp. 785–794. KDD 2016, Association for Computing Machinery, New York, NY, USA (2016). https://doi.org/10.1145/2939672.2939785
6. Chua, K., Calandra, R., McAllister, R., Levine, S.: Deep reinforcement learning in a handful of trials using probabilistic dynamics models. In: Bengio, S., Wallach, H., Larochelle, H., Grauman, K., Cesa-Bianchi, N., Garnett, R. (eds.) Advances in Neural Information Processing Systems, vol. 31. Curran Associates, Inc. (2018). https://proceedings.neurips.cc/paper/2018/file/3de568f8597b94bda53149c7d7f5958c-Paper.pdf
7. Dereszynski, E., Hostetler, J., Fern, A., Dietterich, T., Hoang, T.T., Udarbe, M.: Learning probabilistic behavior models in real-time strategy games. In: Seventh Artificial Intelligence and Interactive Digital Entertainment Conference (2011)
8. Espeholt, L., Marinier, R., Stanczyk, P., Wang, K., Michalski, M.: Seed rl: scalable and efficient deep-RL with accelerated central inference. In: International Conference on Learning Representations (2020). https://openreview.net/forum?id=rkgvXlrKwH
9. Espeholt, L., et al.: Impala: scalable distributed deep-RL with importance weighted actor-learner architectures. In: International Conference on Machine Learning, pp. 1407–1416. PMLR (2018)
10. Fornberg, B.: Generation of finite difference formulas on arbitrarily spaced grids. Math. Comput. (1988). https://doi.org/10.1090/S0025-5718-1988-0935077-0
11. Greydanus, S., Koul, A., Dodge, J., Fern, A.: Visualizing and understanding Atari agents. In: Proceedings of the 35th International Conference on Machine Learning. Proceedings of Machine Learning Research, vol. 80, pp. 1792–1801. PMLR, Stockholmsmässan, Stockholm Sweden (2018)

12. Haarnoja, T., Zhou, A., Abbeel, P., Levine, S.: Soft actor-critic: off-policy maximum entropy deep reinforcement learning with a stochastic actor. In: Dy, J., Krause, A. (eds.) Proceedings of the 35th International Conference on Machine Learning. Proceedings of Machine Learning Research, vol. 80, pp. 1861–1870. PMLR (2018). https://proceedings.mlr.press/v80/haarnoja18b.html

13. Hayes, B., Shah, J.A.: Improving robot controller transparency through autonomous policy explanation. In: 2017 12th ACM/IEEE International Conference on Human-Robot Interaction (HRI), pp. 303–312 (2017)

14. Heuillet, A., Couthouis, F., Díaz-Rodríguez, N.: Explainability in deep reinforcement learning. Knowl. Based Syst. **214**, 106685 (2021). https://doi.org/10.1016/j.knosys.2020.106685

15. Hoffman, R.R., Mueller, S.T., Klein, G., Litman, J.: Metrics for explainable AI: challenges and prospects (2018). https://doi.org/10.48550/ARXIV.1812.04608

16. Hostetler, J., Dereszynski, E., Dietterich, T., Fern, A.: Inferring strategies from limited reconnaissance in real-time strategy games. In: Conference on Uncertainty in Artificial Intelligence (UAI) (2012)

17. Huang, S.H., Bhatia, K., Abbeel, P., Dragan, A.D.: Establishing appropriate trust via critical states. In: 2018 IEEE/RSJ International Conference on Intelligent Robots and Systems (IROS), pp. 3929–3936 (2018). https://doi.org/10.1109/IROS.2018.8593649

18. Huang, S.H., Held, D., Abbeel, P., Dragan, A.D.: Enabling robots to communicate their objectives. Auton. Robot. **43**(2), 309–326 (2019). https://doi.org/10.1007/s10514-018-9771-0

19. Janner, M., Fu, J., Zhang, M., Levine, S.: When to trust your model: model-based policy optimization. In: Wallach, H., Larochelle, H., Beygelzimer, A., d' Alché-Buc, F., Fox, E., Garnett, R. (eds.) Advances in Neural Information Processing Systems, vol. 32. Curran Associates, Inc. (2019). https://proceedings.neurips.cc/paper/2019/file/5faf461eff3099671ad63c6f3f094f7f-Paper.pdf

20. Kaufman, L., Rousseeuw, P.J.: Agglomerative nesting (program agnes). In: Finding Groups in Data: An Introduction to Cluster Analysis, pp. 199–252. Wiley (1990)

21. Kostal, L., Marsalek, P.: Neuronal jitter: can we measure the spike timing dispersion differently? Chin. J. Physiol. **53**(6), 454–464 (2010). https://doi.org/10.4077/cjp.2010.amm031

22. Koul, A., Fern, A., Greydanus, S.: Learning finite state representations of recurrent policy networks. In: International Conference on Learning Representations. ICLR 2019 (2019). https://openreview.net/forum?id=S1gOpsCctm

23. Lage, I., Lifschitz, D., Doshi-Velez, F., Amir, O.: Exploring Computational User Models for Agent Policy Summarization. In: Proceedings of the Twenty-Eighth International Joint Conference on Artificial Intelligence, pp. 1401–1407. International Joint Conferences on Artificial Intelligence Organization, California (2019). https://doi.org/10.24963/ijcai.2019/194

24. Leik, R.K.: A measure of ordinal consensus. Pac. Sociol. Rev. **9**(2), 85–90 (1966). https://doi.org/10.2307/1388242

25. Liang, E., et al.: RLlib: abstractions for distributed reinforcement learning. In: Dy, J., Krause, A. (eds.) Proceedings of the 35th International Conference on Machine Learning. Proceedings of Machine Learning Research, vol. 80, pp. 3053–3062. PMLR (2018). https://proceedings.mlr.press/v80/liang18b.html

26. Lundberg, S.M., Lee, S.I.: A unified approach to interpreting model predictions. In: Guyon, I., Luxburg, U.V., Bengio, S., Wallach, H., Fergus, R., Vishwanathan, S., Garnett, R. (eds.) Advances in Neural Information Processing Systems, vol.

30. Curran Associates, Inc. (2017). https://proceedings.neurips.cc/paper/2017/file/8a20a8621978632d76c43dfd28b67767-Paper.pdf

27. Madumal, P., Miller, T., Sonenberg, L., Vetere, F.: Explainable reinforcement learning through a causal lens. In: Proceedings of the AAAI Conference on Artificial Intelligence, vol. 34, no. 03, pp. 2493–2500 (2020). https://doi.org/10.1609/aaai.v34i03.5631

28. Mnih, V., et al.: Human-level control through deep reinforcement learning. Nature **518**(7540), 529–533 (2015). https://doi.org/10.1038/nature14236

29. Naeem, M., Rizvi, S.T.H., Coronato, A.: A gentle introduction to reinforcement learning and its application in different fields. IEEE Access **8**, 209320–209344 (2020). https://doi.org/10.1109/ACCESS.2020.3038605

30. Olson, M.L., Khanna, R., Neal, L., Li, F., Wong, W.K.: Counterfactual state explanations for reinforcement learning agents via generative deep learning. Artif. Intel. **295**, 103455 (2021). https://doi.org/10.1016/j.artint.2021.103455

31. Berner, C., et al.: Dota 2 with Large Scale Deep Reinforcement Learning (2019). https://doi.org/10.48550/arXiv.1912.06680

32. Pathak, D., Gandhi, D., Gupta, A.: Self-supervised exploration via disagreement. In: Chaudhuri, K., Salakhutdinov, R. (eds.) Proceedings of the 36th International Conference on Machine Learning. Proceedings of Machine Learning Research, vol. 97, pp. 5062–5071. PMLR (2019). https://proceedings.mlr.press/v97/pathak19a.html

33. Pielou, E.: The measurement of diversity in different types of biological collections. J. Theor. Biol. **13**, 131–144 (1966). https://doi.org/10.1016/0022-5193(66)90013-0

34. Puiutta, E., Veith, E.M.S.P.: Explainable reinforcement learning: a survey. In: Holzinger, A., Kieseberg, P., Tjoa, A.M., Weippl, E. (eds.) CD-MAKE 2020. LNCS, vol. 12279, pp. 77–95. Springer, Cham (2020). https://doi.org/10.1007/978-3-030-57321-8_5

35. Puterman, M.L.: Markov Decision Processes: Discrete Stochastic Dynamic Programming, 1st edn. Wiley, New York (1994)

36. Rousseeuw, P.J.: Silhouettes: a graphical aid to the interpretation and validation of cluster analysis. J. Comput. Appl. Math. **20**, 53–65 (1987). https://doi.org/10.1016/0377-0427(87)90125-7

37. Salvador, S., Chan, P.: Toward accurate dynamic time warping in linear time and space. Intel. Data Anal. **11**(5), 561–580 (2007). https://doi.org/10.3233/IDA-2007-11508

38. Schaul, T., Quan, J., Antonoglou, I., Silver, D.: Prioritized experience replay (2015). https://doi.org/10.48550/arxiv.1511.05952

39. Schulman, J., Wolski, F., Dhariwal, P., Radford, A., Klimov, O.: Proximal policy optimization algorithms (2017). https://doi.org/10.48550/arxiv.1707.06347

40. Sequeira, P., Elenius, D., Hostetler, J., Gervasio, M.: A framework for understanding and visualizing strategies of RL agents (2022). https://doi.org/10.48550/arxiv.2208.08552

41. Sequeira, P., Gervasio, M.: Interestingness elements for explainable reinforcement learning: understanding agents' capabilities and limitations. Artif. Intell. **288**, 103367 (2020). https://doi.org/10.1016/j.artint.2020.103367

42. Sequeira, P., Yeh, E., Gervasio, M.: Interestingness elements for explainable reinforcement learning through introspection. In: Joint Proceedings of the ACM IUI 2019 Workshops, p. 7. ACM (2019)

43. Shyam, P., Jaśkowski, W., Gomez, F.: Model-based active exploration. In: Chaudhuri, K., Salakhutdinov, R. (eds.) Proceedings of the 36th International Conference on Machine Learning. Proceedings of Machine Learning Research, vol. 97, pp. 5779–5788. PMLR (2019). https://ngs.mlr.press/v97/shyam19a.html

44. Silver, D., et al.: A general reinforcement learning algorithm that masters chess, shogi, and go through self-play. Science **362**(6419), 1140–1144 (2018). https://doi.org/10.1126/science.aar6404

45. Sutton, R.S., Barto, A.G.: Reinforcement Learning: An Introduction. Adaptive Computation and Machine Learning, 2nd edn. MIT Press, Cambridge (2018)

46. Todorov, E., Erez, T., Tassa, Y.: Mujoco: a physics engine for model-based control. In: 2012 IEEE/RSJ International Conference on Intelligent Robots and Systems, pp. 5026–5033. IEEE (2012). https://doi.org/10.1109/IROS.2012.6386109

47. Vinyals, O., et al.: Grandmaster level in starcraft ii using multi-agent reinforcement learning. Nature **575**(7782), 350–354 (2019). https://doi.org/10.1038/s41586-019-1724-z

48. Vinyals, O., et al.: Starcraft II: a new challenge for reinforcement learning. arXiv preprint arXiv:1708.04782 (2017)

49. van der Waa, J., van Diggelen, J., Bosch, K.V.D., Neerincx, M.: Contrastive explanations for reinforcement learning in terms of expected consequences. In: IJCAI Workshop on Explainable AI, vol. 37, no. 03 arXiv (2018). https://doi.org/10.48550/arxiv.1807.08706

50. Yeh, E., Sequeira, P., Hostetler, J., Gervasio, M.: Outcome-guided counterfactuals for reinforcement learning agents from a jointly trained generative latent space (2022). https://doi.org/10.48550/arxiv.2207.07710

51. Zahavy, T., Ben-Zrihem, N., Mannor, S.: Graying the black box: understanding DQNs. In: Proceedings of The 33rd International Conference on Machine Learning. Proceedings of Machine Learning Research, vol. 48, pp. 1899–1908. PMLR, New York, New York, USA (2016)

The Co-12 Recipe for Evaluating Interpretable Part-Prototype Image Classifiers

Meike Nauta[1]([⊠]) [iD] and Christin Seifert[2,3]([⊠]) [iD]

[1] University of Twente, Enschede, The Netherlands
m.nauta@utwente.nl
[2] University of Duisburg-Essen, Duisburg, Germany
[3] University of Marburg, Marburg, Germany
christin.seifert@uni-marburg.de

Abstract. Interpretable part-prototype models are computer vision models that are explainable by design. The models learn prototypical parts and recognise these components in an image, thereby combining classification and explanation. Despite the recent attention for intrinsically interpretable models, there is no comprehensive overview on evaluating the explanation quality of interpretable part-prototype models. Based on the Co-12 properties for explanation quality as introduced in [42] (e.g., correctness, completeness, compactness), we review existing work that evaluates part-prototype models, reveal research gaps and outline future approaches for evaluation of the explanation quality of part-prototype models. This paper, therefore, contributes to the progression and maturity of this relatively new research field on interpretable part-prototype models. We additionally provide a "Co-12 cheat sheet" that acts as a concise summary of our findings on evaluating part-prototype models.

Keywords: Explainable AI · Interpretability · Evaluation · Prototypes

1 Introduction

The goal of Explainable AI (XAI) is to make the reasoning of a machine learning model accessible to humans, such that users of an AI system can understand the underlying model [2]. Over the last years, many methods and approaches to explain (mostly deep) learning models were proposed [20].

A machine learning model maps an input x to an output $\hat{y}$, and can be described as function $\hat{y} = f(x)$. XAI develops explanation methods e for machine learning models, thus an XAI method represents $e(f(x))$. In the case of intrinsically interpretable models, such as decision trees, e equals the predictive model f since $e(x) = f(x)$. The key aspect of this formalism is that, generally, the user facing output is a combination $e(f)$ of model and explanation. While the community has built a de-facto standard for evaluating machine learning models

© The Author(s), under exclusive license to Springer Nature Switzerland AG 2023
L. Longo (Ed.): xAI 2023, CCIS 1901, pp. 397–420, 2023.
https://doi.org/10.1007/978-3-031-44064-9_21

(e.g., cross-validation, train/validation/test splits, standard evaluation metrics), there is no common agreement on the evaluation of XAI methods [42].

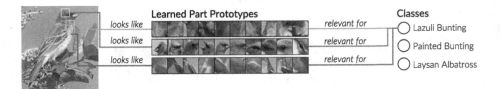

Fig. 1. Part-prototype models learn prototypical parts that can be visualised as image patches. The decision layer learns which prototypes are relevant for which classes. Classification depends on the presence of part-prototypes in an input image.

A promising type of interpretable-by-design models are part-prototype models, which base their reasoning on the recognition-by-components theory [3]. Specifically, part-prototype models use deep neural networks to learn semantically meaningful components (*prototypical parts*), without relying on additional part annotations. Subsequently, an image is classified by automatically testing whether patches in an input image look similar to a learned prototypical part. Thus, the presence or absence of specific parts in the image determines the decision process, as visualised in Fig. 1. Part-prototype models are globally interpretable since the learned part-prototypes can be visualised as image patches, and their decision layer is an interpretable model linking prototypes to classes, such as a decision tree [43] or linear layer [8,41]. Apart from their development using benchmark data, part-prototype models are applied in the medical domain, e.g., on X-rays [53], MRI-scans [37], mammograms [7,57] or CT-scans [52].

The majority of XAI evaluation methods are designed for explanation types produced by post-hoc XAI methods, which separate e from f, such as heatmaps and feature importance scores [42]. In contrast, there is little work on evaluating interpretable-by-design models where $e = f$, as also observed by [31].

In this paper, we collected work that evaluates interpretable part-prototype models and summarise its findings. Moreover, we outline future approaches for evaluating the explanation quality of part-prototype models. For a comprehensive view on the quality of an explanation (method), we organise the existing and suggested evaluation methods for part-prototype models per Co-12 property as introduced in [42] and outlined in Table 1. The Co-12 properties are a high-level decomposition of explanation quality, including Correctness and Compactness. By addressing the Co-12 properties individually, we identify research gaps and we conceptualise how the Co-12 properties can be put in practice for a thorough evaluation of interpretable image classifiers based on prototypical parts, including ProtoPNet [8], ProtoTree [43], ProtoPShare [50], ProtoPool [49], TesNet [58], ProtoPFormer [62] and PIP-Net [41]. We provide an overview of existing methods to evaluate part-prototype models and hope that our identification of future research opportunities serves as a 'recipe' for further evaluation.

Table 1. Summary of the Co-12 explanation quality properties [42].

Property	Describes ...
CONTENT	
Correctness	how faithful the explanation is w.r.t. prediction model
Completeness	how much of the model behaviour is described in the explanation
Consistency	how deterministic and implementation-invariant the explanation method is
Continuity	how continuous and generalisable the explanation is
Contrastivity	how discriminative the explanation is w.r.t. other events
Covariate complexity	how complex the (interactions between) features in the explanation are
PRESENTATION	
Compactness	the size of the explanation
Composition	the presentation and organisation of the explanation
Confidence	the presence and accuracy of probability information in the explanation
USER	
Context	how relevant the explanation is to the user
Coherence	how accordant the explanation is with prior knowledge and beliefs
Controllability	how interactive or controllable the explanation is

Paper Outline: In the following, we review each Co-12 evaluation property in the order of Table 1. We dedicate one section to each property, starting with a general description, reviewing related work w.r.t. this property and finally derive evaluation recommendations. We discuss the evaluation of part-prototype models from a broader perspective in Sect. 3 and conclude our work in Sect. 4.

2   Evaluating Co-12 Properties

In this section, we discuss the Co-12 properties, review related work for each property and provide recommendations towards a more comprehensive evaluation of interpretable part-prototype models. Table 2 supports readers by providing a "Co-12 cheat sheet" that acts as a concise summary of our findings on evaluating part-prototype models.

2.1   Correctness

Part-prototype models are interpretable by design: explanation method e is incorporated in predictive model f. Since a part-prototype model is simultaneously making predictions *and* providing explanations, the correctness of the reasoning process is fulfilled by design. The only part of the explanation that is not guaranteed to be faithful to f is the prototype visualisation for converting

Table 2. "Cheat sheet" for evaluating part-prototype models along Co-12 properties.

Property	Evaluation Approaches
CONTENT	
Correctness $f \stackrel{?}{=} e$	– Classification process of part-prototype models is correct by design since $f(x) = e(x)$ – Evaluate prototype visualisation with synthetic data or incremental deletion/addition of image patches
Completeness	– Output-complete by design – Evaluate human-output-completeness with simulatibility user studies
Consistency $e = e$	– Implementation invariance and nondeterminism
Continuity $e \approx e$	– Stability for slight variations
Contrastivity $e \leftrightarrow e'$	– Contrastive by design; can answer counterfactual questions – Pragmatism and compactness for optimal contrastive explanation – Target-sensitivity for location of prototypes – Target-discriminativeness to evaluate prototypes
Covariate complexity	– Prototype homogeneity / purity with annotated data – Perceived homogeneity with user studies (subjective) – Intruder detection for objective homogeneity evaluation
PRESENTATION	
Compactness	– Number of prototypes (local & global) – Number of unique prototypes (redundancy)
Composition	– Compare different explanation formats with the same content – User study on how to present part-prototypes – User study on classification format (e.g. linear layer or decision tree)
Confidence	– Reliability of classification confidence – Reliability of explanation confidence – Out-of-distribution detection confidence
USER	
Context	– User studies (lab and field)
Coherence	– Anecdotal evidence by visualising reasoning with prototypes – Alignment with domain knowledge from annotated data – Subjective satisfaction with user studies
Controllability	– GUI for interactive and personalised explanations – Explanatory debugging to manipulate prototypes and model's reasoning

latent representations to visual natural image patches. To evaluate the correctness of the visualisation in part-prototype models, one could apply a *controlled synthetic data check* [35, 42] where the discriminative features are known a-priori. If one can safely assume that the model is following a particular reasoning (e.g. when the classifier has near-perfect accuracy), it can be checked whether the prototypes reveal the ground-truth important features. Additionally, correctness can be evaluated with *single deletion* where one important image patch or set of pixels is removed, or *incremental deletion* or *addition*, where image pixels or patches are removed one by one. Correct prototype importance scores should result in an Area under the Deletion Curve (AUDC) that is lower than an AUDC for random rankings. With incremental *addition*, image pixels or patches are added one by one to an initially empty image based on their similarity with a prototype. When starting with the image patch with the highest similarity to a prototype, only one image patch could already be sufficient to activate that prototype and therefore influence the reasoning of the model.

Related Work. Yeh et al. [64] applied the controlled synthetic data check by constructing a set of synthetic images with coloured shapes, and only a few of those shapes were relevant for the ground-truth class. Since their interpretable concept-based classifier obtained near-perfect accuracy, it could be safely assumed that the model had learned the intended reasoning, such that it could be evaluated whether those discriminative shapes are indeed included in the explanation. Similarly, Gautam et al. [15] added a yellow square to images to evaluate whether prototypes reveal the added artefact.

Xu-Darme et al. [61] applied the incremental deletion metric to ProtoTree [43] and ProtoPNet [8]. They find that the AUDC is decreasing when more pixels are removed, and that the decline is steeper for the improved visualisation method Prototypical Relevance Propagation (PRP) [15], hence confirming the faithfulness of part-prototype explanations. Compared to ProtoPNet, the AUDC drops slower for ProtoTree, and the authors hypothesise that this could be explained by the fact that ProtoTree shares prototypes between classes and therefore focuses less on small details [61]. Gautam et al. [15] perform the incremental addition test for ProtoPNet, starting from a random image and incrementally adding the most relevant pixels for a prototype. They find that similarity scores for a prototype indeed increase after adding more pixels, and that their improved visualisation approach, called PRP [15], results in a steeper slope, implying that fewer pixels are needed to obtain a certain similarity score and that the visualisation with PRP is more faithful to the model's reasoning.

Recommendations. Although part-prototype models are interpretable by design, the correctness of approaches for *visualising* part-prototypes can be further evaluated. In addition to the original visualisation approach with bicubic upsampling, we recommend to evaluate new methods, such as the recently introduced PRP method [15] for more precise localisation of prototypical parts. Controlled Synthetic Data Checks could be performed to evaluate the correctness of the visualised prototypes. In addition to simplistic synthetic data, more advanced datasets can be used for this purpose, such as Animals with Attribute [34], BAM [63], NICO [24] and a recent set of synthetic benchmarks for XAI [35]. Evaluating with synthetic data checks may in turn lead to further insights for improving prototype visualisation.

We also recommend to apply existing deletion and addition methodology, usually applied to heatmaps, to part-prototype models. Important here is to take the specific nature of part-prototype models into account. Features in prototype explanations are not single pixels, but rather object parts that can occur more than once in an image. For instance, a prototype that represents a car tyre will still be detected when only one of four tyres is masked. Therefore, not only the image pixel/patch with the highest similarity score to the prototype should be removed or perturbed, but *all* pixels/patches with a sufficiently high similarity score to that particular prototype. Additionally, an often-raised criticism for deletion methods is that naively removing or perturbing image pixels in an input image could lead to out-of-distribution (OoD) data. Moreover, it was found that the *shape* of a mask could leak class information to the model [47,60]. Various approaches are recently presented to circumvent these OoD and shape-leakage issues, e.g. [23,47], and we encourage the research community to adapt and apply these improved evaluation methods to part-prototype models.

2.2 Completeness

Completeness describes how much of the black box behaviour is described in the explanation. We can distinguish between *reasoning*-completeness, which is generally not quantified but rather a property of the model, and *output*-completeness. Reasoning-completeness indicates the extent to which the explanation describes the entire *internal* workings of the model. Part-prototype models transparently show the relation between prototypes and classes, but intentionally abstract away all matrix multiplications and other calculations of the neural network backbone by showing prototypical parts. Output-completeness addresses the extent to which the explanation covers the output of a predictive model f. Evaluating output-completeness is highly relevant for post-hoc explanation methods where explanation method e is applied to a trained model f, as it measures whether the explanation is sufficient for explaining the output of model f. Instead, prototypical part models are designed to be intrinsically interpretable, such that $e = f$, implying that output-completeness is fulfilled by design.

One could also evaluate *human*-output-completeness with the *forward simulatability* evaluation method [42], which measures whether a user can simulate the model's reasoning by letting the user predict the model's output based on the input and the explanation. A human-output-complete explanation with understandable prototypes should be sufficient for a user to follow the model's reasoning and hence end up with the same prediction. Also the *counterfactual simulatability* can be measured [12], where the user is given the input, explanation and output, after which the user should predict what the model will output for a perturbed version of the initial input.

Related Work. Hase & Bansal [22] evaluated the forward and counterfactual simulatability of a prototype model for text and tabular data, and found that prototype models are effective in counterfactual simulation tests. Although the prototypes were full data samples rather than prototypical *parts*, and not evaluated on image data, their result is promising and a motivation for further studies on human-output-completeness of part-prototype models. Kim et al. [31] evaluated the forward simulatability of part-prototypes (ProtoTree and ProtoPNet) and heatmaps (BagNet [5] and GradCAM [51]). They conclude that participants have difficulties in predicting the model's output based on the explanations, as participants predict between 43% (for ProtoTree) to 48% (for GradCAM) of the outputs correctly when the model predicted the correct class label, and 33% (BagNet and ProtoTree) to 36% (GradCAM) when the model was incorrect.

Recommendations. Model-output-completeness is fulfilled by design in part-prototype models. Simulatability studies for measuring human-output-completeness is related to other Co-12 properties such as Correctness, Covariate complexity and Coherence. We think that the forward simulatability performance for part-prototype models can be improved by addressing other Co-12 properties. Specifically, improving the Correctness of the visualisation (e.g. by applying recently introduced visualisation methods that locate prototypes more precisely [15,61]) and the Covariate complexity of the visualised prototypes, such as showing multiple image patches rather than one (c.f. Sect. 2.6) can have a positive impact on human-output-completeness.

2.3 Consistency

Consistency addresses the idea that identical inputs should have identical explanations and that explanations should be implementation invariant. Where most XAI publications already report predictive performance across multiple runs, this property focuses on the consistency of *explanations*. Existing part-prototype models are in principle deterministic as there is no source of randomness built into their design. At test time, identical images should thus result in identical explanations. However, even though part-prototype models do not have intentionally added random components in their designs, nondeterminism can still occur from their neural network backbones, such as model initialisation and random seeds. The evaluation method *implementation invariance* quantifies consistency in more detail, in order to analyse experiment repeatability [38,42].

Related Work. The implementation invariance of explanations from part-prototype models can be evaluated by comparing explanations from models trained with different initialisations or with a different shuffling of the training data. For example, the latent distances of prototypes in ProtoTree [43] are evaluated across different runs. [49] specifically analysed for ProtoPool the distribution of how prototypes are shared between classes and reported negligible differences between different runs.

Recommendations. Implementation invariance is not only important for explanation consistency, but also for experiment replicability in order to fairly validate part-prototype models and to be able to quantify improvements of new methods. While the most salient factors of nondeterminism are model initialisation and random seeds, it is important to be aware of other sources of randomness, including data augmentation, shuffling of training data, dropout, batch normalisation, tooling and hardware [55,66]. [66] report for standard neural networks that top-line evaluation metrics as top1-accuracy are not much impacted by randomness, but that models are far more sensitive on certain parts of the data distribution. For future work, we think it would be interesting to quantify to what extent classification decisions and explanations are influenced by nondeterminism in part-prototype models, taking inspiration from existing experiments on nondeterminism and randomness [55,66]. Additionally, a comparison can be made between the implementation invariance of standard black box classifiers and interpretable part-prototype models. Lastly, we would like to emphasise that most of the nondeterminism can be eliminated with the right code implementations, although with potentially significant overhead [66]. Ensuring Consistency will therefore be a trade-off with computation speed and resources, and may depend on the criticality of the application.

2.4   Continuity

Continuity describes how continuous and generalisable the explanation function is, targeting that similar inputs should have similar explanations. For part-prototype models, *stability for slight variations* [42] is relevant, as it quantifies whether slightly perturbed inputs lead to the same explanation, given that the model makes the same classification. Such stability is especially relevant for generalisability, as input data might be collected from different data sources with slightly different image characteristics [26].

Related Work. The evaluation method *stability for slight variations* was implemented by [26] with image compression and adding adversarial human-imperceptible noise to images, after which they found that ProtoPNet [8] assigns drastically lower similarity scores to prototypes for these perturbed images. They conclude that there is a semantic gap between ProtoPNet's understanding of similarity (in latent space) and that of humans (in input space). To address this shortcoming, Hoffmann et al. [26] found that the continuity of ProtoPNet can be improved with adversarial training and data augmentation, albeit at the cost of classification accuracy. Adding a regularisation mechanism to ProtoPNet can also improve its robustness to adversarial attacks [39]. The "transformation invariance" of ProtoTree and ProtoPNet is evaluated in [54], arguing that prototypes should capture a semantic meaningful concept "irrespective of their variability in scale, translation, or rotation angle across different samples". They evaluated transformation invariance by forwarding a cropped or rotated test image through the prototype model and analysing whether similar prototypes are found. They found that ProtoPNet detects different prototypes, even from different classes, in the transformed test sample, whereas the prototypes and hence the decision path in ProtoTree did not change after the transformation, "indicating ProtoTree to be more robust to image transformations than ProtoPNet" [54]. Rymarczyk et al. [50] evaluated ProtoPNet's and their ProtoPShare model's resistance to perturbations by modifying brightness, contrast, saturation, hue and perspective of images. They found that the accuracy of both models decreases only slightly for large perturbations.

PIP-Net incorporates continuity already *during* training with its contrastive learning of prototypes. PIP-Net is optimised to assign the same prototype similarity scores to two augmented views of the same image. As such, human perception of similarity is indirectly encoded in the data augmentation, and thus in the training process. Also noise and image compression as used by [26] can be included in PIP-Net's data augmentation.

Recommendations. Continuity of predictive models is important to ensure their robustness and generalisability. It also contributes to the predictability of explanations and may in turn influence the user's trust in part-prototype models. Recent work has shown that the continuity of prototype-based explanations can be improved with extended data augmentation and adversarial training, and we therefore recommend to include image variations that might occur in the intended application in the training process of part-prototype models. Since adversarial attacks and defence mechanisms are an active research area [36], we also support further research that would investigate whether more advanced adversarial defence methods can be incorporated in the training process of part-prototype models. Follow-up research could then analyse whether prototype-based models are more continuous and robust than standard black box classifiers.

2.5   Contrastivity

Contrastivity describes how discriminative the explanation is with respect to other events or targets, and contrastive explanations help to answer counterfactual questions as "why not?" and "what if?". The *target sensitivity* evaluation method captures that explanations should differ between classes and is mostly evaluated for heatmaps [42], since a heatmap for one class should be different from a heatmap that explains another class [1,48]. Part-prototype models have their interpretability incorporated into their prediction model, so the local explanation is by design output-complete (c.f. Sect. 2.2). As a result, a different classification corresponds to a different reasoning and hence to a different explanation. Contrastivity is thus by design incorporated in part-prototype models.

Related Work. Sinhamahapatra et al. [54] evaluated *subjective* target discriminativeness with a small-scale user study by analysing whether users could guess the class that a set of prototypes belongs to. The class prediction accuracy for ProtoPNet was higher than ProtoTree (98% vs 55%), which is, as the authors also note, expected since ProtoPNet learns class-specific prototypes, whereas

ProtoTree's prototypes are shared between classes such that the set of proto-types on one decision path will not necessarily correspond to a single class [54]. Goyal et al. [19] specifically developed an approach for answering counterfactual questions by generating images in which a specific region is adapted such that the model's classification is changed. Whereas they do an exhaustive search to find the best counterfactual spatial region, we think that the prototypical parts learned by part-prototype models inherently provide the model's discriminative regions. They report that presenting counterfactual visualisations in *addition* to representative training samples helps teaching users in classification tasks [19].

Recommendations. Contrastivity is inherently incorporated in part-prototype models. But rather than looking at *which* prototypes are found in an input image, we see a research opportunity to also evaluate target-sensitivity by analysing *where* prototypes are detected. For perfect target sensitivity, a part-prototype model should find different prototypes at different locations in the test image. E.g., a prototype of a bird's red beak should be detected at a different location than a prototype of a long tail. A fruitful idea for future work would be to anal-yse to what extent evidence for one prototype is found at a different location in a test image than evidence for another prototype, averaged over all images in a test set. Additionally, contrastivity can be measured with the *target dis-criminativeness* method, which captures whether another, external model can predict the right class label from the explanation. It was found that this method is mostly applied to generative explanation methods that produce for example text or synthesised images [42]. We see multiple ways to automatically quantify the target discriminativeness of prototypes visualised as image patches. The sim-ilarity scores per prototype can be organised in a tabular format, and provided as input to standard machine learning algorithms, such as linear classifiers. A high classification accuracy of the external model would indicate that the prototype similarity scores contain relevant discriminative information about the target. Alternatively, the prototype image patches can be provided to an external neu-ral network, after which the deep classifier should be able to predict either the right prototype or the right class label. Interestingly, if the external classifier finds that a prototype is not discriminative for the target, it might be an indication that the prototype is also unnecessary in the part-prototype model. Removing it from the part-prototype model might then improve the compactness of the explanation, potentially without hurting predictive performance.

Lastly, the built-in contrastivity also allows to answer counterfactual ques-tions by identifying which prototypes should have been present or absent in an image for a different decision. E.g., a user can follow a decision path in ProtoTree bottom-up, starting at the actual class leaf, and find the crucial node that would have led to ending up in a different leaf and hence a different classification. Given the promising results of counterfactuals in a previous user study [19], we encour-age further experiments that use part-prototype models to generate counterfac-tual explanations. Since there are usually different counterfactual explanations available, the cost or size of the counterfactual change can be considered, as quantified by e.g. *pragmatism* and *counterfactual compactness* [42].

2.6 Covariate Complexity

Covariate complexity describes how complex it is for users to understand the features in an explanation. In part-prototype models, the prototypical parts visualised as image patches are the explanation covariates. Quantifying the complexity or understandability of these visual features requires evaluation with human subjects, or relying on automated evaluation based on annotations made by humans. The main approach for evaluating the covariate complexity of prototypes is to evaluate their *homogeneity*, which indicates how consistently a prototype represents a human-interpretable concept. In part-prototype models, a prototype ideally only gets high similarity scores for one semantically meaningful concept. Hence, the purity of the cluster with all image patches that have a high similarity with a particular prototype should be high. Lakkaraju and Leskovec [33] also aim for what they call "inverse purity", meaning that ideally all image patches that encode a particular meaningful concept are in one cluster, indicating the cluster's completeness. These terms were introduced for evaluating clusters for time series data, where a prototype was defined as a representative data point for a cluster [33], but we think that the purity and inverse purity metrics are also applicable to clusters with image patches. Evaluation will require a ground-truth, either provided by human judgements (*perceived homogeneity*) or with annotations, such as predefined concepts [14] or object part annotations.

Applying the *intruder detection* evaluation method to prototype visualisations would be a more objective evaluation of perceived homogeneity. In this user study, participants are shown a set of image patches that all, except one, have a high similarity to one particular prototype. If a prototype is homogeneous and interpretable, participants should be able to discover the odd one out.

Related Work. Borowski et al. [4] found that exemplary natural images are more informative than generated synthetic images for predicting CNN activations, both for lay and expert participants [4]. Additionally, participants were also faster and more confident for natural images. Their results are already a promising indication that image patches are understandable to humans. Sinhamahapatra et al. [54] evaluate with manual inspection how well learned part-prototypes of ProtoTree and ProtoPNet correspond to a "distinct human-relevant entity". They confirm earlier findings [43] that prototypes in the top layers of the tree can be difficult to interpret as they are shared between many classes [54]. For ProtoPNet, they report that understanding the meaning of a single image patch can be difficult, but that the context where prototypes are located improves the understanding. The method from [40] addresses these ambiguities and can clarify the meaning of a prototype by quantifying the influence of colour hue, shape, texture, contrast and saturation. Such an additional explanation of what the prototype represents can thus reduce covariate complexity.

To quantify covariate complexity, the purity of PIP-Net's prototypes can be measured by calculating whether the same ground-truth object part is shown in a prototype's top-10 most similar image patches, reporting a purity of up to 93% for the CUB birds dataset [41]. Ghorbani et al. [16] instead did an intruder detection experiment with human subjects for evaluating the coherency of learned visual concepts, and found that 97% to 99% of the provided answers were correct. They also asked participants to describe a set of image segments, representing a learned *concept*, with one word and evaluated how many participants provided the same word. They found that 56% of the participants described the concept with the most frequent word and its synonyms, and therefore concluded that the learned concepts are semantically and verbally meaningful to humans. Das et al. [11] asked participants to select one out of six image patches that best explains an image and its class label. They then compared to users' selections with their ProtoPFormer's model selections and found that most of the post-hoc prototypes generated by their surrogate model are in line with human preferences, thereby concluding that their prototypes are human understandable [11].

Recommendations. Measuring covariate complexity with annotated data is more accessible and scalable than doing user studies. Although we think that measuring the correspondence of prototypical parts with ground-truth annotations (e.g. object parts) is valuable, it is important to be aware of its limitations. A meaningful prototype may not correspond to an annotated concept in the dataset, but could still have a semantic meaning, such as representing a particular colour, texture or shape. Hence, these automated purity metrics relate closely to the Coherence property (Sect. 2.11). User studies or manual visual inspection could complement automated evaluation. For example, intruder detection experiments can be organised. The high detection accuracy in the user study by [16] confirm that their shown image segments were coherent to humans, but also indicate that an intruder detection experiment might be too straightforward. We see possibilities to make the evaluation more insightful by showing e.g. image patches with a lower but still sufficiently high similarity score for a prototype, or by showing an intruder that has a low but non-zero similarity to the prototype. Such experiments will give more insights into the perceived 'decision boundaries' of humans regarding visual similarity and prototype complexity.

2.7   Compactness

Compactness describes the size of the explanation since an explanation should not overwhelm the user. For prototypical part models, compactness is usually evaluated by counting the number of prototypes. E.g. ProtoTree [43] and ProtoPool [49] have roughly 10× fewer prototypes than ProtoPNet. It is important to distinguish between the number of prototypes in a *local* and *global* explanation. The global explanation shows the full classification model, while the local explanation shows the model's reasoning for a particular input image. A local explanation of a part-prototype model is thus always a subset of the global explanation. E.g., a local explanation in ProtoTree is a particular path in the tree and hence substantially reduces explanation size compared to showing the whole tree. The most suitable explanation size can depend on the user and the intended task. E.g., Kim et al. [31] only showed the last two prototypes in a decision path of ProtoTree to its participants in a user study, to reduce their cognitive workload. In addition to measure the size of the explanation, also *redundancy* of the explanation can be evaluated [42]. For part-prototype models, it is desired that prototypes complement each other and are not redundant.

Related Work. Sinhamahapatra et al. [54] manually evaluate the redundancy between prototypes and they argue that prototypes should be "semantically disentangled", meaning that "each prototype should represent distinctly different semantic units". They evaluate this disentanglement with a manual visual inspection of the prototypes, and find that ProtoPNet contains many redundant prototypes, whereas ProtoTree avoids redundancy due to the substantially lower number of prototypes, resulting in prototypes that are "quite semantically disentangled over the whole dataset" [54]. This is in line with other findings, which quantified that over 200 prototypes in ProtoPNet are identical or visually similar [40]. ProtoPFormer [62] and PIP-Net [41] explicitly optimise for the diversity between prototypical parts in order to prevent redundancy.

Recommendations. Compact explanations are desired, although the optimal size may depend on the number of discriminative features needed for the classification task, and the cognitive load and time availability of the user. However, evaluating compactness alone would be insufficient for quantifying explanation quality, since also the interpretability of the prototypes should be taken into account. Consider the simple example where a classifier should detect whether there is a 'sun or dog' present in the image [41]. The resulting classifier could theoretically contain a single prototype that encodes both the sun *and* the dog. Such a model would score high in terms of compactness, but the prototypes do not encode clear, unambiguous semantically meaningful concepts and would therefore conflict with the Coherence property. Rather, a model with two prototypes (one for sun and one for dog) would be easier to understand. This example hence motivates again that explainability is a multi-faceted property that should be evaluated from multiple dimensions.

2.8 Composition

Composition evaluates the presentation format and organisation of the explanation, and focuses on *how* something is explained rather than *what* is explained. Composition can be evaluated by comparing different explanation formats with the same content, or by asking users about their preferences regarding the presentation and structure of the explanation.

Related Work. The comprehensibility of decision tables, trees and rule-based models was compared by [27], and Jeyakumar et al. [29] did a large-scale user study to determine which explanation style users prefer for understanding DNN model decisions. Although they did not evaluate *part*-prototype models, they compared heatmaps and feature importance methods with an explanation method that presents full data samples from the dataset as representative samples [29]. They found that this explanation-by-example style was most preferred for image classification, which is a promising result for part-prototype models. Also Kim et al. [31] evaluated explanation forms and compared part-prototypes from ProtoTree [43] and ProtoPNet [8] with heatmaps from GradCAM [51] and BagNet [5]. They found that participants self-rated their level of understanding similarly, between 3 (fair) and 4 (good), for both explanation formats.

Recommendations. In addition to comparing explanation styles, future research could study how part-prototypes can be best presented to the user. For ProtoPNet, it was reported that a 'standalone' prototype, visualised as a single image patch, can be difficult to interpret [54]. Instead, PIP-Net [41] visualises a prototype as a set of multiple image patches. In addition to assessing the most suitable composition for visualising a part-prototype, a future study could analyse how these prototypes can be best structured and included in the reasoning process. For part-prototype models, we can distinguish between a fully-connected linear layer of prototypes as used in ProtoPNet, a sparse linear layer in PIP-Net and a decision tree with prototypes as in ProtoTree. A future research question would be which format a user prefers when the part-prototypes are the same.

2.9 Confidence

Confidence describes whether there is probability information in the explanation regarding the confidence or uncertainty of the explanation or model output. The confidence property is mostly a tick mark indicating whether the predictive model and/or the explanation provide confidence estimates. The accuracy and reliability of these confidence/uncertainty estimates can be evaluated by comparing with random confidence estimates, and by calculating the correlation with feature deletion metrics [42].

Related Work. Most part-prototype models are trained with softmax and cross-entropy loss, such that the model's classification confidence can be reported. E.g., ProtoPNet [8] and ProtoPShare [50] use softmax to normalise raw output logits to probabilities, and ProtoTree [43] applies softmax for the class distributions in the leaves. Instead, PIP-Net [41] does not provide classification probabilities at inference, but rather generates unnormalised scores.

Recommendations. We recommend to distinguish between *classification* confidence, *explanation* confidence, and *out-of-distribution detection* confidence, which can all be evaluated in future work. Softmax is known to provide over-confident class probabilities [21], motivating a future study that analyses the reliability of a model's classification probabilities. Additionally, it would be relevant to extract *explanation* confidence that indicates how confident the explanation generation method is, e.g. of the similarity calculation or visualisation process. Prototype similarity scores may reveal information about the model's uncertainty, and we are in favour of further research that would investigate whether explicit explanation confidence values can be generated *in addition* to classification confidence. A user would then get a deeper understanding of the model's uncertainty, and can take over automated decisions when the model is not confident enough.

Additionally, softmax probabilities can fail to decrease for input data that is far from the training distribution [46]. We therefore expect that most part-prototype models will be overconfident for out-of-distribution (OoD) data, which should be assessed by a future study. Instead, PIP-Net [41] does not provide classification probabilities and is specifically designed to handle OoD data by using a scoring-sheet reasoning and outputting near-zero scores for OoD images. Other models with scoring-sheet reasoning, such as ProtoPNet and ProtoP-Share [50], normalise output logits with softmax and will therefore not be able to detect OoD data and accurately generate confidence estimates. However, we hypothesise that the scale of the raw output scores might be an indication of the model's classification confidence. Tree-shaped reasoning such as ProtoTree might be more problematic, since an OoD image provided to ProtoTree will be classified according to the most-left leaf when no prototype was found in the image. A 'quick fix' might be to make the most-left leaf untrainable such that the model abstains from classifying images in that leaf. However, we think more suitable approaches to let part-prototype trees deal with OoD data and provide precise uncertainty estimates would be possible. Concluding, further research should investigate the reliability of different confidence outputs, and analyse to what extent part-prototype models can handle OoD data. We are convinced that reliable uncertainty estimates will contribute to more intuitive and trustworthy explanations.

2.10   Context

Context addresses the extent to which the user and their needs are taken into account for comprehensible explanations that are relevant to the user's needs and level of expertise. Most evaluation methods are quantitative and do not consider the end-user in their relevant context [42]. Quoting Colin et al. [10]: "it is not yet clear (1) how useful current explainability methods are in real-world scenarios; and (2) whether current performance metrics accurately reflect the usefulness of explanation methods for the end user". Evaluation approaches addressing the Context property are therefore highly relevant for "application-grounded" [12] evaluation, especially since different types of users may have different perceptions and explanatory values [13].

Related Work. Colin et al. [10] conducted psychophysics experiments to evaluate the usefulness of heatmaps in multiple real-world scenarios and found that heatmaps can help end-users in detecting biases and identifying a model's classification strategy but are not helpful for understanding failures. In a user study with 15 participants on usefulness of prototypes learned by ProtoTree and ProtoPNet, it was found that only 20% of the prototypes of ProtoTree and 27% of the prototypes of ProtoPNet were found totally useful for identifying the class [54]. Kim et al. [31] performed a more objective user study (50 participants per experiment) to evaluate the usefulness and practical effectiveness of visual explanations, including ProtoTree and ProtoPNet, in AI-assisted decision making. Concretely, they investigated how useful explanations are for detecting whether a model's prediction is correct, and found that participants score above the random baseline but are far from the perfect score, indicating room for improvement. Participants were however lay crowdworkers, and evaluating with domain experts or end-users in a real-world application was left for future work. Nguyen et al. [44] did a user study to evaluate whether explanations can successfully assist users with image classification and model debugging, and compared heatmaps with showing nearest training-set examples. They found that AI-experts performed substantially better with nearest neighbour explanations than heatmaps, which is a promising result for part-prototype image patches.

Recommendations. We identify research opportunities to evaluate part-prototype models with application-grounded user studies, similar to evaluation with heatmaps [10]. These evaluations can be subjective or objectively measured. An often applied evaluation method is to ask users to self-rate explanations on properties as usefulness, trust and relevance [42]. However, cognitive biases and response biases often lead to discrepancies between self-reported results and findings from behavioural experiments [59], and this has also been observed in the context of XAI. E.g., Hase and Bansal [22] collected subjective ratings for the quality of explanations from a prototype model for text and tabular data, and found that participant's ratings were not predictive for their performance on forward or counterfactual simulatability tasks. Moreover, Kim et al. [31] warn for a *confirmation bias* where participants prefer a model with explanations over a model without explanations, and tend to believe that a model's prediction is correct when explanations are provided. Also [30] found that the existence of explanation can already lead to over-trust, although user's trust after showing explanations may depend on the accuracy of the predictive model [45]. Results from a user study should therefore be carefully interpreted, and ideally these risks are already taken into account when setting up the study design.

2.11   Coherence

Coherence describes how coherent the explanation is with prior knowledge and beliefs, and addresses the plausibility or reasonableness of explanations to users. Coherence is often evaluated with anecdotal evidence by visualising example prototypes, as done by e.g. ProtoTree [43], PIP-Net [41], ProtoPNet [8] and ProtoPool [49]. For a more objective evaluation, annotated data can be used to automatically evaluate how well prototypes align with domain knowledge.

Related Work. Goyal et al. [18] calculated how often discriminative regions in counterfactual visual explanations lie near object part keypoints, and concluded that the selected counterfactual image patches are often "semantically meaningful". Similarly, the purity of prototypes in PIP-Net [41] is evaluated by calculating the overlap between prototypical image patches and object part annotations. Xu-Darme et al. [61] did not evaluate with prototypical *parts* but rather measured the intersection of prototypical image patches with the segmentation of the main object. They find that the original visualisation method of ProtoPNet and ProtoTree (bicubic upsampling) results in 35% of the prototypes in ProtoTree not having overlap with a bird object segmentation mask[1]. However, when applying the new PRP visualisation method [15], only 0.5% of ProtoTree's prototypes do not have any overlap, outperforming ProtoPNet. Rather than only evaluating how well prototypes align with a certain object, prototypes can be constrained to concentrate on foreground patches [62], to optimise for Coherence and Covariate Complexity directly. However, these automated evaluation methods for calculating the correspondence with data annotations have been shown to correlate poorly with participant's behaviour in user studies [10,31,44]. For example, Kim et al. [31] found near zero correlation between the localisation quality of heatmaps and participant's confidence in forward simulatability experiments. These discrepancies again underline the importance of evaluating explanation quality from multiple dimensions and complementing automated evaluation with application-grounded evaluation with user studies.

ProtoTree and ProtoPNet were also applied on a synthetic dataset to *manually* evaluate whether the model's reasoning was similar to human logic [54]. One of their findings is that ProtoTree classifies a class based on *absence* of prototypes, which can be different from a human's classification process. Rymarczyk et al. [49] asked participants how certain they were that a prototypical image patch was discriminative for classifying a given object. We emphasise that such questions do not evaluate the correctness of the model's reasoning, but only quantify whether the shown image patches are in line with expectations and prior knowledge of the participants. They reported that users found prototypes from their ProtoPool method (including their "focal similarity") often more distinctive than prototypes from ProtoTree [49].

Recommendations. Prototypes are often evaluated based on anecdotal evidence, with automated evaluation with an annotated dataset, or with manual evaluation. Other quantitative evaluation methods with user studies would be to measure *subjective satisfaction* and *subjective comparison*, where participants

---

[1] In ProtoPNet, only 2% of the prototypes have no overlap with an object, since ProtoPNet uses cropped images which makes it less likely to entirely miss the object.

can rate their satisfaction, preference and trust for part-prototypes [42]. Future work could therefore more extensively capture the subjective dimension of XAI evaluation to address the Coherence property, supported by e.g. already developed XAI questionnaires [25]. The resulting insights could in turn provide suggestions to improve part-prototype models further.

2.12   Controllability

Controllability describes how interactive/controllable an explanation is to a user. Existing part-prototype models are in principle static models that are user-independent. Of course a designer, or users themselves, can choose which prototypes are shown (e.g. a global or local explanation, or only the top-k relevant prototypes). For an improved user experience, a graphical user interface can be added for visualising the reasoning of a part-prototype model. Such an interface could also enable personalised explanations where users can interact with the model and ask counterfactual questions. A promising direction that exploits the interpretability of part-prototype models, is that the user would have the possibility to directly *manipulate* the explanation and, in turn, the model's reasoning.

Related Work. Kulesza et al. [32] introduced *explanatory debugging*, an approach where the user can personalise a prediction model by means of its explanations. Allowing a user to disable undesired prototypes would be a concrete and promising example of explanatory debugging for part-prototype models.

Recommendations. Since part-prototype models are interpretable by design, adapting the explanation implies that also the model's reasoning is adapted. We identify research opportunities to enable users to suppress or modify learned prototypes, ideally supported by a graphical user interface. Such a human-in-the-loop approach may allow 'fixing' the model by removing spurious correlations and aligning it more with human reasoning. The *human feedback impact* [42] evaluation method can then measure whether the model accuracy and explanation quality improve after human involvement. Being able to directly control and manipulate a model's reasoning is a strong benefit of part-prototype models, and is therefore a promising direction that should be investigated further.

3   Discussion and Broader Impact

Importance of Part-Prototype Models. Explainable and interpretable models are important for responsible AI, especially in high-risk decision domains [6]. Explainable AI could reveal that an accurate prediction model is right for the *wrong* reasons due to biases or shortcuts [42,48]. Where most explanations only give an approximation of the reasoning, part-prototype models are interpretable by design and give insight into their full decision making process [41]. More and more use cases for interpretable-by-design models in the medical domain are emerging, e.g. part-prototype models are used for breast cancer detection in mammograms [7,57], COVID-19 detection in CT-scans [52] and Alzheimer detection in MRI scans [37]. Explanations for automated decisions can also become a legal requirement, such as the European GDPR law demanding "meaningful information about the logic involved" [17], and the upcoming EU AI act.

Due to the built-in interpretability of part-prototype models, the relatively new research area of part-prototype models holds promise for many applications. The literature on part-prototype models is however fragmented. In this work, we collect and organise findings from existing work that evaluate particular aspects of part-prototype models using a bottom-up analysis. This work therefore acts as a roadmap for researchers seeking to explore existing part-prototype literature.

Evaluation Paradigm. Evaluation of explainable AI methods is important to ensure that explanations are truthful, relevant and understandable. As opposed to other communities, such as information retrieval and machine learning, the XAI community does not have an agreement on evaluating those methods. Recently, multiple suggestions for evaluating XAI have been proposed [9,25,42,56,65]. XAI evaluation papers mostly address post-hoc XAI methods, that approximate an already trained prediction model. Since part-prototype models are interpretable by design, existing evaluation methods for post-model XAI may not be directly applicable to in-model explainability methods. We fill a gap in the XAI evaluation landscape by providing a detailed analysis of XAI evaluation for interpretable part-prototype models.

Our contribution on part-prototype model evaluation is three-fold. First, we assess evaluation methods in XAI more broadly and discuss their applicability to part-prototype models. Our structured approach along the Co-12 properties puts existing works in a framework, shows that part-prototype models can be evaluated from various dimensions, and helps to identify research gaps. Second, we take the specific nature of part-prototype models into account by outlining how existing evaluation methods should be adapted to make them compatible and relevant for part-prototype models, and also suggest new evaluation methods for part-prototype models such as the target-sensitivity of the location of part-prototypes. Thorough evaluation of part-prototype models can reveal their strengths and limitations, and in turn accelerate progress and innovation. Third, we contribute to consistency, awareness and clarity in terminology for XAI evaluation. For example, we distinguish between three types of confidence, and discuss both model-output-completeness and human-output-completeness.

In this way, we facilitate effective communication, efficiently guide future work for a more comprehensive evaluation and contribute to a solid foundation for further advancements in the field. Our evaluation cheat sheet (Table 2) is a concise overview of evaluation methods for part-prototype models, which can serve as a guideline for method developers and as a discussion point for the community for future improvements. Our suggested evaluation approaches include both content-related, presentation-related and user-related experiments, and are therefore relevant for various disciplines, including computer science, human-computer interaction (HCI) and user experience design.

4   Conclusion

We have discussed recent work that has evaluated various Co-12 properties for part-prototype models, and have also made concrete recommendations for further evaluation, as summarised in our Co-12 cheat sheet in Table 2. We agree with Jacovi & Goldberg [28] that interpretable methods should be held to the same standards as post-hoc explanation methods. With the Co-12 recipe presented in this paper, we aim to contribute to the progression and maturity of the relatively new research field on interpretable part-prototype learning.

References

1. Adebayo, J., Gilmer, J., Muelly, M., Goodfellow, I., Hardt, M., Kim, B.: Sanity checks for saliency maps. In: Bengio, S., Wallach, H., Larochelle, H., Grauman, K., Cesa-Bianchi, N., Garnett, R. (eds.) Advances in Neural Information Processing Systems (2018)
2. Barredo Arrieta, A., et al.: Explainable Artificial Intelligence (XAI): concepts, taxonomies, opportunities and challenges toward responsible AI. Inf. Fusion **58** (2020)
3. Biederman, I.: Recognition-by-components: a theory of human image understanding. Psychol. Rev. **94**(2), 115 (1987)
4. Borowski, J., et al.: Exemplary natural images explain CNN activations better than state-of-the-art feature visualization. In: Proceedings of the International Conference on Learning Representations (2021)
5. Brendel, W., Bethge, M.: Approximating CNNs with bag-of-local-features models works surprisingly well on ImageNet. In: Proceedings of the International Conference on Learning Representations (2019)
6. Bruckert, S., Finzel, B., Schmid, U.: The next generation of medical decision support: a roadmap toward transparent expert companions. Front. Artif. Intell. **3**, 507973 (2020)
7. Carloni, G., Berti, A., Iacconi, C., Pascali, M.A., Colantonio, S.: On the applicability of prototypical part learning in medical images: breast masses classification using ProtoPNet. In: Rousseau, J.J., Kapralos, B. (eds.) ICPR 2022. LNCS, vol. 13643, pp. 539–557. Springer, Cham (2023). https://doi.org/10.1007/978-3-031-37660-3_38
8. Chen, C., Li, O., Tao, D., Barnett, A., Rudin, C., Su, J.: This looks like that: deep learning for interpretable image recognition. In: Wallach, H.M., Larochelle, H., Beygelzimer, A., d'Alché-Buc, F., Fox, E.B., Garnett, R. (eds.) Advances in Neural Information Processing Systems, pp. 8928–8939 (2019)
9. Clement, T., Kemmerzell, N., Abdelaal, M., Amberg, M.: XAIR: a systematic metareview of explainable AI (XAI) aligned to the software development process. Mach. Learn. Knowl. Extr. **5**(1), 78–108 (2023)
10. Colin, J., Fel, T., Cadene, R., Serre, T.: What I cannot predict, I do not understand: a human-centered evaluation framework for explainability methods. In: Advances in Neural Information Processing Systems (2022)
11. Das, S., Xu, P., Dai, Z., Endert, A., Ren, L.: Interpreting deep neural networks through prototype factorization. In: Fatta, G.D., Sheng, V.S., Cuzzocrea, A., Zaniolo, C., Wu, X. (eds.) Proceedings of the International Conference on Data Mining Workshops, ICDM Workshops, pp. 448–457. IEEE (2020)

12. Doshi-Velez, F., Kim, B.: Considerations for evaluation and generalization in interpretable machine learning. In: Escalante, H.J., et al. (eds.) Explainable and Interpretable Models in Computer Vision and Machine Learning. TSSCML, pp. 3–17. Springer, Cham (2018). https://doi.org/10.1007/978-3-319-98131-4_1

13. Ehsan, U., et al.: The who in explainable AI: how AI background shapes perceptions of AI explanations. arXiv preprint arXiv:2107.13509 (2021)

14. Fong, R., Vedaldi, A.: Net2Vec: quantifying and explaining how concepts are encoded by filters in deep neural networks. In: Proceedings of the IEEE Conference on Computer Vision and Pattern Recognition, pp. 8730–8738. IEEE Computer Society (2018)

15. Gautam, S., Höhne, M.M.-C., Hansen, S., Jenssen, R., Kampffmeyer, M.: This looks more like that: enhancing self-explaining models by prototypical relevance propagation. Pattern Recogn. **136**, 109172 (2023)

16. Ghorbani, A., Wexler, J., Zou, J.Y., Kim, B.: Towards automatic concept-based explanations. In: Wallach, H.M., Larochelle, H., Beygelzimer, A., d'Alché-Buc, F., Fox, E.B., Garnett, R. (eds.) Advances in Neural Information Processing Systems, pp. 9273–9282 (2019)

17. Goodman, B., Flaxman, S.: European union regulations on algorithmic decision-making and a "right to explanation". AI Mag. **38**(3), 50–57 (2017)

18. Goyal, Y., Feder, A., Shalit, U., Kim, B.: Explaining classifiers with causal concept effect (CaCE). arXiv preprint arXiv:1907.07165 (2019)

19. Goyal, Y., Wu, Z., Ernst, J., Batra, D., Parikh, D., Lee, S.: Counterfactual visual explanations. In: Chaudhuri, K., Salakhutdinov, R. (eds.) Proceedings of the International Conference on Machine Learning, ICML 2019, Long Beach, California, USA, 9–15 June 2019, vol. 97, pp. 2376–2384. PMLR (2019)

20. Guidotti, R., Monreale, A., Ruggieri, S., Turini, F., Giannotti, F., Pedreschi, D.: A survey of methods for explaining black box models. ACM Comput. Surv. (CSUR) **51**(5), 1–42 (2018)

21. Guo, C., Pleiss, G., Sun, Y., Weinberger, K.Q.: On calibration of modern neural networks. In: Precup, D., Teh, Y.W. (eds.) Proceedings of the International Conference on Machine Learning, vol. 70, pp. 1321–1330. PMLR (2017)

22. Hase, P., Bansal, M.: Evaluating explainable AI: which algorithmic explanations help users predict model behavior? In: Jurafsky, D., Chai, J., Schluter, N., Tetreault, J.R. (eds.) Proceedings of the Annual Meeting of the Association for Computational Linguistics, ACL 2020, Online, 5–10 July 2020, pp. 5540–5552. Association for Computational Linguistics (2020)

23. Hase, P., Xie, H., Bansal, M.: The out-of-distribution problem in explainability and search methods for feature importance explanations. In: Ranzato, M., Beygelzimer, A., Dauphin, Y., Liang, P., Vaughan, J.W. (eds.) Advances in Neural Information Processing Systems, vol. 34, pp. 3650–3666. Curran Associates Inc. (2021)

24. He, Y., Shen, Z., Cui, P.: Towards non-IID image classification: a dataset and baselines. Pattern Recogn. **110**, 107383 (2021)

25. Hoffman, R.R., Mueller, S.T., Klein, G., Litman, J.: Metrics for explainable AI: challenges and prospects. arXiv:1812.04608 [cs] (2019)

26. Hoffmann, A., Fanconi, C., Rade, R., Kohler, J.: This looks like that... does it? Shortcomings of latent space prototype interpretability in deep networks. arXiv preprint arXiv:2105.02968 (2021)

27. Huysmans, J., Dejaeger, K., Mues, C., Vanthienen, J., Baesens, B.: An empirical evaluation of the comprehensibility of decision table, tree and rule based predictive models. Decis. Support Syst. **51**(1) (2011)

28. Jacovi, A., Goldberg, Y.: Towards faithfully interpretable NLP systems: how should we define and evaluate faithfulness? In: Jurafsky, D., Chai, J., Schluter, N., Tetreault, J.R. (eds.) Proceedings of the Annual Meeting of the Association for Computational Linguistics, ACL 2020, Online, 5–10 July 2020, pp. 4198–4205. Association for Computational Linguistics (2020)

29. Jeyakumar, J.V., Noor, J., Cheng, Y., Garcia, L., Srivastava, M.B.: How can I explain this to you? An empirical study of deep neural network explanation methods. In: Larochelle, H., Ranzato, M., Hadsell, R., Balcan, M., Lin, H. (eds.) Advances in Neural Information Processing Systems (2020)

30. Kaur, H., Nori, H., Jenkins, S., Caruana, R., Wallach, H., Wortman Vaughan, J.: Interpreting interpretability: understanding data scientists' use of interpretability tools for machine learning. In: Proceedings of the CHI Conference on Human Factors in Computing Systems, pp. 1–14. Association for Computing Machinery, New York (2020)

31. Kim, S.S.Y., Meister, N., Ramaswamy, V.V., Fong, R., Russakovsky, O.: HIVE: evaluating the human interpretability of visual explanations. In: Avidan, S., Brostow, G., Cissé, M., Farinella, G.M., Hassner, T. (eds.) ECCV 2022. LNCS, vol. 13672, pp. 280–298. Springer, Cham (2022). https://doi.org/10.1007/978-3-031-19775-8_17

32. Kulesza, T., Burnett, M., Wong, W.-K., Stumpf, S.: Principles of explanatory debugging to personalize interactive machine learning. In: Proceedings of the International Conference on Intelligent User Interfaces, pp. 126–137. Association for Computing Machinery, New York (2015)

33. Lakkaraju, H., Leskovec, J.: Confusions over time: an interpretable Bayesian model to characterize trends in decision making. In: Lee, D.D., Sugiyama, M., von Luxburg, U., Guyon, I., Garnett, R. (eds.) Advances in Neural Information Processing Systems, pp. 3261–3269 (2016)

34. Lampert, C.H., Nickisch, H., Harmeling, S.: Learning to detect unseen object classes by between-class attribute transfer. In: 2009 IEEE Conference on Computer Vision and Pattern Recognition, pp. 951–958 (2009)

35. Liu, Y., Khandagale, S., White, C., Neiswanger, W.: Synthetic benchmarks for scientific research in explainable machine learning. In: NeurIPS Datasets and Benchmarks Track (2021)

36. Michel, A., Jha, S.K., Ewetz, R.: A survey on the vulnerability of deep neural networks against adversarial attacks. Progress Artif. Intell. **11**, 131–141 (2021). https://doi.org/10.1007/s13748-021-00269-9

37. Mohammadjafari, S., Cevik, M., Thanabalasingam, M., Basar, A.: Using ProtoPNet for interpretable Alzheimer's disease classification. In: Canadian Conference on AI (2021)

38. Montavon, G.: Gradient-based vs. propagation-based explanations: an axiomatic comparison. In: Samek, W., Montavon, G., Vedaldi, A., Hansen, L.K., Müller, K.-R. (eds.) Explainable AI: Interpreting, Explaining and Visualizing Deep Learning. LNCS (LNAI), vol. 11700, pp. 253–265. Springer, Cham (2019). https://doi.org/10.1007/978-3-030-28954-6_13

39. Nakka, K.K., Salzmann, M.: Towards robust fine-grained recognition by maximal separation of discriminative features. In: Ishikawa, H., Liu, C.-L., Pajdla, T., Shi, J. (eds.) ACCV 2020. LNCS, vol. 12627, pp. 391–408. Springer, Cham (2021). https://doi.org/10.1007/978-3-030-69544-6_24

40. Nauta, M., Jutte, A., Provoost, J., Seifert, C.: This looks like that, because ... explaining prototypes for interpretable image recognition. In: Kamp, M., et al.

(eds.) ECML PKDD 2021. CCIS, vol. 1524, pp. 441–456. Springer, Cham (2021). https://doi.org/10.1007/978-3-030-93736-2_34

41. Nauta, M., Schlötterer, J., van Keulen, M., Seifert, C.: PIP-Net: patch-based intuitive prototypes for interpretable image classification. In: Proceedings of the IEEE/CVF Conference on Computer Vision and Pattern Recognition (CVPR), pp. 2744–2753 (2023)

42. Nauta, M., et al.: From anecdotal evidence to quantitative evaluation methods: a systematic review on evaluating explainable AI. ACM Comput. Surv. (2023)

43. Nauta, M., van Bree, R., Seifert, C.: Neural prototype trees for interpretable fine-grained image recognition. In: Proceedings of the IEEE/CVF Conference on Computer Vision and Pattern Recognition (CVPR), pp. 14933–14943 (2021)

44. Nguyen, G., Kim, D., Nguyen, A.: The effectiveness of feature attribution methods and its correlation with automatic evaluation scores. In: Ranzato, M., Beygelzimer, A., Dauphin, Y., Liang, P., Vaughan, J.W. (eds.) Advances in Neural Information Processing Systems, vol. 34, pp. 26422–26436. Curran Associates Inc. (2021)

45. Papenmeier, A., Kern, D., Englebienne, G., Seifert, C.: It's complicated: the relationship between user trust, model accuracy and explanations in AI. ACM Trans. Comput.-Hum. Interact. **29**(4) (2022)

46. Pearce, T., Brintrup, A., Zhu, J.: Understanding softmax confidence and uncertainty. arXiv preprint arXiv:2106.04972 (2021)

47. Rong, Y., Leemann, T., Borisov, V., Kasneci, G., Kasneci, E.: A consistent and efficient evaluation strategy for attribution methods. In: Chaudhuri, K., Jegelka, S., Song, L., Szepesvari, C., Niu, G., Sabato, S. (eds.) Proceedings of the International Conference on Machine Learning, vol. 162, pp. 18770–18795. PMLR (2022)

48. Rudin, C.: Stop explaining black box machine learning models for high stakes decisions and use interpretable models instead. Nat. Mach. Intell. **1**(5), 206–215 (2019)

49. Rymarczyk, D., Struski, Ł, Górszczak, M., Lewandowska, K., Tabor, J., Zieliński, B.: Interpretable image classification with differentiable prototypes assignment. In: Avidan, S., Brostow, G., Cissé, M., Farinella, G.M., Hassner, T. (eds.) ECCV 2022. LNCS, pp. 351–368. Springer, Cham (2022). https://doi.org/10.1007/978-3-031-19775-8_21

50. Rymarczyk, D., Struski, L., Tabor, J., Zieliński, B.: ProtoPShare: prototypical parts sharing for similarity discovery in interpretable image classification. In: Proceedings of the ACM SIGKDD Conference on Knowledge Discovery & Data Mining, pp. 1420–1430. Association for Computing Machinery, New York (2021)

51. Selvaraju, R.R., Cogswell, M., Das, A., Vedantam, R., Parikh, D., Batra, D.: Grad-CAM: visual explanations from deep networks via gradient-based localization. In: IEEE International Conference on Computer Vision, ICCV, pp. 618–626. IEEE Computer Society (2017)

52. Singh, G.: Think positive: an interpretable neural network for image recognition. Neural Netw. **151**, 178–189 (2022)

53. Singh, G., Yow, K.-C.: An interpretable deep learning model for Covid-19 detection with chest X-ray images. IEEE Access **9**, 85198–85208 (2021)

54. Sinhamahapatra, P., Heidemann, L., Monnet, M., Roscher, K.: Towards human-interpretable prototypes for visual assessment of image classification models. arXiv preprint arXiv:2211.12173 (2022)

55. Summers, C., Dinneen, M.J.: Nondeterminism and instability in neural network optimization. In: Meila, M., Zhang, T. (eds.) Proceedings of the International Conference on Machine Learning, vol. 139, pp. 9913–9922. PMLR (2021)

56. Vilone, G., Longo, L.: Notions of explainability and evaluation approaches for explainable artificial intelligence. Inf. Fusion **76** (2021)
57. Wang, C., et al.: Knowledge distillation to ensemble global and interpretable prototype-based mammogram classification models. In: Wang, L., Dou, Q., Fletcher, P.T., Speidel, S., Li, S. (eds.) MICCAI 2022. LNCS, vol. 13433, pp. 14–24. Springer, Cham (2022). https://doi.org/10.1007/978-3-031-16437-8_2
58. Wang, J., Liu, H., Wang, X., Jing, L.: Interpretable image recognition by constructing transparent embedding space. In: Proceedings of the IEEE/CVF International Conference on Computer Vision (ICCV), pp. 895–904 (2021)
59. Williams, P.A., Jenkins, J., Valacich, J., Byrd, M.D.: Measuring actual behaviors in HCI research-a call to action and an example. AIS Trans. Hum.-Comput. Interact. **9**(4), 339–352 (2017)
60. Xie, W., Li, X.-H., Cao, C.C., Zhang, N.L.: ViT-CX: causal explanation of vision transformers. arXiv preprint arXiv:2211.03064 (2022)
61. Xu-Darme, R., Quénot, G., Chihani, Z., Rousset, M.-C.: Sanity checks and improvements for patch visualisation in prototype-based image classification. working paper or preprint (2023)
62. Xue, M., et al.: ProtoPFormer: concentrating on prototypical parts in vision transformers for interpretable image recognition. arXiv preprint arXiv:2208.10431 (2022)
63. Yang, M., Kim, B.: Benchmarking attribution methods with relative feature importance. CoRR, abs/1907.09701 (2019)
64. Yeh, C., Kim, B., Arik, S.Ö., Li, C., Pfister, T., Ravikumar, P.: On completeness-aware concept-based explanations in deep neural networks. In: Advances in Neural Information Processing Systems (2020)
65. Zhou, J., Gandomi, A.H., Chen, F., Holzinger, A.: Evaluating the quality of machine learning explanations: a survey on methods and metrics. Electronics **10**(5) (2021)
66. Zhuang, D., Zhang, X., Song, S., Hooker, S.: Randomness in neural network training: characterizing the impact of tooling. In: Marculescu, D., Chi, Y., Wu, C. (eds.) Proceedings of the Machine Learning and Systems, vol. 4, pp. 316–336 (2022)

Reason to Explain: Interactive Contrastive Explanations (REASONX)

Laura State[1,2]([✉]) [iD], Salvatore Ruggieri[1] [iD], and Franco Turini[1] [iD]

[1] University of Pisa, Pisa, Italy
laura.state@di.unipi.it
[2] Scuola Normale Superiore, Pisa, Italy

Abstract. Many high-performing machine learning models are not interpretable. As they are increasingly used in decision scenarios that can critically affect individuals, it is necessary to develop tools to better understand their outputs. Popular explanation methods include contrastive explanations. However, they suffer several shortcomings, among others an insufficient incorporation of background knowledge, and a lack of interactivity. While (dialogue-like) interactivity is important to better communicate an explanation, background knowledge has the potential to significantly improve their quality, e.g., by adapting the explanation to the needs of the end-user.

To close this gap, we present REASONX, an explanation tool based on Constraint Logic Programming (CLP). REASONX provides interactive contrastive explanations that can be augmented by background knowledge, and allows to operate under a setting of under-specified information, leading to increased flexibility in the provided explanations. REASONX computes factual and contrastive decision rules, as well as closest contrastive examples. It provides explanations for decision trees, which can be the ML models under analysis, or global/local surrogate models of any ML model.

While the core part of REASONX is built on CLP, we also provide a program layer that allows to compute the explanations via Python, making the tool accessible to a wider audience. We illustrate the capability of REASONX on a synthetic data set, and on a well-developed example in the credit domain. In both cases, we can show how REASONX can be flexibly used and tailored to the needs of the user.

Keywords: explainable AI · Contrastive Explanations · Background Knowledge · Interactivity · Constraint Logic Programming

1 Introduction

Contrastive (counterfactual) explanations (CEs)[1] are a popular method to provide insights into not interpretable machine learning (ML) models. Signifi-

---

[1] In this paper, we refer to *contrastive* over counterfactual explanations, in order to avoid confusion with the concept of counterfactuals as understood in causality, and following [28].

© The Author(s), under exclusive license to Springer Nature Switzerland AG 2023
L. Longo (Ed.): xAI 2023, CCIS 1901, pp. 421–437, 2023.
https://doi.org/10.1007/978-3-031-44064-9_22

cant efforts are made to provide CEs for different data types such as tabular data [49], images [9] or text [53], based on numeric [31,49], causal [24] or other approaches [38,48]. However, some open challenges remain, such as the integration of background knowledge [5,45], and interactivity [28,29,51].

To tackle these shortcomings, we present REASONX (REASON to eXplain). We display an exemplary dialogue between a fictional end-user and REASONX below. The dialogue is situated in the context of a credit application example, therefore the user of the tool is a natural person whose credit application has been rejected by an Automated Decision-Making (ADM) system. Please note that while the information content of the displayed dialogue is exactly what REASONX can provide, we enhanced the dialogue to mimic better a realistic interaction by reporting questions and answers in natural language.[2]

USER: I want to understand the decision better. Can I see the rule that led to the denial of my credit application?

REASONX: Your credit application was rejected, because your income is lower than 60,000 EUR/year, and you still have to pay back the lease of your car.

USER: Ok. Can you present me two different options that will lead to a change of the decision outcome? Please take into consideration that I need a credit of at least 10,000 EUR. I would like to see options that require as little change as necessary.

REASONX: You have the following two options: you pay back the lease on the car, or you increase your age by 10 years (from 35 to 45 years).

USER: The second option presented is a bit strange. I am wondering whether this is something salient in the model. Can I please see the options to obtain credit for an individual with the same properties as me, for a credit of at least 10,000 EUR, but with the feature age at 35 years or less (i.e., young applicant), instead of fixed?

REASONX: For the given profile, the credit is always rejected.

USER: Can you please show how to reverse the decision, under as few changes as possible, for the specified profile?

REASONX: Credit can be obtained, if the feature age is set to higher than 35 years.

USER: This is interesting and worth investigating further. There could be bias w.r.t. the age of the person that applies for credit.

This dialogue illustrates the capabilities of REASONX. Our tool addresses the following points:

Background Knowledge. Adding background knowledge to an explanation has the potential to significantly improve its quality, but it is seldom offered [5,45]. Ignoring this knowledge is not necessarily wrong, but can lead to contrastive explanations that ignore the needs of the data subject under decision, or CEs that do not fit the reality of our world - this depends closely on the purpose of the explanation. An example of such knowledge in the credit application example is the minimum credit amount ("a credit of at least 10,000 EUR", see dialogue above). For REASONX, we rely on background knowledge in the form of linear constraints over the features.

---

[2] Adding a layer that implements a natural language communication between the user and REASONX is left for future work.

Interactivity. Interactivity is a property of an explanation that is important, if the explanations should be communicated successfully to the end-user [28,29,51]. However, most eXplainabe AI (XAI) tools do not account for this. Interactivity arises naturally in REASONX: the end-user can flexibly query the explanation tool, choosing answers that best fit her questions, adding and removing constraints, and thereby building her own, personalized explanation.

Under-Specified Information. REASONX allows computing CEs under under-specified information. For example, it is not necessary to fix all features of the data instance of interest to compute a matching CE but provide only bounds ("feature age at 35 years or less", see dialogue above). This property is implicitly in the use of CLP, and leads to a wider flexibility in provided explanations. Further, there is a loose connection to the notion of *group contrastive explanations*, which have been shown to be beneficial to the end-user via user studies [50].

1.1 Contributions and Structure of the Paper

With this paper, we make the following contributions

- *Explanation tool.* We propose REASONX, a novel explanation tool that provides contrastive interactive explanations, that can incorporate background knowledge, and that works under under-specified information. To the best of our knowledge, this is one of the first tools using constraint logic programming to generate contrastive explanations.
- *Synthetic data set illustration.* A first illustration of REASONX is based on a well-defined synthetic data set. We demonstrate step-by-step how REASONX operates under different (constraint) settings, including some graphical representations.
- *Credit application example.* We demonstrate the capabilities of REASONX on the Adult Income data set. This data set can be used as an approximation to determine the income of a natural person, we assume here that this approximation relates directly to a decision about credit allocation. We provide this demonstration together with an in-depth discussion of the relevant context (credit domain). We chose this context, as ADM systems for credit applications are an important and recurring topic. Further, as they are classified as "high-risk" according to the proposed AI Act of the European Union [16], they have to be considered particularly carefully.

This paper is structured as follows. In Sect. 2, we discuss background and related work. In Sect. 3, we introduce REASONX, followed by the illustration on synthetic data in Sect. 4 and the credit application example in Sect. 5. We close our paper by discussing limitations of this work in Sect. 6, and a conclusion in Sect. 7.

We provide our code (REASONX and experiments) via a public repository.[3] In-depth theory and implementation details of REASONX will be provided in a companion paper.

---

[3] https://github.com/lstate/REASONX.

2   Background and Related Work

2.1   Explanations

Explanations for opaque ML models ("black box models") can be divided into two categories [19]: *global* methods, explaining the full model at once, or *local* methods, producing explanations that are only valid for a single data instance (data subject). Further, we can distinguish between *model-agnostic* and *model-specific* methods - the first can be applied to any ML model, the second only to the ML model type it was developed for.

Contrastive (Counterfactual) Explanations. Contrastive explanations (CEs) are local, model-agnostic explanations. They are computed *after* the model was trained (post-hoc), and based only on input-output pairs.

Wachter et al. [49] introduced the idea of contrastive explanations in the field of XAI. Following them, a contrastive explanation can be described as an optimization problem of the following form:

$$\arg \min_{x_{ce}} \max_{\lambda} \lambda(f_w(x_{ce}) - y_{ce})^2 + d(x_f, x_{ce}) \tag{1}$$

x_{ce} denotes the contrastive data point, x_f the original data point, $f_w(x_{ce})$ the prediction of the contrastive example and y_{ce} the desired prediction. Further, λ denotes a tuning parameter, and $d(\cdot, \cdot)$ a distance measure, usually the Manhattan distance, weighted by the median absolute deviation. Equation 1 minimizes the distance between the factual and the contrastive data point. The intuition underlying a CE is that to be realistic, it should be as close as possible to the original data point, while at the same time making sure that the prediction of the CE aligns with the desired prediction.

Contrastive explanations are well received by the community. However, they do not only have support from the technical side. While [49] is discussing the legal basis for contrastive explanations, with a focus on the European General Data Protection Regulation (GDPR), [7] argues in favor of CEs from a psychological point of view. Further, both [28] and [30] make clear that explanations in a contrastive form in general, i.e., explanations outlining why other events did not occur and differences to the actual outcome, are highly desirable for the (lay) end-user. Finally, we point to a number of surveys: [23] focusing on the computational side of CEs and actionable recourse, a closely related field, [25], critically analyzing the lack of evaluation methodology for CE methods, and two additional surveys [17, 46].

Technically Related Approaches. The approach taken in this work is inspired by two strands of research, focusing either on solving CE queries by (a) using SAT, or causality-based frameworks [22, 24] or (b) using ILP/MILP approaches [13, 21, 38, 48]. However, our approach is different in two main points: first, our focus is clearly on creating explanations for *any* ML model. Approaches (a) are generally agnostic, but the model internals need to be known, in (b) only linear or additive models are considered. Second, to the best of our knowledge, this is one of the first approaches using CLP to generate CEs.

Group Contrastive (Counterfactual) Explanations. The notion of group contrastive explanations is relatively new and refers to a small body of work that has not yet converged on a common definition. A definition of group contrastive explanations that is based on common "feature differences", i.e., the idea that different but similar data points share the same contrastive example is proposed in [50]. Their approach builds on a simple extension of the traditional approach for the generation of CEs such as [31]. Further, the paper benchmarks its approach via a user study, showing its usefulness. Other works include [2], focusing on explanations that refer to an ensemble of decisions, and [34], connecting group CEs to actionable recourse.

Background Knowledge. Adding background knowledge to an explanation has the potential to significantly improve its quality [5,45]. In this work, we refer to background (or prior) knowledge as to any information that is relevant in the decision context but that does not emerge through the decision pipeline. Not only do simple facts count as such, but we would also consider a natural law as such knowledge, or as in our example in the introduction, a specific restriction a customer has related to her living reality (e.g., a minimum credit amount). However, we have to restrict ourselves to knowledge that can be formalized and thus used by the explainer.

REASONX incorporates knowledge in the form of linear constraints. Other examples of knowledge integration include the following. A local explanation tool for medical data that incorporates an ontology (the ICD-9-CM) to generate a meaningful, local neighborhood for explanation generation [33]. A discrimination discovery approach [37], where knowledge in the form of association rules is used to detect cases of indirect discrimination. Explanations are also historically connected to knowledge and logic reasoning - the first systems offered to explain AI models were expert systems [11].

Interactivity. Interactivity as property of an explanation aligns closely with our working definition: "an explanation, or explainability is about an interaction, or an exchange of information", where it crucially matters to *whom* the explanation is given, and for *what* purpose [45].

While being acknowledged as an important property of an explanation that is successfully communicated to the end-user [28,29,51] - interactivity is only in very few cases incorporated into XAI methods. Sokol and Flach [44] outline the usefulness of interactivity prominently in their paper: "Truly interactive explanations allow the user to tweak, tune and personalise them (i.e., their content) via an interaction, hence the explainee is given an opportunity to guide them in a direction that helps to answer selected questions" Also, they present a first solution (the glass-box tool [42]): an interactive explanation tool that provides

426   L. State et al.

explanations in natural language and that can be queried either by voice or via a chat. Similar to our work, it relies on a decision tree to generate the explanations. The tool was tested in different environments, this helped the authors to also develop a mapping of desiderata of interpretable explanations.

We further point to [27], presenting an interview study with practitioners that revealed that interactivity for explanations is strongly preferred, and discussing some ideas about how to achieve this. As a last example, we point to the what-if tool, a commercial application provided by Google.[4]

2.2 (Constraint) Logic Programming

Logic programming (LP) is a declarative approach to problem-solving, based on logic rules in the form of (Horn) clauses [1]. It supports reasoning under various settings, i.e., deductive, inductive, abductive and meta-reasoning [12,39]. Starting with the Prolog programming language [10], programming in logic has been extended in several directions, as per expressivity and efficiency [26]. Constraint logic programming (CLP) augments logic programming with the ability to solve constrained problems in some domain [20]. We rely on CLP(R), which consists of linear constraints over the reals, as implemented in the SWI Prolog system [52]. CLP(R) adds to logic programming rules the ability to test for linear constraint satisfiability, entailment, equivalence, and projection, as well as for solving MILP optimization problems.

(C)LP for XAI Logic programming is considered symbolic reasoning - contrary to what is commonly referred to as sub-symbolic reasoning, or ML. While the first set of approaches is inherently transparent, most ML models are not, but come with other advantages, such as the ability to work on large amounts of data. Combining both is a promising synergy - exactly what we do in this paper.

A related approach to our work is a body of papers by Sokol et al. [41–43]. While the first introduces explanations for decision trees (among others, through contrastive explanations), the second generalizes it to be used as a local surrogate model. In the third paper, the focus is explicitly set on interactivity. Our work is closely linked to that. The main difference is in methodology, i.e., we rely on CLP in our computations, thus allowing for the integration of background knowledge, interactivity, and operation under under-specified information, making REASONX unique against previous approaches. Another related work is [6]. It provides CEs - but treats them from the angle of (actual) causality. Methodologically, it relies on answer set programming (ASP), and uses also its straightforward ability to integrate knowledge into the explanations.

A survey that discusses how to combine both symbolic (logic) and sub-symbolic systems, with a specific focus on explainable AI is [8]. Further, [47] adopts ASP to compute both local and global explanations for tree ensemble models. While it is methodologically related to our approach (relying on logic programming and on tree structures), it does not discuss the notion of

---

[4] https://pair-code.github.io/what-if-tool/.

CEs. There are also a few approaches using logic rules as explanations, but that methodologically do not rely on LP, e.g., [18] and [40].

3 REASONX: Reason to Explain

We propose REASONX, a novel tool to generate contrastive explanations that can account for background knowledge, that works under under-specified information and is highly interactive. REASONX can be used to obtain factual and contrastive decision rules about the classification of the data point (or profile) of interest, and provides the closest CE (via optimization). In all settings, background knowledge can be added in the form of linear constraints.

REASONX is strongly guided by a decision tree model, called the *base model*. Such a decision tree can be: (a) the model to be explained and reasoned about; (b) a global surrogate model of a black box; (c) a local surrogate model of a black box decision in the neighborhood of an instance to explain. In cases (b) and (c), the surrogate model is assumed to have good fidelity in reproducing the black box decisions. This is reasonable for local models, i.e., in case (c), by learning the tree over a localized neighborhood as common in perturbation-based explanation methods such as LIME [35]. Regarding case (b), we point out that our approach works with any type of decision tree, including axis-parallel, oblique, and complete decision trees – the last one offering very good performances. For presentation purposes, we assume the case (a), in order to disentangle the properties of REASONX in detail under no gap in fidelity between the surrogate model and the black box that should be explained.

The base model is translated into a set of Prolog facts, one for each path in the decision tree. In fact, a split in a decision tree is a linear constraint over features $\mathbf{x}$ of the form $c^T\mathbf{x} \geq b$ or $c^T\mathbf{x} < b$. A path from the root to a leaf is then a conjunction of linear constraints, represented by a Prolog fact such as:

$$path(m, [\mathbf{x}], [c_1^T\mathbf{x} \geq b_1, \ldots, c_k^T\mathbf{x} \geq b_k], c, p).$$

where m is an id of the path, $[\mathbf{x}]$ the list of features, c the class predicted at the leaf, p the confidence of the prediction, and $[c_1^T\mathbf{x} \geq b_1, \ldots, c_k^T\mathbf{x} \geq b_k]$ the list of k splits from the root to the leaf. Such linear constraints can be combined with constraints on data types (modeling for instance one-hot encoded features), on distance functions (modeling norms[5] to be used in computing contrastive examples), and user-provided ones (the background knowledge). Further, a constraint φ can be reasoned about in the following forms:

- checking satisfiability, i.e., whether $\exists_\mathbf{x}\ \varphi$ holds, also considering some features from $\mathbf{x}$ over the domain of integers, e.g., the one-hot encoded features or ordinal features;
- projecting over some features $\mathbf{w} \subseteq \mathbf{x}$, i.e., computing $\exists_{\mathbf{x}\setminus\mathbf{w}}\ \varphi$, as a way to express φ w.r.t. features in $\mathbf{w}$ only;

---

[5] REASONX currently implements the L1 norm.

- checking entailment, i.e., whether they entail some other linear constraint, e.g., in order to test if solutions of φ satisfy some property;
- solving a MILP minimization problem $\min f(\mathbf{x}) s.t. \varphi$ where $f(\cdot)$ is a linear function, e.g., in the distance minimization when computing contrastive instances.

The reasonings above are implemented through the $CLP(R)$ functionalities. However, to allow for wider accessibility of REASONX, we build a Python layer on top of the $CLP(R)$ core, which translates the base model and the user queries into Prolog queries, and translates back the results into Python data structures. Python also adds some syntactic sugar to express more concisely a few categories of constraints, such as the immutability of features, or to generate constraints from the features of an instance.

4   Synthetic Data Set Illustration

To illustrate the capabilities of REASONX, we introduce a simple synthetic data set, comprised of two classes with each 1,000 data instances. These were sampled from different random normal distributions over two independent features. The distributions were generated to be almost separable by an axis-parallel decision tree. We choose a data instance from class 0, called the *factual instance* ("factual" in the figures), to illustrate a few of the functionalities of REASONX.

As a first operation, we use REASONX to provide us with the factual rule (plotted as factual region in Fig. 1, left) that is satisfied by the data instance. Next, we ask for the contrastive rules, i.e., admissible contrastive regions where potential contrastive examples are located (plotted as contrastive regions in Fig. 1, right). In this example, three of those regions exist.

In Fig. 2 we demonstrate the capability of REASONX to account for background knowledge. We use a constraint that ensures that feature 2 stays constant between the factual instance and the contrastive example (Fig. 2, left), or a constraint that ensures that instead feature 1 stays constant (Fig. 2, right). While the first leads to an admissible contrastive region in the form of a region (a line), the second constraint suppresses any solution (no solution exists).

Now, we extend the example along two dimensions: asking for the *closest* contrastive example under a specified constraint setting, and admitting underspecified information in the factual instance. In Fig. 3, left, we run REASONX under a linear constraint between the two features (feature 1 and feature 2 have to be equal to each other). Instead of solving for admissible contrastive regions, we ask for the *closest* CE. The solution is provided as red dots. We observe the following: first, all solutions lie on the line that marks the linear constraint as introduced. Second, REASONX provides not only one but three solutions with a different distance to the factual instance. This stems from the fact that in this example, three admissible contrastive regions (see also Fig. 1, right) are given.

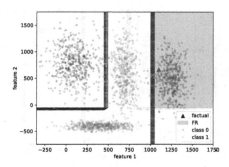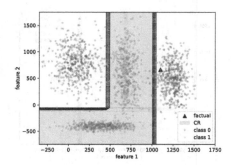

Fig. 1. Left: factual region (FR) as provided by REASONX. Right: contrastive regions (CR) as provided by REASONX. Grey lines refer to the decision boundary of the tree.

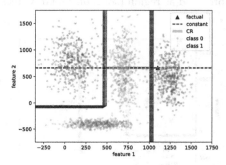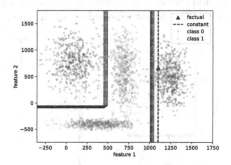

Fig. 2. Left: contrastive region (CR) as provided by REASONX, and given a constraint on feature 2. Right: given the constraint on feature 1, no solution provided by REASONX. The dashed line refers to the enforced constraint. Grey lines refer to the decision boundary of the tree.

REASONX solves the optimization for each of those independently, and provides us therefore not with the global optimum (one solution), but three local optima. This can be an advantage over conventional tools that provide contrastive explanations, as it leaves more flexibility to the end-user. A further refinement of the results, e.g. filtering for the global optimum, can be implemented.

In Fig. 3, right, we re-initialize the factual instance and allow feature 2 to be under-specified, i.e., setting it to a region instead of a fixed value. We omit all constraints, and solve again for the *closest* CE. We display one solution of this query in Fig. 3, right. For the same reasons as above, there exist three solutions (other two solutions in Fig. 4). We observe that the provided solution is also a region in the data space.

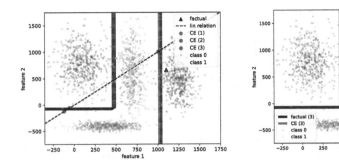

Fig. 3. Left: closest CEs as provided by REASONX, given a constraint on feature 1 and feature 2. The dashed line refers to the enforced constraint. Right: one closest CE as provided by REASONX, feature 2 of factual is provided as region (solution 1). Grey lines refer to the decision boundary of the tree.

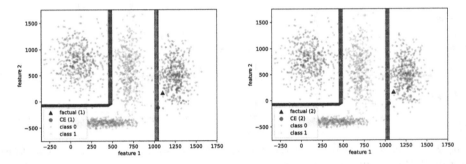

Fig. 4. Closest CE as provided by REASONX, feature 2 of factual is provided as region (solution 2 and 3). Grey lines refer to the decision boundary of the tree.

5   Credit Application Example

This example focuses on contrastive explanations for an ADM system that assesses credit applications, for example, provided by a bank. The main *purpose* of the explanation is for a customer (our imagined end-user) to make sense of the decision, and to receive insights about possible opportunities of action. Secondary purposes are legal compliance of the ADM, as well as increasing the trust of its customers in internal decisions, both in the interest of the bank. Next to demonstrating the capabilities of REASONX, this example serves as a (qualitative) *validation* of the tool. This is justified by the strong qualitative nature of REASONX, and ties closely to the fact that an explanation tool always has to be discussed in context [32].

We run the example on a processed version of the Adult Income data set[6], which has a binary response variable. It contains twelve features, and we restrict ourselves to a subset: three categorical features (workclass, race, sex), one

---

[6] https://archive.ics.uci.edu/ml/datasets/Adult.

ordinal (education) and four continuous (age, capitalgain, capitalloss, hoursperweek). Categorical features are one-hot encoded. The queries as displayed below work iteratively, i.e., background knowledge that is added to the program is always kept (but can be retracted). The verbose parameter determines how the output of the query is displayed. The project parameter is used to map results of the set of variables onto a subset.

After initializing REASONX with the base decision tree trained on a subset of available data, we turn towards a first question of the user (corresponding to the factual instance): *Why was my application rejected?* We answer it by showing the rule behind the decision. This requires naming an instance ('F' in the code below, for 'factual') and passing the feature values (InstFeatures) and the decision of the base model (InstDecision).

```
USER:     r.instance('F', features=InstFeatures, label=InstDecision)
          r.solveopt(verbose=2)
REASONX: Rule satisfied by F:
          IF F.capitalgain<=5119.0,F.education<=12.5,F.age<=30.5
          THEN <=50K [0.9652]
```

The rule as returned by REASONX explains the classification of the factual instance. It refers to a specific region in the data input space as characterized by the base decision tree. A second answer can be given by comparing the factual instance against a contrastive rule, using the differences as an explanation. This requires naming a second instance ('CE' in the code below, for 'contrastive example'), and possibly a minimum confidence of the rule leading to the contrastive decision. We obtain two rules by running the following query:

```
USER:     r.instance('CE', label=1-InstDecision, minconf=0.8)
          r.solveopt(verbose=2)
REASONX: Rule satisfied by CE:
          IF CE.capitalgain>5119.0,CE.capitalgain<=5316.5
          THEN >50K [1.0],
          Rule satisfied by CE:
          IF CE.capitalgain>7055.5,CE.age>20.0
          THEN >50K [0.9882]
```

By comparing this output with the answer to the previous question, the user can understand the factual decision of the ADM better. This is especially relevant to answer a second question: *What are my options to change the outcome of the ADM, and receive the credit?* For example, comparing the first contrastive with the factual rule, an increase of the feature capitalgain will lead to a change in the predicted outcome of the ADM. Similarly, an increase in the capitalgain, and a change in the age (from 19 to 20 or higher) will alter it.

In the next step, we add some background knowledge to the explanations. We apply an immutability constraint on the feature age:

```
USER:     r.constraint('CE.age = F.age')
          r.solveopt(verbose=2)
REASONX: Rule satisfied by CE:
          IF CE.capitalgain>5119.0,CE.capitalgain<=5316.5
          THEN >50K [1.0]
```

As expected, the solution has changed: by adding the above-stated constraint, the admissible region for CEs becomes smaller, and only one contrastive rule remains. Last, we ask for the CE that is *closest* to the factual instance:

```
USER:     r.solveopt(minimize='l1norm(F, CE)', project=['CE'],
          verbose = 2)
REASONX: Answer constraint:
          CE.race=Black, CE.sex=Male,
          CE.workclass=Private,
          CE.education=10.0,
          CE.age=19.0,
          CE.capitalgain=5119.0,
          CE.capitalloss=0.0,
          CE.hoursperweek=40.0
```

REASONX returned the *closest* CE. This corresponds to the most common notion of a CE in the literature. However, REASONX also took care of the specified background knowledge - the CE is returned under the above specified constraints on the feature **age**. This is a similar case as described in Sect. 4, Fig. 3, left. We extend the example to account for under-specified information. E.g., it can be interesting to ask for the *closest* CE in the case the feature **age** is not fixed, but restricted to 19 years or lower.

```
USER:     r.retract('F.age=19.0')
          r.constraint('F.age<=19.0')
          r.solveopt(minimize='l1norm(F, CE)', project=['CE', 'F.age'],
          verbose = 2)
REASONX: Answer constraint:
          CE.race=Black, CE.sex=Male,
          CE.workclass=Private,
          CE.education=10.0,
          CE.age=F.age,
          CE.capitalgain=5119.0,
          CE.capitalloss=0.0,
          CE.hoursperweek=40.0
```

The returned solution of REASONX is similar to the previous one, but we observe that also in the CE, the feature **age** is not fixed to a single value but is provided as an equality region. This is a nice demonstration of how both in the input and the output, REASONX does work under under-specified information. For a similar example based on the synthetic data set, see Sect. 4, Fig. 3, right.

Since queries work iteratively, the flow of the above corresponds exactly to how an *interaction* with REASONX could look like, forming what we call an explanation (dialogue). Repeated specification of background knowledge and querying are a central part of this dialogue between the end-user and REASONX, allowing to build individual, personalized explanations.

6   Limitations

Evaluation So far, we demonstrated the capabilities of REASONX via a synthetic illustration and an example in the credit domain, and - by surveying relevant literature - we showed how REASONX is novel against other XAI tools. The most prominent difference between REASONX and other XAI methods is that it relies on symbolic reasoning, based on CLP capabilities, to generate (contrastive) explanations. This is exactly what makes it possible for REASONX to combine a set of useful properties: background knowledge integration, interactivity, and operation under under-specified knowledge. However, a thorough evaluation of REASONX is currently *missing* from this paper. While there is yet no fixed consensus on how to evaluate an explanation, in the case of REASONX, a qualitative and quantitative evaluation is especially tricky: no method exists so far for explanation tools utilizing CLP. Developing a proposal of a set of suitable methods is therefore a priority for future work. We also point out the possibility of user studies for evaluation [36], or validation via real-world data [32].

Technical. We demonstrated the capabilities of REASONX on (nominal, ordinal, and continuous) tabular data, and for a binary decision problem. While an extension to multi-class problems is straightforward, the extension to unstructured data, such as text and images, needs to be strictly formalized. In the domain of images, a solution can be the integration of concepts, as demonstrated by [14].

Social. We discussed the delivery of explanations to enable the end-user to understand the decision better. Another reason to compute explanations is to understand algorithmic harms such as bias. An important question is: *Is the protected attribute (e.g., gender, race, age [15]) determining the decision outcome?* The answer can be given by e.g., comparing a factual instance and the CE, with a focus on whether only protected attributes alter the decision outcome.

Another important point to consider is the fairness of explanations. For two popular model-agnostic, local methods it has been shown that explanations can be unfair: different fidelity values can apply for different subgroups [3].

Last, we would like to discuss two basic assumptions of REASONX that *must* be taken care of in social application contexts. We do not explicitly talk about recommendations based on contrastive explanations but must consider this as a secondary application, as discussed under the keyword of *algorithmic recourse* [23]. First, we assume that our model is *stable over time*, making it possible not only to obtain several contrastive explanations but proposing that the CE suggests a change that indeed alters the outcome of the ML model. While this might hold in a toy setting, it likely does not in practice and can create some wrong promises [4,45]. Second, by querying the *closest* CE, there is often the implicit assumption that the closer such a CE, the easier the proposed change. This does not necessarily hold in practice, as pointed out already [23]. While an extension of REASONX to account for a variety of norms in the optimization is possible and part of future work, we acknowledge the importance of the choice of a suitable distance function, depending on the context of the application.

7   Conclusion

We presented REASONX, an explanation tool that interactively provides con-trastive explanations that can account for background knowledge in the form of constraints, and that works under-specified information. Background knowledge has the potential to significantly improve the quality of an explanation, while interactivity is an important aspect of explanations to be communicated to the end-user. Further, our tool works on under-specified information (profiles) which leads to increased flexibility. REASONX provides explanations for decision trees, which can be the ML models under analysis, or global/local surrogate models of any ML model. We demonstrated REASONX both on a synthetic data set, and an example in the credit domain.

We aim at extending REASONX along several directions: i) the implementa-tion of more constraints, ii) an extension to account for more expressive trees such as oblique/optimal decision trees, iii) the application to local explanations. Implementing other constraints (e.g., diversity of a set of CEs, or sparsity of changes from the factual instance to the CE) will lead to a more flexible tool, and possibly better explanations, depending on the context that will necessitate these constraints. Relying on oblique/optimal decision trees instead of standard decision trees that use axis-parallel splits will allow to better fit the model onto the data, for higher accuracies, and therefore improved quality of the explana-tions, while not departing from reasoning over linear constraints. Last, REASONX can be easily adapted as a local explanation tool. The necessary changes include learning the tree not over the input data but a local neighborhood, which can, for example, be generated using random perturbations as in LIME [35].

We would also like to refer to the option to extend REASONX in a direction that allows a tighter integration between symbolic and sub-symbolic approaches. One possibility is an extension that allows REASONX to extract the rules which are fundamental to REASONX not via a tree, but directly from an underlying sub-symbolic structure.

Acknowledgments. Work supported by the European Union's Horizon 2020 research and innovation programme under Marie Sklodowska-Curie Actions for the project NoBIAS (g.a. No. 860630), and under the Excellent Science European Research Coun-cil (ERC) programme for the XAI project (g.a. No. 834756). This work reflects only the authors' views and the European Research Executive Agency (REA) is not responsible for any use that may be made of the information it contains.

References

1. Apt, K.: From Logic Programming to Prolog. Prentice Hall, London New York (1997)
2. Artelt, A., Vrachimis, S.G., Eliades, D.G., Polycarpou, M.M., Hammer, B.: One explanation to rule them all - ensemble consistent explanations. CoRR abs/2205.08974 (2022)

3. Balagopalan, A., Zhang, H., Hamidieh, K., Hartvigsen, T., Rudzicz, F., Ghassemi, M.: The road to explainability is paved with bias: measuring the fairness of explanations. In: FAccT, pp. 1194–1206. ACM (2022)

4. Barocas, S., Selbst, A.D., Raghavan, M.: The hidden assumptions behind counterfactual explanations and principal reasons. In: FAT*, pp. 80–89. ACM (2020)

5. Beckh, K., et al.: Explainable machine learning with prior knowledge: an overview. CoRR abs/2105.10172 (2021)

6. Bertossi, L.E.: Declarative approaches to counterfactual explanations for classification. CoRR abs/2011.07423 (2020)

7. Byrne, R.M.J.: Counterfactuals in explainable artificial intelligence (XAI): evidence from human reasoning. In: IJCAI, pp. 6276–6282. ijcai.org (2019)

8. Calegari, R., Ciatto, G., Omicini, A.: On the integration of symbolic and subsymbolic techniques for XAI: a survey. Intelligenza Artificiale 14(1), 7–32 (2020)

9. Chang, C., Creager, E., Goldenberg, A., Duvenaud, D.: Explaining image classifiers by counterfactual generation. In: ICLR (Poster). OpenReview.net (2019)

10. Clocksin, W.F., Mellish, C.S.: Programming in Prolog. Using the ISO Standard. Springer, Heidelberg (2003). https://doi.org/10.1007/978-3-642-55481-0

11. Confalonieri, R., Coba, L., Wagner, B., Besold, T.R.: A historical perspective of explainable artificial intelligence. WIREs Data Mining Knowl. Discov. 11(1), e1391 (2021)

12. Cropper, A., Dumancic, S.: Inductive logic programming at 30: a new introduction. J. Artif. Intell. Res. 74, 765–850 (2022)

13. Cui, Z., Chen, W., He, Y., Chen, Y.: Optimal action extraction for random forests and boosted trees. In: KDD, pp. 179–188. ACM (2015)

14. Donadello, I., Dragoni, M.: Sexai: introducing concepts into black boxes for explainable artificial intelligence. In: XAI.it@AI*IA. CEUR Workshop Proceedings, vol. 2742, pp. 41–54. CEUR-WS.org (2020)

15. European Union: Charter of Fundamental Rights of the European Union (2007)

16. European Commission: Proposal for a regulation of the European Parliament and the Council laying down harmonized rules on artificial intelligence (Artificial Intelligence Act) and amending certain union legislative acts (2021)

17. Guidotti, R.: Counterfactual explanations and how to find them: literature review and benchmarking. Data Mining and Knowledge Discovery (2022). https://doi.org/10.1007/s10618-022-00831-6

18. Guidotti, R., Monreale, A., Giannotti, F., Pedreschi, D., Ruggieri, S., Turini, F.: Factual and counterfactual explanations for black box decision making. IEEE Intell. Syst. 34(6), 14–23 (2019)

19. Guidotti, R., Monreale, A., Ruggieri, S., Turini, F., Giannotti, F., Pedreschi, D.: A survey of methods for explaining black box models. ACM Comput. Surv. 51(5), 93:1–93:42 (2019)

20. Jaffar, J., Michaylov, S., Stuckey, P.J., Yap, R.H.C.: The CLP(R) language and system. ACM Trans. Program. Lang. Syst. 14(3), 339–395 (1992)

21. Kanamori, K., Takagi, T., Kobayashi, K., Arimura, H.: DACE: distribution-aware counterfactual explanation by mixed-integer linear optimization. In: IJCAI, pp. 2855–2862. ijcai.org (2020)

22. Karimi, A., Barthe, G., Balle, B., Valera, I.: Model-agnostic counterfactual explanations for consequential decisions. In: AISTATS. Proceedings of Machine Learning Research, vol. 108, pp. 895–905. PMLR (2020)

23. Karimi, A., Barthe, G., Schölkopf, B., Valera, I.: A survey of algorithmic recourse: definitions, formulations, solutions, and prospects. CoRR abs/2010.04050 (2020)

24. Karimi, A., Schölkopf, B., Valera, I.: Algorithmic recourse: from counterfactual explanations to interventions. In: FAccT, pp. 353–362. ACM (2021)
25. Keane, M.T., Kenny, E.M., Delaney, E., Smyth, B.: If only we had better counterfactual explanations: five key deficits to rectify in the evaluation of counterfactual XAI techniques. In: IJCAI, pp. 4466–4474. ijcai.org (2021)
26. Körner, P., et al.: Fifty years of Prolog and beyond. Theory Pract. Log. Program. **22**(6), 776–858 (2022)
27. Lakkaraju, H., Slack, D., Chen, Y., Tan, C., Singh, S.: Rethinking explainability as a dialogue: a practitioner's perspective. CoRR abs/2202.01875 (2022)
28. Miller, T.: Explanation in artificial intelligence: insights from the social sciences. Artif. Intell. **267**, 1–38 (2019)
29. Miller, T., Howe, P., Sonenberg, L.: Explainable AI: beware of inmates running the asylum or: how I learnt to stop worrying and love the social and behavioural sciences. CoRR abs/1712.00547 (2017)
30. Mittelstadt, B.D., Russell, C., Wachter, S.: Explaining explanations in AI. In: FAT, pp. 279–288. ACM (2019)
31. Mothilal, R.K., Sharma, A., Tan, C.: Explaining machine learning classifiers through diverse counterfactual explanations. In: FAT*, pp. 607–617. ACM (2020)
32. Murdoch, W.J., Singh, C., Kumbier, K., Abbasi-Asl, R., Yu, B.: Interpretable machine learning: definitions, methods, and applications. CoRR abs/1901.04592 (2019)
33. Panigutti, C., Perotti, A., Pedreschi, D.: Doctor XAI: an ontology-based approach to black-box sequential data classification explanations. In: FAT*, pp. 629–639. ACM (2020)
34. Rawal, K., Lakkaraju, H.: Beyond individualized recourse: interpretable and interactive summaries of actionable recourses. In: NeurIPS (2020)
35. Ribeiro, M.T., Singh, S., Guestrin, C.: "Why should I trust you?": explaining the predictions of any classifier. In: KDD, pp. 1135–1144. ACM (2016)
36. Rong, Y., et al.: Towards human-centered explainable AI: user studies for model explanations. CoRR abs/2210.11584 (2022)
37. Ruggieri, S., Pedreschi, D., Turini, F.: Data mining for discrimination discovery. ACM Trans. Knowl. Discov. Data **4**(2), 9:1–9:40 (2010)
38. Russell, C.: Efficient search for diverse coherent explanations. In: FAT, pp. 20–28. ACM (2019)
39. Russell, S.J., Norvig, P.: Artificial Intelligence: A Modern Approach, 2nd edn. Pearson Education, London (2003)
40. Setzu, M., Guidotti, R., Monreale, A., Turini, F., Pedreschi, D., Giannotti, F.: GLocalX - from local to global explanations of black box AI models. Artif. Intell. **294**, 103457 (2021)
41. Sokol, K.: Towards intelligible and robust surrogate explainers: a decision tree perspective. Ph.D. thesis, School of Computer Science, Electrical and Electronic Engineering, and Engineering Maths, University of Bristol (2021)
42. Sokol, K., Flach, P.A.: Glass-box: explaining AI decisions with counterfactual statements through conversation with a voice-enabled virtual assistant. In: IJCAI, pp. 5868–5870. ijcai.org (2018)
43. Sokol, K., Flach, P.A.: LIMEtree: interactively customisable explanations based on local surrogate multi-output regression trees. CoRR abs/2005.01427 (2020)
44. Sokol, K., Flach, P.A.: One explanation does not fit all. Künstliche Intell. **34**(2), 235–250 (2020)
45. State, L.: Logic programming for XAI: a technical perspective. In: ICLP Workshops. CEUR Workshop Proceedings, vol. 2970. CEUR-WS.org (2021)

46. Stepin, I., Alonso, J.M., Catalá, A., Pereira-Fariña, M.: A survey of contrastive and counterfactual explanation generation methods for explainable artificial intelligence. IEEE Access **9**, 11974–12001 (2021)
47. Takemura, A., Inoue, K.: Generating explainable rule sets from tree-ensemble learning methods by answer set programming. In: ICLP Technical Communications. EPTCS, vol. 345, pp. 127–140 (2021)
48. Ustun, B., Spangher, A., Liu, Y.: Actionable recourse in linear classification. In: FAT, pp. 10–19. ACM (2019)
49. Wachter, S., et al.: Counterfactual explanations without opening the black box. Harv. JL Tech. **31**, 841 (2017)
50. Warren, G., Keane, M.T., Guéret, C., Delaney, E.: Explaining groups of instances counterfactually for XAI: a use case, algorithm and user study for group-counterfactuals. CoRR abs/2303.09297 (2023)
51. Weld, D.S., Bansal, G.: The challenge of crafting intelligible intelligence. Commun. ACM **62**(6), 70–79 (2019)
52. Wielemaker, J., Schrijvers, T., Triska, M., Lager, T.: SWI-Prolog. Theory Pract. Log. Program. **12**(1–2), 67–96 (2012)
53. Wu, T., Ribeiro, M.T., Heer, J., Weld, D.S.: Polyjuice: generating counterfactuals for explaining, evaluating, and improving models. In: ACL/IJCNLP (1), pp. 6707–6723. Association for Computational Linguistics (2021)

Sanity Checks for Saliency Methods Explaining Object Detectors

Deepan Chakravarthi Padmanabhan[1] , Paul G. Plöger[1],
Octavio Arriaga[2], and Matias Valdenegro-Toro[3]

[1] Bonn-Rhein-Sieg University of Applied Sciences, Sankt Augustin, Germany
[2] University of Bremen, Bremen, Germany
arriagac@uni-bremen.de
[3] University of Groningen, Groningen, The Netherlands
m.a.valdenegro.toro@rug.nl

Abstract. Saliency methods are frequently used to explain Deep Neural Network-based models. Adebayo *et al.*'s work on evaluating saliency methods for classification models illustrate certain explanation methods fail the model and data randomization tests. However, on extending the tests for various state of the art object detectors we illustrate that the ability to explain a model is more dependent on the model itself than the explanation method. We perform sanity checks for object detection and define new qualitative criteria to evaluate the saliency explanations, both for object classification and bounding box decisions, using Guided Backpropagation, Integrated Gradients, and their Smoothgrad versions, together with Faster R-CNN, SSD, and EfficientDet-D0, trained on COCO. In addition, the sensitivity of the explanation method to model parameters and data labels varies class-wise motivating to perform the sanity checks for each class. We find that EfficientDet-D0 is the most interpretable method independent of the saliency method, which passes the sanity checks with little problems.

Keywords: Object detectors · Saliency methods · Sanity checks

1 Introduction

Localizing and categorizing different object instances is pivotal in various real-world applications such as autonomous driving [7], healthcare [4], and text detection [9]. Recent advances with Deep Neural Network-based (DNN) object detectors demonstrate remarkable performances both in terms of robustness and generalization across practical use cases [3]. Even though detectors are extensively needed in safety-critical applications, the heavily parameterized DNN-based detectors limit understanding the rationale behind the detections made by such detectors. In addition, object detectors are prone to non-local effects as a slight change in the object position can affect the detector prediction [20]. Therefore, explaining detector decisions is imperative to earn user trust and

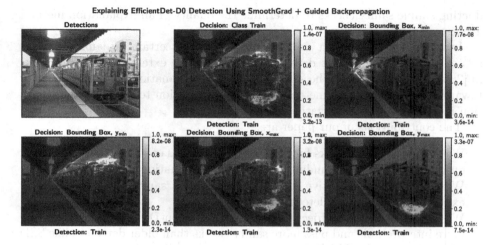

Fig. 1. Sample detection explanations using EfficientDet-D0 and SGBP, considering one saliency explanation for classification and bounding box regression decisions. We find that EfficientDet-D0 provides high quality explanations that pass sanity checks. For all figures in this paper, the saliency maps are overlaid on the corresponding original image after min-max normalization with the minimum and maximum value indicated in the corresponding heatmap.

understand the reason behind predictions to a certain extent in safety-critical situations, overall improving system safety.

Explaining a DNN decision-making process has been addressed prominently [6,23,24,34]. The explanations are useful for debugging the model, reveal the spurious effects and biases learned by a model as well as underpins regulatory requirements (like GDPR). Furthermore, such explanations boost transparency and contribute towards safety of the associated DNN-based systems [11,29]. Among the methods explaining DNNs, saliency methods are popular explanation methods [16,21], which provide the input feature attribution that highlights the most relevant pixels responsible for the model prediction. Despite extensive study of employing saliency methods to classification tasks, only handful of works explain detector decisions [8,18,30]. Moreover, the evaluation metrics used to quantitatively assess the detector explanations fail certain sanity checks as well and prove to be statistically unreliable [28].

Sanity checks are basic procedures to test the ability of an explanation method to correctly explain a model decision [2] or test the ability of an evaluation metrics to correctly assess the explanation method [28] that generates a saliency map. In this paper, we are concerned with the former, where we check the ability of an explanation method to generate relevant saliency map based explanations for detections made by an object detector. However, there is limited work studying object detector explainability, and in particular basic sanity checks have not been performed to the best of our knowledge. Therefore, conducting simple sanity checks to determine the quality of an explanation method is extremely important.

In this paper we conduct simple sanity checks for certain explanation methods explaining three object detector predictions. We extend the sanity checks in [2] to object detectors. The sanity checks test explanation method sensitivity towards the detectors parameters (model randomization test) and data generation method (data randomization test) (Fig. 1).

The contributions of our paper are:

- We evaluate sanity checks for saliency explanations of object detectors, both on classification and bounding box decision explanations.
- We define clear qualitative evaluation criteria for sanity checks in saliency explanations for object detectors.
- We find that Modern object detectors like EfficientDet-D0 [27] seem to be more interpretable and pass more sanity checks than older detectors like SSD [15] and Faster R-CNN [19].

We expect that our work helps advance our understanding of object detector explainability and increases the use of explanations in computer vision.

2   Related Work

Adebayo *et al.* [2] are the pioneers to propose sanity checks for explanation methods based on randomization tests. The authors identify that various widely used explanation methods provide saliency map explanations that are independent of the model parameters and the data used to develop the model. The widely-used gradient-based explanation methods such as guided backpropagation [24] and Guided GradCAM [22] fail both model and data randomization sanity checks. In this related work, the sanity checks are performed on classifier models such as Inception v3, CNN, and MLP trained using ImageNet, Fashion MNIST, and MNIST datasets respectively. However, Yona *et al.* [33] posit that the randomization tests are distribution-dependent and modify the sanity checks proposed in [2] with a causal perspective. The model sensitivity test is performed by combining the original images with multiple or partial objects to generate saliency maps for random and trained model. This reformulation is an attempt to spatially control the relevant features for a particular class and extract visually distinct saliency maps. The methods failing the sanity checks in [2] such as vanilla and guided backpropagation pass this reformulated version. Kindermans *et al.* [13] proposes input invariance property as a sanity check for saliency methods. The saliency method output should not be affected by the transformations done to the input, mirroring the model sensitivity to the specific transformation. Experiments on MNIST illustrate the possibility to forcefully manipulate the explanations. The literature on interpretability cover certain axioms such as completeness [6], implementation invariance, and sensitivity [26] are considered as indicators of reliability for saliency methods. Kim *et al.* [12] develop a synthetic benchmark and enable a ground-truth-based evaluation procedure. Various evaluation metrics to assess the explanation method with regards to factors such as faithfulness, robustness, and fairness of explanation is provided by [10]. Tomsett *et al.* [28] conclude the evaluation metrics assessing the faithfulness of the explanations are unreliable by conducting certain sanity checks on the metrics. In this paper, we extend the sanity checks performed by [2] based on randomization to detectors and report our findings.

3 Sanity Checks for Object Detection Saliency Explanations

We use two kinds of sanity checks as defined by Adebayo *et al.* [2]. The model parameter and data randomization tests have been proposed to evaluate the explanation methods for classification tasks.

Model Randomization. The model parameter randomization test analyzes the saliency method output for a trained classifier model against the saliency method output for a model parameter initialized with random values [2]. The saliency maps help to understand the explanation method sensitivity to model parameters and to model properties, in general. A similar saliency map signifies that the saliency method will not be helpful to debug a model as the saliency method is invariant to the model parameters.

Data Randomization. In the data randomization test, the saliency maps for a model trained on a correctly labeled dataset and model trained using randomly permuted labels are compared [2].

A similar saliency map between the two outputs illustrates the relationship insensitivity between labels and input images. The saliency maps will not reflect the reason behind label and input image relationship captured by the data generation process. If the explanations are indifferent to a random label assigned to a mammogram image, for instance, the saliency map fails to explain the real reason for a diagnosis output.

The tests serve as sanity checks to assess the scope of a particular explanation method for explaining models performing certain tasks. These are very basic assumptions made on saliency explanations and many methods fail these basic tests in classification tasks.

In this paper, we use the two randomization tests on pre-trained object detectors, for a certain set of saliency explanation methods, and we test if those detectors and explanation methods pass the basic sanity checks.

3.1 Quantitative Evaluation Criteria

For quantitative evaluation, in order to assess the change in saliency maps when randomizing the model parameters, the similarity between the classification decision saliency maps generated from each randomized model instance and the true model is computed using Structural Similarity (SSIM). This allows for visual changes to the saliency map to be compared and tracked.

Table 1. Summary of the subjective analysis for the model randomization test. The score is computed as explained in Sect. 3.2. The higher the score the more sensitive is the method for the detector model parameters. Each column indicates an aspect considered to evaluate the change in the saliency map which is produced for the randomized model. The table is generated by scoring the majority characteristic illustrated by each detector and explanation method combination over 15 randomly sampled detections from the COCO test 2017 split.

OD	IM	Edge Detector	Highlight only Interest Object	Focus more than One Object	Texture Change	Illustrate Artifacts	Intensity range change	Score
ED0	GBP	✗	✗	✗	✓	✗	✓	7
	SGBP	✗	✗	✗	✓	✗	✓	7
	IG	✗	✗	✗	✓	✗	✓	7
	SIG	✗	✗	✗	✓	✗	✓	7
SSD	GBP	✓	✗	✗	✓	✗	✓	5
	SGBP	✓	✗	✗	✓	✗	✓	5
	IG	✓	✗	✗	✓	✗	✓	5
	SIG	✓	✗	✗	✓	✗	✓	5
FRN	GBP	✗	✗	✗	✗	✓	✓	1
	SGBP	✗	✗	✗	✗	✓	✓	1
	IG	✗	✗	✓	✓	✓	✓	5
	SIG	✗	✗	✓	✓	✓	✓	5

3.2   Qualitative Evaluation Criteria

This section reports on the subjective analysis carried out to understand the differences in sensitivity of explanation methods across various detectors. Table 1 illustrates clearly that the ability to explain is more model-dependent than the ability of the explanation method to interpret a particular model.

A comparison is developed by visually inspecting certain aspects of the saliency map obtained using a completely randomized model and also by comparing it with the saliency map generated using the trained model. The various aspects considered to indicate the magnitude of sensitivity are provided below with the a scoring guide. A visual illustration of these aspects is shown in Table 2. In the negative scenarios, the methods are awarded a score $-1 \times$ (score awarded below). A score 1 is added to the total score if the method scores 1 for any one aspect. This indicates that the method passes the sanity test.

Now we define criteria to evaluate a saliency map made by explaining an object detector output.

1. **Edge detector**. Saliency methods sometimes act as an edge detector which does not depend on the input image, which is undesirable [2]. A method acting as an edge detector is scored -1 because the explanations should be meaningful rather than simply behaving like an edge detector.

Table 2. Visual illustrations of saliency map sanity check properties. This table compares explanation patterns made by different detectors and saliency explanation methods against a randomly trained model. These results complement the qualitative evaluation we perform in this paper.

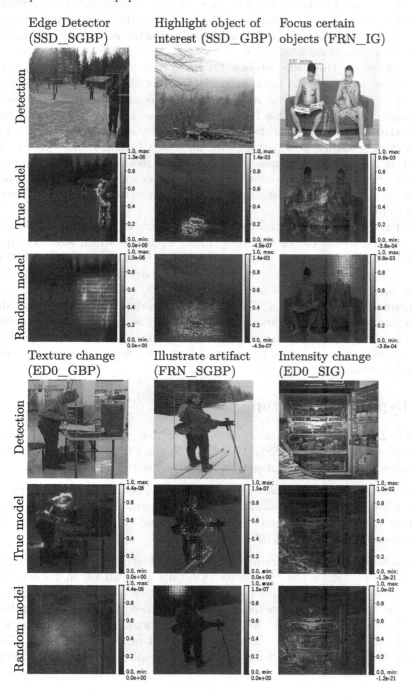

2. **Highlight only interest object**. Saliency explanations should be focused on the interest object inside the bounding box, assuming that that model performs adequately and is not fooled by context or background [20]. A model with randomized should not have this behavior as information was destroyed and the saliency map should reflect this. When the saliency map generated using the randomized model only highlights the interest object explained, the method is awarded a −1 score.
3. **Focus more than one object**. Opposite from the previous criteria, a randomized model should focus in more than one object as there is no object-specific information in the model. Score of 1 is awarded to the method producing a saliency map that highlights more than a single object in the image.
4. **Texture change**. The texture of a saliency map denotes the spatial arrangement of intensity in a pattern over an image region. If the texture of the saliency map obtained using the randomized model varies from that of the saliency map of the true model, the method is awarded a score 1. For instance, the randomized model map can be a smoothened version without sharp features or completely hazy.
5. **Illustrate artifacts**. Artifacts in saliency maps are also undesirable as they show bias in the model structure and/or equations which affect the quality of a saliency map. If the saliency map from the randomized model displays certain image artifacts such as checkerboard artifacts and sharp parallel lines, the method is awarded −1.
6. **Intensity range change**. The range of pixel values in a saliency map should change as the model is randomized, reflecting the destruction in information when weights are randomized. Score of 1 is awarded if the saliency map intensity range changes before normalizing between 0 to 1 across the randomized and true model.

4   Experimental Setup

Object Detectors. In this study we evaluate three pre-trained object detectors: Faster R-CNN (FRN) [19], SSD512 (SSD) [15], and EfficientDet-D0 (EDO0) [27], all trained on the COCO dataset [14]. Detailes are provided in Table 3.

Explanation Methods. We evaluate several gradient-based saliency methods, namely Guided Backpropagation (GBP) and Integrated Gradients (IG), as well as their variations using SmoothGrad (SGBP and SIG). Mathematical details for these methods are provided in the appendix.

Datasets. The detectors trained on common objects are used to perform the model randomization test. The detector details are available in Table 3. Therefore, the model randomization test is carried out for all the 12 combinations of detectors and explanation methods. The dataset used for the model randomization study is the COCO test 2017 split [14]. 15 randomly sampled images from the COCO test 2017 split is analyzed for model randomization test. The test split is chosen because the train and validation splits are used in training the detectors.

Table 3. Summary of object objector implementations used in this work. The detectors are trained to detect common objects using COCO dataset. The mAP reported is at 0.5 IoU threshold. val35k represents 35k COCO validation split images. minival is the remaining images in the validation set after sampling val35k.

COCO split						
Detector	Stage	Train set	Test set	mAP (%)	Weights	Code
Faster R-CNN	Two	train+val35k 2014	minival2014	54.4	[1]	[1]
SSD512	Single	train+val35k 2014	test-dev 2015	46.5	[15]	[5]
EfficientDet-D0	Single	train 2017	test-dev 2017	53.0	[27]	[5]

Table 4. Details about the marine debris objector used in this work. The mAP reported is at 0.5 IoU threshold.

SSD Backbones	mAP (%)	Input Image Size
VGG16	91.69	300×300
ResNet20	89.85	96×96
MobileNet	70.30	96×96
DenseNet121	73.80	96×96
SqueezeNet	68.37	96×96
MiniXception	71.62	96×96

In order to perform the data randomization test, the Marine Debris dataset [31,32] is used. This study uses two versions of SSD trained on the Marine Debris dataset. Details and performance of detectors trained on Marine Debris Dataset are shown in Table 4. The two versions are true and random SSD models with VGG16 backbone trained using the true and random labels respectively. The additional details about the true SSD-VGG16 model is provided in Table 4. The random detector is trained using random class labels and adding random noise to the ground truth box coordinates. The random detector is trained until the mAP@[IoU = 0.5] on the train set is 80%. The explanations are generated for the test set images. The Marine Debris dataset is used for this experiment to overcome the time taken to train a detector on a complex COCO dataset. In addition, the Marine debris dataset aids in studying the applicability of explaining detectors in a real-world application.

5 Results and Discussion

Model Randomization Test: The saliency maps are investigated for both the bounding box and classification decisions corresponding to a detection. The model parameter randomization randomizes the weight variables starting from the last layers. The left-most column after the interest detection with 0% represents the saliency map generated using the trained model with none of the

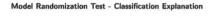

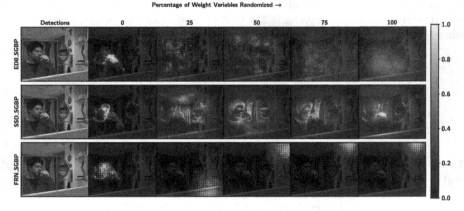

Fig. 2. Model randomization test for classification explanations (red-colored box) across different models using SGBP. The first column is the detection of interest that is explained in the consecutive columns. The second column is the saliency map generated using the trained model without randomizing any parameters, which highlights the important parts such as hands, eyes, and face. The last column is the saliency map generated using a model with all parameters randomized. Note how FRN fails the randomization test. (Color figure online)

weight variables randomized. 100% in the last column is the saliency maps generated using a randomly initialized model with all weight variables completely randomized. Figure 2 illustrates the effect of classification explanations to the model parameters. In the case of the EfficientDet-D0 classification explanation with SGBP, the saliency map is completely noisy without highlighting any specific feature. SSD with SGBP acts like an edge detector by sharply highlighting certain features as the number of weight variables randomized changes. However, the saliency map highlights feature other than the person object. Figure 4 illustrate the sensitivity of box coordinate x_{min} explanations using SGBP to the model characteristics. The saliency maps highlight regions of the person at a certain randomization level for SIG as shown in Fig. 3.

The magnitude of change between the saliency maps of true and randomized model is different for each model as the weight variables are randomized. It clearly illustrates model randomization tests should be performed for each model and method combinations as stated in the related work. Section 3.2 discusses subjectively the magnitude of the change in sensitivity across detectors and explanation method combinations. Therefore, the ability to explain models are more dependent on the model than the ability of the explanation method to explain the model.

The explanation using GBP for EfficientDet-D0 is noisy because the GBP method acts similar to the Gradients method in the case of EfficientDet-D0. Gradients estimate the gradient of the output target neuron with the input. Since

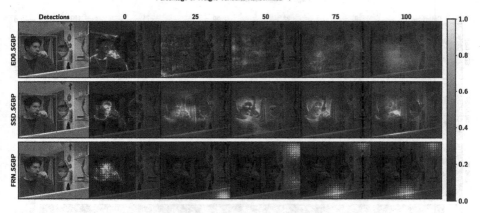

Fig. 3. Comparison of explanations using different explanation methods for the classification decision corresponding to EfficientDet-D0 detections. The first column is the detection (red-colored box) explained by the methods. The second column is the saliency map generated using the trained model without randomizing any parameters. The last column is the saliency map generated using the model with all parameters randomized. SIG after randomizing 75% of the weight variables visually highlight certain regions of the person detection. However, the magnitude is relatively very less and texture of the map is considerably different to the true model explanation. (Color figure online)

there are no ReLU activations for EfficientDet-D0 the negative contributions are not retarded and the prime usage of GBP is relaxed to work as Gradients method.

The SSIM in Fig. 5 is the average SSIM across different percentage of weight variables randomized for a set of 15 images randomly sampled from the COCO test set. Since the explanations have changed in terms of the important pixels highlighted, saliency map texture, and SSIM metric with regards to the explanations using the true model, all the explanation methods pass the model randomization test for detectors.

The gradient attribution maps for the two-stage detector, Faster R-CNN, illustrate checkerboard artifact on randomizing weights as shown in Fig. 2. There are various reasons for the gradient artifacts as discussed in [17,25].

In the case of using GBP and SGBP with Faster R-CNN, the higher SSIM between the classification decision saliency maps of completely randomized model and true model is because of the checkerboard artifact shown in Fig. 2. Even though the center of mass of the grid pattern shifts over the image, the SSIM provides a higher score due to similarity in the pattern. This observation is in agreement with the subjective analysis in Sect. 3.2 with low sensitivity scores for Faster R-CNN - GBP as well as Faster R-CNN - SGBP compared to other detector and explanation method combinations.

Model Randomization Test - Classification Explanation

Percentage of Weight Variables Randomized →

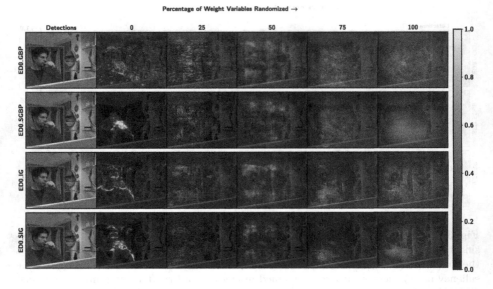

Fig. 4. Model randomization test for x_{min} explanations (red-colored box) across different models using SGBP. The first column is the detection of interest that is explained in the consecutive columns. The second column is the saliency map generated using the trained model without randomizing any parameters. The second column highlights the important parts such as hands, eyes, and face. The last column is the saliency map generated using a model with all parameters randomized. Note how FRN fails the randomization test.

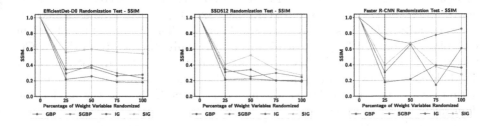

Fig. 5. A quantitative assessment using SSIM of the change in classification saliency map features during model randomization test across explanation methods and detectors is provided. SSIM is the average SSIM computed across a subset of test images sampled from the COCO test 2017.

Data Randomization Test: Figure 6 illustrate the differences in the saliency maps explaining classification decision of SSD-VGG16. The attribution map intensity levels are largely different. The texture of the explanations from the random model looks smoothed. However, the explanations generated using the true model illustrate sharp features. There are substantial differences in the

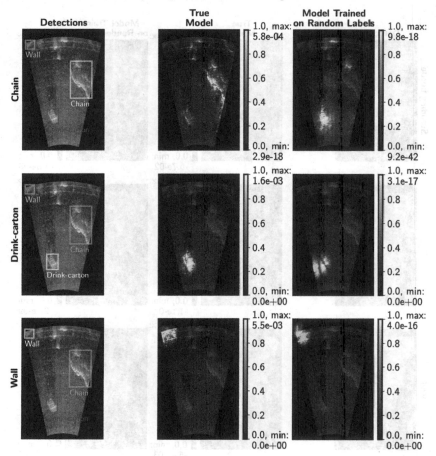

Fig. 6. Data randomization test using SSD-VGG16 and SIG. The saliency maps explains the classification decision. The first column depicts the detections, the detection of interest is highlighted in white. The true and random model classification explanations differ in terms of the features highlighted, attribution intensity, and the explanation texture.

saliency map generated using SIG for the chain detection in Fig. 6. In addition, the drink-carton classification explanations for the random model illustrates patches, where as, the drink-carton is relatively sharper in the explanation from the true model. However, the difference for other detection is only at the level of attribution intensity and texture. Therefore, this opens up the possibility to perform sanity checks at the class level. The methods should remain sensitive for each class predicted by the model. The findings is consistent in Fig. 7 for explanations generated using GBP. In addition, all the explanation methods provide different saliency maps for both classification and bounding box explanations in

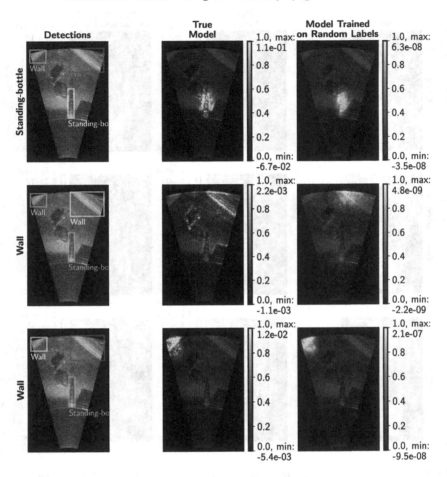

Fig. 7. Data randomization test using SSD-VGG16 and GBP. The saliency maps explains the classification decision. The first column depicts the detections, the detection of interest is highlighted in white. The true and random model classification explanations differ in terms of the features highlighted, attribution intensity, and the explanation texture.

terms of features highlighted, saliency map texture, and the attribution intensity. Therefore, none of the selected explanation methods fail the data randomization test for the SSD-VGG16 detector.

6   Conclusions and Future Work

In this work we have evaluated standard sanity checks for saliency explanations in object detectors, considering both object classification and bounding box regression explanations, through data and weight randomization. We defined new qualitative criteria to systematically evaluate saliency maps visually, and we find that overall, more modern object detectors like EfficientDet-D0 pass more sanity checks and provide higher quality saliency explanations than older detectors like SSD and Faster R-CNN.

Our conclusions hold under multiple gradient-based saliency methods, we tested Guided Backpropagation and Integrated gradients, as well as their Smooth Gradient combinations.

When Faster R-CNN fails to be explained using gradient-based saliency maps, there are large checkerboard artifacts in the explanation, which stay even as weights are randomized. SSD does not produce checkboard patterns but the explanation is insensitive to weights being randomized. Only EfficientDet-D0 produces explanations that pass both data and weight randomization checks.

We expect that our work can increase interest in object detector explanations, and provide additional ways to empirically validate these explanations. We believe that our work provides additional insights not covered by [2], specially using multiple and more complex models like object detectors.

Limitations. On a broader note, our work can focus on a larger evaluation set with more defined evaluation metrics to assess the saliency maps. The evaluation set is limited due to the high computation time to generate saliency maps for each detection in an image for all coordinates, category decision, and randomization levels.

In addition, we consider that certain models are not explainable based solely on the fact that a few explanation methods fail in effectively explaining certain detector decision. To make informed decisions, more explanation methods should be evaluated together with sanity checks. Our work only provides a limited view on this problem, but we do show that explainability depends both on model and saliency explanation method.

A   Additional Sanity Check Results

(See Figs. 8, 9 and 10).

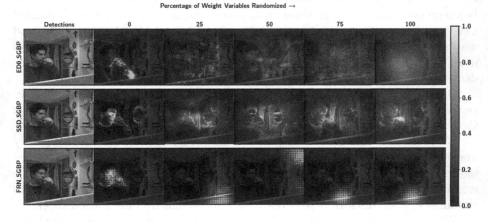

Fig. 8. Model randomization test for x_{max} explanations (red-colored box) across different models using SGBP. The first column is the detection of interest that is explained in the consecutive columns. The second column is the saliency map generated using the trained model without randomizing any parameters. The second column highlights the important parts such as hands, eyes, and face. The last column is the saliency map generated using a model with all parameters randomized. Note how FRN fails the randomization test.

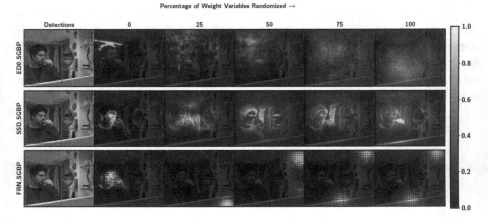

Fig. 9. Model randomization test for y_{min} explanations (red-colored box) across different models using SGBP. The first column is the detection of interest that is explained in the consecutive columns. The second column is the saliency map generated using the trained model without randomizing any parameters. The second column highlights the important parts such as hands, eyes, and face. The last column is the saliency map generated using a model with all parameters randomized. Note how FRN fails the randomization test.

Model Randomization Test - Bounding Box y_{max} Explanation

Percentage of Weight Variables Randomized →

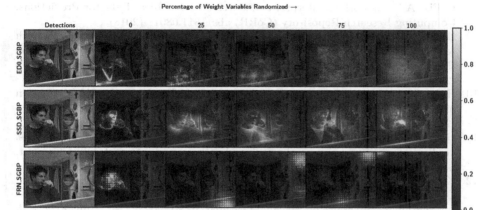

Fig. 10. Model randomization test for y_{max} explanations (red-colored box) across different models using SGBP. The first column is the detection of interest that is explained in the consecutive columns. The second column is the saliency map generated using the trained model without randomizing any parameters. The second column highlights the important parts such as hands, eyes, and face. The last column is the saliency map generated using a model with all parameters randomized. Note how FRN fails the randomization test.

References

1. Abdulla, W.: Mask R-CNN for object detection and instance segmentation on Keras and TensorFlow. GitHub (2017). Accessed 20 Sept 2021
2. Adebayo, J., Gilmer, J., Muelly, M., Goodfellow, I.J., Hardt, M., Kim, B.: Sanity Checks for Saliency Maps. In: Bengio, S., Wallach, H.M., Larochelle, H., Grauman, K., Cesa-Bianchi, N., Garnett, R. (eds.) Advances in Neural Information Processing Systems (NeurIPS), vol. 31, pp. 9525–9536. Curran Associates, Inc. (2018)
3. Arani, E., Gowda, S., Mukherjee, R., Magdy, O., Kathiresan, S.S., Zonooz, B.: A comprehensive study of real-time object detection networks across multiple domains: a survey. Trans. Mach. Learn. Res. (2022). survey Certification
4. Araújo, T., Aresta, G., Galdran, A., Costa, P., Mendonça, A.M., Campilho, A.: UOLO - automatic object detection and segmentation in biomedical images. In: Stoyanov, D., et al. (eds.) DLMIA/ML-CDS -2018. LNCS, vol. 11045, pp. 165–173. Springer, Cham (2018). https://doi.org/10.1007/978-3-030-00889-5_19
5. Arriaga, O., Valdenegro-Toro, M., Muthuraja, M., Devaramani, S., Kirchner, F.: Perception for autonomous systems (paz). computing research repository (CoRR) abs/2010.14541 (2020)
6. Bach, S., Binder, A., Montavon, G., Klauschen, F., Müller, K., Samek, W.: On pixel-wise explanations for non-linear classifier decisions by layer-wise relevance propagation. PLOS ONE **10**(7), 1–46 (2015)
7. Feng, D., et al.: Deep multi-modal object detection and semantic segmentation for autonomous driving: datasets, methods, and challenges. IEEE Trans. Intell. Transp. Syst. (TITS) **22**(3), 1341–1360 (2021)

8. Gudovskiy, D.A., Hodgkinson, A., Yamaguchi, T., Ishii, Y., Tsukizawa, S.: Explain to Fix: A Framework to Interpret and Correct DNN Object Detector Predictions. Computing Research Repository (CoRR) abs/1811.08011 (2018)

9. He, P., Huang, W., He, T., Zhu, Q., Qiao, Y., Li, X.: Single shot text detector with regional attention. In: 2017 IEEE International Conference on Computer Vision (ICCV), pp. 3066–3074. Institute of Electrical and Electronics Engineers (IEEE) (2017)

10. Hedström, A., et al.: Quantus: an explainable AI toolkit for responsible evaluation of neural network explanations and beyond. J. Mach. Learn. Res. **24**(34), 1–11 (2023)

11. Huang, X., et al.: A survey of safety and trustworthiness of deep neural networks: verification, testing, adversarial attack and defence, and interpretability. Comput. Sci. Rev. **37**, 100270 (2020)

12. Kim, J.S., Plumb, G., Talwalkar, A.: Sanity simulations for saliency methods. In: Chaudhuri, K., Jegelka, S., Song, L., Szepesvári, C., Niu, G., Sabato, S. (eds.) International Conference on Machine Learning, ICML 2022, 17–23 July 2022, Baltimore, Maryland, USA. Proceedings of Machine Learning Research, vol. 162, pp. 11173–11200. PMLR (2022)

13. Kindermans, P.-J., et al.: The (un)reliability of saliency methods. In: Samek, W., Montavon, G., Vedaldi, A., Hansen, L.K., Müller, K.-R. (eds.) Explainable AI: Interpreting, Explaining and Visualizing Deep Learning. LNCS (LNAI), vol. 11700, pp. 267–280. Springer, Cham (2019). https://doi.org/10.1007/978-3-030-28954-6_14

14. Lin, T.-Y., et al.: Microsoft COCO: common objects in context. In: Fleet, D., Pajdla, T., Schiele, B., Tuytelaars, T. (eds.) ECCV 2014. LNCS, vol. 8693, pp. 740–755. Springer, Cham (2014). https://doi.org/10.1007/978-3-319-10602-1_48

15. Liu, W., et al.: SSD: single shot multibox detector. In: Leibe, B., Matas, J., Sebe, N., Welling, M. (eds.) ECCV 2016. LNCS, vol. 9905, pp. 21–37. Springer, Cham (2016). https://doi.org/10.1007/978-3-319-46448-0_2

16. Marcinkevics, R., Vogt, J.E.: Interpretability and explainability: a machine learning zoo mini-tour. computing research repository (CoRR) abs/2012.01805 (2020)

17. Odena, A., Dumoulin, V., Olah, C.: Deconvolution and checkerboard artifacts. Distill **1**, e3 (2016)

18. Petsiuk, V., et al.: Black-box explanation of object detectors via saliency maps. In: Proceedings of the IEEE/CVF Conference on Computer Vision and Pattern Recognition (CVPR), pp. 11443–11452 (2021)

19. Ren, S., He, K., Girshick, R.B., Sun, J.: Faster R-CNN: towards real-time object detection with region proposal networks. IEEE Trans. Pattern Anal. Mach. Intell. (PAMI) **39**(6), 1137–1149 (2017)

20. Rosenfeld, A., Zemel, R.S., Tsotsos, J.K.: The elephant in the room. computing research repository (CoRR) abs/1808.03305 (2018)

21. Samek, W., Montavon, G., Lapuschkin, S., Anders, C.J., Müller, K.: Explaining deep neural networks and beyond: a review of methods and applications. Proc. IEEE **109**(3), 247–278 (2021)

22. Selvaraju, R.R., Cogswell, M., Das, A., Vedantam, R., Parikh, D., Batra, D.: Grad-CAM: visual explanations from deep networks via gradient-based localization. Int. J. Comput. Vision **128**(2), 336–359 (2020)

23. Simonyan, K., Vedaldi, A., Zisserman, A.: Deep inside convolutional networks: visualising image classification models and saliency maps. In: Bengio, Y., LeCun, Y. (eds.) 2nd International Conference on Learning Representations (ICLR) Workshop Track Proceedings (2014)

24. Springenberg, J.T., Dosovitskiy, A., Brox, T., Riedmiller, M.A.: Striving for simplicity: the all convolutional net. In: Bengio, Y., LeCun, Y. (eds.) 3rd International Conference on Learning Representations (ICLR) Workshop Track Proceedings (2015)
25. Sugawara, Y., Shiota, S., Kiya, H.: Checkerboard artifacts free convolutional neural networks. APSIPA Trans. Signal Inf. Process. **8**, e9 (2019)
26. Sundararajan, M., Taly, A., Yan, Q.: Axiomatic attribution for deep networks. In: Precup, D., Teh, Y.W. (eds.) Proceedings of the 34th International Conference on Machine Learning (ICML) 2017. Proceedings of Machine Learning Research, vol. 70, pp. 3319–3328. Proceedings of Machine Learning Research (PMLR) (2017)
27. Tan, M., Pang, R., Le, Q.V.: EfficientDet: scalable and efficient object detection. In: 2020 IEEE/CVF Conference on Computer Vision and Pattern Recognition (CVPR), pp. 10778–10787. Institute of Electrical and Electronics Engineers (IEEE) (2020)
28. Tomsett, R., Harborne, D., Chakraborty, S., Gurram, P., Preece, A.D.: Sanity checks for saliency metrics. In: Proceedings of the AAAI conference on artificial intelligence, pp. 6021–6029. AAAI Press (2020)
29. Toner, H., Acharya, A.: Exploring clusters of research in three areas of AI safety. Center for Security and Emerging Technology (2022)
30. Tsunakawa, H., Kameya, Y., Lee, H., Shinya, Y., Mitsumoto, N.: Contrastive relevance propagation for interpreting predictions by a single-shot object detector. In: 2019 International Joint Conference on Neural Networks (IJCNN), pp. 1–9. Institute of Electrical and Electronics Engineers (IEEE) (2019)
31. Valdenegro-Toro, M.: Deep neural networks for marine debris detection in sonar images. Computing Research Repository (CoRR) abs/1905.05241 (2019)
32. Valdenegro-Toro, M.: Forward-looking sonar marine debris datasets. GitHub (2019). Accessed 01 Dec 2021
33. Yona, G., Greenfeld, D.: Revisiting sanity checks for saliency maps. CoRR abs/2110.14297 (2021)
34. Zeiler, M.D., Fergus, R.: Visualizing and understanding convolutional networks. In: Fleet, D., Pajdla, T., Schiele, B., Tuytelaars, T. (eds.) ECCV 2014. LNCS, vol. 8689, pp. 818–833. Springer, Cham (2014). https://doi.org/10.1007/978-3-319-10590-1_53

Relating the Partial Dependence Plot and Permutation Feature Importance to the Data Generating Process

Christoph Molnar[1,4] , Timo Freiesleben[2] , Gunnar König[1,3] ,
Julia Herbinger[1,7], Tim Reisinger[1], Giuseppe Casalicchio[1,7(✉)] ,
Marvin N. Wright[4,5,6] , and Bernd Bischl[1,7]

[1] Department of Statistics, LMU Munich, Munich, Germany
giuseppe.casalicchio@stat.uni-muenchen.de
[2] Cluster of Excellence Machine Learning, Tübingen, Germany
[3] University of Vienna, Vienna, Austria
[4] Leibniz Institute for Prevention Research and Epidemiology, Bremen, Germany
[5] University of Bremen, Bremen, Germany
[6] University of Copenhagen, Copenhagen, Denmark
[7] Munich Center for Machine Learning (MCML), Munich, Germany

Abstract. Scientists and practitioners increasingly rely on machine learning to model data and draw conclusions. Compared to statistical modeling approaches, machine learning makes fewer explicit assumptions about data structures, such as linearity. Consequently, the parameters of machine learning models usually cannot be easily related to the data generating process. To learn about the modeled relationships, partial dependence (PD) plots and permutation feature importance (PFI) are often used as interpretation methods. However, PD and PFI lack a theory that relates them to the data generating process. We formalize PD and PFI as statistical estimators of ground truth estimands rooted in the data generating process. We show that PD and PFI estimates deviate from this ground truth not only due to statistical biases, but also due to learner variance and Monte Carlo approximation errors. To account for these uncertainties in PD and PFI estimation, we propose the learner-PD and the learner-PFI based on model refits and propose corrected variance and confidence interval estimators.

Keywords: XAI · Interpretable Machine Learning · Permutation Feature Importance · Partial Dependence Plot · Statistical Inference · Uncertainty Quantification

---

C. Molnar, T. Freiesleben and G. König—Equal contribution.

L. Longo (Ed.): xAI 2023, CCIS 1901, pp. 456–479, 2023.
https://doi.org/10.1007/978-3-031-44064-9_24

1   Introduction

Statistical models such as linear or logistic regression models are frequently used to learn about relationships in data. Assuming that a statistical model reflects the data generating process (DGP) well, we may interpret the model coefficients in place of the DGP and draw conclusions about the data. An important part of interpreting the coefficients is the quantification of their uncertainty via standard errors, which allows separation of random noise (non-significant coefficients) from real effects.

Increasingly, machine learning (ML) approaches – such as gradient-boosted trees, random forests or neural networks – are being used in science instead of or in addition to statistical models as they are able to learn highly-non linear relationships and interactions automatically. Applications range from modeling volunteer labor supply [4], mapping fish biomass [17], analyzing urban reservoirs [36], identifying disease-associated genetic variants [8], to inferring behavior from smartphone use [43]. However, in contrast to statistical models, machine learning approaches often lack a mapping between model parameters and properties of the DGP. This is problematic, since in scientific applications the model is only the means to an end: a better understanding of the DGP, in particular to learn what features are predictive of the target variable.

Interpretation methods [41] are a (partial) remedy to the lack of interpretable parameters of more complex models. Model-agnostic techniques, such as partial dependence (PD) plots [20] and permutation feature importance (PFI) [9,18] can be applied to any ML model and are popular methods for describing the relationship between input features and model outcome on a global level. PD plots visualize the average effect that features have on the prediction, and PFI estimates how much each feature contributes to the model performance and therefore how relevant a feature is.

Scientists who want to use PD and PFI to draw conclusions about the DGP face a problem as these methods have been designed to describe the prediction function, but lack a theory linking them to the DGP. In particular, the uncertainty of PD and PFI with respect to the DGP is not quantified, making it hard for scientists to assess the extent to which it is justified to draw conclusions based on the PD and PFI.

Contributions. We are the first to treat PD and PFI as statistical estimators of ground truth properties in the DGP. We introduce two notions, model-PD/PFI and learner-PD/PFI, which allow to analyze the uncertainty due to Monte-Carlo integration and uncertainty due to the training data/process, respectively. We perform bias-variance decompositions and propose theorems of unbiasedness, standard estimators, and confidence intervals for both PD and PFI. In addition, we leverage a variance correction approach from model performance estimation [35] to adjust for variance underestimation due to sample dependency.

Structure. We start with a motivating example (Sect. 1.1) and a discussion of related work (Sect. 1.2). In the methods section (Sect. 2), we introduce PD and

PFI formally, relate them to the DGP, and provide bias-variance decompositions, variance estimators and confidence intervals. In the simulation study in Sect. 3, we test our proposed methods in various settings and compare them to alternative approaches. In the application in Sect. 4, we revisit the motivating example to demonstrate how our confidence intervals for PD/PFI may help scientists to draw more justified conclusions about the DGP. Finally, we discuss the limitations of our work in Sect. 5.

1.1 Motivating Example

Imagine a researcher who wants to use machine learning methods and the publicly available UCI heart disease dataset [15] ($n = 918$) not only to predict heart disease, but also to understand how the disease is associated with sociological and medical indicators.

To select the model class, she compares the performance w.r.t. the predicted probabilities of a logistic regression model, a decision tree (CART) [10], and a random forest classifier [9] using 5-fold cross validation measured by the Brier score on the dataset; the mean losses for the different models are 0.130 (logistic regression), 0.258 (tree), and 0.125 (random forest). Since the random forest outperforms the linear model and decision tree, she uses a random forest for further analysis; she fits the model on 60% of the data and uses the remaining 40% as test set.[1]

To learn about the associations in the data, she applies the PD and PFI. To get interpretations that are true to the data and that avoid extrapolation, she employs conditional sampling based versions of PD and PFI (for a discussion of marginal versus conditional sampling, we refer to the literature [13,19], Sect. 2.1, and Sect. 2.3). The conditional PD corresponds to the expected prediction and therefore indicates how the probability of having heart disease varies with the feature of interest [19]. Conditional feature importance quantifies the surplus contribution of each feature over the remaining features (and can be linked to conditional dependence with the prediction target [28,45]).[2]

The results (Fig. 1) match the researcher's intuition. Many conditional PFI values are small, indicating that the features could be replaced with the remaining features. The most important features are the slope of the ECG segment (STSlope), the type of chest pain (ChestPainType), and cholesterol level (Cholesterol). Furthermore, the researcher is interested in the relationship between heart disease and age. Thus, she inspects the corresponding conditional PD plot. She observes that the probability of having chronic heart disease increases with age and that there is a small bump around the age of 55.

---

[1] All code is publicly available as part of the supplementary material.
[2] Conditional interpretation methods require sampling from conditional distributions. She samples categorical variables using a log-loss optimal classifier, and samples continuous variables by predicting the conditional mean and resampling residuals (thereby assuming homoscedasticity). She fits a random forest once on the dataset for all sampling tasks. To model multivariate mixed distributions, she employs a sequential design [5,7].

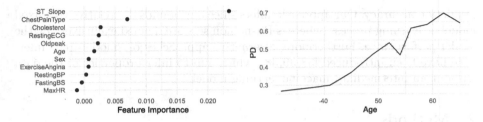

Fig. 1. Left: Conditional Feature Importance. Right: Conditional Partial Dependence Plot for the feature `Age`. The values are difficult to interpret since it is unclear how uncertainties in model fitting and IML method estimation influence them.

Although the researcher finds the results plausible, she is unsure whether her conclusions extend to the data generating process (DGP). Are features with nonzero feature importance actually relevant, or are the values nonzero by chance? Does the shape of the PDP really reflect the data? After all, various uncertainties could influence her result: The feature importance and conditional PD results vary when they are recomputed - even for the same model; and the random forest fit itself is a random variable as well.

Throughout this paper, we propose confidence intervals for partial dependence and feature importance values that take the uncertainties from the estimation of the interpretability method and the model fitting into account. We will return to this example in Sect. 4 and Fig. 6, where we show how our approach can help the researcher to evaluate the uncertainty in her estimates.

1.2 Related Work

PD: For models with inherent variance estimators (such as Bayesian additive regression trees) it is possible to construct model-based confidence intervals [11]. Moosbauer et al. [34] introduced a variance estimator for PD which is applicable to all probabilistic models that provide information on posterior (co)variance, such as Gaussian Processes (GPs). Furthermore, various applied articles contain computations of PD confidence bands [4,16,17,22,36,37]. These approaches either quantify only the error due to Monte Carlo approximation or do not account for underestimation of the variance when covering learner variance. This demonstrates the need for a theoretical underpinning of this inferential tool for practical research.

PFI: Various proposals for confidence intervals and variance estimation exist. Many of them are specific to the random forest PFI [3,26,27], for which Altmann et al. [1] propose a test for null importance. There are also model-agnostic accounts that are more similar to our work [45–47], however, unlike these other proposals, we additionally correct for variance underestimation arising from resampling [35] and relate the estimators to the proposed ground truth PFI. An alternative approach for providing bounds on PFI is proposed by Fisher et al. [18] via Rashomon sets, which are sets of models with similar near-optimal prediction accuracy. Our approach differs since our bounds are relative to a fixed model or learning process, whereas Rashomon sets are defined exclusively by the model performance. Furthermore, alternative approaches of "model-free" inference have been introduced [38,39,48], which aim to infer properties of the data without an intermediary machine learning model.

2 Methods

In this section, we present our formal framework: We introduce notation and background on PD and PFI (Sect. 2.1); formulate PD and PFI as estimators of (proposed) ground truth estimands in the DGP (Sect. 2.3); apply bias and variance decompositions and separate different sources of uncertainty (Sect. 2.4); and propose variance estimators and confidence intervals for the model-PD/PFI (which only takes the variance from Monte-Carlo integration into account, see Sect. 2.5) and the learner-PD/PFI (which also takes learner variance into account, see Sect. 2.6).

2.1 Notation

We denote the joint distribution induced by the data generating process as $\mathbb{P}_{XY}$, where X is a p-dimensional random variable and Y a 1-dimensional random variable. We consider the case where we aim to describe the true mapping from X to the target Y with $f(X) = E[Y \mid X = x]$.[3] We denote a single random draw from the DGP with $x^{(i)}$ and $y^{(i)}$, and a dataset consisting of n draws $\mathcal{D}_n$.

A machine learning model $\hat{f}$ is a function ($\hat{f} : \mathcal{X} \to \mathcal{Y}$) that maps a vector x from the feature space $\mathcal{X} \subseteq \mathbb{R}^p$ to a prediction $\hat{y}$ (e.g. in $\mathcal{Y} = \mathbb{R}$ for regression). The model $\hat{f}$ is induced based on a dataset $\mathcal{D}_n$, using a loss function $L : \mathcal{Y} \times \mathbb{R}^p \to \mathbb{R}_0^+$. The model $\hat{f}$ is induced by the learner algorithm $I : \Delta \to \mathcal{H}$ that maps from the space of datasets Δ to the function hypothesis space $\mathcal{H}$. The learning process contains an essential source of randomness, namely the training data. Since the model $\hat{f}$ is induced by the learner fed with data, it can be seen as a realization of a random variable F with distribution $\mathbb{P}_F$. We assume that the model is evaluated with a risk function $\mathcal{R}(\hat{f}) = \mathbb{E}_{XY}[L(Y, \hat{f}(X))] = \int L(y, \hat{f}(x)) d\mathbb{P}_{XY}$. The dataset $\mathcal{D}_n$ is split into $\mathcal{D}_{n_1}$ for model training and $\mathcal{D}_{n_2}$ for evaluation. The empirical risk is estimated with $\hat{\mathcal{R}}(\hat{f}_{\mathcal{D}_{n_2}, \lambda}) := \frac{1}{n_2} \sum_{i=1}^{n_2} L\left(y^{(i)}, \hat{f}_{\mathcal{D}_{n_2}, \lambda}(x^{(i)})\right)$.

Many interpretation techniques require perturbing variables by resampling from marginal or conditional distributions. We use ϕ to denote a sampler, which can formally be seen as a density function. A dataset drawn with a marginal sampler (denoted ϕ_{marg}) follows $P(X_j)$, and a dataset drawn with a conditional sampler (denoted ϕ_{cond}) follows $P(X_j|X_C)$. The choice of the sampler affects the interpretation of PD and PFI [2,18,32,33,45] and should depend on the

---

[3] This choice for f is motivated by the fact that the conditional expectation is the Bayes-optimal predictor for the L2 loss and for the log-loss optimal predictor in binary classification [24].

modeler's objective. Under certain conditions, the marginal sampler allows to estimate causal effects [49], but for correlated input features, the marginal sampler may create unrealistic data and the conditional sampler may be a better choice to draw inference [19] (see online Appendix A [31] for details).

2.2 Interpretation Techniques

Partial Dependence Plot. The PD of a feature set X_S, $S \subseteq \{1, \ldots, p\}$ (usually $|S| = 1$) for a given $x \in X_S$, a model $\hat{f}$ and a sampler $\phi : \mathcal{X}_S \to \{\psi \mid \psi$ density on $\mathcal{X}_C\}$ is:

$$PD_{S,\hat{f},\phi}(x) := \mathbb{E}_{\tilde{X}_C \sim \phi(x)}[\hat{f}(x, \tilde{X}_C)] = \int_{\tilde{x}_c \in \tilde{\mathcal{X}}_C} \phi(x)(\tilde{x}_c)\hat{f}(x, \tilde{x}_c)\, d\tilde{x}_c, \quad (1)$$

where $\tilde{X}_C$ is a random variable distributed with density $\phi(x)$, and C denote the indices of the remaining features so that $S \cup C = \{1, \ldots, p\}$ and $S \cap C = \emptyset$.

To estimate the PD for a specific function $\hat{f}$ using Monte Carlo integration, we draw $r \in \mathbb{N}$ samples for every $x \in \mathcal{X}_S$ from $\phi(x)$ and denote the corresponding dataset by $B_{\phi(x)} = (\tilde{x}_C^{(i,x)})_{i=1,\ldots,r}$. The estimation is given by:

$$\widehat{PD}_{S,\hat{f},\phi}(x) = \frac{1}{r} \sum_{i=1}^{r} \hat{f}(x, \tilde{x}_C^{(i,x)}). \quad (2)$$

By partial dependence plot (PDP) we denote the graph that visualizes the PDP. The PDP consists of a line connecting the points $\{(x^{(g)}, \widehat{PD}_{S,\hat{f},\phi}(x^{(g)})\}_{g=1}^{G}$, with G grid points that are usually equidistant or quantiles of $\mathbb{P}_{X_S}$. See Fig. 1 for an example of a PDP.

For the marginal sampler, the PDP of a model $\hat{f}$ visualizes the expected effect of a feature after marginalizing out the effects of all other features [20]. For the conditional sampler, the PDP is also called M-plot and visualizes the expected prediction given the features of interest, taking into account its associative dependencies with all other features [2,20].

Permutation Feature Importance. The PFI of a feature set X_S (usually just one feature) for a model $\hat{f}$ and a sampler $\phi : \mathcal{X}_C \to \{\psi \mid \psi$ density on $\mathcal{X}_S\}$ is defined by:

$$PFI_{S,\hat{f},\phi} := \mathbb{E}_{X_C,Y}[\mathbb{E}_{\tilde{X}_S \sim \phi(X_C)}[L(Y, \hat{f}(\tilde{X}_S, X_C))]] - \mathbb{E}_{XY}[L(Y, \hat{f}(X))], \quad (3)$$

where $\tilde{X}_S$ is a random variable distributed with density $\phi(X_C) \sim P(X_S|X_C)$, and X_C are the remaining features $\{1, \ldots, p\} \setminus S$. To estimate the PFI for a specific function $\hat{f}$ and a sampler ϕ using Monte Carlo integration, we draw $r \in \mathbb{N}$ samples for every datapoint $x_C^{(i)} \in \mathcal{X}_C$ ($x_C^{(i)}$ describes the feature values in C of the i-th instance in the evaluation[4] dataset D_{n_2}) from $\phi(x_C^{(i)})$ and denote

---

[4] The estimation of $\widehat{PFI}$ requires unseen data, so that the loss estimates deliver unbiased results [14,29].

the corresponding datasets by $B_{\phi(x_C^{(i)})} = (\tilde{x}_S^{(k,i)})_{k=1,...,r}$. The estimation is given by:

$$\widehat{PFI}_{S,\hat{f},\phi} = \frac{1}{n_2} \sum_{i=1}^{n_2} \left(\frac{1}{r} \sum_{k=1}^{r} L(y^{(i)}, \hat{f}(\tilde{x}_S^{(k,i)}, x_C^{(i)})) - L(y^{(i)}, \hat{f}(x^{(i)})) \right). \quad (4)$$

We restrict PFI to losses that can be computed per instance.[5] See Fig. 1 for a PFI example.

If we resample the perturbed variables from the marginal distribution, the PFI of a model $\hat{f}$ describes the change in loss if the feature values in X_S are randomly sampled from X_S i.e. the possible dependence to X_C and Y is broken (extrapolation) [9,18]. If we sample X_S conditional on the remaining variables X_C, PFI is also called the conditional PFI and may be interpreted as the *additional* importance of a feature *given that we already know the other feature values* [12,25,32,45].

Indices. To avoid indices overhead and because PDP/PFI and their respective estimations are always relative to a fixed feature set S and sampler ϕ, we will abbreviate $PD_{S,\hat{f},\phi}, \widehat{PD}_{S,\hat{f},\phi}, PFI_{S,\hat{f},\phi}, \widehat{PFI}_{S,\hat{f},\phi}$ with $PD_{\hat{f}}, \widehat{PD}_{\hat{f}}, PFI_{\hat{f}}, \widehat{PFI}_{\hat{f}}$ respectively.

2.3   Relating the Model to the Data Generating Process

The goal of statistical inference is to gain knowledge about DGP properties via investigating model properties. For example, under certain assumptions, the coefficients of a generalized linear model (i.e. model properties) can be related to parameters of the respective conditional distribution defined by the DGP, such as conditional mean and covariance structure (i.e. DGP properties). Unfortunately, machine learning models such as random forests or neural networks lack such a mapping between learned model parameters and DGP properties. Interpretation methods such as PD and PFI provide **external descriptors** of how features affect the model predictions. However, PD and PFI are estimators that lack a counterpart estimand in the DGP.

We define the ground truth version of PD and PFI, we call them *DGP-PD* and the *DGP-PFI*, as the PD and PFI applied to the true function f instead of the trained model $\hat{f}$:

Definition 1 (DGP-PD).   *The DGP-PD is the PD applied to function* f : $\mathcal{X} \mapsto \mathcal{Y}$ *of the DGP with sampler* $\phi : \mathcal{X}_S \to \{\psi \mid \psi$ *density on* $\mathcal{X}_C\}$.

$$DGP\text{-}PD(x) := PD_f(x)$$

---

[5] This excludes losses such as the area under the receiver operating characteristic curve (AUC).

Definition 2 (DGP-PFI). *The DGP-PFI is the PFI applied to function f :* $\mathcal{X} \mapsto \mathcal{Y}$ *of the DGP with sampler* $\phi : \mathcal{X}_C \rightarrow \{\psi \mid \psi$ *density on* $\mathcal{X}_S\}$.

$$DGP\text{-}PFI := PFI_f$$

Note that the DGP-PD and DGP-PFI may not be well-defined for all possible samplers. The DGP $f(x) = \mathbb{E}[Y \mid X = x]$ for instance is undefined for $x \in \mathcal{X}$ with zero density $(\psi_X(x) = 0)$. For the marginal sampler, for instance, DGP-PD and DGP-PFI might not be defined if the input features show strong correlations [25]. Conditional samplers, on the other side, do not face this threat as they preserve dependencies between features and therefore do not create unrealistic inputs [2,18,32,45].[6] However, under certain conditions, it can still be useful to also use other samplers than the conditional samplers to gain insight into the DGP. For example, under certain conditions, the marginal PDP allows to estimate causal effects [49] or recover relevant properties of linear DGPs [23].

Clearly, the function f is unknown in most applications, which makes it impossible to know the DGP-PD and DGP-PFI for these cases. However, Definitions 1 and 2 enable, at least in theory, to compare the PD/PFI of a model with the PD/PFI of the DGP **in simulation studies** and to research statistical biases. More importantly, the ground truth definitions of DGP-PD and DGP-PFI allow us to treat PD and PFI as statistical estimators of properties of the DGP.

In this work, we study PD and PFI as statistical estimators of the ground truth DPG-PD and DGP-PFI – including bias and variance decompositions – as well as confidence interval estimators. DGP-PD and DGP-PFI describe interesting properties of the DGP concerning the associational dependencies between the predictors and the target [19]; however, practitioners must decide whether these properties are relevant to answer their question or if different tools of model-analysis provide more interesting estimands.

2.4 Bias-Variance Decomposition

The definition of DGP-PD and DGP-PFI gives us a ground truth to which the PD and PFI of a model can be compared – at least in theory and simulation. The error of the estimation (mean squared error between estimator and estimand) can be decomposed into the systematic deviation from the true estimand (statistical bias) and the learner variance. PD and PFI are both expectations over the (usually unknown) joint distribution of the data. The expectations are therefore typically estimated from data using Monte Carlo integration, which adds another source of variation to the PFI and PD estimates. Figure 2 visualizes the chain of errors that stand between the estimand (DGP-PD, DGP-PFI) and the estimates $(\widehat{PD}, \widehat{PFI})$.

---

[6] To illustrate the idea of unrealistic data points, think of two strongly correlated features such as the weight and height of a person. Not every combination of feature values is possible – a person with a weight of 4kg and a height of 2m is from a biological perspective inconceivable.

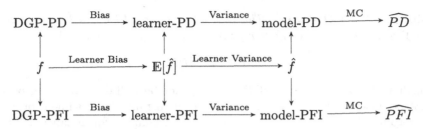

Fig. 2. A model $\hat{f}$ deviates from f due to learner bias and variance. Similarly, $\widehat{PD}$ and $\widehat{PFI}$ estimates deviate from their ground truth versions DGP-PD and DGP-PFI due to bias, variance, and Monte Carlo integration (MC).

For the PD, we compare the mean squared error (MSE) between the true DGP-PD (PD_f as defined in Eq. 1) with the theoretical PD of a model instance $\hat{f}$ ($PD_{\hat{f}}$) at position x.

$$\mathbb{E}_F[(PD_f(x) - PD_{\hat{f}}(x))^2] = \underbrace{(PD_f(x) - \mathbb{E}_F[PD_{\hat{f}}(x)])^2}_{Bias^2} + \underbrace{\mathbb{V}_F[PD_{\hat{f}}(x)]}_{Variance}$$

Here, F is the distribution of the trained models, which can be treated as a random variable. The bias-variance decomposition of the MSE of estimators is a well-known result [21]. For completeness, we provide a proof in online Appendix B [31]. Figure 3 visualizes bias and variance of a PD curve, and the variance due to Monte Carlo integration.

Similarly, the MSE of the theoretical PFI of a model (Eq. 3) can be decomposed into squared bias and variance. The proof can be found in online Appendix C [31].

$$\mathbb{E}_F[(PFI_{\hat{f}} - PFI_f)^2] = Bias_F^2[PFI_{\hat{f}}] + \mathbb{V}_F[PFI_{\hat{f}}]$$

The learner variance of PD/PFI stems from variance in the model fit, which depends on the training sample. When constructing confidence intervals, we must take into account the variance of PFI and PDP across model fits, and not just the error due to Monte Carlo integration. As we show in an application (Sect. 4), whether PD and PFI are based on a single model or are averaged across model refits can impact both the interpretation and especially the certainty of the interpretation. We therefore distinguish between model-PD/PFI and learner-PD/PFI, which are averaged over refitted models. Variance estimators for model-PD/PFI only account for variance due to Monte Carlo integration.

2.5   Model-PD and Model-PFI

Here, we study the model-PD and the model-PFI, and provide variance and confidence interval estimators. With the terms model-PD and model-PFI, we refer to the original proposals for PD [20] and PFI [9,18] for fixed models. Conditioning on a given model $\hat{f}$ ignores the learner variance due to the learning process. Only the variance due to Monte Carlo integration can be considered in this case.

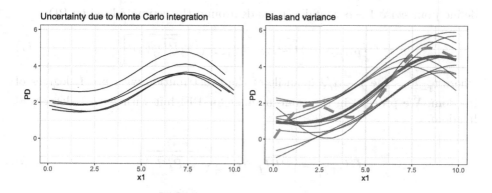

Fig. 3. Illustration of bias, variance and Monte Carlo approximation for the PD with marginal sampling. Left: Various PDPs using different data for the Monte Carlo integration, but keeping the model fixed. Right: The green dashed line shows the DGP-PDP of a toy example. Each thin line is the PDP for the model fitted with a different sample, and the thick blue line is the average thereof. Deviations of the DGP-PDP from the expected PDP are due to bias. Deviations of the individual model-PDPs from the expected PDP are due to learner variance. (Color figure online)

The model-PD estimator (Eq. (2)) is unbiased regarding the theoretical model-PD (Eq. (1)). Similarly, the estimated model-PFI (Eq. 4) is unbiased with respect to the theoretical model-PFI (Eq. 3). These findings rely on general properties of Monte Carlo integration, which state that Monte Carlo integration converges to the integral due to the law of large numbers. Proofs can be found in online Appendix D and F [31]. Moreover, under certain conditions, model-PD and model-PFI are unbiased estimators of the DGP-PD (Theorem 1) and DGP-PFI (Theorem 2), respectively.

To quantify the variance due to Monte Carlo integration and to construct confidence intervals, we calculate the variance across the sample. For the model-PD, the variance can be estimated with:

$$\widehat{\mathbb{V}}(\widehat{PD}_{\hat{f}}(x)) = \frac{1}{r(r-1)} \sum_{i=1}^{r} \left(\hat{f}(x, \tilde{x}_C^{(i,x)}) - \widehat{PD}_{\hat{f}}(x) \right)^2. \tag{5}$$

Similarly for the model-PFI, the variance can be estimated with:

$$\widehat{\mathbb{V}}(\widehat{PFI}_{\hat{f}}) = \frac{1}{n_2(n_2-1)} \sum_{i=1}^{n_2} \left(L^{(i)} - \widehat{PFI}_{\hat{f}} \right)^2, \tag{6}$$

where $L^{(i)} = \frac{1}{r} \sum_{k=1}^{r} L(y^{(i)}, \hat{f}(\tilde{x}_S^{(k,i)}, x_C^{(i)})) - L(y^{(i)}, \hat{f}(x^{(i)}))$.

The model-PD and model-PFI are mean estimates of independent samples with estimated variance. As such, they can be modelled approximately with a t-distribution with $r-1$ and n_2-1 degrees of freedom, respectively. This allows us to construct point-wise confidence bands for the model-PD and confidence intervals for the model-PFI that capture the Monte Carlo integration uncertainty. We define point-wise $1 - \alpha$-confidence bands around the estimated model-PD:

$$CI_{\widehat{PD}_{\hat{f}}(x)} = \left[\widehat{PD}_{\hat{f}}(x) \pm t_{1-\frac{\alpha}{2}} \sqrt{\widehat{\mathbb{V}}(\widehat{PD}_{\hat{f}}(x))} \right]. \tag{7}$$

where $t_{1-\frac{\alpha}{2}}$ is the $1 - \alpha/2$ quantile of the t-distribution with $r - 1$ degrees of freedom. We proceed in the same manner for PFI but with $n_2 - 1$ degrees of freedom:

$$CI_{\widehat{PFI}_{\hat{f}}} = \left[\widehat{PFI}_{\hat{f}} \pm t_{1-\frac{\alpha}{2}} \sqrt{\widehat{\mathbb{V}}(\widehat{PFI}_{\hat{f}})} \right]. \tag{8}$$

Confidence intervals for model-PD and model-PFI ignore the learner variance. Therefore, the interpretation is limited to variance regarding the Monte Carlo integration, and we cannot generalize results to the DGP. The model-PD/PFI and their confidence bands/intervals are applicable when the focus is a fixed model.

2.6   Learner-PD and Learner-PFI

To account for the learner variance, we propose the learner-PD and the learner-PFI, which average the PD/PFI over m model fits $\hat{f}_d$ with $d \in \{1, \ldots, m\}$. The models are produced by the same learning algorithm, but trained on different data samples, denoted by training sample indices B_d and the remaining test data B_{-d} so that $B_d \cap B_{-d} = \emptyset$ and $B_d \cup B_{-d} = \mathcal{D}_n$. The learner-variants are averages of the model-variants, where for each model-PD/PFI, the model is repeatedly "sampled" from the distribution of models F.

The learner-PD is therefore the expected PD over the distribution of models generated by the learning process, i.e. $\mathbb{E}_F[PD_{\hat{f}}(x)]$. We estimate the learner-PD with:

$$\overline{\overline{PD}}(x) = \frac{1}{m} \sum_{d=1}^{m} \frac{1}{r} \sum_{i=1}^{r} \hat{f}_d \left(x, x_C^{i,x,d} \right), \tag{9}$$

where $\hat{f}_d$ is trained on sample indices B_d and the PD estimated with data $B_{\phi(x),d}$ using a sampler ϕ m-times.

Following the PD, the learner-PFI is the expected PFI over the distribution of models produced by the learner: $\mathbb{E}_F[PFI_{\hat{f},\phi}]$. We propose the following estimator for the learner-PFI:

$$\overline{\overline{PFI}} = \frac{1}{m} \sum_{d=1}^{m} \frac{1}{n_2} \sum_{i=1}^{n_2} \left(\tilde{\bar{L}}_d^{(i)} - L_d^{(i)} \right), \tag{10}$$

where losses $L_d^{(i)} = L(y^{(i)}, \hat{f}_d(x^{(i)}))$ and $\tilde{\bar{L}}_d^{(i)} = \frac{1}{r} \sum_{k=1}^{r} L(y^{(i)}, \hat{f}_d(\tilde{x}_S^{(k,i,d)}, x_C^{(i)}))$ are estimated with data B_{-d} and m-times sampled data $B_{\phi(x),d}$ for a model trained on data B_d. A similar estimator has been proposed by Janitza et al. [27] for random forests.

Bias of the Learner-PD. The learner-PD is an unbiased estimator of the expected PD over the distribution of models F, since

$$\mathbb{E}_F[\overline{\widehat{PD}}(x)] = \mathbb{E}_F\left[\frac{1}{m}\sum_{d=1}^{m}\widehat{PD}_{\hat{f}_d}(x)\right] = \frac{m}{m}\mathbb{E}_F[PD_{\hat{f}_d}(x)] = \mathbb{E}_F[PD_{\hat{f}_d}(x)].$$

The bias of the learner-PD *regarding the DGP-PD* is linked to the bias of the learner. If the learner is unbiased, the PDs are unbiased as well.

Theorem 1. *Learner unbiasedness implies PD unbiasedness:*
$$\mathbb{E}_F[\hat{f}(x)] = f(x) \implies \mathbb{E}_F[PD_{\hat{f}}(x)] = PD_f(x)$$

Proof Sketch 1. *Applying Fubini's Theorem allows us to switch the order of integrals. Further replacing $\mathbb{E}_F[\hat{f}(x)]$ with f proves the unbiasedness. A full proof can be found in online Appendix E [31].*

By learner bias, we refer to the expected deviation between the estimated $\hat{f}$ and the true function f. Particularly interesting in this context is the inductive bias (i.e. the preference of one generalization over another) that is needed for learning ML models that generalize [30]. A wrong choice of inductive bias, such as searching models $\hat{f}$ in a linear hypotheses class when f is non-linear, leads to deviations of the expected $\hat{f}$ from f. But there are also other reasons why a bias of $\hat{f}$ from f may occur, for example if using an insufficiently large sample of training data. We discuss the critical assumption of learner unbiasedness further in Sect. 5.

Bias of the Learner-PFI. The learner-PFI is unbiased regarding the expected learner-PFI over the distribution of models F, since the learner-PFI is a simple mean estimate. However, unlike the learner-PD, learner unbiasedness does not generally imply unbiasedness of the learner-PFI *regarding the DGP-PFI*. This is generally only the case, if we use the conditional sampler.

Theorem 2. *If the learner is unbiased with $\mathbb{E}_F[\hat{f}] = f$ and the L2-loss is used, then the conditional model-PFI and conditional learner-PFI are unbiased estimators of the conditional DGP-PFI.*

Proof Sketch 2. *Both L and $\tilde{L}$ can be decomposed into bias, variance, and irreducible error. Due to the subtraction, the irreducible error vanishes, and the differences of biases and variances remain. Model unbiasedness sets the bias terms to zero and variance becomes zero due to conditional sampling. The extended proof can be found in online Appendix G [31].*

Intuitively, the model-PFI and learner-PFI should tend to have a negative bias and therefore underestimate the DGP-PFI. A model cannot use more information about the target than what is encoded in the DGP. However, as Theorem 3 shows, under specific conditions, the PFI using conditional sampling can be larger than the DGP-PFI.

Theorem 3. *The difference between the conditional model-PFI and the conditional DGP-PFI is given by:*

$$PFI_f - PFI_{\hat{f}} = 2\mathbb{E}_{X_C}\left[\mathbb{V}_{X_S|X_C}[f] - Cov_{X_S|X_C}[f, \hat{f}]\right].$$

Proof Sketch 3. *For the L2 loss, the expected loss of a model $\hat{f}$ can be decomposed into the expected loss between $\hat{f}$ and f and the expected variance of Y given X. Due to the subtraction, the latter term vanishes. The remainder can be simplified using that $Y \perp\!\!\!\perp \tilde{X}_S \mid X_C$ and $P(\tilde{X}_S, X_C) = P(X_S, X_C)$ due to the conditional sampling. The extended proof can be found in online Appendix H [31].*

However, for an overestimation of the conditional PFI to occur, the expected conditional variance of $\hat{f}$ must be greater than the one of f. Moreover, $\hat{f}$ and f must have a large expected conditional covariance, meaning that $\hat{f}$ has learned something about f.

Variance Estimation. The learner-PD and learner-PFI vary not only due to learner variance (refitted models), but also due to using different samples each time for the Monte Carlo integration. Therefore, their variance estimates capture the entire modeling process. Consequently, learner-PD/PFI along with their variance estimators bring us closer to the DGP-PD/PFI, and only the systematic bias remains unknown.

We can estimate this point-wise variance of the learner-PD with:

$$\widehat{\mathbb{V}}(\overline{\widehat{PD}}(x)) = \left(\frac{1}{m} + c\right) \cdot \frac{1}{(m-1)} \sum_{d=1}^{m} (\widehat{PD}_{\hat{f}_d}(x) - \overline{\widehat{PD}}(x))^2$$

And equivalently for the learner-PFI:

$$\widehat{\mathbb{V}}(\overline{\widehat{PFI}}) = \left(\frac{1}{m} + c\right) \cdot \frac{1}{(m-1)} \sum_{d=1}^{m} (\widehat{PFI}_{\hat{f}_d} - \overline{\widehat{PFI}})^2$$

The correction term c depends on the data setting. In simulation settings that allow us to draw new training and test sets for each model, we can use $c = 0$, yielding the standard variance estimators. In real world settings, we usually have a fixed dataset of size n, and models are refitted using resampling techniques. Consequently, data are shared by model refits, and variance estimators will underestimate the true variance [35]. To correct the variance estimate of the generalization error for bootstrapped or subsampled models, Nadeau and Bengio [35] suggested the correction term $c = \frac{n_2}{n_1}$ (where n_2 and n_1 are sizes of test and training data). However, the correction remains a rough correction, relying on the strongly simplifying assumption that the correlation between model refits depends only on the number of shared observations in the respective training datasets and not on the specific observations that they share. While this assumption is usually wrong, we show in Sect. 3.1 that the correction term offers a vast improvement for variance estimation – compared to using no correction.

Confidence Bands and Intervals. Since the learner-PD and learner-PFI are means with estimated variance, we can use the t-distribution with $m - 1$ degrees of freedom to construct confidence bands/intervals, where m is the number of model fits. The point-wise confidence band for the learner-PD is:

$$CI_{\overline{\widehat{PD}}(x)} = \left[\overline{\widehat{PD}}(x) \pm t_{1-\frac{\alpha}{2}} \sqrt{\widehat{\mathbb{V}}(\overline{\widehat{PD}}(x))} \right],$$

where $t_{1-\frac{\alpha}{2}}$ is the respective $1 - \alpha/2$ quantile of the t-distribution with $m - 1$ degrees of freedom. Equivalently, we propose a confidence interval for the learner-PFI:

$$CI_{\overline{\widehat{PFI}}} = \left[\overline{\widehat{PFI}} \pm t_{1-\frac{\alpha}{2}} \sqrt{\widehat{\mathbb{V}}(\overline{\widehat{PFI}})} \right].$$

Taking the learner variance into account can affect the interpretation, as we show in the application in Sect. 4. An additional advantage of the learner-PD and learner-PFI is that they make better use of the data, since a larger share of the data is employed as test data compared to only using a small holdout set.

3   Simulation Studies

In this Section, we study the coverage of the confidence intervals for the learner-PD/PFI on simulated examples (Sect. 3.1) and compare our proposed refitting-based variance estimation with model-based variance estimators (Sect. 3.2).

3.1   Confidence Interval Coverage Simulation

In simulations, we compared confidence interval performance between bootstrapping and subsampling, with and without variance correction. We simulated two DGPs: a *linear* DGP was defined as $y = f(x) = x_1 - x_2 + \epsilon$ and a *non-linear* DGP as $y = f(x) = x_1 - \sqrt{1 - x_2} + x_3 \cdot x_4 + (x_4/10)^2 + \epsilon$. All features were uniformly sampled from the unit interval $[0; 1]$, and for both DGPs, we set $\epsilon \sim N(0, 1)$. We studied the two settings "simulation" and "real world" as described in Sect. 2.1. In both settings, we trained linear models (lm), regression trees (tree) and random forests (rf) each 15 times, and computed confidence intervals for the learner-PD and learner-PFI across the 15 refitted models. In the "simulation" setting, we sampled $n \in \{100, 1000\}$ fresh data points for each model refit, where 63.2% of the data were used for training and the remaining 36.8% for PDP and PFI estimation.[7]

In the "real world" setting, we sampled $n \in \{100, 1000\}$ data points **once** per experiment, and generated 15 training data sets using a bootstrap (sample size n with replacement, which yields $0.632 \cdot n$ unique data points in expectation) or subsampling (sample size $0.632 \cdot n$ without replacement). In both settings, the learner-PD and learner-PFI as well as their respective confidence intervals were

---

[7] We choose this training size (63.2%) to match the expected number of unique samples when using bootstrapping, which allows to compare bootstrapping and subsampling.

Table 1. Coverage Probability of the 95% Confidence Bands/Intervals for PDP and PFI. boot = bootstrap, subs = subsampling, * = with adjustment.

dgp	model	n	PD					PFI				
			boot	boot*	subs	subs*	ideal	boot	boot*	subs	subs*	ideal
linear	lm	100	0.41	0.89	0.34	0.82	0.95	0.27	0.70	0.23	0.63	0.94
linear	lm	1000	0.41	0.89	0.33	0.80	0.95	0.25	0.68	0.21	0.60	0.95
linear	rf	100	0.39	0.86	0.36	0.83	0.95	0.44	0.92	0.39	0.88	0.95
linear	rf	1000	0.38	0.87	0.35	0.83	0.95	0.42	0.90	0.38	0.86	0.95
linear	tree	100	0.54	0.96	0.47	0.92	0.95	0.52	0.97	0.42	0.90	0.95
linear	tree	1000	0.57	0.96	0.48	0.91	0.95	0.42	0.90	0.34	0.81	0.95
non-linear	lm	100	0.43	0.90	0.36	0.84	0.95	0.31	0.81	0.25	0.72	0.94
non-linear	lm	1000	0.41	0.89	0.33	0.81	0.95	0.25	0.67	0.21	0.59	0.95
non-linear	rf	100	0.39	0.87	0.36	0.84	0.95	0.47	0.94	0.43	0.91	0.95
non-linear	rf	1000	0.38	0.86	0.36	0.83	0.95	0.41	0.89	0.38	0.86	0.95
non-linear	tree	100	0.58	0.98	0.51	0.95	0.95	0.68	0.99	0.56	0.96	0.94
non-linear	tree	1000	0.59	0.97	0.51	0.94	0.95	0.58	0.97	0.46	0.92	0.95

computed over the 15 retrained models. We repeated the experiment 10,000 times and counted how often the estimated confidence intervals covered the expected PD or PFI ($\mathbb{E}_F[PD_{\hat{f}}]$ and $\mathbb{E}_F[PFI_{\hat{f}}]$) over the distribution of models F.[8] These expected values were computed using 10,000 separate runs. The coverage estimates were averaged across features per scenario and for PD also across grid points ($\{0.1, 0.3, 0.5, 0.7, 0.9\}$) for all features.

Table 1 shows that in the "simulation" setting ("ideal"), we can recover confidence intervals using the standard variance estimation with the desired coverage probability. However, in the "real world" setting, the confidence intervals for both the learner-PD and learner-PFI are too narrow across all scenarios and both resampling strategies when the intervals are based on naive variance estimates. Some coverage probabilities are especially low, such as for linear models with 30%–40%.

The coverage probabilities drastically improve when the correction term is used (see Fig. 4a). However, in the simulated scenarios, these probabilities are still somewhat too narrow. For the linear model, the confidence intervals were the narrowest, with coverage probabilities of around 80%–90% for PD and 60%–80% for PFI across DGPs and sample sizes. The PD confidence bands were not heavily affected by increasing sample size n, but the PFI estimates became slightly narrower in most cases. In the case of decision trees, the adjusted confidence intervals were sometimes too large, especially for the adjusted bootstrap.

Except for trees on the *non-linear* DGP, the bootstrap outperformed subsampling in terms of coverage, i.e. the coverage was closer to the 95% level and rather erred on the side of "caution" with wider confidence intervals (see Fig. 4b).

---

[8] The coverage does not refer to the DGP-PD/PFI, but rather to the expected learner-PD/PFI, as we studied the choices of resampling and correction for the learner variance.

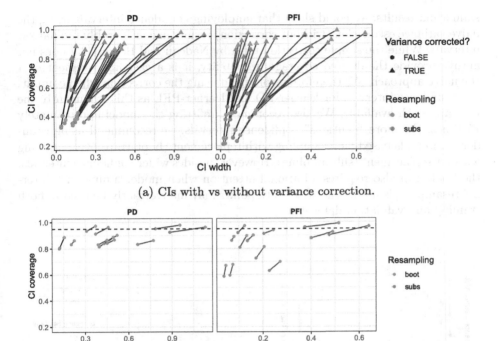

(a) CIs with vs without variance correction.

(b) Bootstrapping- vs subsampling-based CIs (with variance correction).

Fig. 4. Confidence interval width vs. coverage for bootstrapping (boot) and subsampling (subs), segments connect identical scenarios.

As recommended by Nadeau and Bengio [35], we used 15 refits. We additionally analyzed how the coverage and interval width changed by increasing refits from 2 to 30 and noticed that the coverage worsened with more refits while the width of the confidence intervals decreased. Increasing the number of refits incurs an inherent trade-off between interval width and coverage: The more refits are considered, the more accurate the learner-PFI and learner-PD become, and also the more certain the variance estimates become, scaling with $1/m$. However, there is a limit to the information in the data, such that additional refits falsely reduce the variance estimate and the confidence intervals become too narrow. To refit the model 10–20 times seemed to be an acceptable trade-off between coverage and interval width, as demonstrated in Fig. 5. Below ~10 refits, the confidence intervals were large and the mean PD/PFI estimates have a high variance. Above ~20 refits, the widths no longer decreased substantially. The figures for the other scenarios can be found in online Appendix I [31].[9] With our

---

[9] The CI coverage and width: for PD with n = 100 can be found in Figure I.1 and Figure I.2; for PD with n = 1000 can be found in Figure I.3 and Figure I.4; for PFI with n = 100 can be found in Figure I.5 and Figure I.6; for PFI with n = 1000 can be found in Figure I.7 and Figure I.8.

simulation results, we could show that employing confidence intervals using the naive variance estimation (without correction) results in considerably too narrow intervals. While the simple correction term by Nadeau and Bengio [35] does not always provide the desired coverage probability, it is a vast improvement over the naive approach. We therefore recommend using the correction when computing confidence intervals for learner-PD and learner-PFI, as this is currently the best approach available. We also recommend refitting the model approximately 15 times. For more "cautious" confidence intervals, we recommend using confidence intervals based on resampling with replacement (bootstrap) over sampling without replacement (subsampling). However, besides wider confidence intervals, the bootstrap also requires additional attention when model-tuning with internal resampling is used; otherwise, data points may inadvertently be used in both training and validation datasets.

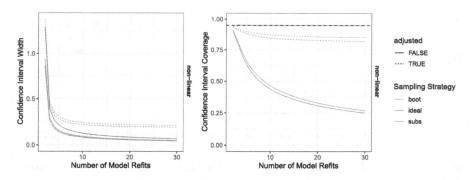

Fig. 5. Average PD confidence band width (left) and coverage (right) as a function of the number of refitted models for the random forest on the *non-linear* DGP.

3.2   Comparison to Model-Based Approaches

While our methods based on model-refits provide confidence intervals for PD and PFI in a model-agnostic manner, it is also possible to exploit (co)variance estimates of probabilistic models to construct confidence intervals. Here, we will, for the case of PD[10], compare our approach with the model-based approach of Moosbauer et al. [34] applied to a Gaussian Process (GP) and a linear model (LM).[11] We find that our approach more reliably delivers better coverages that are closer to the $1 - \alpha$ confidence level; this can be explained by the fact that the model-based approach ignores the variance in Monte Carlo integration.

---

[10] We do not know of any application of Moosbauer et al.'s [34] approach to PFI of probabilistic models.

[11] More details on the approach of Moosbauer et al. [34] are provided in online Appendix J [31].

We consider the following simulation setting:

$$\text{DGP:} \quad Y = 4X_1 - 2X_2 + 2X_3 - X_4 + X_5 + \epsilon$$

with $X_j \overset{i.i.d.}{\sim} U(0,1)$ for all $j \in \{1, ..., 5\}$. Given a DGP of the form $y = f(x) + \epsilon$ the distribution of ϵ is set to $\epsilon \sim N(0, (0.2\, \sigma(f(x)))^2)$.

We calculate the DGP-PD analytically. The experiments are performed 1000 times for $n = 200$ and $n = 1000$, where a random sample of $n_1 = 0.632 \cdot n$ is used to fit the models and the remaining $n_2 = 0.368 \cdot n$ observations are used to calculate the PD. Since model-based variance estimates for linear models can be derived analytically based on the variance of their coefficients, we additionally compare these estimates to our resampling-based approach (i.e. the learner-PD) for a correctly specified linear model. The model-based variance estimates can be calculated by one model fit per repetition. In contrast, we use 15 refits on subsampled data sets per repetition to compute the variance estimate for the resampling-based approach.[12][13] We choose the grid points $\{0.1, 0.3, 0.5, 0.7, 0.9\}$ and a confidence level of 0.95 to evaluate the mean and variance estimates of the PDs. Table 2 shows the results for both the model-based (mod) and the adjusted subsampling-based (subs) approach. While the subsampling-based approach shows almost perfect coverages for the different settings, the model-based approach is far off the nominal level with values around 0.35 for the correctly specified linear model. This gap can be explained by the MC integration variance which is not incorporated in the model-based approaches. Hence, if the MC error is relatively high compared to the model variance, coverages are bad. To illustrate this relationship, we calculated the average standard deviation of the MC integration variance estimator (see Eq. (5)) for the model-based approaches (see Table 2). Since the confidence bands of these approaches only cover the model variance, the confidence width is directly proportional to the model variance. If we compare the "MC se" column with the average widths of the model-based approach, it is observable that coverages are rather low (e.g., 0.34 for LM with $n = 200$) in the case where "MC se" divided by width is rather high (e.g., $0.15/0.15 = 1$) and vice versa.

Thus, if the main goal is to quantify both uncertainty sources inherent in the PD estimation and thus to receive reasonable coverages, the model-based approach cannot be recommended since only one of two sources of variability are covered by the estimates. Even for the linear model, which is commonly used for inferential purposes, the confidence bands for the PD estimates might be far too conservative as shown in Table 2. The subsampling-based variance estimates we proposed in this work however cover both the learner variance and the MC error and provide satisfying coverage values.

---

[12] We use a marginal sampler for perturbations (since we assume uncorrelated features in all scenarios).

[13] We did not consider the bootstrapping approach in our experiments as we encountered numerical issues in the invertability of the covariance matrix (due to duplicated values introduced by bootstrap) [42].

Table 2. Coverage probabilities for 95% confidence bands of PD estimates for model-based (mod) and subsampling-based (subs) approaches. Results are averaged over all features and grid points for the GP and LM. The experiments were conducted on two different sample sizes n. Furthermore, mean (standard deviation) of confidence width are reported for both approaches. The last column contains the standard deviation of the MC error for the model-based approach.

dgp	model	n	coverage		width (sd)		
			mod	subs	mod	subs	mod
1	gp	200	0.66	0.95	0.36 (0.19)	0.48 (0.11)	0.15
1	gp	1000	0.71	0.97	0.28 (0.31)	0.24 (0.07)	0.07
1	lm	200	0.34	0.95	0.15 (0.03)	0.41 (0.10)	0.15
1	lm	1000	0.35	0.95	0.06 (0.01)	0.19 (0.05)	0.07

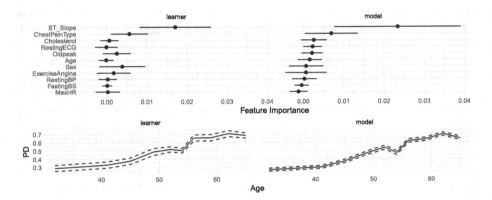

Fig. 6. Top: Conditional Learner-PFI and model-PFI with point-wise 95%-confidence intervals for the random forest. Bottom: Conditional Learner-PDP and model-PDP with point-wise 95%-confidence bands for the random forest and feature `Age`.

4   Application

We apply our proposed estimators to the motivational example from Sect. 1.1. We supposed that a researcher predicted chronic heart disease [15] ($n = 918$) from sociological and medical indicators such as age, blood pressure and maximum heart rate. She fitted one random forest and estimated conditional PFI and conditional PDPs to interpret the result.

Instead of only computing the conditional PFI and conditional PDP for one model, we estimate the proposed conditional model-PFI and conditional learner-PFI along with the proposed confidence intervals. For the learner-based insights, we therefore refitted the model 15 times on resampled training sets.

Figure 6 shows model and learner based conditional PFI and conditional PDP with the corresponding confidence intervals ($\alpha = 0.05$).

Learner-PFI and model-PFI disagree on the ordering of the features: they agree that slope of the ECG segment (STSlope) and the type of chest pain (ChestPainType) are the most important features; but learner-PFI ranks sex (Sex) and ST depression induced by exercise relative to rest (Oldpeak) next, while model-PFI ranks cholesterol (Cholesterol) second and resting state ECG (RestingECG) third. For both model-PFI and learner-PFI all except two confidence intervals include zero, namely STSlope and ChestPainType. The confidence intervals for model-PFI and learner-PFI indicate that both learner variance and the uncertainty stemming from the Monte Carlo integration are relatively high. The model-PFI cannot tell us to what extent the estimate varies due to learner variance; only the learner-PFI can quantify the learner variance.

Figure 6, bottom row, shows both the conditional model-PDP and the conditional learner-PDP for age (Age). Model-PDP and learner-PDP agree that individuals of higher age are more likely to have heart disease with a strong increase in prevalence around the age of 55. However, the confidence bands of the learner-PDP are wider than those of the model-PDP. Furthermore, the bump that can be observed in the model-PDP around the age of 50 is smoother in the learner PDP and should partly be attributed to uncertainties involved in model fitting. Neglecting the learner variance would mean being overconfident about the partial dependence curve. In particular, the Monte Carlo approximation error decreases with $1/n$ as the sample size n for PD and PFI estimation increases. Wrongly interpreted, this can lead to a false sense of confidence in the estimated effects and importance since only one model is considered and learner variance is ignored.

5   Discussion

We related the PD and the PFI to the DGP, proposed variance and confidence intervals, and discussed conditions for inference. Our derivations were motivated by taking an external view of the statistical inference process and postulating that there is a ground truth counterpart to PD/PFI in the DGP. To the best of our knowledge, statistical inference via model-agnostic interpretable machine learning is already used in practice, but under-explored in theory.

A critical assumption for inference of effects and importance using interpretable machine learning is the unbiasedness of the learner. The learner bias is difficult to test, and can be introduced by e.g. choice of model class, regularization, and feature selection. For example, regularization techniques such as LASSO introduce a small bias *on purpose* [44] to decrease learner variance and improve predictive performance. We must better understand how specific biases affect the prediction function and consequently PD and PFI estimates.

Another crucial limitation for inference of PD and PFI is the underestimation of variance due to data sharing between model refits. While we could show that a simple correction of the variance [35] vastly improves the coverage, a proper estimation of the variance remains an open issue. A promising approach relying on repeated nested cross validation to correctly estimate the variance was recently proposed by Bates et al. [6]. However, this approach is more computationally intensive by a factor of up to 1,000.

Furthermore, samplers are not readily available. Especially conditional sampling is a complex problem, and samplers must be trained using data. Training samplers even introduces another source of uncertainty to our estimates that we neglected in our work. It is difficult to separate this source of uncertainty from the uncertainty of the model learner, since trained samplers are correlated not only with each other, but possibly also with the trained models. We see integrating sampler uncertainty as an important step in providing reliable uncertainty estimates in practice, but we leave this to future work.

Statements and Declarations

Funding. This project is supported by the Bavarian State Ministry of Science and the Arts, the Bavarian Research Institute for Digital Transformation (bidt), the German Federal Ministry of Education and Research (BMBF) under Grant No. 01IS18036A, by the German Research Foundation (DFG) – Emmy Noether Grant 437611051 to MNW, and the Carl Zeiss Foundation (project on "Certification and Foundations of Safe Machine Learning Systems in Healthcare"). The authors of this work take full responsibilities for its content.

Availability of Data, Code, and Online Appendix. The data used in the application is openly available and referenced in this paper. The code for visualizations, simulations and the application is written in the R programming language [40] and is publicly available via https://github.com/gcskoenig/paper_inference_code. The online Appendix is available via [31].

References

1. Altmann, A., Toloşi, L., Sander, O., Lengauer, T.: Permutation importance: a corrected feature importance measure. Bioinformatics **26**(10), 1340–1347 (2010)
2. Apley, D.W., Zhu, J.: Visualizing the effects of predictor variables in black box supervised learning models. J. R. Stat. Soc.: Ser. B (Stat. Methodol.) **82**(4), 1059–1086 (2020)
3. Archer, K.J., Kimes, R.V.: Empirical characterization of random forest variable importance measures. Comput. Stat. Data Anal. **52**(4), 2249–2260 (2008)
4. Bair, E., et al.: Multivariable modeling of phenotypic risk factors for first-onset TMD: the OPPERA prospective cohort study. J. Pain **14**(12), T102–T115 (2013)
5. Bates, S., Candès, E., Janson, L., Wang, W.: Metropolized knockoff sampling. J. Am. Stat. Assoc. **116**(535), 1413–1427 (2021)
6. Bates, S., Hastie, T., Tibshirani, R.: Cross-validation: what does it estimate and how well does it do it? J. Am. Stat. Assoc. 1–12 (2023)
7. Blesch, K., Watson, D.S., Wright, M.N.: Conditional feature importance for mixed data. AStA Adv. Stat. Anal. 1–20 (2023)
8. Boulesteix, A.L., Wright, M.N., Hoffmann, S., König, I.R.: Statistical learning approaches in the genetic epidemiology of complex diseases. Hum. Genet. **139**(1), 73–84 (2020)

9. Breiman, L.: Random forests. Mach. Learn. **45**(1), 5–32 (2001)
10. Breiman, L., Friedman, J., Stone, C.J., Olshen, R.: Classification and Regression Trees. CRC Press, Cambridge (1984)
11. Cafri, G., Bailey, B.A.: Understanding variable effects from black box prediction: quantifying effects in tree ensembles using partial dependence. J. Data Sci. **14**(1), 67–95 (2016)
12. Candes, E., Fan, Y., Janson, L., Lv, J.: Panning for gold: 'model-X'knockoffs for high dimensional controlled variable selection. J. R. Stat. Soc.: Ser. B (Stat. Methodol.) **80**(3), 551–577 (2018)
13. Chen, H., Janizek, J.D., Lundberg, S., Lee, S.I.: True to the model or true to the data? arXiv preprint arXiv:2006.16234 (2020)
14. Chernozhukov, V., et al.: Double/debiased machine learning for treatment and structural parameters. Economet. J. **21**(1), C1–C68 (2018)
15. Dua, D., Graff, C.: UCI machine learning repository (2017). http://archive.ics.uci.edu/ml
16. Emrich, E., Pierdzioch, C.: Public goods, private consumption, and human capital: using boosted regression trees to model volunteer labour supply. Rev. Econ./Jahrbuch für Wirtschaftswissenschaften **67**(3) (2016)
17. Esselman, P.C., Stevenson, R.J., Lupi, F., Riseng, C.M., Wiley, M.J.: Landscape prediction and mapping of game fish biomass, an ecosystem service of Michigan rivers. North Am. J. Fish. Manag. **35**(2), 302–320 (2015)
18. Fisher, A., Rudin, C., Dominici, F.: All models are wrong, but many are useful: learning a variable's importance by studying an entire class of prediction models simultaneously. J. Mach. Learn. Res. **20**(177), 1–81 (2019)
19. Freiesleben, T., König, G., Molnar, C., Tejero-Cantero, A.: Scientific inference with interpretable machine learning: analyzing models to learn about real-world phenomena. arXiv preprint arXiv:2206.05487 (2022)
20. Friedman, J.H.: Greedy function approximation: a gradient boosting machine. Ann. Stat. 1189–1232 (2001)
21. Geman, S., Bienenstock, E., Doursat, R.: Neural networks and the bias/variance dilemma. Neural Comput. **4**(1), 1–58 (1992)
22. Grange, S.K., Carslaw, D.C.: Using meteorological normalisation to detect interventions in air quality time series. Sci. Total Environ. **653**, 578–588 (2019)
23. Groemping, U.: Model-agnostic effects plots for interpreting machine learning models. Reports in Mathematics, Physics and Chemistry, Department II, Beuth University of Applied Sciences Berlin. Report 1/2020 (2020)
24. Hastie, T., Tibshirani, R., Friedman, J.H., Friedman, J.H.: The Elements of Statistical Learning: Data Mining, Inference, and Prediction, vol. 2. Springer, Heidelberg (2009)
25. Hooker, G., Mentch, L., Zhou, S.: Unrestricted permutation forces extrapolation: variable importance requires at least one more model, or there is no free variable importance. Stat. Comput. **31**, 1–16 (2021)
26. Ishwaran, H., Lu, M.: Standard errors and confidence intervals for variable importance in random forest regression, classification, and survival. Stat. Med. **38**(4), 558–582 (2019)
27. Janitza, S., Celik, E., Boulesteix, A.L.: A computationally fast variable importance test for random forests for high-dimensional data. Adv. Data Anal. Classif. **12**(4), 885–915 (2018)
28. König, G., Molnar, C., Bischl, B., Grosse-Wentrup, M.: Relative feature importance. In: 2020 25th International Conference on Pattern Recognition (ICPR), pp. 9318–9325. IEEE (2021)

29. Zheng, W., van der Laan, M.J.: Cross-validated targeted minimum-loss-based estimation. In: Zheng, W., van der Laan, M.J. (eds.) Targeted Learning. SSS, pp. 459–474. Springer, New York (2011). https://doi.org/10.1007/978-1-4419-9782-1_27
30. Mitchell, T.M.: The need for biases in learning generalizations. Citeseer (1980)
31. Molnar, C., et al.: Online appendix for "Relating the Partial Dependence Plot and Permutation Feature Importance to the Data Generating Process" (2023). https://doi.org/10.6084/m9.figshare.23294945.v1
32. Molnar, C., König, G., Bischl, B., Casalicchio, G.: Model-agnostic feature importance and effects with dependent features: a conditional subgroup approach. Data Min. Knowl. Discov. 1–39 (2023)
33. Molnar, C., et al.: General pitfalls of model-agnostic interpretation methods for machine learning models. In: Holzinger, A., Goebel, R., Fong, R., Moon, T., Müller, K.R., Samek, W. (eds.) xxAI 2020. LNCS, vol. 13200, pp. 39–68. Springer, Cham (2022). https://doi.org/10.1007/978-3-031-04083-2_4
34. Moosbauer, J., Herbinger, J., Casalicchio, G., Lindauer, M., Bischl, B.: Explaining hyperparameter optimization via partial dependence plots. In: Advances in Neural Information Processing Systems, vol. 34, pp. 2280–2291 (2021)
35. Nadeau, C., Bengio, Y.: Inference for the generalization error. Mach. Learn. **52**(3), 239–281 (2003)
36. Obringer, R., Nateghi, R.: Predicting urban reservoir levels using statistical learning techniques. Sci. Rep. **8**(1), 1–9 (2018)
37. Page, W.G., Wagenbrenner, N.S., Butler, B.W., Forthofer, J.M., Gibson, C.: An evaluation of NDFD weather forecasts for wildland fire behavior prediction. Weather Forecast. **33**(1), 301–315 (2018)
38. Parr, T., Wilson, J.D.: A stratification approach to partial dependence for codependent variables. arXiv preprint arXiv:1907.06698 (2019)
39. Parr, T., Wilson, J.D., Hamrick, J.: Nonparametric feature impact and importance. arXiv preprint arXiv:2006.04750 (2020)
40. R Core Team: R: A language and environment for statistical computing. R Foundation for Statistical Computing, Vienna, Austria (2018). https://www.R-project.org/
41. Ribeiro, M.T., Singh, S., Guestrin, C.: Model-agnostic interpretability of machine learning. ICML WHI 2016 (2016). arXiv preprint arXiv:1606.05386
42. Roustant, O., Ginsbourger, D., Deville, Y.: DiceKriging, DiceOptim: two R packages for the analysis of computer experiments by kriging-based metamodeling and optimization. J. Stat. Softw. **51**(1), 1–55 (2012)
43. Stachl, C., et al.: Predicting personality from patterns of behavior collected with smartphones. Proc. Natl. Acad. Sci. **117**(30), 17680–17687 (2020)
44. Tibshirani, R.: Regression shrinkage and selection via the lasso. J. Roy. Stat. Soc.: Ser. B (Methodol.) **58**(1), 267–288 (1996)
45. Watson, D.S., Wright, M.N.: Testing conditional independence in supervised learning algorithms. Mach. Learn. **110**, 2107–2129 (2021)
46. Williamson, B.D., Gilbert, P.B., Carone, M., Simon, N.: Nonparametric variable importance assessment using machine learning techniques. Biometrics (2019)

47. Williamson, B.D., Gilbert, P.B., Simon, N.R., Carone, M.: A general framework for inference on algorithm-agnostic variable importance. J. Am. Stat. Assoc. 1–14 (2021)
48. Zhang, L., Janson, L.: Floodgate: inference for model-free variable importance. arXiv preprint arXiv:2007.01283 (2020)
49. Zhao, Q., Hastie, T.: Causal interpretations of black-box models. J. Bus. Econ. Stat. **39**(1), 272–281 (2021)

Explainable AI in Finance, Cybersecurity, Health-Care and Biomedicine

Evaluating Feature Relevance XAI in Network Intrusion Detection

Julian Tritscher[1(✉)], Maximilian Wolf[2], Andreas Hotho[1], and Daniel Schlör[1]

[1] University of Würzburg, Am Hubland, 97074 Würzburg, Germany
`{tritscher,hotho,schloer}@informatik.uni-wuerzburg.de`
[2] Coburg University of Applied Sciences, 96450 Coburg, Germany
`m.wolf@informatik.uni-wuerzburg.de`

Abstract. As machine learning models become increasingly complex, there is a growing need for explainability to understand and trust the decision-making processes. In the domain of network intrusion detection, post-hoc feature relevance explanations have been widely used to provide insight into the factors driving model decisions. However, recent research has highlighted challenges with these methods when applied to anomaly detection, which can vary in importance and impact depending on the application domain. In this paper, we investigate the challenges of post-hoc feature relevance explanations for network intrusion detection, a critical area for ensuring the security and integrity of computer networks. To gain a deeper understanding of these challenges for the application domain, we quantitatively and qualitatively investigate the popular feature relevance approach SHAP when explaining different network intrusion detection approaches. We conduct experiments to jointly evaluate detection quality and explainability, and explore the impact of replacement data, a commonly overlooked hyperparameter of post-hoc feature relevance approaches. We find that post-hoc XAI can provide high quality explanations, but requires a careful choice of its replacement data as default settings and common choices do not transfer across different detection models. Our study showcases the viability of post-hoc XAI for network intrusion detection systems, but highlights the need for rigorous evaluations of produced explanations.

Keywords: Anomaly detection · Feature relevance · Explainable AI

1 Introduction

Explainable artificial intelligence (XAI) is a rapidly growing research field that has recently gained particular attention in the security-critical application domain of network intrusion detection [16]. In this domain, the increasing complexity of detection systems has led to a growing use of post-hoc explainability methods that can shed light on the decision-making process of trained machine learning models [1,10,12,15,18,20,25,26,32–34]. Despite the widespread use of post-hoc XAI for explaining network intrusion detection systems (NIDS), there

L. Longo (Ed.): xAI 2023, CCIS 1901, pp. 483–497, 2023.
https://doi.org/10.1007/978-3-031-44064-9_25

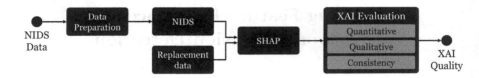

Fig. 1. Experimental setup for the XAI evaluation of SHAP within NIDS. We investigate XAI performance across multiple NIDS and across different choices of replacement data.

is a lack of quantitative evaluation of the resulting explanations, as most studies are limited to small qualitative discussions of single data point explanations.

As intrusion attacks are usually rare and not always known ahead of time, a subfield of NIDS models the task as anomaly detection [3]. Within the field of anomaly detection, however, recent research finds that the application of popular post-hoc XAIs to machine learning models poses significant challenges [30]. These challenges arise from the selection of replacement data (also called reference, background or baseline data in literature), a common hyperparameter of popular post-hoc XAIs, that is used to contrast observed feature values with alternative observations. This hyperparameter is often overlooked in applications and can have domain-specific impact on the performance of various XAI techniques, vastly decreasing explanation quality if set inappropriately.

In this paper, we address the lack of quantitative evaluation of post-hoc XAIs when applied to NIDS by building an expert-annotated dataset. We conduct a comprehensive quantitative and qualitative evaluation of the impact of replacement data on the performance of SHAP [14], a commonly used post-hoc XAI method in anomaly-based NIDS [1,10,12,15,18,20,25,26,32–34]. We evaluate SHAP across multiple NIDS and multiple established choices of replacement values[1]. Our experimental setup is illustrated in Fig. 1. Our study shows that the choice of replacement data is critical for obtaining good explanations and that the optimal selection strategy for replacement data not only depends on the application domain but also on the model being explained. We further demonstrate that commonly used replacement values do not always lead to good explanations, making quantitative evaluations of explanations an essential step in building new explainable NIDS.

In summary, our contributions are as follows: (1) We rigorously evaluate the popular post-hoc XAI method SHAP when applied to NIDS both qualitatively and quantitatively using ground truth explanations, finding that SHAP can indeed provide high-quality explanations for NIDS. (2) We systematically investigate the impact of replacement data and show that common choices do not always result in good explanations. This emphasizes the importance of this often overlooked hyperparameter and demonstrates the need for quantitative evaluation of XAI in practice.

---

[1] Code and annotations are available under https://professor-x.de/xai-nids.

The remainder of this paper is structured as follows. In Sect. 2, we first outline related work in terms of explainable NIDS. We then describe the methodology in Sect. 3, covering the dataset and preprocessing, anomaly detection and XAI methodology, as well as our evaluation protocol. In Sect. 4, we outline our experimental setup and report and discuss intrusion detection performance, as well as XAI performance qualitatively and quantitatively before we conclude this work in Sect. 5.

2   Related Work

The majority of research literature, as well as commercial NIDS, is based on two main approaches: misuse detection, and anomaly detection. Misuse detection is typically modeled as supervised classification task that detects known threats based on predefined patterns, making it the most commonly used approach in NIDS [4]. In contrast, anomaly detection-based NIDS is an unsupervised or semi-supervised task that identifies anomalies which deviate from a well-defined normal behavior.

A survey of current methods, challenges, and opportunities for explainable intrusion detection systems (X-IDS) has been conducted by Neupane et al. [16], providing a comprehensive overview of the state-of-the-art in a variety of different modeling approaches with respect to explainability technique and machine learning methodology. When developing X-IDS, a black-box approach is often recommended [16]. This is reflected in the significant amount of research that incorporates SHapley Additive exPlanations (SHAP) [14] in NIDS, allowing to explain arbitrary black-box models [1,10,12,15,18,20,25,26,32–34]. All of these approaches include SHAP as post-hoc XAI approach to generate explanations for misuse detection, which are then exemplarily discussed with respect to the specific features that the authors would expect to explain different types of attacks. In addition to these distinct interpretations of selected examples, none of these studies investigates the quality of explanations from a quantitative perspective.

The study by Dang [5] stands out as one of the few that quantitatively evaluates explainability for intrusion detection. It applies partial dependence plots and SHAP and compares pre- and post-explainability-based feature selection. In contrast, our work models NIDS as anomaly detection task and incorporates ground truth annotations to directly evaluate explainability of a specific model, instead of relying on an indirect evaluation that assesses whether relevant features give sufficient prediction quality with a new model. Although misuse detection models are common in studies on explainable NIDS, only few proposed works focus on explainability of anomaly detection-based NIDS. The Gradient-based Explainable Variational Autoencoder (GEE) [17] is a framework to detect and explain anomalies in network traffic, which analyzes the gradients contributed by each feature of the data point to explain anomalies. However, their evaluation of these gradient fingerprints as explanation is limited to a discussion of examples and their clustering. The most similar related work to our study is presented by Antwarg et al. [2]. In their study, an Autoencoder is used together with SHAP for explainable anomaly detection. They investigate the quality of explanations on an artificial dataset quantitatively, whereas the evaluation on real-world datasets is limited to the surrogate task of reducing anomality similar to [5] and expert interviews. Additionally, they highlight the potential influence of replacement data on explanation quality but leave evaluations as future work.

With our study, we extend the existing work in two aspects. First, in absence of an "application-grounded evaluation" with real humans and the real task [8], we collect ground truth explanations from three domain experts in the domain of network intrusion detection for quantitative evaluation. Second, we address the issue of replacement data as raised by Antwarg et al. [2] and systematically evaluate several approaches to select these replacement data for different anomaly detection models applied to the CIDDS-001 dataset [23] in a quantitative and qualitative evaluation.

3 Methodology

To study the performance of post-hoc feature relevance explanations in NIDS, we first obtain ground truth explanations through an annotation process with three domain experts. We train multiple machine learning models in an anomaly detection setting through a hyperparameter study, and apply post-hoc feature relevance explanations to the resulting best performing models. The ground truth explanations allow us to then follow the experimental setting of [31] for XAI evaluation. In the following, we present the used data, pre-processing steps, machine learning models, XAI approach, and XAI evaluation setup.

3.1 Data and Labeling Process

To validate explanations within multiple NIDS, we use the established CIDDS-001 dataset [24], which we additionally augment with ground truth explanations of attacks. CIDDS-001 features network traffic of a simulated computer network of virtual machines, where clients interact within the network via scripted normal actions or in different attack scenarios. Attacks included within the dataset are denial-of-service (dos) attacks that target available services within the local network, port scans that test for open ports of nodes within the local network, ping scans that sweep the local network to discover IP addresses in use, and brute force attacks that attempt to establish a password-protected ssh connection to an internal node by repeatedly trying passwords using a brute force algorithm.

The total dataset consists of 4 weeks of traffic, with attacks included in week 1 and week 2. In our experiments we use anomaly-based NIDS that train on the exclusively normal data of week 3 and 4 (train), validating hyperparameters on week 2 (valid) and testing on week 1 (test).

For the XAI evaluation, 20 attacks are sampled randomly from each of the available dos, port scan, ping scan, and brute force attacks within the test set, obtaining 80 attack data points in total. To gain ground truth explanations, we conduct an annotation process with three intrusion detection experts. All three experts are given a brief introduction to the data, and are then tasked to independently annotate the 80 attacks. Annotations are created on a per-data basis, where experts assess each feature of a given attack data point regarding whether it is indicative of the underlying attack. Experts are tasked with marking all indicative features within the attack, creating a binary ground truth of relevant features. Overall, the three experts achieved an inter-annotation agreement of 88%, based on Krippendorff's alpha coefficient [11]. Differences in annotation were then discussed among the experts and unified to obtain the ground truth.

3.2 Pre-processing

Network data processed by NIDS commonly consists of both numerical (e.g. packet sizes) and categorical features (e.g. IP addresses and ports) [7].

Categorical features with small numbers of observed combinations, such as the type of network traffic, are commonly encoded using a one-hot representation. For categorical features such as IP addresses or ports, that may contain large numbers of observed values, direct one-hot encoding is undesirable to prevent an explosion in feature space. Common representations are one-hot encoding after replacing specific value groups with dummy tokens to reduce feature space (e.g., modeling all external IP addresses through one token [29]), modeling IP addresses and ports as numerical variables, bit-wise encoding, or learning of vector representations [22]. In this work, we utilize one-hot encoding for all categorical variables, using aggregation for IP addresses and ports to retain the categorical nature of these features while limiting the increase in feature space that would result from direct one-hot encoding. For IP addresses, we aggregate external IPs into one token as the CIDDS-001 dataset is focused on internal private network traffic. For ports, we focus on standardized ports, aggregating all ports above 1024 into one token, and additionally grouping all ports that occur less than 10 times within the training data.

Numerical features are commonly standardized to prevent machine learning models from showing sensitivity to feature value ranges. Possible standardization techniques include min-max scaling, z-score scaling, or quantization. In our experiments, we follow [31] by using quantization for all numerical features. We create buckets with equal value frequency according to the training data, and additionally limit the out-most buckets to only 1% of the data to capture outlier values and highlight them for the machine learning models.

Since we investigate anomaly-based NIDS that cannot model sequential dependencies within the data, we further add an additional feature that aggregates the number of flows that were registered within the last 10 min for a specific IP address and port combination, which is a common preprocessing approach [7]. Aggregating this information for source and destination IPs/ports gives detection systems access to a simple representation of usual traffic frequencies when learning the normal network behavior.

3.3 Intrusion Detection

In our evaluation we focus on anomaly-based NIDS, evaluating the explanation process of attacks detected by three well-established anomaly detection models that have been successfully used as NIDS [17,19,29].

Autoencoders (AEs) [9] are under-complete neural networks that learn a simplified data representation of normal behavior by reproducing their inputs at the output layer. Isolation Forests (IFs) [13] are ensemble-based models that use the concept of isolation to identify anomalies using multiple decision trees. One-class Support Vector Machines (OC-SVMs) [27] are maximum margin classifiers that detect anomalies by constructing a hyperplane which separates the given data from the origin in the feature space. For computational efficiency, the used OC-SVM is trained on a random slice of 0.1% of the available training data.

We evaluate the suitability of these methods through a parameter study, and report our results on multiple random seeds during our experiments to capture the statistical variation in the non-deterministic IF and AE, as well as the random training data sampling for the OC-SVM. Results are reported on the established area under the precision recall curve (PR) and area under the receiver operator characteristic curve (ROC) scores. We report all results on both metrics, but rely on the PR score to select hyperparameters, as it is known to be more suited to unbalanced settings such as anomaly detection [6].

3.4 XAI: SHAP

Kernel SHapley Additive exPlanations (SHAP) [14] is a model-agnostic post-hoc XAI approach, that assigns each feature a score which represents how much it contributed to a single model decision. These feature relevance explanations are obtained by repeatedly removing feature combinations from the input and monitoring the model output. Since many machine learning models can not handle missing feature values, SHAP instead replaces values using replacement data that may be chosen as hyperparameter.

For this replacement data, multiple choices exist in literature. Next to SHAP's default implementation using cluster center points of *k-means* clustering from training data, and the use of the *zero-vector* or overall *mean* of training data established in classification settings, replacements that are conditional on the data point to explain can be used in anomaly detection [30]. The latter replacement option may be chosen to prevent the creation of new anomalies when placing normal replacement values into the potentially unfitting context of the data point to explain. Possible options are the use of nearest neighbors (*NN*) from normal data, or gradient-based optimization procedures (*opt*) that generate a normal data point in the proximity of the point to explain [28].

While the choice of replacement values was found to have great influence on the explanations of anomaly detection models [30], current works that employ SHAP in NIDS currently either do not mention replacement values at all [1,10,12,15,20,25,26,32] or use SHAP's default implementation [18], which motivates the investigation of replacement values for explaining NIDS.

3.5 XAI Evaluation

For qualitative inspection of their explanations, SHAP provides visualizations that show the contribution of features to a model decision. While applications of SHAP in NIDS perform brief qualitative inspections using these plots [1, 10, 12, 15, 18, 20, 25, 26, 32], they do not conduct a rigorous quantitative evaluation, which proves difficult due to the lack of ground truth explanations.

Using the binary ground truth obtained through our expert labeling process described in Sect. 3.1, we are able to evaluate SHAP explanations with established metrics. This evaluation is based on the observation that well performing NIDS systems need to rely on features that are indicative of an attack to successfully separate attacks from normal behavior. Since the binary ground truth marks features that are indicative of an attack and detection performance can be assessed prior to explanation quality, established metrics can be used to assess whether indicative features are rated as more relevant than other features [31]. Following [31], we use two metrics to compare the feature relevance scores of a single data point with the ground truth explanations. ROC scores favor correctly identifying anomalous features within the highest ranking results over identifying all anomalies with decent scores. Cosine similarity (COS), on the other hand, favors a complete match of the entire ground truth explanation, showing how well the XAI highlighted all anomalous features. We report both metrics, but focus our evaluation on ROC scores, as machine learning models do not need to find all suspicious features to identify an attack.

Finally, we also conduct the consistency evaluation of [31] that aims to discover whether similar attacks are detected and explained in a consistent way. This may, for example, be used in practice to generate attack fingerprints based on common explanation patterns, as illustrated in [17]. To showcase the similarity of explanations, we remove all features with an impact of less than 25% of the most influencing feature to remove noise and calculate the Hamming distance between all fraudulent samples. The resulting distances may be visualized as a heatmap, where data points are ordered by their attack type.

Table 1. Hyperparameter grid with tested parameter sets for investigated NIDS.

approach	parameters
OC-SVM	kernel $\in$ [rbf], $\gamma \in$ [1e3, 1e2, 1e1, 1e0, 1e−1, 1e−2, 1e−3], $\nu \in$ [0.2, 0.4, 0.6, 0.8]
AE	neurons $\in$ {[32, 16, 8, 16, 32], [64, 32, 16, 32, 64], [128, 64, 32, 64, 128], [64, 32, 16, 8, 16, 32, 64], [128, 64, 32, 16, 32, 64, 128], [256, 128, 64, 32, 64, 128, 256], [128, 64, 32, 16, 8, 16, 32, 64, 128], [256, 128, 64, 32, 16, 32, 64, 128, 256], [512, 256, 128, 64, 32, 64, 128, 256, 512]}, learning rate $\in$ [1e-2, 1e-3, 1e-4], batch size $\in$ [2048]
IF	trees $\in$ [16, 32, 64, 128], max samples $\in$ [0.4, 0.6, 0.8, 1.0], max features $\in$ [0.4, 0.6, 0.8]

Table 2. Best results of each approach on evaluation and test set, reporting mean and standard deviation of scores across 10 random seeds.

model	PR^{eval}	PR^{test}	ROC^{eval}	ROC^{test}
OC-SVM	**98.6 ± 0.2**	**99.5 ± 0.1**	**99.9 ± 0.0**	**99.9 ± 0.0**
AE	98.4 ± 1.1	99.2 ± 0.5	99.8 ± 0.1	**99.9 ± 0.0**
IF	98.0 ± 1.4	99.3 ± 0.5	99.7 ± 0.2	99.9 ± 0.1

4   Experiments

In this section, we discuss the anomaly detection results, as well as the results from an XAI perspective.

4.1   Anomaly Detection Results

To ensure that explanations are generated for models that are capable of detecting intrusion attacks, we conduct a parameter study through grid search. The investigated parameter sets are reported in Table 1. The best models are chosen through PR score on the *eval* split, and performance is reported on both *eval* and the independent *test* split in Table 2. All models score highly on attacks within the test dataset on both PR and ROC score, with little statistical fluctuation across different random seeds. This shows that the models are suited to detect attacks within the netflow data, and allows us to use a model with these hyperparameter settings for generating explanations.

4.2   XAI Results

For our explanation evaluation, we run SHAP on all anomaly detection models, explaining the 80 attack data points labeled as described in Sect. 3.1. To capture the impact of different replacement data choices within SHAP, we use SHAP with the replacement options discussed in Sect. 3.4, namely the *zero-vector*, *k-means* cluster centers, overall *mean*, *NN*, and *opt*. All replacement methods that require data were fitted only on the training data. We additionally use the gradient-based optimization process to explain AE, as it is the only differentiable architecture. To contrast SHAP's XAI results, we calculate baseline explanations. As baselines we report the explanation scores of uniform random noise sampled from $[-1, 1]$, as well as random noise multiplied with the input anomaly (noise × input). Further, for AE we report the scores obtained through using the reconstruction error of individual features as explanation, which is another option to extract explanations from AE [21].

Quantitative Results. XAI results are reported through ROC and COS scores for each individual attack, as discussed in Sect. 3.5. We report the mean and standard deviation of these scores across all 80 labeled attacks for our baselines in Table 3, and for the SHAP explanations in Table 4. While almost all combinations of detection models and replacement values are able to surpass the random baselines, we observe large variation across models and replacements. The highest explanation scores both in ROC and COS are similar for all models, suggesting that explaining NIDS through SHAP is feasible. However, we observe that no coherent best replacement choice exists across anomaly detection models. Additionally, we find that *NN* replacements perform poorly across all models, which may be caused by its use of proximity. When replacement features are identical to the features they are replacing, by construction, SHAP assigns a feature relevance score of zero. Since *NN* selects data points that are close to the anomaly, and may therefore share feature values with the anomaly, these features can not be recognized by SHAP. In application scenarios where anomalies are not easily identified through simple distance measures, this can introduce a bias into SHAP explanations, leading to poor performance.

Table 3. Baselines for quantitative explanation scores.

Baseline	ROC_{XAI}	COS_{XAI}
uniform noise	49.4 ± 21.7	-1.7 ± 38.1
noise×input	49.8 ± 19.2	-0.2 ± 26.4
AE reconstruction	$\mathbf{87.9 \pm 10.3}$	$\mathbf{72.7 \pm 14.8}$

Table 4. Quantitative explanation scores using different reference values.

Replacement	OC-SVM		AE		IF	
	ROC_{XAI}	COS_{XAI}	ROC_{XAI}	COS_{XAI}	ROC_{XAI}	COS_{XAI}
k-means	88.1 ± 8.7	68.6 ± 12.6	$\mathbf{91.3 \pm 8.7}$	$\mathbf{71.8 \pm 15.9}$	73.5 ± 19.3	52.8 ± 23.1
zeros	85.2 ± 9.2	48.1 ± 13.9	51.9 ± 11.7	-20.7 ± 16.6	$\mathbf{87.2 \pm 8.7}$	$\mathbf{65.9 \pm 13.2}$
mean	$\mathbf{90.1 \pm 7.5}$	$\mathbf{71.0 \pm 12.9}$	82.6 ± 12.7	57.4 ± 19.6	65.8 ± 18.7	33.4 ± 25.7
k-NN	71.3 ± 11.9	56.4 ± 18.1	75.4 ± 11.6	61.1 ± 15.7	68.8 ± 11.7	43.8 ± 22.7
opt	N/A	N/A	88.5 ± 8.7	68.9 ± 14.3	N/A	N/A

For OC-SVM, all replacement values beside *NN* work comparably well, with highest scores achieved through *mean* replacement. For AE, *k-means* and *opt* show high explanation scores, while *mean* performs decently. The *zero-vector* replacements, on the other hand, show problematic behavior. The *zero-vector* itself obtains higher anomaly scores for AE than attacks within the dataset. This causes issues, as SHAP constructs its explanations relative to the model prediction obtained on the replacement data. When the replacement is rated as more anomalous than the data point to explain, SHAP scores highlight features that change the model output away from the anomalous replacement values, as opposed to showing the desired features that move the model output away from normal behavior. As a consequence, the resulting explanations are entirely unsuitable for identifying anomalous feature values, as reflected in the obtained ROC and COS scores. Low performance on *mean* can be explained by the same observation in a weakened form, as the mean data point obtains similar anomaly scores to those of the attacks within the test set. The replacements drawn from the multiple *k-means* cluster centers, however, appear to stabilize this behavior, being scored by AE as less abnormal than attacks and producing high explanation scores. IF exhibits similar behavior on different replacements, obtaining poor explanations when using *k-means*, *mean*, and *NN* replacements. Again, we find that these replacements obtain anomaly scores from IF that are in the same value range as the attacks within the dataset. IF only achieves good explanation performance using the *zero-vector* as replacement, which for IF obtains smaller anomaly scores compared to the attacks.

Qualitative Results. To gain a more in-depth understanding of the observed explanation behavior, we investigate the individual explanations obtained by different models and replacement values in detail. We utilize SHAP plots to visualize and closely inspect the annotated explanations. Exemplary SHAP plots for different NIDS on a dos attack can be seen in Fig. 2.

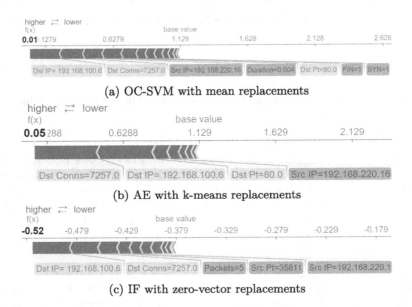

(a) OC-SVM with mean replacements

(b) AE with k-means replacements

(c) IF with zero-vector replacements

Fig. 2. SHAP explanations for each NIDS with best performing replacement values on a single non-cherry-picked dos attack. Bar width corresponds to feature influence, and features that are indicative of an attack (green) or non-indicative (red) are highlighted according to ground truth. OC-SVM distributes relevance to many different features. AE and IF highlight relevant features well, while IF additionally highlights irrelevant packet size. (Color figure online)

Across all replacement options we make the following observations. We find that for dos attacks OC-SVM correctly identifies high connection frequencies of unusual IP addresses, but also highlights flow duration. Port scans are mainly detected over suspicious IPs and ports, with anomalously high connection frequencies of the attacker also highlighted in some data points. In ping scans, the atypical ICMP protocol in combination with the two IP addresses is found, but not without highlighting some irrelevant packet size related features. Finally, brute force attacks are explained through the anomalous combination of the port used by ssh, together with the IP addresses, as well as through frequent connections to the ssh port. Overall, we find OC-SVM explanations to assign relevance to many different features, a similar behavior to that observed in [31]. While OC-SVM assigns a large amount of relevance to truly anomalous features, this also produces a lot of noise, since many irrelevant features obtain a smaller but not negligible amount of relevance.

AE reliably highlights dos attacks through high connection frequencies and corresponding IP address and port of the attack victim. Port scans are detected mainly through the unusual combination of IP addresses and the victim's port. On ping scans, explanations successfully highlight uncommon ICMP traffic, but do not highlight further indicative features. Brute force attacks are identified by the atypical combination of ssh port and IP addresses, but also contain some noise with highlighted irrelevant TCP flags.

IF finds the anomalous combination of high connection frequency and IP address for the dos victim, but also highlights some irrelevant TCP flags and packet sizes. It successfully identifies port scans through high usage frequency of the attacker's port in combination with the corresponding attacker IP, but also highlights packet sizes. Ping scans are detected through identifying unusual ICMP traffic between attacker and victim IPs and ports. Finally, it identifies brute force attacks through the combination of ssh port and IP addresses, while also highlighting few TCP flags. Overall, IF using *zero-vector* replacement successfully identifies many relevant attack characteristics, and shows a slight preference for highlighting irrelevant TCP flags and packet sizes. Other replacements result in highlighting many irrelevant TCP flags and irrelevant IP address entries.

Consistency Results. As a final step in our evaluation, we investigate whether the obtained SHAP explanations show consistent patterns across specific attack scenarios, which might allow for pattern matching and detection of common attack scenarios through explanations. We construct heatmaps as described in Sect. 3.5 for each anomaly detection model using their best performing replacement values, and visualize the heatmaps in Fig. 3. OC-SVM consistently highlights similar features across ping scan attacks, with some clear patterns showing on dos attacks. On port scans and brute force attacks, patterns are less pronounced with multiple points showing very low similarity of their most relevant features. Compared to the other models, OC-SVM's similarities are also lower across all groups of attacks, which again highlights OC-SVM's behavior to split relevance between many individual features, causing noisy explanations. Both AE and IF explanations show similar patterns with clear similarity between dos, port scan, and brute force attacks, with highlighted features varying more on port scans and IF explanations being slightly more consistent throughout.

Discussion. Overall, we observe that the direct application of SHAP to popular anomaly detection techniques can indeed provide strong explanations within NIDS, validating the popular use of SHAP within this domain. However, we find that the selection of replacement values within SHAP is critical for explanation quality, and there is no apparent replacement that consistently performs well across models. This highlights the need for incorporating quantitative XAI evaluations into the development of explainable NIDS, as the use of common default values for SHAP replacement data does not guarantee high quality explanations.

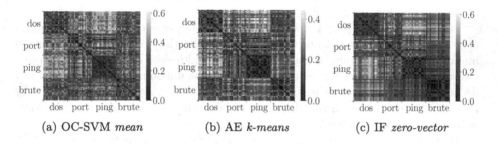

(a) OC-SVM *mean*   (b) AE *k-means*   (c) IF *zero-vector*

Fig. 3. Heatmaps showing the similarity of feature relevance explanations.

5   Conclusion

In this paper we constructed ground truth explanations for multiple attack scenarios within an established network intrusion detection dataset through expert annotation. We used these annotations to conduct an in-depth quantitative evaluation of multiple anomaly-based approaches for NIDS when explained by the popular SHAP post-hoc XAI approach and specifically investigated the impact of choosing different replacement strategies.

Our findings indicate that SHAP can produce high-quality explanations for all investigated detection models, but the choice of replacement values significantly impacts the quality of the resulting explanations. Our findings also emphasize the importance of considering the selection of replacement values during the design of explainable NIDS, as well as the systematic evaluation of post-hoc XAI techniques used in the pipeline, since we have demonstrated that SHAP's default replacement choice may not always produce satisfactory explanations for all models.

While this paper yields a positive result for the use of SHAP in NIDS, it is subject to several limitations that provide potential opportunities for future work. Beyond the investigation of XAI quality across multiple NIDS and replacement data, evaluations could be extended to investigate the impact of data preprocessing schemes and different XAI approaches. Additionally, while we quantitatively validate that SHAP successfully identifies anomalous features within NIDS attacks when using appropriate replacement data, the benefit of SHAP from a user perspective is also worthy of investigation. Finally, our work highlights that a consistent choice for replacement values is desirable for anomaly-based NIDS, marking the construction of model-invariant replacement values as relevant future work.

References

1. Alani, M.M., Miri, A.: Towards an explainable universal feature set for IoT intrusion detection. Sensors **22**(15), 5690 (2022). https://doi.org/10.3390/s22155690
2. Antwarg, L., Miller, R.M., Shapira, B., Rokach, L.: Explaining anomalies detected by autoencoders using Shapley Additive Explanations. Expert Syst. Appl. **186**, 115736 (2021). https://doi.org/10.1016/j.eswa.2021.115736
3. Buczak, A.L., Guven, E.: A survey of data mining and machine learning methods for cyber security intrusion detection. IEEE Commun. Surv. Tutor. **18**(2), 1153–1176 (2016). https://doi.org/10.1109/COMST.2015.2494502
4. Casas, P., Mazel, J., Owezarski, P.: Unsupervised network intrusion detection systems: detecting the unknown without knowledge. Comput. Commun. **35**(7), 772–783 (2012). https://doi.org/10.1016/j.comcom.2012.01.016
5. Dang, Q.V.: Improving the performance of the intrusion detection systems by the machine learning explainability. Int. J. Web Inf. Syst. **17**(5), 537–555 (2021). https://doi.org/10.1108/IJWIS-03-2021-0022
6. Davis, J., Goadrich, M.: The relationship between precision-recall and ROC curves. In: Proceedings of the 23rd International Conference on Machine Learning, pp. 233–240 (2006)
7. Davis, J.J., Clark, A.J.: Data preprocessing for anomaly based network intrusion detection: a review. Comput. Secur. **30**(6), 353–375 (2011)
8. Doshi-Velez, F., Kim, B.: Towards a rigorous science of interpretable machine learning (2017)
9. Goodfellow, I., Bengio, Y., Courville, A.: Deep Learning. MIT Press (2016). http://www.deeplearningbook.org
10. Houda, Z.A.E., Brik, B., Khoukhi, L.: "Why should i trust your IDS?": an explainable deep learning framework for intrusion detection systems in internet of things networks. IEEE Open J. Commun. Soc. **3**, 1164–1176 (2022). https://doi.org/10.1109/OJCOMS.2022.3188750
11. Krippendorff, K.: Content Analysis: An Introduction to Its Methodology, pp. 145–154. Sage Publications, Beverly Hills (1980)
12. Le, T.T.H., Kim, H., Kang, H., Kim, H.: Classification and explanation for intrusion detection system based on ensemble trees and SHAP method. Sensors **22**(3), 1154 (2022). https://doi.org/10.3390/s22031154
13. Liu, F.T., Ting, K.M., Zhou, Z.H.: Isolation forest. In: 2008 Eighth IEEE International Conference on Data Mining, pp. 413–422. IEEE (2008)
14. Lundberg, S., Lee, S.I.: A unified approach to interpreting model predictions. CoRR abs/1705.07874 (2017)

15. Mane, S., Rao, D.: Explaining network intrusion detection system using explainable AI framework. arXiv preprint arXiv:2103.07110 (2021)
16. Neupane, S., et al.: Explainable intrusion detection systems (X-IDS): a survey of current methods, challenges, and opportunities (2022)
17. Nguyen, Q.P., Lim, K.W., Divakaran, D.M., Low, K.H., Chan, M.C.: GEE: a gradient-based explainable variational autoencoder for network anomaly detection. In: 2019 IEEE Conference on Communications and Network Security (CNS), pp. 91–99 (2019)
18. Oseni, A., et al.: An explainable deep learning framework for resilient intrusion detection in IoT-enabled transportation networks. IEEE Trans. Intell. Transp. Syst. **24**(1), 1000–1014 (2023). https://doi.org/10.1109/TITS.2022.3188671
19. Patel, D., Srinivasan, K., Chang, C.Y., Gupta, T., Kataria, A.: Network anomaly detection inside consumer networks—a hybrid approach. Electronics **9**(6), 923 (2020)
20. Pawlicki, M., Zadnik, M., Kozik, R., Choraś, M.: Analysis and detection of DDoS backscatter using NetFlow data, hyperband-optimised deep learning and explainability techniques. In: Rutkowski, L., Scherer, R., Korytkowski, M., Pedrycz, W., Tadeusiewicz, R., Zurada, J.M. (eds.) ICAISC 2022. LNCS, vol. 13588, pp. 82–92. Springer, Cham (2023). https://doi.org/10.1007/978-3-031-23492-7_8
21. Ravi, A., Yu, X., Santelices, I., Karray, F., Fidan, B.: General frameworks for anomaly detection explainability: comparative study. In: 2021 IEEE International Conference on Autonomous Systems (ICAS), pp. 1–5 (2021)
22. Ring, M., Schlör, D., Landes, D., Hotho, A.: Flow-based network traffic generation using generative adversarial networks. Comput. Secur. **82**, 156–172 (2019)
23. Ring, M., Wunderlich, S., Grüdl, D., Landes, D., Hotho, A.: Creation of flow-based data sets for intrusion detection. J. Inf. Warfare **16**, 40–53 (2017)
24. Ring, M., Wunderlich, S., Grüdl, D., Landes, D., Hotho, A.: Flow-based benchmark data sets for intrusion detection. In: Proceedings of the 16th European Conference on Cyber Warfare and Security (ECCWS), pp. 361–369. ACPI (2017)
25. Sarhan, M., Layeghy, S., Portmann, M.: Evaluating standard feature sets towards increased generalisability and explainability of ML-based network intrusion detection (2021)
26. Sauka, K., Shin, G.Y., Kim, D.W., Han, M.M.: Adversarial robust and explainable network intrusion detection systems based on deep learning. Appl. Sci. **12**(13), 6451 (2022). https://doi.org/10.3390/app12136451
27. Schölkopf, B., Platt, J.C., Shawe-Taylor, J., Smola, A.J., Williamson, R.C.: Estimating the support of a high-dimensional distribution. Neural Comput. **13**(7), 1443–1471 (2001)
28. Takeishi, N., Kawahara, Y.: On anomaly interpretation via shapley values. arXiv preprint arXiv:2004.04464 (2020), http://arxiv.org/pdf/2004.04464.pdf
29. Torabi, H., Mirtaheri, S.L., Greco, S.: Practical autoencoder based anomaly detection by using vector reconstruction error. Cybersecurity **6**(1), 1 (2023)
30. Tritscher, J., Krause, A., Hotho, A.: Feature relevance XAI in anomaly detection: reviewing approaches and challenges. Front. Artif. Intell. **6**, 1099521 (2023)
31. Tritscher, J., Schlör, D., Gwinner, F., Krause, A., Hotho, A.: Towards explainable occupational fraud detection. In: Koprinska, I., et al. (eds.) ECML PKDD 2022. CCIS, vol. 1753, pp. 79–96. Springer, Cham (2023). https://doi.org/10.1007/978-3-031-23633-4_7
32. Wali, S., Khan, I.: Explainable AI and random forest based reliable intrusion detection system (2021). https://doi.org/10.36227/techrxiv.17169080.v1

33. Wang, M., Zheng, K., Yang, Y., Wang, X.: An explainable machine learning framework for intrusion detection systems. IEEE Access **8**, 73127–73141 (2020)
34. Zebin, T., Rezvy, S., Luo, Y.: An explainable AI-based intrusion detection system for DNS over HTTPS (DoH) attacks. IEEE Trans. Inf. Forensics Secur. **17**, 2339–2349 (2022). https://doi.org/10.1109/TIFS.2022.3183390

Cost of Explainability in AI: An Example with Credit Scoring Models

Jean Dessain[1,2]([✉]) [ID], Nora Bentaleb[2], and Fabien Vinas[3]

[1] IESEG School of Management, Univ. Lille, 59000 Lille, France
j.dessain@ieseg.fr
[2] Reacfin, Place de l'Université. 25, 1348 Louvain-la-Neuve, Belgium
[3] Allianz Trade, Tour First, 1 Pl. des Saisons, 92400 Courbevoie, France

Abstract. This paper examines the cost of explainability in machine learning models for credit scoring. The analysis is conducted under the constraint of meeting the regulatory requirements of the European Central Bank (ECB), using a real-life dataset of over 50,000 credit exposures. We compare the statistical and financial performances of black-box models, such as XGBoost and neural networks, with inherently explainable models like logistic regression and GAMs. Notably, statistical performance does not necessarily correlate with financial performance. Our results reveal a difference of 15 to 20 basis points in annual return on investment between the best performing black-box model and the best performing inherently explainable model, as cost of explainability. We also find that the cost of explainability increases together with the risk appetite.

To enhance the interpretability of explainable models, we apply isotonic smoothing of features' shape functions based on expert judgment. Our findings suggest that incorporating expert judgment in the form of isotonic smoothing improves the explainability without compromising the performance. These results have significant implications for the use of explainable models in credit risk assessment and for regulatory compliance.

Keywords: Explainable AI · Credit Risk · Credit Scoring · Interpretability · Economic Performance

1 Introduction

1.1 Framework

In recent years, the field of artificial intelligence (AI) has experienced an explosive growth in academic research, resulting in the development of increasingly complex AI systems used in high-stakes applications. As a result, demand has grown for AI models that can provide clear and interpretable explanations of their decision-making processes, leading to the emergence of explainable AI (XAI) as a hot topic in AI research [1]. XAI can be achieved through two main approaches: utilizing models that are intrinsically explainable, such as generalized linear models (GLM) or generalized additive models (GAM), or applying a set of techniques to provide ex-post transparency and understanding of how black-box models arrive at their decisions.

L. Longo (Ed.): xAI 2023, CCIS 1901, pp. 498–516, 2023.
https://doi.org/10.1007/978-3-031-44064-9_26

As the drive for explainability continues, concerns are growing about the potential impact of inherent explainability on model performance. This trade-off [2, 3] between performance and explainability means that the most performant models are often less explainable (black-boxes) than intrinsically explainable but less performant ones (glass-boxes). Credit scoring is no exception to this, given the growing role of AI and the need for interpretability. In this article, we explore and discuss the potential cost of explainability as a trade-off that could reduce model performance when using inherently explainable models.

Credit Scoring with AI. Credit scoring is a key application of artificial intelligence that aims to predict the creditworthiness of actual or potential debtors based on various features. These features can be directly linked to the debtor or to external elements such as the economic environment. Credit scoring models attribute a score or a grade that reflects the default probability of a borrower over a time horizon, usually a year (one-year PD) or the maturity of the credit exposure (lifetime PD). They are used for underwriting and pricing credit, managing credit risk, or computing capital requirements for financial institutions under regulations like Basle IV or Solvency II.

The importance of credit risk within financial institutions has spurred the development of numerous credit scoring models. In recent years, there has been a growing interest in using AI for its ability to capture complex relationships between variables and improve prediction accuracy. Several systematic reviews, including [4–14] provide a comprehensive analysis of AI methods for credit scoring. Additionally, [7] offers a review of the main models and of the articles that present these models.

Interpretable or Explainable. Explainability is a crucial consideration in credit scoring models, given their commercial significance for underwriting, pricing, and solvency computation. Internal rating-based (IRB) models must comply with strict constraints, which insurers must follow as per the Solvency II Commission Delegated Regulation (EU) 2015/35 of 10 October 2014, and banks as per the EU Delegated Regulation 2022/439 supplementing the Capital Requirements Regulation (CRR) with regard to Regulatory Technical Standards (RTS) for using the Internal Ratings Based Approach. One such constraint is the interpretability of models, which is mandated by regulatory requirements. These requirements have limited the use of advanced machine learning algorithms for IRB models, as highlighted in the EBA discussion [15].

AI-based credit scoring models can either be intrinsically interpretable or benefit from post-hoc techniques to enhance their understandability. Models that are intrinsically interpretable are often referred to as "white-box" or "glass-box" models, such as generalized linear models (GLMs) or generalized additive models (GAMs). In [16], GAMs, GLMs, and their respective strengths are discussed in detail, and the statistical cost of misclassification is assessed when using GAMs that capture non-linear relationships, as compared to GLMs. [17] investigates the interpretability and trustworthiness of GAMs through quantitative and qualitative analyses and generally confirm their inherent interpretability.

There are also models in credit scoring that are referred to as "black-box", meaning that they lack intrinsic interpretability and require ex-post techniques to improve their interpretability. A detailed review of the main methods can be found in [18]. In addition,

[19] provide an updated taxonomy of explainable AI, where they explicit the difference between "*global interpretability*" (the whole logic of a model and the reasoning leading to all possible outcomes) versus "*local interpretability*" of a single prediction. They differentiate between intrinsically interpretable models and non-intrinsically interpretable models that can benefit from interpretation techniques such as Shapley values, local interpretable model-agnostic explanations (LIME), partial dependence plots (PDP), individual conditional expectation plots (ICE), attention maps, and others. Although these interpretation techniques have their respective strengths and weaknesses, a detailed description of them is beyond the scope of this research. Interested readers can refer to to [18–23] for more information.

It is worth noting that recent developments such as [3, 24–26] attempt to overcome some limitations of traditional interpretation methods and to approach closer to the level of interpretability of inherently interpretable models.

In the remaining sections of this work, we will use the term "explainable model" to refer to a model that is intrinsically or inherently interpretable, and the term "interpretable model" to refer to a black-box model that can be interpreted ex-post using appropriate techniques.

In recent years, there has been a growing interest in developing algorithms that combine the performance of black-box techniques like Gradient Boosting [27, 28] or neural networks [29, 30], with the explainability of generalized linear or additive models (GAMs). These hybrid models aim to strike a balance between interpretability and performance. They have shown promising results.

Measuring Credit Scoring Performance. The assessment of credit risk models involves a wide range of evaluation metrics, as summarized by [31]. The most used statistical measures include AUROC and F-measures derived from the confusion matrix.

However, the effectiveness of statistical metrics in capturing financial results has been questioned in a different context by [32], suggesting that relying solely on such statistical measures may not be sufficient. While most studies use statistical metrics to evaluate credit risk models, only a few have applied some sort of financial measurements. For example, [33] and [34] compute a possible loss, assuming a loss given default (LGD) of 100%, without considering funding costs for the LGD computation. [35] measures the expected loan profitability instead of default risk, using the loan lifetime internal rate of return (IRR), but do not account for LGD. [36] proposes a financial approach that considers LGD for the principal amount only but does not incorporate the link between predicted PD and coupon rate.

In addition to assessing the effectiveness of credit scoring, financial regulation requires that predictive ability, discriminatory power, and stability of model outputs meet certain standards, particularly for IRB models used in solvency computations. Although the banking framework[1] provides detailed guidelines for model acceptability, it has received relatively little attention in academic research. While [37] refers to this regulatory framework, they do not measure compliance with the regulatory rules.

---

[1] EU Delegated Regulation 2022/439, EBA RTS/2016/03 Final Draft RTS, EBA/Op/2020/20 Opinion on RTS/2016/03, EBA Guidelines EBA/GL/2017/16, ECB Guide to Internal Models version 2.2 (Oct 2019).

1.2 Original Contribution

Our paper makes a threefold contribution. First, we compare the standard AI models, both the explainable and the black-box ones, with two newly developed explainable models that use black-box techniques to produce a GAM, which aim at balancing performance and interpretability.

Second, we evaluate the models for their regulatory compliance and financial performance, considering the lender's credit risk appetite, funding costs, predicted PD, and LGD. Third, we introduce the concept of *"cost of explainability"* to measure the financial cost of using inherently explainable models. Therefore, we compare their achieved economic performance with that of the most performant black-box models.

The rest of the paper is organized as follows: Sect. 2 describes the dataset and data management. Section 3 presents the methodology, including the models' construction, evaluation metrics, and financial measures. Section 4 reports the empirical results, discusses the models' performance, regulatory compliance, and financial cost. Finally, Sect. 5 concludes and provides some perspectives for future research.

2 Data

2.1 Description

Our study evaluates various credit scoring models using a dataset supplied by the world leader in trade credit insurance, covering the period from 2019 to 2022. The dataset consists of an anonymized limited and representative set of one-year credit exposures on a group of European borrowers reporting legal and financial information, with total assets above 1 million euros. In total, there are 55 explanatory variables, including 14 balance sheet items, 4 income statement figures, 9 financial ratios, and 9 legal and company descriptive features, plus one year lagged financial information. For confidentiality reasons, we cannot disclose details on the explanatory variables.

We use a training set of 2019 data (76089 rows), and test sets from 2020 to 2022, with 44151, 61406, and 59074 rows, respectively.

2.2 Data Management

Missing Data. The dataset we use for our analysis contains missing values. While some machine learning algorithms can handle missing data, most cannot. Therefore, we test several imputation techniques on the training data to handle the missing values. For univariate imputation, we replace missing values with the median values from the training set. For multivariate imputation, we use KNN, as introduced by [38], which selects the k-nearest neighbors' to determine the imputation value. We also employ a Bayesian Ridge algorithm with a round-robin iterative process, as described in [39]. We analyze the data drift induced by the imputations in the training data using four different tests: the Population Stability Index (PSI), Kolmogorov-Smirnov (KS), Kullback-Leibler divergence (KL), and Jensen-Shannon divergence (JS) tests. Based on the tests results, we decide to use the KNN imputation method with k set to 4.

Data Quality. To improve the quality of our credit scoring models, we apply several data preprocessing techniques.

Imbalance Management: First, we address the class imbalance issue by including all 1,346 defaults from 2017–2018 data in our 2019 training set.

Outliers Management: Second, we apply a 0.5%-99.5% univariate winsorization to financial variables to remove outliers that could negatively impact model performance.

Features Selection: Finally, we conduct a feature selection to reduce the dimensionality of the data. Starting from the original set of 55 features, we remove 20 highly correlated variables and ended up with a set of 35 features: 16 balance sheet or cash features (including their 1-year evolution), 5 income statement features (including their evolution), 5 financial ratios, and 9 descriptive, administrative or legal features.

Standardization or Normalization: To ensure consistency in the analysis of the financial features, we apply either standardization or min-max normalization. We compute the standardization and normalization parameters for each financial feature of the training set and applied them to standardize/normalize the training, validation and test sets. The logistic regression, elastic-net regression, naïve Bayes, linear discriminant analysis, random forest, and support vector machine models use the features standardization, the other models models use min-max normalization. The choice between standardization and normalization has been made following the most common practice for each algorithm. These models are described in Sect. 3.

3   Methodology

3.1   Models

Models Tested. In this section, we describe the credit scoring models that we test for their predictive ability using explanatory variables directly linked to the debtor or external elements such as the economic environment.

We examine twelve different models, which are detailed in [4–14].

Of these models, four are considered inherently 'explainable': Logistic Regression (LR), Elastic Net applied to a logistic regression (ELN), Naïve Bayes (NB), and Linear Discriminant Analysis (LDA).

Six models are classified as black-boxes interpretable ex-post: Support Vector Machine (SVM), Random Forest (RF), Gradient Boosting (GB), Light GBM (LGBM), eXtreme gradient Boosting (XGB), and Multi-Layer Perceptron (MLP).

In addition to these models, we also test two recent explainable Generalized Additive Models (GAM), which we add to the group of inherently explainable models. One model is powered with gradient boosting: the Explainable Boosting machine (EBM) [27, 28]. The other model is based on neural networks: Gami-net (GAMI) [30, 40]. Both models have a GAM form:

$$g(E[y]) = \beta_0 + \sum f_j(x_j) \tag{1}$$

that learns the shape function f_j of each explanatory feature x_j. EBM is using a gradient boosting technique. To learn the features functions and their respective contributions to the model's predictive capacity, the boosting procedure is restricted to train one feature at a time using a "round-robin cycle". Gami-net is a GAM of the same format as EBM that relies on a neural network rather to learn the features' function f_j.

Both models allow pairwise interactions. However, for this exercise, we do not consider pairwise interactions to keep the models sparse and avoid heredity issues related to the hierarchical structure between the main effects and the interactions. As such, we maximize their intelligibility and inherent explainability.

It is worth noting that we do not consider convolutional neural networks (CNN) or long-short-term memory model (LSTM) due to the nature of the available data and the lack of deep historical information, although these models are typically good performers for this type of task.

GAM Isotonicity. Isotonicity can be incorporated in GAM^2 models such as GAMI or EBM by constraining some or all of the f_j in Eq. (1) to be increasing or decreasing, on their entire range or on part of it. This approach has several benefits. By enforcing isotonicity, outliers can be managed effectively, thereby reducing or excluding their impact on the model's predictions. To illustrate this, consider a feature like the debt-to-equity ratio (D/E) in a GAM. Expert judgment suggests that lower D/E ratios correspond to lower default risk. If the training set includes one or more defaulted companies with specific low D/E ratio, the $f_{D/E}$ value for the corresponding bin might be abnormally high, which would distort the model's predictive ability. By imposing a monotonic decrease to $f_{D/E}$, the model's predictive power can be improved by addressing the outlier's issue in the training set.

Not only does isotonicity help manage outliers but it can also enhance the explainability of GAMI or EBM models by aligning each f_j more closely with expert judgement. This can improve the models' interpretability and facilitate effective human supervision. Relying on standard expert judgment in credit risk, we test EBM Isotonic and GAMI Isotonic, forcing isotonicity for 10 of the 35 features of the trained EBM to be isotonic. It is worth noting that the expert judgment only imposes increasingness or decreasingness for f_j, not the values themselves within f_j. Introducing expert judgment to obtain an isotonic GAM increases the interpretability of the model but might come at a cost in terms of accuracy or financial performance.

Hyper-parameters Tuning^3. To secure an efficient use of each model, we perform a hyper-parameters tuning, using a two-step grid search strategy. We start with a wide grid and take into consideration the non-linearities detected during the first grid search, which allows us to better determine the second more narrowly focused grid search.

Reproducibility and Replicability. To ensure the reproducibility and replicability of our tests, we take several measures. First, we fix the seed for Python, Numpy, and Pytorch. Second, we enforce Pytorch to work with deterministic CUDNN. Furthermore,

---

^{2} Isotonicity could also be incorporated in some black-box algorithms like random forest, tree by tree before combining the trees, but that does not improve the explainability of these black-box models.

^{3} Hyper-parameters and computer configurations and versioning are available upon request.

we perform both training and testing on two different computers and confirm that we obtain identical results. To verify the robustness of each model, we conduct additional training and testing using marginally modified hyper-parameters.

3.2 Performance Analysis

Model Calibration. For each borrower in the test sets and for each year, the models generate a probability of default (PD) between 0% and 100%. To standardize the PDs across the different models, we apply a calibration method based on the BIS IFC conference paper [41]. Specifically, we use the predicted PDs to construct a master scale for each model, which produces a normal distribution of grades while ensuring positive monotonicity of the scale.

Using the estimated PDs and constructed master scale per model, we assign a grade to each borrower for each year and create transition matrices. Our PDs, gradings, and transition matrices are then evaluated against ECB regulatory requirements prior to analyzing their statistical and financial performance.

Regulatory Requirements. Our analysis adheres to the ECB's IRB model requirements [42]. We evaluate the applied algorithms for their predictive accuracy and discriminatory power. We examine the stability of the resulting transition matrices. To ensure compliance with ECB standards, we only consider models whose master scales consist of at least 7 grades of not-defaulted credits (ECB required minimum), with a minimum of 0.01% PD distance between two grades.

Predictive Ability: We use the Jeffreys' test [43] to assess the prudence of our PD estimates at both the portfolio and individual grading levels. This involves testing whether the forecasted defaults are greater than the observed defaults, assuming a binomial model with independent observations. In addition to the Jeffrey's test, we conducted a binomial test using confidence interval testing to provide further evidence of the prudent levels of the predicted default probabilities.

Discriminatory Power: We use the AUROC as a metric to evaluate the discriminatory power of the models. The AUROC measures the ability of the model to distinguish between good and bad credit risks by calculating the area under the receiver operating characteristic (ROC) curve. To ensure that the models accurately separate risky borrowers from less risky ones, we evaluate their rank-ordering performance using the Mann-Whitney U statistic. A higher Mann-Whitney U statistic indicates better rank-ordering performance and, therefore, a more effective model. Unlike the parametric AUROC, which assumes that the predicted probabilities follow a certain distribution, the Mann-Whitney U statistic does not require any assumptions about the shape of the distribution. This makes it a more robust measure for assessing model performance on imbalanced datasets.

Stability: The analysis of the grading stability over time includes three different perspectives based on borrowers' grade transition matrices: (i) borrower migrations through matrix weighted bandwidth (MWB), (ii) grades dispersions through the Herfindahl Index (HI) [44], and (iii) the monotonicity of off-diagonal transition frequencies through pairwise z-tests.

MWBs allow us to summarize the downgrades and upgrades and assess whether the models are potentially biased upwards or downwards in their grading, over time.

The HI permits to assess the dispersion in grades by benchmarking the concentration level in grades from a current period to grades from a test period. Hypothesis testing is based on the normal approximation assuming a deterministic HI at current time. The null hypothesis being that the HI of the test year is lower than the current HI, meaning there is no significant increase in the dispersion.

To identify possible portfolio shifts, the monotonicity of off-diagonal transition frequencies in the transition matrix is assessed by means of pairwise z-tests, exploiting the asymptotic normality of the test statistic. The null hypothesis of the tests is that a transition frequency $p_{i,j} \geq p_{i,j-1}$ or $p_{i,j-1} \geq p_{i,j}$ depending on whether the (i,j) entry in the migration matrix is below or above the main diagonal.

We conduct all tests described above with a 5% confidence interval to ensure the reliability of our findings [42].

Explainability: When testing the performance of credit scoring models, explainability is an important consideration. While it is difficult to test explainability directly, we can compare and scrutinize models with varying degrees of interpretability. In our analysis, we focus on comparing the explainability of native GAM models with isotonic GAM models that incorporate expert judgment. Isotonic GAM models provide greater interpretability by allowing an expert to enforce monotonicity constraints on the model's features, for part of the feature shape function or for the entire function. This can hence help ensure that the model's predictions are aligned with the expert's expectations and domain knowledge. Accordingly, we can select a model that strikes an appropriate balance between interpretability and accuracy for a specific use case.

Statistical Performance. The discriminatory power analysis required among the ECB tests includes the computation of the AUROC to which we refer.

Financial Results. To evaluate the financial performance of the models, we simulate an investment of 100 EUR in each credit proposal with a predicted grade below a defined risk appetite threshold. We assume that if a loan is approved, the borrower agrees to pay a coupon consisting of four elements: (i) a one-year risk-free rate (rfr), (ii) a margin (ftp) for funding and liquidity determined by the Fund Transfer Pricing policy (FTP) set by the ALM department and based on market conditions, (iii) a credit risk premium equal to the PD determined for loan i by each model m ($cs_{i,m}$), and (iv) a commercial margin (cm) to remunerate the capital and the commercial and back-offices departments.

We define a risk appetite based on the maximum acceptable grade, whereby any credit with a grade equal to or lower than the threshold would be approved, and credit with a higher grade would be rejected. We are aware that for a real-life implementation, the risk appetite of the model retained would most likely be based on the expected PD rather than the grade, as this would allow a more granular definition of the risk appetite.

For each approved loan i on a given year, whose PD has been assessed with model m, we compute a financial result:

If the loan defaults, the loss is equal to the principal amount plus the expected coupon times the LGD: $result_i = -(1 + rfr + ftp + cs_{i,m} + cm) * LGD$ (or $EAD * LGD$);

If the loan is repaid at maturity, the result is equal to the sum of the credit spread and the commercial margin: $result_i = (cs_{i,m} + cm)$;

where rfr is the 1-year risk free rate, ftp is the cost of funding determined by the ALM, $cs_{i,m}$ is the credit spread for loan i defined by model m and cm is the commercial margin defined by the financial institution. We set the LGD[4] at 45% and assume that the recovery costs are included in the LGD.

This analysis assumes different coupon rates for the same loan since each model might output a different PD. To cope with possible abnormal PD prediction and the competitive environment, we cap the credit spread $cs_{i,m}$ at the level of a commonly accepted *"reference master scale"*[5]. This prevents models outputting very high PDs from artificially benefitting from non-conform credit spread levels (if a grade 5 credit of model j assumes an expected PD of 1.65% while the breakpoint of the reference master scale is 1.15%, the credit spread is set at 1.15% instead of 1.65% generated by the model).

Eventually, we reject models predicting a 100% acceptance rate due to a lack of predictive ability: in such case we do not compute any return and set it to 0%. We acknowledge that with this dataset, we have one-year credit exposures, so the one-year PD is equal to the lifetime PD. For a similar analysis including credits with longer maturities, we should consider the difference between one-year PDs and lifetime PDs.

We can compute the percentage of accepted loans and the return on invested amount for each model. We perform the base case with rfr = 3.25%, ftp = 0.75%, cm = 0.50%, and the risk appetite threshold set at grade 6 on a scale from 0 to 9, corresponding to the breakpoint of 4.33% in the reference master scale. We then test the sensitivity of the returns to a change in the risk appetite threshold.

4   Empirical Results

4.1   Regulatory Requirements[6]

The results of our empirical analysis indicate that three models are unable to produce a master scale with sufficient grades at a minimum distance of 0.01% PD. Specifically, the random forest model results in a master scale with only four grades, while the naive Bayes and support vector machine models produce scales with only five grades. Given that the ECB requires a minimum of seven grades plus an additional grade for defaulted borrowers, these three models are automatically excluded from further analysis. Consequently, we are able to analyze ten models that successfully meet this criterion.

Predictive Ability: Table 1 shows the number of observations and defaults in our test data.

At portfolio level, we find that all the investigated models predict prudent PD estimates for all test years, based on Jeffreys test results. At individual grade levels, all

---

[4] 45% is the LGD for senior unsecured credit to corporates in foundation IRB regulation in Basel Committee on Banking Supervision explicated in CRE 32.5. Rating agencies apply a 40% LGD for rated senior corporate debt.

[5] We use a standard 10 grades public master scale as *"reference master scale"*, that is very close to what the major rating agencies have published based on historical data.

[6] Synthetic results are provided herewith. Detailed ones are available upon request with the corresponding author.

Table 1. Number observations and defaults in the test data, per year.

	2020	2021	2022
Observations	44151	61406	59064
Defaults	582	335	275
Default rate (%)	1.32%	0.55%	0.47%

models pass Jeffreys test for a minimum of 7 grades and a maximum of all (9) grades, for all years. ELN, EBM, EBM Isotonic, XGB and GB are found to have prudent PD estimates for all grades, over all test years. Closely follow LGBM, GAMI and GAMI Isotonic which have at least 8 prudent PD estimates at PD level. The Binomial test consistently confirms the prudence of the PD estimates found through Jeffreys test. LDA and LR are producing the least prudent PD estimates based on Jeffreys test, with only 7 grades that have prudent estimates for two consecutive years.

Discriminatory Power: Figure 1 shows the AUROC values for the 10 models analyzed. AUROC is used to assess the discriminatory power and is the most common statistical metric for assessing credit scoring models' performance.

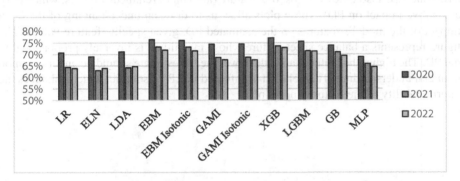

Fig. 1. AUROC per model per year.

XGB achieves the highest AUROC across all three years, closely followed by EBM, which also exhibited the best performance for inherently explainable AI. EBM Isotonic and GAMI Isotonic have similar statistical results than native EBM and GAMI respectively, suggesting that enforcing isotonicity does not affect the statistical performance.

Although we notice a downward trend in the AUROC values across time for all models, we do not have enough evidence to assess the time consistency of the discriminatory power across time, because of the limited test sample.

Stability: The over-time stability analysis indicates that all models predict meaningful grades in terms of stability, over all periods. The Coefficients of variation for the 2020–2021 and 2021–2022 periods, used to calculate the HI, range between [1.27, 1.34] and

[1.33, 1.43] respectively. As a result, all the HI tests pass and the upper and lower MWBs are relatively close to each other, meaning that grade dispersion is meaningful and none of the models has transition matrices biased towards downgrading or upgrading.

Significant grade transitions during the one-year observation periods affect the stability of the scoring model. Nevertheless, it must be considered that (i) the investigated period is short and (ii) that both observation periods fall within the COVID-19 pandemic period. It follows that significant downgrades and upgrades are to be expected and might not directly relate to the stability of the model but rather to its capacity to adequately adapt to changes in underlying features.

A model's stability might be questioned when both the number of significant grade transitions and the size of the transitions are material compared to the actual number of transitions. Moreover, this stability analysis enables the model used to further investigate those borrowers for which material grade transitions are identified. We have identified a maximum of 3 significant shifts per period, per model. The highest jumps are resulting from LDA and MLP, with jump sizes of 4,7 and 4,6 respectively. All other significant jump sizes are between 1 and 3. Due to restricted information on the data, we could not perform any further analysis.

Explainability: Explainable GAMs provide the importance and impact of the features. They also provide the detailed shape of f_j. Figure 2 shows the feature impact plots of EBM and EBM isotonic of the bs_012 feature (amount of retained earnings, which have a negative impact on PD). These plots allow us to draw an understanding of the main impact of the model's features on the estimated PD, given specific feature values. The figure represents a balance sheet feature whose magnitude is inversely proportional to the PD. The higher the feature value, the lower the PD estimate should be under common financial understanding. This relation is enforced in EBM isotonic, which enhances the interpretability of the feature impact plot.

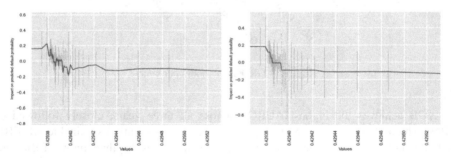

Fig. 2. Feature impact plots resulting from EBM (left) and EBM isotonic (right).

The standard deviation of PD estimates for each region of the feature's space is used to compute error bars on top of the main effects. These are rough estimates of the model uncertainty in each region of the feature space, which are determined by the amount of training data in each region. The larger the error, the higher the uncertainty and hence the more unstable the model predictions such that the interpretability potential lowers.

4.2 Statistical Analysis

For the statistical analysis results, we refer to the AUROC metric from the discriminatory power analysis performed under the regulatory requirements.

4.3 Financial Analysis

We evaluate the performance of the credit scoring models based on their return and acceptance rate for two risk appetite scenarios with different credit grade thresholds. The first scenario is a low-risk appetite with a threshold at grade 6 whereby all credit exposures with grade 6 or lower are accepted, and those with a grade of 7 to 9 are rejected. The second one is a high-risk appetite with the threshold at grade 7. We also compute a baseline return, for which we assume no model, with all credits accepted and an average credit spread corresponding to grade 5 (above the median of all accepted credit with each model).

Financial Performance: The results for 2020–2021 are respectively presented in Tables 2 and 3, with models regrouped by their degree of explainability. 2022 results are very similar and add no significant element[7]. The best models per category in term of generated return are highlighted in bold. The "no model" presents the return if all credits are accepted with a credit spread equivalent to grade 5 of the reference master scale.

MLP is consistently the best performer among all models, while EBM and GAMI are the best performers among the intrinsically explainable models.

Table 2. Credit acceptance rate and return of credit scoring models for 2020.

Model	Threshold Grade 6		Threshold Grade 7	
	Accepted	Return	Accepted	Return
LR	88.53%	1.34%	97.76%	1.52%
ELN	88.67%	1.31%	97.60%	1.49%
LDA	88.30%	1.20%	97.98%	1.38%
EBM	89.09%	1.46%	97.56%	1.64%
EBM Isotonic	*89.11%*	*1.46%*	*97.46%*	*1.65%*
GAMI	88.45%	**1.47%**	96.84%	**1.66%**
GAMI Isotonic	*88.28%*	*1.45%*	*96.88%*	*1.64%*
XGB	88.78%	1.43%	97.55%	1.60%
LGBM	87.44%	1.08%	97.43%	1.31%
GB	88.16%	1.38%	96.61%	1.57%
MLP	88.33%	**1.61%**	96.95%	**1.83%**
No model	*100.00%*	*0.55%*	*100.00%*	*0.55%*

---

[7] Results 2022 are available with the corresponding author upon request.

Table 3. Credit acceptance rate and return of credit scoring models for 2021.

Model	Threshold Grade 6		Threshold Grade 7	
	Accepted	Return	Accepted	Return
LR	90.43%	1.55%	98.21%	1.78%
ELN	90.74%	1.53%	98.25%	1.74%
LDA	90.23%	1.40%	98.27%	1.64%
EBM	91.09%	1.65%	98.29%	1.87%
EBM Isotonic	*91.16%*	*1.66%*	*98.20%*	*1.87%*
GAMI	90.81%	1.64%	97.94%	**1.88%**
GAMI Isotonic	*90.81%*	*1.62%*	*97.97%*	*1.86%*
XGB	90.76%	1.60%	98.25%	1.83%
LGBM	89.33%	1.28%	98.08%	1.58%
GB	90.62%	1.58%	97.67%	1.81%
MLP	90.65%	**1.82%**	97.81%	**2.06%**
No model	*100.00%*	*0.90%*	*100.00%*	*0.90%*

Adding expert judgment through the isotonicity constraint does not alter the financial performance of isotonic models.

Sensitivity Analysis: To evaluate the return sensitivity to credit risk appetite, we analyze the rejection rate as determined by the grade threshold. As we impose a Gaussian grade distribution, the rejection rate follows a quasi-cumulative normal shape, as shown in Table 4.

Table 4. Average rejection rate per risk appetite threshold.

Threshold	Grade 4	Grade 5	Grade 6	Grade 7	Grade 8
Rejection	65.3%	30.9%	9.1%	1.8%	0.2%

As we lower the threshold to reduce the risk appetite, the rejection rate becomes very high, causing the vanishing of differences between models.

The difference between financial performance increases between models with higher risk appetite. Notably, the spreads between models become more visible above grade 5. Figure 3, which presents the return for each model with thresholds between 5 and 8, shows that GAMI is the best performer with a threshold at 5, but MLP becomes the most efficient model from grade 6 and above, followed by EBM and GAMI. LDA does not reject any credit at the grade 8 threshold, so, following our methodology, we reject it and set the return to zero. These results are consistent across all three years analyzed.

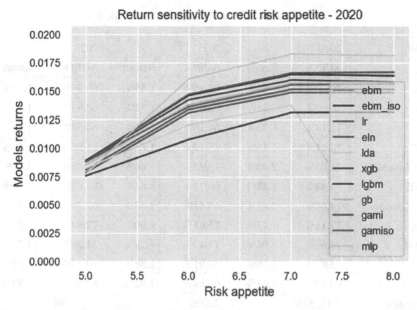

Fig. 3. Return per model as function of the risk appetite of the lender per grade threshold

Statistical Versus Financial Performance: The statistical performance of all models shows a rapid deterioration (around -5% over two years) and could support the need for re-training the models on a yearly basis. Nevertheless, the resilience of financial performance tend to indicate that models are stable and could be re-trained less frequently.

When we compare the AUROC with the returns of each model for each year in Table 5, we find no evidence of a positive correlation between the statistical and financial performances. This lack of positive correlation would require an in-depth analysis that exceeds the framework of this paper.

These results suggest that statistical tests may not be reliable in selecting the most profitable model, a conclusion previously drawn by [33] for AI models predicting asset returns. This highlights the importance of assessing financial performance to consider the practical implications of using a particular model in a real-world setting.

4.4 Cost of Explainability

We compare the financial return generated by (i) the best financially performing model ("best model") with (ii) the best inherently explainable model ("best XAI model"). We find that there is a cost associated with explainability. With GAM models, the cost ranges from 14 to 21bp (Table 6) depending on the risk appetite and time horizon. When we allow human supervision with the isotonicity, we increase the explainability of GAM models at no financial cost. This cost will drop to 0 if we exclude neural networks from the panel for the comparison and if we compare EBM and GAMI solely with decision trees.

Table 5. AUROC and return per year – Grade 6.

Model	2020		2021		2022	
	AUROC	Return	AUROC	Return	AUROC	Return
LR	70.70%	1.34%	64.35%	1.55%	63.87%	1.52%
ELN	68.99%	1.31%	62.95%	1.53%	63.89%	1.49%
LDA	71.14%	1.20%	64.16%	1.40%	64.68%	1.38%
EBM	76.41%	1.46%	73.19%	1.65%	71.86%	1.56%
EBM Isotonic	*76.05%*	*1.46%*	*73.18%*	***1.66%***	*71.48%*	***1.57%***
GAMI	74.48%	**1.47%**	68.78%	1.64%	67.62%	1.56%
GAMI Isotonic	*74.62%*	*1.45%*	*68.61%*	*1.62%*	*67.74%*	*1.55%*
XGB	**77.11%**	1.43%	**73.61%**	1.60%	**72.94%**	1.52%
LGBM	75.63%	1.08%	71.45%	1.28%	71.28%	1.23%
GB	73.81%	1.38%	70.91%	1.58%	69.37%	1.54%
MLP	68.82%	**1.61%**	65.84%	**1.82%**	64.46%	**1.77%**
Correlation	−11. 57%		2.68%		−25.69%	
AUROC- return (excl. Isotonic models)						

The cost of explainability becomes more significant when we limit ourselves to historically predominant models such as LR and exclude EBM and GAMI. In such case, the cost can increase by around 25bp to 30bp, compared to MLP performance.

Table 6. Cost of explainability per year and pet risk appetite (without Isotonic GAM).

		2020	2021	2022
Low risk (threshold 6)	Best XAI model	1.47%	1.66%	1.57%
	Best model	1.61%	1.82%	1.77%
	Cost of XAI	0.14%	0.16%	0.20%
High risk (threshold 7)	Best XAI model	1.66%	1.88%	1.73%
	Best model	1.83%	2.06%	1.94%
	Cost of XAI	0.17%	0.18%	0.21%

The importance of the cost of explainability is to be considered in respect of the specific situation of the lender and the purpose of the model: a commercial model for underwriting and pricing, a risk management model or an internal model for capital requirement measurement.

5 Conclusion and Perspectives

5.1 Conclusion

In this study, we compare machine learning models for credit scoring that pass the bar of ECB minimum requirements. We evaluate their statistical and financial performance on a specific dataset. Our analysis reveals that traditional models like LR, ELN, and LDA perform poorly in both statistical and financial terms. MLP is the best financial performer but among the worst statistical one, while LGBM is a good statistical model with poor financial performance. This highlights the importance of computing the financial performance. We also examine the performance of newly developed explainable models, such as EBM and GAMI, which rely on black-box algorithms to derive GAM outputs. These models demonstrate excellent statistical and financial performance, with the ability to compete with and even outperform decision tree models like XGB in financial terms.

We compute the cost of explainability associated with these inherently explainable models compared with best performing black-box MLP, and find a 0.14% to 0.21% cost of explainability, depending on the risk appetite.

Our study further investigates a way to improve explainability by introducing isotonicity as human supervision. By introducing expert judgment to obtain isotonic GAMs, we improve the explainability of the GAM without compromising the financial or statistical performance. If confirmed with other datasets, these findings could further enhance the attractiveness of GAM models and contribute to their acceptability from a regulatory point of view.

In summary, our findings demonstrate that explainable models, such as EBM and GAMI, are promising alternatives to traditional models, and that isotonicity that expresses expert judgment can be used to enhance their interpretability while preserving their financial and statistical performance.

5.2 Perspectives

While the proposed approach shows promising results, it has only been tested on a single dataset over a limited period, with a low granularity in the risk appetite threshold. Further analysis with different datasets, longer periods, and more granular risk appetite threshold would help confirm or challenge these initial findings. Longer periods would allow the use of more complex neural network architectures and, hence, a possibly higher cost of explainability. Additionally, exploring the use of explainable models for feature selection could be a valuable avenue for future research.

It is also worth noting that the study highlights inconsistencies between statistical and economic results that warrant further investigation. As academic research mostly relies on statistical measures, improving the understanding of how statistical measures reflect or not the economic performance of a model could enhance the application and adoption of academic research in the financial world.

CRediT Authorship Contribution Statement
Dessain Jean: Conceptualization, Methodology, Software, Formal analysis, Investigation, Data curation, Writing - original draft, Supervision, Project administration.

Nora Bentaleb: Validation, Formal analysis, Writing - review & editing, Visualization.
Fabien Vinas: Resources, Writing - review & editing.

Declaration of Competing Interest. The authors declare that they have no known competing financial interests or personal relationships that could have appeared to influence the work reported in this paper.

References

1. Ariza-Garzon, M.J., Arroyo, J., Caparrini, A., Segovia-Vargas, M.J.: Explainability of a machine learning granting scoring model in peer-to-peer lending. IEEE Access **8**, 64873–64890 (2020). https://doi.org/10.1109/ACCESS.2020.2984412
2. Linardatos, P., Papastefanopoulos, V., Kotsiantis, S.: Explainable AI: a review of machine learning interpretability methods. Entropy **23**(1), 18 (2020). https://doi.org/10.3390/E23 010018
3. Bussmann, N., Giudici, P., Marinelli, D., Papenbrock, J.: Explainable AI in fintech risk management. Front. Artif. Intell. **3**, 26 (2020). https://doi.org/10.3389/FRAI.2020.00026/ BIBTEX
4. Assef, F.M., Steiner, M.T.A.: Ten-year evolution on credit risk research: a systematic literature review approach and discussion. Ing. Investig. **40**(2), 50–71 (2020). https://doi.org/10.15446/ ING.INVESTIG.V40N2.78649
5. Wang, Y., Zhang, Y., Lu, Y., Yu, X.: A comparative assessment of credit risk model based on machine learning—a case study of bank loan data. Procedia Comput. Sci. **174**, 141–149 (2020). https://doi.org/10.1016/J.PROCS.2020.06.069
6. Fitzpatrick, T., Mues, C.: How can lenders prosper? Comparing machine learning approaches to identify profitable peer-to-peer loan investments. Eur. J. Oper. Res. **294**(2), 711–722 (2021). https://doi.org/10.1016/j.ejor.2021.01.047
7. Shi, S., Tse, R., Luo, W., D'Addona, S., Pau, G.: Machine learning-driven credit risk: a systemic review. Neural Comput. Appl. **34**(17), 14327–14339 (2022). https://doi.org/10.1007/ S00521-022-07472-2
8. Tripathi, D., et al.: Credit scoring models using ensemble learning and classification approaches: a comprehensive survey. Wirel. Pers. Commun. **123**, 785–812 (2022). https:// doi.org/10.1007/s11277-021-09158-9
9. Ruyu, B., Mo, H., Haifeng, L.: A comparison of credit rating classification models based on spark- evidence from lending-club. Procedia Comput. Sci. **162**, 811–818 (2019). https://doi. org/10.1016/J.PROCS.2019.12.054
10. Moscato, V., Picariello, A., Sperlí, G.: A benchmark of machine learning approaches for credit score prediction. Expert Syst. Appl. **165**, 113986 (2021). https://doi.org/10.1016/j.eswa.2020. 113986
11. Markov, A., Seleznyova, Z., Lapshin, V.: Credit scoring methods: latest trends and points to consider. J. Financ. Data Sci. **8**, 180–201 (2022). https://doi.org/10.1016/J.JFDS.2022.07.002
12. Li, Y., Chen, W.: A comparative performance assessment of ensemble learning for credit scoring. Math. **8**(10), 1756 (2020). https://doi.org/10.3390/MATH8101756
13. Lessmann, S., Baesens, B., Seow, H.-V., Thomas, L.C.: Benchmarking state-of-the-art classification algorithms for credit scoring: an update of research. Eur. J. Oper. Res. **247**, 124–136 (2015). https://doi.org/10.1016/j.ejor.2015.05.030
14. Kim, H., Cho, H., Ryu, D.: Corporate default predictions using machine learning: literature review. Sustainable **12**(16), 6325 (2020). https://doi.org/10.3390/SU12166325

15. EBA: Discussion paper on machine learning for IRB models (2021)
16. Lohmann, C., Ohliger, T.: The total cost of misclassification in credit scoring: A comparison of generalized linear models and generalized additive models. J. Forecast. **38**(5), 375–389 (2019). https://doi.org/10.1002/for.2545
17. Chang, C.-H., Tan, S., Lengerich, B., Goldenberg, A., Caruana, R.: How interpretable and trustworthy are GAMs?, p. 11 (2021). https://doi.org/10.1145/3447548.3467453
18. Guidotti, R., Monreale, A., Ruggieri, S., Turini, F., Giannotti, F., Pedreschi, D.: A survey of methods for explaining black box models. ACM Comput. Surv. **51**(5) (2018). https://doi.org/10.1145/3236009
19. Schwalbe, G., Finzel, B.: A comprehensive taxonomy for explainable artificial intelligence: a systematic survey of surveys on methods and concepts. Data Min. Knowl. Discov. **2023**, 1–59 (2023). https://doi.org/10.1007/S10618-022-00867-8
20. Misheva, B.H., Osterrieder, J., Hirsa, A., Kulkarni, O., Lin, S.F.: Explainable AI in credit risk management. SSRN Electron. J. (2021). https://doi.org/10.2139/ssrn.3795322
21. Ribeiro, M.T., Singh, S., Guestrin, C.: 'Why should i trust you?' explaining the predictions of any classifier. In: NAACL-HLT 2016 - 2016 Conference on North American Chapter of the Association for Computational Linguistics Human Language Technology Proceedings of the Demonstration Session, pp. 97–101 (2016). https://doi.org/10.18653/v1/n16-3020
22. Graziani, M., et al.: A global taxonomy of interpretable AI: unifying the terminology for the technical and social sciences. Artif. Intell. Rev. 1–32 (2022). https://doi.org/10.1007/S10462-022-10256-8/TABLES/6
23. Theissler, A., Spinnato, F., Schlegel, U., Guidotti, R.: Explainable AI for time series classification: a review, taxonomy and research directions. IEEE Access **10**, 100700–100724 (2022). https://doi.org/10.1109/ACCESS.2022.3207765
24. Giudici, P., Raffinetti, E.: Shapley-Lorenz eXplainable artificial intelligence. Expert Syst. Appl. **167**, 114104 (2021). https://doi.org/10.1016/j.eswa.2020.114104
25. Frye, C., Ai, C.F., Rowat, C., Feige, I., Ai Faculty, I.: Asymmetric shapley values: incorporating causal knowledge into model-agnostic explainability. In: 34th Conference on Neural Information Processing Systems (2020)
26. Munoz, C., Modenesi, B., Koshiyama, A.: Local and global explainability metrics for machine learning predictions a preprint. arXiv:2302.12094v1 (2023)
27. Nori, H., Caruana, R., Bu, Z., Shen, J.H., Kulkarni, J.: Accuracy, interpretability, and differential privacy via explainable boosting (2021). https://github.com/interpretml/interpret. Accessed 12 Nov 2022
28. Nori, H., Jenkins, S., Koch, P., Caruana, R.: InterpretML: a unified framework for machine learning interpretability (2019)
29. Yang, Z., Zhang, A., Sudjianto, A.: GAMI-net: an explainable neural network based on generalized additive models with structured interactions. Pattern Recognit. **120** (2020). https://doi.org/10.48550/arxiv.2003.07132
30. Agarwal, R., et al.: Neural additive models: interpretable machine learning with neural nets. In: 35th Conference on Neural Information Processing Systems (2021)
31. Dastile, X., Celik, T., Potsane, M.: Statistical and machine learning models in credit scoring: a systematic literature survey. Appl. Soft Comput. J. **91**, 106263 (2020). https://doi.org/10.1016/j.asoc.2020.106263
32. Dessain, J.: Machine learning models predicting returns: Why most popular performance metrics are misleading and proposal for an efficient metric. Expert Syst. Appl. **199**, 116970 (2022). https://doi.org/10.1016/J.ESWA.2022.116970
33. Aleksandrova, Y., Parusheva, S.: Performance evaluation of machine learning models for credit risk prediction. Izvestia J. Union Sci. (2021)

34. Altman, E.I., Iwanicz-Drozdowska, M., Laitinen, E.K., Suvas, A.: A race for long horizon bankruptcy prediction. Appl. Econ. **52**(37), 4092–4111 (2020). https://doi.org/10.1080/000 36846.2020.1730762
35. Lyócsa, Š, Vašaničová, P., Hadji Misheva, B., Vateha, M.D.: Default or profit scoring credit systems? Evidence from European and US peer-to-peer lending markets. Financ. Innov. **8**(1), 1–21 (2022). https://doi.org/10.1186/S40854-022-00338-5
36. de Lange, P.E., Melsom, B., Vennerød, C.B., Westgaard, S.: Explainable AI for credit assessment in banks. J. Risk Financ. Manag. **15**(12), 556 (2022). https://doi.org/10.3390/JRFM15 120556
37. Ala'raj, M., Abbod, M.F.: Classifiers consensus system approach for credit scoring. Knowl.-Based Syst. **104**, 89–105 (2016). https://doi.org/10.1016/j.knosys.2016.04.013
38. Troyanskaya, O., et al.: Missing value estimation methods for DNA microarrays. Bioinformatics **17**(6), 520–525 (2001). https://doi.org/10.1093/BIOINFORMATICS/17.6.520
39. van Buuren, S., Groothuis-Oudshoorn, K.: Mice: multivariate imputation by chained equations in R. J. Stat. Softw. **45**(3), 1–67 (2011). https://doi.org/10.18637/JSS.V045.I03
40. Yang, Z., Zhang, A., Sudjianto, A.: Enhancing explainability of neural networks through architecture constraints. IEEE Trans. Neural Netw. Learn. Syst. **32**(6), 2610–2621 (2021). https://doi.org/10.1109/TNNLS.2020.3007259
41. Nehrebecka, N., Polski, N.B.: Probability-of-default curve calibration and validation of internal rating systems 1 Probability-of-default curve calibration and the validation of internal rating systems (2016)
42. European Central Bank: Instructions for reporting the validation results of internal models - IRB Pillar I models for credit risk (2019). https://www.bankingsupervision.europa.eu/ban king/tasks/internal_models/shared/pdf/instructions_validation_reporting_credit_risk.en.pdf
43. Brown, L.D., Cai, T.T., Das Gupta, A.: Interval estimation for a binomial proportion, vol. 16, no. 2, pp. 101–133 (2001). https://doi.org/10.1214/SS/1009213286
44. Miller, G.E.: Asymptotic test statistics for coefficients of variation. Commun. Stat. - Theory Methods **20**(10), 3351–3363 (1991). https://doi.org/10.1080/03610929108830707

Lorenz Zonoids for Trustworthy AI

Paolo Giudici[ID] and Emanuela Raffinetti[(✉)][ID]

Department of Economics and Management, University of Pavia, Via San Felice al
Monastero 5, Pavia, Italy
{paolo.giudici,emanuela.raffinetti}@unipv.it

Abstract. Machine learning models are boosting Artificial Intelligence
(AI) applications in many domains, such as finance, health care and
automotive. This is mainly due to their advantage, in terms of predictive
accuracy, with respect to "classic" statistical learning models. However,
although complex machine learning models may reach high predictive
performance, their predictions are not explainable and have an intrinsic
black-box nature. Accuracy and explainability are not the only desirable characteristics of a machine learning model. The recently proposed
European regulation on Artificial Intelligence, the AI Act, attempts to
regulate the use of AI by means of a set of requirements of trustworthiness for high risk applications, to be embedded in a risk management
model. We propose to map the requirements established for high-risk
applications in the AI Act in four main variables: Sustainability, Accuracy, Fairness and Explainability, which need a set of metrics that can
establish not only whether but also how much the requirements are satisfied over time. To the best of our knowledge, there exists no such set
of metrics, yet.

In this paper, we aim to fill this gap, and propose a set of four integrated metrics, aimed at measuring Sustainability, Accuracy, Fairness
and Explainability (S.A.F.E. in brief), which have the advantage, with
respect to the available metrics, of being all based on one unifying statistical tool: the Lorenz curve. The Lorenz curve is a well known robust
statistical tool, which has been employed, along with the related Gini
index to measure income and wealth inequalities. It thus appears as a
natural methodology on which to build an integrated set of trustworthy
AI measurement metrics.

Keywords: Artificial Intelligence methods · Lorenz Zonoids tools ·
S.A.F.E. approach

1 Introduction

Machine learning models are boosting Artificial Intelligence (AI) applications
in many domains, such as finance, health care and automotive. This is mainly
due to their advantage, in terms of predictive accuracy, with respect to "classic"
statistical learning models. However, although complex machine learning models

© The Author(s), under exclusive license to Springer Nature Switzerland AG 2023
L. Longo (Ed.): xAI 2023, CCIS 1901, pp. 517–530, 2023.
https://doi.org/10.1007/978-3-031-44064-9_27

may reach high predictive performance, their predictions are not explainable, and have an intrinsic black-box nature.

Accuracy and explainability are not the only desirable characteristics of a machine learning model. The recently proposed European regulation on Artificial Intelligence, the AI Act [9], attempts to regulate the use of AI by means of a set of requirements of trustworthiness for high risk applications, to be embedded in a risk management model.

We propose to map the requirements established for high-risk applications in the AI Act in four main variables: Sustainability, Accuracy, Fairness and Explainability, which need a set of metrics that can establish not only whether but also how much the requirements are satisfied over time. To the best of our knowledge, there exists no such set of metrics, yet.

In this paper, we aim to fill this gap, and propose a set of four integrated metrics, aimed at measuring Sustainability, Accuracy, Fairness and Explainability (S.A.F.E. in brief), which have the advantage, with respect to the available metrics, of being all based on one unifying statistical tool: the Lorenz curve (see, e.g. [16]). The Lorenz curve is a well known robust statistical tool, which has been employed, along with the related Gini index (see [10]) to measure income and wealth inequalities. It thus appears as a natural methodology on which to build an integrated set of trustworthy AI measurement metrics.

Indeed, a recent work by [12] has shown how to measure Accuracy and Explainability, using the notion of Lorenz Zonoids, based on the Lorenz curve. The result is a metric that can, differently from other available measures, such as Shapley values, jointly measures accuracy and explainability, and that is also robust to data variations, being based on the mutual variability, instead on the variability from the mean, as other accuracy measures, such as the mean square error.

We propose to extend the methodology developed in [12] to the measurement of Accuracy, Fairness and Sustainability, providing an overall joint measure for all S.A.F.E. AI requirements.

The requirement of explainability is fulfilled "by design" through classic statistical models, such as logistic and linear regression. However, in complex data analysis problems, classical statistical models may have a limited predictive accuracy, in comparison with "black-box" machine learning models, such as neural networks and random forests. This suggests to empower machine learning models with post-modelling tools that can "explain" them. Recent attempts in this direction, based on the cooperative game theory work by Shapley (see [19]), have led to promising applications of explainable AI methods in finance, among which [5] and [6].

Shapley values have the advantage of being agnostic: independent on the underlying model with which predictions are computed; but have the disadvantage of not being normalised and, therefore, they are difficult to interpret and compare between different models. To overcome this limitation, [12] proposed Shapley-Lorenz values, which combine Shapley values with Lorenz Zonoids, obtaining a global measure of the contribution of each explanatory variable to the predictive accuracy of the response, rather than to the value of the predictions, as is the case for Shapley values.

The requirement of accuracy is well known in the literature, typically referring to the measurement of the difference between the predicted and the actually observed values of a response variable. However, although several metrics to measure accuracy are available, they depend on the nature of the response variable to be predicted. When the response variable is continuous, euclidean distance measures, such as the mean square of the prediction errors are considered; when the response variable is binary, measures based on the classification error, such as sensitivity, specificity, and the area under the ROC curve are considered.

The requirement of sustainability implies the model outputs are stable under variations in the data and, in particular, when extreme data, resulting from stress scenarios and/or from cyber data manipulations, enter the available database.

To improve the sustainability of AI applications, we aim to extend variable selection methods, available for probabilistic models, such as linear and logistic regression, to non-probabilistic models, such as random forests and neural network models, developing statistical tests based on the comparison between the Lorenz Zonoids of the predictions. This extension will provide a model selection criterion for machine learning models, not available in the literature at the moment. The extension will also allow to measure sustainability comparing the predictions from the selected model in different subsets of the data, from those easier to predict to those that contain extreme and/or cyber injected anomalous data.

The requirement of fairness implies that the predictions of AI applications do not present biases among different population groups, that typically derive from lack of representativeness and/or lack of quality of group specific data.

To measure the fairness of AI applications, we derive metrics based on the Lorenz Zonoids of the predictions, obtained separately for each population group, such as the Gini variability measure. This will lead to metrics for fairness that are, differently from the available metrics, model agnostics, thereby allowing comparison of fairness between different machine learning models.

An important advantage of our proposal is that all four metrics are based on the same notion of variability, derived from the Lorenz curve, and they can therefore be similarly normalised to $[0, 1]$ and integrated in a single measure that can assess the trustworthiness of any AI application.

Although our proposal can be applied to all possible applications of AI, we will focus our attention on finance, the application field to which we are most familiar with. Among high risk applications of AI in finance, the European AI act explicitly mentions the assessment of the creditworthiness of individuals or companies, also known as credit scoring.

2   Proposal: a S.A.F.E. indicator

Lorenz Zonoids were originally proposed by [15] as a generalisation of the ROC curve in a multidimensional setting, based on the Lorenz curve. When referred to the one-dimensional case, the Lorenz Zonoid coincides with the Gini coefficient, a measure typically used for representing the income inequality or the wealth inequality within a nation or a social group (see, e.g. [10]). Both the Gini coefficient and the Lorenz Zonoid measure statistical dispersion in terms of the mutual variability among the observations, a metric that is more robust to extreme data than the standard variability from the mean.

Given n observations of a target response variable Y, a Lorenz Zonoid can be defined from the Lorenz and the dual Lorenz curves (see [16]). The Lorenz curve for a variable Y, denoted with L_Y is obtained by re-ordering the Y values in a non-decreasing sense. It is built joining the set of points with coordinates $(i/n, \sum_{j=1}^{i} y_{r_j}/(n\bar{y}))$, for $i = 1, \ldots, n$, where r_j and $\bar{y}$ indicate the (non-decreasing) ranks of Y and the Y mean value, respectively. Similarly, the dual Lorenz curve of Y, pointed out as L'_Y, is obtained by re-ordering the Y values in a non-increasing sense. Its coordinates are specified as $(i/n, \sum_{j=1}^{i} y_{d_j}/(n\bar{y}))$, for $i = 1, \ldots, n$, where d_j indicates the (non-increasing) ranks of Y. The area lying between the L_Y and L'_Y curves is the Lorenz Zonoid (see Fig. 1).

The Lorenz Zonoid fulfills some attractive properties. An important one is the "inclusion" of the Lorenz Zonoid of the predicted values $\hat{Y}$ into the Lorenz Zonoid of the observed values of Y. The "inclusion property" allows to interpret the ratio between the Lorenz Zonoid of a learning model $\hat{Y}$ and the Lorenz Zonoid of Y as the mutual variability of the response "explained" by the predictor variables that give rise to $\hat{Y}$, similarly to what occurs in the well known variance decomposition that leads to the R^2 measure.

A second important property concerns the practical implementation of the Lorenz Zonoid calculation. It can be shown that the Lorenz Zonoid-value of a generic variable $\cdot$ (such as the response variable, or the predicted response variable) is calculated as

$$LZ(\cdot) = \frac{2Cov(\cdot, r(\cdot))}{nE(\cdot)}, \tag{1}$$

where $r(\cdot)$ are the ranks of $\cdot$ and $E(\cdot)$ is the expected value of $\cdot$.

Equation (1) provides a simple method to implement a Lorenz Zonoid and, consequently, to calculate the share of the Lorenz Zonoid response explained by a model, defined by a function of a set of predictors learned from the data.

A third important property of Lorenz Zonoids is obtained ordering the Y response values not in terms of their ranks, r_j, but with respect to $\hat{r}_j$, the ranks of the predicted $\hat{Y}$ values. This leads to a concordance curve defined by the pairs: $(i/n, \sum_{j=1}^{i} y_{\hat{r}_j}/(n\bar{y}))$, where $\hat{r}_j$ indicates the (non-decreasing) ranks of $\hat{Y}$.

To visually describe the concordance curve, Fig. 1 reports, for a given test set D_{test}, the Lorenz curve, the dual Lorenz curve and the concordance C curve, together with the 45-degree line.

From Fig. 1, note that the Lorenz curve and its dual are symmetric around the 45-degree line, and that the concordance curve lies between them. When $\hat{r}_i = r_i$, for all $i = 1, \ldots, n$, we have a perfect concordance: the concordance curve is equal to the Lorenz curve. When $\hat{r}_i = r_{n+1-i}$, for all $i = 1, \ldots, n$, we

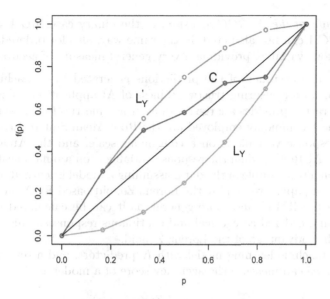

Fig. 1. The L_Y and L'_Y Lorenz curves and the concordance curve C, where p (on the x-axis) and $f(p)$ (on the y-axis) are the cumulative values of the x and y coordinates of the L_Y, L'_Y and C curves.

have a perfect discordance: the concordance curve is equal to the dual Lorenz curve. In general, for any given point, the distance between the concordance curve and the Lorenz curve reveals how the rank of the predicted value differs from that of the best case, which is equal to the rank of the observed value. And, for any given point, the distance between the concordance curve and the dual Lorenz curve reveals how rank of the predicted value differs from that of the worst case, which is equal to the rank of the inversely ordered value. A summary measure for the C curve of a model can be obtained considering the area between the dual Lorenz curve and the concordance curve, and dividing it by its maximum possible value: the area between the dual Lorenz curve and the Lorenz curve. A new measure, called Rank Graduation Accuracy (RGA) measure, can be defined by the following expression:

$$RGA = \frac{\sum_{i=1}^{n}\left\{\frac{1}{n\bar{y}}\left(\sum_{j=1}^{i} y_{r_{n+1-j}} - \sum_{j=1}^{i} y_{\hat{r}_j}\right)\right\}}{\sum_{i=1}^{n}\left\{\frac{1}{n\bar{y}}\left(\sum_{j=1}^{i} y_{r_{n+1-j}} - \sum_{j=1}^{i} y_{r_j}\right)\right\}}. \tag{2}$$

Our preliminary studies (see, e.g.. [18]) indicate that the RGA measure has some important properties and, in particular:

Normalisation: $0 \leq RGA \leq 1$, with $RGA = 1$ in the best case of a perfectly concordant model; $RGA = 0$ in the worst case of a perfectly discordant model; $RGA = 0.5$ in the case of random predictions.

Generalisation of the AUROC Measure: in the binary case, $RGA = AUROC$. However, RGA can be calculated, in the same way, also for ordered categorical and continuous variable, providing a very general measure of accuracy.

Accuracy. The accuracy of the predictions generated by a machine learning model is crucial for ensuring trustworthiness of AI applications. The statistical learning literature provides a large set of accuracy metrics (for a review see, e.g. [14]): the most commonly employed are the Root Mean Square Error (RMSE), when the response variable is on a continuous scale, and the Area Under the ROC curve (AUROC), when the response variable is on a binary scale. Both are calculated on a test sample of the data, assuming a model is learned on a training sample. In the paper, we employ the Lorenz Zonoid based RGA measure, more robust than the RMSE and more general, as it can be calculated in the same way for binary, ordered categorical and continuous responses. This generality is a clear further advantage of the Lorenz Zonoid.

Given a machine learning model with K predictors, and a test sample from the dataset, we can measure the accuracy score of a model as:

$$Ac\text{-}Score = \frac{LZ(\hat{Y}_{X_1,\dots,X_k})}{LZ(Y_{test})}, \tag{3}$$

where $LZ(\hat{Y}_{X_1,\dots,X_k})$ is the Lorenz Zonoid of the predicted response variable, obtained using k predictors on the test set, and $LZ(Y_{test})$ is the Y response variable Lorenz Zonoid value computed on the same test set.

Sustainability. The sustainability of a machine learning depends on its robustness (resilience) to perturbations of the data, either coming from "internal" anomalies or from "external" data injections. In both cases, sustainability improves when a model is parsimonious, that is, when it is the result of a variable selection process aimed at reducing the number of variables without significantly reducing predictive accuracy.

In this respect, a significance test for the difference in Lorenz Zonoids, which can extend [8] for continuous responses and [7] for binary response into a unifying criterion, would provide the basis for a stepwise model comparison algorithm which may lead to a parsimonious model, with $k \leq K$ predictors that, while not significantly losing accuracy, improves robustness and simplifies the computational effort necessary to measure explainability.

In this paper, we develop a stepwise procedure, which starts with the construction of K models, each one depending on only one predictor. The application of formula (1) to all such univariate models will provide a ranking of the candidate predictors, in terms of their (marginal) importance, which can be used to determine insertion into the model. The first explanatory variable to be considered is that with the highest Lorenz Zonoid value. At the second step, a model with the second ranked variable is fitted and a predictive gain, measured as the additional contribution to predictive accuracy determined by the second variable can be calculated as:

$$pay\text{-}off(X_k) = LZ(\hat{Y}_{X' \cup X_k}) - LZ(\hat{Y}_{X'}), \tag{4}$$

where $LZ(\hat{Y}_{X' \cup X_k})$ and $LZ(\hat{Y}_{X'})$ describe the Lorenz Zonoid of the response variable Y explained by the models which, respectively, include $X' \cup X_k$ predictors or only X' predictors.

The procedure can continue until the predictive gain defined in (4) is found not significant. To test for significance, a statistical test is developed by determining the related probability distribution, through a bootstrap procedure.

The above comparison of Lorenz Zonoids can be employed not only to select a parsimonious model by means of variable selection, but also to develop a sustainability score of a machine learning model.

To this extent, we will assess sustainability of a model comparing its predictive accuracy, as measured by the Lorenz Zonoid, in different ordered subset of the data, possibly altered by anomalous or cyber manipulated data.

More precisely, conditionally on a machine learning model, the predicted response values (in the test set) are ordered in terms of their predictive accuracy, from the most accurate to the lowest. The ordered predictions are divided in $g = 1, \ldots, G$ equal size groups (such as the deciles of the distribution). We can build a vector including the sum of the Shapley-Lorenz values of the predictors composing the final model, i.e. $V_G^{SL*} = \{v_1^{SL*}, \ldots, v_g^{SL*}, \ldots, v_G^{SL*}\}$, where $v_g^{SL*} = v_{gX_1}^{SL} + \ldots + v_{gX_{k*}}^{SL}$ represents the sum of the Shapley-Lorenz values related to the predictors $X_1, \ldots, X_{k*}$, where $k^* = 1, \ldots, k$ is such that $k^* < K$ and corresponds to the number of predictors which compose the final model derived from the selection procedure based on the Lorenz Zonoids.

The score for sustainability can then be defined as:

$$Sust\text{-}Score = 1 - LZ(V_G^{SL*}), \tag{5}$$

where $LZ(V_G^{SL*})$ indicates the Lorenz Zonoid (Gini coefficient) calculated on the vector V_G^{SL*}, whose elements correspond to the cumulative sum of the selected predictors' Shapley-Lorenz values in each group.

Explainability. In [12], the Lorenz Zonoid approach has been combined with the Shapley framework, to obtain a metric of explainability that measures the additional contribution of each explanatory variable to the Lorenz Zonoid of the predictions.

Given K predictors, the Shapley-Lorenz contribution associated with the additional variable X_k was defined as:

$$LZ^{X_k}(\hat{Y}) = \sum_{X' \subseteq \mathcal{C}(X) \setminus X_k} \frac{|X'|!(K - |X'| - 1)!}{K!} \cdot [LZ(\hat{Y}_{X' \cup X_k}) - LZ(\hat{Y}_{X'})], \tag{6}$$

where: $\mathcal{C}(X) \setminus X_k$ is the set of all the possible model configurations which can be obtained excluding variable X_k; $|X'|$ denotes the number of variables included in each possible model; $LZ(\hat{Y}_{X' \cup X_k})$ and $LZ(\hat{Y}_{X'})$ describe the (mutual) variability of the response variable Y explained by the models which, respectively, include the $X' \cup X_k$ predictors and only the X' predictors.

The application of formula (6) leads to the Shapley-Lorenz value, a measure of the response variable mutual variability explained by each predictor, normalised in the interval $[0, 1]$. Normalisation is an important advantage of the Shapley-Lorenz measure, with respect to the standard Shapley values. Another important advantage is that the Shapley-Lorenz measure can be calculated for any response variable in the same manner, following (1), differently from measures based on the variance decomposition. And, finally, being based on the mutual variability, it is highly robust to extreme observations.

Given a machine learning model with K predictors, a score for explainability can then be calculated (on the whole sample) as:

$$Ex\text{-}Score = \frac{\sum_{k=1}^{K} SL_k}{LZ(Y)}, \tag{7}$$

where $LZ(Y)$ corresponds to the response variable Y Lorenz Zonoid-value, and SL_k denotes the Shapley-Lorenz values associated with the k-th predictor.

Fairness. Fairness is a property that essentially requires that AI applications do not present biases among different population groups. To measure fairness, we extend the Gini coefficient, originally developed to measure the concentration of income in a population, to the measurement of the concentration of the model predictions. Doing so, we aim to identify the groups which may be affected by bias: those with Shapley-Lorenz values that differ from the rest of the population.

Our proposal can be illustrated as follows. Let $m = 1, \ldots, M$ be the considered population groups and let K the number of the available predictors. Denote with $v_{mX_k}^{SL}$ the Shapley-Lorenz value associated with the k-th predictor in the m-th population.

As well as for the sustainability condition measurement, suppose that the model selection procedure based on the application of the Lorenz Zonoid comparisons leads to choose a subset of all the available explanatory variables as the most parsimonious model for a given level of accuracy. Denote with k^* the number of predictors which compose the selected model, and consider the vector V_M^{SL*} defined as $V_M^{SL*} = \{v_1^{SL*}, \ldots, v_m^{SL*}, \ldots, v_M^{SL*}\}$, where $v_m^{SL*} = v_{mX_1}^{SL} + \ldots + v_{mX_{k^*}}^{SL}$ represents the sum of the Shapley-Lorenz values related to the predictors $X_1, \ldots, X_{k^*}$.

The Gini coefficient can be applied to the vector V_M^{SL*}, obtaining a measure of concentration of the variables' importance among different population groups. For a given set of selected explanatory variables, Shapley-Lorenz values which are similar in the M populations lead to a Gini coefficient close to 0, indicating that the effect of these variables is fair across the different population groups. On the other hand, a Gini coefficient close to 1 indicates that the variables' effect largely depend on some groups, highlighting biasness.

Given a machine learning model with k^* and M population groups, we can obtain a fairness score as:

$$Fair\text{-}Score = 1 - LZ(V_M^{SL*}), \tag{8}$$

where $LZ(V_M^{SL*})$ denotes the Lorenz Zonoid (Gini coefficient) computed on the vector V_M^{SL*} whose elements correspond to the cumulative sum of the selected predictors' Shapley-Lorenz values in each population.

3   Application

To gain insight into features of the proposed set of S.A.F.E. metrics, an example of its possible applications to real data is here discussed. Specifically: Subsect. 3.1 describes the considered data and provides details about the model adopted for the analysis; Subsect. 3.2 discusses the findings, highlighting the advantages derived from our proposal to the evaluation of the AI trustworthiness condition.

3.1   Data and Model

The considered data are described in [11] and are aimed to understand whether and how bitcoin price returns vary as a function of a set of classical financial explanatory variables.

A further investigation of the data was carried out in a work by [12], who introduced a normalised Shapley measure for the assessment of the contribution of each additional predictor, in terms of Lorenz Zonoids.

To the sake of coherence with the aforementioned contributions, here we focus on the same time series observations, where the bitcoin prices from the Coinbase exchange are selected as the target variable to be predicted. The candidate financial predictors are represented by the time series observations describing the prices of Oil, Gold and SP500. In addition, the exchange rates USD/Yuan and USD/Eur are also included as possible further explanatory variables.

Our purpose is to exploit the Lorenz Zonoid tool as a unified criterion for measuring the trustworthiness of AI methodologies.

To better interpret the results obtained from the proposed approach, we investigated the behavior of the involved variables. Specifically, the bitcoin price referred to the Coinbase exchange market appears quite stable until the beginning of 2017 and then begins to progressively increasing reaching its maximum value at the end of the same year. This dynamics is followed by a downtrend, which starts in January 2018. The trend of the SP500 increases overtime contrary to the prices of Gold and Oil, which are characterised by uptrend and downtrend. Finally, the trend of the exchange rates USD/Eur and USD/Yuan is quite similar overtime.

In order to be more exhaustive, we provide some summary statistics in Table 1.

The results in Table 1 highlight that the bitcoin price mean value, as well as the standard deviation, is largely different with respect to those of the classical assets and exchange rates. It also arises that the exchange rates are much less volatile than the bitcoin, SP500 and Oil prices.

The purpose is to apply an explainable machine learning model for the prediction of the bitcoin prices. Although prices and returns are alternative ways to present information on financial markets, as discussed by [20], for the sake of the stationarity condition the price series are transformed into returns.

We select as our candidate model, a neural network with five hidden layers. A cross-validation procedure is carried out with a training dataset, including

Table 1. Summary statistics for: bitcoin prices in the Coinbase exchange market; SP500 index; Gold and Oil prices; exchange rates

Predictors	Mean	Standard deviation	Coefficient of variation
Coinbase bitcoin	3919.05	4318.98	1.10
SP500	2399.17	212.31	0.09
Gold	1275.58	52.34	0.04
Oil	49.36	3.37	0.07
USD/Eur	0.88	0.04	0.05
USD/Yuan	6.68	0.19	0.03

the time series until December 31st, 2017, and as test dataset based on the 2018 time series.

3.2 Discussion of Findings

Our proposed approach provides a series of predictions for the 2018 returns which are compared with the actual price returns, leading to measures of trustworthiness for the applied neural network model.

More precisely, we now present the results that concern the explainability, accuracy, fairness and sustainability scores. In Table 2, we show the Shapley Lorenz measure of explainability (see [12]), which is a normalised extension of the classic Shapley values, for all the considered explanatory variables of the daily bitcoin returns.

Table 2. Explainability in terms of Shapley-Lorenz values

Predictors	Gold	SP500	USD/Eur	USD/Yuan	Oil
Shapley-Lorenz values	0.3500	0.1095	0.0759	0.0237	0.0123

Based on Table 2, it arises that the price return of Gold is the most important variable that explains bitcoin price return variations. The *Ex-Score*, computed on the full model, is defined as the sum of all the Shapley-Lorenz values and equals 0.5714. It derives that more than the 57% of the whole variability associated with the bitcoin price returns is explained by the considered predictors, over all the possible model configurations.

As well known, the Shapley-Lorenz decomposition approach results computationally intensive. For this reason, especially when dealing with a large set of independent variables, a simplification of the model may be needed. To this purpose, we apply our proposed model selection, based on the comparison between Lorenz Zonoids. The procedure inserts Gold and SP500 returns as the relevant predictors, giving rise to a neural network model containing only the above two variables. It is worth noting that, contrary to what done for the determination of the explainability score, where the different neural network model configurations were fitted on the whole dataset, for the accuracy score computation we fitted the model on the training dataset and then we computed the predictions on the test dataset.

The *Acc-Score* is equal to 0.3280, which corresponds to the percentage of the bitcoin return variability explained by the model (in the test dataset).

To measure fairness we have ordered the test data response in terms of the corresponding trading volumes (from the lowest to the highest) and, accordingly, subdivided it into ten deciles. We have then calculated the sum of the Shapley-Lorenz values of the two variables (Gold and SP500) in the final model, separately in each decile. The *Fair-Score* is equal to 0.8617, indicating a high fairness and denoting that the bitcoin price return variability is not due to the corresponding trading volumes.

Similarly, we assessed the sustainability of the selected model by ordering the test data response according to how well it is predicted by the model (from the best to the worst predictions) and, accordingly, subdivided it into ten deciles. We have then calculated the Shapley-Lorenz values of the model, separately in each decile. The *Sust-Score* is equal to 0.8314, highlighting a high sustainability.

For the sake of clarity, the S.A.F.E. scores are reported in Table 3.

Table 3. S.A.F.E. scores

Ex-Score	Ac-Score	Fair-score	Sust-score
0.5714	0.3280	0.8617	0.8314

4   Conclusions

From an operational point of view, the obtained findings allow to understand: the advantages of our proposed generalised accuracy score over existing alternatives (such as the RMSE and AUROC statistics); the advantage of our proposed Shapley-Lorenz approach for explainability (with respect to Shapley values). It also shows how to obtain metrics for Sustainability and Fairness, currently not available in the research literature: Fairness can be measured applying the Gini inequality coefficient to the Shapley Lorenz values of the model, separately calculated in the different population groups; Sustainability can be measured applying the Gini inequality coefficient to the Lorenz Zonoids of the model, separately calculated in the ordered (by accuracy) deciles of the population. The exemplification also shows that all four metrics are normalised in [0,1], and that they can be integrated in a single score. It also shows how to evaluate their significance with an appropriate statistical test.

Our method seems to be well fitted with the requirements of the regulation of AI which is being proposed. For example, the European Artificial Intelligence Act

introduces a risk-based approach to AI applications, classifying them in four risk
categories: unacceptable, high risk (acceptable, but subject to risk management),
limited risk (acceptable, but subject to disclosure), and minimal risk (always
acceptable). Several applications of AI in finance and, in particular, those that
require estimation of creditworthiness of individuals or of companies, can be
considered at high risk and, therefore, require an appropriate risk management
model. To develop such a model, we can express the requirements of the AI
Act in terms of statistical variables, to be measured by appropriate statistical
metrics: Sustainability, Accuracy, Fairness and Explainability.

A similar context arose when the Basel II capital framework was released
(see [3]): market, credit and operational risk were identified as key statistical
variables to assess the capital adequacy of a financial institution and, later,
with the Basel III revision (see [4]) it was the turn of systemic risk. Meanwhile,
statistical metrics such as the Value at Risk and the Expected Shortfall (see,
e.g. [2]) and, later, the CoVaR (see, e.g. [1]) have been proposed by researchers
and, subsequently, integrated by banks and regulators into an integrated measure
aimed at monitoring financial risks and their coverage by banks? internal capital.

In a similar vein, we have desumed from the AI Act four main statistical variables to measure: Sustainability, Accuracy, Fairness and Explainability, which
require the development of appropriate statistical metrics, eventually leading to
an integrated measure of trustworthiness for a specific AI application, similarly
to the integrated financial risk of a financial institution in the Basel regulations.
The development of such metrics, following what we propose, allows to establish not only whether an AI application is trustworthy, but also to monitor the
condition of trustworthiness over time, within a risk management model. To the
best of our knowledge, there exists no such metrics, yet.

We suggest to fill this gap with our approach, which we believe to be ground
breaking for the AI research community and with a high potential impact for AI
developers, users and regulators.

The S.A.F.E. metrics will have two main applications. A first one, mainly
addressed to regulators and supervisors, is to assess the compliance of AI applications in finance to regulations such as the European AI Act, which require
them to be trustworthy. A second one, mainly addressed to the providers and
the users of AI applications, is to develop a risk management model, able to measure the distance from non compliance, and to consequently prioritise mitigation
actions addressed at reducing it.

The proposed metrics will consist of agnostic statistical tools, able to post-
process the predictive output of a machine learning model in a general way,
independently on the underlying data structure and statistical model. To this
aim, we have extended our recent paper [12], which has proposed to employ
Lorenz Zonoids (see [15]), the multidimensional version of the Gini index (see
[10]), to improve Shapley values (see [19]), one of the most employed methodology to achieve explainability of an otherwise black-box machine learning model.
The research in [12] shows that the employment of "Shapley-Lorenz" values
allows to obtain measures of explainability of each predictor in a machine learn-

ing model which, differently from Shapley values, are normalised between 0 and 1, and are expressed as a percentage of the overall predictive accuracy, rather than as a distance from the mean of the predictions, as the classical Shapley values proposed by [19], adapted to the machine learning context by [17].

From an applied viewpoint, in the paper we have focused on the application to bitcoin price prediction. However, what presented for the context of cryptocurrencies can be extended, without loss of generality, to other financial problems in which trustworthiness plays a crucial role: for example, in the assessment of credit rating (see, e.g. [6]) and in the detection of cyber attacks (see, e.g. [13]). It can also be extended to other fields, such as health care and automotive, in which trustworthiness also plays a key role.

Acknowledgements. The authors acknowledge support from the European xAIM (eXplainable Artificial Intelligence in healthcare Management) project supported by the CEF Telecom under Grant Agreement No. INEA/CEF/ICT/A2020/2276680.

References

1. Adrian, T., Brunnermeier, M.: CoVaR. Am. Econ. Rev. **106**, 1705–1741 (2016)
2. Artzner, P., Delbaen, F., Eber, J.M., Heath, D.: Coherent measures of risk. Math. Financ. **9**, 203–228 (2001)
3. Bank for International Settlements: Basel II: International Convergence of Capital Measurement and Capital Standards: a Revised Framework. Basel Committee on Banking Supervision, 10 June 2004 (2004)
4. Bank for International Settlements: Basel III: A global regulatory framework for more resilient banks and banking systems. Basel Committee on Banking Supervision, 1 June 2011 (2011)
5. Bracke, P., Datta, A., Jung, C., Shayak, S.: Machine learning explainability in finance: an application to default risk analysis (2019). https://www.bankofengland.co.uk/working-paper/2019/machine-learning-explainability-in-finance-an-application-to-default-risk-analysis
6. Bussmann, N., Giudici, P., Marinelli, D., Papenbrock, J.: Explainable machine learning in credit risk management. Comput. Econ. **57**, 203–216 (2020)
7. DeLong, E.R., DeLong, D.M., Clarke-Pearson, D.L.: Comparing the areas under two or more correlated receiver operating characteristic curves: a nonparametric approach. Biometrics **44**, 837–845 (1988)
8. Diebold, F., Mariano, R.: Comparing predictive accuracy. J. Bus. Econ. Stat. **13**, 253–263 (1995)
9. European Commission: Proposal for a Regulation of the European Parliament and of the Council laying down harmonised rules on artificial intelligence (Artificial Intelligence Act) and amending certain Union Legislative Acts). European Commission, Brussels, 21 April 2021 (2021)
10. Gini, C.: On the measure of concentration with special reference to income and statistics. Gener. Ser. **208**, 73–79 (1936)
11. Giudici, P., I, Abu-Hashish.: What determines bitcoin exchange prices? A network VAR approach. Financ. Res. Lett. **28**, 309–318 (2019)
12. Giudici, P., Raffinetti, E.: Shapley-Lorenz eXplainable Artificial Intelligence. Expert Syst. Appl. **167**, 1–9 (2021)

13. Giudici, P., Raffinetti, E.: Explainable AI methods in cyber risk management. Qual. Reliab. Eng. Int. **38**, 1318–1326 (2022)
14. Gneiting, T.: Making and evaluating point forecasts. J. Am. Stat. Assoc. **106**, 746–762 (2011)
15. Koshevoy, G., Mosler, K.: The Lorenz Zonoid of a multivariate distribution. J. Am. Stat. Assoc. **91**, 873–882 (1996)
16. Lorenz, M.O.: Methods of measuring the concentration of wealth. Publ. Am. Stat. Assoc. **70**, 209–219 (1905)
17. Lundberg, S.M., Lee, S.I.: A unified approach to interpreting model predictions. In: Advances in Neural Information Processing Systems, pp. 4765–4774 (2017)
18. Raffinetti, E.: A rank graduation accuracy measure to mitigate artificial intelligence risks. Qual. Quant. (2023)
19. Shapley, L.S.: A value for n-person games. In: Contributions to the Theory of Games II, pp. 307–317. Princeton University Press (1953)
20. Tsay, R.S.: Analysis of Financial Time Series, 2nd edn. Wiley, Hoboken (2005)

Explainable Machine Learning for Bag of Words-Based Phishing Detection

Maria Carla Calzarossa[1]([✉]) [ID], Paolo Giudici[2] [ID], and Rasha Zieni[1] [ID]

[1] Department of Electrical, Computer and Biomedical Engineering, University of Pavia, Pavia, Italy
mcc@unipv.it , rasha.zieni01@universitadipavia.it
[2] Department of Economics and Management, University of Pavia, Pavia, Italy

Abstract. Phishing is a fraudulent practice aimed at convincing individuals to reveal sensitive information, such as account credentials or credit card details, by clicking the links of malicious websites. To reduce the impacts of phishing, the timely identification of these websites is essential. For this purpose, machine learning models are often devised. In this paper, we address the problem of website phishing detection by proposing an explainable machine learning model based on bag of words features extracted from the content of the webpages. To select the most important features to be used in the model, we propose to employ the Lorenz Zonoid, the multidimensional generalization of the Gini coefficient. The resulting model is characterized by a good accuracy and it provides explanations of which words are most likely associated with phishing websites. In addition, the number of features retained is significantly reduced, thus making the model parsimonious and easier to interpret.

Keywords: Explainable machine learning · Phishing detection · Lorenz Zonoid

1 Introduction

Phishing is a fraudulent practice that has been around for many years because of its straightforward implementation and of its large potential financial benefits.

The main goal of this practice is to manipulate individuals and convince them to reveal various types of sensitive data, such as bank account credentials, credit card details or other important financial or personal information. As a consequence, individuals and companies might suffer monetary losses, identity thefts and reputation damages. In fact, attackers often leverage the hijacked accounts for performing illegal online transactions or simply sell the collected data on the marketplace.

The implementation of phishing campaigns requires some simple operations, such as:

© The Author(s), under exclusive license to Springer Nature Switzerland AG 2023
L. Longo (Ed.): xAI 2023, CCIS 1901, pp. 531–543, 2023.
https://doi.org/10.1007/978-3-031-44064-9_28

- Creation of websites that look similar to the legitimate counterparts attackers are trying to impersonate;
- Dissemination of the links of the malicious websites using spoofed email messages or other communication media;
- Creation of a sense of urgency in the individuals targeted by the attacks.

Phishing is a very active phenomenon as indicated in the Phishing Activity Trends Reports[1] periodically published by Anti-Phishing Working Group (APWG). For example, a total of 1,350,037 phishing attacks has been observed in the fourth quarter of 2022. This was up slightly from the third quarter, which, with 1,270,883 attacks, represents a new record and the worst quarter for phishing observed by APWG. These numbers are partly due to the large number of attacks from persistent phishers against several specific targets.

To protect individuals from the risks deriving from phishing attacks, the detection of phishing websites is of paramount importance (see, e.g., Zieni et al. [22] for a detailed review). Approaches based on machine learning are particularly suitable for classifying sites as either phishing or legitimate. Features are typically extracted from the links used to reach the websites, i.e., the Uniform Resource Locators (URLs), and from the page source codes. These features have to take into account the characteristics that differentiate the two classes of websites as well as the strategies implemented by attackers to deceive individuals.

In the context of machine learning, explainability plays a fundamental role to understand the decisions taken by the learning algorithms. In this paper, we address this issue by proposing a methodology and an application that allow us to identify the most important features able to explain a machine learning model for bag of words-based phishing detection, thus extending the recent work of Calzarossa et al. [4] which was based on structured data.

The rest of the paper is organized as follows. After this introduction, the state of the art is analyzed in Sect. 2. Section 3 describes the considered unstructured textual data and feature extraction. Section 4 focuses on the methodology proposed to make machine learning models explainable, based on Lorenz Zonoids, while the experimental results are presented in Sect. 5. Finally, after a summary of the main findings given in Sect. 6, some concluding remarks are offered in Sect. 7.

2   Related Work

As already mentioned, approaches based on machine learning have been extensively investigated in the literature for detecting phishing websites. In fact, machine learning models are particularly effective since they cope well with zero-hour attacks and allow on-the-fly detection of phishing webpages. In what follows, we review the state of the art in the contexts of phishing detection and of explainable Artificial Intelligence.

---

[1] https://docs.apwg.org/reports/apwg_trends_report_q4_2022.pdf.

2.1 Phishing Detection

The machine learning approaches applied in the context of phishing detection mainly differ in terms of the features chosen to describe the properties of the websites and of the learning algorithms applied for the classification.

Features can be extracted from the page source codes or from the page URL. For example, features can be generated by analyzing the textual and visual properties of the source codes, the relationships among their components, and the visual appearance of the page (see, e.g., [5,9,15]).

Concerning URL features, these mainly refer to the lexical properties of the URL strings as well as to the patterns existing in these strings considered either at the character or at the word level (see, e.g., [1,11,13,14,20,21]). For example, for analyzing the composition of URL strings, Ma et al. [12] consider the words URLs consist of and extract features according to the bag of words representation. In detail, a bag of words representation is derived for each of the identified URL components, namely, hostname, second level domain, top level domain, pathname and file extension. As a results, tens of thousands of features are generated.

We recall that a bag of words is a representation of text that describes and maps the occurrence of words within a document into a vector. This model, often used for extracting features from unstructured textual data, is motivated by the intuition that documents containing similar words have similar meanings.

Despite the good predictive power of bag of words features, we outline that these representations have not been used frequently in the framework of phishing website detection because of two main limitations, namely, the high dimensionality of the feature vectors combined with their sparsity.

The methodology proposed in this paper overcomes these limitations since it significantly reduces the number of features without significantly affecting the performance of the machine learning model. In addition, our approach makes the model explainable, that is, it clearly identifies the words most likely associated with phishing websites.

2.2 Explainable AI

Machine learning models are boosting Artificial Intelligence (AI) applications in many domains. Although complex machine learning models may reach high predictive performance, their predictions are not explainable: they cannot be understood and overseen by humans in terms of their drivers (see, e.g., [2]).

The requirement of explainability is fulfilled "by design" through classic statistical models, such as logistic and linear regression. However, in complex data analysis problems, classical statistical models may have a limited predictive accuracy, in comparison with "black-box" machine learning models, such as neural networks and Random Forests.

This suggests to empower machine learning models with post-modelling tools that can "explain" them. Recent attempts in this direction, based on the cooperative game theory work by Shapley [17], have led to promising applications of explainable AI methods (see, e.g., [2] and [3]). Shapley values have the advantage of being agnostic: independent on the underlying model with which predictions are computed, although they have the disadvantage of not being normalised and, therefore, they make it difficult the interpretation and comparison between different models.

A recent work [8] has shown how to overcome this issue by means of Shapley-Lorenz values, which combine Shapley values with Lorenz Zonoids [7], obtaining a global measure of the contribution of each explanatory variable to the predictive accuracy of the response, rather than to the value of the predictions, as is the case for Shapley values.

The Shapley Lorenz metrics has so far been applied only to structured data. With this paper we contribute to the state of the art on explainable AI by proposing and implementing a Shapley Lorenz based explainable AI method for textual data.

Numerous attempts at explaining bagging ensembles (by model reduction, model simplification, etc.) have been proposed, see e.g., [16]. Most of these models rely on explainability notions that are model dependent. A noticeable example is the feature importance plot, which can be used for tree models, but cannot be employed for other types of machine learning models. In general, to achieve a full explainability, agnostic tools, independent on the underlying model, are necessary.

In the context of phishing detection, explainable AI is very important for ensuring transparency, providing trust in the decisions made by machine learning models and enhancing cybersecurity practices. Nevertheless, the research on model agnostic explainable AI models in this field is rather limited (see, e.g., [4,6]). In particular, in [6] two explanatory techniques, namely, Local Interpretable Model-agnostic Explanations and Explainable Boosting Machine, are applied for explaining the models developed for detecting phishing URLs, whereas in [4], the Lorenz Zonoid approach is applied to detect phishing websites described by structured data.

3   Data Collection and Feature Extraction

The dataset used in this study is part of a publicly available dataset consisting of about 1.6 million observations of legitimate and phishing webpages [18,19]. One target response variable and ten explanatory attributes referring to various properties of the page URL and source code are associated with each observation.

To keep our dataset manageable, we extract from it 70,000 observations, each described by one attribute, namely, the raw content of filtered text and JavaScript code, and the target variable. We remark that these observations are equally distributed between legitimate and phishing webpages, thus, unlike the original dataset, our dataset is balanced.

To generate the features, we represent the raw content of each webpage using the bag of words model. In detail, from the content we extract words, i.e., tokens delimited by spaces, and we associate with each word its frequency: the number of times a word appears in a webpage.

A preliminary analysis of the raw content of each webpage shows that some words (e.g., those related to the JavaScript code) do not clearly differentiate phishing and legitimate pages, thus, it is better to discard them. To this aim, we apply multiple filters created using regular expressions and we remove the tokens referring to JavaScripts function names (e.g., `eval()`, `find()`, `lastIndex()`) and to English stopwords. In addition, we discard one character words as well as the numbers and any character that does not belong to the English alphabet. Finally, all words are transformed into lower cases using case folding process.

As a result of these pre-processing steps, we obtain a bag of words consisting of 21,156 words, which will be the candidate explanatory features.

4   Methods

In this section we present our proposed methodology: an explainable machine learning procedure based on Lorenz Zonoids for bag of words feature selection.

It is well known that non linear machine learning models, such as ensemble trees and neural networks, can lead to highly accurate predictions, typically better than those obtained with linear models.

Bag of words phishing detection is a classification problem, for which a Random Forest model could be an appropriate model to consider. A Random Forest model averages the classifications obtained from a set of tree models, each of which is based on a bootstrap sample of training data and of feature variables. In a tree, the feature variables determine the splitting rules, and a statistical measure of variability (such as the one dimensional Gini measure of variability) determines when to stop splitting.

A Random Forest model increases the predictive accuracy of the trees of which it is the average, at the expense of explainability. To overcome this weakness, a variable importance plot can be used. However, such a plot is not fully agnostic, as it cannot be applied for models differerent from ensemble models. For this reason, explainable Artificial Intelligence methods need to be employed, such as methods based on Shapley values [8, 17].

Variable importance plots associate with each predictor the corresponding reduction in the Gini index, averaged over all tree models. Although useful from a descriptive viewpoint, the variable importance plot has the additional disadvantage of not choosing the most significant predictors. In this paper, we fill this gap by proposing a variable selection procedure based on Lorenz Zonoids, which extends the Gini coefficient.

Lorenz Zonoids were proposed in [10] as a multidimensional generalization of the ROC curve. In the one-dimensional case, the Lorenz Zonoid coincides with the Gini coefficient, a well known measure in the study of income inequality or wealth inequality within a nation or a social group. The Lorenz Zonoid measures statistical dispersion in terms of mutual variability among the observations, a metric that is more robust to anomalous and extreme data, with respect to the variance, which measures statistical dispersion in terms of variability from the mean.

For a given set of n observations of a response variable Y to be predicted, the Lorenz Zonoid can be defined as the area between the Lorenz and the dual Lorenz curves.

More formally, given a response variable Y, the Lorenz Zonoid L_Y is obtained ordering the Y values in a non-decreasing sense: joining the points with coordinates $(i/n, \sum_{j=1}^{i} y_{r_j}/(n\bar{y}))$, for $i = 1, \ldots, n$, where r_j and $\bar{y}$ indicate the (non-decreasing) ranks of Y and the Y mean value, respectively. Similarly, the dual Lorenz curve L_Y' is obtained ordering the Y values in a non-increasing sense: joining the points with coordinates $(i/n, \sum_{j=1}^{i} y_{d_j}/(n\bar{y}))$, for $i = 1, \ldots, n$, where d_j indicates the (non-increasing) ranks of Y. The area lying between the L_Y and L_Y' curves is the Lorenz Zonoid.

Giudici and Raffinetti [7] introduced Lorenz Zonoids in the field of machine learning, for model comparison and selection of a parsimonious model. They showed that, given a set of K explanatory variables, and letting $\hat{Y}_{X' \cup X_k}$ and $\hat{Y}_{X'}$ be, respectively, the predicted values obtained from a model – which includes a covariate X_k – and the predicted values obtained from a model – which excludes covariate X_k – the additional contribution of a covariate X_k can be obtained as:

$$\frac{LZ(\hat{Y}_{X' \cup X_k}) - LZ(\hat{Y}_{X'})}{LZ(Y) - LZ(\hat{Y}_{X'})},$$

where $LZ(\hat{Y}_{X' \cup X_k})$, $LZ(\hat{Y}_{X'})$ and $LZ(Y)$ are, respectively: the Lorenz Zonoids computed on the predictions obtained including covariate X_k; the Lorenz Zonoids computed on the predictions obtained excluding covariate X_k; and the Lorenz Zonoids computed on the Y response variable values.

Model comparison can then be implemented associating with each additional variable (feature) the term $LZ(\hat{Y}_{X' \cup X_k}) - LZ(\hat{Y}_{X'})$, which measures its relative importance in terms of its additional contribution to the predictive accuracy of a model.

To implement model comparison, it remains to choose in which order inserting the variables in a model. To save computational time, we suggest to follow a forward stepwise procedure, which starts from the null model (containing no variables) and proceeds inserting one variable at a time, following the ranking determined by the variable importance plot.

We remark that the variable importance plot is a well known explainability tool employed in the context of ensemble tree models, based on the notion of reduction in Gini variability, strictly related to Lorenz Zonoid. We cannot rely exclusively on the variable importance plot, for explainability purposes, as we cannot use it for models different from ensemble trees (such as neural networks or regression models). However, given its relationship with Lorenz Zonoids, it is worth employing its results as a pre-processing step to Lorenz Zonoid model comparison, to determine the order in which to insert variables. This can substantially help in reducing computational complexity.

5 Experimental Results

This section presents the experimental results obtained by applying the proposed methodology to the bag of words representation of phishing and legitimate webpages described in Sect. 3.

An exploratory analysis of the words extracted from each webpage provides some preliminary insights on the variables of interest. A first interesting result refers to the composition of phishing and legitimate pages in terms of the number of words they include, reported in Table 1.

Table 1. Statistics of the composition of the webpages expressed in terms of number of words they include.

Webpage	Mean	Std dev	Max	1st Quartile	Median	3rd Quartile	Number of pages
Phishing	201	94.9	458	126	207	270	35,000
Legitimate	58	45.3	431	32	49	71	35,000
All	129	103.2	458	45	84	214	70,000

From the table we observe that phishing pages differ significantly, and contain more words with respect to legitimate ones. On average, a phishing page includes 201 words compared to 58 words of a legitimate page. The frequency distributions of the words, in both phishing and legitimate pages, are shown in Fig. 1.

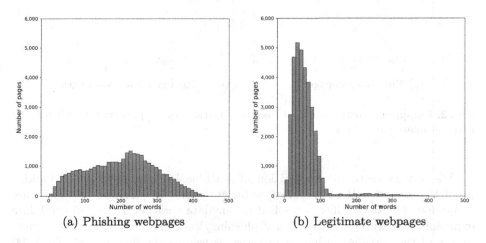

(a) Phishing webpages   (b) Legitimate webpages

Fig. 1. Distributions of frequency of the words appearing in phishing (a) and legitimate (b) webpages

The figure confirms the difference in word frequency between phishing and legitimate pages: the former not only contains, on average, more words, but it is also much more variable. From an interpretational viewpoint, the identified differences could be seen as a specific strategy of the attackers, who tend to insert longer texts to confuse users.

A second result that can be obtained from the exploratory analysis is that the number of unique words appearing in phishing and legitimate pages also differs. As expected, while many unique words are used in phishing pages (i.e., 19,720 out of the 21,156 words extracted from the dataset), the text of legitimate pages is not as rich, as only 12,253 unique words appear in their content.

Another important aspect that can be explored is related to the concentration of the words. For this purpose, Fig. 2 plots the cumulative distributions of the frequency of the words used in phishing and legitimate pages. We can easily notice that the two distributions are quite different. For the phishing pages a very small fraction of the words, that is, 1,375 words, accounts for about 90% of the overall frequency of all words, and a large fraction of all words (about 51%) appears only once. On the contrary, for legitimate pages, 6,700 words are required to account for 90% of the overall frequency, whereas very few words (838) appear only once. From an interpretational result, the previous findings demonstrate that attackers tend to use the same words, leading to a highly concentrated distribution.

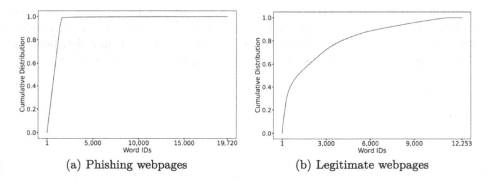

(a) Phishing webpages   (b) Legitimate webpages

Fig. 2. Cumulative distributions of frequency of the words appearing in phishing (a) and legitimate (b) webpages

We now move to the application of machine learning models. To build a predictive model able to recognize webpages either as phishing or legitimate, a Random Forest classifier is applied to our data considering 21,156 candidate explanatory features for the binary phishing/legitimate response. The performance of the classifier, using all features, as well as the first 10,000 and 5,000 most important features (plus a case with nine features that will be explained later) is illustrated in Table 2.

The table clearly shows that the predictive performance of the classifier with all features is very good: the accuracy is about 95%. Similarly, precision, recall

Table 2. Random Forest performance as a function of the number of features used by the classifier.

Features	Accuracy	Precision	Recall	F1-score
21,156 (all)	0.9506	0.95	0.95	0.95
10,000	0.9510	0.95	0.95	0.95
5,000	0.9512	0.95	0.95	0.95
9	0.8904	0.90	0.89	0.89

and F1-score are also rather good. Reducing the number of features to 10,000 and 5,000 does not significantly reduce such performance.

Figure 3 shows a snapshot of the Random Forest feature importance plot, in which the first 32 most important features are displayed. These features are the words that strongly differentiate phishing and legitimate webpages. Note that in the figure we do not explicitly name the words because they are generally dirty words. In fact, our conjecture is that most phishing pages refer to fake adult websites.

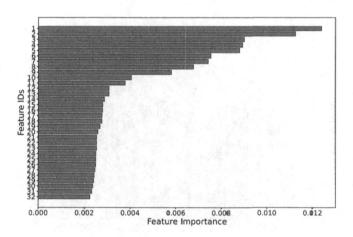

Fig. 3. Random Forest feature importance plot

The figure shows that much of feature importance is captured by the first five words, suggesting that the Random Forest model may be simplified without losing too much accuracy. Indeed, this figure is the basis for selecting the most important features to be retained, while making the model explainable, by means of our proposed Lorenz Zonoid feature selection procedure.

To this end, the Lorenz Zonoid is calculated for the most important features by adding one of them at a time, following the order described by the feature importance plot: starting from the feature with the highest importance, then with that with the second highest importance, and so on.

In more detail, the Random Forest model is first trained using only the most important word. On the basis of such a model, predictive scores of phishing are calculated for all observations in the validation set. The Lorenz Zonoid is applied to the obtained predictive scores, leading to a first accuracy measure, based on a model with only one feature. The procedure is repeated using both the first and the second most important variables, leading to a second Lorenz Zonoid accuracy measure which is likely to have a higher value than the first one, because of the inclusion property of Lorenz Zonoid. The process of adding features, in the order indicated by the feature importance plot, is then repeated, leading to progressively greater values of the Lorenz Zonoids, until a stopping point is reached.

As a stopping point we suggest to follow the "elbow rule" employed in determining the optimal number of principal components in factor analysis: stop when the second derivative of the plot of the Lorenz Zonoid measures changes sign.

The Lorenz Zonoids selection procedure, applied to our data, is shown in Fig. 4. As can be seen, the Lorenz Zonoid measure, which is approximately equal to 10% using only the first word feature, rapidly increases until the first nine words are considered, although with a declining acceleration. The elbow rule, applied to Fig. 4, suggests that a good stopping point is to consider nine features.

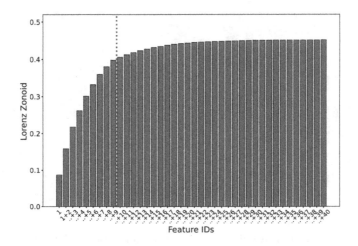

Fig. 4. Lorenz Zonoid for the most important features. The plot reports the Lorenz Zonoid values for models of increasing size, obtained adding one feature at a time, in the order described by the feature importance plot.

6 Discussion of Findings

The findings outlined in this section explain why we have inserted in Table 2 also a model with nine features: it is exactly the model selected by our Lorenz Zonoid procedure.

Indeed, from Table 2 we can observe that, if we drastically reduce the number of words necessary for the predictive classifiers, from as many as 21,156 to only 9, the accuracy only reduces by 6%. A similar behavior is obtained for the other performance measures: the precision reduces only by 5 basis points, from 0.95 to 0.90, the recall only by 6 basis points, from 0.95 to 0.89, and similarly the F1-score.

Altogether, the accuracy measures indicate that a model with 9 features is only slightly less accurate than a model with 21,156 features. On the other hand, a model with only 9 features is much better explained than a model with 21,156 features. It is also very likely that a model with 9 variables is more robust to data variations with respect to a model with 21,156 variables.

We finally remark that a simpler alternative to the Shapley Lorenz method is the variable importance plot, often employed to achieve explainability in ensemble tree models. While variable importance plots are useful, and we make use of them in the paper, they are not fully agnostic as they cannot be employed to other types of learning models, thereby limiting model comparison.

7   Conclusion

In this paper we dealt with the problem of building an explainable machine learning model, that is able to correctly classify, in advance, whether a certain website is phishing or legitimate. We have shown how to tackle the problem in the realistic case of data consisting of unstructured documents.

To build a machine learning model, we have first proposed a bag of words representation of the data. We have given some intuition on how phishing operates, by means of exploratory data analysis.

We have then applied a Random Forest model to a set of 21,156 candidate explanatory feature words. Given the high complexity of the full model, we have shown that our proposed Lorenz Zonoid selection procedure can lead to a drastic reduction of complexity, without significantly affecting the model accuracy: we are able to reduce the important features to 9 feature words, losing only 6% of the predictive accuracy.

Our contribution to the explainable AI field is twofold. From a methodological viewpoint, we have proposed a feature selection method, based on Lorenz Zonoid comparisons, which can drastically simplify a bag of words model, without losing much predictive accuracy. From an applied viewpoint, we have shown how our proposed methods can lead to a model explained by a limited set of features, that can be oversight to monitor and detect on time possible phishing attacks.

Our results indicate that bag of words phishing detection could lead to very useful insights on the nature of phishing websites, and can help not only to identify a priori suspicious websites, but also to understand the words that identify and explain them. These are important results for end users of websites and also for the authorities aimed at monitoring cyber attacks and implementing cyber security measures.

Future research is needed in the extension of what presented here to similar data problems. Indeed, our approach is very general and can be applied to any machine learning model based on unstructured data analysis. The advantage of our proposal will be particularly evident, in terms of a gain in explainability and a reduction in computational costs, in problems in which the number of available feature variables is large.

Finally, we remark that, although our results clearly demonstrate the effectiveness of our proposed methodology, further comparative analyses should be conducted with existing and novel techniques to provide a more robust assessment.

References

1. Blum, A., Wardman, B., Solorio, T., Warner, G.: Lexical feature based phishing URL detection using online learning. In: Proceedings of the ACM Conference on Computer and Communications Security, pp. 54–60 (2010)
2. Bracke, P., Datta, A., Jung, C., Shayak, S.: Machine learning explainability in finance: an application to default risk analysis. Staff Working Paper, Bank of England (816) (2019)
3. Bussmann, N., Giudici, P., Marinelli, D., Papenbrock, J.: Explainable AI in credit risk management. Comput. Econ. **57**(1), 203–216 (2021)
4. Calzarossa, M., Giudici, P., Zieni, R.: Explainable machine learning for phishing feature detection. Qual. Reliab. Eng. Int. (2023)
5. Corona, I., et al.: DeltaPhish: detecting phishing webpages in compromised websites. In: Foley, S.N., Gollmann, D., Snekkenes, E. (eds.) ESORICS 2017. LNCS, vol. 10492, pp. 370–388. Springer, Cham (2017). https://doi.org/10.1007/978-3-319-66402-6_22
6. Galego Hernandes, P., Floret, C., Cardozo De Almeida, K., Da Silva, V., Papa, J., Pontara Da Costa, K.: Phishing detection using URL-based XAI techniques. In: Proceedings of the IEEE Symposium Series on Computational Intelligence - SSCI. IEEE (2021)
7. Giudici, P., Raffinetti, E.: Lorenz model selection. J. Classif. **37**(2), 754–768 (2020)
8. Giudici, P., Raffinetti, E.: Shapley-Lorenz explainable artificial intelligence. Expert Syst. Appl. **158**(895), 1–9 (2021)
9. Jain, A., Gupta, B.: A machine learning based approach for phishing detection using hyperlinks information. J. Ambient. Intell. Humaniz. Comput. **10**, 2015–2028 (2019)
10. Koshevoy, G., Mosler, K.: The Lorenz Zonoid of a multivariate distribution. J. Am. Stat. Assoc. **91**(434), 873–882 (1996)
11. Le, A., Markopoulou, A., Faloutsos, M.: PhishDef: URL names say it all. In: Proceedings of the 30th IEEE International Conference on Computer Communications - INFOCOM, pp. 191–195. IEEE (2011)
12. Ma, J., Saul, L., Savage, S., Voelker, G.: Beyond blacklists: learning to detect malicious web sites from suspicious URLs. In: Proceedings of the 15th ACM SIGKDD International Conference on Knowledge Discovery and Data Mining - KDD, pp. 1245–1254. ACM (2009)
13. Ma, J., Saul, L., Savage, S., Voelker, G.: Learning to detect malicious URLs. ACM Trans. Intell. Syst. Technol. **2**(3) (2011)
14. Marchal, S., Francois, J., State, R., Engel, T.: PhishStorm: detecting phishing with streaming analytics. IEEE Trans. Netw. Serv. Manage. **11**(4), 458–471 (2014)

15. Rao, R., Pais, A., Anand, P.: A heuristic technique to detect phishing websites using TWSVM classifier. Neural Comput. Appl. **33**(11), 5733–5752 (2021)
16. Sagi, O., Rokach, L.: Explainable decision forest: transforming a decision forest into an interpretable tree. Inf. Fusion **61**, 124–138 (2020)
17. Shapley, L.: A value for n-person games. In: Contributions to the Theory of Games II, pp. 307–317 (1953)
18. Singh, A.: Dataset of malicious and benign webpages. Mendeley Data (2020). https://data.mendeley.com/datasets/gdx3pkwp47/2
19. Singh, A.: Malicious and benign webpages dataset. Data Brief **32**, 106304 (2020)
20. Tupsamudre, H., Singh, A.K., Lodha, S.: Everything is in the name – a URL based approach for phishing detection. In: Dolev, S., Hendler, D., Lodha, S., Yung, M. (eds.) CSCML 2019. LNCS, vol. 11527, pp. 231–248. Springer, Cham (2019). https://doi.org/10.1007/978-3-030-20951-3_21
21. Verma, R., Dyer, K.: On the character of phishing URLs: accurate and robust statistical learning classifiers. In: Proceedings of the 5th ACM Conference on Data and Application Security and Privacy - CODASPY, pp. 111–122. ACM (2015)
22. Zieni, R., Massari, L., Calzarossa, M.: Phishing or not phishing? A survey on the detection of phishing websites. IEEE Access **11**, 18499–18519 (2023)

An Evaluation of Contextual Importance and Utility for Outcome Explanation of Black-Box Predictions for Medical Datasets

Avleen Malhi[1,2]([⊠]) and Kary Främling[1,3]

[1] Aalto University, Helsinki, Finland
avleen.malhi@aalto.fi,amalhi@bournemouth.ac.uk, kary.framling@cs.umu.se
[2] Bournemouth University, Poole, UK
[3] Umeå University, Umeå, Sweden

Abstract. Contextual Importance and Utility (CIU) is a model-agnostic method for producing situation- or instance-specific explanations of the outcome of so-called black-box systems. A major difference between CIU and other outcome explanation methods (also called *post-hoc* methods) is that CIU produces explanations without producing any intermediate interpretable model. CIU's notion of *importance* is similar as in Decision Theory but differs from how importance is defined for other outcome explanation methods. *Utility* is also a well-known concept from Decision Theory that is largely ignored in current Explainable AI research. CIU is here validated by providing explanations for the two popular medical data sets - heart disease and breast cancer in order to show the applicability of CIU explanations on medical predictions and with different black-box models. The explanations are compared with corresponding ones produced by the Local Interpretable Model-agnostic Explanations (LIME) method [17], which is currently one of the most used post-hoc explanation methods. The paper's main contribution is to provide new CIU results and insights on several benchmark data sets and showing in what way CIU differs from LIME-based explanations.

Keywords: Explainable AI · Contextual Importance · Contextual Utility · Multiple Criteria Decision Making · Heart disease · Breast cancer data

1 Introduction

Explainable Artificial Intelligence (XAI) is a research domain with an ambition to make the results of AI systems interpretable, explainable and understandable to humans. Recently, XAI research area has gained increased attention from academic researchers with an exceptional resurgence of XAI research interest. In reality, XAI is a relatively old domain with a relatively active period in the 1990's

L. Longo (Ed.): xAI 2023, CCIS 1901, pp. 544–557, 2023.
https://doi.org/10.1007/978-3-031-44064-9_29

as shown by [19] for instance. However, a vast majority of the work performed then was focusing on so-called *intrinsic interpretability* or *interpretable model extraction*, i.e. extract rules or other interpretable forms of knowledge from the trained neural network and then use that representation for explainability. The XAI was proposed by Van Lent et al. [20] in 2004 for describing a system's ability to interpret the AI-controlled entities' behaviour in simulated game environments but, with the significant progress of ML, as AI reaches an inflection point, the pace of solving this problem has slowed down. Since then, the attention of artificial intelligence research has shifted to implementing models and algorithms, which emphasize predictive capabilities, while the ability to explain the decision-making process ranks second. Actually, XAI term is more inclined to the efforts and initiatives which have been made in retaliation to AI transparency and trust issues, compared to a more formal and technical definition. Hence, to add some elucidation about this concept, we quote some definitions: According to DARPA [1], XAI focuses to 'produce more explainable models, while maintaining a high level of learning performance (prediction accuracy); and enable human users to understand, appropriately, trust, and effectively manage the emerging generation of artificially intelligent partners". A structured and unified perspective of the important concepts used in XAI research has been illustrated in Fig. 1 based on the above term analysis.

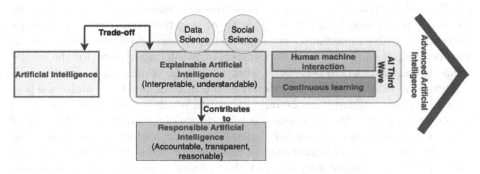

Fig. 1. XAI related concepts [2]

1.1 Motivation

As pointed out by many researchers and notably Miller [14], current XAI research tends to focus on developing methods that allow AI and Machine Learning (ML) researchers to analyze and understand the results of their own models, rather than providing explanations that could be understandable by true end-users. In practice, the concept of explainability and how humans define and understand an explanation should probably be guided by domains such as social sciences, psychology, cognitive sciences and even philosophy. One domain that seems largely neglected in current XAI research is *Decision Theory* and related sub-areas such as *Multiple Criteria Decision Making (MCDM)*. The Merriam-Webster dictionary defines 'Decision Theory' as "a branch of statistical theory concerned with quantifying the process of making choices between alternatives". Nevertheless, Decision Theory is by definition closely related with the domains mentioned above (social science, data science and human machine interaction) since the intention is to produce Decision Support Systems (DSS) understandable and usable by humans. MCDM provide clear definitions of what is meant by the *importance* of an input, as well as what is the *utility* of a given input value towards the outcome of a DSS. A simple linear DSS model is the weighted sum, where a numerical weight expresses the importance of an input and a numerical score expresses the utility of the current value of that input.

Rather than attempting to address explainability with gradient-based linear approximations such as LIME or SHAP [13], this paper studies a non-linear extension to the notions of importance and utility used in linear models. The extension is called **Contextual Importance and Utility (CIU)** and was initially proposed in [9] [10] [8]. This paper provides a comparative study of the performance, model fidelity and explainability of CIU in comparison with LIME. Generated explanations are studied for several UCI data sets for predictions generated by typical ML models.

The authors are also concerned with the current use of the term 'importance' by the XAI community, where it is often indicated as being 'positive/favorable/typical' or 'negative/non-favorable/non-typical'. By definition, the term 'importance' cannot be positive or negative, i.e. saying that something has 'positive importance' or 'negative importance' does not make sense. A feature or input can have 'great importance' or 'weak importance' for the results of an AI reasoner, which reflects to what extent the result can be modified by changing the value of the feature. However, the value of a feature can have a positive or negative influence on the outcome value, which is often called the *utility* of that value. In real-life situations, the importance of a feature and the utility of different feature values can change depending on the *context*. As an illustrating example, there is great importance of the outdoor temperature on a person's comfort but only considering the fact that person is outdoor. As soon as the person goes inside, the context changes and outdoor temperature has minimal effect on the comfort level of the person. Regarding utility, a warm temperature is good if the person is wearing a T-shirt but bad if the person is wearing winter clothes. The combined use of importance and utility is demonstrated in Sect. 5, where they allow richer visual explanations than methods that do not take the separation between importance and utility into account.

2 Understanding XAI

2.1 Need for XAI

The existing literature explores the need for explainable artificial intelligence systems for many reasons which can typically be categorized in the four main grounds for capturing the motivation behind explainability.

1. *Explanations to discover:* It is always considerate to ask for explanations for learning new facts, gathering information and hence gaining knowledge.
2. *Explanations to Justify:* There has been an ever increasing demand for explanations to ensure trust in AI based decisions.
3. *Explanations to Control:* Explanations help to understand if anything goes wrong.
4. *Explanations to Improve:* They help in improving and making the model more strong by getting the feedback from the users on the understanding of the system.

Not as long ago, ML models were used for understanding of the system rather than for predictions. The recent research on employing more complicated ML models has redirected the expectations of model from understandability to the prediction due to the model complexity which hinders understandability. The new models are becoming more efficient in predictions leading to emergence of multitude accurate algorithms but overlooking the challenge imposed by black-box behaviour of the models. Now the question is: why can't we trust the ML model which is performing with higher accuracy ignoring why it reached at a particular decision? "The problem is that a single metric, such as classification accuracy, is an incomplete description of most real-world tasks." [5]. Why the model interpretability is considered as crucial is because the predictions might be enough in some instances giving a good performance while in other instances, knowing the reason will help in auditing and debugging purposes to know about the problem. There are already some models which can be interpreted such as decision trees, but the interpretation is at generic level rules and are not very specific to any instances. While interpretability models provide explanations of model's decisions for all instances. These provide feature importance for individual instance of decision while decision tree generates the generic rules for all instances.

Generally, linear models are often not considered good at predictive performance, as the learned relationships are so restricted leading to oversimplification of the complex reality. Logistic regression, an extension of the linear regression model also fail in scenarios with nonlinear relationship between features and outcome or where features interact with each other. The interpretation is more difficult in the logistic regression model due to multiplicative weights rather than additive. Again, in Neural Networks (NN), the input data flows through the multiple multiplication layers with the learned weights and through non-linear transformations. Even one prediction can be associated with millions of mathematical operations depending on the NN architecture used. It is not possible for humans to follow the exact input data mapping to prediction. To interpret the neural network behavior and predictions, specific interpretation methods are required. These networks use their hidden layers to learn features, concepts and special tools required to reveal them [15].

2.2   Enabling XAI: The Technical Challenge

ML models are built to provide the simplifications of reality. Although the predictive capability of the ML model may be very high but it may still not seem easy for human to understand. Hence, having explanations for the ML models need evaluations at first place which can be majorly done with two methods [11]: *interpretability* and *completeness*. The *interpretability* aims in describing the internal functionality of the system in a manner that humans can understand. Hence, the interpretibility success and failure totally depends on user's perception and knowledge to examine the result. On contrary, *completeness* refers to description of the internal functioning of the system in detailed manner. An explanation of a system is considered more complete if its behaviour can be forecasted in advance for a different scenario. For instance, deep neural network's complete explanation can be attained by proclaiming all the underlying mathematical operations and parameters. An ideal XAI model focuses on development of interpretable and complete explanations.

Generally, explanations can be classified into local and global. Local explanations which usually rely on local surrogate models contribute to each single prediction using the surrogate interpretable models rather than considering whole ML model at once. Local interpretations assist in understanding model's predictions for a single data row or similar group rows by drawing the inferences in close proximity with the selected instance. On Contrary, global explanations help to increase the understanding of the inputs and the model relationship with predictor target but these often can lead to higher approximation at times in some instances. Hence, we use another models on top of these models to make these complex models simple and understandable and these models are known as surrogate models. These surrogate models try to emulate the prediction behaviour of the black box model with respect to a distinct consideration that the surrogate models should be interpretable. Hence these surrogate models, often termed as explainers require to be easily interpretable (like linear regression) and may not have the flexibility and adaptability of the initial black box model they tend to explain.

3   Contextual Importance and Utility (CIU)

Contextual Importance and Utility (CIU) uses the contributing features of the dataset in generating the explanations and interpretations. The idea of contextual importance and contextual utility was introduced by Kary Främling in his PhD thesis [6] for justifying the black box models' recommendations which was one of the earliest work in addressing this. The proposed method helped in the context of multiple criteria decision making (MCDM) in explanations of the preferences of the neural networks [9]. This approach can be used for both linear and non-linear models for explaining the model predictions for a particular test instance by the calculation of each feature's contextual importance and utility. The capabilities of these explanations are *contextual* since one feature might be important for taking a decision in one circumstance but can be irrelevant in another circumstance [3].

CI is the ratio of output range obtained by varying the input values for a certain feature x_1 throughout its whole range from minimum to maximum. The output range lies between the lowest possible output value (C_{min}) by varying feature values and the highest possible output value (C_{max}). The contextual importance (CI) of an input is defined by the inputs' current values and range. The contextual importance $CI_j(\vec{C}, \{i\})$ of a given set of inputs $\{i\}$ for a certain output j in the context $\vec{C}$. The definition of CI is

$$CI_j(\vec{C}, \{i\}) = \frac{Cmax_j(\vec{C}, \{i\}) - Cmin_j(\vec{C}, \{i\})}{absmax_j - absmin_j} \tag{1}$$

where $absmax_j$ is the maximal possible value for output j and $absmin_j$ is the minimal possible value for output j. $Cmax_j(\vec{C}, \{i\})$ is the maximal value of output j observed when modifying the values of inputs $\{i\}$ and keeping the values of the other inputs at those specified by $\vec{C}$. Correspondingly, $Cmin_j(\vec{C}, \{i\})$ is the minimal value of output j observed. The estimation of $Cmax_j(\vec{C}, \{i\})$ and $Cmin_j(\vec{C}, \{i\})$ is done by using the input value ranges defined by the minimum and maximum input values in the training set and we use Monte-Carlo simulation with uniformly distributed, randomly generated values within the provided value ranges of inputs $\{i\}$.

The contextual utility (CU) is defined by the output range and current output value. The definition of CU is

$$CU_j(\vec{C}, \{i\}) = \frac{out_j(\vec{C}) - Cmin_j(\vec{C}, \{i\})}{Cmax_j(\vec{C}, \{i\}) - Cmin_j(\vec{C}, \{i\})} \tag{2}$$

where $out_j(\vec{C})$ is the value of the output j for the context $\vec{C}$. CU refers to the position of the predicted output y_i for the selected test instance with context to the output range calculated by CI i.e. if the y_i is close to (C_{max}), it is having high utility and if it is close to (C_{min}), it is having low utility.

4   Methods

CIU has been applied for providing explanations to black-box ML model predictions on medical datasets. We have used neural networks and random forest in generating the predictions for medical datasets [12] and provided the explanations using CIU and compared it with the current state-of-the-art method, LIME. We have generated explanations for the classification tasks. Random forest and neural network have been used as black-box models, as illustrated in Fig. 2. For the two datasets studied in detail (heart disease and breast cancer), classical feature importance has been calculated for the entire data set in order to illustrate how it differs from instance-specific outcome explanations produced by CIU and LIME. Additionally, to illustrate how CIU explanations are generated on different scenarios, we present CIU results on a selection of medical datasets from the UCI repository [4]. CIU values and explanations can be calculated for any combination of inputs, including the combination of all inputs. Such results have been included in Table 3 for informative purposes. However, since LIME and other state-of-the-art XAI methods for outcome explanation do not provide such functionality, a detailed analysis on them has not been included in this paper. The use of such combined inputs as 'intermediate concepts' is proposed e.g. in [6] and [7].

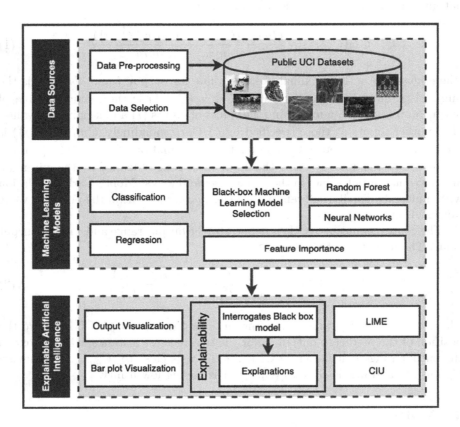

Fig. 2. Explanation workflow

5   Experiments

This section details the results obtained for medical UCI datasets. The datasets used for the experimental evaluation are: heart disease, breast cancer and Table 1 gives the description of the datasets. The experiments were implemented in "R". The CIU implementation used is on Github at the address

The ML models used here are Random Forest and Neural Net and the source code for producing all the results of this paper are available at {*hidden for anonymous review*}

Table 1. The benchmark datasets of Heart disease and Breast cancer

Name	Heart	Breast
# Instances	303	699
# Inputs	13	9
# Output classes	5	2

5.1 Heart Disease

The heart disease dataset has 5 possible output classes, with class 0 depicting no heart disease and classes 1–4 giving the severity of the heart disease. As usual for this dataset, we have converted the four "heart disease present" classes 1,2,3,4 into one single class, while class 0 corresponds to not having heart disease. A random forest model was trained using the heart disease dataset. First, the feature importance is calculated for the trained random forest using the 'varImp()' function of the *caret* package, which is shown in Table 2. If the model learned by the random forest would be linear, then the feature importances indicated in Table 2 should be identical also for the outcome explanations produced by LIME and CIU. However, the whole idea of black-box outcome explanation is to deal with the case of non-linear models, where the importance of a feature, and the utility of the feature value for a specific instance, depends on the other feature values for the studied instance. Therefore, the expectation is that for most instances the instance-specific feature importances calculated by CIU and LIME should **not** be identical to those in Table 2 for non-linear models.

Finally, a Recursive Feature Elimination analysis with 10-fold cross validation using the 'rfe()' function from *caret* package indicates that the top features are 'ca', 'thal' and 'cp', which give a higher prediction accuracy (0.845) than using more features. It is interesting to notice that this result differs slightly from the result of 'varImp()' because 'rfe' has 'ca' as a top feature, whereas it is only fifth in importance given by 'varImp()'. This indicates that those top features ('ca', 'thal', 'cp') are expected to have a high importance for most instances also in CIU and LIME explanations, despite non-linearity.

For comparing CIU and LIME, we take a single $heart_{data}$ instance selected from the data set that is classified as 'heart disease present'. The corresponding input values of the specific instance are indicated between parentheses in Fig. 3 of CIU results, where visual explanations are shown for CIU and LIME for that specific instance.

Table 2. The feature importance calculated by the random forest model for the heart disease data

Variable	Importance
cp	13.8909
thal	13.3055
thalach	12.2028
oldpeak	11.5130
ca	8.1884
chol	7.7483
trestbps	7.0494
age	6.8000
slope	5.7956
exang	5.3617
sex	3.4640
restecg	1.6067
fbs	0.9787

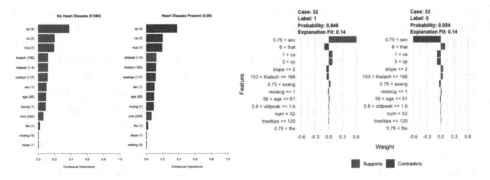

Fig. 3. Bar plot visualisation for heart disease classes (present and not present) based on CIU explanations and LIME explanations. Bar length corresponds to CI value. CU values are indicated by a continuous red-yellow-green colour scale, where CU=0 is red (worst), CU=0.5 is yellow (neutral) and CU = 1 is dark green (best). (Color figure online)

In the CIU plots, the bar length corresponds to CI (the contextual importance), whereas CU (contextual utility) is visualised using a continuous red-yellow-green colour scale, where CU = 0 corresponds to red (worst), CU = 0.5 to yellow (neutral) and CU = 1 to dark green (best). In LIME plots, bar lengths also correspond to the estimated feature importance. However, LIME does not have a 'utility' notion. Since LIME uses a locally linear model (similar to a gradient), a feature can only 'support' or 'contradict' the result, based on the sign of the partial gradient. When comparing CIU and LIME explanations in Fig. 3,

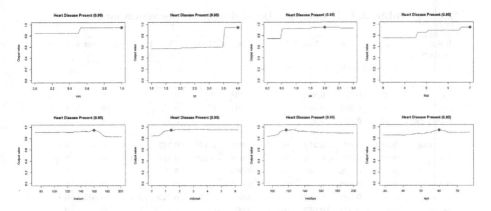

Fig. 4. Output values of Heart Disease classes as a function of selected inputs for random forest model

there are clear differences, which raises the question about which explanation is correct and why? Major differences are at least the following:

1. LIME indicates that 'sex' is by far the most important feature, whereas CIU ranks 'sex' 7th in importance.
2. CIU indicates that all feature values support this result, whereas LIME indicates that several features contradict the result. Notably the 'thal' feature is significant for this instance.

The Fig. 3 depicts how the explanations are provided by CIU and LIME where explanations provided by CIU also take utility into consideration whereas the LIME only gives the feature importance in local context without considering how the model behaves corresponding to the whole training data. The CIU plots give the feature utility of each input feature in determining the probability of a particular class. The probabilities of each class are given on top of each graph and the input values for each feature are given in () sorted in the increasing order of feature importance. The explanations are also added with the help of a local surrogate model LIME. The output of LIME comprises the explanation which reflects each feature's contribution to the prediction made by the black-box model. LIME explanations give the feature importance for the test class and these features have weights defined internally by the algorithm which help to define their feature importance which is either in favor of particular class or contrasts it. The values of these attributes help calculating the weights internally based for the prediction probability for a particular class. LIME is a local linear model which can provide and estimate how much small changes in an input attribute might affect the output but they do not explain the scenario when the input value is changed slightly more. Hence, it does not take into account the utility of the input. Furthermore, LIME explanations are still confusing and not giving very clear understanding of the feature utility and importance as well as the concept of new variables generation for providing feature importance is not interpretable from end-user point of view.

Table 3. CIU values for Heart disease classes versus inputs

Input Feature	Class 0	Class 1	Class 2	Class 3	Class 4	Class 0	Class 1	Class 2	Class 3	Class 4
CIU Values for single inputs										
	CI					CU				
Age	0.052	0.09	0.348	0.226	0.048	0	0	1	0	0.083
Sex	0.042	0.002	0.108	0.068	0.004	0	0	1	0	1
Chest pain type	0.45	0.19	0.48	0.088	0.01	0	0	1	1	0
trestbps	0.072	0.08	0.272	0.286	0.036	0.166	0.375	1	0.03	0.22
chol	0.044	0.09	0.208	0.05	0.098	0.227	0.155	0.92	0.12	0.04
fbs	0.002	0.086	0.046	0.038	0.004	1	0	1	1	1
restecg	0.012	0.098	0.08	0.014	0.004	1	0	1	0.714	0
thalach	0.032	0.308	0.352	0.118	0.06	0.25	0.012	0.971	0.203	0.1
exang	0.03	0.004	0.052	0.018	0.008	0	1	1	0	0
oldpeak	0.09	0.114	0.23	0.122	0.1	0.22	0.017	0.982	0.114	0.02
Slope	0.012	0.032	0.088	0.042	0.026	1	0	1	0	0
ca	0.38	0.102	0.446	0.048	0.048	0	0	0.95	1	0.125
thal	0.036	0.136	0.172	0.02	0.02	0	0	1	1	0
CIU Values for 2 inputs combined										
	CI					CU				
age and sex	0.246	0.232	0.044	0.028	0.02	0.09	0.905	1	0.285	0
cp and trestbps	0.468	0.37	0.184	0.06	0.012	0.247	0.967	0.01	0.2	0
chol and fbs	0.116	0.112	0.062	0.008	0.002	0.94	0.321	0.032	0.25	0
restecg and thalach	0.256	0.176	0.058	0.074	0.012	0.187	1	0.586	0.081	0
exang and oldpeak	0.324	0.186	0.118	0.038	0.162	0.944	0.225	0.508	0.105	0
slope and ca	0.214	0.064	0.08	0.128	0.018	1	0.562	0.15	0.015	0
CIU Values for all inputs combined										
	CI					CU				
all inputs	0.736	0.548	0.484	0.42	0.394	0.65	0.609	0.103	0.009	0.005

The plots in Fig. 4 will be studied in detail for understanding the differences. Figure 4 shows how the value of the output 'Heart Disease Present' changes as a function of the eight most relevant features, as well as their estimated feature importance. The red dot the input and output value for the studied instance, e.g. the graph for 'cp' feature clearly depicts that the 'cp' value is typical for 'Heart Disease Present'. The prediction made for 'Heart Disease Present' is given on top of the graphs as 0.95, indicating that there is 0.95 probability of heart disease being present for that instance. CIU explanations correspond to the plots of Fig. 4 'by definition', i.e. how CI and CU are calculated based on them is clear from Eqs. 1 and 2. The corresponding CI and CU values are shown in Table 3. Since CIU doesn't create any intermediate 'interpretable model', CIU explanations correspond exactly to the behaviour of the underlying black-box model.

Regarding LIME explanations, it is difficult to understand why 'sex' is given great importance by LIME. There is a warning message given by LIME *"Warning message: sex does not contain enough variance to use quantile binning. Using standard binning instead."* feature. In practice, Fig. 4 clearly indicates a class separation at 0.5 between 'female' and 'male', as well as an indication that 'male' value increases the probability for 'Heart Disease Present'. What comes to the 'thal' feature, it is clear from Fig. 4 that a high value (7) is clearly typical for 'Heart Disease Present'. Without going further into details, based on this analysis it seems clear that *the LIME explanation does not correspond to the actual black-box model.* This conclusion is in line with earlier claims that LIME also lacks consistency in repeated explanations for a single prediction, which is one of the most desirable properties in building trust in AI [16,18].

Finally, as mentioned already, CIU is not restricted to one input or feature. CIU is defined for any combination of inputs, as well as for all inputs simultaneously. Table 3 shows CI and CU for combined features such as 'age and sex' (inputs one and two) and 'cp and trestbps' (inputs three and four) and so on, as well as CI and CU when calculated for all inputs.

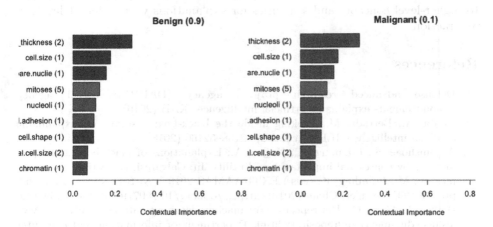

Fig. 5. CIU bar plot visualisation for Breast cancer classes where CU=0 is red (worst), CU=0.5 is yellow (neutral) and CU=1 is dark green (best). (Color figure online)

5.2   CIU Results for Breast Cancer Dataset

It appears that existing literature hasn't presented results on the use of CIU for different benchmark datasets with varied complexity. This is why a similar breast cancer dataset has been selected, for which CIU bar graph visualizations have been created. The bar graph visualisations for breast cancer dataset are shown in Fig. 5 where the contextual importance and utility for the benign and malignant classes in shown in the order of importance and the corresponding utility.

6   Conclusion and Future Work

As shown by the experimental results of the paper, it is justified to question to what extent LIME explanations actually correspond to the behaviour of the underlying black-box model. LIME belongs to the family of XAI methods for outcome explanation that can be considered gradient-based, which seems to be the main approach taken by the XAI community for the moment. However, the results presented here show that the use of gradient-based methods for outcome explanation of black-box models may not be well-founded. Furthermore, it is questionable if the current use of the 'importance' concept is justified and if only two levels of 'utility' ('supports' vs. 'contradicts') is sufficient.

CIU is entirely model-agnostic and constructs explanations directly based on observations of input and output values of black-box models. Contrary to most XAI methods for outcome explanation, CIU does not construct any intermediate 'interpretable model', which guarantees that CIU-based explanations correspond exactly to the behaviour of the underlying model. CIU also deals with the 'utility' notion in a non-binary and clearly defined manner. Finally, CIU is applicable for any number of combined features, which opens possibilities to apply CIU to higher-level concepts and semantics for explanations with different levels of abstraction.

References

1. Defense advanced research projects agency (DARPA): Broad agency announcement- explainable artificial intelligence (XAI) (2016)
2. Adabi, A., Berrada, M.: Peeking inside the black-box: a survey on explainable artificial intelligence. IEEE Access **6**, 52138–52160 (2018)
3. Anjomshoae, S., Främling, K., Najjar, A.: Explanations of black-box model predictions by contextual importance and utility. In: Calvaresi, D., Najjar, A., Schumacher, M., Främling, K. (eds.) EXTRAAMAS 2019. LNCS (LNAI), vol. 11763, pp. 95–109. Springer, Cham (2019). https://doi.org/10.1007/978-3-030-30391-4_6
4. Blake, C., Merz, C.: Uci repository of machine learning databases. http://www.ics.uci.edu/mlearn/mlrepository.html. Department of information and computer science. University of California, Irvine, CA 55 (1998)
5. Doshi-Velez, F., Kim, B.: Towards a rigorous science of interpretable machine learning. arXiv preprint arXiv:1702.08608 (2017)
6. Främling, K.: Modélisation et apprentissage des préférences par réseaux de neurones pour l'aide à la décision multicritère. Phd thesis, INSA de Lyon (1996), https://tel.archives-ouvertes.fr/tel-00825854
7. Främling, K.: Explainable AI without interpretable model (2020)
8. Främling, K.: Contextual importance and utility: a theoretical foundation. In: Long, G., Yu, X., Wang, S. (eds.) AI 2022. LNCS (LNAI), vol. 13151, pp. 117–128. Springer, Cham (2022). https://doi.org/10.1007/978-3-030-97546-3_10
9. Främling, K., Graillot, D.: Extracting explanations from neural networks. In: Proceedings of the ICANN, vol. 95, pp. 163–168. Citeseer (1995)
10. Främling, K., Westberg, M., Jullum, M., Madhikermi, M., Malhi, A.: Comparison of contextual importance and utility with LIME and shapley values. In: Calvaresi, D., Najjar, A., Winikoff, M., Främling, K. (eds.) EXTRAAMAS 2021. LNCS

(LNAI), vol. 12688, pp. 39–54. Springer, Cham (2021). https://doi.org/10.1007/978-3-030-82017-6_3

11. Gilpin, L.H., Bau, D., Yuan, B.Z., Bajwa, A., Specter, M., Kagal, L.: Explaining explanations: an overview of interpretability of machine learning. In: 2018 IEEE 5th International Conference on Data Science and Advanced Analytics (DSAA), pp. 80–89. IEEE (2018)

12. Knapič, S., Malhi, A., Saluja, R., Främling, K.: Explainable artificial intelligence for human decision support system in the medical domain. Mach. Learn. Knowl. Extr. 3(3), 740–770 (2021)

13. Lundberg, S.M., Lee, S.I.: A unified approach to interpreting model predictions. In: Guyon, I., et al. (eds.) Advances in Neural Information Processing Systems, vol. 30, pp. 4765–4774. Curran Associates, Inc. (2017). http://papers.nips.cc/paper/7062-a-unified-approach-to-interpreting-model-predictions.pdf

14. Miller, T.: Explanation in artificial intelligence: insights from the social sciences. Artif. Intell. **267**, 1–38 (2019). https://arxiv.org/abs/1706.07269

15. Molnar, C.: Interpretable machine learning. In: Interpretable Machine Learning: A Guide for Making Black Box Models Explainable. Creative Commons License (2020). https://christophm.github.io/interpretable-ml-book/simple.html

16. Rehman Zafar, M., Mefraz Khan, N.: Dlime: A deterministic local interpretable model-agnostic explanations approach for computer-aided diagnosis systems. arXiv pp. arXiv-1906 (2019)

17. Ribeiro, M.T., Singh, S., Guestrin, C.: Why should i trust you?: explaining the predictions of any classifier. In: Proceedings of the 22nd ACM SIGKDD International Conference on Knowledge Discovery and Data Mining, pp. 1135–1144. ACM (2016)

18. Shankaranarayana, S.M., Runje, D.: ALIME: autoencoder based approach for local interpretability. In: Yin, H., Camacho, D., Tino, P., Tallón-Ballesteros, A.J., Menezes, R., Allmendinger, R. (eds.) IDEAL 2019. LNCS, vol. 11871, pp. 454–463. Springer, Cham (2019). https://doi.org/10.1007/978-3-030-33607-3_49

19. Towell, G.G., Shavlik, J.W.: Extracting refined rules from knowledge-based neural networks. Mach. Learn. **13**(1), 71–101 (1993). https://doi.org/10.1007/BF00993103

20. Van Lent, M., Fisher, W., Mancuso, M.: An explainable artificial intelligence system for small-unit tactical behavior. In: Proceedings of the National Conference on Artificial Intelligence, pp. 900–907, Menlo Park, CA. AAAI Press, MIT Press 1999 (2004)

Evaluating Explanations
of an Alzheimer's Disease 18F-FDG Brain
PET Black-Box Classifier

Lisa Anita De Santi[1,2]([envelope]) [iD], Filippo Bargagna[1,2] [iD],
Maria Filomena Santarelli[3] [iD], and Vincenzo Positano[2] [iD]

[1] Department of Information Engineering, University of Pisa, Pisa, Italy
lisa.desanti@phd.unipi.it
[2] U.O.C. Bioingegneria, Fondazione G. Monasterio CNR-Regione Toscana,
Pisa, Italy
[3] CNR Institute of Clinical Physiology, Pisa, Italy

Abstract. eXplainable Artificial Intelligence (XAI) has been increasingly applied to interpret Deep Neural Networks (DNN) in medical imaging applications, but a general consensus about the best interpretation strategy is missing. This is also due to the absence of a validated framework to assess the quality of the explanations/interpretations produced by different XAI methods. This work aims to quantify the ability of interpretation techniques of producing good explanations and non-misleading representations of what a black-box model has learned. We selected a DNN which classifies 18F-FDG PET images according to the cognitive decline in Alzheimer's disease, and we applied two different interpretability methods commonly employed in bioimaging: attribution maps (Backpropagation, GradCAM++, Layerwise Relevance Propagation), and latent space interpretation (t-SNE, UMAP, TriMAP, PaCMAP). We evaluated the interpretations using different literature frameworks: evaluation of attribution maps with imaging biomarkers and region perturbation, and preservation of data local and global structure of the latent space. Results suggested that we are not able to observe a clear relationship between the PET signal and attribution maps, highlighting the importance of not assuming that XAI explanations should reflect the human's reasoning. Layerwise Relevance Propagation best explains the classifier's decisions according to the region-perturbation evaluation, confirming literature results. Finally, the UMAP and the TriMAP embedding respectively reported the best result for the preservation of the local and the global data structure, which is, to the best of our knowledge, the first systematic assessment in the medical imaging domain, and in line with theoretical background of the methods employed.

Keywords: Medical Imaging · Black-box DL · Posthoc Explanations · Attribution Maps · Latent Space Interpretation · Evaluating XAI

© The Author(s), under exclusive license to Springer Nature Switzerland AG 2023
L. Longo (Ed.): xAI 2023, CCIS 1901, pp. 558–581, 2023.
https://doi.org/10.1007/978-3-031-44064-9_30

1 Introduction

Deep Learning (DL) models such as Convolutional Neural Networks (CNN) have been successfully applied in different medical imaging tasks, but their *"black-box"* nature makes their application in systems that involve high-stakes decisions controversial from a legal, ethical, safety, and trustworthiness point of view [3,17,29,33,40]. Factors such as their complex multilayer architectures, characterized by thousands or millions of parameters and non-linear elements, and the multidimensionality of input data make DL models opaque and not interpretable by a human observer, so it's difficult to explain how and why a DL model maps inputs to outputs. The research field of eXplainable Artificial Intelligence (XAI) aims to overcome the obscure nature which characterizes this kind of system.

The issue of interpretability and transparency is also gaining the attention of regulatory bodies. It's often reported by the XAI community the so-called *"right to explanation"* outlined by The General Data Protection Regulation (EU) 2016/679 (GDPR) [15,41,47]. In the more recent AI Act Proposal, the European Commission is discussing the issue of the black-box nature of certain AI models. The European Parliament proposed a proportional risk-based approach with a series of requirements for high-risk AI systems [13,53]. Medical devices, like medical imaging software including AI algorithms, according to the AI Act classification, are considered high-risk systems. Hence, the black-box nature of DL models may pose controversial during the process of certificate of conformity of the device. Despite The European Medical Devices Regulation (EU) 2017/745 (EU MDR) does not explicitly preclude manufacturers from placing "inexplicable" devices on the market to date, its potential integration with the AI Act may suggest that XAI research will directly impact the industrial development of medical devices.

XAI has been increasingly applied in the medical imaging domain, and several XAI techniques have been proposed in this field. Available approaches focus on developing new classes of predictors which can be considered inherently interpretable, producing post-hoc explanations to the prediction returned by an obscure model or trying to inspect certain characteristics of the model. To date, each strategy presents its strength and limitation, and there is still no unique approach to deal with the *"open the black-box"* problem. An extensively used method in deep learning-based medical imaging analysis is Attribution Maps [41], often also referred to as Visual Explanations [47] or Saliency-based methods [6], which consists in the generation of a heatmap to explain single prediction which has the same dimension of the input image, indicating the importance of each voxel for the final classification decision returned by an AI model. Heatmap generation can be exploited as an intuitive and immediate investigation tool to explain what drives and contributes to the predictor's decisions [34]. As the feature space of the CNN consists of hundreds of features, it is not possible to interpret them to visualize intra-class and inter-class similarities, outliers, and other data structure information. It may be helpful to visualize extracted data features in a low-dimensional space where the significant structure of the data is preserved [41] to provide a depiction/intuition of how they are arranged in the representation learned by the network [6]. In this way, we can visualize how DL models change the representation of input data through the network layers: that is visualize the *"deep-features"* in a reduced space. This approach, referred to in the literature as Latent Space Interpretation [41], involves the usage of dimensionality reduction (DR) techniques.

Several works that examined the interpretability of Deep Neural Networks (DNN) for medical imaging applications drew attention to the question of the evaluation of explanations [6,41,45,47]. The usage of quantitative metrics to evaluate explanations is a fundamental step to verify that the explanations produced are robust, sensitive to model and data, and consistent [47]. However, the definition itself of the quality of explanation produced can be non-trivial, for example, because can be subjective to the specific problem faced and area of expertise of the model's user, so it's still considered an open discussion. Furthermore, the absence of available ground truth to compare the explanations generated makes the evaluation and quantification of the quality of explanations a great challenge [41]. Salahuddin et al. [41] grouped the evaluation strategies of interpretability methods for explaining Deep Learning models for medical imaging analysis tasks into: (1) Evaluation in a clinical setting; (2) Evaluation using imaging biomarkers; (3) Evaluation against adversarial perturbation. The *evaluation in a clinical setting* assesses the satisfaction with the provided explanations of the end-users, that is the medical doctor. The peculiarities of high-stakes decision systems make the involvement of domain expert users a key issue in the evaluation process of explanation strategies, in order to assess the effective impact of XAI methods on diagnostic performance. Due to this aspect, the XAI research is closely tied to the field of human-computer interaction (HCI) and human-centered AI, which considers real-world scenarios where users collaborate with the AI system with a *human-in-the-loop* paradigm [4,8,45]. The *evaluation using imaging biomarkers* is defined as the usage of quantifiable features or structure in an image suitable for the diagnosis and prognosis of disease to check if the DL model uses clinically relevant features [41]. This can be considered an evaluation strategy based on prior knowledge/experience of what is regarded as being relevant [42]. However, when assessing explanations' quality according to prior knowledge, we should be aware that an explanation like an attribution heatmap always represents the classifier's view: there is no guarantee that classifier explanations match human intuition nor focus on the object of interest. Explanation produced may strongly depend on the type and quality of the classifier: a model trained on flawed data may learn nonsensical relations, which are in turn shown by the explanations, but which can be perceived as being wrong although they are truthfully reflecting the model's reasoning [37,42]. Consequently, alternative approaches, which may fall under the *evaluation against adversarial perturbation*, suggested the execution of a certain perturbation process of the input data signal, data labels of model parameters, and the usage of evaluation metrics to quantify the faithfulness of the explanation to the AI model's internal decision process [1,16,42].

Practitioners should be aware in assuming that explanations produced by XAI techniques always accurately replicate the model's logic [37]. Despite attribution maps are the most commonly employed method to explain prediction returned by a medical imaging black-box classifier [47], several studies have pointed out several criticisms [1,6,9,12,16,41,46,47]. Adebayo et al. [1] developed a general evaluation framework based on a statistical randomization test and discovered that the explanations produced are unrelated neither to the model's parameter nor data. Ghorbani et al. [16] developed a perturbation scheme to systematically characterize the robustness of interpretation methods. They generated for each image a perceptively indistinguishable image equally classified by the model, and they observed that their corresponding attribution maps substantially differ from each other. This highlighted the vulnerability of visual explanation to adversarial attacks. Rudin has furthermore pointed out [9] that visual explanation techniques are able to produce only incomplete explanation: they can determine what part of the image a black-box model "looks", but they still do not provide information about how the classifier uses the relevant information to return their predictions. Providing only partial insights about the model's behaviour may be misleading and can instil a false sense of confidence both in the model and in the explanation method. The evaluation of visual explanation is also gaining attention in the medical imaging domain and we can find different recent works in literature where authors developed new guidelines and/or applied evaluation frameworks to assess the appropriateness of attribution maps in depicting the logic implemented by the medical diagnostic decision-making system [22,23,35,45]. Jin et al. [22] defined five different clinical XAI desiderata in this context: (1) Understandability to the clinical users; (2) Clinical relevance according to the physicians' decision-making process; (3) Truthfulness in reflecting the black-box's decision-making process (which can be also referred to as faithfulness); (4) Informative plausibility according to the user's judgement; (5) Computational efficiency in generating explanations. The approaches employed differ from research to research, confirming how the evaluation of XAI can still be considered as a developing field.

As concerns the latent space interpretation, despite manifold learning being believed to be good at handling nonlinear data and discovering their intrinsic local geometry in the low-dimensional embedding, rigorous theory and techniques to evaluate its efficiency in maintaining the data structure are rarely investigated in the existing literature [18]. To perform DR, manifold learning techniques introduce information loss, and existing approaches can be distinguished into global and local methods. Global methods focus on preserving distances between points farther away from each other in high-dimensional data, but they generally cannot capture complex nonlinear structures. On the other hand, local methods are typically able to preserve the set of high-dimensional neighbours for each point and their relative distances, that is the composition of each cluster [49]. Due to the information loss, manifold learning algorithms can be misleading. For instance, they can display cluster structures not present in the original data or show observation as far when they are actually close in the original space [49]. Consequently, supporting manifold learning with quantitative metrics could improve the ability to systematically analyze all the different methods.

This work aims to quantitatively evaluate the ability of several interpretation techniques commonly employed in medical imaging analysis of producing good explanations and non-misleading representations of what a black-box model has learned. We selected a trained CNN, which we refer to as ADNINet, that takes ad input 3D 18F-FDG Brain PET images and classifies them according to the clinical cognitive decline of the patient in Alzheimer's disease: Cognitively Normal (CN), Mild Cognitive Impairment (MCI), and Alzheimer's Disease (AD). To give more insight into the prediction returned by ADNINet we applied two different classes of interpretability methods for DNN [41]: (1) Attribution Maps produced using Backpropagation (BP) [24], Gradient-weighted Class Activation Mapping (GradCAM++) [39], and Layerwise Relevance Propagation (LRP) [44]); and (2) Latent Space Interpretation performed using t-distributed Stochastic Neighbor Embedding (t-SNE) [26], Uniform Manifold Approximation and Projection (UMAP) [30], TriMap [2], and Pairwise Controlled Manifold Approximation Projection (PaCMAP) [49]. As a unified framework to assess results produced by interpretation techniques is still missing, we applied different evaluation strategies proposed in relevant literature: evaluation of attribution maps with imaging biomarkers and region perturbation process and preservation of data global and local structure in latent space interpretation.

2   Materials and Methods

2.1   Clinical Context: 18F-FDG PET in Alzheimer's Disease Diagnosis

Alzheimer's disease (AD) is a neurodegenerative disorder and the most common form of dementia. Current diagnostic criteria involve clinical and neuropsychological tests, but these have shown several limitations for its early detection and lack of objectivity of the final diagnosis [10,21,50,52]. A curative treatment is still missing, and actual regimen therapies aim at delaying the cognitive decline of the patient into a more severe form of dementia. MCI represents a transitional condition between normal ageing and early dementia, but its detection is challenging [32]. Neuroimaging examinations like Positron Emission Tomography (PET) may be useful in AD detection and monitoring. In particular, 18F-FDG PET uses Fluorodeoxyglucose (FDG) marked with a 18F radionuclide to mimic brain cells' glucose metabolism. This technique may highlight brain regions with a reduced glucose metabolism characteristic of AD. Hypometabolic patterns in the early stage of AD typically involve the parietotemporal association cortices, posterior cingulate cortex, and precuneus. With disease progression, areas affected also involved the frontal cortices and expand to the sensorimotor cortex and occipital region [7,19,28].

2.2 Data Collection

Data used in the preparation of this article was obtained from the Alzheimer's Disease Neuroimaging Initiative (ADNI) database (adni.loni.usc.edu). The ADNI was launched in 2003 as a public-private partnership, led by Principal Investigator Michael W. Weiner, MD. The primary goal of ADNI has been to test whether serial magnetic resonance imaging (MRI), positron emission tomography (PET), other biological markers, and clinical and neuropsychological assessment can be combined to measure the progression of MCI and early AD.

We selected 3D 18F-FDG PET images pre-processed by the ADNI team with the highest level of preprocessing (Co-reg, Avg, Std Img and Vox Siz, Uniform Resolution). Scans collected are constituted by $160 \times 160 \times 96$ 1.5 mm isotropic voxels. Complete details about acquisition protocols and pre-processing steps can be found on the ADNI website (http://www.adni-info.org/).

Images used to produce and evaluate explanations belong to a subset of the ADNI 18F-FDG PET database randomly sampled by maintaining the original exams' class distribution. We collectively selected 510 exams as follow: 183 CN, 230 MCI, and 97 AD. As we employed a publicity available dataset, for reproducibility purposes, we reported as supplementary material the comprehensive list of all the exams selected. We selected an already trained CNN architecture from the work of De Santi et al. [43] that we refer to as ADNINet. The developed model is publicly available and can be downloaded at https://github.com/Alzheimer-PET-XAI/3DCNN-SM-LRP.

2.3 Black-Box Interpretation Techniques

Attribution Maps. Attribution maps can be produced using different methods [47]. We selected three different techniques which belong to the so-called *Backpropagation-based* (or even *Gradient-based*) methods: explanation heatmaps generation is based in computing the gradient of the prediction score respects to the input features (that is, the pixels of input image). In particular, we performed: (1) Backpropagation (BP), [24]; (2) Gradient-weighted Class Activation Mapping (GradCAM++), [39]; and (3) Layerwise Relevance Propagation (LRP), [44]. Further details about theoretical backgrounf of each algorithm are reported in Appendix in Table 5. For each PET scan, we generated a single heatmap for all the class scores predicted by the black-box model. This results in 9 attribution maps for every input image (a CN heatmap, an MCI heatmap, and an AD heatmap produced using BP, GradCAM++, and LRP). We produced explanations both for the images that had been correctly classified by the network and for those misclassified.

Latent Space Interpretation. We used manifold learning to dimensionally reduce the features extracted by ADNINet in the layer before the final classification. The original features space consists of 32 dimensions (number of neurons in the inspected layer). We selected four different techniques to produce this kind of embedded representation of the ADNINet's feature space: (1) t-distributed Stochastic Neighbor Embedding (t-SNE), [26]; (2) Uniform Manifold Approximation and Projection (UMAP), [30]; (3) TriMap, [2]; and (4) Pairwise Controlled Manifold Approximation Projection (PaCMAP), [49]. t-SNE and UMAP are traditionally considered as local methods, while TriMap belong to the class of global method. PaCMAP is a recently proposed approach designed to preserve both local and global data structure [49]. All the algorithms are based on the construction of a graph where nodes correspond to the observations x_i in the high-dimensional space, and weighted edges represent the similarity between nodes according to a certain metric [49]. Then, a loss function based on the graph structure is defined and optimized to find the low-dimensional data representation y_i. More insights are reported in Appendix in Table 6.

2.4 Quantitative Assessment of Interpretation

As previously mentioned, the development of general metrics to evaluate the quality of XAI approaches is still an open challenge and to date, there is no quantitative metrics applicable for all interpretability methods. Due to this, we decided to assess the different XAI methods using different evaluation frameworks found in the literature: Evaluation of attribution maps using (1) imaging biomarkers and (2) region perturbation, and assessment of (3) local and (4) global data structure preservation by manifold learning techniques for DNN's latent space interpretation.

Attribution Maps

Evaluation Using Imaging Biomarkers. We performed the evaluation of the attribution maps using imaging biomarkers starting from the work of De Santi et al. [43] to inspect their characteristics and the relationship between them and the PET signal.

We registered all the input images and the corresponding attribution maps explanations with the Cerebrum Atlas (CerebrA) along with the MNI-ICBM2009c average template [27]. We selected a brain atlas with a finer level of anatomical details compared to De Santi et al. [43]. For all the exams we evaluated the average PET signal of the registered images and the average importance highlighted by the registered attribution maps in every region of the anatomic atlas. For each type of attribution map ((1) BP CN; (2) BP MCI; (3) BP AD; (4) GradCAM++ CN; (5) GradCAM++ MCI; (6) GradCAM++ AD; (7) LRP CN; (8) LRP MCI; (9) LRP AD) we averaged the importance assigned to each brain region between the subjects, and we sorted the regions in descending order the brain regions according to their average importance.

We used statistical inference to test where the average PET signal significantly differs between subjects with a different level of cognitive decline. All the details about the statistical tests performed were reported in the "Statistical Methods" section. For each class, we selected brain regions where statistical tests highlighted a significant difference in the average signal with at least one of the other classes. We computed the Point-biserial Correlation Coefficient (PbCC) to evaluate if the magnitude of the average importance assigned to the brain regions for a certain class correlates with the presence of a significant statistical difference in the averaged PET signal within the regions with respect to the other classes. In other words, we tested if the regions considered most relevant for the prediction of a certain class by an attribution mapping technique are those where statistical inference had highlighted a significant difference in the PET signal of the selected class of subjects.

Evalution Using Region Perturbation. We performed the evaluation of attribution maps using region perturbation applying the methodology proposed by Samek et al. [42]. This kind of evaluation framework is based on a greedy perturbation process: we assessed how the score of the label predicted disappears when we progressively perturb information from the input image following the ordering induced by the heatmapping function. Input images were perturbed following the *Most Relevant First (MoRF)* criteria. Given: (i) x : Input image; (ii) f : Black-box classifier; (iii) r_p : Encoded location of pixel p on the input image's grid of pixels; and (iv) $h_p = H(x, f, r_p)$: Heatmapping function; the score h_p indicate how important the pixel p at the location r_p of the image is for representing the image class $H(.)$ e.g. BP, GradCAM++, LRP. The heatmapping function induce an ordering $O = (r_1, r_2, ..., r_L)$ such that locations in the image that are most relevant for the class encoded by the classifier f will be found at the beginning of the sequence O: $(i < j) \Leftrightarrow (H(x, f, r_i) > H(x, f, r_j))$ The perturbation recursive formula is: (1) $x_{MoRF}^{(0)} = x$; (2) $\forall 1 \leq k \leq L : x_{MoRF}^{(k)} = g(x_{MoRF}^{(k-1)}, r_k)$.

We progressively replaced the pixels in the input image in a 9×9 neighborhood around the first 100 location (they focused only on the most relevant regions). Where $g(.)$ is a function which perturb information of the image $x_{MoRF}^{(k-1)}$ in a 9×9 neighborhood of location r_k. Pixel's perturbation was performed sampling from a random uniform distribution. Each perturbation step defines a point in the *MoRF* perturbation curve, which is computed by assessing the difference between the score associated with a certain class by the classification function for the original input image and the classification output returned for the image at $k - th$ perturbation step. The quantity of interest used to compare different heatmapping methods is the Area Over the *MoRF* Perturbation Curve $(AOPC)$. The $AOPC$ value is computed by averaging over all the images in the dataset and repeating the perturbation process 10 times in order to reduce the effect of randomness. $AOPC$ is defined as: $AOPC = \frac{1}{L+1} \left\langle \sum_{k=0}^{L} f\left(x_{MoRF}^{(0)}\right) - f\left(x_{MoRF}^{(k)}\right) \right\rangle_{p(x)}$ Where $\langle . \rangle_{p(x)}$ denotes the average over all images in the dataset. Heatmaps which rank first the most sensitive regions will have a steep decrease of the *MoRF* graph and thus larger $AOPC$.

Latent Space Interpretation. We assessed the quality of the four manifold methods considering the framework proposed by Wang et al. [49].

Preservation of Data Local Structure. We measured the preservation of data local structure using K-Nearest Neighbors (KNN) accuracy and Support Vector Machine (SVM) accuracy. The baseline is computed in the original high-dimensional (32-dimensional) feature space. KNN Accuracy is computed by applying leave-one-out cross-validation using the KNN classifier and tuning for the number of neighbors k. When the manifold method does not preserve neighborhoods, the prediction accuracy of KNN should deviate from the baseline. The SVM accuracy is still a measure of the neighborhoods' cohesiveness, with the ability to more flexibly manage data distribution compared to the KNN accuracy. We trained an SVM model with a radial basis function (RBF) kernel using 5-fold cross-validation.

Preservation of Data Global Structure. We measured the preservation of global structure using Random Triplet (RT) Accuracy. RT Accuracy is constituted by the percentage of triplets whose relative distance in the high- and low-dimensional spaces maintain their relative order. We used a random sample of triplets for numerical tractability, applied this metric five times, and reported the mean value and standard deviation.

2.5 Statistical Methods

We used statistical inference to identify atlas brain regions in which the average PET signal significantly differs according to the clinical cognitive decline. Firstly, we tested if the averaged PET signal in the selected region belong to a Gaussian distribution for all three classes of subjects. Then, we performed Bartlett's test to verify if all the distributions are characterized by equal variances. If the three distributions of the average PET signal inside the brain region are homoscedastic Gaussian populations, we used one-way ANOVA to identify if we have at least one distribution that differs from the others; otherwise, we applied the non-parametric Kruskal Wallis test. If ANOVA/Kruskal Wallis identified at least one group of samples which differs from the others, we performed a posthoc comparison using respectively pairwise t-test and Dunn test. All Statistical Test has been executed using a significance $\alpha = 0.05$.

2.6 Hardware and Software Specification

The proposed XAI methods was implemented using Python utilities (version 3.9) on an Intel Core i7 5.1 MHz PC, 32 Gb RAM, equipped with an NVIDIA RTX3090 GPU with 24 Gb of embedded RAM. We produced the attribution maps using the keras-vis package (version 0.8.1) [25] for both BP and Grad-CAM++, while for the LRP Maps we used the implementation of Bohle et al. [34]. Image registration was performed using SimpleITK interface [5] while statistical inference was implemented using Python library SciPy [48]. To perform the dimensionality reduction with manifold learning, we employed the following package publicly available: t-SNE [38], UMAP [31], TriMAP [2], and PaCMAP [49].

3   Results

3.1   Attribution Maps

Evaluation Using Imaging Biomarkers. In Table 1, Table 2, and Table 3 we reported the 15 most important brain regions for every attribution mapping method. Brain regions where statistical inference highlighted a significant difference in the average PET signal are reported as Supplementary Material. In Fig. 1 we reported the PbCC between the average level of importance assigned to each brain region and the presence of a relevant difference in PET signal according to the cognitive decline.

Table 1. Top 15 regions for the CN, MCI, and AD BP attribution maps. RH states for Right Hemisphere and LH states for Left Hemisphere

Backpropagation, (BP)		
Class CN	Class MCI	Class AD
Caudate RH	Pars Orbitalis RH	Pars Orbitalis RH
Pars Orbitalis LH	Caudate RH	Caudate RH
Putamen LH	Inferior temporal RH	Pars Triangularis RH
Thalamus LH	Rostral Middle Frontal LH	Putamen LH
Thalamus RH	Middle Temporal RH	Middle Temporal RH
Pars Triangularis LH	Pars Triangularis RH	Pars Orbitalis LH
Rostral Middle Frontal LH	Pars Triangularis LH	Thalamus LH
Pars Orbitalis RH	Pars Orbitalis LH	Rostral Middle Frontal RH
Accumbens Area LH	Accumbens Area RH	Inferior temporal RH
Lateral Orbitofrontal LH	Lateral Orbitofrontal RH	Accumbens Area LH
Isthmus Cingulate RH	Putamen LH	Rostral Middle Frontal LH
Inferior temporal RH	Rostral Middle Frontal RH	Pars Triangularis LH
Isthmus Cingulate LH	Thalamus RH	Thalamus RH
Inferior Parietal RH	Lateral Orbitofrontal LH	Inferior Parietal RH
Accumbens Area RH	Accumbens Area LH	Lateral Orbitofrontal RH

Evaluation Using Region Perturbation. In Fig. 2 we reported the AOPC of the three different heatmapping methods.

3.2   Latent Space Interpretation

Figure 3 reported the 2-dimensional projection applying all the different manifold learning strategies to the 32-dimensional feature space extracted by the ADNINet's layer before the final classification. Figure 4, and Table 4 show the average KNN, SVM, and RT accuracies to measure the embeddings' quality of the ADNINet latent space before the final classification layer.

Table 2. Top 15 regions for the CN, MCI, and AD GradCAM++ attribution maps. RH states for Right Hemisphere and LH states for Left Hemisphere

GradCAM++		
Class CN	Class MCI	Class AD
Fourth Ventricle RH	Transverse Temporal LH	Fourth Ventricle RH
Fourth Ventricle LH	Rostral Middle Frontal RH	Fourth Ventricle LH
Vermal lobules I-V RH	Thalamus RH	Vermal lobules I-V RH
Cerebellum White Matter RH	Rostral Anterior Cingulate RH	Cerebellum White Matter RH
Parahippocampal LH	Lingual RH	Parahippocampal LH
Lingual RH	Lateral Ventricle RH	Lingual RH
Vermal lobules I-V LH	Middle Temporal LH	Vermal lobules I-V LH
Pericalcarine LH	Parahippocampal RH	Pericalcarine LH
Transverse Temporal LH	Hippocampus RH	Transverse Temporal LH
Vermal lobules VI-VII RH	Cuneus RH	Vermal lobules VI-VII RH
Lateral Orbitofrontal LH	Fusiform RH	Lateral Orbitofrontal LH
Parahippocampal RH	Lateral Occipital RH	Parahippocampal RH
Medial Orbitofrontal LH	Ventral Diencephalon RH	Medial Orbitofrontal LH
Lateral Occipital RH	Lateral Occipital LH	Lateral Occipital RH
Pericalcarine RH	Cerebellum Gray Matter RH	Pericalcarine RH

Table 3. Top 15 regions for the CN, MCI, and AD LRP attribution maps. RH states for Right Hemisphere and LH states for Left Hemisphere

Layerwise Relevance Propagation, (LRP)		
Class CN	Class MCI	Class AD
Putamen LH	Putamen LH	Putamen LH
Thalamus LH	Thalamus LH	Thalamus LH
Rostral Middle Frontal RH	Rostral Middle Frontal RH	Rostral Middle Frontal RH
Pars Orbitalis LH	Pars Orbitalis LH	Pars Orbitalis LH
Putamen RH	Putamen RH	Putamen RH
Lateral Orbitofrontal LH	Lateral Orbitofrontal LH	Lateral Orbitofrontal LH
Lateral Occipital RH	Lateral Occipital RH	Lateral Occipital RH
Rostral Middle Frontal LH	Rostral Middle Frontal LH	Rostral Middle Frontal LH
Thalamus RH	Thalamus RH	Thalamus RH
Pars Orbitalis RH	Pars Orbitalis RH	Pars Orbitalis RH
Lateral Orbitofrontal RH	Lateral Orbitofrontal RH	Lateral Orbitofrontal RH
Accumbens Area LH	Accumbens Area LH	Accumbens Area LH
Pars Triangularis LH	Pars Triangularis LH	Pars Triangularis LH
Lateral Occipital LH	Lateral Occipital LH	Lateral Occipital LH
Pericalcarine RH	Pericalcarine RH	Pericalcarine RH

Pointwise-biserial Correlation Coefficient (PbCC)

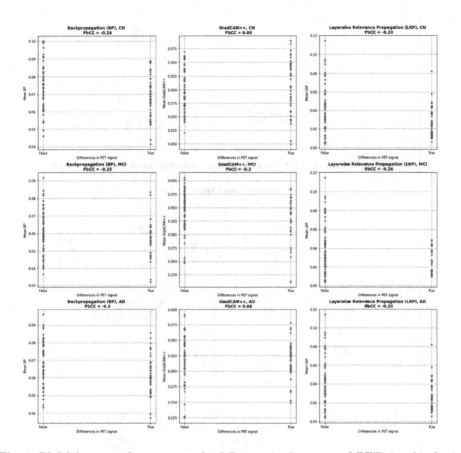

Fig. 1. PbCC between the presence of a difference in the averaged PET signal in brain regions for a certain class of subjects (False = No difference; True = Difference) and the importance assigned to the brain region by the heatmapping technique. We want to verify if the attribution maps recognize as most important the brain regions where the PET signal varies according to the subject's class.

4   Discussion

In this work, we applied several frameworks to quantitatively evaluate different interpretation techniques of an Alzheimer's disease 18F-FDG PET black-box classifier. We assessed the explanation's performances of two different types of XAI methods commonly employed in the medical imaging field: attribution maps and latent space interpretation. We evaluated the attribution map explanations produced by comparing them with imaging biomarkers and performing a region-based perturbation process. As concerns the latent space interpretation of the features extracted by the CNN, we assessed the preservation of the local and

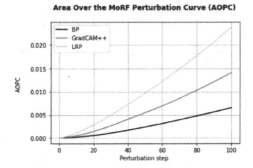

Fig. 2. Comparison of AOPC of the three different heatmapping methods

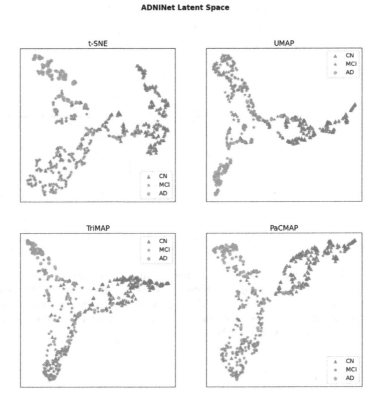

Fig. 3. Dimensionality reduction of features extracted by ADNINet using manifold learning. Each point represents a different PET scan.

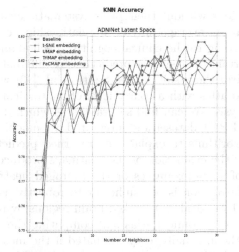

Fig. 4. Local Structure Preservation computed using KNN Accuracy. The best mani-fold representation of latent space according KNN accuracy (that one with KNN accu-racy closest to the baseline) is the UMAP embedding.

Table 4. Original data structure preservation computed using SVM Accuracy (preser-vation of local structure) and RT Accuracy (preservation of global structure)

Metric	Baseline	t-SNE	UMAP	TriMAP	PaCMAP
SVM Accuracy	0.83 ± 0.02	0.82 ± 0.03	0.82 ± 0.02	0.82 ± 0.02	0.82 ± 0.02
RT Accuracy	-	0.88 ± 0.00	0.91 ± 0.01	0.92 ± 0.01	0.90 ± 0.00

global data structure of the original data. We applied all the evaluation frame-works to the case study of Alzheimer's diagnosis from neuroimaging exams, but this analysis can be generalized to other settings.

We performed a quantitative evaluation of attribution maps with imaging biomarkers by applying the evaluation framework proposed by De Santi et al. [43]. From Table 1, 2, and 3 we observed that different heatmapping methods considered as most important different brain regions. This means that differ-ent attribution mapping techniques explain the same predictions returned by the same black-box model in a different way. For example, according to BP, ADNINet considered the Pars Orbitalis RH as the most important region for the prediction of the AD class, while according to LRP the most important brain region for the prediction of AD is the Putamen LH. An attribution map should indicate which part of the input image the black-box model "looks" to produce the output, but such results highly vary according to the attribution mapping technique employed, we should be careful in considering these heatmaps as reliable explanations without their prior systematic evaluation. This evaluation did not reveal, on average, any clear relationship between the difference in PET signal according to the clinical cognitive decline and the brain regions considered as important for the class prediction by different heatmapping techniques. These confirm the results of De Santi et al. [43] which were obtained using an anatomical atlas with a coarse level of anatomical details, which may affect the final analysis. We can find several works which developed a DNN on the ADNI 18F-FDG PET dataset and integrated the model with different attribution mapping algorithms to explain the returned predictions [11,14,20,51]. Most of them based the evaluation of the heatmaps produced on a visual qualitative inspection of single examples or the averaged heatmap. However, this kind of anecdotal inspection is not sufficient to robustly assess the validity of XAI methods [37]. Jyoti et al. [20] ranked brain regions by registering the attribution maps with an anatomical atlas and computing the average importance inside each one of them. Finally, they evaluated if the most important regions according to the attribution maps match with regions typically affected by brain hypometabolism in AD according to the medical literature.

However, we should be aware that explanations do not necessarily reflect the human's reasoning but the classifier's view, which may use a different method of deduction [37,42]. This aspect suggests to do not limiting the explanations assessment to an image biomarker-based evaluation, so we decided to expand our research including an evaluation step based on a perturbation process. In particular, we implemented the framework developed by Samek et al. [42]: we computed the AOPC, which measures the decrease of the score of the predicted class by altering pixels of input images considered as most important by different attribution mapping methods. Larger AOPC implies that the most sensitive regions are ranked first by the heatmap, that is, by altering the pixels considered as most important we obtain a higher decay in the score of the predicted class. Our results suggested that LRP attribution maps, computed using ϵ−rule, performed significantly better compared to BP and GradCAM++ according to the *AOPC* method. These findings are in line with those obtained by Samek et al., which performed the same evaluation on different public datasets. The quantitative assessment of XAI explanations is also gaining attention in the medical imaging domain, and we can find some recent works which evaluated different attribution map algorithms in this field. Muddamsetty et al. [35] tested two different visual explanation methods, Grad-CAM and SIDU [36], to explain predictions of an AI system that classifies retinal fundus images using an evaluation in a clinical setting approach. They generated ground truth heatmaps collecting eye fixation points of ophthalmologist experts which inspected input images using an eye-tracker. Then, they compared explanation heatmaps with the ground truth using the Area Under ROC Curve (AUC) and the Kullback-

Leibler Divergence (KL-DIV). They observed that SIDU performs better than GradCAM for both metrics. Jin et al. [23] systematically evaluated faithfulness (how accurately the explanation reflects the model's true decision process) and plausibility (how explanations agreed with users' prior knowledge) of 16 different XAI visual explanations techniques applied on a multi-modal brain tumor classification tasks in the BraTS 2020 dataset. They proposed two metrics: Modality Importance (MI) correlation and Modality-Specific Feature Importance (MSFI) which evaluated respectively the importance of different modalities in the model and the ability of heatmaps in localizing modality-dependent important features, which can both be considered as modality specific evaluations. They also performed a perturbation experiment in input images according to the heatmaps' importance to quantify the degree of performance deterioration using the difference of AUC (diffAUC) with respect to a random perturbation. They observed that all XAI methods produced poor and unstable explanations according to the evaluations performed, highlighting the risk of applying visual explanations in medical imaging tasks. Jin et al. [22] expand their work by defining five different clinical XAI guidelines and assessing truthfulness (equivalent to faithfulness in this context) using the MI correlation and the ΔAUPC. Authors computed the ΔAUPC performing a similar perturbation experiment compared to their previous work [23] and evaluated the difference of the area under the feature perturbation curve of the XAI heatmapping method and a random perturbation. The ΔAUPC measurement differs from the metric employed in our work such we did not compute the difference with respect to the random baseline. The evaluation results showed that heatmaps did not fulfil truthfulness and informative plausibility suggesting their inadequacy for clinical use. Our attribution maps analysis is closely linked to the truthfulness measurement performed by Jin et al. [22, 23]. Despite the evaluation metrics are not directly comparable, both experiments confirm our concerns in considering visual explanations as a faithful reproduction of the model's reasoning without assessing them with proper evaluation criteria.

As concerns the latent space interpretation, we can find several applications of manifold learning to enhance the model's interpretability; however, most of them limit their analysis to a qualitative visual inspection of the visual cluster projected, and to the best of our knowledge this is the first work that applied this systematic evaluation in the medical imaging domain. Ding et al. [11] applied PCA followed by t-SNE to visualize the features extracted from the training set by a CNN (Inception V3 network) which predict the cognitive decline of the patient from 18F-FDG PET scans. t-SNE dimension reduction highlighted three main clusters and from a visual inspection cluster's purity correlates with CNN's sensitivity and precision. Etminani et al. [14] trained a CNN which performed an almost similar classification task and uses UMAP to project both the original input data and the extracted features by the CNN model before the classification layer both for the training and test set. The UMAP projection of extracted features was able to separate the four classes of the model, CN, MCI due to AD, AD, and Dementia with Lewy Bodies (DLB), well enough. In particular, UMAP projections show that features in DLB cases have been well separated compared to the original data, which may partially explain the good performance of the model. Also in this case authors limited their evaluation to visual analysis. Such there is still no rigorous theory to evaluate the efficiency of manifold techniques in maintaining the intrinsic data structure [18] we decided to apply the framework proposed by Wang et al. [49], to support a systematic evaluation of the outputs produced by different methods. In particular, we used t-SNE, UMAP, TriMAp, and PaCMAP to dimensionally reduce the 32-dimensional features extracted by the ADNINet's layer before the final classification. According to the KNN Accuracy, the UMAP embedding better maintained the original data local structures, while we did not observe significant differences in performances between different methods according to the SVM Accuracy. For the data global structure's preservation, the TriMap method obtained the best results according to the RT Accuracy. These results are in line with the relevant literature, as the UMAP belongs to the class of local methods, while the TriMap to the global methods.

Several limitations can be recognized in the present study. As previously mentioned, we performed our evaluation on a subset of the ADNI database. We chose this configuration as a trade-off between the results' representativeness and computing time, and future work will include an extension of the evaluation to the entire dataset. As concerns the image biomarker-based evaluation of explanations, we performed a global evaluation according to the clinical cognitive decline. This average analysis may lose subject-specific characteristics eventually present both in brain PET scans and attribution maps. So, we plan to extend our work in order to be able to capture all the individual patients' patterns. We chose an evaluation strategy based on region-perturbation following the work of Samek et al. [42] and our results are in line with those obtained by the authors of the work. Setup depends on several experimental choices, e.g. dimension of the perturbed regions, the perturbation function employed, etc. which may affect the final results. We planned to repeat the evaluation by changing the experimental setup in order to assess how this changes the final AOPC metric. In addition, this is only one of the possible evaluation strategies based on a perturbation process, so we plan to extend our research by applying different frameworks, e.g. sensitivity of explanations to the model's parameter and input data [1], and robustness to adversarial attacks [16]. In addition, in order to build AI systems which integrate explanation feedback that enables better diagnostic performance, the evaluation of the explanations' impact should inevitably involve the end-user feedback [4,8]. This human-centered perspective defines another promising research direction of XAI evaluation techniques, which is the assessment of their effectiveness in a clinical setting. Finally, we applied different manifold learning strategies to only dimensionally reduced and visualize in a 2D plane the features extracted by the ADNINet in the layer before the final classification. As manifold algorithms depend on several hyperparameters, we are going to evaluate how their changes affect the performances of the preservation of local and global data structures.

5   Conclusion

In our research, we selected a publicity available DNN which classifies 18F-FDG PET scans for Alzheimer's disease, and we applied two different interpretation strategies for black-box models in medical imaging: attribution maps (BP, GradCAM++, LRP), and latent space interpretation (t-SNE, UMAP, TriMAP, PaCMAP). Finally, we evaluated the interpretations using different literature frameworks: evaluation of attribution maps with imaging biomarkers and region perturbation, and preservation of data local and global structure of the latent space. With our research, we wanted to enhance the importance of systematically assessing the quality of explanations and interpretations of black-box models.

The evaluation of XAI is a controversial and still developing field. In the medical imaging domain, most work performed a systematic assessment of XAI attribution maps techniques and, to the best of our knowledge, this is the first work that applied different quantitative evaluation strategies for the latent space interpretation of a black-box model. We would also like to emphasize that the usage of a public dataset and black-box model, the supplementary materials provided, and the definition of all the experimental settings make our work fully reproducible. Results did not highlight, on average, a clear relationship between the PET signal and the attribution maps produced using different techniques. With the region-perturbation evaluation, LRP obtained the highest AOPC, so it best explains the classifier's decisions according to this metric. Finally, in performing dimensionality reduction of the features extracted by the ADNINet in the layer before the final classification, the UMAP better preserved the data local structure while the TriMAP obtained the best results for the global data structure. These findings confirm the literature's results reported and furthermore pointed out the importance of not assuming that outputs produced by XAI's method should reflect human reasoning.

A   Appendix

Table 5. Theoretical details of the different heatmapping methods implemented.

Backpropagation (BP)

$$H_{BP}^c = \frac{\partial y_c}{\partial I}\bigg|_{I_0} \tag{1}$$

Where:

- y_c : Class score function
- I : Input image
- I_0 : Input point where the model is evaluated, that is, the input image for which we want to generate the explanation

---

Gradient-weighted Class Activation Mapping (GradCAM++)

$$\alpha_k^c = \frac{1}{Z} \sum_i \sum_j \frac{\partial y^c}{\partial A_{ij}^k} \tag{2}$$

$$H_{GradCAM}^c = ReLU\left(\sum_k \alpha_k^c A^k\right) \tag{3}$$

Where:

- y_c : Class score function
- A^k : Feature maps of the last convolutional layer
- α_k^c : Importance weight of feature map k for the class c
- $\frac{1}{Z} \sum_i \sum_j (.)$: Global-average-pooling operation, Z is the feature map dimension

---

Layerwise Relevance Propagation (LRP)

$$y_c \approx \sum_{d=1}^V R_d \tag{4}$$

Where:

- y_c : Class score
- R_d : Relevance
- V : Input dimension

Conservation law: $y_c = ... = \sum_{d \in l+1} R_d^{(l+1)} = \sum_{d \in l} R_d^{(l)} = ... = \sum_{d \in 1} R_d^{(1)}$

Relevance of the $i - th$ neuron in the $l - th$ layer: $R_i^{(l)} = \sum_k R_{i \leftarrow k}^{(l,l+1)}$

Where i is the input for neuron k direction during classification time

$$R_i^{(l+1)} = \sum_i R_{i \leftarrow k}^{(l,l+1)} \tag{5}$$

$$\epsilon - rule : R_j = \sum_k \frac{a_j w_{jk}^+}{\epsilon + \sum_j a_j w_{jk}^+} R_k \tag{6}$$

Where:

- a_j : Neuron's activation
- w_{ij} : Model's parameters

$$H_{LRP,\epsilon-rule}^c = R_j \tag{7}$$

LRP technique was implemented using the $\epsilon-$rule. By changing ϵ we modulate the resulting explanation, in our work we left ϵ to its default implementation value of 10^{-6}

Table 6. Theoretical details of the different manifold learning methods implemented.

---

t-distributed Stochastic Neighbor Embedding (t-SNE)

$$Loss_{i,j}^{t-SNE} = \sum_i \sum_j p_{ij} log \frac{p_{ij}}{q_{ij}} \tag{8}$$

Where:

– (i,j) : graph's edges
– p_{ij} : function representing affinities of data points in the original space
– q_{ij} : affinities of data points in the low dimensional space

---

Uniform Manifold Approximation and Projection (UMAP)

$$Loss_{i,j}^{UMAP} = \begin{cases} \overline{w}_{i,j} log(1 + a(||y_i - y_j||_2^2)^b)^{-1} & i,j \text{ neighbors} \\ (1 - \overline{w}_{i,j}) log(1 - (1 + a(||y_i - y_j||_2^2)^b)^{-1}) & \text{otherwise} \end{cases} \tag{9}$$

Where:

– (i,j) : graph's edges
– $\overline{w}_{i,j}$: edge weight function of data points in the original space
– a, b : UMAP's hyperparameters

TriMap

$$Loss_{i,j,k}^{TM} = w_{i,j,k} \frac{s(y_i, y_k)}{s(y_i, y_j) + s(y_i, y_k)} \tag{10}$$

Where:

– $s(y_i, y_j) = (1 + ||y_i - y_j||^2)^{-1}$
– (i,j,k) : graph's edges to that $Distance_{i,j} \leq Distance_{i,k}$
– $w_{i,j,k}$: function of data points in the original space

---

Pairwise Controlled Manifold Approximation Projection (PaCMAP)

$$Loss^{PaCMAP} = w_{NB} \cdot Loss_{NB} + w_{MN} \cdot Loss_{MN} + w_{FP} \cdot Loss_{FP} \tag{11}$$

Where:

– $Loss_{NB} = \sum_{i,j \in n_{NB}} \frac{\tilde{d}_{ij}}{10 + \tilde{d}_{ij}}$

With Near pairs, NB: i's nearest neighbors according $d_{ij}^{2,select} = \frac{||x_i - x_j||^2}{\sigma_{ij}}$ where σ_i is the average distance between i and its Euclidean nearest fourth to sixth neighbors. We selected the $min(n_{NB} + 50, N)$ nearest neighbors according to the Euclidean distance, where N is the total number of observations.

– $Loss_{MN} = \sum_{i,k \in n_{MN}} \frac{d_{ik}}{10000 + d_{ik}}$

With Mid-near pairs, MN: i's second closest observation from 6 samples. We select $n_{MN} = \lfloor n_{NB} \times MN_{ratio} \rfloor$, where default $MN_{ratio} = 0.5$.

– $Loss_{FP} = \sum_{i,l \in n_{FP}} \frac{1}{1 + d_{il}}$

With Further pairs, FP: We sample a number of $n_{FP} = \lfloor n_{NB} \times FP_{ratio} \rfloor$, where default $FP_{ratio} = 2$.

– $\tilde{d}_{ab} = ||y_a - y_b||^2 + 1$
– w_{NB}, w_{MN}, w_{FP} change during iteration, prioritizing the preservation of mid-near pairs in early iteration and resorting local neighborhood in later ones

---

References

1. Adebayo, J., Gilmer, J., Muelly, M., Goodfellow, I., Hardt, M., Kim, B.: Sanity checks for saliency maps (2018). http://arxiv.org/abs/1810.03292
2. Amid, E., Warmuth, M.K.: Trimap: large-scale dimensionality reduction using triplets (2019). http://arxiv.org/abs/1910.00204
3. Amina, A., Mohammed, B.: Peeking inside the black-box: a survey on explainable artificial intelligence (XAI). IEEE Access **6**, 52138–52160 (2018). https://doi.org/10.1109/ACCESS.2018.2870052

4. Bansal, G., Wu, T., Zhou, J.: Does the whole exceed its parts? The effect of AI explanations on complementary team performance. Association for Computing Machinery (2021). https://doi.org/10.1145/3411764.3445717
5. Beare, R., Lowekamp, B., Yaniv, Z.: Image segmentation, registration and characterization in R with simpleitk. J. Stat. Softw. **86**(8), 1–35 (2018). https://doi.org/10.18637/jss.v086.i08. https://www.jstatsoft.org/index.php/jss/article/view/v086i08
6. Borys, K., et al.: Explainable AI in medical imaging: an overview for clinical practitioners – beyond saliency-based XAI approaches. Eur. J. Radiol. 110786 (2023). https://doi.org/10.1016/j.ejrad.2023.110786. https://linkinghub.elsevier.com/retrieve/pii/S0720048X23001006
7. Brown, R.K.J., Bohnen, N.I., Wong, K.K., Minoshima, S., Frey, K.A.: Brain pet in suspected dementia: patterns of altered FDG metabolism. RadioGraphics **34**(3), 684–701 (2014). https://doi.org/10.1148/rg.343135065. PMID: 24819789
8. Cabitza, F., et al.: Rams, hounds and white boxes: investigating human-AI collaboration protocols in medical diagnosis. Artif. Intell. Med. **138** (2023). https://doi.org/10.1016/j.artmed.2023.102506
9. Cynthia, R.: Stop explaining black box machine learning models for high stakes decisions and use interpretable models instead. Nat. Mach. Intell. **1**(5), 206–215 (2019). https://doi.org/10.1038/s42256-019-0048-x
10. DeTure, M.A., Dickson, D.W.: The neuropathological diagnosis of Alzheimer's disease. Mol. Neurodegener. **14**(1), 32 (2019). https://doi.org/10.1186/s13024-019-0333-5
11. Ding, Y., et al.: A deep learning model to predict a diagnosis of Alzheimer disease by using 18F-FDG pet of the brain. Radiology **290**(2), 456–464 (2019). https://doi.org/10.1148/radiol.2018180958. PMID 30398430
12. Doshi-Velez, F., Kim, B.: Towards a rigorous science of interpretable machine learning (2017). http://arxiv.org/abs/1702.08608
13. Ebers, M., Hoch, V.R.S., Rosenkranz, F., Ruschemeier, H., Steinrötter, B.: The european commission's proposal for an artificial intelligence act-a critical assessment by members of the robotics and AI law society (rails). J **4**, 589–603 (2021). https://doi.org/10.3390/j4040043
14. Etminani, K., et al.: A 3D deep learning model to predict the diagnosis of dementia with Lewy bodies, Alzheimer's disease, and mild cognitive impairment using brain 18F-FDG PET. Eur. J. Nucl. Med. Mol. Imaging **49**, 563–584 (2022). https://doi.org/10.1007/s00259-021-05483-0
15. The European Parliament and the Council of the European Union: I (legislative acts) regulations regulation (EU) 2016/679 of the European parliament and of the council of 27 April 2016 on the protection of natural persons with regard to the processing of personal data and on the free movement of such data, and repealing directive 95/46/EC (general data protection regulation) (text with EEA relevance)
16. Ghorbani, A., Abid, A., Zou, J.: Interpretation of neural networks is fragile (2019). https://www.aaai.org/
17. Guidotti, R., Monreale, A., Ruggieri, S., Turini, F., Giannotti, F., Pedreschi, D.: A survey of methods for explaining black box models. ACM Comput. Surv. **51**(5) (2018). https://doi.org/10.1145/3236009
18. Han, H., Li, W., Wang, J., Qin, G., Qin, X.: Enhance explainability of manifold learning. Neurocomputing **500**, 877–895 (2022). https://doi.org/10.1016/j.neucom.2022.05.119

19. Hnilicova, P., et al.: Imaging methods applicable in the diagnostics of Alzheimer's disease, considering the involvement of insulin resistance. Int. J. Mol. Sci. **24** (2023). https://doi.org/10.3390/ijms24043325
20. Islam, J., Zhang, Y.: Understanding 3D CNN behavior for Alzheimer's disease diagnosis from brain pet scan (2019). https://doi.org/10.48550/ARXIV.1912.04563. https://arxiv.org/abs/1912.04563
21. Jack, C.R., et al.: NIA-AA research framework: toward a biological definition of Alzheimer's disease. Alzheimer's Dement. **14**(4), 535–562 (2018). https://doi.org/10.1016/j.jalz.2018.02.018
22. Jin, W., Li, X., Fatehi, M., Hamarneh, G.: Guidelines and evaluation of clinical explainable AI in medical image analysis. Med. Image Anal. **84** (2023). https://doi.org/10.1016/j.media.2022.102684
23. Jin, W., Li, X., Hamarneh, G.: Evaluating explainable AI on a multi-modal medical imaging task: can existing algorithms fulfill clinical requirements? (2022). http://arxiv.org/abs/2203.06487
24. Karen, S., Andrea, V., Andrew, Z.: Deep inside convolutional networks: visualising image classification models and saliency maps. Preprint (2013)
25. Kotikalapudi, R., contributors: keras-vis (2017). https://github.com/raghakot/keras-vis
26. Maaten, L.V.D., Hinton, G.: Visualizing data using t-SNE (2008)
27. Manera, A.L., Dadar, M., Fonov, V., Collins, D.L.: Cerebra, registration and manual label correction of mindboggle-101 atlas for mni-icbm152 template. Scientific Data **7** (2020). https://doi.org/10.1038/s41597-020-0557-9
28. Marcus, C., Mena, E., Subramaniam, R.M.: Brain pet in the diagnosis of Alzheimer's disease. Clin. Nucl. Med. **39**(10) (2014)
29. Mauricio, R., et al.: On the interpretability of artificial intelligence in radiology: challenges and opportunities. Radiol. Artif. Intell. **2**(3) (2020). https://doi.org/10.1148/ryai.2020190043. PMID: 32510054
30. McInnes, L., Healy, J., Melville, J.: UMAP: uniform manifold approximation and projection for dimension reduction (2018). http://arxiv.org/abs/1802.03426
31. McInnes, L., Healy, J., Saul, N., Grossberger, L.: UMAP: uniform manifold approximation and projection. J. Open Source Softw. **3**(29), 861 (2018)
32. McKhann, G., Knopman, D., Chertkow, H.: The diagnosis of dementia due to Alzheimer's disease: recommendations from the national institute on aging-Alzheimer's association workgroups on diagnostic guidelines for Alzheimer's disease. Alzheimer's Dement. **7**(3), 263–269 (2011). https://doi.org/10.1016/j.jalz.2011.03.005
33. Montavon, G., Samek, W., Müller, K.R.: Methods for interpreting and understanding deep neural networks. Digit. Signal Process. **73**, 1–15 (2018). https://doi.org/10.1016/j.dsp.2017.10.011. https://www.sciencedirect.com/science/article/pii/S1051200417302385
34. Moritz, B., Fabian, E., Martin, W., Kerstin, R.: Layer-wise relevance propagation for explaining deep neural network decisions in MRI-based Alzheimer's disease classification. Front. Aging Neurosci. **11** (2019). https://doi.org/10.3389/fnagi.2019.00194. https://www.frontiersin.org/article/10.3389/fnagi.2019.00194
35. Muddamsetty, S.M., Jahromi, M.N.S., Moeslund, T.B.: Expert level evaluations for explainable AI (XAI) methods in the medical domain. In: Del Bimbo, A., et al. (eds.) ICPR 2021. LNCS, vol. 12663, pp. 35–46. Springer, Cham (2021). https://doi.org/10.1007/978-3-030-68796-0_3

36. Muddamsetty, S.M., Mohammad, N.S.J., Moeslund, T.B.: SIDU: similarity difference and uniqueness method for explainable AI. In: 2020 IEEE International Conference on Image Processing (ICIP), pp. 3269–3273 (2020). https://doi.org/10.1109/ICIP40778.2020.9190952
37. Nauta, M., et al.: From anecdotal evidence to quantitative evaluation methods: a systematic review on evaluating explainable AI. ACM Comput. Surv. (2023). https://doi.org/10.1145/3583558
38. Pedregosa, F., et al.: Scikit-learn: machine learning in Python. J. Mach. Learn. Res. **12**, 2825–2830 (2011)
39. Selvaraju, R.R., Michael, C., Abhishek, D., Ramakrishna, V., Devi, P., Dhruv, B.: Grad-cam: visual explanations from deep networks via gradient-based localization. In: 2017 IEEE International Conference on Computer Vision (ICCV), pp. 618–626 (2017). https://doi.org/10.1109/ICCV.2017.74
40. Panayides, A.S., et al.: AI in medical imaging informatics: current challenges and future directions. IEEE J. Biomed. Health Inform. **24**(7), 1837–1857 (2020). https://doi.org/10.1109/JBHI.2020.2991043
41. Salahuddin, Z., Woodruff, H.C., Chatterjee, A., Lambin, P.: Transparency of deep neural networks for medical image analysis: a review of interpretability methods. Comput. Biol. Med. **140** (2022). https://doi.org/10.1016/j.compbiomed.2021.105111
42. Samek, W., Binder, A., Montavon, G., Bach, S., Müller, K.R.: Evaluating the visualization of what a deep neural network has learned (2015). http://arxiv.org/abs/1509.06321
43. Santi, L.D., Pasini, E., Santarelli, M., Genovesi, D., Positano, V.: An explainable convolutional neural network for the early diagnosis of Alzheimer's disease from 18F-FDG PET. J. Digit. Imaging **36** (2023). https://doi.org/10.1007/s10278-022-00719-3
44. Sebastian, B., Alexander, B., Montavon, G., Frederick, K., Klaus-Robert, M., Wojciech, S.: On pixel-wise explanations for non-linear classifier decisions by layer-wise relevance propagation. PLoS ONE **10**(7), 1–46 (2015). https://doi.org/10.1371/journal.pone.0130140
45. Sheu, R.K., Pardeshi, M.S.: A survey on medical explainable AI (XAI): recent progress, explainability approach, human interaction and scoring system (2022). https://doi.org/10.3390/s22208068
46. Tomsett, R., Harborne, D., Chakraborty, S., Gurram, P., Preece, A.D.: Sanity checks for saliency metrics (2019). http://arxiv.org/abs/1912.01451
47. van der Velden, B.H., Kuijf, H.J., Gilhuijs, K.G., Viergever, M.A.: Explainable artificial intelligence (XAI) in deep learning-based medical image analysis. Med. Image Anal. **79**, 102470 (2022). https://doi.org/10.1016/j.media.2022.102470. https://www.sciencedirect.com/science/article/pii/S1361841522001177
48. Virtanen, P., et al.: SciPy 1.0: fundamental algorithms for scientific computing in python. Nat. Methods **17**, 261–272 (2020). https://doi.org/10.1038/s41592-019-0686-2
49. Wang, Y., Huang, H., Rudin, C., Shaposhnik, Y.: Understanding how dimension reduction tools work: an empirical approach to deciphering t-SNE, UMAP, TriMAP, and PaCMAP for data visualization. J. Mach. Learn. Res. **22**(201), 1–73 (2021). http://jmlr.org/papers/v22/20-1061.html
50. Weiner, M.W., et al.: The Alzheimer's disease neuroimaging initiative: progress report and future plans. Alzheimer's Dement. **6**(3), 202–11.e7 (2010). https://doi.org/10.1016/j.jalz.2010.03.007

51. Yee, E., Popuri, K., Beg, M.F., Initiative, A.D.N.: Quantifying brain metabolism from FDG-PET images into a probability of Alzheimer's dementia score. Hum. Brain Mapp. **41**(1), 5–16 (2020). https://doi.org/10.1002/hbm.24783. https://pubmed.ncbi.nlm.nih.gov/31507022
52. Young, P.N.E., et al.: Imaging biomarkers in neurodegeneration: current and future practices. Alzheimer's Res. Therapy **12**(1), 49 (2020). https://doi.org/10.1186/s13195-020-00612-7
53. Zanca, F., Brusasco, C., Pesapane, F., Kwade, Z., Beckers, R., Avanzo, M.: Regulatory aspects of the use of artificial intelligence medical software. Semin. Radiat. Oncol. **32**, 432–441 (2022). https://doi.org/10.1016/j.semradonc.2022.06.012

The Accuracy and Faithfullness of AL-DLIME - Active Learning-Based Deterministic Local Interpretable Model-Agnostic Explanations: A Comparison with LIME and DLIME in Medicine

Sarah Holm[✉][iD] and Luis Macedo[iD]

Center for Informatics and Systems of the University of Coimbra, University of Coimbra, Coimbra, Portugal
sarahjholm@gmail.com, macedo@dei.uc.pt

Abstract. The goal of this paper is twofold. Firstly, it aims to introduce a novel eXplainable Artificial Intelligence (XAI) model, AL-DLIME (Active Learning-based Deterministic Local Interpretable Model-Agnostic Explanations), that integrates Active Learning (AL) into the DLIME framework. Secondly, it aims to perform a detailed comparison of LIME, DLIME, and AL-DLIME for medical diagnosis applications, with a focus on assessing the impact of DLIME and AL-DLIME's deterministic behavior on their overall performance. For the purposes of this study, four datasets were selected within some of the areas of medicine that are considered to have the least accuracy in terms of diagnosis, oncology and cardiovascular diseases. As LIME, DLIME, and AL-DLIME are post-hoc XAI algorithms, Random Forest (RF) was selected to serve as the underlying black box model due to its popularity and overall good performance. Furthermore, we employ a Decision Tree (DT) model in order to address the accuracy-explainability tradeoff, more specifically, if the use of a black box model is strictly necessary. The performance of each model was evaluated using several metrics, including accuracy, F1-score, faithfulness to the black box model, single and incremental deletion, and stability measured through Jaccard's distance. Our RF model outperformed DT on all accounts of both accuracy and F1-score, with its highest score of accuracy, 99%, being on par with other state of the art Machine Learning (ML) models. DLIME and AL-DLIME managed to outperform RF on several datasets, with AL-DLIME achieving the best results of accuracy and F1-score overall among all XAI models. However, LIME obtained the overall highest scores of faithfulness to RF, with results consistently above 60%. The study provides insights into the strengths and weaknesses of each XAI model and their suitability for medical diagnosis applications.

This research was supported by the Portuguese Recovery and Resilience Plan (PRR) through project C645008882-00000055, Center for Responsible AI.

L. Longo (Ed.): xAI 2023, CCIS 1901, pp. 582–605, 2023.
https://doi.org/10.1007/978-3-031-44064-9_31

Keywords: Local interpretability and explainability · Active
Learning · LIME · DLIME · XAI metrics · Faithfullness · Accuracy ·
Random Forest · XAI and Medicine

1   Introduction

In recent years, the field of Artificial Intelligence (AI) has evolved tremendously,
garnering significant interest and expanding to include numerous subfields, such
as machine learning (ML), deep learning, natural language processing, and
many more [33, p.16-29]. Nevertheless, many concerns have been raised over
the ethics of AI, especially when considering its most sensitive areas of application [27,30,39]. Some of these concerns, such as those related to privacy, data
protection, bias, and safety, are rooted in real-life events that have shown the
potential danger of AI [13,27,39]. Reliability, accountability, and traceability are
all topics of interest when it comes to discussions of how AI should be regulated.
The common thread among all of these concepts is transparency, and through
transparency there is hope to achieve trust in AI [16,18].

In a study published in 2019 by the High Level Expert Group on AI (AI
HLEG) [16], they determined that, in order to achieve trustworthy AI, the technology should follow four ethical principles: respect for human autonomy, prevention of harm, fairness, and explicability. While the first three are self-explanatory,
serving as a clear reflection of fundamental human rights, the final concept is
something more inherent to AI. When it comes to applications that may have
catastrophic consequences given an instance of misclassification, or even a single
flaw in the algorithm, it is of utmost importance that we understand the origin
of any potential issues. Given the current popularity of algorithms which are,
for all intents and purposes, black boxes, this issue becomes more complex [17].
Therefore, explainability has been proposed to mitigate these concerns, and with
it, the subfield of XAI was formed [22,25].

There are many different fields where AI could be an important asset. However, one of the most critical areas of application is perhaps in medicine, where
any single mistake may cost the life of a patient [38]. Yet, despite the potential benefits of AI in healthcare being vast, good performance is simply seen as
insufficient in regards to garnering approval for use in real life scenarios - or,
more specifically, trust [4,7]. Thus, the potential explainability could offer to
such areas is unparalleled.

One of the most cited XAI models is LIME [32], due to its impressive performance and faithfulness to the underlying black box model. However, despite
its prevalence, the non-deterministic nature of the algorithm means that there
may be differences between explanations regarding the same instance. For applications such as medical diagnoses, where the end-users have no obligation to
understand how these algorithms work, this may cause tension and, therefore,
a loss of trust. It is for this reason that Zafar and Khan proposed DLIME [41],
a deterministic model based on LIME. In their original paper [42], they demonstrated the stability of their proposed model through the use of Jaccard's dis-

tance among a select array of medical-based datasets. However, the lack of evaluation metrics in their original paper limited the comparison between DLIME and LIME. To address this gap, they published a more comprehensive comparison [41], which showed DLIME outperforming LIME in terms of stability and classification quality. However, LIME performed better in terms of faithfulness.

Across both of Zafar and Khan's articles, we recognize that there is still scope for experimentation within the DLIME framework, and despite a lack of metrics to assess the quality of explanations, DLIME's potential for improving medical diagnoses should not be dismissed. As such, in this study we propose AL-DLIME, a novel XAI model that implements Active Learning (AL) within the DLIME framework. By proposing and evaluating AL-DLIME, we hope to contribute to the development of XAI models that can be applied in sensitive and critical domains, such as medicine, with improved performance and transparency. While DLIME is a modified version of LIME that avoids non-determinism and thereby promotes a more stable generation of explanations, AL-DLIME is in turn a modified DLIME in that the clustering stage is substituted by an AL stage, thereby selecting the most informative instances to train the surrogate model (ridge linear regression in our case). Thus, AL-DLIME not only offers the benefit of determinism, an important feature for critical domains such as medicine, but also the possibility of training the surrogate model with a limited number of instances, specifically those that provide the most valuable information. The latter property, in particular, is also of extreme importance in domains where data exists in large quantities, though it is mostly, if not completely, unlabeled, as is the case with medicine. In order to evaluate AL-DLIME, we employed a few metrics, including the faithfulness metric from Ribeiro et al. [32], the metric of stability from Zafar and Kahn [41], and the single and incremental deletion metrics [3,11,19,34]. These measures provide a comprehensive evaluation of the quality of the explanations generated by both XAI models, including their accuracy, consistency, and faithfulness. The results obtained with these metrics by AL-DLIME in four datasets from the field of medicine are confronted with those of the XAI models of LIME and DLIME.

The next section (Sect. 2) describes the related work. In Sect. 3, we present AL-DLIME, with special focus on the differences to DLIME, as well as all the experimental methodology used to assess the accuracy and faithfulness of AL-DLIME, including the datasets and the baseline models with which AL-DLIME is confronted. The results, including their comparison to those of LIME and DLIME, are presented and discussed in Sect. 4. Finally, we draw some conclusions, including the limitations of AL-DLIME, in Sect. 5.

2   Related Work

2.1   AI and Healthcare

With the ability to detect and exploit underlying relationships in vast amounts of data that would otherwise go unnoticed by the human eye, AI is an excellent candidate to be applied to the area of medicine. This becomes especially clear in time-sensitive cases such as cancer and cardiovascular diseases (CVDs), when even the slightest detail may count towards the survival of the patient. As such, many ML models have been developed over the years with the goal of aiding in the diagnostic process.

Several studies have compared different ML models for cancer diagnosis. Lu et al. [23] found that Decision Trees (DT) outperformed ROMA (a mathematical algorithm built for calculating the probability of ovarian cancer) and logistic regression for ovarian cancer prediction, achieving an accuracy, sensitivity, and specificity of 0.921, 1, and 0.899 on the testing data, respectively.

Setiawan et al. [40] also compared DT against logistic regression, with the area of application in this instance being pancreatic cancer diagnosis. Once again, DT outperformed the latter in all evaluation metrics.

Osmanovic et al. [29] compared two DT models from the WEKA tool (more specifically, the J48 and LMT models) with a multilayer perceptron for ovarian cancer detection. In their study, they found that the DT models outperformed the perceptron.

Shan et al. [36] also chose the diagnosis of breast cancer for their study. Among all the models used, Random Forest (RF) outperformed DT, artificial neural networks, and Support Vector Machines (SVM) for breast cancer diagnosis, while SVM achieved a higher value for AUC.

Simegn et al. [37] developed a web-based application for CVD diagnosis, which is composed of three modules: the first, for processing ECG data, the second for predicting heart disease, and, lastly, a multiclassification module for the different types of CVD. Of the two classification modules, RF managed to outperform all other selected ML models.

Ahamad et al. [2] compared several ML models and found that RF, alongside gradient boosting machine and light gradient boosting machine, achieved the best results for accuracy, sensitivity, and AUC. Moreover, the authors provided a calculation of feature importance for each of the models, which may be viewed as a kind of global explainability, as it permits an overall look at one of the most important aspects the ML algorithms used to reach their predictions.

Massafra et al. [24] also focused on feature importance. They found that RF performed well for the prediction of breast cancer recession amid both scopes presented in the study (recession within 5 years, and 10 years).

While all of these studies demonstrate promising results for AI in healthcare, only Ahamad et al. provided some approximation of explainability. Additionally, none of the authors evaluated their models in terms of their target audience, healthcare professionals, which raises concerns about the acceptance of such solutions in the healthcare industry.

2.2   Explainable AI

LIME. With the overall purpose of facilitating trust between humans and black box algorithms, Ribeiro et. al [32] proposed the novel explanation technique of LIME. This XAI algorithm is locally explainable and model agnostic, providing support for both text and image-based datasets, and therefore offering a large realm of application.

In their paper, Ribeiro et. al denote the model being explained as $f : IR_d \rightarrow IR$, with $x \in IR_d$ serving as the representation of an instance to be explained.

The explanation model, with a domain of $\{0,1\}^{d'}$, is described through $g \in G$, wherein G represents a collection of possible XAI models. As a means to measure the explanation's complexity, Ribeiro et. al define $\Omega(g)$.

The model samples instances around x' uniformly and at random, which are denoted by $z' \in \{0,1\}^{d'}$. From these perturbed instances, the original values of $z \in R^d$ are obtained, which are then used to determine $f(z)$, or, in other words, the probability of that instance belonging to a certain class. These samples are weighted by $\pi_x(z)$, which serves as a measure of the proximity between the original instance, x, and the sampled one, z. Through these perturbations, the model aims to observe changes in prediction and, consequently, determine which attributes contribute the most to the model's classifications.

The objective of the LIME algorithm, therefore, is the minimization of the measure $\mathcal{L}(f, g, \pi_x)$, which serves to assess g's unfaithfulness in approximating f in the locality defined by π_x, while maintaining a value of $\Omega(g)$ that is low enough so that g may be interpretable. This is described through Formula 1.

$$\xi(x) = \arg\min_{g \in G} \mathcal{L}(f, g, \pi_x) + \Omega(g) \tag{1}$$

DLIME. Despite LIME's far reach in success and popularity, it is necessary to evaluate how it might be perceived in different situations. Namely, for the purpose of this work, in a medical setting. Due to its non-deterministic nature, in the sense that the surrogate model is trained on randomly perturbed data points, there is always the possibility that LIME may present different explanations for the same instance. This, of course, could place the relationship between the XAI model and health professionals in a precarious situation, as consistency is key to any well-grounded explanation. It is due to this reason that Zafar and Khan proposed DLIME, a deterministic approach to the LIME model [41].

There are two main differences between the LIME and DLIME frameworks. Firstly, DLIME initially utilizes agglomerative hierarchical clustering (AHC) to partition the training dataset into clusters. Originally, all data points correspond to distinct clusters; then, each of these N clusters are merged until only a C number of clusters remain, with C corresponding to the number of classes the original dataset presents (i.e., for a binary dataset, $C = 2$).

Instead of selecting samples in the local proximity to the test instance (x) through random perturbations, DLIME uses the k-nearest neighbors algorithm. In other words, the euclidean distance between x and the surrounding instances is computed, from which the k-nearest instances are selected. Of the instances that are selected, DLIME then determines the most prevalent cluster among them, and the samples with the majority cluster label are used to train the chosen regression model. In this case, the authors chose ridge linear regression.

Following the selection of samples, LIME and DLIME follow the same path of weighting the samples and training the interpretable surrogate model.

2.3 Evaluation Metrics

From the topics addressed in previous sections, we may assume that there is still much to be explored in the field of XAI, namely, evaluation metrics. The "goodness" of an explanation is highly subjective, which lends itself to an equally high difficulty in determining how to evaluate such constructs. Thus, as of yet, there is no gold standard for evaluation metrics regarding XAI models [1,9,14, 26]. Recent strides have been taken to formulate some semblance of a baseline for such purposes, however.

As a more popular example, we have the proposal put forth by Doshi-Velez and Kim [9]. In their article, they define three possible avenues through which XAI evaluation may take place: application-grounded, human-grounded, and functionally-grounded. Application-grounded evaluations involve domain experts who perform an experiment using XAI-generated explanations to determine their quality. Human-grounded evaluations involve laypeople and provide a more general evaluation of explanation quality. Finally, functionally-grounded evaluations aim to evaluate XAI models through formal definitions of explainability, with the ultimate goal of approximating various characteristics through proxies.

Overall, both categories involving humans are costly, though between the two, human-grounded scenarios might be more cost-effective. This may show through tangible expenses to compensate for their involvement, or time spent explaining the experiments, as well as time spent performing them.

In a similar vein, Murdoch et al. [26] present the predictive, descriptive and relevant (PDR) framework. Likewise to Doshi-Velez and Kim, this framework presents three categories - predictive accuracy, descriptive accuracy, and relevancy - through which XAI models may be evaluated. Furthermore, the PDR framework serves also as a guide for the selection and construction of such models.

Predictive accuracy measures how accurately a black box model approximates underlying data relationships. This evaluation aims to assess the performance of the algorithm before it is used for XAI. If the algorithm performs poorly, any explanation derived from it cannot be considered reliable. Descriptive accuracy assesses how well the XAI model approximates the base model, an approach which is most appropriate for post-hoc methods. Finally, relevancy refers to how well the model's explanation fits its application. Similarly to Doshi-Velez and Kim's approaches, relevancy can only be evaluated with human involvement.

A comprehensive survey published by Nauta et al. [28] provides an in-depth view of quantitative evaluation metrics. As a result of an extensive review of 361 papers, the authors define 12 categories for XAI evaluation metrics, which they denominate as the Co-12 properties. These properties were then aligned along three different dimensions: content, presentation, and user. However, it is important to emphasize that the authors recognize that trade-offs may need to be realized, as some categories oppose one another. Therefore, not unlike other aspects of XAI, researchers must carefully consider what aspects are most important to the end-goal of their models, and evaluate them appropriately.

As for concrete metrics, those proposed by the authors of LIME and DLIME are perhaps of most interest. Thus, they will now be explained in further detail.

LIME and DLIME Evaluation Metrics. For the purposes of their paper, Ribeiro et al. [32] defined a few metrics in order to fully evaluate their model. They employed both functionally and human-grounded metrics. For our study, from these metrics we selected that of faithfulness to the model.

In the case of surrogate models such as LIME and DLIME, any explanation that is generated becomes meaningless if the instance it is explaining has no correlation to the original classifier. By training an interpretable classifier with a maximum of 10 features to be used for any individual instance, the authors are left with a gold standard of features for that model. After applying LIME on the test set, they compute the fraction of gold standard features that are used in the XAI model's explanations.

With the aim of measuring the stability of their model, Zafar and Khan [42] used Jaccard's distance in their original paper. Thereafter, they also applied a metric of faithfulness to the black box model [41]. In terms of performance related to DLIME's classifications, they used precision, recall, accuracy, balanced accuracy, and F1-score.

3   Materials and Methods

In order to evaluate the performance of AL-DLIME, we performed a few experiments. The generic AI pipeline we followed is described in the next subsection.

3.1   General Methodology

Our research methodology comprised of the following stages: dataset selection, pre-processing, model optimization, and the application of the post-hoc models LIME, DLIME, and AL-DLIME to the RF algorithm, as well as an evaluation of the performance of their results. With this aim, two experiments were conducted: the first involved the standardization of each dataset, which permitted the addition of two evaluation metrics (single and incremental deletion); as for the second, there was no process of standardization in the pre-processing stage, which, therefore, left only accuracy, F1-score, faithfulness, and Jaccard's distance for evaluation metrics. The subsequent sections of this paper will provide a more thorough explanation of each step.

3.2   Datasets

We considered only tabular datasets, due to DLIME's current limitation to this kind of data. Given the high mortality and misdiagnosis rate of both cancer and CVDs, we selected datasets from these domains. The next sections describe the datasets selected: the breast cancer dataset (BCD), ovarian cancer dataset (OCD), pancreatic cancer dataset (PCD), and heart disease dataset (HDD).

Breast Cancer Dataset. The Wisconsin breast cancer dataset is commonly used for the purpose of evaluating ML classifiers. Available through the UCI ML repository[1], it comprises 569 instances and 30 features, with a binary target (benign, or malignant).

A fine needle aspirate was taken of a breast mass, from which the authors computed 10 core features from each cell nucleus present in the digitized image. These core features are the radius, texture, perimeter, area, smoothness, compactness, concavity, concave points, symmetry, and fractal dimension. Following this, the authors then calculated the mean, standard error, and worst of each core feature, resulting in a total of 30 features. In other words, for each core feature, there exists three different variations (for example, there is a mean radius, standard error radius, and worst radius).

Ovarian Cancer Dataset. This dataset[2], published alongside the study carried out by Lu et al. [23], was constructed with the purpose of ovarian cancer classification, and has a total of 349 instances and 47 features.

The majority of features consist of biomarkers, with the addition of demographic information, such as age, and whether or not the patient has gone through menopause. Once again, the dataset is binary, with classes differentiating between benign ovarian tumors, and malignant ones.

Pancreatic Cancer Dataset. Debernardi et al. [8] collected samples from multiple sources[3], resulting in a dataset containing 590 instances and 12 features. Similarly to the previous dataset, several demographic features are included, such as age and sex, with the remaining features corresponding to various biomarkers.

This is the sole multiclass dataset, with 3 classes to consider: healthy patients; patients with non-cancerous pancreatic conditions (such as pancreatitis); patients with pancreatic cancer, more specifically, pancreatic ductal adenocarcinoma.

Heart Failure Dataset. Finally, we selected the following dataset for CVD classification[4], or, heart disease classification. It is composed of five different heart disease datasets that have been published in the UCI ML repository (all

---

[1] https://archive.ics.uci.edu/ml/datasets/Breast+Cancer+Wisconsin+%28Diagnostic%29.

[2] https://data.mendeley.com/datasets/th7fztbrv9.

[3] https://www.kaggle.com/datasets/johnjdavisiv/urinary-biomarkers-for-pancreatic-cancer.

[4] https://www.kaggle.com/datasets/fedesoriano/heart-failure-prediction.

available under the index of heart disease datasets[5]), with a total of 918 unique instances, and 11 features. The data includes categorical and continuous values, with demographic information regarding the patients, such as age and sex, as well as information resulting from routine tests, such as chest pain type, resting blood pressure, and so forth. Once more, the dataset is binary, describing either healthy individuals, or patients with some sort of heart disease.

3.3 Data Pre-processing

After selecting the datasets, preprocessing was necessary to ensure the data was ready for modeling. Since the majority of the data had been used previously in scientific studies, minimal preprocessing was required. The steps required were data balancing for the OCD and PCD, data cleaning for the PCD, BCD, and HDD, and the standard train-test split of 80-20. Furthermore, once these steps were complete, a copy was made of all datasets, which were then standardized (or, normalized) for use in the first experiment. This is necessary for some models which perform best on data that behaves like standard normally distributed data, as is the case for ridge linear regression [15, p.82].

3.4 AL-DLIME

One of the main contributions of this study is the proposal of AL-DLIME. As aforementioned in Sect. 1, this model is based on the DLIME framework, with one key difference: the use of AL in place of AHC and KNN. This alteration preserves the original model's determinism while exploring an entirely different branch of AI, one which we hope will improve the transparency and interpretability of complex ML models or, at the very least, lend some interest towards future research involving the same concepts. AL is a subfield of ML that focuses on minimizing the amount of labeled instances that is necessary to achieve a good performance [35]. It does so by selecting the most informative instances according to the model's current state of knowledge, and then queries a human oracle or pre-existing, labeled dataset for the correct labels. In the case of the area of medicine, where there is a common problem of large datasets being mostly (or completely) unlabeled due to the medical professionals' lack of time [12,20], AL is understandably an attractive choice [10,31].

There are three main scenarios for the queries made by AL models: membership query synthesis, stream-based selective sampling, and pool-based AL [35]. Membership query synthesis involves the learner generating its own instances from the dataset to query the oracle. Stream-based selective sampling allows the learner to decide whether to query unlabeled instances drawn one at a time using informative measures or query strategies. Pool-based sampling, on the other hand, utilizes the entire pool of unlabeled instances and selects the most informative one for the learner to query.

---

[5] https://archive.ics.uci.edu/ml/machine-learning-databases/heart-disease/.

For the purposes of AL-DLIME, pool-based sampling was selected due to its popularity [6]. However, in cases of limited memory or processing power, stream-based or membership synthesis scenarios are the more preferable option [35]. As for the query strategy, uncertainty sampling was selected. The idea behind this measure is simple, as it focuses on the instances on which the learner is most uncertain about. In the case of probabilistic models in binary settings, this is quite simple. Given the model's predictions, the AL learner need only select those of which present a probability of around 50% of belonging to a certain class. This is the measure that was selected, with logistic regression being the preferred model for probability extraction due to its presence in all of the XAI models used in this study.

The basis of AL-DLIME, therefore, is quite simple. Firstly, a logistic regression model is trained on a small set of labeled data. Following this, the probabilities for class distribution are obtained on a larger, unlabeled set of data through the logistic regression model. A range of uncertainty is selected, which depends on how strict you wish the process of sampling to be. In the case of this study, a range of 47% to 53% was used, as we believed it to be an acceptable representation of the degree of uncertainty we wished to explore. All instances from the previously collected set of probabilities which belonged to this range were then selected as the most informative instances. This process may be viewed in Algorithm 1.

Algorithm 1. Selection of the Most Informative Instances

    Input: Dataset D_{train}, Dataset D_{test}, Labels L_{test}
1: Initialize $S \leftarrow \{\}$
2: Initialize $S_{labels} \leftarrow \{\}$
3: Initialize $ind \leftarrow \{\}$
4: C_{lr} = Create new Logistic Regression model
5: Train C_{lr} with D_{test}
6: y = Probabilities regarding all instances from D_{train} to belong to class 0
7: $p = 0.47$ (uncertainty interval from 0.47 to 0.53)
8: **for** i from 0 to (number of rows in D_{train})-1 **do**
9:     **if** instance i from y is between p and $(1 - p)$ inclusive **then**
10:       $ind_i \leftarrow \{i\}$
11:     **end if**
12: **end for**
13: $S \leftarrow$ Get instances from D_{train} with indices ind
14: $S_{labels} \leftarrow$ Get instances from L_{train} with indices ind
15: **return** S, S_{labels}

Once AL-DLIME has selected a set of instances with the highest level of uncertainty, it proceeds in much the same way as DLIME and LIME (Fig. 1). These instances are then weighted and labeled using the chosen black box model (which, in the case of our paper, is RF), thereafter being used to train a weighted and interpretable white box model, the surrogate model (in the case of this study,

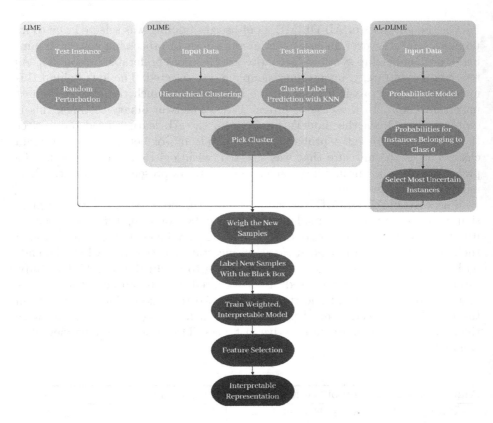

Fig. 1. Flowchart which depicts the general pipeline of all XAI models used in this study, and how they relate to one another.

ridge linear regression). Feature selection is then achieved through the newly trained white box model, and an interpretable representation is generated.

3.5   Baseline Explainable Models

We have chosen LIME [32] as a model for explainability due to its robustness and high popularity in the area of XAI. Due to our interest in exploring applications of XAI in medicine, DLIME was also selected as an interesting juxtaposition to LIME. We hope to achieve a more comprehensive comparison between these models, and AL-DLIME.

3.6   Baseline Black and White Box Models

Seeing as how the selected XAI models are post-hoc, it was necessary to choose a baseline black box model. Owing to the limitations of the procured datasets (namely, their size), algorithms such as neural networks were deemed unfeasible, as they require substantial amounts of data in order to perform effectively. The

RF algorithm was selected primarily due to its superior performance against different models in a number of different articles, as discussed in Sect. 2. Additionally, a DT model was utilized as a control for the black box model. Specifically, the DT model serves to verify the necessity of utilizing a black box model, by comparing its performance against the RF model with the evaluation metrics discussed later on in Sect. 3.7.

During the construction of ML models, it is vital to take into account the impact each hyperparameter may have on model performance, and adjust them accordingly. This process of adjusting hyperparameters to optimize the performance is known as model optimization [5, p.98-99] [21]. One of the most widely used methods is the Grid Search method, which determines the optimal set of hyperparameters through an exhaustive search, or brute force. More specifically, the Grid Search method constructs an algorithm for every possible combination of hyperparameters within a given grid of hyperparameters to test, and compares them against each other with a certain metric, such as accuracy. This process can be time-consuming and computationally intensive, depending on the number of combinations to consider.

In the case of the work reported in this paper, the Grid Search method was used to find the optimal set of hyperparameters for both the RF and DT models, in relation to both the standardized and non-standardized datasets. The final set of parameters for RF and DT for both experiments may be found in Table 1 and 2.

Table 1. Optimized hyperparameters for RF and DT on the standardized datasets.

Model	Dataset	Parameters				
		nEstimators	criterion	minSamplesLeaf	minSamplesSplit	maxFeatures
Random Forest	BCD	20	gini	1	3	sqrt
	OCD	95	gini	1	4	sqrt
	PCD	90	entropy	2	3	log2
	HDD	85	entropy	2	6	log2
Decision Tree	BCD	-	entropy	2	6	log2
	OCD	-	entropy	3	3	sqrt
	PCD	-	entropy	1	3	log2
	HDD	-	gini	1	6	sqrt

3.7 Evaluation Metrics

In order to evaluate an XAI algorithm, we need to consider not only the performance of the underlying model, but also the quality of the explanation. This has proven to be difficult to achieve, for reasons explored in Sect. 2.3. However, although there may not currently be a gold set of metrics used to evaluate XAI, there is also no lack of proposed metrics to choose from.

The performance of the DT and RF algorithms was evaluated through accuracy and F1-score.

Table 2. Optimized hyperparameters for RF and DT on the non-standardized datasets.

Model	Dataset	Parameters				
		nEstimators	criterion	minSamplesLeaf	minSamplesSplit	maxFeatures
Random Forest	BCD	40	gini	1	3	sqrt
	OCD	15	gini	1	7	sqrt
	PCD	55	entropy	3	6	log2
	HDD	75	gini	2	4	log2
Decision Tree	BCD	-	entropy	1	5	sqrt
	OCD	-	entropy	3	5	sqrt
	PCD	-	entropy	1	6	sqrt
	HDD	-	gini	1	4	sqrt

By considering both precision and recall, the F1-score is able to provide a more accurate perspective of the algorithm's performance, regardless of the imbalance in the dataset.

Beyond the evaluation of the DT and RF classifiers, we found it pertinent to measure LIME, AL-DLIME, and DLIME's performances with the same metrics. Due to the nature of both LIME, AL-DLIME, and DLIME as post-hoc models, it is important to determine if the approximated models are comparable to the RF algorithm. Thus, through the use of accuracy and F1-score, it is possible to assess the effectiveness of LIME, AL-DLIME, and DLIME in approximating the RF classifier.

To evaluate the quality of the explanations provided by the XAI models, several metrics were employed, including: the faithfulness metric from Ribeiro et al. [32], the metric of stability from Zafar and Kahn [41], and the single and incremental deletion metrics. These measures provide a comprehensive evaluation of the quality of the explanations generated by both XAI models, including their consistency and faithfulness.

In regards to faithfulness, Ribeiro et al. [32] originally suggested using a maximum of 10 features for the gold set. This was possible for all datasets except the PCD, which, as previously stated, has only 8 features. Thus, in this instance, we set the number of gold standard features to 6. We based our selection of the gold set of features on the results from our RF model's feature importance, choosing those that presented the highest values.

The single deletion metric [3,34] is used to evaluate the accuracy of XAI algorithms in approximating a black box model. The metric involves removing one feature at a time and assessing the impact on the algorithm's classification, replacing that feature and selecting the next at the end of each iteration. There are two variations with the feature selection: most important to least important, or least important to most important. In this study, we chose the first approach, and selected two features at a time in order to preserve computational power.

Juxtaposed to the single deletion metric, there is incremental deletion [11,19]. The basis of this metric is very similar to single deletion, in that it involves the removal of features in order to determine how the XAI model reacts. However, in this case, this removal is successive. In other words, once a feature has been removed, it will not be replaced. This would normally imply an even larger perturbation in the resulting classifications. Once again, if the XAI model demonstrates this behavior, it may be deemed faithful to the black box.

4   Results and Discussion

In this section, the results of this study will be presented alongside their interpretative analysis and discussion.

4.1   Standardized Datasets

As explained in Sect. 3.3, this experiment consisted of the use of an additional step in preprocessing, standardization.

Beginning with the results of accuracy and F1-Score shown in Table 3, it is clear, first and foremost, that AL-DLIME performed the best on each dataset across all models, including RF. In fact, AL-DLIME even outperformed RF in both accuracy and F1-score with the OCD and HDD. However, it is necessary to state that both instances were only small improvements upon the black box model's performance. In contrast, DLIME performed slightly better than RF on only one account, the F1-score obtained with the OCD. Finally, LIME proved to be the least faithful to RF in terms of classifier performance, obtaining the highest discrepancy between results from the PCD and HDD.

Overall, the XAI models all performed most similarly to RF through the BCD. Moreover, RF outperformed DT on all accounts across all datasets, which was to be expected.

Table 3. Accuracy and F1-Score results for all models on the standardized datasets. Best results for accuracy and F1-Score for each dataset are highlighted through bold text.

Model	Accuracy				F1-Score			
	BCD	OCD	PCD	HDD	BCD	OCD	PCD	HDD
RF	**0.982**	0.767	**0.576**	0.870	**0.977**	0.722	**0.574**	0.896
DT	**0.982**	0.558	0.534	0.766	0.929	0.537	0.517	0.804
LIME	0.956	0.767	0.492	0.647	0.940	0.737	0.415	0.775
DLIME	0.947	0.767	**0.576**	0.870	**0.977**	0.762	**0.574**	0.896
AL-DLIME	**0.982**	**0.791**	**0.576**	**0.875**	**0.977**	**0.780**	**0.574**	**0.900**

Table 4 shows the results of faithfulness between each XAI model, and the RF classifier. It is apparent that LIME performed overall the best out of all the XAI algorithms, despite AL-DLIME boasting the best overall best result across all datasets. All models performed the best with the PCD and HDD, and DLIME and AL-DLIME performed notably worse with the BCD and OCD, while LIME consistently achieved values above 0.600.

Table 4. Faithfulness of the XAI models on the standardized datasets. Best results for each dataset are highlighted through bold text.

	Faithfulness			
Model	BCD	OCD	PCD	HDD
LIME	**0.600**	**0.700**	**0.833**	0.900
DLIME	0.272	0.300	0.667	0.900
AL-DLIME	0.349	0.219	0.668	**0.935**

In Table 5, the results for the single deletion metric are shown. As for the PCD, there are no results for rounds 4 and 5 due to the reduced number of features available, compounded with the fact that we removed two features at a time. From all models, LIME obtained the overall best results, consistently across round 1 of removal. To reiterate a previous point, we hoped to achieve low results for similarity, as that would signify the model is faithful to the choice of the most important features. As we began with removing the most important features, it was to be expected that we would see the lowest results in round 1. However, LIME was the only model which obtained values below 0.600. In fact, the results from RF are nearly all above 0.900 with the exception of the values obtained through the PCD, which range from 0.780 to 0.873, and a single instance obtained through the OCD, with a value of 0.860. Both DLIME and AL-DLIME performed similarly, with the lowest results of similarity being through the PCD. However, DLIME and AL-DLIME also achieved the lowest value in regards to the BCD, despite this result being relatively high, regardless (0.965).

Finally, Table 6 shows the results for the incremental deletion metric. Once again, there are no results for the PCD for rounds 4 and 5 due to the reduced number of features Overall, it appears that DLIME and AL-DLIME both achieved the lowest results for two datasets (BCD and HDD, and BCD and OCD, respectively), while LIME and RF achieved the lowest results for the PCD and HDD, respectively. Furthermore, there was further variability between results, which was to be expected to the nature of the metric – successively removing features from the datasets. However, as for the BCD, no value below 0.940 was achieved across all rounds, from all models. Finally, the lowest results that were obtained were nearly all from round 5, which further aligns with our predictions.

For this first experiment, the results for accuracy and F1-score from the ML models were satisfactory, with the exception of those obtained with the PCD. As aforementioned, RF outperformed DT on every occasion which was consistent with the findings in Sect. 2.1. This provides a more robust defense for the use of black box models in this area of application, though a more comprehensive study may be executed in the future, with a larger array of both black box and white box models. Within the scope of this paper, the results of the model optimization through the grid search method lead us to believe that RF is preferable over DT among the selected datasets. When compared to performance of AL-

Table 5. Results for single deletion across all five rounds. Lowest values across all rounds for each dataset are highlighted through bold text.

Model	Dataset	Round 1	Round 2	Round 3	Round 4	Round 5
RF	BCD	0.991	0.991	0.982	0.969	0.991
	OCD	0.930	0.930	0.930	0.930	0.860
	PCD	0.873	0.763	0.780	-	-
	HDD	0.902	0.967	0.967	0.973	0.973
LIME	BCD	1.000	0.991	0.991	0.991	0.982
	OCD	**0.721**	0.884	0.930	0.907	0.884
	PCD	**0.508**	0.797	0.669	-	-
	HDD	**0.446**	0.984	0.598	1.000	0.951
DLIME	BCD	0.991	0.991	0.982	**0.965**	0.982
	OCD	0.930	0.930	0.930	0.930	0.860
	PCD	0.873	0.763	0.780	-	-
	HDD	0.902	0.967	0.967	0.973	0.973
AL--DLIME	BCD	0.991	0.991	0.982	**0.965**	0.982
	OCD	0.930	0.907	0.930	0.930	0.860
	PCD	0.873	0.763	0.780	-	-
	HDD	0.886	0.973	0.973	0.967	0.967

Table 6. Results for incremental deletion across all five rounds. Lowest values across all rounds for each dataset are highlighted through bold text.

Model	Dataset	Round 1	Round 2	Round 3	Round 4	Round 5
RF	BCD	0.965	0.982	0.991	0.965	0.956
	OCD	0.884	0.744	0.884	0.884	0.674
	PCD	0.907	0.500	0.619	-	-
	HDD	0.891	0.625	0.690	0.821	**0.054**
LIME	BCD	0.982	0.991	1.000	1.000	0.991
	OCD	0.721	0.721	0.791	0.791	0.721
	PCD	0.788	0.449	**0.407**	-	-
	HDD	0.495	0.435	0.500	0.582	0.582
DLIME	BCD	0.965	0.982	0.991	0.965	**0.947**
	OCD	0.884	0.744	0.884	0.884	0.674
	PCD	0.907	0.441	0.619	-	-
	HDD	0.891	0.625	0.690	0.821	**0.054**
AL--DLIME	BCD	0.965	0.982	0.991	0.965	**0.947**
	OCD	**0.651**	0.907	0.860	0.860	0.721
	PCD	0.907	0.441	0.619	-	-
	HDD	0.875	0.625	0.690	0.804	0.065

DLIME, however, the question remains: are black box algorithms strictly necessary? Despite the fact that the instances in which AL-DLIME outperformed RF were merely slight improvements, the fact remains that its performance exceeded RF. This could be another potential avenue for future research.

In terms of faithfulness to the black box model, the results for both DLIME and AL-DLIME were surprisingly low, though all XAI models performed well on the HDD. Beyond this, there is an especially interesting correlation between the results of accuracy and F1-score, and faithfulness. All models performed the best in terms of accuracy and F1-score on the BCD and OCD, while, in stark contrast, obtaining their worst results in regards to faithfulness. Moreover, LIME's results of accuracy and F1-score showed the biggest discrepancy to those of RF through the HDD, while it obtained its best result for faithfulness on that same dataset. This would seem to suggest that a higher faithfulness to the black box model comes at a cost of performance. However, in the case of AL-DLIME, the opposite occurred: on the HDD, not only did it outperform RF, it also obtained the best result for faithfulness out of all XAI models, from all utilized datasets.

The trend of high results for similarity regarding the single deletion metric was yet another point of interest. It is important to note that the overall lowest results were obtained through the PCD, the dataset with the smallest amount of features and, thus, the smallest "gold set", consisting of only 6 features. The removal of 2 out of 6 of these features would, in theory, have a greater impact, which could explain the low results. As for the results of the incremental deletion metric, a larger discrepancy was noted, though still less than expected. The lowest results for similarity were obtained through the PCD, as well as the HDD, while the results for the BCD were overall the highest. Once again, this outcome may be due to the difference in terms of number of features among the datasets. The BCD and OCD, with the largest amount of features, are more likely to have multiple features with similar values of importance, than the PCD and HDD, both of which contain under 15 features. However, despite the results not being in accordance with what was expected, it should be emphasized that, overall, all XAI models performed closely to RF, with DLIME and AL-DLIME obtaining the closest results to the black box model.

In regards to the values obtained for Jaccard's distance, through Fig. 2 we may see the results regarding a random instance from the BCD. The results of Jaccard's distance are represented through confusion matrices, from which we may view the variety of values through their color representation, depicted in the color bars on the right side of each matrix. Therefore, DLIME and AL-DLIME, whose matrices (Figs. 2a and 2b, respectively) are solid colors depicting the value 0, demonstrate the utmost stability. In contrast, LIME's confusion matrix (Fig. 2c) depicts a wide variety of different values, which translates into less stability. Further examples will be available posteriorly.

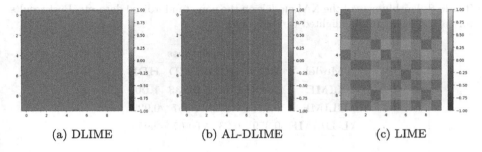

(a) DLIME	(b) AL-DLIME	(c) LIME

Fig. 2. Results for Jaccard's distance across ten iterations on a single, random instance from the standardized BCD, presented in confusion matrices.

4.2 Non-standardized Datasets

For the second experiment, the process of standardization was omitted, thus resulting in the exclusion of the single and incremental deletion metrics. The remaining process, as explained in Sect. 3, was much the same.

From Table 7, we may find the results of accuracy and F1-Score obtained for the ML and XAI models in this experiment. Once again, AL-DLIME demonstrated a strong performance, although it did not dominate as in the previous experiment. In fact, the performance of DLIME and AL-DLIME was similar, with both models managing once again to outperform RF. DLIME, however, performed in the most similar manner to RF, with the biggest discrepancy in terms of accuracy and F1-score being 0.011. Comparatively, LIME was the least faithful to RF in regards to these metrics, with the biggest discrepancy between both models' values being 0.063. Beyond this, it is worth noting that the datasets with which these models performed most similarly to RF were the OCD and HDD, in regards to LIME and DLIME, and the PCD and HDD for AL-DLIME.

Table 7. Accuracy and F1-Score results for all models on the non-standardized datasets. Best results for accuracy and F1-Score for each dataset are highlighted through bold text.

Model	Accuracy				F1-Score			
	BCD	OCD	PCD	HDD	BCD	OCD	PCD	HDD
RF	**0.991**	0.767	0.703	**0.870**	**0.989**	0.762	0.707	**0.897**
DT	0.956	0.698	0.585	0.804	0.943	0.629	0.589	0.830
LIME	0.982	0.767	0.644	0.864	0.976	0.737	0.644	0.893
DLIME	0.982	0.767	**0.712**	**0.870**	0.977	0.762	**0.716**	**0.897**
AL-DLIME	0.982	**0.791**	0.703	**0.870**	0.977	**0.780**	0.707	**0.897**

Table 8. Faithfulness of the XAI models on the non-standardized datasets. Best results for each dataset are highlighted through bold text.

Model	Faithfulness			
	BCD	OCD	PCD	HDD
LIME	**0.800**	**0.600**	**0.833**	**1.000**
DLIME	0.344	0.272	0.667	0.929
AL-DLIME	0.379	0.237	0.667	0.955

Regarding faithfulness, which may be viewed in Table 8, LIME once again demonstrated the strongest performance. In fact, LIME achieved the overall highest faithfulness score (1.000) among all XAI models, which was attained through the HDD. While the remaining models performed similarly, AL-DLIME outperformed DLIME marginally across all datasets. Moreover, it is worth noting that all models obtained their highest scores with the HDD, while their lowest scores were obtained with the OCD. This is most certainly due to the difference between the amount of features present in either dataset: while the OCD contains the largest amount at 47 features, the HDD only contains 11, of which 10 were selected for classification. Following this logic, it is unsurprising that the second highest scores were obtained with the PCD, which only contains 8 features, 5 of which were used at any point in time for classification. Despite this, there is a considerable difference between the results of faithfulness from the PCD between LIME, and both DLIME and AL-DLIME, which, in addition to LIME's overall high scores, suggests that LIME is a better candidate when considering the aspect of faithfulness to the underlying black box model.

In spite of the high scores of faithfulness, in combination to the close performance to RF of the XAI models regarding accuracy and F1-score, through the HDD, it is necessary to highlight the effect of the dataset's small size of features. Instead, it is perhaps more productive to consider the relation between the scores attained through the PCD: all models performed closely to RF, in terms of accuracy and F1-score, while at the same time obtaining their lowest overall scores for faithfulness.

Finally, DLIME and AL-DLIME once again outperform LIME in regards to the stability of their explanations, as shown by Fig. 3. As demonstrated by the lighter colors, moreover, we may conclude that in this instance, LIME demonstrated even further instability than the previous example with the standardized data. Of course, it is important to stress once again that these are only random, singular instances from one of the four selected datasets. However, the stability of DLIME and AL-DLIME in comparison to LIME remains undeniable.

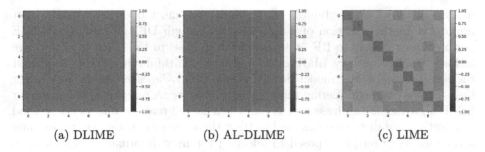

| (a) DLIME | (b) AL-DLIME | (c) LIME |

Fig. 3. Results for Jaccard's distance across ten iterations on a single, random instance from the non-standardized BCD, presented in confusion matrices.

4.3 Comparative Analysis

In both experiments, RF outperformed DT by a significant enough margin to justify its use over the transparent model, especially when one considers the scores from the standardized OCD, and the non-standardized PCD. Beyond this, the scores themselves were satisfactory for the area of application in question. However, it is noteworthy to mention that there was an improvement in results with the use of the non-standardized datasets. In fact, RF managed an impressive score of 0.991 in accuracy with the BCD, which is on par with many state of the art models. This dataset is very widely used, and an important benchmark for training and testing many ML algorithms; thus, attaining such a score is not only testament to an optimized model, but also a well constructed dataset.

One of the main arguments for XAI is the perceived superiority of black box models over white box models. The results of the experiments conducted in this thesis in regards to RF and DT initially appear to support this claim. However, it was observed on several occasions that both DLIME and AL-DLIME achieved higher accuracy and F1-score RF in both experiments, albeit with small margins. Future research could investigate a wider range of both black box and white box models to reach a consensus on this issue. Nonetheless, given the results of this work, it may be more advantageous in certain cases to use a simpler, more explainable model such as logistic regression, which is the surrogate model used in the selected XAI models, instead of a more complicated model such as RF.

Regarding the performance of the XAI models, the results showed that DLIME and AL-DLIME consistently outperformed LIME in relation to accuracy and F1-score across both experiments. Moreover, on several instances, AL-DLIME performed slightly better than its predecessor, though the difference was negligible. When viewing these results from the perspective of the scores for faithfulness, however, a trend was noted. The scores of accuracy and F1-score that are the closest to those of RF correlate with the XAI model's lowest results in faithfulness. As explained before, the fact that 10 out of 11 features were used for the classification of the HDD skewed the results of faithfulness for this dataset, and thus should not be considered. In addition to this, it is important to note that LIME performed significantly better than the remaining XAI models in terms of faithfulness. As a result, one must question what is most important in the selection of a XAI model. Though DLIME and AL-DLIME perform most closely to RF, in terms of faithfulness to the black box, they are lacking. On the contrary, LIME offers a generally faithful representation of what the selected black box model deems as important, however, there is a larger discrepancy when considering accuracy and F1-score. A possible explanation for LIME's greater faithfulness to the black box model may be due to its method of selecting instances that are used to train the surrogate model. By performing a random selection (as opposed to selecting the most informative instances, in the case of AL-DLIME), it is possible that LIME rids itself of any bias towards the data, thus approximating a more faithful representation.

Given the origin of XAI is based on the value of trust, we would propose that faithfulness should be viewed above accuracy and F1-score; additionally, the discrepancy noted never surpassed 0.250 across both experiments, and therefore may still be considered as acceptable. However, the stability of DLIME and AL-DLIME is undeniable in comparison to the explanations generated through LIME.

5   Conclusions

The present study served, first and foremost, to present a novel XAI model based on the DLIME framework. This was achieved through the use of AL, applying pool-based sampling and a query strategy in order to select the most informative examples. Beyond this, we aimed to provide a comprehensive comparison between our proposed model, AL-DLIME, and DLIME and LIME, across four datasets related to medicine. Several metrics were selected, including faithfulness to the black box model, Jaccard's distance to measure stability of the explanations, single and incremental deletion, and, finally, accuracy and F1-Score.

Our proposed model obtained satisfactory results in terms of accuracy and F1-Score, managing to outperform RF on several instances in both experiments. DLIME performed similarly to AL-DLIME in regards to accuracy and F1-Score, though AL-DLIME managed to outperform its predecessor ever so slightly. However, despite their strong performance related to classifications, AL-DLIME and DLIME's scores of faithfulness were lacking on both the BCD and OCD when compared to LIME through either experiment, with results as low as 0.219. As for the single and incremental deletion metrics, there was not as much perturbation as expected, including the scores from RF. However, despite this, all models behaved similarly to RF, with AL-DLIME and DLIME performing the most similarly. Finally, AL-DLIME and DLIME both received perfect scores of stability, as demonstrated through the Jaccard's distance scores, while LIME's explanations proved a considerable degree of instability, especially in the case of the second experiment.

Overall, the results are satisfying, as well as exciting, due to the plethora of possibilities for future research. In terms of future directions, several areas stand out: exploring different sampling scenarios and query strategies for AL;

incorporating other black box models such as SVMs or neural networks to enable a comprehensive comparison of the accuracy and F1-Score between AL-DLIME and alternative models; considering various potential variations for the proposed model; investigating the application of additional XAI evaluation metrics, including human-based metrics; incorporating other relevant metrics like specificity and sensitivity, commonly used in evaluating classification models in the medical field; and extending the approach to accommodate image-based datasets, which are widespread in the medical domain.

References

1. Adadi, A., Berrada, M.: Peeking inside the black-box: a survey on explainable artificial intelligence (XAI). IEEE Access **6**, 52138–52160 (2018). https://doi.org/10.1109/ACCESS.2018.2870052
2. Ahamad, M.M., et al.: Early-stage detection of ovarian cancer based on clinical data using machine learning approaches. J. Pers. Med. **12**, 39–54 (2022). https://doi.org/10.3390/jpm12081211
3. Alvarez-Melis, D., Jaakkola, T.S.: Towards robust interpretability with self-explaining neural networks. CoRR abs/1806.07538 (2018). https://doi.org/10.48550/arXiv.1806.07538
4. Amann, J., Blasimme, A., Vayena, E., Frey, D., Madai, V.I.: Explainability for artificial intelligence in healthcare: a multidisciplinary perspective. BMC Med. Inform. Decis. Mak. **20** (2020). https://doi.org/10.1186/s12911-020-01332-6
5. Brownlee, J.: Machine Learning Mastery with Python: Understand Your Data, Create Accurate Models and Work Projects End-to-end. Jason Brownlee (2016)
6. Budd, S., Robinson, E.C., Kainz, B.: A survey on active learning and human-in-the-loop deep learning for medical image analysis. Med. Image Anal. **71**, 102062 (2021). https://doi.org/10.1016/j.media.2021.102062
7. Cutillo, C.M., Sharma, K.R., Foschini, L., Kundu, S., Mackintosh, M., Mandl, K.D.: Machine intelligence in healthcare-perspectives on trustworthiness, explainability, usability, and transparency. NPJ Digit. Med. **3** (2020). https://doi.org/10.1038/s41746-020-0254-2
8. Debernardi, S., et al.: A combination of urinary biomarker panel and pancrisk score for earlier detection of pancreatic cancer: a case-control study. PLoS Med. **17**, 1–23 (2020). https://doi.org/10.1371/journal.pmed.1003489
9. Doshi-Velez, F., Kim, B.: Towards a rigorous science of interpretable machine learning. arXiv (2017). https://doi.org/10.48550/arXiv.1702.08608
10. Faria, B., Perdigão, D., Brás, J., Macedo, L.: The joint role of batch size and query strategy in active learning-based prediction - a case study in the heart attack domain. In: Marreiros, G., Martins, B., Paiva, A., Ribeiro, B., Sardinha, A. (eds.) EPIA 2022. LNCS, vol. 13566, pp. 464–475. Springer, Cham (2022). https://doi.org/10.1007/978-3-031-16474-3_38
11. Fong, R.C., Vedaldi, A.: Interpretable explanations of black boxes by meaningful perturbation. In: 2017 IEEE International Conference on Computer Vision (ICCV), pp. 3449–3457 (2017). https://doi.org/10.1109/ICCV.2017.371
12. Gaillochet, M., Desrosiers, C., Lombaert, H.: Active learning for medical image segmentation with stochastic batches (2023). https://doi.org/10.48550/arXiv.2301.07670

13. Gerke, S., Minssen, T., Cohen, G.: Ethical and legal challenges of artificial intelligence-driven healthcare. In: Artificial Intelligence in Healthcare, pp. 295–336 (2020). https://doi.org/10.1016/B978-0-12-818438-7.00012-5
14. Guidotti, R., Monreale, A., Ruggieri, S., Turini, F., Giannotti, F., Pedreschi, D.: A survey of methods for explaining black box models. ACM Comput. Surv. **51**(5) (2018). https://doi.org/10.1145/3236009
15. Hastie, T., Tibshirani, R., Friedman, J.: The Elements of Statistical Learning: Data Mining, Inference, and Prediction, 2nd edn. Springer, New York (2009). https://doi.org/10.1007/978-0-387-84858-7
16. High-Level Expert Group on Artificial Intelligence: Ethics guidelines for trustworthy AI (2019). https://digital-strategy.ec.europa.eu/en/library/ethics-guidelines-trustworthy-ai
17. Holzinger, A.: Explainable AI and multi-modal causability in medicine. I Com **19**, 171–179 (2021). https://doi.org/10.1515/icom-2020-0024
18. Holzinger, A.: The next frontier: AI we can really trust. In: Kamp, M., et al. (eds.) ECML PKDD 2021. CCIS, vol. 1524, pp. 427–440. Springer, Cham (2021). https://doi.org/10.1007/978-3-030-93736-2_33
19. Hooker, S., Erhan, D., Kindermans, P., Kim, B.: Evaluating feature importance estimates. CoRR abs/1806.10758 (2018). https://doi.org/10.48550/arXiv.1806.10758
20. Kholghi, M., Sitbon, L., Zuccon, G., Nguyen, A.: Active learning: a step towards automating medical concept extraction. J. Am. Med. Inform. Assoc. **23**(2), 289–296 (2015). https://doi.org/10.1093/jamia/ocv069
21. Liashchynskyi, P., Liashchynskyi, P.: Grid search, random search, genetic algorithm: a big comparison for NAS. CoRR abs/1912.06059 (2019). https://doi.org/10.48550/arXiv.1912.06059
22. Longo, L., Goebel, R., Lecue, F., Kieseberg, P., Holzinger, A.: Explainable artificial intelligence: concepts, applications, research challenges and visions. In: Holzinger, A., Kieseberg, P., Tjoa, A.M., Weippl, E. (eds.) CD-MAKE 2020. LNCS, vol. 12279, pp. 1–16. Springer, Cham (2020). https://doi.org/10.1007/978-3-030-57321-8_1
23. Lu, M., et al.: Using machine learning to predict ovarian cancer. Int. J. Med. Inform. **141**, 104–195 (2020). https://doi.org/10.1016/j.ijmedinf.2020.104195
24. Massafra, R., et al.: A clinical decision support system for predicting invasive breast cancer recurrence: preliminary results. Front. Oncol. **11** (2021). https://doi.org/10.3389/fonc.2021.576007
25. Molnar, C.: Interpretable Machine Learning, 2 edn. (2022). https://christophm.github.io/interpretable-ml-book
26. Murdoch, W.J., Singh, C., Kumbier, K., Abbasi-Asl, R., Yu, B.: Definitions, methods, and applications in interpretable machine learning. Proc. Natl. Acad. Sci. **116**(44), 22071–22080 (2019). https://doi.org/10.1073/pnas.1900654116
27. Müller, V.C.: Ethics of artificial intelligence and robotics. In: Zalta, E.N. (ed.) The Stanford Encyclopedia of Philosophy. Metaphysics Research Lab, Stanford University, Summer 2021 edn. (2021)
28. Nauta, M., et al.: From anecdotal evidence to quantitative evaluation methods: a systematic review on evaluating explainable AI. ACM Comput. Surv. (2023). https://doi.org/10.1145%2F3583558
29. Osmanović, A., Abdel-Ilah, L., Hodžić, A., Kevric, J., Fojnica, A.: Ovary cancer detection using decision tree classifiers based on historical dataof ovary cancer patients. In: CMBEBIH 2017. IP, vol. 62, pp. 503–510. Springer, Singapore (2017). https://doi.org/10.1007/978-981-10-4166-2_77

30. Fox-Skelly, J., et al.: The ethics of artificial intelligence: issues and initiatives, p. 13. European Parliament (2020). https://doi.org/10.2861/6644
31. Pinto, C., Faria, J., Macedo, L.: An active learning-based medical diagnosis system. In: Marreiros, G., Martins, B., Paiva, A., Ribeiro, B., Sardinha, A. (eds.) Progress in Artificial Intelligence. LNCS, vol. 13566, pp. 207–218. Springer, Cham (2022). https://doi.org/10.1007/978-3-031-16474-3_18
32. Ribeiro, M.T., Singh, S., Guestrin, C.: Why should i trust you?: explaining the predictions of any classifier (2016). https://doi.org/10.1145/2939672.2939778
33. Russel, S.J., Norvig, P.: Artificial Intelligence: A Modern Approach, 3rd edn. Pearson Education, Upper Saddle River (2010)
34. Selvaraju, R.R., Das, A., Vedantam, R., Cogswell, M., Parikh, D., Batra, D.: Gradcam: why did you say that? Visual explanations from deep networks via gradient-based localization. CoRR abs/1610.02391 (2016). https://doi.org/10.48550/arXiv.1610.02391
35. Settles, B.: Active learning literature survey. Computer Sciences Technical report 1648, University of Wisconsin-Madison (2009)
36. Shan, J., Alam, S.K., Garra, B., Zhang, Y., Ahmed, T.: Computer-aided diagnosis for breast ultrasound using computerized BI-RADS features and machine learning methods. Ultrasound Med. Biol. **42**(4), 980–988 (2016). https://doi.org/10.1016/j.ultrasmedbio.2015.11.016
37. Simegn, G.L., Gebeyehu, W.B., Degu, M.Z.: Computer-aided decision support system for diagnosis of heart diseases. Res. Rep. Clin. Cardiol. **13**, 39–54 (2022). https://doi.org/10.2147/RRCC.S366380
38. Singh, H., Schiff, G.D., Graber, M.L., Onakpoya, I., Thompson, M.J.: The global burden of diagnostic errors in primary care. BMJ Qual. Saf. **26**, 484–494 (2017). https://doi.org/10.1136/bmjqs-2016-005401
39. Stahl, B.C.: Ethical issues of AI. In: Stahl, B.C. (ed.) Artificial Intelligence for a Better Future. SRIG, pp. 35–53. Springer, Cham (2021). https://doi.org/10.1007/978-3-030-69978-9_4
40. Wibowo, V.V.P., Rustam, Z., Laeli, A.R., Sa'id, A.A.: Logistic regression and logistic regression-genetic algorithm for classification of liver cancer data. In: 2021 International Conference on Decision Aid Sciences and Application (DASA), pp. 244–248. IEEE (2021)
41. Zafar, M.R., Khan, N.: Deterministic local interpretable model-agnostic explanations for stable explainability (2021). https://doi.org/10.3390/make3030027
42. Zafar, M.R., Khan, N.M.: Dlime: a deterministic local interpretable model-agnostic explanations approach for computer-aided diagnosis systems (2019). https://doi.org/10.48550/arXiv.1906.10263

Understanding Unsupervised Learning Explanations Using Contextual Importance and Utility

Avleen Malhi[1,2]($\boxtimes$), Vlad Apopei[1], and Kary Främling[1,3]

[1] Aalto University, Helsinki, Finland
vlad.apopei@aalto.fi
[2] Bournemouth University, Bournemouth, UK
amalhi@bournemouth.ac.uk
[3] Umeå University, Umeå, Sweden
kary.framling@cs.umu.se

Abstract. While the concept of Explainability has advanced significantly in the past decade, many areas remain unexplored. Although XAI implementations have historically been employed in attempting to 'open' the traditional black-box model of supervised learning implementation aiming to extract human-understandable information, there are no successful attempts at tackling unsupervised learning. This paper aims to tackle the challenge of using an XAI approach, specifically Contextual Importance and Utility (CIU), in order to provide an explainability layer for unsupervised learning models. The paper introduces the current XAI approaches of CIU as well as the other state-of-the-art implementations such as Lime or Shapley. The challenges posed by the unsupervised learning problem are explored and discussed, both on a conceptual and technical level. A relatively novel approach using a CIU implementation on unsupervised clustering techniques is presented along with the brief comparison with another state-of-the-art method called LIME.

Keywords: Unsupervised learning · Explainability · Contextual importance and utility · Machine learning

1 Introduction

The interpretibility in AI systems is quite a challenging technical issue. There has always been an imperative demand for explainability of intelligent systems as a shift from traditional systems which are explainable but hard to use and inflexible, to black box models which are highly efficient but hard to interpret from inside. One of the foundations of XAI has been attempting to open, explore and understand the black-box model of machine learning implementations. Rather than attempting to address explainability with gradient-based linear approximations such as LIME or SHAP [10], this paper studies a non-linear extension to the notions of importance and utility used in linear models. The extension is

L. Longo (Ed.): xAI 2023, CCIS 1901, pp. 606–617, 2023.
https://doi.org/10.1007/978-3-031-44064-9_32

called Contextual Importance and Utility (CIU) and was initially proposed in [4] and many works have been proposed so far using this method [8,12].

Many approaches have been presented throughout the years for supervised learning implementations. Methods such as LIME, Shapley or CIU have provided adequate solutions in time. While the LIME and Shapley have been the more popular solutions, they exhibit significant limitations which proved them unsuitable for unsupervised learning models. The necessity to create a surrogate classifier model as well as relying on pre-existing support for the various types make it infeasible to implement on unsupervised models.

As pointed out by many researchers and notably Miller [13], current XAI research tends to focus on developing methods that allow AI and Machine Learning (ML) researchers to analyze and understand the results of their own models, rather than providing explanations that could be understandable by true end-users. In practice, the concept of explainability and how humans define and understand an explanation should probably be guided by domains such as social sciences, psychology, cognitive sciences and even philosophy. One domain that seems largely neglected in current XAI research is *Decision Theory* and related sub-areas such as *Multiple Criteria Decision Making (MCDM)*. The Merriam-Webster dictionary defines 'Decision Theory' as "a branch of statistical theory concerned with quantifying the process of making choices between alternatives". Nevertheless, Decision Theory is by definition closely related with the domains mentioned above (social science, data science and human machine interaction) since the intention is to produce Decision Support Systems (DSS) understandable and usable by humans. MCDM provide clear definitions of what is meant by the *importance* of an input, as well as what is the *utility* of a given input value towards the outcome of a DSS. A simple linear DSS model is the weighted sum, where a numerical weight expresses the importance of an input and a numerical value expresses the utility of the current value of that input.

There have been many studies proposed in the past discussing about the explainability of the unsupervised learning methods [15]. Kauffmann et al. [7] proposed a framework to explain cluster assignments in terms of input features which is based on the novel idea of rewriting clustering models as neural networks. The cluster predictions of these neural networks can be used to attribute to the input features accurately. However they don't use any different explainability method. Further, there was label free explainability method proposed for unsupervised models [1]. The authors introduce label-free feature importance to highlight influential features and label-free example importance to highlight training examples for a black-box to construct representations. These explanations generated undergo a qualitative and quantitative comparison of representation spaces which are learned by the autoencoders trained on disparate unsupervised tasks but it does not help in explaining the cluster prediction outcomes to assist the users with decision making. There are some works who also tend to provide a scalar explanation for clustering algorithms which means it is a dot product-based similarity in the representation space to the sample being explained but the interpretation of the predictions still remains opaque. Hence, a novel approach called contrastive corpus similarity was proposed for semantically meaningful scalar explanation output based on a contrasting foil set of samples and a reference corpus [9]. There are also approaches defined for the explainability of k-medians and k-means but these methods don't provide the explanations based on the context and they don't generate user specific explanations [11].

For the purposes of this study we will use clustering algorithms such as *k-means*, which in turn have been used on well-established 'benchmark' data-sets as a direct comparison with pre-existing implementations of supervised methods. Current work attempting to provide an explainability layer to such clustering algorithms by employing decision trees as the primary clustering method [14]. This method can however lead to clustering with relatively high cost. Furthermore the explainability method strays from the optimal clustering approach by considering single features rather than all the present ones. CIU while has only been used to tackle supervised learning models and this paper discusses its further expansion into the unsupervised learning based problems.

2   Theory of Contextual Importance and Contextual Utility

Decision Theory proposes a set of quantitative methods for reaching optimal, or at least rational, decisions. A decision problem needs to be formulated in terms of initial conditions and outcomes or courses of action, with their consequences. Each outcome is assigned a *utility value* based on the *preferences* of the decision maker(s). An optimal decision is one that maximizes the expected outcome utility. The concepts of importance and utility can be explained in their simplest form by the following example: The average grade of a university student is calculated as a normalized weighted sum, where the importance corresponds to the number of credits given for the course, so $k_i = \frac{nbr\_credits}{total\_credits}$. The grades of the courses are also normalized so then $x_i = course\_grade$ and $u_i(x_i) = \frac{course\_grade}{max\_course\_grade}$ where i represents each data instance.

In this example, all utility functions are linear and all attributes are additive-independent. In practice, course grades might be calculated as a function of points from many different examinations, where the examination grading quite often is not an linear function of the points. The function is typically monotonically increasing but it might also be decreasing or even non-monotonous. Such non-linearity can not be represented by a simple n-attribute utility function. If the importance (number of credits) or utility (grade) of one or more courses would depend on the grade of one or more other courses, then the attributes are no longer additive-independent but rather become contextual in the sense meant by CIU.

CIU respects additive-independence as long as the underlying model is linear. However, the objective of CIU is not to provide a rank-ordering but providing an explanation for the outcome of an underlying model that is typically non-linear and where input features are rarely independent in practice. Therefore, CIU ensures that u and the u_i are normalized to the range $[0, 1]$. *Contextual*

Importance (CI) of a set of inputs $x_{\{i\}}$ with indices $\{i\}$ relative to the importance of a set of inputs $x_{\{I\}}$ with indices $\{I\}$ is defined as:

$$CI_j(C, \{i\}, \{I\}) = \frac{umax_j(C, \{i\}) - umin_j(C, \{i\})}{umax_j(C, \{I\}) - umin_j(C, \{I\})}, \tag{1}$$

where $\{i\} \subseteq \{I\}$ and $\{I\} \subseteq \{1, \ldots, n\}$. C is the current instance/context to be explained and defines the values of input features that do not belong to $\{i\}$ or $\{I\}$. When $\{I\} = \{1, \ldots, n\}$, CI is calculated relative to the output utilities u_j. For instance, $CI_j(C, \{2\}, \{1, \ldots, n\})$ is the contextual importance of input x_2, whereas $CI_j(C, \{1, 2, 3\}, \{1, \ldots, n\})$ is the **joint** contextual importance of inputs x_1, x_2, x_3 and $CI_j(C, \{1, \ldots, n\}, \{1, \ldots, n\})$ is the joint contextual importance of **all** inputs. $umin_j$ and $umax_j$ are the minimal and maximal utility values u_j observed for output j for all possible $x_{\{i\}}$ and $x_{\{I\}}$ values in the context C, while keeping other input values at C. This corresponds to using the *caeteris-paribus* or 'other things held constant' principle. The values of $umin_j$ and $umax_j$ can only be calculated exactly if all input features are categorical and the number of input value combinations remains reasonable. In all other cases, $umin_j$ and $umax_j$ need to be estimated.

Equation 1 is applicable to any black-box model because it only requires modifying input values x and observing the corresponding output values y, assuming that the utility function $u_j(y_j)$ is known. In classification tasks, the utility function is simply $u_j(y_j) = y_j$ because the output is already a probability/utility value in the range $[0, 1]$. In regression tasks, the y_j value is rarely a utility value in itself and at least requires an affine transformation of the form $u_j(y_j) = Ay_j + b$. For the well-known Boston Housing data set, for instance, the y_j value is the median value of owner-occupied homes in \$1000's and is in the range $[5, 50]$. $u_j(y_j) = \frac{1}{45}y_j - \frac{1}{9}$ transforms y_j into a $u_j \in [0, 1]$, assuming that the preference is to have a higher value. However, from a buyer's point of view, the preference might be for lower prices and then the transformation would rather be $[50, 5] \mapsto [0, 1]$. In this paper, we assume that $u_j(y_j) = Ay_j + b$, which also applies to classification tasks[1]. In practice, $u_j(y_j)$ does not need to be known for producing CIU explanations because when applying $u_j(y_j) = Ay_j + b$ to Eq. 1, CI can be directly calculated as:

$$CI_j(C, \{i\}, \{I\}) = \frac{ymax_j(C, \{i\}) - ymin_j(C, \{i\})}{ymax_j(C, \{I\}) - ymin_j(C, \{I\})}, \tag{2}$$

where $ymin_j$ and $ymax_j$ are the minimal and maximal y_j values observed for output j. Equation 2 is identical to the CI definitions in [2,3].

Estimating $ymin_j$ and $ymax_j$ becomes increasingly challenging when the number of input features in $\{i\}$ and $\{I\}$ increases. In practice, those challenges can be avoided in most cases. To begin, we will define $absmin_j =$

---

[1] $u_j(y_j)$ could have any shape as long as it produces values in the range $[0, 1]$ but that case goes beyond the scope of the current paper (and theory).

$ymin_j(C, \{1, \ldots, n\})$ and $absmax_j = ymax_j(C, \{1, \ldots, n\})$, the minimal and maximal values that y_j can get when modifying the values of **all** input features within 'reasonable' bounds. Fortunately, $absmin_j$ and $absmax_j$ can be defined without any calculations for most practical cases. In classification tasks, $absmin = 0$ and $absmax = 1$ for all j. In regression tasks, the minimal and maximal values of output j in the training set are usually good choices for $absmin_j$ and $absmax_j$.

3   Proposed Method

Conceptually the explainability process undertaken by any of the explainable methods involves using the pre-existing labelling of a data-set. For example, the CIU method analyses the importance of each feature for a given label by taking one feature into consideration in the given data and measuring the resulting strength of the prediction. Clearly this approach is not suitable for a clustering problem considering the absence of any labelling. Contrary to the previous work on this method, we propose a *post-modelling* solution, akin to a supervised learning approach. Attempting to provide the pre-requisite conditions for a successful CIU implementation, there are a number of missing factors. While this method does not rely on any surrogate models, there is still the necessity of data labelling. Unsupervised methods, such as the *k-means* used in this study, can provide the aforementioned labelling *post-clustering*. Assuming successful division into k clusters, there are a k number of centroids, representing the central values for the clusters, ergo the logically ideal representation of a resulting 'label'.

A CIU implementation on the resulting centroids would allow us to extract their relatively defining features. This in turn allows for a *human-understandable* labelling of each cluster based on the aforementioned features. While the theoretical aspect is promising, this relies on the assumption that we can measure how good a "prediction" is in order to extract the features. In the case of the state-of-the-art classifiers, a prediction function is provided, however that is not the case for unsupervised clustering models. Simulating the inner workings of a *k-means* clustering algorithm attempting to derive a prediction function would output a hard-clustering result. In this case, our prediction function simulates the output of a supervised model. For a clustering algorithm this output is characteristic of a fuzzy-clustering method such as *c-means*. This type of method sees an output of points belonging to one or more clusters at once in various gradations of intensity, therefore defining a *membership* percentage for each point in the data-set and each relative cluster. Therefore, a point x has a set of coefficients giving the degree of being in the kth cluster $wk(x)$. In fuzzy c-means, the centroid of a cluster is the mean of all points, weighted by their degree of belonging to the cluster, modified by the parameter m controlling how fuzzy the cluster can be and is given as:

$$c_k = \frac{\sum_x w_k(x)^m x}{\sum_x w_k(x)^m}$$

Consequently for a collection of points $X = \{\mathbf{x}_1, ..., \mathbf{x}_n\}$ the algorithm will produce a set of clusters $C = \{\mathbf{c}_1, ..., \mathbf{c}_c\}$ and a resulting partition $W = w_{i,j} \in [0,1]$, $i = 1, ..., n$, $j = 1, ..., c$, such that w_{ij} denotes the percentage of the aforementioned membership of $\mathbf{x}_i$ to cluster $\mathbf{c}_j$ [6].

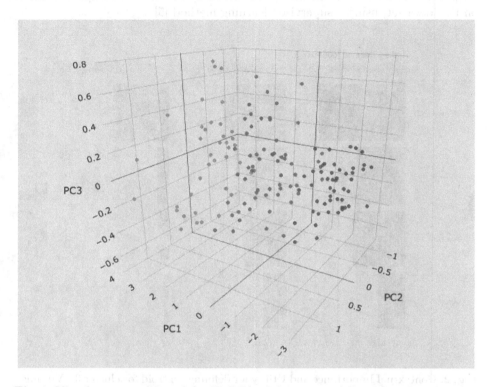

Fig. 1. Visual representation of the 3D PCA of the post-modelling clustering distribution

4   Results

For the purposes of this study the data-set chosen is the Iris flower [16], a simple yet effective data-set that has been used and tested extensively throughout the years. This allows us to have a direct comparison between existing XAI implementations on supervised methods and our proposed CIU implementation on unsupervised methods.

In Fig. 1 we can see the visual representation of the 3D Principal Component Analysis (PCA) of the *post-modelling* clustering distribution. Once a successful clustering is obtained and established, the next step was to implement CIU to obtain an explanation. The output shown in Fig. 2 is quite similar to the output we would see in a supervised model implementation of CIU. From the figure we can see that the most important (CI) features for defining the centroid of cluster number three, and therefore the cluster, are *petal-length* with a value of 5.7 followed by *sepal-length* with a value of 6.9. These values are consistent with the defined characteristics of the *virginica* variety. Likewise, the resulting CIU output is consistent with the output presented by another CIU implementation on this data-set, using a supervised learning method [5].

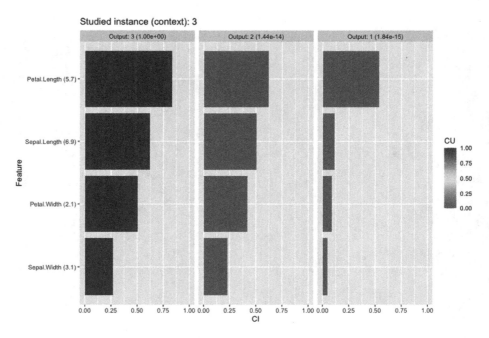

Fig. 2. Contextual Importance and Utility for defining centroid for cluster 3 - Virginica

The explanations provided by CIU also take utility into consideration whereas the LIME only gives the feature importance in local context without considering how the model behaves corresponding to the whole training data. The CIU plots give the feature utility of each input feature in determining the probability of a particular class. The probabilities of each class are given on top of each graph and the input values for each feature are given in () sorted in the increasing order of feature importance. The explanations are also added with the help of a local surrogate model LIME as shown in Fig. 3. The output of LIME comprises the explanation which reflects each feature's contribution to the prediction made by the black-box model. LIME explanations give the feature importance for the test class and these features have weights defined internally by the algorithm which help to define their feature importance which is either in favor of particular class or contrasts it. The values of these attributes help calculating the weights internally based for the prediction probability for a particular class. LIME is a local linear model which can provide and estimate how much small changes in an input attribute might affect the output but they do not explain the scenario when the input value is changed slightly more. Hence, it does not take into account the utility of the input. Furthermore, LIME explanations are still confusing and not giving very clear understanding of the feature utility and importance as well as the concept of new variables generation for providing feature importance is not interpretable from end-user point of view.

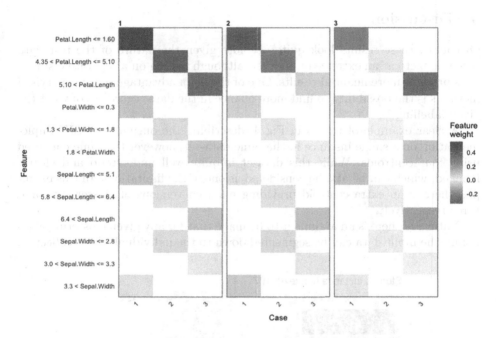

Fig. 3. LIME output shown on the same instance of centroid for cluster 3

The logic of the approach used on within the CIU implementation could theoretically be used with some of the other more popular methods. As per the current state of these methods, there is no support for unsupervised learning models, although some do support custom classifiers to a certain extent. Another state-of-the-art method, LIME, does have this support but one of the main problems here is that this process is not only simply made for supervised methods, but quite tailored to it. This forces us to specify every possible component manually. First, the type of the *k-means* model had to be defined as *"classification"*, however semantically erroneous. Likewise, this method also requires specifying a prediction method. However there are no specific output type requirements, as such the previously defined prediction method can be used. Having provided the model and handling methods, the surrogate *explainer* model is then created.

The graph shown in Fig. 3 describes the output of the surrogate model applied to the dataframe containing the centroids, just as in the CIU example. These results seem consistent with the output of a traditional classification model. Although the differences between the two methods (CIU and LIME) are notable, either implementation can provide a semantically coherent output. It is worth noting that the LIME implementation is rather *forced* since this entire implementation relies on having to implement it as a de-facto classifier. However this certainly shows that with adequate support provided, the LIME algorithm could also evolve to incorporate unsupervised learning methods.

5   Discussion

Of course, these results look quite absolute given the nature of the test data being de-facto at an extreme or another, although testing on a separate instance does produce more nuanced results. One of the main advantages of unsupervised methods is the possibility to find more nuance in the data regardless of what the given labelling is.

A clear example of this is in Fig. 4, describing the output of a CIU implementation on a single instance in the same data-set, however this time clustered using four centroids. While this dataset is quite well understood and clearly labelled, which can be also be considered as one of the limitations. In this example, there is an extra centroid providing nunaced versions of clusters two and three respectively.

Naturally there is an argument to be made that for any given clustering algorithm, the input data can be segmented down to the individual. For a collection

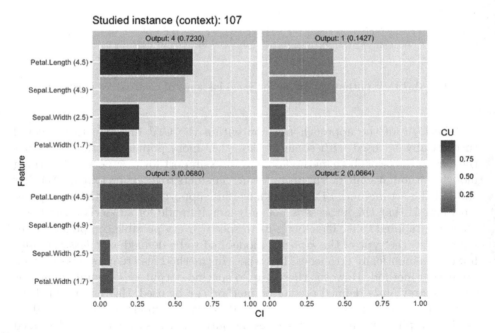

Fig. 4. CIU result of single instance clustered using four centroids

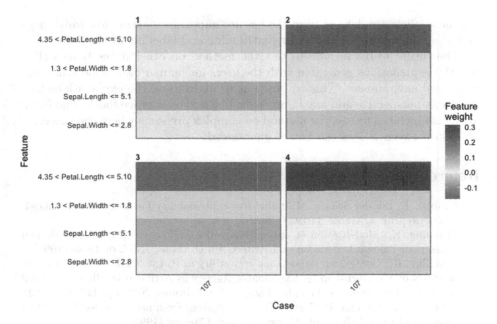

Fig. 5. LIME result of single instance clustered using four centroids

of points $X = \{\mathbf{x}_1, ..., \mathbf{x}_n\}$ there is an equal output of clusters $C = \{\mathbf{c}_1, ..., \mathbf{c}_k\}$, such that $\{\mathbf{n} = \mathbf{k}\}$. However, outside of such extreme cases, we believe that this kind of implementation can provide a more detailed insight into the dataset, allowing the user to interpret their own labelling befitting their needs and the purposes of the specific application. Likewise this type of implementation can be achieved using the LIME approach giving similar results consistent with the initial implementation, Fig. 5. The source code for our proposed method using CIU is available at https://github.com/vladapopei/CIU-Unsupervised.

6 Conclusion

In this paper, we review our recently proposed 'Contextual importance and utility' approach for bringing XAI to workhorses of unsupervised learning such as kernel density estimation and k-means clustering. It investigates the use of explainability approaches in unsupervised learning. The paper proposes a new contextual importance and utility based explainability approach specifically for the unsupervised learning. The method has been tested on the public Iris Flower dataset which shows the feasibility of the approach and also compared with state-of-the-art methods to show the applicability of such a designed method. The approach is showcased on application of iris dataset for analysis of features in the dataset which shows that explanations generated by CIU were clearly labelled and well understood compared to the other most commonly used method, LIME.

The new labels are defined from the feature importance extraction which helps in finding more detailed and niche partitioning and labelling of the dataset.

The future works include to test the method on other datasets as well as test the explanations generated with the users for human evaluation study in a controlled environment. This will help us to understand the explanations from the user's perspective and any improvements based on user feedback. The future work also includes to test the method on complex divisions where the successful division between classes can not be guaranteed.

References

1. Crabbé, J., van der Schaar, M.: Label-free explainability for unsupervised models. arXiv preprint arXiv:2203.01928 (2022)
2. Främling, K.: Modélisation et apprentissage des préférences par réseaux de neurones pour l'aide à la décision multicritère. Ph.D. thesis, INSA de Lyon (1996)
3. Främling, K.: Contextual importance and utility in R: the 'CIU' package. In: Proceedings of 1st Workshop on Explainable Agency in Artificial Intelligence, at 35h AAAI Conference on Artificial Intelligence, 2–9 February 2021, pp. 110–114 (2021)
4. Främling, K., Graillot, D.: Extracting explanations from neural networks. In: Proceedings of the ICANN, vol. 95, pp. 163–168. Citeseer (1995)
5. Främling, K.: Contextual importance and utility in R: the 'CIU' package (2021)
6. Kannan, S., Ramathilagam, S., Chung, P.: Effective fuzzy C-means clustering algorithms for data clustering problems. Expert Syst. Appl. **39**(7), 6292–6300 (2012). https://doi.org/10.1016/j.eswa.2011.11.063
7. Kauffmann, J., Esders, M., Ruff, L., Montavon, G., Samek, W., Müller, K.R.: From clustering to cluster explanations via neural networks. IEEE Trans. Neural Netw. Learn. Syst. (2022)
8. Knapič, S., Malhi, A., Saluja, R., Främling, K.: Explainable artificial intelligence for human decision support system in the medical domain. Mach. Learn. Knowl. Extract. **3**(3), 740–770 (2021)
9. Lin, C., Chen, H., Kim, C., Lee, S.I.: Contrastive corpus attribution for explaining representations. arXiv preprint arXiv:2210.00107 (2022)
10. Lundberg, S.M., Lee, S.I.: A unified approach to interpreting model predictions. In: Guyon, I., et al. (eds.) Advances in Neural Information Processing Systems, vol. 30, pp. 4765–4774. Curran Associates, Inc. (2017). http://papers.nips.cc/paper/7062-a-unified-approach-to-interpreting-model-predictions.pdf
11. Makarychev, K., Shan, L.: Near-optimal algorithms for explainable k-medians and k-means. In: International Conference on Machine Learning, pp. 7358–7367. PMLR (2021)
12. Malhi, A., Madhikermi, M., Huotari, M., Främling, K.: Air handling unit explainability using contextual importance and utility. In: Hara, T., Yamaguchi, H. (eds.) MobiQuitous 2021. Lecture Notes of the Institute for Computer Sciences, Social Informatics and Telecommunications Engineering, vol. 419, pp. 513–519. Springer, Cham (2021). https://doi.org/10.1007/978-3-030-94822-1_32
13. Miller, T.: Explanation in artificial intelligence: Insights from the social sciences. Artif. Intell. **267**, 1–38 (2019). https://arxiv.org/abs/1706.07269
14. Moshkovitz, M., Dasgupta, S., Rashtchian, C., Frost, N.: Explainable k-means and k-medians clustering (2020). http://proceedings.mlr.press/v119/moshkovitz20a.html

15. Scholbeck, C.A., Funk, H., Casalicchio, G.: Algorithm-agnostic interpretations for clustering. arXiv preprint arXiv:2209.10578 (2022)
16. Unwin, A., Kleinman, K.: The iris data set: in search of the source of virginica. Significance **18**, 26–29 (2021)

Color Shadows 2: Assessing the Impact of XAI on Diagnostic Decision-Making

Chiara Natali[1]([✉])[iD], Lorenzo Famiglini[1][iD], Andrea Campagner[1,2][iD],
Giovanni Andrea La Maida[3], Enrico Gallazzi[3][iD], and Federico Cabitza[1,2][iD]

[1] Universitá degli Studi di Milano-Bicocca, Milan, Italy
chiara.natali@unimib.it
[2] IRCCS Istituto Ortopedico Galeazzi, Milan, Italy
[3] Istituto Ortopedico Gaetano Pini—ASST Pini-CTO, Milan, Italy

Abstract. A comprehensive assessment of the impact of eXplainable AI (XAI) on diagnostic decision-making should adopt a socio-technical perspective. Our study focuses on Decision Support Systems (DSS) that provide explanations in the form of Activation Maps, assessing their impact in terms of automation bias and algorithmic aversion. Specifically, we focus on the XAI-assisted task of detecting thoraco-lumbar fractures from X-rays by radiologists, taking into account the complexity of the cases and the experience level of users. Our results show how XAI support has a clear and positive impact on diagnostic performance. By introducing the concepts of technology impact, reliance patterns, and the white box paradox, we highlight the importance of designing Human-AI Collaboration Protocols (HAI-CP) that are specific to the task at hand to optimize the integration of XAI into diagnostic decision-making.

Keywords: eXplainable AI (XAI) · Decision Support Systems (DSS) · Human-AI Collaboration Protocol (HAI-CP)

1 Introduction

The integration of artificial intelligence (AI) into medical imaging analysis is revolutionizing the field of radiology, allowing for faster and more accurate diagnoses and, at least in theory, democratize access to super-specialist capabilities [1–3]. However, concerns have arisen regarding the 'black box' nature of AI systems [4], which can make the algorithmic advice difficult to understand and integrate in clinical decision making. The concept of eXplainable AI (XAI) has gained attention as a way to address this issue and endow AI systems with capabilities to make their output more interpretable and appropriable.

To define explanations, we adopt the simplifying approach recently proposed in [5]: explanations are the *meta-output* of an explainable system that describes, enriches or complements, another main output (usually a piece of advice). This means that explanations, just like any other AI output, can be either right and useful, or wrong and useless, or even harmful, when they are so effective in terms

L. Longo (Ed.): xAI 2023, CCIS 1901, pp. 618–629, 2023.
https://doi.org/10.1007/978-3-031-44064-9_33

of persuasiveness that they mislead users when the advice is wrong, leading to the so called "white-box paradox" [6–8].

This is why we assert that, while previous studies have focused on measuring the accuracy of XAI-assisted decision-making in radiology diagnosis, a comprehensive assessment of the impact of XAI solutions should also embrace a socio-technical perspective [9], which considers the complexity of the cases (hence the difficulty of the diagnostic task), the experience level of the users (i.e., the user-task fit), and the impact of the technology on their decision-making processes.

In this study, we focus on the impact of XAI on diagnostic decision-making in the context of detecting thoraco-lumbar (TL) fractures from X-rays, which is a very complex medical tasks where error rate is still high [10]. We involved 16 orthopaedic professionals aided by a Decision Support System (DSS) providing explanations through various kinds of Activation Maps (AMs) [11], which allow radiologists to visualize the areas of the image that were most influential in the algorithmic decision-making process. Therefore, the XAI support includes both the advice given by the machine in categorical textual terms (presence/absence of fracture) and the activation map with different characteristics.

Specifically, we have assessed the impact of XAI in terms of differential accuracy, by longitudinally comparing pre- and post-XAI performance, automation bias and algorithmic aversion. Automation bias is a possible detrimental effect of algorithmic over-reliance, whereby users become less vigilant [12] and more susceptible to errors of commission [13] when the AI is wrong. Conversely, algorithmic aversion was first defined in [14] as the unsubstantiated preference for human advice over AI advice even when the latter significantly outperforms the former, and is the main detrimental component of the opposite attitude of unjustified non-reliance, [15,16] therefore indicating all of situations where a correct algorithmic advice is discarded by the decision-maker, due to a sort of "prejudice against the machine" [17]. Both algorithmic bias and aversion are measured in terms of the reliance patterns displayed by decision-makers, that is, by the interplay between the initial human judgment (HD1, or Pre-XAI), the AI advice, and the final human decision (HD2, or Post-XAI), obviously affected by the AI response. Specific Human-AI Collaboration Protocols (HAI-CP) [6] ought to be stipulated (and tested) to promote beneficial reliance, by devising which data are made available to the XAI system and in turn which data it provides the user with, at what step of the decision-making process, in which form and in which order with regard to the work of human beings. The decision-making process is thus designed according to evidence-based considerations to promote the best possible configuration for human-AI collaborative effectiveness. These protocols can help optimize the integration of XAI into diagnostic decision-making by guiding radiologists on how to interpret and utilize the explanations provided by the AI system.

Devising, testing (*in vivo* rather than *in laboratory*) and deploying effective HAI-CPs is key to understand which are the best conditions under which AI can actually augment human diagnostic skills, rather than trigger dysfunctional responses and cognitive biases that can undermine decision effectiveness, like in case of the white-box paradox: whenever automation bias is exacerbated by system explanations that fail to provide a degree of transparency that would actually make the system more comprehensible and usable, as reported in [6–8].

To enhance our understanding of phenomena such as AM-induced automation bias and white-box paradoxes in TL fracture detection, we investigated the following research questions:

1. **RQ1** What is the impact of the XAI support on diagnostic performance (i.e., accuracy), also according to **RQ1a** the users' level of radiological expertise and **RQ1b** case complexity?
2. **RQ2** Does the XAI support lead to automation bias?
3. **RQ3** Does the XAI support lead to detrimental algorithmic aversion?

2   Methods

To address the above research questions, we designed and performed a user study in controlled conditions that involved real practitioners, who were called to read x-rays and make a diagnosis of a set of retrospective real cases chosen for their representativeness, both before and after receiving an heterogeneous set of XAI aids, in terms of activation maps that differed both in terms of emphasized features (low and high-level) and coloring schema, as outlined in the following sections.

2.1   The System

The development of the XAI system considered in this study was described in [18]. This system presents its output in both textual/categorical terms (presence/absence of fracture) and visual form in terms of Activation Maps (AM), generated by means of the Class Activation Map technique [19]. This technique produces weight matrices for any given image and associates higher weight values with picture elements and areas of particular importance for the model's classification. For the sake of simplicity, AMs were described to the study participants as "specific heatmaps that, when superimposed on the diagnostic image, emphasize the regions that the classification model deems most significant for determining an accurate diagnosis (presence or absence of fracture)".

Since the main focus of this study is the evaluation of the ability of a XAI system to affect, and possibly enhance, the accuracy of human decision-maker in a complex task of radiological diagnosis, we took into consideration XAI support delivered to each users through one of several different forms of AMs, with this heterogeneity aimed at making the study as representative as possible. The AMs we deployed consisted of four different combinations of coloring and levels of detail, namely *Features detail level: high*, *Features detail level: low*, *Heat map coloring: traditional* (red-blue gradient denoting the importance of pixels) and *Heat map coloring: semantic* (red-blue gradient resulting from the AI model classification, with red used for suggested fracture, and blue for absence of fractures, with brightness as an indicator of pixel relevance).

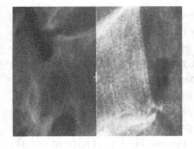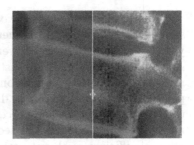

Fig. 1. Two examples of x-rays and their corresponding activation map. On the left-hand side the low-level AMs is used, while on the right-hand side is shown the high-level AM.

Users were provided an image comparison tool, depicted in Fig. 1, to allow for simultaneous examination of the X-rays and AMs. Users could manipulate a sliding control horizontally to overlay one image onto the other, facilitating a comprehensive understanding of the internal anatomical structures.

2.2   The User Study

After generating the AMs for the whole test set, two physicians chose 18 X-rays from a random portion of the test dataset, with half of the AMs belonging to the high-level and half to the low-level detail category (Fig. 2). They carefully selected these X-rays to ensure that these were clear enough for interpretation despite the lower resolution (i.e., 800 × 800 pixels) compared to typical original X-rays. Additionally, we designed the sampling approach to maintain an even distribution of positive and negative examples, considering the complexity of each case to ensure a comprehensive variety of situations for assessment.

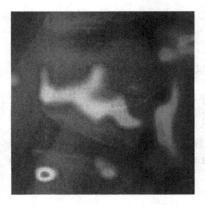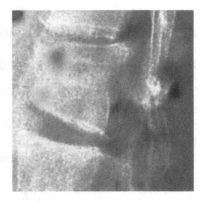

Fig. 2. Two examples of AM, based on the lower level of detail (left-hand side: traditional coloring, right-hand side: semantic coloring)

The study encompassed two x-ray reading sessions, which both involved the same 16 orthopaedics: 8 of them were residents or specialists with less than 5 years of work experience, 8 were specialists or sub-specialists. In the first session, the participants could just consult the 18 x-rays, in random order for each reader, through a multi-page online questionnaire developed on the LimeSurvey platform[1], and give their best diagnosis (either presence or absence of fracture), the level of confidence and perceived level of complexity on an ordinal scale, with no AI nor XAI support. The second session was performed three weeks later, to allow a sufficient wash-out period to pass and to ensure that participants could not recall any particular case (of which they did not receive the correct diagnosis anyway), and performed on a similar platform, which again conveyed the cases in random order. In this second session, the platform provided the participants with both the AI-generated classification and the XAI AMs, asking then each user to provide their definitive diagnosis, level of confidence and perceived utility of the XAI support. As for the color of the AM, the participants were randomly shown either the traditional or semantic coloring, using a Javascript-based comparison element[2], similar to what is demonstrated in Fig. 1. As for the typology of the XAI output, the participants were provided the XAI binary classification ('fracture' or 'no fracture') directly in the form of the color coding of the AM.

After having collected the responses, a comparative analysis was carried out to compare the performance in the pre-XAI and the post-XAI sessions, and hence to evaluate the impact of the XAI support. Considering as a whole the semantic and traditional coloring methods, as well as the AMs displaying moderate and high level of detail[3], we compared the diagnostic accuracy of orthopaedists with respect to their baseline judgment (pre-XAI) stratified by case complexity (high and low) and the likewise dichotomous orthopedists' level of expertise (lower vs higher).

By evaluating the rate of decision change and accuracy following the exposure to the XAI advice, irrespective of its form (color-coding, level of detail), we aimed to assess the phenomena of automation bias, detrimental algorithmic aversion and technology impact related to explainable aids.

3   Results and Discussion

RQ1. What is the impact of XAI on diagnostic performance?

The Human-AI hybrid decision-making team (Humans+AI) exhibits an average accuracy of .89 [.7, 1]. This is 10% higher than the accuracy of both AI and unaided humans (respectively .77 [.66, .88] and .79 [.58, .97]). In particular, the difference in accuracy between the Humans+XAI judgment and the baseline (pre-XAI) human judgment (i.e.,, human+XAI - human), as shown in

---

[1] https://www.limesurvey.org/.

[2] https://juxtapose.knightlab.com/.

[3] The detailed analysis of each kind of XAI support is the subject of another work currently in preparation. In this paper we report on the longitudinal analysis of the impact of XAI without further distinguishing the type of output.

Fig. 5, is not only significant (P-value .007 for the Wilcoxon test , P-value adj. Benjamini-Hochberg correction: .035), but it also presents a very high effect size (i.e. the entity of the difference in accuracy between those aided or unaided by the XAI system) of 1.23, which was even higher than one standard deviation. This result meets the *Fundamental Theorem of Informatics* [20], postulating that the use of technology is only reasonable when it enhances the performance of unaided humans (i.e., H + A > H). It is also a demonstration of the potential of Human-AI *hybrid* or *collective intelligence* [21,22], even when the AI judgment is similarly accurate with respect to the human one, or even slightly less accurate (see above). This positive impact is shown in the Benefit Diagram depicted in Fig. 3 and the Technology Impact represented in Fig. 4.[4] The benefit diagram provides an intuitive understanding of the benefit caused from providing the XAI support in this study. Each circle denotes a reader accuracy, while the brown lines reflect the average difference in accuracy between the baseline and the human+AI configuration, together with the corresponding 95% confidence interval. In this diagram, as well as in the Technology Impact one, the blue area indicates an improvement in accuracy, and the red area denotes an accuracy reduction. As we see in Fig. 3 we see that accuracy reduction affected two participants (while two participants just did not improve nor worsen), although the average collective effect was significantly positive (i.e., the confidence interval of the difference is clearly above the nil-effect level).

In regards to the Technology Impact diagram, we here recall that this impact is derived by combining the odds ratio of the error rate in case of AI support (AIER) and the error rate without AI support (CER), as defined in [13].

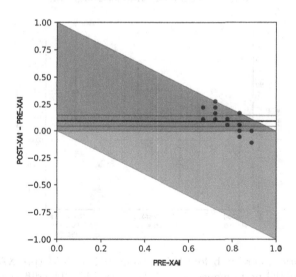

Fig. 3. Benefit diagram comparing the accuracy of the unaided human (pre-XAI) with the effect of the XAI intervention, showing a clear benefit.

---

[4] Both diagrams were generated via the tool available at https://haiiassassessment. pythonanywhere.com/.

RQ1a. What is the impact of XAI on accuracy according to the users' level of radiological expertise?

In the case of lower-expertise radiologists, the p-value associated with the Wilcoxon test (.115, P-value adj. BH correction: .144) leads us to accept the (null) hypothesis of no difference between the baseline and the Human+AI group performance, therefore the effect of the XAI was found to be not significant. However, the effect size is strong (.79), and this means that, with a sufficient number of aided decisions, the difference could become significant. Conversely, for the radiologists with a higher expertise level (more than five years of experience), XAI had a significant effect (P-value .017, P-value adj. BH correction: .042) and the effect size was even higher, being almost equal to two standard deviations (1.76). This huge effect is shown in Fig. 5. We conjecture that the difference between novices and experts could be mainly due to the less-than-trivial interpretations of AMs, which requires a high familiarity with morphological patterns that are suggestive of either negative or positive exams: this suggests that the correct interpretation of AMs should *not* be given for granted, but that rather

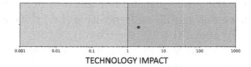

Fig. 4. Technology Impact Diagram.

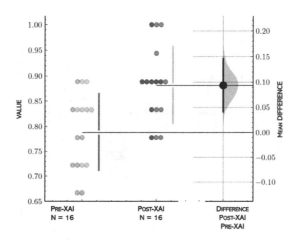

Fig. 5. Diagnostic accuracy, before being supported by XAI (pre-XAI), after (post-XAI) and differential performance (post-XAI - Pre-XAI). The difference is highly significant as the confidence intervals does not cross the 0 line. Each circle represents the accuracy of a single rater. Orange circles represent less expert raters (less or equal than 5 years of expertise), while blue circles represent expert raters (more than 5 years of experience). (Color figure online)

adopting this kind of visual support calls for a specific training of users to make them fully proficient in associating algorithmic saliency, as this is calculated by activation maps algorithms, to visual patterns that are actually relevant for correct diagnosis. In this sense, the provision of XAI support by means of AMs is more akin to a cognitive *catalyst* [23], than a totally unambiguous, and neutral, cognitive aid, which requires users to master a sort of "machine semiotics", as we suggested in a previous study [18] concerning a similar diagnostic settings.

RQ1b. What is the impact of XAI on accuracy according to case complexity?

The impact of XAI on accuracy according to case complexity is shown in Fig. 6. On the left, we see the impact of XAI support on the accuracy in case of high-complexity cases, which is significant (P-value .027 for roportion test, P-value adj. BH correction: .045) and presents a large effect size (1.07). As for low complexity cases, shown on the diagram on the right, we have both a very high p-value (.689) that leads us to accept the null hypothesis of 'no effect' of XAI on decision accuracy compared to the baseline, as well as a weak effect size, equal to 0.14. We conjecture that this lack of differential impact of XAI on the accuracy in the final diagnosis for low-complexity cases is due to the fact that the less complex cases are correctly diagnosed even without any support and therefore it is difficult, especially with relative few decisions, detect a significant incremental effect.

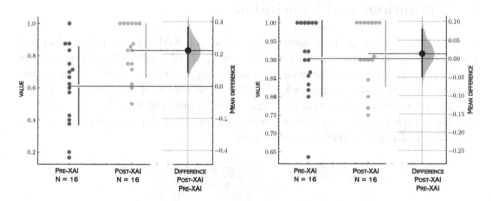

Fig. 6. Diagnostic performance. Left: accuracy rate for high-complexity cases, Right: low-complexity cases. Each diagram represents the pre-XAI, post-XAI and differential accuracy. When the confidence interval of the differential accuracy crosses the 0 line, the post-pre difference cannot be said to be statistically significant.

RQ2. Does XAI lead to automation bias?

The answer to our second research question is presented in the form of benefit diagrams (see Fig. 7). In this measure of automation bias[5], we focused on the ratios and frequencies found in the decision patterns displayed by radiologists engaging with XAI support [13]. We can observe how the measurement of Automation Bias is clearly located in the blue zone, suggesting that XAI has no adverse effects in this case.

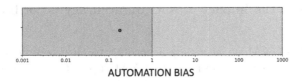

AUTOMATION BIAS

Fig. 7. Benefit diagram related to the phenomenon of automation bias (AB). Red indicates a presence of AB effect, while blue indicates its absence. (Color figure online)

RQ3. Does XAI lead to detrimental algorithmic aversion?

As depicted in Fig. 8, we observed low detrimental algorithmic aversion: this further supports the above finding regarding the beneficial support of XAI in the detection of TL factures.

4   Limitations and Conclusion

In this study, we aimed to assess the impact of XAI on diagnostic decision-making in a radiological task, i.e., the detection of fractures in spine x-rays. Our results demonstrate the feasibility and comprehensiveness of an assessment methodology that determines whether the deployment of XAI systems results in improved accuracy compared to the baseline performance. In our study, we observed a statistically significant positive impact, which is a promising finding, at least for this particular diagnostic task.

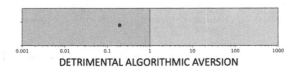

DETRIMENTAL ALGORITHMIC AVERSION

Fig. 8. Benefit diagram related to the phenomenon of detrimental algorithmic aversion (DAA). Red indicates a presence of AB effect, while blue indicates its absence. (Color figure online)

---

[5] Automation bias was calculated via the tool "DSS Quality Assessment" available at https://dss-quality-assessment.vercel.app/?step=4 following the metrics reported in [13].

We observed that the improvement in accuracy was more significant for expert radiologists than for novice radiologists, a finding that deserves further investigations and calls for a profiled, or even personalized, kind of support. Moreover, as expectable, the XAI system proved to be less effective in low-complexity cases, whereas it resulted in a clear and beneficial impact as complexity increases, suggesting that complexity should be a feature to be considered in the optimization of diagnostic support (on this, see also [24]). Finally, the XAI system did not result in automation bias or algorithmic aversion, thus corroborating the finding that the XAI solutions adopted in our user study did have a positive impact on human decision-making: this was verified not only in terms of differential accuracy, but also from the point of view of the impact on psychological attitudes and patterns of reliance.

In light of these promising results, we also acknowledge that this study presents some limitations: these mainly regard the relatively low number of cases considered and the need to distinguish the effect of explanations from that due to only the AI advice. Future research could involve a higher number of participants and cases, and also present a more complex human-AI interaction protocol in which to assess the rate of decision change even at an intermediate level, distinguishing between the effect of presenting the AI advice and its explanation. Additionally, while grouping together several forms of XAI through different AMs proved to be an effective strategy to study the overall impact of XAI in its heterogeneity, future work (already in progress by our research group) could explore the effect of specific features in AM, such as traditional or semantic coloring and high or moderate detail level, on decision accuracy and bias.

By considering socio-technical factors and emphasizing the importance of HAI-CP, we believe not only to have contributed to the literature focusing on how to develop effective and responsible XAI systems that can enhance the accuracy and reliability of radiology diagnoses, but also to promoting a culture of technovigilance [25,26], which ensures that gains in effectiveness do not come at the expense of losses in human oversight and deskilling.

References

1. Liew, C.: The future of radiology augmented with artificial intelligence: a strategy for success. Eur. J. Radiol. **102**, 152–156 (2018)
2. Sogani, J., Allen Jr., B., Dreyer, K., McGinty, G.: Artificial intelligence in radiology: the ecosystem essential to improving patient care (2020)
3. Allen, B., Agarwal, S., Kalpathy-Cramer, J., Dreyer, K.: Democratizing AI. J. Am. Coll. Radiol. **16**(7), 961–963 (2019)
4. Quinn, T.P., Jacobs, S., Senadeera, M., Le, V., Coghlan, S.: The three ghosts of medical AI: can the black-box present deliver? Artif. Intell. Med. **124**, 102158 (2022)
5. Cabitza, F., et al.: Quod erat demonstrandum?-towards a typology of the concept of explanation for the design of explainable AI. Expert Syst. Appl. **213**, 118888 (2023)
6. Cabitza, F., et al.: Rams, hounds and white boxes: investigating human-AI collaboration protocols in medical diagnosis. Artif. Intell. Med. **138**, 102506 (2023)

7. Cabitza, F., Campagner, A., Natali, C., Parimbelli, E., Ronzio, L., Cameli, M.: Painting the black box white: experimental findings from applying XAI to an ECG reading setting. Mach. Learn. Knowl. Extr. **5**(1), 269–286 (2023)
8. Bertrand, A., Belloum, R., Eagan, J.R., Maxwell, W.: How cognitive biases affect XAI-assisted decision-making: a systematic review. In: Proceedings of the 2022 AAAI/ACM Conference on AI, Ethics, and Society, pp. 78–91 (2022)
9. Mumford, E.: A socio-technical approach to systems design. Requirements Eng. **5**, 125–133 (2000)
10. Delmas, P.D., et al.: Underdiagnosis of vertebral fractures is a worldwide problem: the impact study. J. Bone Mineral Res. **20**(4), 557–563 (2005)
11. Vilone, G., Longo, L.: Classification of explainable artificial intelligence methods through their output formats. Mach. Learn. Knowl. Extract. **3**(3), 615–661 (2021)
12. Skitka, L.J., Mosier, K.L., Burdick, M.: Does automation bias decision-making? Int. J. Hum.-Comput. Stud. **51**(5), 991–1006 (1999)
13. Cabitza, F., Campagner, A., Angius, R., Natali, C., Reverberi, C.: AI shall have no dominion: on how to measure technology dominance in AI-supported human decision-making. In CHI 2023: The Proceedings of the 2023 CHI Conference on Human Factors in Computing Systems (2023)
14. Dietvorst, B.J., Simmons, J., Massey, C.: Understanding algorithm aversion: forecasters erroneously avoid algorithms after seeing them err. In: Academy of Management Proceedings, Briarcliff Manor, NY, USA, no. 1, p. 12227. Academy of Management (2014)
15. Jussupow, E., Benbasat, I., Heinzl, A.: Why are we averse towards algorithms? A comprehensive literature review on algorithm aversion. In: Twenty-Eighth European Conference on Information Systems (ECIS2020), Atlanta, GA USA, pp. 1–16. AIS (2020)
16. Sutton, S.G., Arnold, V., Holt, M.: An extension of the theory of technology dominance: understanding the underlying nature, causes and effects. Causes and effects (2022)
17. Cabitza, F.: Biases affecting human decision making in AI-supported second opinion settings. In: Torra, V., Narukawa, Y., Pasi, G., Viviani, M. (eds.) MDAI 2019. LNCS (LNAI), vol. 11676, pp. 283–294. Springer, Cham (2019). https://doi.org/10.1007/978-3-030-26773-5_25
18. Cabitza, F., Campagner, A., Famiglini, L., Gallazzi, E., La Maida, G.A.: Color shadows (part I): exploratory usability evaluation of activation maps in radiological machine learning. In: Holzinger, A., Kieseberg, P., Tjoa, A.M., Weippl, E. (eds.) CD-MAKE 2022. LNCS, vol. 13480, pp. 31–50. Springer, Cham (2022). https://doi.org/10.1007/978-3-031-14463-9_3
19. Zhou, B., Khosla, A., Lapedriza, A., Oliva, A., Torralba, A.: Learning deep features for discriminative localization. In: Proceedings of the IEEE Conference on Computer Vision and Pattern Recognition (CVPR) (2016)
20. Friedman, C.P.: A "fundamental theorem" of biomedical informatics. J. Am. Med. Inform. Assoc. **16**(2), 169–170 (2009)
21. Kamar, E.: Directions in hybrid intelligence: complementing AI systems with human intelligence. In: IJCAI, pp. 4070–4073 (2016)
22. Gupta, P., Woolley, A.W.: Articulating the role of artificial intelligence in collective intelligence: a transactive systems framework. In: Proceedings of the Human Factors and Ergonomics Society Annual Meeting, Los Angeles, CA, USA, vol. 65, pp. 670–674. SAGE Publications (2021)
23. Miller, R.A., Masarie Jr., F.E.: The demise of the "Greek oracle" model for medical diagnostic systems. Methods Inf. Med. **29**(01), 1–2 (1990)

24. Campagner, A., Sternini, F., Cabitza, F.: Decisions are not all equal. Introducing a utility metric based on case-wise raters' perceptions. Comput. Methods Program. Biomed. 106930 (2022)

25. Dixon-Woods, M., Redwood, S., Leslie, M., Minion, J., Martin, G.P., Coleman, J.J.: Improving quality and safety of care using "technovigilance": an ethnographic case study of secondary use of data from an electronic prescribing and decision support system. Milbank Q. **91**(3), 424–454 (2013)

26. Cabitza, F., Zeitoun, J.-D.: The proof of the pudding: in praise of a culture of real-world validation for medical artificial intelligence. Ann. Transl. Med. **7**(8) (2019)

Federated Learning of Explainable Artificial Intelligence Models for Predicting Parkinson's Disease Progression

José Luis Corcuera Bárcena[ID], Pietro Ducange[ID], Francesco Marcelloni[ID],
Alessandro Renda[(✉)][ID], and Fabrizio Ruffini[ID]

Department of Information Engineering, University of Pisa, Largo Lucio Lazzarino 1,
56122 Pisa, Italy
joseluis.corcuera@phd.unipi.it,
{pietro.ducange,francesco.marcelloni,alessandro.renda}@unipi.it,
fabrizio.ruffini@ing.unipi.it

Abstract. Services based on Artificial Intelligence (AI) are becoming increasingly pervasive in our society. At the same time, however, we are also witnessing a growing awareness towards the ethical aspects and the trustworthiness of AI tools, especially in high stakes domains, such as the healthcare one. In this paper, we propose the adoption of AI techniques for predicting Parkinson's Disease progression with the overarching aim of accommodating the urgent need for trustworthiness. We address two key requirements towards trustworthy AI, namely privacy preservation in learning AI models and their explainability. As for the former aspect, we consider the (rather common) case of medical data coming from different health institutions, assuming that they cannot be shared due to privacy concerns. To address this shortcoming, we leverage federated learning (FL) as a paradigm for collaborative model training among multiple parties without any disclosure of private raw data. As for the latter aspect, we focus on highly interpretable models, i.e., those for which humans are able to understand how decisions have been taken. An extensive experimental analysis carried out on a well-known Parkinson Telemonitoring dataset highlights how the proposed approach based on FL of fuzzy rule-based systems allows achieving, simultaneously, data privacy and interpretability. Results are reported for different data partitioning scenarios, also comparing the interpretable-by-design model with an opaque neural network model.

This work has been partly funded by the PNRR - M4C2 - Investimento 1.3, Partenariato Esteso PE00000013 - "FAIR - Future Artificial Intelligence Research" - Spoke 1 "Human-centered AI" and the PNRR "Tuscany Health Ecosystem" (THE) (Ecosistemi dell'Innovazione) - Spoke 6 - Precision Medicine & Personalized Healthcare (CUP I53C22000780001) under the NextGeneration EU programme, and by the Italian Ministry of University and Research (MUR) in the framework of the FoReLab and CrossLab projects (Departments of Excellence). This work was also partially supported by the project "SAFE: Studio e sviluppo di una piAttaForma per la prEvenzione degli infortuni lavorativi" funded by the University of Pisa under the call "PRA 2022–2023".

L. Longo (Ed.): xAI 2023, CCIS 1901, pp. 630–648, 2023.
https://doi.org/10.1007/978-3-031-44064-9_34

Keywords: Federated Learning · Explainable Artificial Intelligence · Linguistic Fuzzy Models · FED-XAI · Parkinson

1 Introduction and Motivations

The enormous development of the Artificial Intelligence (AI) in the last years has encouraged its use in different types of services, that are also employed for everyday life. Since such services are becoming more and more pervasive in our society, they have been receiving the attention of the regulators to ensure that AI can support the prosperity of the society without endangering the fundamental rights of the citizens. As an example, the European Commission considers trustworthy an AI-based system that is: i) lawful - complying with all applicable laws and regulations, ii) ethical - adhering to ethical principles and values and iii) robust - both from a technical perspective and taking its social environment into account [1]. The adhesion to the ethical principles established by the European Commission is contingent upon several requirements. Two of them are i) transparency and ii) data privacy and governance. In this context, transparency means that "AI systems and their decisions should be explained in a manner adapted to the stakeholder concerned".

The quest for trustworthy AI concerns several industrial sectors and application domains; among them, the health sector is one of those where the protection of (patients') sensitive data is most urgent. This often results in very small datasets available to a single medical center for data mining purposes, hindering the goodness of results achievable by AI-systems. Additionally, the health sector is one of the most impacted by data breaches (78% of breaches in primary sectors are related to healthcare [10], and since 2010 the average cost of data breaching in healthcare has been the largest with respect to all other industries [2]).

Several approaches can be used to guarantee data privacy. They include, for instance, pseudoanonymization and encryption techniques, for which a given datum, albeit modified, leaves the original institution and is shared with a third party. As a remarkable alternative, the recently proposed Federated Learning (FL) paradigm [29] is specifically designed to enable collaborative AI model training, still ensuring that raw data are not disclosed to any third party. The intuition behind FL is that each participating entity (also referred to as client or node) shares only the model parameters (and/or aggregated statistics) with a central entity that takes care of building a federated model. This model is based on, and benefit from, all the informative content embedded in the local contributions.

The aspect of explainability is also of paramount importance in the healthcare sector. In fact, all the stakeholders involved (e.g., patients, doctors, hospital governance, insurance companies) are very interested in knowing and understanding how a certain output has been generated, for different and intuitive reasons. Explainable AI (XAI) is the field of AI-related research studying the possibility to explain how an AI system works. Following the terminology in [4], "explainability" refers to the details and reasons a model gives to make its functioning clear or easy to understand to a certain audience. Schematically, two methodologies can be employed to explain how an AI model works: the exploitation of transparent by-design models or the application of post-hoc techniques [4]. Transparency, in this context, is the property of a model to be inherently understandable for a human, since its way of working resembles very closely the human reasoning: decision trees (DTs), rule-based systems (RBSs) or case-based reasoning systems are generally recognised among the most transparent models. Post-hoc explainability techniques are applied to those models, such as Neural Networks (NNs) and ensemble models, that are not designed with the idea of being understandable by humans, but can be explained a-posteriori: for this reason, these models are generally referred to as "opaque". Examples of post-hoc techniques include local explanations, feature relevance, explanations by simplification, explanations by example, text explanations and visualizations [4]. In general, model explainability and model performance are conflicting goals, depending on the complexity of the involved phenomenon: usually, opaque methods such as complex deep NNs (DNNs) provide more accurate results, at the cost of explainability. Thus, in scenarios where interpretability and performance are equally relevant, it is important to understand how to achieve an optimal trade-off.

While the FL approach addresses, in principle, the problem of data privacy preservation for decentralized machine learning, it is seldom coupled with solutions for the explainability issue. Rather, FL was originally proposed for models optimized through stochastic gradient descent (SGD) and specifically for DNNs. However the synergy between FL and XAI is of major relevance and it is at the core of a branch of FL referred to as Fed-XAI (Federated Learning of eXplainable AI models) [6]: one of its main objectives is to adapt the learning procedure of interpretable by-design models to the FL setting.

The present study concerns the adoption of an Fed-XAI approach in the healthcare context, for predicting Parkinson's Disease (PD) progression as a regression task. We assume a plausible case where sensitive raw data of patients come from different medical centers and cannot be shared for centralized learning. The present analysis is not focused on optimizing the overall accuracy of prediction, but in finding a balanced trade-off between performance and trustworthiness, intended as the simultaneous achievement of explainability and privacy preservation. More in detail, we employ a Takagi-Sugeno-Kang Fuzzy Rule-Based system (TSK-FRBS) [36] which is considered as a transparent model to be learnt in a federated fashion. The goodness of results is evaluated also in comparison with an "opaque" model, namely a Multi Layer Perceptron NN (MLP-NN) model, where FL is performed with the well-known federated averaging method [29].

This work entails the following contributions:

1. we simulate feasible scenarios where several medical centers decide to cooperate in creating a PD prediction model with an Fed-XAI approach;
2. we extend the approach for FL of TSK-FRBS with a novel federated feature selection procedure;

3. we compare the Fed-XAI approach with an opaque approach based on an NN, used as reference for the prediction accuracy evaluation;
4. we discuss about the interpretability of the proposed TSK-FRBS, as an asset to be leveraged by domain experts in the decision making process.

The rest of the paper is organized as follows: in Sect. 2 we briefly discuss some relevant works in the adoption of AI tools in the context of PD. Then, we describe some fundamental concepts of FL and XAI in Sect. 3, reporting the details of the model used in the considered regression task. Our specific case study and the experimental setup are described in Sect. 4 and in Sect. 5, respectively. In Sect. 6 we report and discuss the experimental results. Finally, in Sect. 7 we draw the conclusions.

2 Related Works on AI Application in Parkinson's Disease

PD is a progressive neurodegenerative disorder [32], with no medical cure available at the moment. The disease is observed in 1% of population aged 60 years and over [25]. Typical manifestations of PD are related to resting tremor (usually in a frequency of 4–7 Hz), rigidity, bradykinesia (slowness of movement), and impaired postural instability [33]. Other symptoms involve dysphonia and speech disorders [13], which can be observed as five years before the diagnosis [18]. The Unified PD Rating Scale (UPDRS) introduced in 1987 [8] is a score indicator commonly used to measure the severity of PD symptoms. The motor-UPDRS describe the motor symptoms, while the total-UPDRS is related to the disease overall symptoms. Beside age, also sex, ethnicity, heredity, and exposure to environment are known to be PD indicators.

Different approaches and several datasets have been exploited since the 90 s to predict the UPDRS scores or classify the severity of the disease. Several evaluation methods are used, from k-fold cross-validation to leave one out cross-validation or leave one subject out tests. The data types considered for this purpose include speech signals, kinetic data (e.g., coming from wearable sensors) and images (e.g., tomography). Several techniques have been used, spanning from linear regressions, DTs [35,43], k-nearest neighbors, and support vector machines [43] to fuzzy classification or regression methods [9,31] and Random Forests [23,42]. More recently, also DNN models [16] have been used, even though the amount of training data available is generally rather limited in this domain [19]. This is a typical problem of datasets related to the health sector. Thus, also in this context, FL has been employed for PD detection (classification task) using DNNs on tomographic images [10] and on signals from wearable devices [20].

To the best of our knowledge, none of the proposed studies on application of AI models on PD-related tabular data consider the requirement of privacy preservation, but rather adopt a traditional "centralized" learning scheme. Moreover, the majority of approaches focus on models performance, while only few works contain discussion on their explainability. As an example, authors of [28] discuss the adoption of the post-hoc methods for generating explanations from DNN for classifying images from Single Photon Emission Computed Tomography scanning (SPECT) and distinguishing healthy from not-healthy subjects. Similarly, authors in [21] use post-hoc explainability techniques on a multiclass classification task.

Unlike existing works, our approach jointly considers model performance, transparency and data privacy issue. To this aim, we exploited the Parkinson Telemonitoring dataset (described in Sect. 4), which enables a regression task for disease progression prediction from voice measurements. We analyzed two realistic scenarios involving 10 medical centers with the constraint that raw data cannot be shared. This dataset has been exploited in other works, both for classification [16,17] and regression tasks [31,34,42]. However none of the approaches proposed in the literature considers the issue of privacy and transparency.

3   Background

In this section, we first provide some background information about FL and then discuss the approach adopted in this work for FL of TSK-FRBS, which can be framed under the umbrella of Fed-XAI.

3.1   Federated Learning

FL [3,6,22,24,30,44] has been recently introduced as a paradigm to accommodate collaborative training of ML models among multiple participants. The fundamental concept of FL lies in the preservation of privacy of data owners, as only model updates or aggregated statistics (and not local raw data) are shared during the learning process. Yet, FL applications come in different nuances, depending on the data partitioning scheme and the scale of the federation. Data partitioning can be roughly classified into horizontal and vertical: in the *horizontal* setting, the training instances from different participants are described by the same set of features, whereas in the *vertical* setting, it is the feature set that is partitioned among the participants. Scale of federation refers to the number of participants involved in the process and is typically categorized into cross-silo FL and cross-device FL. In *cross-silo* FL the participants are represented by (typically a low number of) organizations or data centers, for which one can generally assume high availability of data and computational power. In *cross-device* FL the number of participants (represented, e.g., by smartphones or personal equipment) is typically large and each of them may feature a relatively small amount of data and computational power.

From an algorithmic point of view, most FL approaches adopt or extend the federated averaging (FedAvg) protocol, which is an iterative, round-based, procedure consisting of the following steps: at each round the server shares the global model to the participants; each participant updates the model through SGD on its local dataset and shares the updated model to the server; finally, the server computes the average of the locally updated models, weighted according to the cardinality of the local datasets, to obtain a new global model. As a consequence, it is quite straightforward to translate from the *local* to the *federated* setting the learning process of models optimized through SGD or its variants. For example, Deep Learning and NN models typically exploit this kind of optimization procedure and have been widely considered in the context of FL. Conversely, FedAvg is not immediately suitable for FL of other classes of models, such as DTs and RBSs, which are not typically learned through the optimization of a differentiable global objective function.

3.2   Fed-XAI: *Federated Learning of XAI* models

Fed-XAI [6] has been recently conceived as a branch of FL focused on the explainability of the ML model learned in a, privacy preserving, federated fashion. Research efforts are proliferating in this domain, either pursuing post-hoc [5,11,12,27,38] or ex-ante [7,26,39,41,45] explainability. In this work, pursuing transparency and inherent interpretability of the ML model as key enablers towards XAI, we exploit TSK-FRBS and resort on a recently proposed procedure for FL of such models [7].

A TSK-FRBS consists of a set of *if-then* rules and has proven to achieve adequate levels of performance in regression tasks. The rule base is constructed in a data-driven fashion: during the structure identification stage the number of rules and the antecedent (*if*) part of the rules are determined either with grid-partitioning of the input space or exploiting fuzzy clustering methods. During the model parameter identification stage, local linear models for the consequent (*then*) part are fitted on the subspaces determined in the first stage. The generic k^{th} rule of a first-order TSK-FRBS has the following form:

$$R_k : \textbf{IF} \quad X_1 \textit{ is } A_{1,j_{k,1}} \quad \textbf{AND} \quad \ldots \quad \textbf{AND} \quad X_F \textit{ is } A_{F,j_{k,F}}$$

$$\textbf{THEN} \quad y_k = \gamma_{k,0} + \sum_{i=1}^{F} \gamma_{k,i} \cdot x_i \tag{1}$$

where F is the number of input variables, $A_{i,j_{k,i}}$ identifies the jth fuzzy set of the fuzzy partition over the ith input variable X_i, and $\gamma_{k,i}$ (with $i = 0, \ldots, F$) are the coefficients of the linear model, which is used to compute the associated output y_k.

Given an input pattern $\mathbf{x} = [x_1, x_2, \ldots, x_F]^T$, the inference stage operates as follows. First, the strength of activation of each rule is computed as:

$$w_k(\mathbf{x}) = \prod_{f=1}^{F} \mu_{f,j_{k,f}}(x_f) \quad \text{for} \quad k = 1, \ldots, K \tag{2}$$

where $\mu_{f,j_{k,f}}(x_f)$ is the membership degree of x_f to the fuzzy set $A_{f,j_{k,f}}$. Then, the output is evaluated either as the average of the outputs associated with the activated rules (weighted by their firing strengths) or coincides with that of the highest firing strength rule (maximum matching policy).

TSK-FRBSs are generally considered among the most transparent models for regression tasks: the inference process, based on application of simple *if-then* rules, resembles in fact a human way of reasoning. Moreover, the adoption of concepts from fuzzy set theory, such as the linguistic representation of numerical variables, fosters the semantic interpretability of the model itself.

Here we leverage a recently proposed approach for learning TSK-FRBS [7], which provides enhanced interpretability. First, a strong uniform fuzzy partition is defined over each input variable. Notably, the geometric properties of such kind of partitions make them more interpretable as they satisfy the criteria of coverage, completeness, distinguishability and complementarity [14]. Furthermore, the maximum matching policy is adopted as inference process: high *local* interpretability is ensured as only one rule is considered for generating the output. Specifically, the antecedent of the rule identifies a specific region of the attribute space and, within this region, the output is computed as a linear combination of the input attributes. As per the *global* interpretability, it is determined by the number of rules and parameters of the system: evidently, more compact rule bases are generally deemed as easier to interpret.

The FL approach for building TSK-FRBSs proposed in [7] considers horizontally partitioned data and can be summarized as follows: each client generates a local TSK-FRBS and shares it with the server. Then, the server aggregates the received rule bases by juxtaposing the rules received from clients and resolving possible conflicts. A conflict arises when rules from different FRBSs identify the same specific region of the attribute space (i.e., they have the same antecedent) but have different consequents. Conflict resolution consists indeed in the generation of a single rule from each set of conflicting rules: the new rule retains the common antecedent and it has, as new consequent, the average of consequent coefficients from the conflicting rules.

4   Case Study: Progress Prediction of Parkinson's Disease in the Federated Setting

In this section, we first describe the dataset considered for the evaluation of PD Progression. Then, we introduce the data distribution scenarios considered in our case study: our objective is to learn a regression model under the hypothesis that the instances of the dataset come from different hospitals and cannot be shared to a single entity for centralized processing and training. FL is indeed well suited to deal with this setting, but its performance may vary depending on the actual distribution of data across the participating nodes.

4.1   Parkinson Telemonitoring Dataset

We consider the Parkinson Telemonitoring dataset, a well-known regression dataset available within the UCI Machine Learning Repository [37]. It is composed of biomedical voice measurements from 42 patients with early-stage PD, acquired remotely during a six-month trial. Each of the 5875 instances corresponds to one voice recording, characterized by 22 attributes (described in Table 1). In the present study, the regression objective is to predict the total Unified Parkinson's Disease Rating Scale (total_UPDRS) score.

Table 1. Dataset description

Feature name	Brief description
subject#	patient identifier
age	Subject age
sex	Subject gender '0' - male, '1' - female
test_time	Time since recruitment into the trial.
motor_UPDRS	Clinician's score, linearly interpolated
total_UPDRS	Clinician's score, linearly interpolated
Jitter[%, Abs, RAP, PPQ5, DDP]	Measures of variation in fundamental frequency
Shimmer, Shimmer[dB, APQ3, APQ5, APQ11, DDA]	Measures of variation in amplitude
NHR, HNR	Two measures of ratio of noise to tonal components in the voice
RPDE	A nonlinear dynamical complexity measure
DFA	Signal fractal scaling exponent
PPE	A nonlinear measure of fundamental frequency variation

4.2 Data Distribution Scenarios

The FL setting assumes that data are scattered over participating nodes. In this work, we consider the case of horizontal cross-silo FL and simulate two realistic data distribution scenarios across ten hospitals. Let $P_h(\mathbf{x}, y)$ be the local distribution of input features $\mathbf{x}$ and associated target values y (total_UPDRS) for the hospital h, and $P(\mathbf{x}, y)$ the overall data distribution. The two scenarios are defined as follows:

– **Scenario 1 (S1).** It represents the independent and identically distributed *i.i.d.* setting: $P_h(\mathbf{x}, y) \sim P(\mathbf{x}, y) \ \forall h$. In other words, the ten hospital has roughly the same training data distributions. Each hospital has a local test set which follows the same data distribution.
– **Scenario 2 (S2).** It represents the *non-i.i.d.* setting: $P_i(\mathbf{x}, y) \neq P_j(\mathbf{x}, y)$ for any pair (i, j) of hospitals. Specifically we force a severe feature distribution skew [22] in which each hospital contains data from only a specific range of ages (e.g., 56 to 57, 58 to 59, ..., more than 75 years old). Each hospital has

a local test set which follows the overall data distribution, equal to the one considered in S1. In other words, it is representative of all age groups.

The test set is therefore the same in the two scenarios and constitutes 10% of the entire dataset. Table 2 summarizes the two data distribution scenarios. Note that data on a particular patient come always from a single hospital.

Table 2. Scenarios description

	S1: training set		S2: training set		test set	
client	age range	samples	age range	samples	age range	samples
0	[36,85]	529	[36,55]	561	[36,85]	59
1	[36,85]	529	[56,57]	473	[36,85]	59
2	[36,85]	529	[58,59]	655	[36,85]	59
3	[36,85]	529	[60,62]	487	[36,85]	59
4	[36,85]	529	[63,65]	506	[36,85]	59
5	[36,85]	529	[66,66]	380	[36,85]	59
6	[36,85]	529	[67,71]	689	[36,85]	59
7	[36,85]	528	[72,72]	279	[36,85]	59
8	[36,85]	528	[73,74]	591	[36,85]	58
9	[36,85]	528	[75,85]	666	[36,85]	58
tot.		5287		5287		588

5   Experimental Setup

In this section, we first describe the experimental setup in terms of regression task and evaluation strategies. Then, we detail on the configuration of the regression models adopted in the experimental campaign, namely a TSK-FRBS and an MLP-NN, adopted as an "opaque" baseline.

5.1   Total_UPDRS Prediction as a Regression Problem

We formulate the PD progress prediction as a regression problem, where the target variable is the Total_UPDRS value. The following preprocessing steps have been applied: i) a robust scaling (using 0.025, 0.975 quantiles) is applied to the input features to remove outliers and clip the distribution in the range $[0,1]$, ii) the output variable is normalized in the range $[0,1]$, iii) a feature selection procedure is applied in a federated fashion.

To implement federated feature selection, we slightly modify the FL scheme proposed in [7] as follows: let $\hat{F}$ be the desired number of features to be selected, which can be indicated by the orchestrating server; in a preliminary communication round, each client determines the $\hat{F}$ features to be selected based on some importance criterion and shares such a candidate list with the server. Then, the server selects the most popular $\hat{F}$ features based on the votes of the participants and transmits such information to the nodes. At this point, the traditional FL process starts considering only the relevant subset of features.

In our experiment the local feature selection is based on Decision Tree (DT) [15]: the importance of each feature is obtained as its associated Gini impurity determined by inducing a DT regressor. Furthermore, we set $\hat{F} = 4$ in order to achieve a reasonable trade-off between model complexity and generalization capability. A thorough investigation of different trade-offs represents an interesting development of this work. Ultimately, the following features have been selected: age, test_time, Jitter(Abs), DFA.

5.2 Evaluation Strategies

The evaluation of the suitability of FL approach is carried out by comparing it with two baseline learning settings, namely Local Learning and Centralized Learning. Figure 1 schematizes the three learning settings.

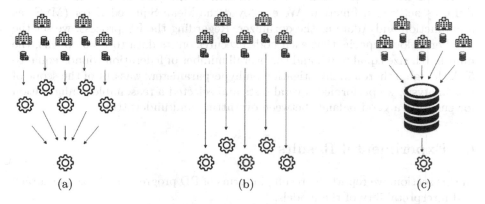

Fig. 1. Schematized representation of three learning settings: (a) federated learning (FL), (b) local learning (LL), (c) centralized learning (CL).

The essence of the three learning settings can be summarised as follows:

- FL: the hospitals collaborate in obtaining a single federated model without sharing their raw data.
- LL: each hospital locally learns a model from its private data only. As a consequence, the privacy of sensitive data is preserved, as in the federated case, but there is no collaboration among different hospitals.
- CL: data from all hospitals are first collected and stored in a single central repository (e.g., a cloud server) and then they are exploited to learn a global model. CL implies indeed maximum collaboration among hospitals, but evidently violates users privacy, as private data need to be transmitted elsewhere.

The assessment of the performance of an FL approach entails, on the one hand, measuring the gain with respect to the LL setting, thus pointing out the benefits of participating in the federation. On the other hand, CL can be used as a reference approach, although in real applications it is not viable due to privacy concerns.

To assess the quality of the predictions obtained by the regression models, two popular metrics are employed, namely Root Mean Squared Error (RMSE) and Pearson correlation coefficient (r).

5.3   Regression Models

For each data distribution scenario, we trained a TSK-FRBS model and an MLP-NN model according to FL, LL, and CL settings. As for the first order TSK-FRBS model (described in Sect. 3.2), we employed a strong uniform fuzzy partition on the features with five fuzzy sets. The five fuzzy sets can be labelled with the following linguistic terms for the purpose of describing linguistically a given rule: *VeryLow*, *Low*, *Medium*, *High* and *VeryHigh*, .

As for the MLP, we consider two hidden layers with 64 neurons each and ReLu as activation function. We employed the Mean Squared Error (MSE) as loss function and Adam as the optimizer. Regarding the FL process, we set the number of local epochs that each node executes on its data to E=5 epochs, the mini-batch size equal to 64, and the overall number of federation rounds equal to 5. Although a thorough investigation on hyperparameters was out of the scope of this analysis, we performed several tests and selected a reasonable configuration for ensuring a good balance between overfitting and underfitting.

6   Experimental Results

In this section, we report the results in terms of PD progress prediction accuracy and interpretability of the models.

6.1   PD Progress Prediction Accuracy

Table 3 reports the average values of RMSE and r coefficient obtained in the proposed experimental setup after transforming the total_UPDRS values back to the unscaled range. Specifically, for both Scenario 1 (S1, iid) and Scenario 2 (S2, non-iid) and for each learning setting (LL, FL, CL), we report the average values of the metrics both on the training and on the test sets. The left-hand side of the table refers to the TSK-FRBS, whereas the right-hand side refers to the MLP-NN.

Table 3. Average values of RMSE and pearson-r (r) on the training and test sets, obtained with the three learning settings, for each of the models used. (left) TSK-FRBS, (right) MLP-NN.

TSK	RMSE		r		MLP	RMSE		r	
	train	test	train	test		train	test	train	test
S1 - LL	6.165	11.214	0.820	0.448	**S1 - LL**	8.981	9.122	0.553	0.490
S1 - FL	7.907	8.657	0.677	0.622	**S1 - FL**	9.492	9.192	0.472	0.476
S1 - CL	7.790	7.850	0.688	0.660	**S1 - CL**	7.651	7.722	0.704	0.675
S2 - LL	3.221	91.832	0.919	-0.064	**S2 - LL**	5.243	18.108	0.799	0.180
S2 - FL	13.166	14.807	0.509	0.470	**S2 - FL**	10.047	10.150	0.203	0.353
S2 - CL	7.477	7.850	0.641	0.660	**S2 - CL**	7.477	7.657	0.599	0.682

The analysis of the results covers all the dimensions of the investigation.

First, it can be observed that the interpretable-by-design TSK-FRBS is able to achieve a prediction accuracy comparable to the one of the MLP-NN on the considered dataset. This specifically holds in the CL setting, regardless of the data distribution scenario (obviously, as the "gathered" training sets are consistent). It is worth highlighting that other works report better performance metrics on the same dataset but they have been obtained considering different dataset splits and/or different input attributes [31,42]: in our case, we are not pursuing state of art performances on the PD Telemonitoring dataset, but rather focusing on the suitability of the Fed-XAI approach w.r.t. other learning setting and in the comparison with a non-inherently interpretable model.

Second, the FL approach generally outperforms the LL setting, in terms of generalization capability on the test set. This outcome is particularly noticeable in the non-iid scenario (S2), where local models lack of generalization capability due to the feature distribution skew. However it can be appreciated also in the case of iid data (S1) where knowledge aggregation in the federated model still brings an improvement over the local setting, especially in the case of TSK-FRBS. It is also interesting to notice that the TSK-FRBS learnt in a federated fashion achieves similar results compared to the NN counterpart: in S1 it slightly outperforms, on average, the MLP-NN both in terms of RMSE (8.657 vs 9.192 , the lower the better) and r (0.622 vs 0.476, the higher the better); in S2, TSK-FRBS achieves a worse RMSE value (14.807 vs 10.150) but a better r (0.470 vs 0.353). This also indicates that RMSE and r capture different aspects, namely how much the prediction deviates from the true value and how much predicted and true values are correlated, respectively.

Third, the LL models are more prone to overfitting, compared to the FL and CL ones. Considering the difference between the accuracy measured on the corresponding training and test sets, we can conclude that overfitting is particularly severe in the non-iid scenario (S2). Local models are able to adequately fit training data, which, however, represent only a slice of the population (split by age); consequently, they cannot generalize on the entire population. However, overfitting also emerges in the iid scenario (S1), especially for the TSK-FRBS, for the LL models: surprisingly, although the MLP-NN consists of several layers of non-linear information processing and entails a greater complexity compared to TSK-FRBS, it is less affected by overfitting.

Fourth, the performance of the FL setting is worse than (although quite close) the one obtained by the CL setting, both for TSK-FRBS and MLP-NN. The better performance of the centralised model was expected, since it exploits all data for training a model in a traditional fashion, but at the same time it represents an unfeasible approach when privacy preservation is an imperative need.

Table 3 provides only a general overview of the results, reporting average values of the metrics. A more insightful picture of the results can be obtained by analysing the actual performance experienced by each hospital. For the sake of compactness, such fine-grained results are shown in Fig. 2 in the form of empirical cumulative distribution function (ECDF) for the RMSE metric.

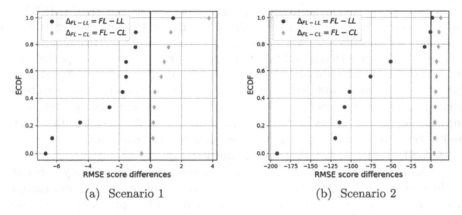

(a) Scenario 1   (b) Scenario 2

Fig. 2. Empirical cumulative distribution function (ECDF) of the differences of RMSE scores obtained by the TSK-FRBS between FL and LL (Δ_{FL-LL}, dark blue) and between FL and CL (Δ_{FL-CL}, light blue) for Scenario 1 (a) and Scenario 2 (b).

The ECDF is reported for the values of the difference, for each hospital, of the RMSE score between the FL setting and the LL setting (Δ_{FL-LL}, dark blue circles) and between the FL setting and the CL setting (Δ_{FL-CL}, cyan diamonds) for S1 (Fig. 2a) and S2 (Fig. 2b). Each curve has 10 points, coherently with the number of hospitals considered in our setting. Whenever a point lies in the negative half-plane (negative RMSE difference) it indicates that the RMSE value of the FL model is lower (and therefore better) compared to the other one (either CL or LL). It can be immediately noticed that FL setting outperforms the LL setting in 9 out of 10 hospitals for both data distribution scenarios. Furthermore, the difference is limited in the case of S1 ($[-7, +2]$) and extremely large in the case of S2 ($[-192, +2]$): this confirms the unsuitability of the local models in the non-iid setting. As expected, the CL setting outperforms the FL setting with a difference in $[-1, +4]$ for S1 and $[+3, +12]$ for S2.

Although the ECDF curves already suggest the existence of significant differences, we have also executed a pairwise Wilcoxon signed-rank test [40] to assess if there is statistical evidence of such differences in performances (both in terms of RMSE and r) between the FL setting and the other ones: specifically, we select the *FL* setting as the control one and compare it separately with *LL* and *CL*. Table 4 reports the results of the test in terms of p-value.

Table 4. Results of the Wilcoxon Signed-Rank test on the performance metrics measured on the test sets (RMSE and r), in terms of p-value. A p-value lower than the significance level ($\alpha = 0.05$) is highlighted in bold.

Comparison	RMSE		r	
	Scenario 1	Scenario 2	Scenario 1	Scenario 2
TSK-FRBS				
FL vs LL	**0.0098**	**0.0059**	**0.0020**	**0.0020**
FL vs CL	**0.0195**	**0.0020**	**0.0488**	**0.0020**
MLP-NN				
FL vs LL	0.4316	**0.0020**	0.4316	**0.0488**
FL vs CL	**0.0020**	**0.0020**	**0.0020**	**0.0020**

The statistical hypothesis of equivalence can be rejected whenever the p-value is lower than the level of significance α. As for the TSK-FRBS, results confirm that, with $\alpha = 0.05$, there is statistical evidence of a difference in performance between FL and LL, and between FL and CL, regardless of the metric and the data distribution scenario considered. Same considerations apply for the MLP-NN model with the exception of the comparison between FL and LL in the iid case: in this case the null hypothesis of equivalence cannot be rejected.

6.2   TSK-FRBS Interpretability

Global interpretability is primarily related to the structural properties of the model. In the case of TSK-FRBS, the number of rules can be regarded as a proxy for assessing the model complexity and, therefore, its interpretability. Table 5 reports the number of rules of the LL (average value), FL and CL models.

Table 5. Model complexity: number of rules of the TSK-FRBSs.

	LL	FL	CL
Scenario 1	217.8	419.0	419.0
Scenario 2	71.7	419.0	419.0

The federated TSK-FRBS and the centralized TSK-FRBS have the same number of rules since in both cases all the training instances spread on the various hospitals are considered for the rule antecedent generation. As expected, such models are more complex than the locally learned ones by a factor of around 2 in the iid scenario (S1) and of around 6 in the non-iid scenario (S2). In Sect. 6.1 we have shown that the FL approach (and CL, as well) significantly outperforms the LL one: here we observe that this is achieved at the cost of an increased complexity (i.e., lower global interpretability) of the TSK-FRBSs. The choice of the most appropriate trade-off between these two conflicting objectives (accuracy and interpretability) may depend on the specific application case and can be left to an end-user.

Local interpretability is instead associated with the inference process and focuses on how the prediction is computed for any single input instance. As discussed in Sect. 3.2, the adopted TSK-FRBS model adopts the maximum matching policy, for which only the rule with the highest activation strength is considered for making a prediction. An example rule extracted from the federated TSK-FRBS in Scenario 1 is reported in the following:

$$
\begin{aligned}
R_k : &\textbf{IF } age \text{ is } VeryHigh \textbf{ AND } test\_time \text{ is } Low \\
&\textbf{AND } Jitter(Abs) \text{ is } High \textbf{ AND } DFA \text{ is } VeryHigh \\
&\textbf{THEN} : Total\_UPDRS = 0.269 + 0.210 \cdot age+ \\
&+ 0.347 \cdot test\_time + 0.014 \cdot Jitter(Abs) - 0.020 \cdot DFA
\end{aligned}
\tag{3}
$$

The antecedent part of the rule entails a good semantic interpretability thanks to the adoption of just 5 fuzzy sets, which are distinguishable and complementary by design. The rule can be interpreted as follows: with very high *age* and *DFA*, high *Jitter(Abs)* and low *test_time*, the predicted output is mostly affected by *age* and *test_time* (relatively high positive coefficient), while *Jitter(Abs)* and *DFA* have lower and opposite impact (positive and negative, respectively). The explanation can be provided to clinicians and operators, in order to motivate a certain outcome, as well as monitored by the developer for possible debugging of the model.

7   Conclusions

In this paper, we report on the application of Fed-XAI methods to the healthcare sector and, specifically, to the prediction of Parkinson's Disease progression. The adoption of TSK-FRBS models learnt according to the FL paradigm is motivated by the necessity to simultaneously meet the trustworthy requirements of data privacy and transparency. On one hand, in fact, each medical center can often benefit of small-sized datasets, since collecting raw patients' data from other entities is typically not feasible. Small datasets usually hamper accurate analytics based on ML tools, as locally learned models feature poor generalization capability: hence, the need to resort to the FL paradigm. On the other hand, the adoption of interpretable by design models provides, in principle, more interpretable results.

To assess the performance of the Fed-XAI approach, we devised two experimental scenarios featuring 10 hospitals: the former considers an iid setting, where all hospitals have consistent data distributions; the latter considers a non-iid setting, where each hospital contains training data from only a specific age-range, simulating a scenario in which each hospital is specialized in a specific group of patients but is interested in obtaining a federated model with better generalization capability. Results of the regression task suggest that the models learnt in a federated fashion have higher generalization capability compared to locally learned ones. This is particularly noticeable in the non-iid scenario. Furthermore, the performance obtained by TSK-FRBS are comparable to those of an opaque MLP-NN, considered as a non-interpretable by-design reference model. This confirms the capability of the Fed-XAI model to reach an adequate level of accuracy in the proposed experiment, while providing also a high level of interpretability by-design. Further developments of this work include the refinement and extension of the Fed-XAI approach with other interpretable by-design models (e.g., decision trees), the investigation of other data distribution scenarios and the comparison, in terms of explainability, with post-hoc techniques.

References

1. Ethics Guidelines for Trustworthy AI, Technical Report. European Commission. High Level Expert Group on AI (2019). https://ec.europa.eu/digital-single-market/en/news/ethics-guidelines-trustworthy-ai
2. Cost of a Data Breach report. IBM (2022). https://www.ibm.com/account/reg/us-en/signup?formid=urx-51643
3. Aledhari, M., Razzak, R., Parizi, R.M., Saeed, F.: Federated learning: a survey on enabling technologies, protocols, and applications. IEEE Access **8**, 140699–140725 (2020)
4. Barredo Arrieta, A., et al.: Explainable Artificial Intelligence (XAI): concepts, taxonomies, opportunities and challenges toward responsible AI. Inf. Fusion **58**, 82–115 (2020)
5. Chen, P., Du, X., Lu, Z., Wu, J., Hung, P.C.: EVFL: an explainable vertical federated learning for data-oriented Artificial Intelligence systems. J. Syst. Arch. **126**, 102474 (2022). https://doi.org/10.1016/j.sysarc.2022.102474. https://www.sciencedirect.com/science/article/pii/S1383762122000583
6. Corcuera Bárcena, J.L., et al.: Fed-XAI: federated learning of explainable artificial intelligence models. In: XAI.it 2022: 3rd Italian Workshop on Explainable Artificial Intelligence, Co-located with AI*IA 2022 (2022). https://ceur-ws.org/Vol-3277/paper8.pdf
7. Corcuera Bárcena, J.L., Ducange, P., Ercolani, A., Marcelloni, F., Renda, A.: An approach to federated learning of explainable fuzzy regression models. In: 2022 IEEE International Conference on Fuzzy Systems (FUZZ-IEEE), pp. 1–8 (2022). https://doi.org/10.1109/FUZZ-IEEE55066.2022.9882881
8. Daneault, J.F., Carignan, B., Sadikot, A.F., Duval, C.: Are quantitative and clinical measures of bradykinesia related in advanced Parkinson's disease? J. Neurosci. Methods **219**(2), 220–223 (2013). https://doi.org/10.1016/j.jneumeth.2013.08.009
9. Niousha, D.K., Sert, O.C., Ozyer, T., Reda, A.: Fuzzy classification methods based diagnosis of Parkinson's disease from speech test cases. Curr. Aging Sci. **12**, 100–120 (2019). https://doi.org/10.2174/1874609812666190625140311

10. Dipro, S.H., Islam, M., Al Nahian, A., Sharmita Azad, M., Chakrabarty, A., Reza, T.: A federated learning based privacy preserving approach for detecting Parkinson's disease using deep learning. In: 2022 25th International Conference on Computer and Information Technology (ICCIT), pp. 139–144 (2022). https://doi.org/10.1109/ICCIT57492.2022.10055787

11. Fiosina, J.: explainable federated learning for taxi travel time prediction. In: VEHITS (2021)

12. Fiosina, J.: Interpretable privacy-preserving collaborative deep learning for taxi trip duration forecasting. In: International Conference on Vehicle Technology and Intelligent Transport Systems, International Conference on Smart Cities and Green ICT Systems, pp. 392–411. Springer, Heidelberg (2022). https://doi.org/10.1007/978-3-031-17098-0_20

13. Franciscatto, M.H., et al.: Towards a speech therapy support system based on phonological processes early detection. Comput. Speech Lang. **65**, 101130 (2021). https://doi.org/10.1016/j.csl.2020.101130. https://www.sciencedirect.com/science/article/pii/S0885230820300632

14. Gacto, M., Alcalá, R., Herrera, F.: Interpretability of linguistic fuzzy rule-based systems: an overview of interpretability measures. Inf. Sci. **181**(20), 4340–4360 (2011). https://doi.org/10.1016/j.ins.2011.02.021. https://www.sciencedirect.com/science/article/pii/S0020025511001034

15. Grabczewski, K., Jankowski, N.: Feature selection with decision tree criterion. In: Fifth International Conference on Hybrid Intelligent Systems (HIS 2005), p. 6 (2005). https://doi.org/10.1109/ICHIS.2005.43

16. Grover, S., Bhartia, S., Akshama, Yadav, A., K.R., S.: Predicting severity of Parkinson's disease using deep learning. Procedia Comput. Sci. **132**, 1788–1794 (2018). https://doi.org/10.1016/j.procs.2018.05.154. https://www.sciencedirect.com/science/article/pii/S1877050918308883

17. Gunduz, H.: Deep learning-based Parkinson's disease classification using vocal feature sets. IEEE Access **7**, 115540–115551 (2019). https://doi.org/10.1109/ACCESS.2019.2936564

18. Harel, B., Cannizzaro, M., Snyder, P.J.: Variability in fundamental frequency during speech in prodromal and incipient Parkinson's disease: a longitudinal case study. Brain Cogn. **56**(1), 24–29 (2004). https://doi.org/10.1016/j.bandc.2004.05.002. https://www.sciencedirect.com/science/article/pii/S0278262604001393

19. Hlavica, J., Prauzek, M., Peterek, T., Musilek, P.: Assessment of Parkinson's disease progression using neural network and ANFIS models. Neural Netw. World **26**, 111–128 (2016). https://doi.org/10.14311/nnw.2016.26.006

20. Jorge, J., et al.: Applying federated learning in the detection of freezing of gait in Parkinson's disease. In: 2022 IEEE/ACM 15th International Conference on Utility and Cloud Computing (UCC), pp. 195–200 (2022). https://doi.org/10.1109/UCC56403.2022.00037

21. Junaid, M., Ali, S., Eid, F., El-Sappagh, S., Abuhmed, T.: Explainable machine learning models based on multimodal time-series data for the early detection of Parkinson's disease. Comput. Methods Prog. Biomed. **234**, 107495 (2023). https://doi.org/10.1016/j.cmpb.2023.107495. https://www.sciencedirect.com/science/article/pii/S016926072300161X

22. Kairouz, P., et al.: Advances and open problems in federated learning. arXiv preprint arXiv:1912.04977 (2019)

23. Karan, B., Sahu, S.S., Mahto, K.: Parkinson disease prediction using intrinsic mode function based features from speech signal. Biocybern. Biomed. Eng. **40**(1), 249–

264 (2020). https://doi.org/10.1016/j.bbe.2019.05.005. https://www.sciencedirect. com/science/article/pii/S0208521618305564

24. Li, Q., Wen, Z., Wu, Z., Hu, S., Wang, N., He, B.: A survey on federated learning systems: vision, hype and reality for data privacy and protection. arXiv preprint arXiv:1907.09693 (2019)

25. Lin, G., Wang, L., Marcogliese, P.C., Bellen, H.J.: Sphingolipids in the pathogenesis of Parkinson's disease and parkinsonism. Trends Endocrinol. Metab. 30(2), 106–117 (2019). https://doi.org/10.1016/j.tem.2018.11.003. https://www.sciencedirect. com/science/article/pii/S1043276018302030

26. Ludwig, H., et al.: IBM federated learning: an enterprise framework white paper, no. 1, p. 10 (2020). https://doi.org/10.48550/ARXIV.2007.10987. https://arxiv. org/abs/2007.10987

27. Lundberg, S.M., Lee, S.I.: A unified approach to interpreting model predictions. In: Guyon, I., Luxburg, U.V., Bengio, S., Wallach, H., Fergus, R., Vishwanathan, S., Garnett, R. (eds.) Advances in Neural Information Processing Systems, vol. 30. Curran Associates, Inc. (2017)

28. Magesh, P., Myloth, R., Tom, R.: An explainable machine learning model for early detection of Parkinson's disease using LIME on DaTSCAN imagery. Comput. Biol. Med. 126, 104041 (2020). https://doi.org/10.1016/j.compbiomed.2020.104041

29. McMahan, B., Moore, E., Ramage, D., Hampson, S., Arcas, B.A.Y.: Communication-efficient learning of deep networks from decentralized data. In: Singh, A., Zhu, J. (eds.) Proceedings of the 20th International Conference on Artificial Intelligence and Statistics. Proceedings of Machine Learning Research, vol. 54, pp. 1273–1282. PMLR (2017)

30. Mothukuri, V., Parizi, R.M., Pouriyeh, S., Huang, Y., Dehghantanha, A., Srivastava, G.: A survey on security and privacy of federated learning. Future Gener. Comput. Syst. 115, 619–640 (2021)

31. Nilashi, M., Ibrahim, O., Samad, S., Ahmadi, H., Shahmoradi, L., Akbari, E.: An analytical method for measuring the Parkinson's disease progression: a case on a Parkinson's telemonitoring dataset. Measurement 136, 545–557 (2019). https://doi.org/10.1016/j.measurement.2019.01.014. https://www. sciencedirect.com/science/article/pii/S0263224119300144

32. Postuma, R., Montplaisir, J.: Predicting Parkinson's disease - why, when, and how? Parkinsonism Relat. Disord. 15, S105–S109 (2009). https://doi.org/ 10.1016/S1353-8020(09)70793-X. https://www.sciencedirect.com/science/article/ pii/S135380200970793X

33. Renfroe, J., Bradley, M., Okun, M., Bowers, D.: Motivational engagement in Parkinson's disease: preparation for motivated action. Int. J. Psychophysiol. 99, 24–32 (2016). https://doi.org/10.1016/j.ijpsycho.2015.11.014. https://www. sciencedirect.com/science/article/pii/S0167876015300490

34. Shahid, A.H., Singh, M.P.: A deep learning approach for prediction of Parkinson's disease progression. Biomed. Eng. Lett. 10, 227–239 (2020)

35. Sonu, S.R., Prakash, V., Ranjan, R., Saritha, K.: Prediction of Parkinson's disease using data mining. In: 2017 International Conference on Energy, Communication, Data Analytics and Soft Computing (ICECDS), pp. 1082–1085 (2017). https:// doi.org/10.1109/ICECDS.2017.8389605

36. Takagi, T., Sugeno, M.: Fuzzy identification of systems and its applications to modeling and control. IEEE Trans. Syst. Man Cybern. 1, 116–132 (1985)

37. Tsanas, A., Little, M.A., McSharry, P.E., Ramig, L.O.: Accurate telemonitoring of Parkinson's disease progression by noninvasive speech tests. IEEE Trans. Biomed. Eng. 57(4), 884–893 (2010). https://doi.org/10.1109/TBME.2009.2036000

38. Wang, G.: Interpret federated learning with shapley values. arXiv preprint arXiv:1905.04519 (2019)
39. Wilbik, A., Grefen, P.: Towards a federated fuzzy learning system. In: 2021 IEEE International Conference on Fuzzy Systems (FUZZ-IEEE), pp. 1–6. IEEE (2021)
40. Wilcoxon, F.: Individual comparisons by ranking methods. In: Breakthroughs in Statistics, pp. 196–202. Springer, Heidelberg (1992). https://doi.org/10.1007/978-1-4612-4380-9_16
41. Wu, Y., Cai, S., Xiao, X., Chen, G., Ooi, B.C.: Privacy preserving vertical federated learning for tree-based models. Proc. VLDB Endow. **13**(12), 2090–2103 (2020). https://doi.org/10.14778/3407790.3407811
42. Xue, Z., Zhang, T., Lin, L.: Progress prediction of Parkinson's disease based on graph wavelet transform and attention weighted random forest. Expert Syst. Appl. **203**, 117483 (2022). https://doi.org/10.1016/j.eswa.2022.117483. https://www.sciencedirect.com/science/article/pii/S0957417422008132
43. Yadav, G., Kumar, Y., Sahoo, G.: Predication of Parkinson's disease using data mining methods: a comparative analysis of tree, statistical and support vector machine classifiers. In: 2012 National Conference on Computing and Communication Systems, pp. 1–8 (2012). https://doi.org/10.1109/NCCCS.2012.6413034
44. Yang, Q., Liu, Y., Chen, T., Tong, Y.: Federated machine learning: concept and applications. ACM Trans. Intell. Syst. Technol. (TIST) **10**(2), 1–19 (2019)
45. Zhu, X., Wang, D., Pedrycz, W., Li, Z.: Horizontal federated learning of Takagi-Sugeno fuzzy rule-based models. IEEE Trans. Fuzzy Syst. **30**(9), 3537–3547 (2022). https://doi.org/10.1109/TFUZZ.2021.3118733

An Interactive XAI Interface
with Application in Healthcare
for Non-experts

Jingyu Hu[1](✉), Yizhu Liang[1,2], Weiyu Zhao[1], Kevin McAreavey[1](✉),
and Weiru Liu[1](✉)

[1] University of Bristol, Bristol, UK
jingyu-hu@outlook.com,
{dn21257,jm21920,kevin.mcareavey,weiru.liu}@bristol.ac.uk
[2] Bank of China Fintech, Beijing, China

Abstract. Explainable artificial intelligence (XAI) has gained increasing attention in the medical field, where understanding the reasons for predictions is crucial. In this paper we introduce an interactive and dynamic visual interface providing global, local and counterfactual explanations to end-users, with a use case in healthcare. The dataset used in the study is about predicting an individual's coronary heart disease (CHD) within 10 years using the decision tree classification method. We evaluated our XAI system with 200 participants. Our results show that the participants reported an overall good assessment of the user interface, with non-expert users showing a higher satisfaction than users who have some degree of knoweldge of AI.

Keywords: XAI · non-expert users · interactive XAI system · global · local · counterfactual explanation

1 Introduction

1.1 Background

Artificial intelligence (AI), the intelligent technology of machines [30], has made significant progress in performing tasks that traditionally require human intelligence. Recent advances in both hardware and high-performance computing have enabled the development of increasingly complex AI models that achieve high accuracy by continuously turning their parameters.

However, the increasing complexity and the lack of transparency of AI models, especially black-box models, make it difficult to convey security and trustworthiness to users in how and why decisions are made in different applications [9]. The lack of transparency has led to ethical concerns in various fields, such as medical diagnosis and legal judgment. The ability to explain why a certain decision was made, became a vital property of AI systems. Derived from the

L. Longo (Ed.): xAI 2023, CCIS 1901, pp. 649–670, 2023.
https://doi.org/10.1007/978-3-031-44064-9_35

emerging demand for explaining the deployed AI systems, the topic of Explainable Artificial Intelligence (XAI) emerged recently, and has since became an active research area. XAI aims to make AI more understandable by providing details and reasons for its decisions and actions [3].

The Concepts of Explainability and Interpretability: In the community of XAI, the concepts of explainability and interpretability are equated in some cases but there does exist a subtle difference between them. According to the paper by Biran and Cotton [5], systems are interpretable if their operations can be understood by a human, either through introspection or through a produced explanation. In general, the process of interpretation for a model tends to be revealing the working structure and the rationale, while explanation mostly focuses on providing post-hoc explanations for existing machine learning models. The AWS Whitepaper[1] gives a brief summary. Interpretability focuses more on the inner mechanics of models, which are about how and why the predictions are generated, raising the question *How does the model work?*. Explainability is the ability to explain the model's behaviours in human terms, which can usually be achieved by model-agnostic methods, raising *What else can the model tell me?*. There exists a tradeoff between interpretability and model performance given common AI/ML models.

1.2   The Methods of XAI

While there has been an explosive growth of XAI methods, they have two common broad aims: transparency and post-hoc interpretation [23]. Transparency refers to how a model works intrinsically, while post-hoc interpretation concerns how a model behaves after the model training.

Based on a comprehensive and holistic analysis of previous surveys [1], XAI methods are organized into three categories: (1). Complexity-related methods (2). Scope-related methods (3). Model-related methods (Table 1).

In this study, we place emphasis on the following explanation approaches:

- Global explanation: global explanations focus on the overall logic of a model and the entire decision-making process that lead to all the different outcomes. This class of methods are applied when the macro-level decisions are crucial. A general strategy is to display the decision-making process by symbolic and graphical representations. For example, [10] introduced the algorithm of TREPAN, to generate symbolic representations for given neural networks and extract decision-tree structures. Partial Dependence plot (PDP) is a model-agnostic explanation method [12]. PDP displays the marginal effect of attributes to the output of models. Attributes can have either a linear or a more complex effect on the predicted outcome. The limitation of

---

[1] https://docs.aws.amazon.com/whitepapers/latest/model-explainability-aws-ai-ml/interpretability-versus-explainability.html.

Table 1. XAI methods categories

Complexity Related Methods		
Scope Related Methods	Global Methods	
	Local Methods	
Model Related Methods	Model-specific Methods	
	Modelagnostic Methods	Visualization: Surrogate models, Partial Dependence Plot,etc
		Knowledge Extraction: Rule extraction, etc
		Influence Methods: Sensitivity analysis, Feature importance,etc
		Example-based Explanation: Counterfactual explanations, etc

PDP derives from its assumption of independence that the attributes for which partial dependence are computed are not correlated with each other. Also, it is not able to describe the heterogeneous effects of attributes. The method of Individual Conditional Expectation (ICE) extends PDP. ICE plots reveal interactions and individual differences by disaggregating the partial dependence function, which enables a deeper understanding of the level of individual observations [1].

– Local explanation: local explanations aim at explaining why a particular decision was made. [29] presented the algorithm of LIME (Local Interpretable Model-agnostic Explanations), which is a model-agnostic method explaining the local decisions of any interpretable classifier or regressor. It can also approximate black-box models in a local neighborhood of any prediction. Given the goal of exploring the reason why the black-box model made a certain decision, LIME attempts to find out how the outcomes change when variations were added to the input data [24]. It feeds the black-box models by perturbed samples and generates a new dataset of perturbed samples plus the outcomes of models. Based on the new dataset, an interpretable model will be built up, which is weighted by the proximity of perturbed samples to the original [24]. LIME calculates and outputs how much each attribute contributes to the predication of a single sample. Another similar algorithm, Shapley Additive Explanations (SHAP), proposed by [19] in 2017, is a method from cooperative game theory, which assumes that each attribute value of the sample is a player in a game where the prediction outcome is the payout [24]. For each data sample, the algorithm computes the SHAP value of each attribute showing how much effect each attribute has on the prediction.

- Counterfactual explanation: counterfactual explanations describe the minimum alterations to the input data that are needed to obtain a different decision. Counterfactual methods do not touch the overall logic of the model, but focus on explaining individual predictions. Counterfactual explanations are useful when addressing questions such as "why the outcome is P rather than Q?". Therefore, counterfactual explanations can be understood as aiming to find data samples that can produce Q as the outcome while revealing which attributes' values will need to be changed (from the original data sample) in order to achieve this. In this sense, counterfactual explanation approaches can be extended to provide contrastive explanations for non-classification problems.

XAI Tools and Applications: XAI methods have been applied to develop interpretive systems. In many fields, smart systems that incorporate domain knowledge and XAI are mostly used to assist experts. For example, Clinical Decision Support Systems (CDSSs) enhancing communication efficiency and assisting in the diagnosis by physicians [31]. Apart from those systems designed for professional and practitioners, there is a strong need to provide explanations to non-experts to facilitate the adoption and gain the public trust of AI in the wider society. Several interactive interfaces have been developed to address this need, including InterpretML [28], AIX360 [4], which both offer global and local explanations. [11] conducted a user study on eXplanation through Plan Properties (XPP) tools, and the evaluations indicate that these explanations enable users to find better trade-offs.

1.3   What Constitutes a Good Explanation?

Though there are a great many ways to provide explanations, what constitutes a good explanation is still an issue requires considering. Recent works on XAI, which focused on simplified models that approximate the true criteria to make decisions, can lead to a gap of expectations between AI/ML and the fields of philosophy [23]. Given the questions such as "Are the explanations useful?", "Is the model understandable?", or "Is the decision-making sensible", people with different backgrounds may have opposite opinions. A good explanation in the view of a machine learning specialist may be unconvincing to the context of philosophy, sociology and cognitive sciences.

[22] provided a comprehensive review of social sciences on human explanation and discussed if and how these works can be applied to XAI. According to [22], humans have certain biases in their cognitive processes, which means they generate, select and evaluate explanations in a biased manner. When explaining a phenomenon, people are more likely to bias explanations towards inherent attributes, rather than extrinsic attributes. That bias towards inherence is

thought to derive from prior knowledge, cognitive ability and so on [22]. As human explanations are selected, an explanation provider may not provide complete causes of an event, but can still convey useful information by emphasizing the key attributes or evidence in explanation based on their relevance to the recipients' interests. Explanations are social activities involving an interaction between explainers and explainees [23]. Explanations of AI/ML models can be conceived as generated by an iterative process, selected and evaluated based on presuppositions and beliefs [23].

[8] introduced their online experiment where participants use different interfaces to get explanations of an algorithm for making decisions on university admissions. By measuring users' understanding of the algorithm, it is found that interactive explanations are more effective than static explanations while "white-box" explanations are more effective than the "black-box". Those conclusions can be conceived as the design principle of user interfaces, which enable users to explore the system's behaviours freely through interactive explanations and "white-box" (defined as the visualization of the inner working of the system in the paper) [8]. [6] conducted a controlled user study using 4 different systems to investigate if contextualizing and allowing the exploration of explanations based on local attribute importance could improve users' satisfaction. The results of analysis of variance demonstrated that by providing users with missing contextual information (ML knowledge, domain knowledge, external/real-life knowledge), and providing interactive attributes to test their hypotheses (interactive display and example-based explanations), the objective understanding scores of users are increased.

Therefore, those related works provide strong motivations for a user study with an interactive contextualized interface. Interacting with the interface, users engage in the communication through dialogue, textual description and graphical presentation which leads to their own understanding of the model.

2   Preliminaries

2.1   Global and Local Explanation for Decision Trees

Global Explanation: Global explanation is to explain how a model makes decisions by considering all the attributes. Decision tree [27] is a tree-like algorithm that recursively splits the data into smaller subsets and uses the tree leaves to represent the final classification result. In some decision tree algorithms, the maximum depth of the tree can be specified. In our experiments, we set the maximum tree depth to 6. One of the main criterion for splitting a node (D) in a tree into sub-branches (D1, D2, ...) is the GINI index, which calculates the effectiveness of a split based on an attribute at node D.

A commonly used formula for the GINI index is Eq. 1, where $|D|$ (or $|D_i|$) represents the cardinality of set D (or D_i)

$$\text{GiniIndex}(D) = \sum_{i=1}^{n} \frac{D_i}{D} \text{Gini}(D_i) \tag{1}$$

Equation 2 is the definition of GINI, where c_j is the number of records in D_i with class label as j (for total of n class labels)

$$\text{Gini}(D_i) = 1 - \sum_{i=1}^{n} (\frac{c_j}{D_i})^2 \tag{2}$$

Figure 1, referenced from xoriant[2], presents an example of decision tree algorithm. The decision tree considers age, eating habits, and exercise preferences to determine whether a person is fit. The first layer is whether a person's age is less than 30. The second layer decides whether the person eats a lot of pizza or exercises in the morning. The leaf nodes are the final judgment result (fit/unfit).

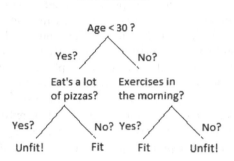

Fig. 1. A simple decision tree determining if a person is fit

Local Explanation: Local explanation is an explanation of how a model predicts a decision for a specific record. In the decision tree model, the specific decision path from the root to the leaf corresponding to that specific record can be regarded as a local explanation. For example, we can draw following local explanations about whether a person is fit or not by following each branch from root to node in the decision tree of Fig. 1.

Example 1: if a person's age < 30 AND person eats lots of pizzas THEN the person is unfit.

Example 2: if a person's age > 30 AND person exercises in the morning THEN the person is fit.

2.2   Counterfactual Explanations

Counterfactual explanations aim to explain why a model predicted one result P instead of another result Q. Some early works in AI are closely related to

---

² https://www.xoriant.com/blog/decision-trees-for-classification-a-machine-learning-algorithm.

counterfactuals, such as [14,32]. However, the explanations provided by these expert-focused or rule-based systems do not offer insight into the internal logic of classifiers. Later counterfactual explanations took an end-to-end integrated approach. For data-driven classification [21], a heuristic method was proposed to explain classified documents. Meanwhile, adversarial perturbations [13], such as Deepfool attacks [25], have been studied for generating counterfactual explanations for deep neural networks. To overcome challenges in interpretability and accountability, researchers like [33] explored unconditional counterfactual explanations of automated decisions. Diverse Counterfactual Explanations(DiCE) [26] extends the work of [33] and provides a method that can be applied to any differentiable machine learning classifier.

Generate Counterfactual Records by DiCE: Equation 3 presents the original counterfactual explanation framework proposed by [33]. Given F as the predictive ML model, it generates a counterfactual record c that has a different predicted outcome than that for the original record x by minimizing the loss function $yloss$.

$$c = \arg\min_c yloss(F(c), F(x)) + Dis(x, c) \tag{3}$$

where $Dis(x, c)$ is the distance between x and c. $Dis(x, c)$ keeps the counterfactual close to the original record and can be achieved with distance measures like Euclidean, Cosine and Manhattan distance.

DiCE introduces diversity and proximity constraints and optimises the above equation by presenting Eq. 4, where $\lambda 1$ and $\lambda 2$ are hyperparameters used for balancing the weights of three parts in the equation.

Proximity and *Diverse* are defined as Eq. 5 and Eq. 6.

$$C(x) = \operatorname*{argmin}_{c_1...,c_k} \frac{1}{k} \sum_{j=1}^{k} yloss\ (F(c_i), F(x)) + \lambda_1 \cdot Proximity + \lambda_2 \cdot Diverse \tag{4}$$

Proximity is quantified as the (negative) distance between the attributes of the original input and the generated record. In DiCE, the proximity of a set of counterfactual records is defined as their average proximity.

$$Proximity = -\frac{1}{k} \sum_{i=1}^{k} Dis(c_i, x) \tag{5}$$

Equation 6 says that the diversity of a set of counterfactuals $\{c_1, c_2, ...c_k\}$ is defined as $det(K)$, where the elements of matrix K equal to $K_{i,j}$. $det(K)$ is the determinant of K. It shows diversity constraints in subset selection problems implemented by Determinantal Point Processes (DPP) [17]. DPP-based diversity facilitates the selection of subsets containing more diverse elements, and results in higher probabilities for these subsets.

$$Diverse = \det(K), K_{i,j} = \frac{1}{1 + Dis(c_i, c_j)} \tag{6}$$

3   XAI System Design and Implementation

3.1   Architecture Design

This paper therefore reports the findings of Interactive Graphical User Interfaces (GUIs) of explainable Artificial Intelligent systems oriented to non-expert users, and to discuss how to improve the quality of explanations by means of user study. Given the dataset of cardiovascular, users are asked to explore a classification problem based on the model of decision tree. The interface provides explanations generated by global, local and counterfactual methods for users, helping them comprehend how and why the decision tree makes predictions. Based on the existing methodologies of XAI and motivated by works that apply cognitive sciences, the design of interface takes advantage of the achievements from previous user studies, conforming to the principles of "interactive", "selective" and "contextualization".

Figure 2 displays the overall structure of the design. The web application is based on the Flask [15] framework. Bootstrap and LayUI templates are used to set the CSS styles. Tree visualizations are generated using Echarts [18] in Javascript. Data interactions are created using Jinja and Ajax requests. The front-end web pages and back-end implementations are packaged as Docker containers and deployed to a cloud server (Ubuntu 20). Nginx acts as a reverse proxy between users and cloud server, forwarding requests to the backend server application and returning its response to the user.

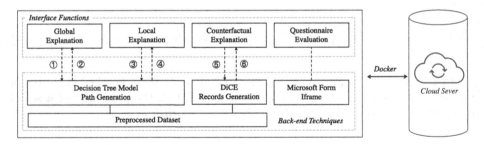

Fig. 2. System overview ((1) Maximum decision tree depth; (2) Decoded global path; (3) Maximum decision tree depth and selected record; (4) Decoded local path; (5) Original data sample and actionable counterfactual attributes; (6) Prediction and counterfactual data samples)

3.2 Dataset

Cardiovascular study[3] is a public data source with 4,237 records. Each record covers 15 attributes, containing information on people's demographic, behavioural, and medical status. We leverage these attributes to predict and explain whether individuals are at risk of developing coronary heart disease (CHD) within 10 years. Table 2 shows the dataset descriptions, where $\mathbb{Z}$ for Integer, $\mathbb{R}$ for real number and *Bool* for Boolean type.

Table 2. Dataset Description

Attribute Name	Description	Value
Sex	Gender of the person	String: **M** for male, **F** for female
Age	Age of the person	$\mathbb{Z}$: An Integer ≥ 0
Is smoking	Whether a current smoker	Bool: 1 for true, 0 for false
Cigs Per Day	Average daily cigarette consumption	$\mathbb{Z}$: An Integer number ≥ 0
BP Meds	Whether on blood pressure medication	Bool: 1 for true, 0 for false
Prevalent Stroke	Whether had previously had a stroke	Bool: 1 for true, 0 for false
Prevalent Hyp	Whether was hypertensive	Bool: 1 for true, 0 for false
Diabetes	Whether had diabetes	Bool: 1 for true, 0 for false
Tot Chol	Total cholesterol level per deciliter	$\mathbb{Z}$: Normal ≤ 200 milligrams
Sys BP	Systolic blood pressure	$\mathbb{R}$: Hypertension ≥ 140 mmHg
Dia BP	Diastolic blood pressure	$\mathbb{R}$: Hypertension ≥ 100 mmHg
BMI	Body Mass Index	$\mathbb{R}$: Normal $18 \sim 25$
Heart Rate	Heart rate per minute	$\mathbb{Z}$: Normal $60 \sim 100$
Glucose	Glucose level	$\mathbb{Z}$: Normal $\leq 200 mg/dL$
10-year CHD	10-year risk of coronary heart disease	Bool: 1 for true, 0 for false

The attributes *age, BMI, cigs/day, cholesterol, diaBP, sysBP, heart rate*, and *glucose* are categorized and encoded using OneHotEncoder. The remaining attributes are processed numerically using StandardScaler. Two of these processes are packaged in a ColumnTransformer and applied to the raw dataset for preprocessing.

3.3 Visualisations of Global and Local Explanations

Decision trees and nodes of a tree produced directly by a decision tree algorithm contain lots of additional information, in addition to the attribute name and its split condition as seen in Fig. 1. The additional information may include for example, GINI values or the number of records reaching a leaf nodes. Such

---

[3] https://www.kaggle.com/datasets/christofel04/cardiovascular-study-dataset-predict-heart-disea.

information is difficult for non-expert users to understand and there is actually
no need to present such information to non-expert users.

Our objective is to provide more straightforward explanations by visualising the decision tree. Figure 3 illustrates the process of converting text into an
interactive graphical decision tree.

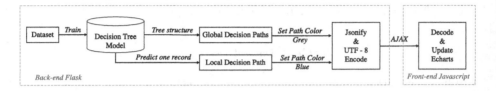

Fig. 3. The process of visualising decision trees

The decision tree model is based on implementation of CART in scikit-learn
[7]. After training, the global decision path is formed by recursively exploring
the 'tree_' attribute in the model. The local decision path can be obtained by
identifying a specific 'node_id' before exploring the 'tree_'. To differentiate
global and local explanations, we set the global paths in a grey line style, while
the local paths are shown in blue lines. After that, we convert the path into a
JSON format and encode it. The encoded string is then passed to the front-end
by Flask [15] and Ajax. In the JavaScript of the HTML webpage, we utilise
'atob' and 'JSON.parse' functions to decode the data into a normal format.
The decision tree is updated whenever we reset the Echarts [18] with the latest
decoded data.

Visualization Optimization: Scalability and selective tree depths are implemented in the tree visualization to enhance user experience. The interface enables
the generation of global explanations with a range of maximum tree depths
between 2 and 6. Based on the tree we described in Sect. 3.2, Fig. 4 shows global
explanations with the tree depths of 2 and 3 respectively.

It's an interactive function that sends an Ajax request back to the model and
returns the corresponding tree model when the user selects a depth and clicks
the 'update depth' button.

The tree structure becomes more complex as the tree gets deeper. To enhance
readability, we hide some nodes when a tree depth exceeds 4. Nodes can be
expanded or hidden by clicking on a particular node. Figure 5 shows the tree
zoom in and out function.

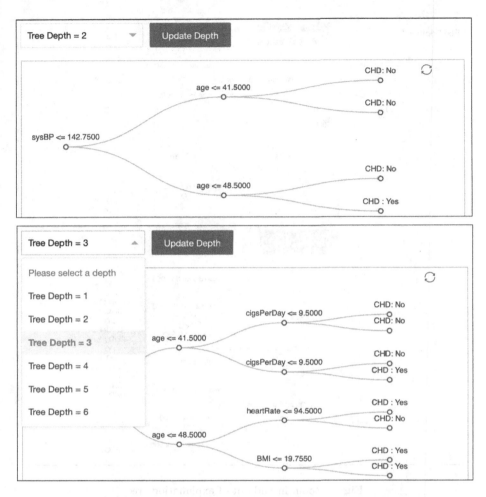

Fig. 4. The global explanation tree of different tree depths, where each node is expandable upon a click.

3.4 Counterfactual Explanation Criteria

Changeable Attributes Selection: The dataset contains 15 attributes and attribute selection can reduce the dimensionality and enhance the computational efficiency of the algorithm. Moreover, some attributes are not actionable, for instance, an individual's age, or gender.

Identifying and focusing on the most important attributes improves the actionability and interpretability of the counterfactual records. We use Shapley Additive Explanations(SHAP) [20] as a reference to select attributes.

SHAP is a method that quantifies attribute contributions for any machine learning model. SHAP calculates the Shapley value for each attribute given a specific record and measures its importance to the final outcome of this record.

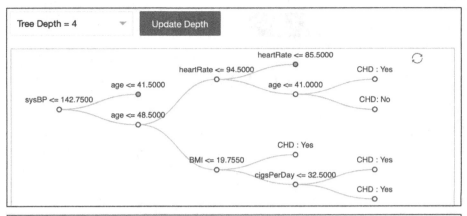

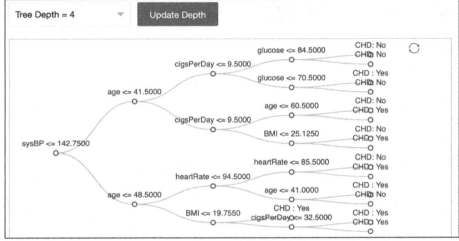

Fig. 5. Zoom in and out of explanation tree

The intuition behind the Shapley value is to calculate the output difference with and without a specific attribute.

$$SHAP_{A(X_S)} = \sum_{S \subseteq F \setminus \{A\}} W * [f_{S \cup \{A\}}(X_{S \cup \{A\}})) - f_S(X_S)] \tag{7}$$

$$W = \frac{|S|!(|F| - |S| - 1)!}{|F|!} \tag{8}$$

In Eqs. 7 and 8, F is the set of all attributes in a dataset, A is an individual attribute, and $F \setminus \{A\}$ means the set of attributes without A. $f_{S \cup \{A\}}$ is a ML model with attribute A present, and f_S is a model without A, and X_S represents the values of attributes in S.

SHAP value for a single attribute of a particular record can be extended to calculate SHAP values for this attribute over all of the records in a dataset. The global importance of this attribute is then obtained by averaging these individual SHAP values for this attribute. The ranking of the attributes based on (global) SHAP values is shown in Fig. 6.

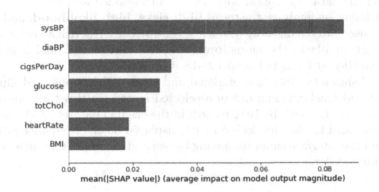

Fig. 6. The SHAP attribute importance plot

In practice, we first select important key attributes referring to the explanation of attributes contributions using SHAP. Then, we opt-out attributes that are not actionable, e.g., gender and age, not possible to change easily. Last, sysBP, diaBP, BMI, HR, cigs per day, glucose are 6 changeable attributes we provide when generating counterfactual records.

Attributes Range Constraints. Range constraints are used for filtering potential infeasible counterfactual records due to real-world limits. Table 3 below lists range constraints of changeable attributes when generating counterfactual explanations.

Table 3. Attributes range constraints

Cigs/Day	Sys BP	Dia BP	Heart Rate	BMI	Glucose
[0, 400]	[0, 300]	[0, 250]	[0, 200]	[10]	[0,250]

4 Interactive XAI System and Its Evaluation

4.1 System Testing

The interface is available to access via weblink[4]. When users access the XAI interactive page for the first time, they will be redirected to the page containing

---

[4] https://med.bristol-xai.uk.

a research introduction and participation ethical terms. Users must click the 'I consent' button to explore following main functions.

Data description, global and local explanation, counterfactual explanation, feedback & questionnaire are the four sections in the application. Most of the content on the data description page has been mentioned in Sect. 3.2.

In the following analysis, the terms **high risks**, **high likelihood**, and **more likely** are used interchangeably to refer to the 10-year CHD risk associated with a **Yes** result. Similarly, the terms **low risks**, **low likelihood**, and **less likely** refer to the 10-year CHD risk associated with a **No** result.

Figure 7 shows the interface of global and local explanations, and illustrate the global and local explanations of a selected record (in this case, we set the tree depth as 3). Each of the 1011 records in the original dataset can be selected on the righ-panel to view its decision path displayed on the left-panel with blue colour, and the interface supports sorting by age and blood pressure in ascending or descending order.

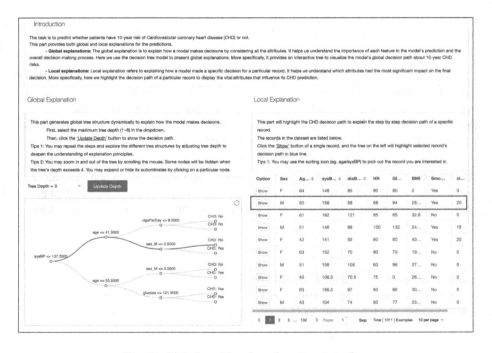

Fig. 7. Global and local explanation interface

Figure 8 presents the counterfactual explanation interface. A brief introduction to counterfactual explanation is provided at the top. Default values have been set to facilitate users in exploring the two panels below more conveniently.

Panel 1 displays how a 10-year CHD risk prediction can be generated when the button "Step 1" is clicked by a user. To aid a user in inputting these values,

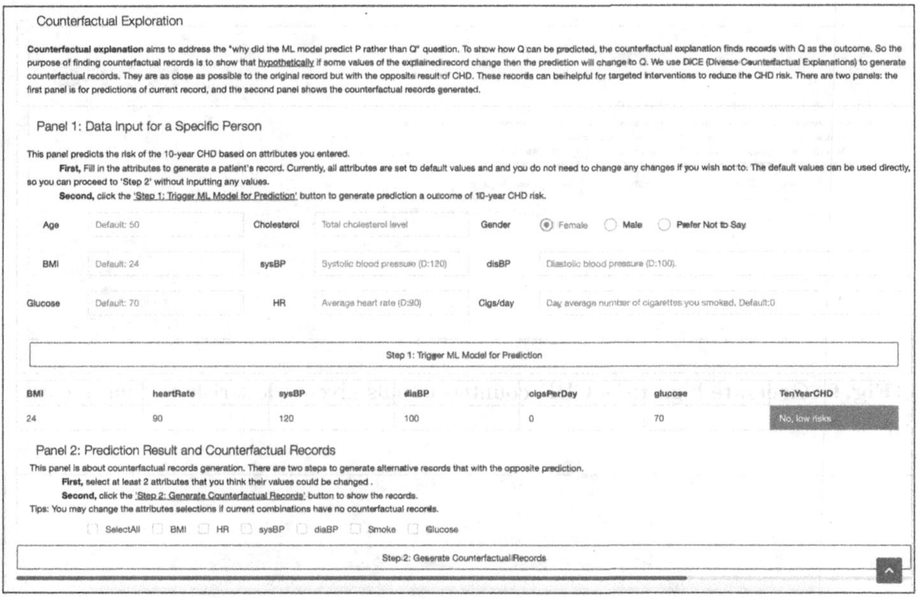

Fig. 8. Counterfactual explanation interface

we provide some default values in these attribute boxes to start with. If a user wishes to alter any of these values, they can do so, and clicked the Step 1: Trigger ML Model for Prediction. The tabular display will appear beneath the button and show the prediction result (far-right in green colour).

For Panel 2, Fig. 9 shows the counterfactual records found for the original record displayed in Panel 1. These counterfactual records are provided by using DiCE and considering the importance of attributes measured by SHAP given in Fig. 6. In the counterfactual records, when the sign "-" is displayed under an attribute name, it means, the value of this attribute is the same as that in the original record. Counterfactual records only display attribute values which are different from original, and these values actually show how changes in some attribute values will contribute to generating a different prediction outcome. This is the essence of counterfactual explanation.

Similarly, if the original record show "Yes, High-risk" and we want to provide counterfactuals to a user, "No, low-risk" records will be produced by DiCE to show how changes in some attribute values can alter the prediction outcome to "No" as shown in Fig. 10. It shall be pointed out that in this case, only two attributes are used to find counterfactuals. Users are provided with a choice of how many attributes they wish to use to find counterfactuals. This is done by selecting attribute names in Panel 2, such as either "Select All", or just select some by clicking on individual attribute names.

Figure 11 shows an example of counterfactual records generated by using 4 attributes.

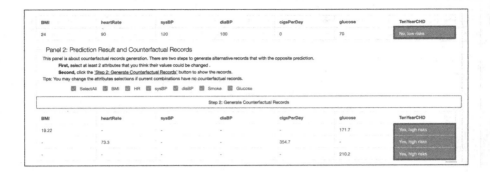

Fig. 9. Generate high risks CHD counterfactuals given a low-risk original record

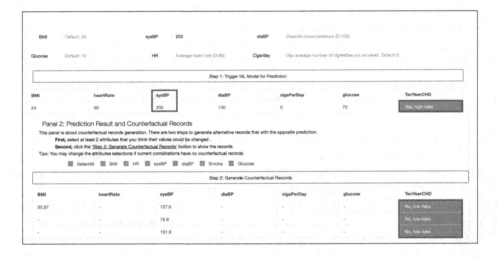

Fig. 10. Generate low risks CHD counterfactuals given a high-risk original record

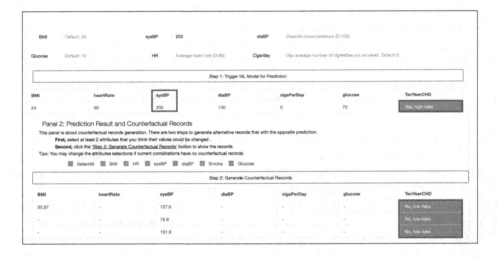

Fig. 11. Counterfactual explanations with 4 changeable attributes

When a counterfactual does not exist if a certain combination of attributes selected. When this happens, the system will prompt 'No Counterfactuals found for the given configuration, perhaps try with different attributes combinations. Recommend: try selectAll attributes for the first attempt'.

4.2 Questionnaire Evaluation

XAI aims to provide decision-makers with explanations of the computing system to help them understand that the entire process is reasonable. It is important to evaluate the effectiveness of the XAI explanation through a questionnaire for participants.

Table 4 shows our 14 questions covering three aspects: basic information, system satisfactory, and overall experience. The designed questions refer to the metrics for explainable AI proposed by [16], including goodness, satisfaction, and understanding.

Result Analysis: In total, 200 participants tried our XAI system after filtering out incomplete questionnaries. 34.5% under 20, 49.5% aged between 20 and 30, and 16% over 30 years old. As for English proficiency, 20% are beginners, 37% are intermediate, and 43% are advanced or native speakers. Additionally, there are 103 non-experts in AI and 120 individuals unfamiliar with healthcare (Fig. 12).

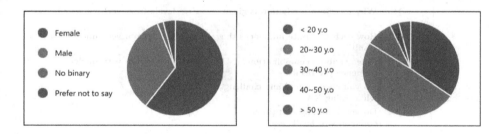

Fig. 12. The distributions of gender and age

Questions related to system satisfaction (Q7 and Q8) receive high ratings, Fig. 13 shows that most of participants believe that the interfaces are helpful in understanding the decision tree classifier.

Table 5 reflects the mean, median, Standard Deviation(SD), Coefficient of Variation(CV) scores of question Q7 to Q12. The mean scores reflect the participants' overall ratings. The median values display central tendency and are robust to skewed distributions. SD and CV scores take into account the dispersion of rating data and can be used to assess the stability and consistency of the scores.

Q7 gains highest average score of 3.705, and the lowest standard deviation of 0.913, suggesting that most participants agreed that decision trees are useful

Table 4. Questions for evaluation

Class	Alias	Question	Options
Basic Information	Q1	Your age	< 20; 20~30; 30~40; 40~50;>50
	Q2	Your gender	Female;Male;No binary;Prefer not to say
	Q3	Do you have any prior Artificial Intelligence experience?	Yes,a STEM related student/worker/researcher; No
	Q4	Do you have any prior Medical Domain experience?	Yes (a medical student/worker/researcher); Yes (been diagnosed with CHD/any related diseases); No (mainly focus on other domains)
	Q5	How do you describe your English proficiency?	Beginner, Intermediate, Advanced, Proficient, Native
System Satisfactory	Q6	Rank the explanations from easiest to least understandable in the list.	Data Description, Global Explaination, Local Explanation, Counterfactuals Explore
	Q7	How useful do you find the decision tree to your understanding the global & local explanations?	Five levels from very unhelpful to very helpful
	Q8	How useful do you find the counterfactual examples it generates to your understanding of counterfactual explanations?	Five levels from very unhelpful to very helpful
The Helpfulness of Explanations	Q9	How the decision tree works	Five levels from very unclear to very clear
	Q10	Why a certain prediction is given.	Five levels from very unclear to very clear
	Q11	How each attribute influences the result.	Five levels from very unclear to very clear
	Q12	How attributes combinations influence the result.	Five levels from very unclear to very clear
Overall Feedback	Q13	Do you encountered any challenges while using XAI	Optional
	Q14	Do you have any additional comments or feedback	Optional

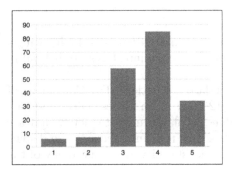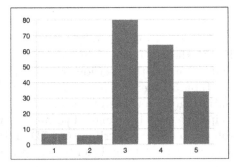

Fig. 13. Rates distributions of Q7(left) and Q8(right)

Table 5. Mean, median, SD, CV scores for Q7 to Q12

	Q7	Q8	Q9	Q10	Q11	Q12
Mean	3.705	3.586	3.490	3.469	3.367	3.376
Median	4.000	4.000	4.000	4.000	3.000	4.000
Standard Deviations	0.913	0.941	1.046	1.088	1.061	1.079
Coefficient Variation	24.64%	26.24%	29.97%	31.36%	31.51%	31.96%

for understanding global and local explanations. Although Q8 receive a lower score, the average grade of 3.586 still suggests counterfactual explanations are effective. For the median values, most questions received a score of 4, while Q11 gained a median score of 3.

We further examined the coefficient of variation and found the variation in scores for Q10, Q11, and Q12 was above 31%. This indicates significant differences exist in how participants considered questions related to why a certain prediction is given (Q10), how each attribute influences the result (Q11), and how attribute combinations influence the result (Q12).

These findings show a positive attitude among participants towards our XAI interface but different satisfactory degrees exist for participants with different backgrounds.

To further investigates the effect of participants' background, participants are divided into four groups based on whether they have prior knowledge of the AI field (Q3) and healthcare(Q4). Those with medical knowledge, such as medical students, medical workers, or those previously diagnosed with CHD-related diseases, are considered to have prior knowledge of healthcare, and the distribution for each group are shown in Table 6.

Table 6. Background group description and distribution

Group Names	AI Field	Healthcare Field	Percentage (%)
Group1	No	No	40.1%
Group2	No	Yes	11.2%
Group3	Yes	No	19.3%
Group4	Yes	Yes	29.4%

Figure 14 shows the scores given by each group for questions Q9 to Q12. Groups without AI-related knowledge (Group 1, 2) find the explanation useful and clear, with average scores around 3.5. One interesting finding is that participants with AI but no medical background (Group 3) give the lowest ratings, with average scores around 3.

Also, we read optional feedback (Q13, Q14) from Group 3 and found one possible reason for their critics is their familiarity with the ML model and expect

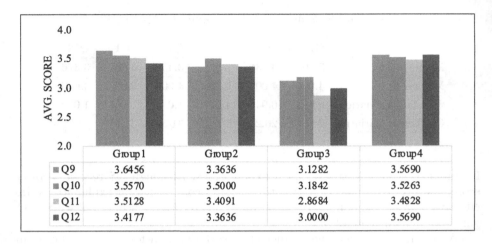

	Group 1	Group 2	Group 3	Group 4
▪ Q9	3.6456	3.3636	3.1282	3.5690
▪ Q10	3.5570	3.5000	3.1842	3.5263
▪ Q11	3.5128	3.4091	2.8684	3.4828
▪ Q12	3.4177	3.3636	3.0000	3.5690

Fig. 14. Comparison of Q9–Q12 Average Scores by Group

more advanced implementations. They provide many helpful suggestions for further improvement including applying the technique to large-scale datasets, using figures like PDP plots to show attribute importance, and focusing on the robustness of the interface. The feedback from other groups is more general, including applying the current technology to other fields and providing support for different languages.

5   Conclusion

This paper presents an interactive web application that provides decision support to non-experts. The system offers intuitive global, local, and counterfactual explanations to visualise how a decision tree classifier works.

Compared to traditional static GUIs, the system provides dynamic explanations that enable users to (1) adjust the maximum depth of the decision tree, (2) personalize predictions based on textual inouts, and (3) generate counterfactuals based on different attribute combinations.

The system is applied in the healthcare field and evaluated through feedback from online participants. The results demonstrate that XAI methods can improve the model's credibility by helping users understand how and why it predicts a specific outcome. Moreover, users can deepen their understanding of the XAI system by experimenting with various inputs and observing changes in dynamic explanations Our work shares similarities with ExpliClas [2]. ExpliClas is a web service that generates global and local explanations after the user selects a dataset and a classifier. The main distinction is that we also offer counterfactual explanations with adjustable attributes. This feature offers a deeper insight into why the ML model predicted P instead of Q. Nonetheless, we are inspired to pursue the following improvements in future research: (1) support multiple datasets for user flexibility, (2) personalize user experience through their inter-actions with the interface, (3) track user browsing duration to assess the XAI system's attractiveness and (4) provide some additional explanations such as attribute-importance plot using DPP or LIME.

Acknowledge. This work is partially funded by the EPSRC CHAI project (EP/T026820/1)

References

1. Adadi, A., Berrada, M.: Peeking inside the black-box: a survey on explainable artificial intelligence. IEEE Access **6**, 52138–52160 (2018)
2. Alonso, J.M., Bugarín, A.: Expliclas: automatic generation of explanations in natural language for weka classifiers. In: 2019 IEEE International Conference on Fuzzy Systems (FUZZ-IEEE), pp. 1–6. IEEE (2019)
3. Arrieta, A.B., et al.: Explainable artificial intelligence (xai): concepts, taxonomies, opportunities and challenges toward responsible AI. Inf. Fusion **58**, 82–115 (2020)
4. Arya, V., et al.: One explanation does not fit all: a toolkit and taxonomy of AI explainability techniques. arXiv preprint arXiv:1909.03012 (2019)
5. Biran, O., Cotton, C.: Explanation and justification in machine learning: a survey. In: IJCAI-17 Workshop on Explainable AI (XAI), vol. 8, no. 1, pp. 8–13 (2017)
6. Bove, C., Aigrain, J., Lesot, M.J., Tijus, C., Detyniecki, M.: Contextualization and exploration of local feature importance explanations to improve understanding and satisfaction of non-expert users. In: Proceedings of 27th International Conference on Intelligent User Interfaces, pp. 807–819 (2022)
7. Buitinck, L., et al.: Api design for machine learning software: experiences from the scikit-learn project. arXiv preprint arXiv:1309.0238 (2013)
8. Cheng, H.F., et al.: Explaining decision-making algorithms through ui: strategies to help non-expert stakeholders. In: Proceedings of the 2019 Chi Conference on Human Factors in Computing Systems, pp. 1–12 (2019)
9. Confalonieri, R., Coba, L., Wagner, B., Besold, T.R.: A historical perspective of explainable artificial intelligence. Wiley Interdisc. Rev. Data Mining Knowl. Disc. **11**(1), e1391 (2021)
10. Craven, M., Shavlik, J.: Extracting tree-structured representations of trained networks. Adv. Neural Inf. Process. Syst. **8** (1995)
11. Eifler, R., Brandao, M., Coles, A.J., Frank, J., Hoffmann, J.: Plan-property dependencies are useful: a user study. In: ICAPS 2021 Workshop on Explainable AI Planning (2021)
12. Friedman, J.H.: Greedy function approximation: a gradient boosting machine. In: Annals of Statistics, pp. 1189–1232 (2001)
13. Goodfellow, I.J., Shlens, J., Szegedy, C.: Explaining and harnessing adversarial examples. arXiv preprint arXiv:1412.6572 (2014)
14. Gregor, S., Benbasat, I.: Explanations from intelligent systems: theoretical foundations and implications for practice. MIS Q., 497–530 (1999)
15. Grinberg, M.: Flask Web Development: Developing Web Applications with Python. O'Reilly Media, Inc., Sebastopol (2018)
16. Hoffman, R.R., Mueller, S.T., Klein, G., Litman, J.: Metrics for explainable ai: challenges and prospects. arXiv preprint arXiv:1812.04608 (2018)

17. Kulesza, A., Taskar, B., et al.: Determinantal point processes for machine learning. Found. Trends® Mach. Learn. **5**(2–3), 123–286 (2012)
18. Li, D., et al.: Echarts: a declarative framework for rapid construction of web-based visualization. Visual Inf. **2**(2), 136–146 (2018)
19. Lundberg, S.M., Lee, S.I.: A unified approach to interpreting model predictions. Adv. Neural Inf. Process. Syst. **30** (2017)
20. Lundberg, S.M., Lee, S.I.: A unified approach to interpreting model predictions. In: Guyon, I., et al. (eds.) Advances in Neural Information Processing Systems, vol. 30, pp. 4765–4774. Curran Associates, Inc. (2017). http://papers.nips.cc/paper/7062-a-unified-approach-to-interpreting-model-predictions.pdf
21. Martens, D., Provost, F.: Explaining data-driven document classifications. MIS Q. **38**(1), 73–100 (2014)
22. Miller, T.: Explanation in artificial intelligence: insights from the social sciences. Artif. Intell. **267**, 1–38 (2019)
23. Mittelstadt, B., Russell, C., Wachter, S.: Explaining explanations in ai. In: Proceedings of the Conference on Fairness, Accountability, and Transparency, pp. 279–288 (2019)
24. Molnar, C.: Interpretable Machine Learning, 2 edn. (2022). https://christophm.github.io/interpretable-ml-book
25. Moosavi-Dezfooli, S., Fawzi, A., Frossard, P., Deepfool: a simple and accurate method to fool deep neural networks. In: Proceedings of the CVPR, pp. 2574–2582
26. Mothilal, R.K., Sharma, A., Tan, C.: Explaining machine learning classifiers through diverse counterfactual explanations. In: Proceedings of the 2020 Conference on Fairness, Accountability, and Transparency, pp. 607–617 (2020)
27. Myles, A.J., Feudale, R.N., Liu, Y., Woody, N.A., Brown, S.D.: An introduction to decision tree modeling. J. Chemometr. J. Chemometr. Soc. **18**(6), 275–285 (2004)
28. Nori, H., Jenkins, S., Koch, P., Caruana, R.: Interpretml: a unified framework for machine learning interpretability. arXiv preprint arXiv:1909.09223 (2019)
29. Ribeiro, M.T., Singh, S., Guestrin, C.: "why should i trust you?" explaining the predictions of any classifier. In: Proceedings of the 22nd ACM SIGKDD International Conference on Knowledge Discovery and Data Mining, pp. 1135–1144 (2016)
30. Stevenson, A.: Oxford Dictionary of English. Oxford University Press, New York City (2010)
31. Sutton, R.T., Pincock, D., Baumgart, D.C., Sadowski, D.C., Fedorak, R.N., Kroeker, K.I.: An overview of clinical decision support systems: benefits, risks, and strategies for success. NPJ Dig. Med. **3**(1), 17 (2020)
32. Swartout, W.R., Buchanan, B.G., Shortliffe, E.H.: Rule-Based Expert Systems: The Mycin Experiments of the Stanford Heuristic Programming Project, p. 702. Addison-wesley, Reading (1984)
33. Wachter, S., Mittelstadt, B., Russell, C.: Counterfactual explanations without opening the black box: automated decisions and the GDPR. Harv. JL Tech. **31**, 841 (2017)

Selecting Textural Characteristics of Chest X-Rays for Pneumonia Lesions Classification with the Integrated Gradients XAI Attribution Method

Oleksandr Davydko[1](✉) [iD], Vladimir Pavlov[2] [iD], and Luca Longo[1] [iD]

[1] Artificial Intelligence and Cognitive Load Research Lab, School of Computer Science, Technological University Dublin, Dublin, Ireland
d22125337@mytudublin.ie
[2] The National Technical University of Ukraine Igor Sikorsky Kyiv Polytechnic Institute, Kyiv, Ukraine

Abstract. Global texture characteristics are powerful tools for solving medical image classification tasks. There are many such characteristics like Grey-Level Co-occurrence Matrices, Grey-Level Run-Length Matrices, Grey-Level Size Zone Matrices, texture matrices and others. However, not all are important when solving particular image classification tasks, while their calculation requires many computational resources. The current work aims to evaluate the importance of each characteristic, taking into account a large dimensionality of the texture characteristics matrices. To achieve this aim, it is proposed to use neural networks and a novel mean integrated gradient eXplainable Artificial Intelligence method to achieve the stated aim. The experiment showed that texture matrices with higher mean integrated gradient values are more important than others while solving pneumonia lesions classification tasks on X-Ray lung images. The result also indicates that classification quality does not degrade and even improves after shrinking the feature set with the proposed method. These facts prove that the mean integrated gradients can be used for solving feature selection tasks for classification purposes.

Keywords: Explainable artificial intelligence · Neural networks · Texture analysis · Medical image processing · Classification

1 Introduction

Various effective tools of intelligent data analysis have been developed to identify pathologies in medical images. In cases where it is possible to identify pathologies through shades and combinations of colour tones in the picture, technologies of texture analysis are recognized as the powerful tool for forming the input field of classification task characteristics [7,10,31]. These methods are often used with

L. Longo (Ed.): xAI 2023, CCIS 1901, pp. 671–687, 2023.
https://doi.org/10.1007/978-3-031-44064-9_36

second-order statistics defined in the same works. Those statistics allow for drastically reducing feature space for classification. But when using texture characteristics matrices in a raw form [6], a need to analyze a significant number of primary statistical features emerges, leading to a high consumption of computational resources. That fact makes a feature importance evaluation a critical task. At the same time, existing feature selection methods cannot provide a sufficient level of performance. The current work discusses a solution to the stated problem using eXplainable Artificial Intelligence (xAI) methods. Here proposed the usage of the Integrated Gradients (IG) attribution method applied to the neural network classifier with texture characteristics matrices as an input. To evaluate feature importance in the dataset context, it is proposed to take IG mean across all records. As there is no way to calculate individual features from texture matrices efficiently, the selection will be performed on the matrices level by analysing the mean integrated gradients set for the whole matrix. The main research question can be stated as follows: how can the IG method be used to select texture feature matrices for classification so classification quality will not worsen?

The remainder of this article is structured as follows: Sect. 2 describes the problem under investigation and state-of-the-art solutions to solve it; Sect. 3 describes the novel implemented pipeline and the methods employed. Section 4 presents the results, followed by a discussion, while Sect. 5 summarises the study and presents possible future work.

2   Related Work

Two primary approaches are employed for feature extraction in image classification. The first approach involves using pixel intensities as inputs for the feature-forming algorithm. Researchers have utilized this approach in various studies to detect COVID-19-induced lesions in X-Ray images, using neural networks trained on pixel intensities [9,15]. The second approach involves a more complex analysis of image texture to extract features. Global texture descriptors such as Grey-Level Co-occurrence Matrices (GLCM), Grey-Level Run-Length Matrices (GLRLM), and Grey-Level Size Zone Matrices (GLSZM) have been identified as effective tools for solving image classification problems. In the work [10] GLCMs are described as the relative frequencies $P(i,j,d,\alpha)$ of the adjacent pixels pairs presence with intensities I, J = 0, 1, ..., 255 (intensity codes), where d - the distance between pixels, α - an angle between pixels (Fig. 1). Work [7] describes grey-level run-length matrices (GLRLM) elements (I, p /α) as the relative frequencies $P(I, p/\alpha)$ of the pixel occurrence with the same intensity I, the number of consecutive p, at an angle direction α (Fig. 2). GLSZM concentrate statistics similar to GLRLM estimating the distribution of 8-connected pixels areas with the same intensity, regardless of direction, as described in [31] (Fig. 3).

Previous works such as [7,10], and [31] describe a method for obtaining aggregated second-order statistics that have been proven effective in classification tasks. Further studies have also demonstrated the effectiveness of these approaches. For example, [24] and [8] demonstrate the effectiveness of these techniques, but they are limited to using only GLCM matrices for feature extraction. Work [19] also uses GLRLM, local binary GLCM, and segmentation-based

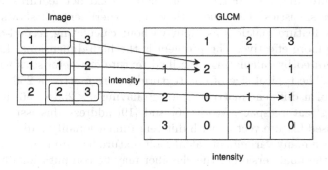

Fig. 1. Visual example of GLCM computation

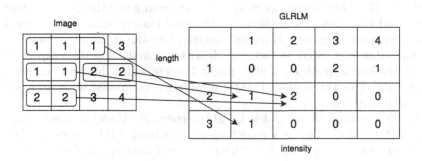

Fig. 2. Visual example of GLRLM computation

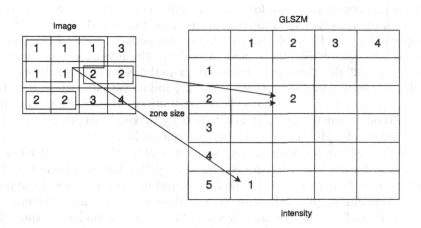

Fig. 3. Visual example of GLSZM computation

fractal texture analysis (SFTA) [5] methods to extract features with further second-order statistics calculation. However, experiment [6] shows that using bare texture feature matrices as input without calculating second-order statistics may be more effective. The problem is the high-dimensional feature space can be generated by calculating described texture characteristics with different parameters. The typical size of one texture feature matrix is 256×256, so the calculation of n different matrices leads to having $n \times 256 \times 256$ dimensions in the resulting feature space. Works [6] and [19] address this issue by generating compressed feature vectors with different dimensionality reduction methods. Still, there are many variants of calculation texture feature matrices and having them all in the final version of the classifier may be computationally inefficient. That fact makes selecting the most important texture feature matrices an actual task. Possible solutions to this issue may lay in the domain of xAI applied to feature selection tasks.

One of the most adopted approaches for feature selection with xAI methods is SHAP [17], which estimates Shapley values from game theory. Here, features are treated like players; a prediction is the total players' gain. This method is a great advantage because it is model-agnostic, but also it has the downside of a low computational speed. In fact, the algorithm complexity grows exponentially to the number of features, and it might become unfeasible to compute their importance. This is the case of textural matrices, composed of many elements, the actual features.

An alternative xAI method is Local Interpretable Model-Agnostic Explanations (LIME) [25], which is a model-agnostic method. LIME relies on the local approximation of the prediction with a simple explainable model which is trained for each data sample. A dataset is generated for each sample by tweaking feature values and becomes an input for the explaining model. However, explaining data samples with a large number of features may be computationally inefficient, because the need to tweak each feature value emerges.

If neural networks are used for image classification based on texture matrices, then attribution methods to evaluate feature importance in the context of a single input object can be employed. Attribution methods are a class of explainable artificial intelligence techniques used to evaluate the importance of input features. Paper [32] describes several attribution methods for neural networks. The popular attribution method is Grad-CAM [27] and its variants, which have been used in works such as [20,34] to generate attributions for neural network input. This method calculates gradient attribution by making backpropagation with zeroed features for all classes in the soft-max output layer except the target one. This method allows for determining the level of activation for input elements. The alternative method is Integrated Gradients [29], which determines the contribution of each input feature to the final neural network response by approximating Aumann-Shapley values but in a model-specific way and by computing the sum of gradients by the path from input feature to model's output. This method is computationally efficient and is suitable for neural networks trained with image-like data, like those used in this research. The Integrated Gradients method has been widely used to explain convolutional neural networks, as shown in works such as [14,22,35]. The main advantage of the integrated gradients over Grad-CAM is the compliance with the sensitivity axiom, described in [29] which leads to more accurate attributions estimations.

However, there is currently no established approach for feature selection using saliency methods. While the previous works focus on explaining classifier decisions for individual objects, feature selection requires analyzing attributions in the context of the entire dataset. This study proposes a method to evaluate the importance of features in the context of the whole dataset based on analysis of mean integrated gradients histograms. It is assumed that if a convolutional neural network is trained to classify chest X-ray scans into three categories (healthy, COVID-19, and pneumonia) based on a set of textural characteristics, then there exists a subset of such attributes with significantly higher mean integrated gradients absolute values than others, indicating a higher impact on classification.

3   Design and Methodology

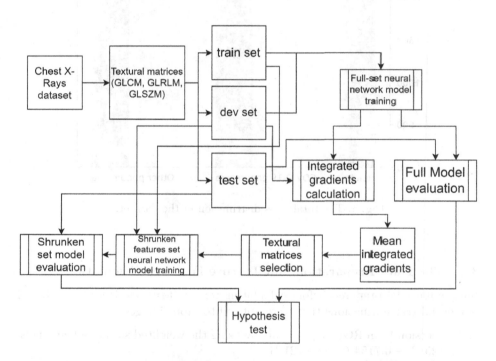

Fig. 4. Flow diagram that describes the process of texture matrices selection for classification of X-Ray images using integrated gradients method. Here squares represent entities while s

Current work discusses selecting the most valuable texture feature matrices to distinguish lung X-Ray images into three classes - healthy, COVID-19, and other pneumonia. The proposed method pipeline is illustrated in the Fig. 4. The dataset [2] was chosen for the classifier training and evaluation. Program code for experiments was implemented using numpy [11], scikit-learn [23] and PyTorch [21] software. Visual materials were generated using matplotlib [13] and seaborn [33] software.

3.1 The Dataset Description

The dataset consists of 6639 images. Radiologists labelled images by three classes: healthy lungs, COVID-19 lesions, and other pneumonia lesions. The dataset was split into the train (90%), development (5%), and test (5%) parts in a stratified manner to guarantee the same class distribution in all parts. The total class distribution is shown in Fig. 5

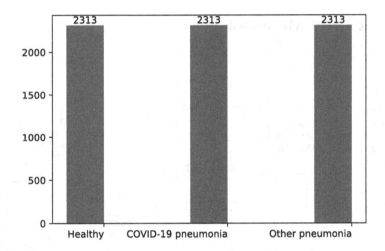

Fig. 5. The total class distribution in the dataset.

3.2 The Data Preparation and Texture Features Calculation

Images must be prepared before calculating texture features. Here is the list of sequential transformations that were applied to input images:

1. Conversion from RGB to grayscale by using the weighted sum of all channels:
   0.2125 R + 0.7154 G + 0.0721 B
2. Resize to 256 × 256

Then, a full set of texture feature matrices is calculated by corresponding algorithms described in [7,10,31]. All calculated texture matrix types are shown in Table 1: Eleven matrices are calculated in the total. The size of each matrix is 256 × 256, which means that 11 × 256 × 256 is calculated for each image tensor of size.

Table 1. Calculated textural characteristics

Textural matrix method	Used parameters
GLCM	Distances: 1, 2, 3; Angles: 0, 45,
GLRLM	Angles: 0, 45, 90, 135; Maximum Length: 256
GLSZM	Maximum zone size: 256

3.3 The Classifier

It is proposed to build a classifier as a neural network that accepts textural feature matrices as input. The neural network to process textural matrices input consists of three main components as described in work [6]. The first component (Fig. 6) consists of a set of parallel convolutional networks designed to compress massive matrix input into a relatively small compressed feature vector (CFV). The next component takes CFVs from the previous layer and condenses them into a single feature vector (Fig. 7). That vector is used as input for the last component - classifier (Fig. 8), which is built as a radial basis functions neural network with Gauss activation functions. The training process features training of all three components simultaneously. The complete structure is shown in Fig. 9.

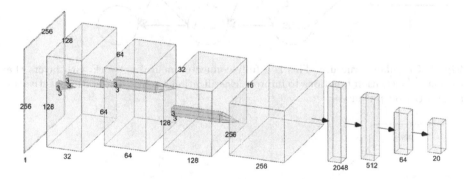

Fig. 6. Texture matrices coder structure. This is the structure of the convolutional neural network for encoding GLCM, GLRLM, and GLSZM matrices into a single compressed vector. It is assumed that the input matrix has a size of 256 by 256. However, it can be changed while using separate encoders for different matrices.

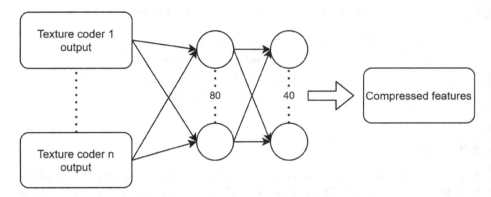

Fig. 7. Features encoder structure. Defines a fully-connected neural network with two hidden layers, which takes as input compressed feature vectors from texture matrices encoders and compresses them into a single combined feature vector.

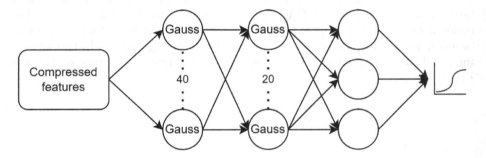

Fig. 8. Classifier structure. This is a fully-connected neural network with layers that use Gauss activation functions to improve classification quality. The softmax activation follows the output layer.

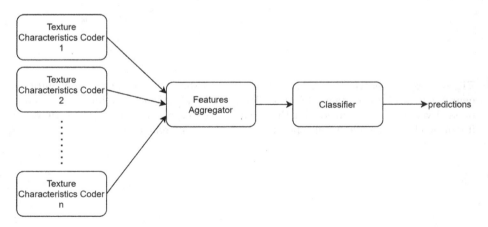

Fig. 9. Whole classification network structure. This figure shows all components of the classifier neural network put together.

3.4   Texture Matrices Selection

It is possible to calculate integrated gradients attribution for each element of texture features matrices. Such attribution is calculated for each image from the development set. The size of the attribution tensor will be the same as the input size (test images count × 11 × 256 × 256). Next, the Mean is calculated for each attribution element across all input images. The resulting tensor size is (11 × 256 × 256). The Mean of the integrated gradients for each component can show how significant a particular feature is. Nevertheless, our goal is to determine the whole texture feature matrix as significant, as there is no efficient way to calculate only a specific matrix element. It is proposed to build a histogram of integrated gradients means separately for each texture feature matrix type, reflecting the distribution of mean gradients' absolute values.

4   Results and Discussion

4.1   Classification and Selection Results

The neural network classifier was trained for 142 epochs until a total classification accuracy of 0.93 on the development set was reached. The neural network was trained with Adam optimiser. 1e-4 was used as the learning rate value. Classification results are shown in the Table 2

Table 2. The classifier results

Dataset	Class	Precision	Recall	F1-Score
Train	Healthy	0.91	0.96	0.94
	COVID-19	0.99	0.97	0.98
	Other pneumonia	0.95	0.91	0.93
	Total accuracy			0.95
Dev	Healthy	0.91	0.93	0.92
	COVID-19	0.95	0.95	0.95
	Other pneumonia	0.94	0.92	0.93
	Total accuracy			0.93
Test	Healthy	0.89	0.91	0.90
	COVID-19	0.96	0.93	0.94
	Other pneumonia	0.90	0.91	0.90
	Total accuracy			0.91

In Figs. 10, 11, 12, and 13 mean integrated gradients histograms are shown for each texture matrix type.

Manual analysis of these histograms and histograms overlap (Fig. 13) shows the highest mean integrated gradients were obtained for the following texture features matrices: GLCM (d = 3, a = 0), GLRLM (d = 256, a = 0,45), and GLSZM

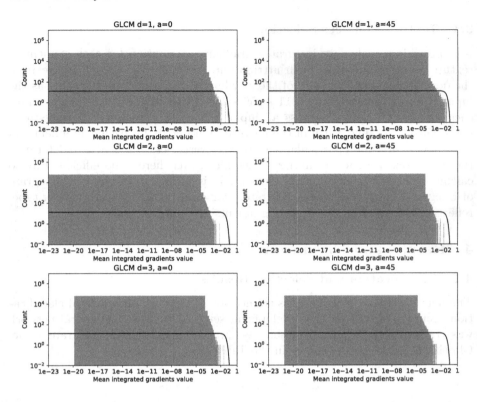

Fig. 10. Mean integrated gradients for GLCM matrices. Blue bars show histogram bins, and the orange plot represents the density function. α and d are GLCM calculation parameters. d is the distance between pixels, and α is the angle between pixels. (Color figure online)

matrices as their histograms show the higher distribution density for the higher values of gradients. Next, the classifier was trained on these four matrices types. The classifier results with the shrunken set of matrices are shown in Table 3. The Kruskall-Wallis test determined statistically significant differences between texture characteristics sets. The test result was equal to 312441.05 with a p-value equal to $< .001$, which indicates the presence of statistically significant differences. Additionally, the Dunn test was run for post-hoc analysis. The presence of differences for pair of texture characteristics matrices are shown in Fig. 14. It can be inferred that all groups of the mean integrated gradients (except GLRLM, $d = 256$, $\alpha = 135$, and GLSZM) have significant differences, allowing the selection of the most significant texture characteristics matrices by ordering them descending by the sum of the mean and standard deviation of their mean integrated gradients.

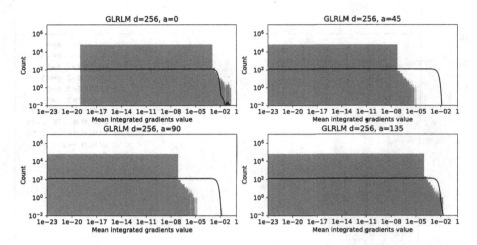

Fig. 11. Mean integrated gradients histograms for GLRLM matrices. Blue bars show histogram bins, and the orange plot represents the density function. α and d are GLRLM calculation parameters. α - the angle between pixels, d - a maximal distance of pixels of the same intensity. (Color figure online)

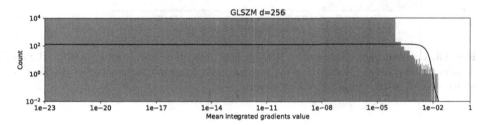

Fig. 12. Mean integrated gradients histograms for GLSZM texture features matrix. Blue bars show histogram bins, and the orange plot represents the density function. (Color figure online)

4.2 Discussion of Results

The noticeable fact is that classification results are not worsening after shrinking the features set when comparing data in Tables 2 and 3. It is also a slight improvement in the accuracy of the test set classification. That proves the correctness of our assumption that matrices with higher mean gradients distribution density on high levels have a higher impact on classification results. Also, at least one texture feature matrix is selected from each type which was crucial to maintain high classification metrics. For example, removing the GLSZM matrix from the final classifier input led to the classification accuracy downgrade to 73% on the development set. This fact leads to the assumption that enrichment of the feature set with the other texture feature matrices types, such as grey-level dependency matrix [28], neighbourhood grey-tone difference matrix [1], grey-level entropy

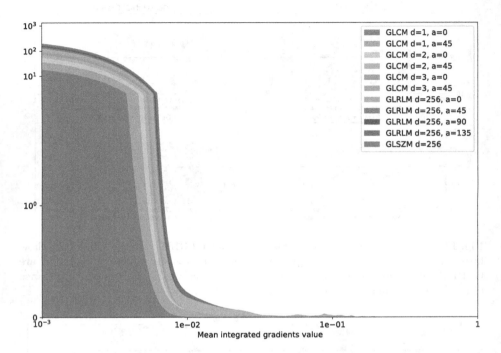

Fig. 13. Overlap of the histograms density functions. Here mean integrated gradients density functions for all matrices are put on a single graph to analyse which have a wider spectrum and higher gradient values.

Table 3. The classifier with shrunken features set results

Dataset	Class	Precision	Recall	F1-Score
Train	Healthy	0.88	0.97	0.92
	COVID-19	0.98	0.96	0.97
	Other pneumonia	0.97	0.89	0.93
	Total accuracy			0.94
Dev	Healthy	0.86	0.97	0.91
	COVID-19	0.96	0.94	0.95
	Other pneumonia	0.98	0.88	0.93
	Total accuracy			0.93
Test	Healthy	0.86	0.97	0.91
	COVID-19	0.98	0.91	0.95
	Other pneumonia	0.94	0.89	0.91
	Total accuracy			0.92

	GLCM d=1, a=0	GLCM d=1, a=45	GLCM d=2, a=0	GLCM d=2, a=45	GLCM d=3, a=0	GLCM d=3, a=45	GLRLM d=256, a=0	GLRLM d=256, a=45	GLRLM d=256, a=90	GLRLM d=256, a=135	GLSZM d=256
GLCM d=1, a=0	0	1	1	1	1	1	1	1	1	1	1
GLCM d=1, a=45	1	0	1	1	1	1	1	1	1	1	1
GLCM d=2, a=0	1	1	0	1	1	1	1	1	1	1	1
GLCM d=2, a=45	1	1	1	0	1	1	1	1	1	1	1
GLCM d=3, a=0	1	1	1	1	0	1	1	1	1	1	1
GLCM d=3, a=45	1	1	1	1	1	0	1	1	1	1	1
GLRLM d=256, a=0	1	1	1	1	1	1	0	1	1	1	1
GLRLM d=256, a=45	1	1	1	1	1	1	1	0	1	1	1
GLRLM d=256, a=90	1	1	1	1	1	1	1	1	0	1	1
GLRLM d=256, a=135	1	1	1	1	1	1	1	1	1	0	0
GLSZM d=256	1	1	1	1	1	1	1	1	1	0	0

Fig. 14. Result of Dunn post-hoc test. Here 1 declares the statistical difference between matrices' mean integrated gradients, 0 - opposite

matrix [18], will lead to increased classification performance due to the broader spectrum of available texture characteristics.

Removal of insignificant texture feature matrices allowed to lower the RAM consumption by 64%. However, using individual features instead of the whole matrices will allow for multiplying these efforts. However, schemes of texture feature matrices' partial calculation is still an open research question. Current research described a successful approach to analyse feature importance in the context of the dataset, but it is necessary to understand approach limitations. The same feature space for all objects is required to take a mean of calculated attribution across all objects correctly. Statistical features extraction methods like texture feature matrices satisfy this condition, but for other texture descriptors, such as local binary patterns (LBP) [16], scale-invariant texture descriptors (SIFT) [12], speeded up robust features (SURF) [3], our approach cannot be applied directly and further work required to resolve this issue. The current method also cannot be used for the raw images for the same reason.

Obtained classification results are comparable to other methods described in [8] but worse than for the most advanced practices described in [4,30] where absolute accuracy on the test set reaches 93–96% when our classifier has reached only 88% accuracy on the test set. Our current research does not focus on obtaining the best classifier structure. However, the enrichment of the input with other texture matrices described above, optimisation of the classifier neural network architecture, and usage of hybrid classification schemes such as in [6] can significantly improve classification quality. However, the explainability of the hybrid classification model is an open research question as recent model agnostic methods [17,25] still do not meet performance requirements while working with a large number of features.

One of the limitations is that the current work performs feature selection only with an integrated gradient method and is limited to neural networks only. Therefore, this study can be extended in many ways by trying different learning methods and various xAI methods. For example, one of the most recent methods called Integrated Grad-CAM (IGC) [26] could be employed. IGC combines the strengths of the IG and Grad-CAM which leads to the assumption that IGC usage can allow better feature selection results.

The current study does not consider selecting features that are strongly associated with some class in the dataset. However, this can be easily implemented in the current framework by calculating mean integrated gradients for data samples in classes rather than for the whole dataset and identifying matrices highly activated to class input. It is assumed that such a technique will allow to reduce selected feature sets even more.

5   Conclusions and Future Work

The current study addressed the feature selection problem using texture characteristics matrices. The solution to conduct feature selection in an ample feature space was introduced. The study presents a novel mean integrated gradients approach for identifying relevant texture feature matrices in medical image classification with neural networks. The efficiency of the proposed method was demonstrated by training a classifier on a reduced set of texture feature matrices, yielding performance metrics equivalent to those achieved with the complete set of features. Future research could explore the usage of alternative attribution methods as IGC, and optimise the structure of the classifier neural network. Additionally, the present approach could be expanded to calculate mean integrated gradients for each class in the dataset, enabling more effective feature selection by identifying the features most strongly associated with specific categories. Furthermore, it is necessary to develop optimised procedures for calculating texture matrices that permit the passage of individual characteristics rather than requiring evaluation of the entire texture matrix.

Acknowledgements. We want to thank Giuliano Anselmi from IBM for granting us access to computing resources and helping us configure the IBM power stations our models were trained on.

References

1. Amadasun, M., King, R.: Textural features corresponding to textural properties. IEEE Trans. Syst. Man Cybern. **19**(5), 1264–1274 (1989). https://doi.org/10.1109/21.44046
2. Asraf, A.: COVID19, pneumonia and normal chest x-ray PA dataset (2021)
3. Bay, H., Tuytelaars, T., Van Gool, L.: SURF: speeded up robust features. In: Leonardis, A., Bischof, H., Pinz, A. (eds.) ECCV 2006. LNCS, vol. 3951, pp. 404–417. Springer, Heidelberg (2006). https://doi.org/10.1007/11744023_32
4. Constantinou, M., Exarchos, T., Vrahatis, A.G., Vlamos, P.: COVID-19 classification on chest x-ray images using deep learning methods. Int. J. Environ. Res. Public Health **20**(3), 2035 (2023). https://doi.org/10.3390/ijerph20032035
5. Costa, A.F., Humpire-Mamani, G., Traina, A.J.M.: An efficient algorithm for fractal analysis of textures. In: 2012 25th SIBGRAPI Conference on Graphics, Patterns and Images, pp. 39–46 (2012). https://doi.org/10.1109/SIBGRAPI.2012.15
6. Davydko, O., Hladkyi, Y., Linnik, M., Nosovets, O., Pavlov, V., Nastenko, I.: Hybrid classifiers based on cnn, lsof, gmdh in covid-19 pneumonic lesions types classification task. In: 2021 IEEE 16th International Conference on Computer Sciences and Information Technologies (CSIT), vol. 1, pp. 380–384 (2021). https://doi.org/10.1109/CSIT52700.2021.9648752
7. Galloway, M.M.: Texture analysis using gray level run lengths. Comput. Graph. Image Process. **4**(2), 172–179 (1975). https://doi.org/10.1016/S0146-664X(75)80008-6
8. Gaudêncio, A.S., et al.: Evaluation of covid-19 chest computed tomography: a texture analysis based on three-dimensional entropy. Biomed. Signal Process. Control **68**, 102582 (2021). https://doi.org/10.1016/j.bspc.2021.102582
9. Hamza, A., et al.: Covid-19 classification using chest x-ray images: a framework of cnn-lstm and improved max value moth flame optimization. Front. Public Health **10** (2022). https://doi.org/10.3389/fpubh.2022.948205
10. Haralick, R.M., Shanmugam, K., Dinstein, I.: Textural features for image classification. IEEE Trans. Syst. Man Cybern. SMC **3**(6), 610–621 (1973). https://doi.org/10.1109/TSMC.1973.4309314
11. Harris, C.R., et al.: Array programming with NumPy. Nature **585**(7825), 357–362 (2020). https://doi.org/10.1038/s41586-020-2649-2
12. Hegenbart, S., Uhl, A., Vécsei, A., Wimmer, G.: Scale invariant texture descriptors for classifying celiac disease. Med. Image Anal. **17**(4), 458–474 (2013)
13. Hunter, J.D.: Matplotlib: a 2d graphics environment. Comput. Sci. Eng. **9**(3), 90–95 (2007). https://doi.org/10.1109/MCSE.2007.55
14. Jha, A., K. Aicher, J., R. Gazzara, M., Singh, D., Barash, Y.: Enhanced integrated gradients: improving interpretability of deep learning models using splicing codes as a case study. Genome Biol. **21**(1) (2020). https://doi.org/10.1186/s13059-020-02055-7
15. Khan, E., Rehman, M.Z.U., Ahmed, F., Alfouzan, F.A., Alzahrani, N.M., Ahmad, J.: Chest x-ray classification for the detection of covid-19 using deep learning techniques. Sensors **22**(3) (2022). https://doi.org/10.3390/s22031211
16. Liu, L., Fieguth, P., Guo, Y., Wang, X., Pietikäinen, M.: Local binary features for texture classification: taxonomy and experimental study. Pattern Recogn. **62**, 135–160 (2017)
17. Lundberg, S., Lee, S.I.: A unified approach to interpreting model predictions (2017)

18. Nielsen, B., et al.: Entropy-based adaptive nuclear features are independent prognostic markers in a total population of uterine sarcomas. Cytometry Part A (2014). https://doi.org/10.1002/cyto.a.22601
19. Öztürk, Ş, Özkaya, U., Barstuğan, M.: Classification of coronavirus (scp-COVID/scp -19) from scpx-ray/scp and scpCT/scp images using shrunken features. Int. J. Imaging Syst. Technol. **31**(1), 5–15 (2020). https://doi.org/10.1002/ima.22469
20. Panwar, H., Gupta, P., Siddiqui, M.K., Morales-Menendez, R., Bhardwaj, P., Singh, V.: A deep learning and grad-cam based color visualization approach for fast detection of covid-19 cases using chest x-ray and ct-scan images. Chaos Solitons Fractals **140**, 110190 (2020). https://doi.org/10.1016/j.chaos.2020.110190
21. Paszke, A., et al.: Pytorch: an imperative style, high-performance deep learning library. In: Wallach, H., Larochelle, H., Beygelzimer, A., d'Alché-Buc, F., Fox, E., Garnett, R. (eds.) Advances in Neural Information Processing Systems, vol. 32, pp. 8024–8035. Curran Associates, Inc. (2019)
22. Patel, S., Lohakare, M., Prajapati, S., Singh, S., Patel, N.: Diaret: a browser-based application for the grading of diabetic retinopathy with integrated gradients. In: 2021 IEEE International Conference on Robotics, Automation and Artificial Intelligence (RAAI), pp. 19–23 (2021). https://doi.org/10.1109/RAAI52226.2021.9507938
23. Pedregosa, F., et al.: Scikit-learn: machine learning in python. J. Mach. Learn. Res. **12**, 2825–2830 (2011)
24. Preethi, G., Sornagopal, V.: Mri image classification using glcm texture features. In: 2014 International Conference on Green Computing Communication and Electrical Engineering (ICGCCEE), pp. 1–6 (2014). https://doi.org/10.1109/ICGCCEE.2014.6922461
25. Ribeiro, M.T., Singh, S., Guestrin, C.: "why should i trust you?" explaining the predictions of any classifier. In: Proceedings of the 22nd ACM SIGKDD International Conference on Knowledge Discovery and Data Mining, pp. 1135–1144 (2016)
26. Sattarzadeh, S., Sudhakar, M., Plataniotis, K.N., Jang, J., Jeong, Y., Kim, H.: Integrated grad-cam: Sensitivity-aware visual explanation of deep convolutional networks via integrated gradient-based scoring. In: ICASSP 2021–2021 IEEE International Conference on Acoustics, Speech and Signal Processing (ICASSP), pp. 1775–1779 (2021). https://doi.org/10.1109/ICASSP39728.2021.9415064
27. Selvaraju, R.R., Cogswell, M., Das, A., Vedantam, R., Parikh, D., Batra, D.: Grad-cam: visual explanations from deep networks via gradient-based localization. In: 2017 IEEE International Conference on Computer Vision (ICCV), pp. 618–626 (2017). https://doi.org/10.1109/ICCV.2017.74
28. Sun, C., Wee, W.G.: Neighboring gray level dependence matrix for texture classification. Comput. Vision Graph. Image Process. **23**(3), 341–352 (1983). https://doi.org/10.1016/0734-189X(83)90032-4
29. Sundararajan, M., Taly, A., Yan, Q.: Axiomatic attribution for deep networks (2017)
30. Sunnetci, K.M., Alkan, A.: Biphasic majority voting-based comparative COVID-19 diagnosis using chest x-ray images. Expert Syst. Appl. **216**, 119430 (2023). https://doi.org/10.1016/j.eswa.2022.119430
31. Thibault, G., et al.: Texture indexes and gray level size zone matrix application to cell nuclei classification (2009)
32. Vilone, G., Longo, L.: Notions of explainability and evaluation approaches for explainable artificial intelligence. Inf. Fusion **76** (2021). https://doi.org/10.1016/j.inffus.2021.05.009

33. Waskom, M.L.: Seaborn: statistical data visualization. J. Open Source Softw. 6(60), 3021 (2021). https://doi.org/10.21105/joss.03021 https://doi.org/10.21105/joss.03021

34. Zhang, Y., Hong, D., McClement, D., Oladosu, O., Pridham, G., Slaney, G.: Gradcam helps interpret the deep learning models trained to classify multiple sclerosis types using clinical brain magnetic resonance imaging. J. Neurosci. Methods **353**, 109098 (2021). https://doi.org/10.1016/j.jneumeth.2021.109098

35. Čík, I., Rasamoelina, A.D., Mach, M., Sinčák, P.: Explaining deep neural network using layer-wise relevance propagation and integrated gradients. In: 2021 IEEE 19th World Symposium on Applied Machine Intelligence and Informatics (SAMI), pp. 000381–000386 (2021). https://doi.org/10.1109/SAMI50585.2021.9378686

Author Index

Printed in the United States
by Baker & Taylor Publisher Services